Paul and Philodemus

# Supplements to
# Novum Testamentum

Editorial Board
C. K. Barrett, Durham
P. Borgen, Trondheim
J. K. Elliott, Leeds
H. J. de Jonge, Leiden
M. J. J. Menknen, Utrecht
J. Smit Sibinga, Amsterdam

Executive Editors
A. J. Malherbe, New Haven
D. P. Moessner, Atlanta

Volume LXXXI

# Paul and Philodemus

## Adaptability in Epicurean and Early Christian Psychagogy

by

Clarence E. Glad

Society of Biblical Literature
Atlanta

Copyright © 1995 by Koninklijke Brill NV, Leiden,
The Netherlands

This edition published under license from Koninklijke Brill NV, Leiden, The Netherlands by the Society of Biblical Literature.

All rights reserved. No part of this work may be reproduced or transmitted in any form or by any means, electronic or mechanical, including photocopying and recording, or by any means of any information storage or retrieval system, except as may be expressly permitted by the 1976 Copyright Act or in writing from the Publisher. Requests for permission should be addressed in writing to the Rights and Permissions Department, Koninklijke Brill NV, Leiden, The Netherlands.

Authorization to photocopy items for internal or personal use is granted by Brill provided that the appropriate fees are paid directly to The Copyright Clearance Center, 222 Rosewood Drive, Suite 910, Danvers, MA 01923, USA. Fees are subject to change.

Library of Congress Cataloging-in-Publication Data

Glad, Clarence E.
 Paul and Philodemus : adaptability in Epicurean and early Christian psychagogy / by Clarence E. Glad.
   p. cm.
 Originally published : Leiden ; New York : Brill, 1995. (Supplements to Novum Testamentum ; v. 81)
   Includes bibliographical references (p.   ) and indexes.
   ISBN 978-1-58983-502-3 (paper binding : alk. paper)
 1. Bible. N. T. Corinthians, 1st, IX, 19–23—Criticism, interpretation, etc. 2. Spiritual formation —Biblical teaching. 3. Adaptability (Pschology)—Biblical teaching. 4. Philodemus, ca. 110–ca. 40 B.C. De libertate dicendi. 5. Epicurus—Influence. I. Title.
  BS2675.6.S65G57  2010
  227'.206—dc22                                    2010031562

*For Kolla*

CONTENTS

Preface .................................................................................. xi
Abbreviations ...................................................................... xiii
Introduction ........................................................................ 1
 Focus and method ............................................................ 1
 Objectives and scope of the study .................................. 4

PART ONE
FLATTERERS AND FRIENDS:
ADAPTABILITY, VERSATILITY, AND PSYCHAGOGY

I. Adaptability, Versatility, and Psychagogy ...................... 15
 1.1 The Concept of "Psychagogy" ................................. 17
 1.2 The Flatterer (κόλαξ), and the Obsequious
  Person (ἄρεσκος) ...................................................... 23
  1.2.1 Adaptability and servility to the great .......... 30
  1.2.2 Flattery: A specious frankness ...................... 33
 1.3 The Genuine Frank Counselor ............................... 36
  1.3.1 Adaptability in the unreserved association
   with all ............................................................ 38
  1.3.2 1 Corinthians 9:19–23. A suggestive
   hypothesis ...................................................... 43
 1.4 Adaptability Valued by Orators, Philosophers,
  and Moralists ............................................................. 45

II. Psychagogy and the Mixed Method of Moral
 Exhortation ........................................................................ 53
 2.1 The Psychagogic Perspective ................................... 53
  2.1.1 The mature guide ............................................. 53
  2.1.2 Psychagogy and moral instruction ................ 58
  2.1.3 The diversity of exhortation .......................... 60
  2.1.4 The recipients of psychagogic guidance
   and the need for versatility ........................... 65
 2.2 Adaptability and the Mixed Method of Praise
  and Blame ................................................................... 69

|  |  |  |  |
|---|---|---|---|
| | 2.2.1 | The "mixed method" proper ........................ | 71 |
| | | 2.2.1.1 The mixture of harsh and gentle means of exhortation ............ | 72 |
| | 2.2.2 | Destructive harshness and the weak and tender students ........................................ | 78 |
| | 2.2.3 | The appropriateness of praise and blame for the progressing person ................... | 81 |
| | 2.2.4 | The philotropeic method and the beneficial use of harshness ............................ | 85 |
| 2.3 | "Harsh" and "Gentle" Philosophers ........................ | | 89 |

PART TWO
EPICUREAN PSYCHAGOGY

III. Epicurean Communal Psychagogy ...................... 101
   3.1 The Nature of Παρρησία. The Debate ............... 104
      3.1.1 The present focus ............................................ 104
      3.1.2 The nature of παρρησία in Philodemus' Περὶ παρρησίας ................................................. 107
   3.2 Epicurean Communal Psychagogy: Philodemus' *On Frank Criticism* ...................... 124
      3.2.1 Mutual participation in edification, admonition, and correction. Openness and concealment; confession and reporting; trust and distrust .......................... 124
      3.2.2 Medical imagery and the stochastic method ........................................................... 133
      3.2.3 Types of students and approaches ............... 137
      3.2.4 Symmetry and/or asymmetry? Authority and obedience ................................ 152

IV. Psychagogy and Friendship .................................... 161
   4.1 Psychagogy and Friendship among Epicureans ........ 161
      4.1.1 Friendship, openness, and trust ................... 162
      4.1.2 Frank criticism and the friendship of many ........................................................... 165
   4.2 The Individual and the Community ...................... 175

## PART THREE
## PAULINE PSYCHAGOGY

V. Pauline Psychagogy .................................................... 185
   5.1  Paul, the Psychagogue, and Pauline Psychagogy ..... 186
   5.2  Pauline Communal Psychagogy ............................... 190
       5.2.1  Pauline psychagogy? ....................................... 190
       5.2.2  Member participation in communal
              psychagogy ...................................................... 192
              5.2.2.1  Reciprocal benefits from a
                        common endeavor .......................... 193
              5.2.2.2  The psychagogic "proxy" ................. 195
              5.2.2.3  Participatory communal
                        psychagogy ....................................... 195
              5.2.2.4  Paul's call for participatory
                        psychagogy ....................................... 200
       5.2.3  Authority and obedience in Pauline
              psychagogy ...................................................... 205
       5.2.4  Symmetry and/or asymmetry in Pauline
              psychagogy? ................................................... 208
   5.3  Pauline Communal Psychagogy and the Function
       of Romans 14:1–15:14 ............................................ 213

VI. Paul's Psychagogic Adaptability and the Weak
    and Recalcitrant Members of the Corinthian
    Community ................................................................. 236
   6.1  Paul's Adaptability in Conduct and Speech ............. 240
   6.2  The Form and Function of 1 Corinthians 9:19–23:
       Adaptability in the Unreserved Association with
       All and in Psychagogy ............................................ 249
       6.2.1  The social grid of patronage and Paul's
              dictum of adaptability .................................... 264
       6.2.2  The psychagogic dimension of
              1 Corinthians 9:19–23 .................................... 272
   6.3  Psychagogic Adaptability and the Weak and
       Tender Students (1 Cor 8:1–13; 10:24–11:1) .......... 277
   6.4  Paul's Psychagogic Approach Towards the
       Recalcitrant Corinthians ......................................... 295
       6.4.1  Paul's characterization of the
              recalcitrant ones ............................................. 297

|  |  |  |
|---|---|---|
| 6.4.2 | Paul's stringent guidance of the recalcitrant students | 304 |
| 6.4.3 | Paul's debate with the recalcitrant Corinthians | 310 |
| | 6.4.3.1 Paul's self-depiction as an open, clear, and consistent guide | 311 |
| | 6.4.3.2 The problem of excessive harshness | 315 |
| 6.5 Pauline Pedagogy | | 326 |

Conclusion .................................................................... 333
Bibliography ................................................................. 337
Index of Authors .......................................................... 355
Index of Passages ......................................................... 361
Index of Subjects ......................................................... 401

# PREFACE

I have written this book with two objectives in mind. Firstly, I want to make available to the scholarly community a discussion of Philodemus' *De libertate dicendi*, which has not been treated extensively in a book before. Secondly, I want to underscore the Greco-Roman context in which the apostle Paul operated and compare and contrast his activities with those of his contemporaries and thereby broaden our horizon when viewing Paul. This I have done by spotlighting a wide range of works by philosophers, rhetoricians, and moralists who concerned themselves with the problem of versatility, including the literature concerning flattery and friendship. Furthermore, I have focused on the Epicureans, because they offer the most appropriate comparative material for an investigation of Paul's psychagogic nurture of the proto-Christian communities.

The book is a revision of my dissertation submitted to the Department of Religious Studies at Brown University in May, 1992. The main thesis remains the same as well as the material on Philodemus but I have substantially revised the Pauline material and the overall structure of the work in order to sharpen my arguments and present an original thesis more lucidly. I would like to express my debts to the director of my dissertation, Professor Stanley K. Stowers, who with insight guided me step by step in a rather arduous three years of research and writing. The origin of my dissertation can be traced to a seminar on *Psychology and Psychagogy in Hellenistic Philosophy and Early Christianity* in the spring semester of 1989, when I read Philodemus for the first time. Here Stowers' innovative approach to the interpretation of New Testament texts was evident, an approach which has and will remain paradigmatic for me. Professor Stowers was instrumental in the shaping of my professional views while at Brown, as were the late Horst Moehring and Professor Giles Milhaven.

I am also indebted to the two readers of my dissertation, David Konstan, Professor of Classics and Comparative Literature at Brown, and Susan Ashbrook Harvey, Associate Professor in Religious Studies at Brown. I am also thankful to Professor John T. Fitzgerald, at the University of Miami, who read my dissertation in its revised version, to Wincie Jóhannsdóttir, teacher, who improved my English style, and to the Icelandic Council of Science, Division of Humanities and Social Sciences, and The Institute of Theology at the University of Iceland, for a three-year post-doctoral grant which has given me the leisure to direct my time and effort to a most enjoyable task. I am also indebted to the director of The Institute of Theology, Professor Jón Sveinbjörnsson, for all of his assistance. Last, but not least, my thanks go to Professor Abraham J. Malherbe, Buckingham Professor Emeritus of New Testament Criticism and Interpretation at Yale Divinity School, who read and responded to selected sections of my dissertation and was responsible for seeing this manuscript through to completion. His writings on the subject matter of this book have been influential from the tentative beginnings of its thesis through the final stages of writing. I also wish to express my gratitude to the editorial board and to the executive editors of the series Supplements to Novum Testamentum at E. J. Brill for including my book in this distinguished series.

Finally, my deepest thanks and affection go to my wife, Kolbrún (Kolla), a licensed psychologist and teacher. She, more than anyone else, has made me realize the importance of a flexible and versatile approach in the care of others. Along with our two daughters Karen Áslaug and Harpa Rún, she has shared in one way or another in making this book. I dedicate it to her.

Clarence E. Glad<br>December 1994

# ABBREVIATIONS

Abbreviations used in the notes follow the guidelines of the Society of Biblical Literature (cf. JBL 107:3 (1988), 579–96) and the reference system used in Liddell-Scott-Jones's *A Greek-English Lexicon* and *The Oxford Classical Dictionary*. Translations of ancient Greek and Latin authors in the *Loeb Classical Library* (LCL) have been used when available. Unless otherwise noted, all translations of Philodemus' *De libertate dicendi* are my own.
Scripture quotations, unless otherwise noted, are from the Revised Standard Version of the Bible, copyright © 1946, 1952, and 1971 by the Division of Christian Education of the National Council of Churches.

| | |
|---|---|
| ABR | *Australian Biblical Review* |
| AJP | *American Journal of Philosophy* |
| AJPh | *American Journal of Philology* |
| AnBib | *Analecta Biblica* |
| ANRW | *Aufstieg und Niedergang der römischen Welt*, ed. H. Temporini and W. Haase (Berlin/New York: Walter de Gruyter, 1972) |
| ARW | *Archiv für Religionswissenschaft* |
| BAA | Walter Bauer, *Griechisch-deutsches Wörterbuch zu den Schriften des Neuen Testaments und der frühchristlichen Literatur*. 6., völlig neu bearbeitete Auflage, herausgegeben von Kurt Aland und Barbara Aland (Berlin/New York: Walter de Gruyter, 1988) |
| BAGD | W. Bauer, *A Greek-English Lexicon of the New Testament and Other Early Christian Literature*, trans. and adapted by W. F. Arndt and F. W. Gingrich; 2nd ed. rev. and adapted by F. W. Gingrich and F. W. Danker (Chicago: University of Chicago Press, 1961) |
| BDF | F. Blass and A. Debrunner, *A Greek Grammar of the New Testament and Other Early Christian Literature*, trans. and rev. by R. W. Funk (Chicago: University of Chicago Press, 1961) |
| BETL | Bibliotheca Ephemeridum Theologicarum Lovaniensium |
| BHT | Beiträge zur historischen Theologie |
| CBQ | *Catholic Biblical Quarterly* |
| CErc | *Cronache Ercolanesi* |
| CPh | *Classical Philology* |
| CQ | *Classical Quarterly* |
| ÉB | Études bibliques |
| EMC | Echos du Monde Classique |
| FRLANT | Forschungen zur Religion und Literatur des Alten und Neuen Testaments |
| GR | *Greece and Rome* |
| GRBS | *Greek, Roman and Byzantine Studies* |
| Herc | *Herculanensium Voluminum* |
| HTR | *Harvard Theological Review* |
| ICS | *Illinois Classical Studies* |
| JAC | *Jahrbuch für Antike und Christentum* |
| JAPA | *Journal of the American Psychological Association* |
| JBL | *Journal of Biblical Literature* |
| JCE | *Journal of Christian Education* |

| | |
|---|---|
| *JEH* | *Journal of Ecclesiastical History* |
| *JHS* | *Journal of Hellenic Studies* |
| *JRH* | *Journal of Religious History* |
| *JSNT* | *Journal for the Study of the New Testament* |
| *JTS* | *Journal of Theological Studies* |
| LCL | Loeb Classical Library |
| LSJ | H. G. Liddell and R. Scott, *A Greek-English Lexicon*, rev. and augmented by H. S. Jones, with the assistance of R. McKenzie (Oxford: Clarendon Press, 1940) |
| *MusHelv* | *Museum Helveticum* |
| *NovT* | *Novum Testamentum* |
| NovTSup | Novum Testamentum Supplements |
| *NTS* | *New Testament Studies* |
| *NTT* | *Nederlands Theologisch Tijdschrift* |
| *PCPS* | *Proceedings of the Cambridge Philological Society* |
| PG | Patrologia Graeca |
| *PIPA* | *Proceedings of the Irish Biblical Association* |
| PW | A. Pauly, G. Wissowa, and W. Kroll, eds., *Real-Encyclopädie der klassischen Altertumswissenschaft* |
| *RAC* | *Reallexikon für Antike und Christentum* |
| *RB* | *Revue biblique* |
| *RhM* | *Rheinisches Museum* |
| *RSR* | *Recherches de science religieuse* |
| SBLDS | Society of Biblical Literature Dissertation Series |
| SBLSBS | Society of Biblical Literature Sources for Biblical Study |
| *SO* | *Symbolae Osloenses* |
| *ST* | *Studia Theologica* |
| Συζήτησις | Συζήτησις: *Studi sull' epicureismo greco e romano offerti a Marcello Gigante*. Biblioteca della Parola del Passato 16 (Naples: Gaetano Macchiaroli, 1983) |
| SVF | *Stoicorum Veterum Fragmenta*, ed. H. von Arnim, 4 vols. (Leipzig: B. G. Teubner, 1903–24) |
| *TAPA* | *Transactions of the American Philological Association* |
| TDNT | G. Kittel and G. Friedrich, eds., *Theological Dictionary of the New Testament*, trans. G. W. Bromiley (Grand Rapids: W. B. Eerdmans, 1964–76) |
| TU | Texte und Untersuchungen zur Geschichte der altchristlichen Literatur |
| *TynBul* | *Tyndale Bulletin* |
| Us. | H. Usener, ed. *Epicurea*. Leipzig, 1887 |
| *VC* | *Vigiliae Christianae* |
| *YClS* | *Yale Classical Studies* |
| *ZNW* | *Zeitschrift für die neutestamentliche Wissenschaft* |
| *ZTK* | *Zeitschrift für Theologie und Kirche* |

# INTRODUCTION

*Focus and method*

Paul's well known dictum, "I have become everything in turn to men of every sort" (1 Cor 9:22b NEB), has called forth a wide variety of responses, ranging from praise of Paul's remarkable flexibility, adaptability, and accommodation, to charges of contemptible opportunism and lack of resolve and steadfastness. These responses resemble to a striking degree those evoked by reflections on Homer's Odysseus. Indeed, a comparison has been drawn between Paul's "quality of being all things to all men" and Odysseus' traditional versatility and resourcefulness.[1] The fundamental ambiguity present in the characters of both Odysseus and Paul has also brought forth negative responses and evaluations, perhaps understandably, since, as W. B. Stanford notes, the border between adaptability and hypocrisy is easily crossed.[2] But noting the apparent similarity between Paul's and Odysseus' versatility and the charges leveled against them both on this score does not do justice to the various interpretive options available to us when considering Paul's dictum. A satisfactory treatment of the interpretive options is our challenge.

My thesis is that 1 Corinthians 9:22b, "I have become everything in turn to men of every sort," is part of a tradition in Greco-Roman society which underscores, in the light of human diversity, the importance of adaptability in conduct and speech in the unreserved association with all and in the psychagogic adaptation to different human dispositions. This twofold focus is evident from the structure of the pericope of 1 Cor 9:19–23. Adaptation in light of human diversity is underscored by Paul in his reference in this pericope to "Jews," "those under the law," and the "lawless ones," and psychagogic adaptation in his reference to the "weak."

---

[1] By W. B. Stanford, *The Ulysses Theme. A Study in the Adaptability of a Traditional Hero* (2nd ed. revised. New York, 1968), p. 91, who traces the fate of, and the various responses to, Homer's traditional hero throughout the centuries. The comparison is continued by A. J. Malherbe in *Paul and the Popular Philosophers* (Minneapolis, 1989), pp. 100–101.

[2] Stanford, *The Ulysses Theme*, p. 91.

I shall argue that this pericope reflects Paul's concern with adaptation in light of human diversity both in the unreserved association with all in recruitment and in the practice of psychagogy or "care of the young."[3] I use the term "psychagogy" or the "guidance of the soul" to describe a mature person's leading of neophytes in an attempt to bring about moral reformation by shaping the neophyte's view of himself and of the world. Such a reshaping demands in many cases a radical reorientation through social, intellectual, and moral transformation. Psychagogic discourse attempts to effect such a transformation. Such a discourse is then a form of paraenesis or moral exhortation having a twofold focus: on dissuasion and on persuasion. Not surprisingly, psychagogic discourse is often embedded in works of deliberative and epideictic genres, which on the one hand make clear what is honorable and what is shameful, and on the other hand prescribe what course of action is expedient or useful in the future.

I focus on the psychagogue's method of exhortation, as well as on his perception of the status of his clients. The latter should not be neglected since ψυχαγωγεῖν (to lead a soul) requires knowledge of the types of souls to be led.[4] It is pertinent to focus on both the psychagogue's methods and perception of his clients, firstly, since the medium of the psychagogue's behavior is considered to be a part of his message; secondly, since charges leveled against ancient psychagogues, including Paul, focus on both words and deeds; thirdly, because of the common demand for consistency between words and deeds; and, fourthly, since the psychagogue's presentation of himself to his clients and his verbal means of exhortation reveal his view of their condition. Form cannot be separated from content. It is thus imperative not to sever the intricate connection between speech and behavior.

The intricate connection between σχῆμα and λόγος has implications for Paul's self-presentation in 1 Cor 9:19–23. Modern scholarship has tended to focus exclusively on inconsistency in Paul's behavior and thereby severing the crucial connection between speech and conduct. However, some of the charges leveled against Paul for inconsistency and concealment arise precisely from his adaptability

---

[3] Or ἐπιμέλεια τῶν νέων. See Epictetus, *Discourse* 3.21.18–24 for a succinct description of the practice of the "care of the young." Compare Isocrates, *To Demonicus* 3 and 6. See pp. 11–12, below.

[4] So argued by Plato in *Phaedrus* 271C. See further pp. 18 and 47, below.

in speech or from his use of different hortatory terms and techniques in light of different dispositions of people. Paul's use of praise and blame, of harsh and gentle means of persuasion, and his often indirect, and polyphonic approach towards the Corinthians should be seen as aspects of a friend's frank speech and psychagogic adaptation to his friends. Such adaptation in speech is a prime source of charges against Paul for his inconsistent conduct.

Since the leadership model affirmed in 1 Cor 9:19–23 has implications for Paul's hortatory practice and guidance of his converts, I investigate Paul's guidance of the Corinthians seen not only in his willingness to associate with people of different moral and social status and in his guidance of the weak but also in his instruction of the wise which forms the setting of Paul's remarks on his versatile approach. Paul gives the wise of Corinth an example of how to treat the weak and suggests that they implement a proper form of psychagogic guidance. After having dealt with the form and function of 1 Cor 9:19–23 in the final chapter of the book, I thus contextualize the leadership model Paul articulates in this pericope both in its immediate and its wider literary context in Paul's nurture of the weak and explore his more stringent supervision of the wise. Retrospective evidence of 2 Corinthians reveals the repercussions of Paul's critique of the wise and the mounting tensions between Paul and his recalcitrant critics due to their differing views on the use of harshness in psychagogic guidance.

Paul's psychagogic guidance has similarities not only to the practice of flatterers and those who have many friends but also to that of the flexible guide. Hence the need to situate such a practice of adaptation in a larger cultural context in view of discussions of the similarities and differences between flatterers and friends. Since Paul's practice will be seen to resemble that of a friend, the need arises to locate it within ancient discussions of friendship. Also, since Paul's psychagogy can be shown to resemble the practices of his philosophic contemporaries, it is important to draw attention to their theory and practice of spiritual guidance. The selection of texts for comparison is determined by an analogical-functional approach. Paul's nurture will be shown to function in many ways analogously to that of his philosophic contemporaries. Here Paul also avails himself of the moralists' classification of students as more or less mature by characterizing some as "strong" or "wise," and others as "weak".

Paul's dictum of adaptation as enunciated in 1 Cor 9:19–23 has indeed affinities to Antisthenes' characterization of Odysseus' adaptability in his attempt to benefit others.⁵ I will argue, however, that despite noticeable affinities with the method of many a moralist, Paul's dictum in its context most clearly resembles the Epicurean "philotropeic method," which emphasizes that particular attention should be paid to the character and disposition of each recipient of the psychagogue's care.⁶ Concerns with psychagogic adaptation are widespread in antiquity, but it is the thesis of this book that, within this tradition of psychagogy, it is in the practices of the Epicureans in Athens, Naples, and Herculaneum less than a century before Paul that we find the closest comparison to Paul's psychagogic nurture of the proto-Christian communities. These practices are witnessed primarily in Philodemus' *On Frank Criticism*. In chapters one and two I discuss various aspects of the tradition of psychagogic nurture and versatility; in chapter three and four I focus on Philodemus and the Epicurean communities; and in chapters five through six I concentrate on Paul and the proto-Christian communities, especially the one in Corinth.

### *Objectives and scope of the study*

I will use the evidence collected in this book to develop a model complementary to the one propounded by Abraham J. Malherbe in several studies. Malherbe has argued that Paul casts his teaching activity and self-understanding in the form of the gentle Cynics in conscious opposition to the rigoristic Cynics. I argue that Epicurean practice is the closest comparison available when we focus on Paul's psychagogy and nurture of the proto-Christian communities. This book agrees though with the presentation of Paul in Malherbe's studies, a Paul who is at once *Paulus christianus* and *Paulus hellenisticus*, one who is thoroughly familiar with the traditions of his philosophic contemporaries and who knows these traditions first-hand.⁷ Malherbe does draw attention to the ways in which Paul differs from his con-

---

⁵ So Malherbe, *Paul and the Popular Philosophers*, pp. 100–101.

⁶ This method is referred to in Philodemus' *De libertate dicendi* fr. 43; A. Olivieri (ed.), *Philodemi* ΠΕΡΙ ΠΑΡΡΗΣΙΑΣ (Leipzig: Teubner, 1914), p. 21. From now on I refer to this work as *On Frank Criticism*. For the reason of this translation of Περὶ παρρησίας, see p. 108, below.

⁷ Malherbe, *Paul and the Popular Philosophers*, p. 8.

temporaries and to his similarities with philosophers other than Cynics as well as to Paul's originality in shaping the traditions he appropriates, but the preponderance of the Cynic material calls for a redressing of the balance in favor of other authors whose methods might be even closer akin to Paul's methods and self-understanding. I shall attempt to align Paul's psychagogic practices with those witnessed in contemporary Epicurean schools.[8]

Malherbe recognizes the congruity between Paul and the Epicureans and the importance of Philodemus for a study of Paul. He has discussed Philodemus under such headings as "The Condition of Converts" and "Nurture Among the Philosophers." Here Philodemus, as well as Seneca, Epictetus, and Plutarch, are seen as examples of how people sought to help each other in a way of life different from that of the larger society. Malherbe notes that Philodemus' *On Frank Criticism* treats in detail the way in which an Epicurean community was to engage in the nurture of its members,

> It was the Epicureans who had developed the system of psychagogy, but what Philodemus says in the first century BC is reflected in the writings of Seneca, Paul's Stoic contemporary, and a generation later by the Platonist Plutarch. In short, the concerns and techniques that interest us were widespread at the time Paul wrote. The Epicureans, however, are of special interest, for, like Paul, they formed genuine communities that engaged in mutual exhortation.[9]

In a similar vein Malherbe explains the rationale for his focus on the

---

[8] Philodemus was born in Gadara in Syria c. 110 BCE and died c. 40/35 BCE. He was probably of Greek parentage and received a Greek education. He was the leader as well as a probable founder of the Epicurean school at Herculaneum. The date of the founding of the Epicurean school at the bay of Naples is uncertain but Philodemus may have arrived in Italy about the year 80 BCE. There is no certain evidence for the school's existence after 50 BCE, although the fact that the Epicurean library at Herculaneum was preserved until the eruption of Mt. Vesuvius in 79 CE strongly suggests that it did not disappear under the early Empire. The evidence shows unequivocally that the Epicurean school in Naples and Herculaneum was an important intellectual and literary center in the first century BCE (See E. A. and P. H. de Lacy, *Philodemus: On Methods of Inference* (2nd ed. Naples, 1978), pp. 145–52). Both Philodemus and Siro, the leader of the Epicurean school at nearby Naples, studied in Athens under Zeno of Sidon, the scholarch of the Epicurean school in Athens, and Demetrius the Laconian. *On Frank Criticism* contains the lecture notes of Zeno of Sidon, copied by Philodemus and preserved at Herculanaeum, in the house of Philodemus' patron, the influential Calpurnius Piso, father-in-law of Julius Caesar. These lecture notes give us evidence of the way in which moral instruction was conducted in the different Epicurean centres in Greece and Italy.

[9] Malherbe, *Paul and the Thessalonians. The Philosophic Tradition of Pastoral Care* (Philadelphia: Fortress Press, 1987), pp. 84, 40–43, 85–88.

Cynics: firstly, the traditions Paul uses are given a hard edge by the Cynics through their sharp formulation of issues; secondly, Cynics have been slighted in earlier scholarly discussions and the balance needs to be redressed; thirdly, they have been lumped uncritically with the Stoics; and fourthly, Paul's practice is seen in "sharper profile" against the background to which the Cynics belong. But Paul is no Cynic, although he addresses some of the issues they raised and uses their language. The Cynics' preoccupation with the individual contrasts with Paul's communal concern; Paul is a founder of communities, "of which the Cynics had none."[10] In his communal concern, Paul is more like the Epicureans, but this proper care of humans approximates that of people like Plutarch and the substance of his teaching reminds us at times of Musonius Rufus; and Paul could use the same devices in his argumentation that Epictetus does. In this way Malherbe, despite his focus on the Cynics, recognizes Paul's affinities with a variety of moralists. In a similar vein, I draw on material from authors of different philosophical convictions but attempt to show that Epicurean practice throws Pauline psychagogy into the sharpest possible relief.

Around the turn of the century Johannes Weiss insisted that students of the New Testament should know Seneca, Epictetus, Plutarch, Lucian, Musonius Rufus, Marcus Aurelius, and Cicero intimately, and that the New Testament should be studied with Hans von Arnim's collection of Stoic texts "at their elbows."[11] Weiss, despite his disclaimer,[12] followed his own advice in his commentary on 1 Corinthians

---

[10] Idem, *Paul and the Popular Philosophers*, pp. 8–9. A school setting has been suggested for the Socratic letters: W. Obens, *Qua aetate Socratis et Socraticorum epistulae, quae dicuntur, scriptae sunt* (Münster i. W. Aschendorff, 1912), p. 6; L. Köhler, *Die Briefe des Sokrates und der Sokratiker herausgegeben, übersetzt und kommentiert* (Philologus suppl. B. 20, 2. Leipzig, 1928), pp. 4–5; B. Fiore, S. J., *The Function of Personal Example in the Socratic and Pastoral Epistles* (Rome, 1986), pp. 108–10, 115–26, 129–30. In *Paul and the Thessalonians* (7–12), Malherbe, in response to S. K. Stowers' protestation (in "Social Status, Public Speaking and Private Teaching: The Circumstances of Paul's Preaching Activity," *NovT* 26 (1984), pp. 59–82) that it is difficult to imagine Paul entering into competition with the Cynics, notes: "more to the point is Stowers's argument that Paul, unlike the field preachers, did not primarily deliver an individualistic challenge to give up vice but aimed at forming a community of those who responded to his proclamation, for which a teacher-student relationship was necessary. Such a relationship required a more secluded setting than the marketplace."

[11] J. Weiss, *Die Aufgaben der neutestamentlichen Wissenschaft in der Gegenwart* (Göttingen, 1908), pp. 4, 11, 55; cf. Malherbe, *Paul and the Popular Philosophers*, p. 3.

[12] The disclaimer referred to is from Weiss's Introduction to his commentary on 1 Corinthians in which he compares himself unfavorably to Georg Heinrici as to

and showed how parallel material, particularly from the Stoic moralists, could throw light on and situate Paul in a larger hellenistic literary and religious context. Abraham J. Malherbe, who more than any other modern author has concerned himself with understanding Paul as he moves within the traditions of his philosophic contemporaries, has called for expansion of the emphasis of Weiss and others, to include not only Cynics and Stoics, but also Platonists, Peripatetics, Epicureans and Pythagoreans, since they all, in some form or shape, aimed at moral reformation in their protreptic endeavors.[13]

Such a wide casting of the net is legitimate since, if the postulate is true that most moralists shared a common protreptic goal, it is not *prima facie* unlikely that the substance of their moral instruction and many of the devices and methods developed and employed to attain this goal were also common. This was the case, for example, with the mixed method of moral exhortation that I discuss in chapter two. But the ubiquitous nature of the requirement of adaptation and accommodation dealt with in chapters one and two requires that we cast the net even wider, since the need to adapt to different audiences, segments of audiences, times and locations, was a commonly valued principle among philosophers, moralists, and orators, as well as some of Paul's Jewish contemporaries and predecessors. This concern was shared by Paul, too.

However, when it comes to the principle of psychagogic adaptation in Paul's nurture of the proto-Christian communities and the practice of participatory psychagogy among its members, the practice of Epicureans of late Republican times presents itself as naturally analogous. Both Paul and Philodemus advocate, as do other moralists, the mixing of praise and blame in moral exhortation, and thus recognize the harsh as well as the more gentle dimensions of παρρησία. Both also emphasize that the bitter-sweet application of frank speech should be administered with good-will and sympathy for all, noble or wicked, with particular attention to the character of

---

breadth of knowledge of Hellenistic literature and modestly claims: "[ich] glaube aber namentlich die stoische Diatribe, insbesondere Teles, Musonius und Epiktet, auch Seneca so weit zu kennen, dass ich sie mit Nutzen zur Erklärung des Paulus heranziehen kann" (J. Weiss, *Der erste Korintherbrief*. MeyerK 5; 9th ed.; Göttingen, 1910, p. 1).

[13] A. J. Malherbe, *Social Aspects of Early Christianity* (Philadelphia, 1983), p. 117; idem, *Paul and the Popular Philosophers*, pp. 3–5; idem "Greco-Roman Religion and Philosophy and the New Testament," *The New Testament and its Modern Interpreters* (Atlanta, Georgia, 1989), pp. 15–17.

each recipient. Most important, however, both place exhortation in a communal context and stress mutual participation in correction and exhortation among members as a feature of the community. Member participation, trust, and openness, are thus intrinsic to the two communities. The social matrix of their common practice of communal, participatory psychagogy, suggests a close knit community integrated by an active member participation. This participatory psychagogy in moral exhortation, edification, and correction, is to be a mechanism of communal solidarity but has inherent elements which are bound to become sources of disunity and mental distraction.

The "religious" aspects of the Epicurean communities, their commemorative festivals and common meals, their submission to the authority of Epicurus, the "sole savior," the diversity and debate among later Epicureans concerning canonization and the attempt to establish the authoritative words of Epicurus, and, finally, the practice of epistolary psychagogy among Epicureans, together provide a great impetus toward a comparison with the proto-Christian communities.[14] There is also, I submit, a basic congruity between the Pauline communities and the Epicureans as it relates to the communal pattern of mutual participation by community members in exhortation, edification, and correction.[15] Paul's directives of communal exhortation and

---

[14] For some of these features among Epicureans, see D. Clay, "The Cults of Epicurus," *CErc* 16 (1986), pp. 11–28. I am not suggesting that all the above elements were somehow uniquely commensurable among early Christians and Epicureans. They were not. To take one example, as D. Sedley has demonstrated, the importance of founding figures as identity markers of philosophical allegiance was common in the Greek philosophical schools ("Philosophical allegiance in the Greco-Roman World," in M. Griffin and J. Barnes (eds.), *Philosophia Togata* (Oxford, 1989), pp. 97–119). N. W. de Witt's overzealous and uncritical comparison between Paul and Epicurus should deter us from seeing Epicurean traces everywhere in Paul (*St. Paul and Epicurus*. Minneapolis, 1954). Note H. Diels' comment on late Epicurean literature as "die Sprache der Schulbibel," and his comparison of it with Peripatetic and "ecclesiastical" literature: "Denn es ist ja bekannt, dass die späteren Epikureer, von deren Schrifttum wir einige Überreste haben, von Metrodor bis zu Demetrios Lakon und Philodem, ja bis zu Diogenes von Oinoanda hinab, alle die Sprache der Schulbibel in einer Weisse sich angeeignet haben, wie wir es nur in der peripatetischen und ekklesiastischen Literatur finden" (in "Ein epikureisches Fragment über Götterverehrung," *Kleine Schriften* (ed. W. Burkert; Darmstadt, 1969), p. 293.

[15] W. Meeks (*The First Urban Christians* (New Haven, 1983), pp. 83–84) rejects the Pythagorean and Epicurean communities as the best available model for the Pauline communities despite noticeable affinities: "they resemble the Pauline communities just to the extent that they take the form of modified households or voluntary associations...." And, "the fact is that none of the four models (scil. the household, the voluntary association, the synagogue, and the philosophic or rhetorical school)... captures the whole of the Pauline ἐκκλησία, although all offer significant analogies."

correction to the various communities he founded gain significance in light of Epicurean practice. Such a congruity might simply be fortuitous, but it does give us a rationale for comparing the hortatory and psychagogic practices of the two communities.

My purpose then is not to demonstrate either a pattern of influence and cultural borrowing or direct influence or reaction, but to highlight a widespread and shared communal practice among Epicureans and early Christians. Also, it is important not to forget that Epicureans and early Christians were often lumped together in the common consciousness of the early Empire. Perhaps one of the reasons for this, besides those traditionally given, is precisely because of known similarities in their communal practices.[16] The thesis of this book is thus closely tied in with the legitimacy of the comparison. The main interest here is the nurturing and growth of the respective communities, not their means and methods of attracting new members through recruitment efforts, but their means and methods of sustaining the community. My study thus attempts to gain an inside look at some operational factors in the communal dynamics of these two communities.[17] Although such a comparative study is to some

---

The psychagogic model, I contend, favors the model of the philosophical school. And, psychagogy is not ancillary, but constitutive, of both early Christian and Epicurean communities.

[16] The two groups were lumped together by outside observers from the second century of the common era onward. Lucian mentions Christians and Epicureans together as opponents of Alexander of Abonouteichos (*Alexander* 25, 38). Both groups were charged with atheism, separateness and secrecy, misanthropy, social irresponsibility, the disruption of families, sexual immorality and general moral depravity. See A. D. Simpson, "Epicureans, Christians, Atheists in the Second Century," *TAPA* 72 (1941), pp. 372–381; and J. J. Walsh, "On Christian Atheism," *VC* 45 (1991), pp. 255–77. The early Christian attitude towards the Epicureans was understandably polemical as they attempted to disassociate themselves from the Epicureans. See W. Schmid, "Epikur," *RAC* 5 (1962), cols. 780–803; R. Jungkuntz, "Epicureanism and the Church Fathers. Diss. Univ. of Wisconsin. Ann Arbor, Mich., 1961; idem, "Fathers, Heretics and Epicureans," *JEH* 17.1 (1966), pp. 3–10.

[17] My methodological presuppositions thus come down squarely among the so-called "verstehende social sciences" which emphasize that beliefs and practices, norms and values, roles and institutions are inherently meaningful, i.e., they stand in some relation to both (subjective) intentions and cultural traditions. The aim is to make human behavior intelligible, to illuminate its rationality in terms of cultural assumptions and subjective intentions. See Karl-Otto Apel, *Understanding and Explanation. A Transcendental-Pragmatic Perspective* (Cambridge, MA, 1984), p. vii, and T. J. Sergiovanni and R. J. Starratt, *Supervision. Human Perspectives* (New York, 1988 (4)), pp. 216–18. For some of the problems of such a comparative study and what justifiably constitutes a "parallel" to the New Testament writers, see A. J. Malherbe, "Hellenistic Moralists and the New Testament," *ANRW* 2.26.1 (Berlin/New York, 1992), pp. 273–78, 299–304, 324–25.

extent a *tour de force*, a growing awareness of the importance of the Greek and Roman moralists for the study of Paul and the nascent Christian groups requires that we start mapping out possible areas of congruence and non-congruence.

In both the Pauline and the Epicurean schools, psychagogy is non-dogmatic and preceptive, aimed at molding and consolidating the recipients for purposes of communal solidarity. Its function is only secondarily for legitimation purposes, i.e., to establish the authoritative status of the "spiritual guides" or to inculcate belief. These two subsidiary functions, though present, are secondary both chronologically and in importance. Trust and submissiveness to persons in authority who are capable of guiding one through life is indeed underlined.[18] The primary function, however, of a psychagogue in these communities is to distinguish neophytes from society at large, to attempt a certain formation of the self, to establish a certain in-group mentality and to highlight the awareness of the recipients in view of the total realignment implicit in their conversion. Participatory psychagogy has thus an important function among both Epicureans and early Christians as a means of unifying the internal life of the group and is probably one of the more important social factors in the longevity of both groups.[19] In this the psychagogic practices of the two communities are commensurable.

The diversity of members in both communities gives an added poignancy to the need for accommodation and communal unity. What unites the friends of the proto-Christian communities and the Epicureans, indeed, what constitutes their "likeness," is not virtue or character but a unity or likeness of purpose. In pursuit of their respective communal goals, participatory psychagogy as a social practice was

---

[18] E. Zeller labelled the Hellenistic age "eclectic," characterized by its decline of intellectual vigor and consisting of a compromise among the doctrines of the warring schools which now emphasized moral edification. In a collection of essays which reevaluates the concept of "eclecticism," its editors note that during this period one can observe "a growth of faith in authority, a seeking for 'ancient' sources (leading to the proliferation of pseudepigrapha)" (J. M. Dillon and A. A. Long (eds.), *The Question of 'Eclecticism'. Studies in Later Greek Philosophy* (Berkeley, 1988), p. 2).

[19] Although I venture to suggest that "participatory psychagogy" is one of the social factors in the longevity of both groups, I am not so presumptuous as to suggest that I have thereby discovered a universal law for the maintenance of community. Contrast M. Weinfeld, who (in his *The Organization Pattern and the Penal Code of the Qumran Sect. A Comparison with Guilds and Religious Associations of the Hellenistic-Roman Period* [Göttingen, 1986], p. 72) claims to have discovered "the universal character of sectarian organizational procedure."

important, not only as a solidarity mechanism but also as a defining characteristic of the community, a *sine qua non* of the fellowship. This communal practice is not ancillary but constitutive of both communities and establishes a form of community ethos which binds members together in their common purpose. Although there is evidence of communal edification and correction among the Pythagoreans,[20] the Essene community,[21] and partially in the school of Epictetus,[22] other factors exclude these three from comparison with the Epicureans and the Pauline communities.

The concern for the nurture of neophytes among Epicureans and Christians is a variation of the common practice of the "care of the young" or a reformatory ethic which in turn is an extension of the practice of the "cultivation of the self." As Michel Foucault notes, ἐπιμέλεια, the care or cultivation of self, constitutes, not an exercise in solitude but a social practice linked intrinsically to "soul service" and a system of reciprocal obligations:

---

[20] Although much in the organization of the Pythagorean school (C. J. de Vogel, *Pythagoras and Early Pythagoreanism* [Assen, 1966], pp. 150–159; W. Burkert, *Lore and Science in Ancient Pythagoreanism* [Cambridge, Mass., 1972], pp. 166–208) could be profitably compared to the Epicureans and early Christians, there is a basic difference between them and the Pythagoreans. According to Iamblichus (*Vit. Pyth.* 17.71–74) young *men* who were personally selected by Pythagoras were inducted after a three-year period of testing (these were the so-called ἀκουσματικοί or "auditors"), followed by a five-year novitiate of silence (these were known as the μαθηματικοί or "students"). The final level was that of the πολιτικοί (E. L. Minar, Jr., "Pythagorean Communism," *TAPA* 75 (1944), pp. 34–46). This contrasts sharply with the evidence in *On Frank Criticism* and the Pauline corpus where the give and take of the teacher-student relationship is apparent. There is no evidence of a testing period for candidates or strict admission procedure in either group.

[21] The Dead Sea community practiced mutual exhortation and correction and valued openness among members (1QS V 20–VI 1). There are four reasons why the Dead Sea community is not comparable to that of the Epicureans and Paul. Firstly, the admission of new members to the community followed clearly defined steps (1QS VI 13–23). Secondly, evaluation and correction was ongoing among the latter two, not periodic (1QS V 24). Thirdly, the community of the latter two was not a community of devout males mainly, as it was among the Essenes who had created an all-male utopia (P. Brown, *The Body and Society. Men, Women and Sexual Renunciation in Early Christianity* (New York, 1988), p. 39). Fourthly, the emphasis on the different ranks of members in view of their respective function was much more pronounced in the Dead Sea community than either among Epicureans or the Pauline communities (1QS V 23; VI 2b, 3b–4, 8–9a). See F. G. Martínez, *The Dead Sea Scrolls Translated. The Qumran Texts in English* (Leiden: E. J. Brill, 1994), pp. 9–11.

[22] Epictetus recognizes several categories of students (B. L. Hijmans, *ΆΣΚΗΣΙΣ: Notes on Epictetus' Educational System* (Assen, 1959), pp. 41–46), but does not accentuate reciprocal participation in corrective discipline. Instead, he individualizes and internalizes blame (cf. *Encheiridion* 5; *Discourses* 4.4.44; 4.8.1–9). R. F. Hock demonstrates that Epictetus was an isolated figure who did not exert much influence as a

It often took form within more or less institutionalized structures. The neo-Pythagorean communities are an example of this, or those Epicurean groups about whose practices we have some information by way of Philodemus: a recognized hierarchy gave the most advanced members the task of tutoring the others (either individually or in a more collective fashion). But there were also common exercises that allowed one, in the attention he gave to himself, to receive the help of others: this was the task defined as to δι' ἀλλήλων σώζεσθαι.[23]

Although, as we shall see, Foucault's description is somewhat misdirected, he has correctly gauged the significance of mutual assistance among the Epicureans. This social practice of *mutual* edification and exhortation as well as that of *mutual* correction is found among the Epicureans in Athens, Naples, and Herculaneum and the proto-Christian communities as among no other comparable group in antiquity. Paul is thus not promoting a new type of community education for adults, but rather conforms to a widespread pedagogical pattern already adopted in contemporary Epicurean schools.[24]

I shall present the evidence for this communal psychagogy among the Epicureans and the Pauline communities in chapters three through six. Before that, in chapters one and two, I shall discuss various aspects of the tradition of psychagogic nurture, of which the communal psychagogy of the two communities is a part, along with the related topics of versatility and beguilement.

---

Stoic teacher: "'By the Gods, it's My One desire to see an actual Stoic': Epictetus' Relations with Students and Visitors in his Personal Network," *Semeia* 56 (1991), pp. 121–42.

[23] M. Foucault, *The Care of the Self* (History of Sexuality, vol. 3; New York, 1988), pp. 51–52.

[24] My thesis agrees with E. A. Judge's recognition that Paul is a participant in adult education, but is at variance with his claim that Paul is promoting a "new kind of community education for adults." See "The Reaction against Classical Education in the New Testament," *JCE* 77 (1983), p. 12. In my emphasis on the social and historical context of Pauline psychagogy, I differ from K. Maly (*Mündige Gemeinde: Untersuchungen zur pastoralen Führung des Apostels Paulus im 1. Korintherbrief.* SBM 2; Stuttgart: Katholische Bibelwerk, 1967), who analyses 1 Cor 2–3, 8–10 and 12–14 both exegetically and offers a theological interpretation of "pastoral guidance" as reflected in these texts. My approach betrays rather a "realgeschichtlich-historisches" interest, congruent with the approach of U. Neymeyr in his *Die Christlichen Lehrer im zweiten Jahrhundert. Ihre Lehrtätigkeit, ihr Selbstverständnis und ihre Geschichte* (SupVC 4; Leiden: E. J. Brill, 1989), pp. 2–8. This book was not available to me until during the final revision of my manuscript. Neymeyr correctly recognizes the "unofficial" psychagogic responsibility of early Christian teachers. On this score, my book suggests a greater continuity between "ur-" and "frühchristlichen" teachers than A. F. Zimmermann would allow for (See *Die urchristlichen Lehrer. Studien zum Tradentenkreis der διδάσκαλοι im frühen Christentum.* WUNT 2, 12; Tubingen: J. C. B. Mohr (Paul Siebeck), 1984).

PART ONE

FLATTERERS AND FRIENDS:
ADAPTABILITY, VERSATILITY, AND PSYCHAGOGY

CHAPTER ONE

ADAPTABILITY, VERSATILITY, AND PSYCHAGOGY

Some have seen 1 Corinthians 9 as the rebuttal of a charge of inconstancy in light of Paul's opportunism. Paul is charged with not acting as a free man should, with behaving in a servile manner (9:15–18). In response, Paul picks up the ridicule and describes his apostleship in terms of servility. 1 Cor 9:22b ("I have become everything in turn to men of every sort") spotlights the charge of Paul as a servile and inconsistent flatterer.[1] Others have emphasized that chapter 9 does not function as a defence, since Paul is not defending his conduct but arguing from it. Chapter 9 shows how "Christians are to express their freedom for the benefit of others" by giving Paul's own conduct as an example; 9:19–23 then sets forth Paul's principles which are the basis of his rejection of support.[2] Regardless of whether 1 Cor 9 is a retrospective or prospective self-defence,[3] the similarities between Paul's description of his conduct and the practice of flatterers need to be addressed. Paul presents his affable and obsequious behavior, considered reprehensible by many, as an example to be emulated (11:1).

Paul's explicit statement that he has "become everything in turn to men of every sort" and "made himself a slave to all," and also his remark that he tries "to please all men in everything" (1 Cor 9:22b; 10:32–33) do indeed remind us of a common trait of both the flatterer and the obsequious person, suggesting that we must incorporate information also about the ingratiating person when explicating Paul's statements. Unlike many others, Paul has no qualms about presenting himself and his practice as that of the affable person who is willing and ready to adapt to, associate with, and please "all."[4]

---

[1] So argued by P. Marshall in *Enmity in Corinth: Social Conventions in Paul's Relations with the Corinthians* (WUNT 2.23; Tübingen, 1987).
[2] E.g. W. Willis, "An Apostolic Apologia? The Form and Function of 1 Corinthians 9," *JSNT* 24 (1985), pp. 33–48. Cf. pp. 38 and 40.
[3] See Margaret M. Mitchell, *Paul and the Rhetoric of Reconciliation: An Exegetical Investigation of the Language and Composition of 1 Corinthians* (HUT 28; Tübingen: Mohr-Siebeck, 1991), pp. 243–50, on problems with the retrospective view.
[4] Some disassociated themselves from charges of being ingratiating. Epicurus thus

Besides recognizing Paul's emphasis on adaptation, one could highlight the use of κερδαίνω in 1 Cor 9:19–22a with its connotations of "gaining something for oneself," and Paul's statement that he wants to secure his (future) participation in (the benefits of) the gospel (9:23b). This does nothing to lessen the impression of Paul as a sychophant, if observers are inclined to interpret Paul's behavior negatively.

The first occurrence of both παρρησία and κολακεία in early Christian literature shows how integrally connected flattery and frank speech were in Paul's mind.[5] In light of the fact that Paul uses this common contrast and since, in his earliest correspondence, he is at pains to disassociate himself from the practices of flatterers, Paul's remarks on his affable approach in 1 Corinthians become all the more intriguing.[6] Paul's statement does, however, look different when seen in light of the practice of psychagogy and the social context of patronage where issues of association with different character types come to the fore. From that perspective v. 22b, "I have become everything in turn to men of every sort," is not an invective utilized by the Corinthians in their charge against Paul as a protean flatterer due to his rejection of their gift and his acceptance of the Philippian gift, but an expression of Paul's own recruitment and psychagogic practice. This is clear from the larger context which underscores both the "preaching of the gospel" (9:12–18) and the solicitous concern for the weak (9:22a; 8:7–12). If the above statement is a kind of "quotation" from Paul's critics one would expect Paul to qualify the charge since this is his practice with other "slogans" referred to in the same letter.[7] Instead, Paul introduces the dictum as an expression of his own affable practice.

Paul's statements do emphasize adaptation and flexible behavior which does indeed resemble the practice of flatterers and obsequious

---

claimed not to have been ingratiating to the multitude (Fr. 187 Us.) and Bion said that it was impossible to please the crowd (Dio Chrysostom, *Discourse* 66.26). Diogenes of Sinope had compared ingratiating speech with "honey used to choke you" (Cf. Diogenes Laertius, *Lives of Eminent Philosophers* 6.51).

[5] See 1 Thess 2:2, 5, "... we had courage in our God (ἐπαρρησιασάμεθα ἐν τῷ θεῷ) to declare to you the gospel of God in spite of great opposition.... We never came with words of flattery..."

[6] Compare also Gal 1:10 with 1 Cor 10:33 and 9:19–23, where the importance of obeying and pleasing only God in contradistinction to that of pleasing humans is present. See P. Richardson, "Pauline Inconsistency: 1 Corinthians 9:19–23 and Galatians 2:11–14," *NTS* 26 (1980), pp. 347–62.

[7] On the Corinthian "slogans," see J. C. Hurd, *The Origin of 1 Corinthians* (New York, 1965), p. 68.

persons; however, I suggest that we view it as a positive enunciation of a versatile approach needed in recruitment and in psychagogy. Because of the blurred boundary between hypocrisy and truthful guidance, there is still a basic ambiguity inherent in Paul's reflections, an ambiguity which aligns a psychagogue in several ways with the flatterer and the obsequious person: is adaptation a form of cunning employed for personal gain or does it reflect a versatile approach used by one who is genuinely concered for the well-being of others? The cultural cues which help us elucidate one of the more important functions of 1 Cor 9:19-23 are to be found precisely in a context where the boundary between "flatterers" and "friends" is blurred, namely, in discussions of versatility and in the behavior of flatterers and friends with their many overlapping characteristics in the social matrix of patronage in the late Republic and the early Empire. Before discussing these cultural cues, I shall briefly introduce the concept of "psychagogy" which, being a form of guidance, also reflects the above ambiguity.

1.1 *The Concept of "Psychagogy"*

I use the term "psychagogy" descriptively to characterize a mature person's leading of others and thus feature the close connection of ψυχαγωγέω and moral exhortation[8] or the "manner of leading the soul through words."[9] The term "psychagogy" is not common in authors of late Republican times or of the early Empire and when it is used, it has a negative undercurrent and characterizes the practice of flatterers. Embedded in the meaning of the term "psychagogy" is a tension between "beguilement" and a more neutral "guidance." Below I introduce some of the recurring terms used to characterize the practice of a psychagoge and accentuate the ambiguous standing of the mature guide and the importance of adaptation, consistency, and openness.

---

[8] As does Clement of Alexandria who says that the benign pedagogue "bestows aid on us in different ways, now offering advice, now reproach" (πολυτρόπως... τὰ μὲν παρῄνεσεν, τὰ δὲ καὶ ὠνείδισεν). In this way, Clement explains, the divine pedagogue holds up to us the dishonor reaped by those who have sinned and reveals their deserved punishment, "both to guide our soul and to admonish us" (ψυχαγωγῶν τε ἅμα καὶ νουθετῶν; *Ped.* 43.2; GCS 261, 21-24 Stählin-Treu).
[9] To use Plato's description in the *Phaedrus* 261A, ψυχαγωγία τις διὰ λόγων. For psychagogy as the art of moving souls, see ibid., 260E-272B; 277BC.

An early meaning of ψυχαγωγεῖν is "to lead departed souls to the nether world." A second metaphorical meaning developed, namely, "to lead or attract the souls of the living, to persuade, or allure," and in a bad sense, "to lead away or delude." Elizabeth Asmis has shown the development in the meaning of the compound ψυχαγωγ- from an earlier meaning of "evoking" souls of the dead and "alluring" the living to that of "guidance of the soul" in Plato's *Phaedrus*. Plato's definition of rhetoric as ψυχαγωγία is a counterproposal to Isocrates' work *Against the Sophists*, already parodied in the *Gorgias* where Socrates claims that rhetoric is not an art but flattery. In the *Phaedrus*, Plato views genuine rhetoric as an art by which a speaker guides another to the truth by adjusting his words to the other's soul. Against Aristophanes' portrait of Socrates as a conjurer of souls, Plato sets a portrait of Socrates as a true rhetorician and a true psychagogue who guides souls to the truth by seeking it himself.[10] Embedded in these early reflections on the term "psychagogy" is a tension between beguilement and truthful guidance.[11]

This ambiguity is also apparent in the terms used to describe the conduct and speech of flatterers and friends. These equivocal terms include ποικίλος, πολύτροπος, πολυφωνός, πολύμορφος, πολυμήχανος, and παντοδαπός. Contrasting terms noting simplicity, such as ἁπλοῦς, also play a role in this ambiguity. Ποικίλος and πολύτροπος, for example, are used both positively or negatively, depending on whether the varied activity in question is valued as resourcefulness or as a manifestation of the duplicity of a trickster. Ποικίλος could thus cover such positive connotations as "resourceful," "versatile," "flexible," "ingenious," "changeable," "protean," and "adaptable," or the negative senses of "vacillating," "inconstant," "volatile," "fickle," "skittish,"

---

[10] E. Asmis, "*Psychagogia* in Plato's *Phaedrus*," *ICS* 11.1/2 (1986), pp. 153–172; cf. pp. 156–57 and 169–70. Aristophanes combines the above noted two senses of ψυχαγωγέω in his portrait of Socrates in the *Birds* (1555) as a conjurer of souls. See Plato, *Gorgias* 463A.

[11] Isocrates notes that those who want to guide the souls of their hearers must abstain from admonition and advice, and must say the kind of things which are most pleasing to the crowd (*To Nicocles* 49). Philodemus takes issue with the view that the clarity of poems is irrelevant for ψυχαγωγία (cf. Polystratus, *On Irrational Contempt* PHerc. 336/1150 col. 18.2–4 Indelli). See D. M. Schenkeveld, "Hoi Kritikoi in Philodemus," *Mnemosyne* 21 (1968), pp. 176–215. Epictetus uses the term for the principles of philosophy leading the soul without the aid of a teacher (*Discourse* 3.21.23), and *Herm. Vis.* 3.6.6, speaks of "their wealth, which leads their souls astray" (αὐτῶν ὁ πλοῦτος ὁ ψυχαγωγῶν αὐτούς). See also Maximus of Tyre, *Discourse* 1.2 (3.1–2 Hobein, ἡ ἐκ μελῶν ψυχαγωγία).

"capricious," "whimsical," "irresolute," "deceitful," "cunning," and "wily."[12] These terms highlight two character types: the *homo duplex* like Odysseus and the flatterer and the *homo simplex* like Achilles and the truthful counselor.

In *The Ulysses Theme*, W. B. Stanford traces the fate of the "man of many turns," Homer's most versatile hero, and demonstrates that the basic ambiguity of Odysseus became the axis around which the Ulysses character vacillated.[13] Odysseus was either criticized for changing his character or hailed for his chameleon-like adaptability in social intercourse. The linguistic ambiguity seen in the above terms receives a sharp focus in the character of Odysseus, already present in the first line of the Odyssey, "Tell me, Muse, of the polytropic man." Etymologically πολύτροπος suggests "of many turns," but the ambiguity still remains.[14] Stanford shows that Odysseus' detractors in the late fifth century BCE interpreted the term pejoratively in the ethical sense of often changing one's character, hence unprincipled and unscrupulous, and how Antisthenes rallied to Odysseus' defence interpreting πολύτροπος as denoting Odysseus' skill in adapting his figures of speech ("tropes") to his hearers at any particular time.[15] On the whole, the scholiasts incline to an ethical interpretation of πολύτροπος in *Odyssey* 1.1, contrasting Odysseus with the ἁπλοῦς type. Achilles is the *homo simplex* type who speaks candidly, opposed to the *homo duplex*, the deceitful Odysseus, who hides his true motives.[16] This

---

[12] See Diogenes Laertius, *Lives of Eminent Philosophers* 4.47, "In truth Bion [of Borysthenes] was in other respects a shifty character, a subtle sophist (πολύτροπος καὶ σοφιστὴς ποικίλος). . . ."

[13] See W. B. Stanford, *The Ulysses Theme. A Study in the Adaptability of a Traditional Hero* (2nd ed. New York, 1968), pp. 7, 17, 26–27 (n. 28), 118–19.

[14] For the two most likely meanings of πολύτροπος (LSJ s.v.), i.e. "much-travelled" or "versatile," see T. Kakridis, "Die Bedeutung von πολύτροπος in der Odyssee," *Glotta* 11 (1921), pp. 288–91, who argues for the former as the most likely for Homer's time. Cf. P. Linde, "Homerische Selbsterläuterungen," *Glotta* 13 (1924), pp. 223–24. LSJ s.v. ποικιλο-/πολυμήτης, ποικιλόφρων.

[15] Antisthenes' views on Odysseus are known from two sophistic speeches on the contest between Ajax and Odysseus. See Stanford, *The Ulysses Theme*, pp. 96–100; R. Hoïstad, *Cynic hero and Cynic king. Studies in the Cynic Conception of Man* (Uppsala, 1948), pp. 25, 94–102; and A. J. Malherbe, *Paul and the Popular Philosophers* (Minneapolis, 1989), pp. 98–101.

[16] Eustathius (12 cent. C. E.) takes πολύτροπος as indicating one who is ποικιλόφρων, comparing it to the adaptability of the chameleon (which is the first use of this analogy in connection with the Ulysses tradition). See Stanford, *The Ulysses Theme*, pp. 18, 249 n. 22; 260–61 n. 28.

contrast is found in Plato's *Lesser Hippias* which discusses the relative merits of Achilles and Odysseus.[17]

Xenophon's *Memorabilia* also discusses deception and uses ἁπλοῦς to describe one's conduct towards a friend.[18] Deceit is an "injustice," but inasmuch as an enemy can be justly deceived in war, justice and injustice hinge on the relationship one has with the person acted upon. Odysseus lies to his enemies but his lies are not to secure his own advantage but that of the Greeks, his comrades and family. He is thus "a great bane to the foe, but a joy to friends," a maxim which, together with "do not deceive your friend," had a long life in Greek thought.[19] Duplicity and frankness recur in later discussions of the flatterer. Ποικίλος is used to describe the flatterer and the friend of many, manipulating the negative connotations of the word with its implications of a conniving character; the flatterer's "language of deception" and the "deceitful and variegated pleasantries" of charmers distort reality by not recognizing the faults of others. But the character of a friend, like the "language of truth," is, as Euripides put it, "simple" (ἁπλοῦς), plain, and unaffected. A friend both commends and reprimands his erring friends, mixing harsh and gentle means of exhortation in the correction of faults.[20] This "variegated" (ποικίλος) method of moral exhortation is not like the "simple method" (τεχνὴ ἁπλῆ) of praise used by the subtle, cunning, and "variable" (ποικίλος) flatterer, but is like the manifold aid administered by physicians.[21]

Significantly, the above terms are used both of conduct and speech. Ἁπλοῦς, in the meaning of *frank* or *open*, is used of words, thoughts, or acts. Πολυμήχανος, *resourceful*, is in later prose applied to words. Ποικίλος, used in the sense of *subtle* or *wily*, is also found in the meaning of "speaking in a double sense." Similarly, παντοδαπός, *of every kind, manifold*, is used in the phrase παντοδαπὸς γίγνεται, *assumes*

---

[17] See Plato, *Lesser Hippias* 364BCE; 365B. Cf. *Theaetetus* 146D.

[18] Xenophon, *Memorabilia* 4.2.14–16. Cf. Aristotle, *Rhetoric* 1416b25, and LSJ s.v. ἁπλοῦς.

[19] Homer, *Odyssey* 6.184; Hesiod, *Works and Days* 353; Sappho, 25.6; Solon, 1.5; Euripides, *Medea* 809–10; Plato, *Gorgias* 492C; *Republic* 362B. See B. Snell, *The Discovery of the Mind in Greek Philosophy and Literature* (New York, 1982), pp. 165–67 and Stanford, *The Ulysses Theme*, pp. 19–22.

[20] Plutarch, *How to Tell a Flatterer from a Friend* 62C. See also ibid., 51C, 59B, 49B, and 56B–D; Diogenes Laertius, *Lives of Eminent Philosophers* 6.72; Seneca, *Epistle* 45.7; Stobaeus, *Anthology* 2.35. See O. Ribbeck, *Kolax. Eine Ethologische Studie* (Leipzig, 1883), pp. 46–48.

[21] Philodemus, *On Frank Criticism* frs. 68.1; 86.6–7; 60.11; Plutarch, *How to Tell a Flatterer from a Friend* 52A–C.

*every shape*, and also of style or poems. And finally, Antisthenes expanded the meaning of πολύτροπος to refer to figures of speech. The tension between beguilement and sincere guidance is, therefore, evident both in behavior and speech.[22]

This ambiguity can be seen in two recurring prerequisites for being a psychagogue, namely, self-scrutiny and consistency of word and deed. This idealized picture of appropriate conduct reveals the holistic view of the psychagogue's self-presentation; speech (λόγος) is an integral part of conduct (σχῆμα). Moralists of the early Empire emphasize the character of the moral director and his knowledge of the recipients as necessary for successful guidance. Epictetus notes that what is needed for the care of the young is both wisdom and a "certain readiness and special fitness for this task, by Zeus, and a particular physique, and above all the counsel of God advising him to occupy this office." The "doctor's office" or "hospital" is the "lecture room of the philosopher."[23] In the use of the medical analogy, Epictetus follows his teacher, Musonius Rufus, who compared the philosopher to the physician. It is necessary to learn to diagnose the condition of one's patients and when and how to apply one's "drugs."[24] Thus a psychagogue must learn before practicing his trade. Also, an antecedent soul-search is essential; the surest means of success is thus a willingness to rectify one's own shortcomings before correcting others.

The proverb "physician, heal yourself" was used from the time of Aeschylus onward to point to the incongruity of a sick doctor who has at his disposal the wherewithal to relieve the suffering of others but not his own. In a moral context, the proverb serves to rebuff someone who has given a moral directive he has not applied to himself, to question another's right to give advice, and to turn a criticism back on its giver.[25] These uses echo the common requirements

---

[22] For information in this paragraph, see LSJ s.v. See Dio Chrysostom, *Discourse* 71.2, on Hippias of Elis composing speeches of divers kinds (λόγοι ποικίλοι) and producing poems of every style (ποιήματα παντοδαπά). Cf. Aelius Aristides, *Oration* 41 (4).2, π. περὶ τοὺς λόγους.

[23] Epictetus, *Discourses* 3.21.17–20 (ἰατρεῖον) and 3.23.27 (τὸ τοῦ φιλοσόφου σχολεῖον).

[24] Musonius Rufus, Fr. 36; Epictetus, *Discourses* 3.23.30–32; 3.21.8–9. Effecting a cure is not a matter of employing or not employing surgery or drugs but of doing so in a certain manner; one must know how and to whom and when to apply them (Aristotle, *Nicomachean Ethics* 1137a14–25).

[25] This proverb has both classical and Rabbinic parallels. See J. Nolland, "Classical and Rabbinic Parallels to 'Physician, heal yourself' (Lk IV 23)" *NovT* 21.3 (1979), pp. 193–209; *Prometheus bound* 469–77; Homer, *Iliad* 11.833–35; Cicero, *Letters to His Friends* 4.5.5; Dio Chrysostom, *Discourse* 49.13–14; Plutarch, *How to Tell a*

of antecedent soul-search and consistency between words and deeds.[26] Maximus of Tyre wrote discourses on both topics, and they are succinctly stated by Musonius when describing different types of pupils; the philosopher should utter words which are most helpful and act consistently with them. This correspondence between speech and conduct was regarded as an "index to [the philosopher's] trustworthiness."[27]

The psychagogue must be honest like the *homo simplex* character type, but adapt in word and deed like the *homo duplex* type in order to be the most effective. These contradictory expectations can be seen in Dio's discourses *On Philosophy* (*Discourse* 70) and *On the Philosopher* (*Discourse* 71). The former discusses the appropriate function of philosophy and the importance of being a philosopher in word and deed in order to distinguish a sham philosopher from a true one. Emphasis falls on consistency in words and deeds, and the absence of deceit and pretence. But the latter discourse eulogizes the versatility and adaptability of Hippias of Elis and Odysseus, and claims that the philosopher should be able to excel all men, including Hippias and Odysseus. The contrast between the *homo duplex* and *homo simplex* character types and the association of consistency in word and deed with the *homo simplex* type is also clear in Philo. No one is wise except when bringing speech, mind, and action into harmony.[28]

This harmonization of speech and behavior, the requirement of consistency in word and deed, and the tendency to view each as a constituent part of the psychagogue's self-presentation, reveal a proclivity to view "behavior" holistically. "Words" and "deeds" are closely intertwined instantiations of the psychagogue's self-presentation. Thus,

---

*Flatterer from a Friend* 71F; 72A; *How to Profit by One's Enemies* 88D; *On Brotherly Love* (481A) connects the proverb to the theme of incongruity of words and deeds.

[26] For the latter see A. J. Festugière, "Lieux communs littèraires et thèmes de folk-lore dans l'Hagiographie primitive," *Wiener Studien* 73 (1960), pp. 140–142. Cf. also R. Helm, *Lucian und Menipp* (Leipzig/Berlin, 1967), pp. 40–41. See Dio Chrysostom, *Discourse* 70.6; 77/78.39; Seneca, *Epistle* 108.35–57; 6.5–6; Lucian, *Demonax* 3; *Peregrinus* 19; Julian, *Oration* 7.214BC.

[27] Malherbe, *Paul and the Popular Philosophers*, pp. 57–58. See Musonius Rufus, *Fragment* 1 (5, 6–11 Hense = 36, 1.1–5 Lutz); Maximus of Tyre, *Discourse* 1, *That the Philosopher's Discourse Is Adapted to Every Subject* and *Discourse* 25, *That Those Discourses are Best Which Correspond to Deeds*.

[28] Dio Chrysostom, *Discourse* 70.7; 71.6; Plato, *Lesser Hippias* 368B–D; Philo, *Every Good Man is Free* 95–6, 99, 126, 155; *On Joseph* 230; *On the Contemplative Life* 31; *The Worse Attacks the Better* 69–78; *Allegorical Interpretation* 1.74–78; *On the Migration of Abraham* 85, 171; *Who is the Heir* 302.

when Dio eulogizes Odysseus' versatility in *Discourse* 71, what receives attention is both intellectual and manual pursuits. This focus on conduct and speech is clear in Maximus of Tyre's *Discourse* 1, *That the Philosopher's Discourse Is Adapted to Every Subject* which, although purportedly dealing with adaptability in speech, also gives examples of Odysseus' adaptability in conduct.[29] Even Dio Chrysostom's *Discourse* 72, *On Personal Appearance*, although purportedly dealing with the σχῆμα of the philosopher, sailor, farmer, and shepherd, emphasizes that the philosopher's function lies in his λόγος to admonish. The philosopher's garb, conduct, and word, are interchangeable variations of his self-presentation, all valid means of evaluating the philosopher.[30] It is when the relative importance of any one of these is contested that disagreements ensue as, for example, in Paul's dealings with the Corinthians.

1.2 *The Flatterer (κόλαξ), and the Obsequious Person (ἄρεσκος)*

Paul's expressed willingness to accommodate himself to others accentuates his chameleon-like qualities. Since Paul's remarks remind us of the practice of the all obliging flatterer, I note some of the flatterers' common features and the related type of the ingratiating person, both because his traits are close to the flatterer and because some of Paul's remarks remind us of him. The overview below should not be seen as an attempt to condense varied traditions into a single type with common characteristics; it is, however, possible to abstract some central and recurring features of the flatterer and the ingratiating person. My interest in culling this information is to draw attention to common characteristics of these character types and to be able to situate Paul's remarks and behavior within this tradition. The following characteristics can be abstracted as recurring features in discussions of the flatterer in Greco-Roman antiquity. The flatterer has only his personal advantage in view. In an attempt to secure his advantage he consents to everything, praises indiscriminately, speaks in order to please, and is charming, affable, and witty. In rendering his services he accommodates himself to those he flatters, and he,

---

[29] Maximus of Tyre, *Discourse* 1 (2, 10–3, 13 Hobein).
[30] Despite the title of the discourse (Περὶ τοῦ σχήματος), Dio uses the terms σχῆμα and στολή interchangeably. Cf. *Discourse* 72.1, 2, 9, and 10.

like the friend of many and the polyp, is cunning in his affable, versatile, and all-adaptable approach. As such the flatterer's behavior was seen as "soft" and servile.

Artotrogus, the parasite of Pyrgopolynices in Plautus' *The Bragging Soldier* and Gnatho, the parasite of Captain Thraso in Terence's *The Eunuch*, capture most of the traits flatterers were accused of displaying. Artotrogus is dishonest, blows things out of proportion, and assents to everything in order to gain personal sustenance; he is servile and affable in his serious attention to his master's need. The same is true of Gnatho, although his position is somewhat more exalted since he acts as Thraso's "advocate." Gnatho is quite candid that the only reason he accepts such a role is out of self-interest, namely, to secure a permanent position in Thraso's household. Otherwise, Gnatho appears as the flattering, all-assenting, all-pleasing, and dishonest person who, despite his personal views, attempts to reinforce Thraso's (false) views of himself. Whatever the master says, to that he assents. In this he is like the flatterer of Eupolis' play who praises everything his master happens to say and claims his master is whatever he wishes to be—an orator, a poet, a painter, a fluteplayer, a swift runner and athlete. In this way rich men select as parasites, "not the finest men, but those best able to play the flatterer and praise them in everything."[31] But Gnatho has no qualms about such a "vocation":

> There is a class of men who set up for being the head in everything and aren't. It's them I track ... I smile on them and stand agape at their intellects. Whatever they say I praise; if again they say the opposite, I praise that too. If one says no, I say no; if one says yes, I say yes. In fact I have given orders to myself to agree with them in everything. That's the trade that pays far the best nowadays.[32]

In addition to all-assenting behavior and indiscriminate praise, personal advantage is the flatterer's most commonly noted feature. Theophrastus emphasizes this in his definition of flattery, agreeing with his teacher, although Aristotle, and later Plutarch, can also speak as if the flatterer only aimed at giving pleasure. When the emphasis is on the profit motive the flatterer is like a parasite who, in Athenaeus' *Sophists at Dinner*, both try to secure a position as dinner partners at

---

[31] This is Athenaeus' charge in his *Sophists at Dinner* 239E. See Plautus, *The Bragging Soldier* 11–12, 20–22, 24–25, 33–37, 70, and Terence, *The Eunuch* 1–3, 254; 391–453, 771–817, 1053–93.

[32] Ibid., 247–49. See Eupolis, *The Flatterers* fr. 159, 9; Plutarch, *How to Tell a Flatterer from a Friend* 58E.

a patron's house. For Aristotle, flatterers and obsequious persons both seek to please people, but the flatterer aims at profit whereas the obsequious person strives to give pleasure.[33] Similarly, Theophrastus defines obsequiousness as "a sort of behavior which provides pleasure, but not with the best of intentions."[34] Philodemus also contrasts obsequiousness and flattery depending on whether personal advantage is in view or not. When dealing with vices akin to flattery, Philodemus concentrates on obsequiousness, thereby yielding evidence concerning the tradition that combined the definitions of the ἄρεσκος and the κόλαξ.[35] The definition of the flatterer as "someone who speaks in order to please" (ὁ πρὸς χάριν λέγων) and does not wish to cause pain but tries to be charming, aligns him closely with the obsequious person. Euripides knows of this definition, as do Nicolaus, Philo, Plutarch, Alciphron, Maximus of Tyre, and Philodemus.[36]

In Plato's view, the art of flattery is a shameful thing which aims at pleasure and is devoid of the good. The pleasant distracts from the good and beneficial, and the painful leads to the good and beneficial. Such views presuppose that the pleasant is not always good;

---

[33] Theophrastus, *Character* 2.1; *Epitome Monacensis descripta a Dielsio* 26, 1–2, 11–12 (in Ribbeck, *Kolax*, pp. 112–113, 17; Theophrastus separated flatterers and obsequious persons both in *On Flattery* and in the *Characters*); Aristotle, *Nicomachean Ethics* 1173b31; 1108a26; 1126b12–15; 1127a7–9; *Eudemian Ethics* 1233b30; Plutarch, *How to Tell a Flatterer from a Friend* 49C; 51B. Athenaeus follows an older meaning of παρασίτος, namely, "one who feeds with": *Sophists at Dinner* 237A; 236D; 248D; Plato, *Laches* 179C; Maximus of Tyre, *Discourse* 14.6 (177, 4–6 Hobein).

[34] *Characters* 5.1. The ἄρεσκος wants to please all: "When he is called to help settle a dispute, his desire is to please the opposite party as well as the friend he stands for, so that he may be thought impartial. He will tell strangers, too, that they are right and his fellow-countrymen wrong" (5.3).

[35] Obsequious persons desire to be liked by all, preferably eminent persons, and are "bound to many people from whom they get no benefit" (PHerc. 1457 col. 5.19–21). See T. Gargiulo, "PHerc. 222: Filodemo sull' Adulazione," *CErc* 11 (1981), p. 124. Athenaeus disagrees with the tradition which combined the definition of flatterers and obsequious persons: "This 'flattery' certain persons, by a perverse use of the term, call 'willingness to oblige'" [*Sophists at Dinner* 255A; Anaxandrides, *The Lady from Samos*, "For this business of flattering now goes by the name of being obliging;" Kock ii. 155]. E. Kondo, "Per l'interpretazione del Pensiero Filodemeo sulla Adulazione nel PHerc. 1457," *CErc* 4 (1974), p. 51; F. Longo Auricchio, "Sulla Concezione Filodemea dell' Adulazione," *CErc* 16 (1986), p. 82; O. Ribbeck, *Kolax*, pp. 17, 110; idem, "Ἀλαζών, Ein Beitrag zur antiken Ethologie," (Leipzig: Teubner, 1882), pp. 55–75.

[36] Athenaeus, *Sophists at Dinner* 238B; Eupolis, fr. 159, 12; Euripides, frs. 362, 364 N (2); Nicolaus, IV 570 M. V. 36; Alciphron, III 44, 2 (Ribbeck, *Kolax*, pp. 38, 43 n. 3); Plutarch, *How to Tell a Flatterer from a Friend* 55A; 55D; Maximus of Tyre, *Discourse* 14.1 (170, 8–172, 9; 173, 2–8 Hobein); Philo, *On Noah's Work as a Planter* 104–06; Philodemus, PHerc. 1457 cols. 1.5–7; 4.7–9.

pain sometimes is. The art of flattery as the paid art of making things pleasant is like tragic poetry which is bent upon the gratification of the spectators.[37] Flattery is like the culinary arts and sophistic rhetoric; it distorts reality, not being able to distinguish between real and apparent good. Similarly, for Aristotle a flatterer distorts reality; he has "the appearance of an admirer and the appearance of a friend."[38] The contrast between the good and beneficial though occasionally unpleasant, and the pleasant and unbeneficial was subsequently commonly exploited and became one of the more important criteria in later attempts to distinguish flatterers and friends.

The social practice of different character types as described in Aristotle's discussion on flattery and obsequiousness is pertinent. Aristotle views flattery and enmity as excesses of which friendship is the mean, and obsequiousness and self-sufficiency as excesses of which dignity is the mean. Aristotle classifies the virtues of character concerned with feelings, external good, and social life, all of which are anchored in his view of the mean. The virtues of social life concern association with others in truth-telling or as a source of pleasure. Both the flatterer and the obsequious person are sources of pleasure in daily life as is the mean which is most like friendship. A person can be friendly in the right way but if he goes to an excess with no further aim, he is ingratiating, and if he does it for his own advantage, he is a flatterer. The deficient person is quarrelsome and does not care in the least about causing pain but ingratiating persons praise everything to please us and think they must cause no pain.[39]

In a response to the question, "Will the just man assimilate himself to the character of those with whom he converses?" Aristotle says,[40] "Surely not. We should deem such conduct that of a flatterer or one who is weakly complaisant." The dignified one neither consorts with all, nor yet with no one, but only with the worthy; he "cannot let anyone else, except a friend, determine his life."[41] But

---

[37] Plato, *Sophist* 222D–223A; *Phaedurs* 240B; *Gorgias* 461B–466A; 500E–501D; 502B–503A; 521D. On τέχνη παρασιτική see Hegesippus fr. 1; 2 (III, 312 K); Sosipater fr. 1 (III, 314 K); Lucian, *The Parasite* 2, 4, 15, 19, 20, 23, and 30; Euripides, fr. 362 N (2).

[38] Aristotle, *Great Ethics* 1208b22; *Rhetoric* 1371a22; *Nicomachean Ethics* 1173b33–1174a2.

[39] Aristotle, *Nicomachean Ethics* 1107a28–1108b10; 1115a25–1128b36; *Eudemian Ethics* 1220b21–1221b27; 1233b30–39; *Great Ethics* 1192b30–39; 1193a20–28.

[40] Ibid., 1100a14–18. Cf. Horace, *Epistle* 1.18.1–16.

[41] Aristotle, *Nicomachean Ethics* 1125a1–3.

the obsequious person consorts with all in every way and under every circumstance and the stubborn person who thinks he is superior to all avoids all intercourse and pays no regard at all to other people. Because of his contemptuous attitude, the self-willed person was seen as harsh, in contrast to the gentle nature of the obsequious person. Flatterers and obsequious persons are inferior to everybody because assent, praise, and speaking in order to please, all display a certain admiration for the one flattered, implying a relationship of inferiority-superiority. In his "voluntary enslavement" the flatterer is willing to associate indiscriminately with anyone.[42] Flattery renders base the characters of flatterers because they will submit to anything, no matter how degrading.

Animal analogies accentuating change sharpen the critique; here the polyp, the chameleon, and the sea-god Proteus, proved helpful analogies.[43] Theognis' advice to Cyrnus was often noted:[44]

> Have the temperament of a complex octopus, who | looks like whatever rock he has clung to. | Now be like this; then, at another time, become someone else in your coloring. | I tell you: resourcefulness is better than not being versatile.

Plutarch also compares the flatterer's changes to the polyp. The term ποικίλος which refers to color and markings when applied to an animal's skin is used to describe the "subtle" and "cunning" flatterer. Athenaeus also records the polyp's ability to change colors, taking on the same hues as the places in which it hides, quoting both Theognis' advice to Cyrnus and Amphiaraus' analogous advice to his son Amphilochus ("With the cunning of the polyp, my son, mighty Amphilochus, adapt thyself to the people into whatsoever country you come"). The flatterer's cunning and versatile approach

---

[42] Ribbeck aptly characterizes the practice of flatterers as a "freiwilligen Knechtschaft" (*Kolax*, 31–2, 38; Clearchus, *Gergithios* fr. 19–20 Wehrli). See Aristotle, *Eudemian Ethics* 1249a27; 1233b34–39; 1239a27, "To be admired implies superiority"; *Great Ethics* 1199a14–18; 1192b30–36.

[43] Philodemus, PHerc. 1573 fr. 12; *Rhetoric* v. 2, 74–75 Sudhaus; Plutarch, *How to Tell a Flatterer from a Friend* 53D; 52F; *On Having Many Friends* 96F–97A; Athenaeus, *Sophists at Dinner* 255C; 258AB; 316A–318F. The flatterer was also likened to worms, a tick, a gadfly, a woodworm, a vulture, a raven, flies, and a puppy or an ape (Longo Auricchio, "Sulla Concezione Filodemea dell' Adulazione," p. 88).

[44] *Elegy* 215–218. Transl. by G. Nagy, "Theognis and Megara: A Poet's Vision of His City," in T. J. Figueira and G. Nagy (eds.), *Theognis of Megara* (Baltimore, 1905), pp. 75–6.

is graphically depicted by reference to his continual changing of coats when he goes to the market.[45]

The flatterer's all-assenting behavior, his speaking in order to please, his indiscriminate praise as well as servility, are all variations of adaptability. The all-changeable flatterer had learned in the art of flattery to "play the second part in word and in deed." This proverbial phrase referred to a mime-player acting a second part, imitating the chief actor in word and gesture (τὰ δευτέρα λέγειν καὶ πράττειν).[46] The flatterer imitates and adapts both in word and deed; he

> obsequiously imitates the posture of those whom he flatters, now crossing his arms, now wrapping himself closely in his ragged cloak. Whence some call him 'arm-crosser,' others, 'posture-magazine.' In fact, the flatterer, in one and the same person, is the very image of Proteus. At any rate, he assumes every kind of shape and of speech as well, so varied are his tones.[47]

What changes in adaptation? The flatterer adapts both in speech and in behavior. He adapts in speech when imitating the "language of friendship."[48] Friends and flatterers differ in figure and voice; both can change.[49] Different Greek terms are used to emphasize change in behavior, namely, τὸ σχῆμα, τὸ ἦθος, ἡ μορφή and πλάσμα.[50] The saying, "a man is by nature an animal readily subject to change," reveals the possibility of improvement and explains one reason for God's delay in punishing humans, namely, to allow those who can be cured a certain period to recover. This is also supported by a reference to changes in the "characters and lives of men" and by an etymology of ἦθος.[51]

---

[45] Plutarch, *How to Tell a Flatterer from a Friend* 52AF; *Alcibiades* 23.4; *On Having Many Friends* 97A; Clearchus, *On Proverbs* = FHG ii.318; Athenaeus, *Sophists at Dinner* 316A–318F; 236EF. Amphiaraus' advice to his son Amphilochus is preserved in a fragment of Pindar (Fr. 43, Snell). Similar advice is found in two verses of the lost "Iphigenia" of Sophocles (Fr. 286 Nauck (2)).

[46] Ribbeck, *Kolax*, p. 49. Cf. Horace, *Epistle* 1.18.14; 1.17.19; Ovid, *The Art of Love* 1.146–162.

[47] Athenaeus, *Sophists at Dinner* 258A = Clearchus, fr. 20 Wehrli (FHG ii.312).

[48] Plutarch, *How to Tell a Flatterer from a Friend* 50F–51D; 51F. See *Precepts of Statecraft* 800A.

[49] Maximus of Tyre, *Discourse* 14.1 (171, 9–10 Hobein). See Philodemus, PHerc. 1089, col. 7.17 (E. A. Méndez, "PHerc. 1089: Filodemo 'Sobre la Adulación'," *CErc* 11 [1981], p. 137).

[50] For change in σχῆμα and μορφή see fns. 48 and 50. For change in ἦθος see Plutarch, *Whether the Affections of the Soul are Worse than Those of the Body* 500CD; *The Dinner of the Seven Wise Men* 155B. For changes in πλάσμα see *Alcibiades* 23.5.

[51] Plutarch, *On the Control of Anger* 463D; *On Tranquility of Mind* 474E; 533B–C; *On*

The difference between flatterers and friends is especially seen in their ἦθος; the examples given are changes in garment, conduct, customs, language and life. Plutarch approvingly notes the flatterers Epaminondas and Agesilaus who "had to do with a very large number of men and cities and modes of life, yet maintained everywhere their own proper character in dress, conduct, language, and life."[52] The friendship of a freeborn is that of "like manners," but a flatterer associates with persons of different manners; he can associate with all and imitates even the base in all things. With one he joins in dancing and singing, with another in wrestling or hunting, with still another in scholarly pursuits, or he joins in drinking with an easy-tempered drinker and a rich man. Similarly, the friend of many can often change himself instantaneously

> from one character to another, reading books with the scholarly, rolling in the dust with wrestlers, following the hunt with sportsmen, getting drunk with topers, and taking part in the canvass of politicians. . . .[53]

The friend of many suddenly shows a liking for conduct and language which used to offend him. He, like the flatterer, thus assumes different σχήματα as he adapts himself to the pursuits and lives of others. Plutarch values a consistency of character, which is sacrificed by the association with many since this entails participation in different practices; such participation requires a change in σχῆμα which bars the development of a healthy and stable ἦθος. Alcibiades displayed many inconsistencies and marked changes in his character, including frivolous jesting, keeping a racing-stable, leading a life full of urbanity and agreeable enjoyment (all in Athens), keeping his hair cropped close, wearing the coarsest clothing, bathing in cold water (in Lacedaemon), fighting and drinking (in Thrace), as well as soft living, luxury, and pretentiousness (in Tissaphernes). By making himself like other people, he tried to conciliate them and win their favor. In Sparta, he bewitched "the multitude" (οἱ πολλοί) by his

---

the *Delays of the Divine Vengeance* 551EF; *On Moral Virtue* 443C; Ps.-Plutarch, *On the Education of Children* 3A; Plato, *Epistle* 13.360D; Aristotle, *Nicomachean Ethics* 1103a17–18. Cf. C. Gill, "The Question of Character-Development: Plutarch and Tacitus," *CQ* 33 (1983), pp. 469–87.

[52] Plutarch, *How to Tell a Flatterer from a Friend*, 52FAB; 51D. In his *Comparison of Alcibiades and Coriolanus* 4.5, Plutarch says of Epaminondas that he had no tendency to "importune or court the favor of the multitude. . . ."

[53] Idem, *On Having Many Friends* 97A. See also *How to Tell a Flatterer From a Friend* 53A–B.

assumption of the Spartan mode of life. Alcibiades could persuade both the multitude and each individual, and he could adapt to the lives of others, assuming more violent changes than the chameleon. He could associate with good and bad alike, and there was nothing he could not imitate and practice.[54] Despite this elasticity,

> it was not that he could so easily pass entirely from one manner of life to another, nor that he actually underwent in every case a change in his character; but when he saw that his natural manners were likely to be annoying to those he happened to meet, he was quick to assume any counterfeit exterior which might in each case be suitable for them.[55]

Alcibiades' adaptation is comparable to that of the chameleon, the cuttlefish, the sea-god Proteus, the flatterer, and the friend of many, because it does not cut deep enough. Alcibiades' change is not in ἦθος or τρόπος, but σχῆμα and πλάσμα.[56]

I have spotlighted features of the flatterer that emphasize his concern with personal advantage, his adaptable and affable approach. The negative undercurrent of this material should not, however, detract from the fact that flatterers and parasites had a valued social function as advisors in ancient Greece. Parasites also had a more honorable role as temple officials whose services to the gods were recompensed by free meals. Later, particularly from the mid-fourth century, a "parasite" is a person who makes himself agreeable at dinner parties in return for a free meal. In this way both flatterers and parasites attached themselves, often as valuable "servants," to the entourage of rich and powerful patrons in order to secure personal sustenance.[57]

### 1.2.1 *Adaptability and servility to the great*

The issues of adaptability and servility to the great, connected with questions of the personal independence of a client, were debated during

---

[54] Idem, *Alcibiades* 2.1; 26.5; 23.4; *Comparison of Alcibiades and Coriolanus* 1.4; 3.2 and 4.5. *How to Tell a Flatterer from a Friend* 52DE, ἐδημαγώγει καὶ καθωμίλει τῷ συναφομοιοῦν καὶ συνοικειοῦν ἑαυτὸν ἅπασιν.... See Menander, 689K.

[55] Plutarch, *Alcibiades* 23.5. I have adjusted the Loeb translation.

[56] Ibid., 2.1; 23.3–5. Alcibiades' change was not deep-rooted enough; a friend assimilates his ἦθος to that of his friend; a flatterer only his σχῆμα and πλάσμα. Plutarch contrasts flatterers who imitate the voices of kings and assimilate themselves to them with the statesman for whom it is not fitting "to imitate the character of his people, but to understand it and to employ for each type those means by which it can be brought under his control" (*Precepts of Statecraft* 800A).

[57] Ribbeck, *Kolax*, pp. 7–8, 52–56; Athenaeus, *Sophists at Dinner* 237B–F; 255B.

the late Republic and the Early Empire; this is seen in Philodemus, Horace, Dio Chrysostom, Plutarch, Lucian, and Maximus of Tyre, all of whom account for the practice of the wise man in his service to a patron. Here, in the social matrix of patronage, the practices of flatterers and friends converge. The main contours of the discussion of how to distinguish flatterers from friends had already been set in the fifth and fourth centuries BCE in discussions of the flatterer and related characters, such as the obsequious person and the pretentious one, focusing on issues of pleasure and pain, the good and the beneficial, personal advantage, and versatility. And yet, although the contrast between flatterers and friends was not new, the fact that independent works were composed discussing the relationship between flatterers and friends shows the resurgence of the topic during late Republican times and under the early Empire.[58]

Horace defensively recognizes the apparent similarities between flatterers and friends in their service to a patron. The theme of servility and personal independence as illustrated in the relationship of a patron and a client, emerges in two Horatian *Epistles* (1.17 and 18). Horace, who was probably influenced by Philodemus both in his *Satires* and the *Epistles*, presents himself as a truthful and versatile friend, an adaptable person who is "able to turn or change easily."[59]

---

[58] On some recurring issues concerning patronage of concern to scholars, see the collection of essays in A. Wallace-Hadrill (ed.), *Patronage in Ancient Society* (London/New York, 1989). For the φίλος—κόλαξ antithesis see Alciphron II 42, 3; 62, 3, Xenophon, *Memorabilia* 2.9 and Antiphon's remark: πολλοὶ δ' ἔχοντες φίλους οὐ γιγνώσκουσιν, ἀλλ' ἑταίρους ποιοῦνται θῶπας πλούτου καὶ τύχης κόλακας (Ribbeck, *Kolax*, pp. 32–33 n. 3). In the view of Heylbut (*de Theophrasti libris περὶ φιλίας*, pp. 28, 33), Theophrastus' work *On Flattery* was part of his *On Friendship* and Plutarch drew on Theophrastus' *Characters* in his *How to Tell a Flatterer from a Friend*. With regard to the text from Xenophon where Archedemus could be either called a flatterer or a friend of Crito, P. Millett says: "This anticipates a common device of Roman patronage: preserving appearances by disguising clients as amici" ("Patronage and its avoidance in classical Athens," in *Patronage in Ancient Society*, p. 33). Plutarch's *How to Tell a Flatterer from a Friend* and Maximus of Tyre's work of the same title, as well as Philodemus' works on flattery, focus on this issue. In late Republican Rome and in the Early Empire the matter is complicated because of the overlapping of "patron-client terminology" and that associated with the "institution of amicitia." See R. P. Saller, *Personal Patronage under the Early Empire* (Cambridge, 1982), pp. 11–15; idem, "Patronage and friendship in early Imperial Rome: drawing the distinction," in *Patronage in Ancient Society*, pp. 49–62; P. White, "Amicitia and the Profession of Poetry," *JRS* 68 (1978), pp. 80–82; P. A. Brunt, "'Amicitia' in the late Roman Republic," *PCPhS* n.s. 11 (1965), pp. 1–20.

[59] As Horace discusses the adaptable person he also draws on Aristotle who had used the term εὐτράπελος for the "witty man" who is midway between the stiff man and the buffoon. Aristotle, *Eudemian Ethics* 1234a4–23; *Nicomachean Ethics* 1108a23–

Horace defends himself as a sycophant of the great and contrasts the Cyrenaic Aristippus, who could adapt to any circumstance, with the less sensible behavior of Diogenes the Cynic, who courted the common people and knew only how to live amid sordid surroundings. Horace plays on the contrast between friends and faithless parasites, saying to Lollius the "most outspoken of men" that he will shrink from "appearing in the guise of a parasite" when he has "professed the friend."[60]

Horace's attempt to account for the practices of the wise man in his service which might be compared to that of the flatterer is like Plutarch's and Maximus' works which delineate criteria by which flatterers and friends could be distinguished. Just as Horace wanted to secure his status with his literary patron, so did Plutarch, who addresses his essay to Antiochus Philopappus of kingly descent, a patron of art and literature, with whom we know Plutarch at one time associated.[61] Plutarch wants to make it clear to his patron that he can be trusted as a faithful friend and advisor who is not on a par with other so-called "friends." The latter are flatterers, who "often overturn kingdoms and principalities," really misleading Philopappus by pandering to his baser appetites.

Friends and flatterers were thus lumped together by some because of their similar behavior—both were accommodating, affable, and pleasant—while others attempted to distinguish the two.[62] This reflects a social matrix of patronage where the practices of "friends" and "flatterers" were similar. The flatterer was the client of a rich and powerful patron, and, one should add, more often than not a valued member of the entourage of the rich. As such his position was not different from that of poets, philosophers, astrologers, social climbers, and other "friends" who attached themselves to the houses

---

26. See R. L. Hunter, "Horace on Friendship and Free Speech (Epistles 1.18 and Satires 1.4)," *Hermes* 113 (1985) pp. 482, 486–88; N. W. de Witt, "Parresiastic Poems of Horace," *CP* 30 (1935), pp. 312–319; and A. K. Michels, "Παρρησία and the Satire of Horace," *CP* 39 (1944), pp. 173–77.

[60] Horace, *Epistle* 1.18.1–16. Horace also criticizes "clownish rudeness" which passes for "simple candour" (libertas dice = παρρησία).

[61] Plutarch, *Table Talk* 628B; *How to Tell a Flatterer from a Friend* 49C; *On Having Many Friends* 94A; *That a Philosopher ought to Converse especially with Men in Power* 776B; 777E–778B.

[62] The close association of flatterers and friends can also be seen in the honorable role flatterers played where they were called φίλοι, ἑταῖροι, συνήθεις and συμβίωτοι. See Ribbeck, *Kolax*, pp. 7–8, 52–56; Millet, "Patronage and its avoidance in classical Athens," *Patronage in Ancient Society*, pp. 30–37.

of the rich. All these were treated in the same fashion and they all accommodated themselves to the demands of a patron.[63] It was then difficult to separate flatterers and friends on the basis of their "gracious services." These resembled each other in the services they rendered, in adaptation, and in being ingratiating and affable.

### 1.2.2 *Flattery: A specious frankness*

The tension between beguilement and truthful guidance is clear in Plutarch's and Maximus of Tyre's attempts to distinguish flatterers from friends. For both, pleasure and pain are important in distinguishing the two. In his use of the Prodicus myth Maximus relates pleasure and pain to questions of leadership.[64] The leaders of the two roads of Virtue and Pleasure are, instead of virtue, a friend, and instead of pleasure, a flatterer. The flatterer uses praise and alluring words; the friend speaks but little, but what he says is true. One should choose the true leader, the friend, as Hercules took virtue for his guide, and not the "fine leader" who through false pleasures leads to real evil. A friend shares everything equally with his friend and can be a bearer of pain: "For the most philanthropic physician causes the greatest pain," like generals, pilots, fathers, teachers, mothers, and nurses, all of whom are sometimes bearers of pain.[65] As mothers and nurses love infants and find pleasure in obsequiously attending them so friendship is not without pleasure. Here Maximus contrasts cooks and physicians. There are indeed some skillful physicians who mingle a short pleasure with the pain of the remedy but imparting pleasure is not the function of Asclepius or his descendants but that of cooks. One must examine whether anything good and useful has grown in the soul from a discourse. The one who uses an intemperate discourse is secretly led to ignorance; he "delights in his wandering, and rejoices in this psychagogy!"[66]

For Plutarch pleasure and pain are also important in distinguishing flatterers and friends. However, pleasure alone cannot show the difference between the two; there is thus no reason why persons who praise should be suspected of being flatterers, "for praise at the right

---

[63] See White, "Amicitia and the Profession of Poetry," pp. 74–92, cf. p. 76.
[64] Maximus of Tyre, *Discourse* 14.1 (170, 8–171, 8 Hobein). Cf. Xenophon, *Memorabilia* 2.1.21–25.
[65] Maximus of Tyre, *Discourse* 14.4 (174, 15–17 Hobein; cf. 171, 10–172, 9; and 173, 2–177, 18 Hobein).
[66] Ibid., 25.4ab (301, 1–12 Hobein); 25.5–6 (303, 4–8, 11–15; 304, 5–13 Hobein).

time is no less becoming to friendship than is censure."⁶⁷ But the one who praises with pleasure blames only when he must. Plutarch's focus on the proper occasion for frank criticism and the legitimate use of harshness reveals the importance of adaptation and harshness in distinguishing the flatterer from the friend. A therapeutic metaphor explicates the matter; a friend

> is like a physician, who, if it be for the good of the patient, administers saffron or spikenard, and indeed oftentimes prescribes a grateful bath or generous diet, but there are cases where he lets all these go and drops in a dose of castor ... or he compounds some hellebore and makes a man drink it down, setting neither in this case the disagreeable nor in the other the agreeable as his final aim, but endeavouring through either course to bring his patient to one state—that which is for his good.⁶⁸

When there is need of reproof, the friend assails with stinging words and all the frankness of a guardian, using the stinging word as a medicine which restores and preserves health. He who implants the sting of repentance by chiding is a true friend. The flatterer knows nothing of words that hurt; he only delivers praise which accustoms a man to treat vice as virtue, and takes away all shame for errors. We must be suspicious of an association that is confined to pleasures, whose complaisance is "unmixed and without a sting."⁶⁹ Indiscriminate praise is as destructive as unrelieved blame. After his discussion of the flatterer's unsalutary praise, Plutarch introduces the topic of παρρησία. The flatterer does not reprimand a person's faults, although one of his most unprincipled tricks is to imitate παρρησία, perceiving that it is "the language of friendship."⁷⁰ Mixing a little admonition with flattery reflects an adulterated frank speech and, if tested, will be seen to be without firmness. True frank speech causes beneficial pain but the flatterer makes a parade of harshness by focusing on trifling shortcomings, like a schoolmaster who scolds a boy about his slate and pencil and disregards his blunders in grammar and diction, and like a man who uses a surgeon's lancet to cut the hair and nails of a person suffering from tumors and abscesses!⁷¹

---

⁶⁷ Plutarch, *How to Tell a Flatterer from a Friend* 49E.
⁶⁸ Ibid., 55AB.
⁶⁹ Ibid., 55DE, τὸ πρὸς χάριν ἔχουσαν ἄκρατον ἀεὶ καὶ ἄδηκτον ὁμιλίαν ὑπονοεῖν. See also ibid., 55F–59A, and Isocrates, *Letter to Philip* 1.1.
⁷⁰ Plutarch, *How to Tell a Flatterer from a Friend* 50B; 51C, ἰδίαν εἶναι φωνὴν ... τῆς φιλίας.
⁷¹ Ibid., 59C–60C, ἡ ... φιλικὴ παρρησία ... σωτήριον ἔχουσα καὶ κηδεμονικὸν τὸ

It is from the nature of his service that one can detect the flatterer, whether its purpose is to give pleasure or help. The flatterer imitates any shameful thing, instead of censuring it. A friend on the other hand neither imitates nor commends everything, but only the best.[72] A friend attempts to turn his friend aside from what is unbecoming, and, if unsuccessful, will retort with Phocion's remark to Antipater, "You cannot use me as both friend and flatterer," assisting both in deed and misdeed.[73] Many think that if they abuse and find fault they use frankness but frank speech must be applied at the proper time so that its "smart" does not cause unsalutary injury.[74] Its application requires skill and there should be reason in it to take away its excess. It should also be devoid of all arrogance and ridicule. A "stinging reproof" should be profitable and not like the many stern rebukes of the comic poets, mixed with "drollery and scurillity," which made their frankness of no profit to the hearers.[75] Frank speech, then, being a form of blame, causes pain and can easily be confused with inconsiderate faultfinding.

The proper occasion is important to Plutarch's views on the nature of frank speech.[76] The focus is on when frank speech can be used and the appropriate degree of harshness. Plutarch takes up a position against the inconsiderate harshness of some Cynics.[77] Most people lack the courage to school their friends when they are prospering, although that is precisely when humans have the most need of friends to speak frankly and reduce their excess of pride. But when they are cast down, there is no use for stinging reproof but only consolation and encouragement. Such circumstances require the gentleness displayed by nurses who, when children fall down, take them up, wash them, straighten their clothes, and then rebuke and discipline them.[78] A friend should be severe in his use of frank speech when checking pleasure, anger and arrogance, abating avarice or

---

λυποῦν.... 60D–61D, μετὰ παρρησίας λαμπρᾶς ἡ κολακεία; 73C and A, μὴ φιλικῶς ἀλλὰ παιδαγωγικῶς προσφέρηται τοῖς συνήθεσιν....

[72] Idem, *On Having Many Friends* 96F–97B; *Alcibiades* 23.4; *How to Tell a Flatterer from a Friend* 53C–D.

[73] Ibid., 64C; 62B–65A; 50C. See also *Advice to Bride and Groom* 142B, and *Life of Agis* 795E.

[74] Idem, *How to Tell a Flatterer from a Friend* 66A ἂν λοιδορῶσι καὶ ψέγωσι, παρρησίᾳ χρῆσθαι. See Philodemus' *On Frank Criticism* fr. 60.

[75] Plutarch, *How to Tell a Flatterer from a Friend* 66B; 67BE; 68AC.

[76] Ibid., 68D–74D. Chps. 27–37 treat the opportune moment or ὁ καιρός.

[77] Ibid., 70B; 69CD, παρρησίαν κυνικὴν καὶ λόγους τραχεῖς.

[78] Ibid., 68F–69C, λόγων βάρος ἐχόντων καὶ δηγμὸν ... ὁ δὲ παρρησία καὶ δηγμὸν ...

curbing inconsiderate heedlessness.⁷⁹ But all admonition and disclosure should be in secret. Admonishing someone inconsiderately when others are present destroys the salutary nature of frank speech. One should show empathy since persons are more wont to yield to those who seem to have like emotions but no feeling of contempt. In addition, one should not use "unmixed admonition" when dealing with a "troubled spirit." In such cases, "among the most useful helps is a light admixture of praise" which "mitigates the harsh and peremptory tone of the censure."⁸⁰

After our friends have been mollified by our commendations, we should give them an application of frank speech like a tempering bath. A kind-hearted physician does indeed prefer to relieve a sick man's ailment by sleep and diet rather than by castor and scammony; so a kindly friend, a good father, and a teacher, take pleasure in using praise rather than blame for the correction of character; for nothing else makes the frank person give so little pain and do so much good by his words, as to approach the erring with kindliness, without sharply censuring them. Again, Plutarch reverts to the analogy of physicians discussing the opportune moment with the aid of the mixed method of praise and blame. By choosing this finale Plutarch accentuates that it is here that the difference between flatterers and friends can be seen most clearly; a friend, like a physician, recognizes the need for the occasional use of pain. As physicians do not leave the part that has been operated upon in its suffering but treat it with soothing lotions, so when using admonition one should not simply apply its bitterness and then run away but should by further converse and gentle words mollify and assuage.⁸¹

## 1.3 *The Genuine Frank Counselor*

The frank counselor had, like the flatterer, precise collocations in Greco-Roman society. The diary of Crates contrasted the following

---

⁷⁹ Ibid., 68EF; 70DE. Opportunity for admonition presents itself also when people have become submissive after having been reviled by others (τὸ μὲν λυπηρὸν τοῦ λοιδοροῦντος, τὸ δ' ὠφέλιμον τοῦ νουθετοῦντος).

⁸⁰ Ibid., 72B–D, καὶ νουθεσίαν ἄκρατον ... ὁ παραμιγνύμενος ἐλαφρὸς ἔπαινος. See also ibid., 70F; 71A–D, 72B; cf. 53F. See Stobaeus, *Anthology* 3.41; Epictetus, *Discourse* 4.13.1.

⁸¹ Plutarch, *How To Tell a Flatterer from a Friend* 74DE. For references in this paragraph see 73DE and 74AC.

"professions": A cook and a physician; a flatterer and a frank counselor; a prostitute and a philosopher. Flatterers were often compared to cooks; frank counselors to physicians.[82] The themes sounded by Maximus and Plutarch are traditional, a continuation of issues discussed by Plato, Aristotle, and Isocrates. Flatterers and charlatans were naturally contrasted with "outspoken men" just as pleasure was with pain. Related to the frank counselor was the simple (ὁ ἁπλοῦς), forthright (ὁ αὐθέκαστος) or truthful person, commonly contrasted with the self-deprecator and the pretentious person.[83] Although the frank counselor resembles the forthright person in the Peripatetic tradition, most Hellenistic schools included truthfulness as a "virtue" and polemicized against flattery and deceit. A person who would sufficiently test a soul as to rectitude of life should go to work with three things, namely, knowledge, goodwill, and frank speech.[84] The correct kind of caring demands frank speech which dares to censure another persons' faults.

The frank counselor resembles Aristotle's character between an obsequious person and a flatterer, on the one hand, and a cantankerous and contentious person, on the other hand. In Book 4.6 of the *Nicomachean Ethics* Aristotle contextualizes his remarks in regard to meeting people, living together, and associating in conversations and actions. The mean is achieved by someone who can accept and object to things in the right way. The character of such a person is what we mean when we speak of a decent friend, except that the friend is fond of us. The "friendship" of such a person does not require any special feeling or any fondness for the people he meets. Such a person will behave thus to both new and old acquaintances, to familiar companions and strangers without distinction, except that he will do what is suitable for each. He will share pleasure and avoid causing pain, but consequences, i.e. what is fine and expedient, take precedence. Thus to secure great pleasure in the future, he will cause

---

[82] Plato, *Gorgias* 464D; 465B; 500B and 501A (culinary art a form of flattery), 520C–522E; *Republic* 404C–D; Philo, *On Joseph* 62; Maximus of Tyre, *Discourse* 14.8g–i (181, 3–11 Hobein).

[83] Plutarch, *On Tranquility of Mind* 472F; *How to Tell a Flatterer from a Friend* 52E; Menander, *Sententiae* 545K; Athenaeus, *Sophists at Dinner* 588A; Dio Chrysostom, *Discourse* 77/78.33; Lucian, *Alexander* 25; *The Fisherman* 19; *The Parliament of the Gods* 2; Philodemus, PHerc. 222, col. 1.3–4; *On Piety* 123, 17. The eulogized attributes of the frank counselor are the same as those of the statesman, also contrasted with flatterers (Plutarch, *Precepts of Statecraft* 799C; 800AB; 808D–809B).

[84] Plato, *Gorgias* 487A.

slight pain. The frank counselor respects the individuality of those he meets and can be the bearer of pain. Such a person values what Aristotle calls "unemotional friendship." It has been noted that this type of friendship and the corresponding vices well suited the political and social circumstances of the Hellenistic and Roman worlds.[85] It provides the context for evaluating the importance of the mature guide in psychagogy.

### 1.3.1 *Adaptability in the unreserved association with all*

The flatterer's versatility was depreciated by some as a form of cunning, graphically depicted by Athenaeus in his reference to the flatterer's two coats. Adaptation thus faced the charge of involving deceit and deliberately adopting a guise. Odysseus' cunning, as Stanford's painstaking study has demonstrated, could also be valued as a form of remarkable versatility. Adopting a guise for the sake of a greater good had a long history in Greek thought and one finds from Homer onwards reflections on a "good type of lying" and deliberate deceit. The "magnificent liar," Odysseus, could then in his voluntary suffering and self-abasement adopt the guise of a slave in order to effect a greater good; this is a "deceit" that was valued positively.[86] Similar motifs were exploited among Jews contemporary with Paul. In the *Testament of Joseph*, for example, Joseph is silent, hides his real status, endures injustice and humiliates himself as he passes himself off as a slave. This he does for the sake of his brothers and Potiphar's wife. Although Philo and Josephus, as well as the *Testament of Joseph*, focus in connection with this story on aspects of silence, self-humiliation, faithfulness, and endurance, they are also aware that Joseph's effort to conceal his identity was a deliberate act of self-disguise for the good of his brothers.[87]

---

[85] R. L. Hunter, "Horace on Friendship and Free Speech (Epistles 1.18 and Satires 1.4)," p. 483. See Aristotle, *Nicomachean Ethics* 1108a26–30; 1126b11–16, 20–29; 1127a3–6. Cf. 1126b36–1127a3.

[86] W. B. Stanford, *The Ulysses Theme* (New York, 1968), pp. 19–24, 95; B. Snell, *The Discovery of the Mind in Greek Philosophy and Literature* (New York, 1982), pp. 164–66, and R. Hoïstad, *Cynic Hero and Cynic King* (Uppsala, 1948), pp. 94–102. The reference to Odysseus as the "magnificent liar" is that of B. Snell. According to the casuistry of the old Stoa, a physician is allowed to lie (SVF 3.513). See also Aristotle, *Nicomachean Ethics* 1146a17–22.

[87] *T. Jos.* 3–9; 9.2–16.6. See H. W. Hollander, "The ethical character of the Patriarch Joseph. A Study in the ethics of the Testaments of the XII Patriarch," G. W. E. Nickelsburg, Jr. (ed.), *Studies in the Testament of Joseph* (Missoula, 1975), pp. 47–104. See also Josephus, *Antiquities* 10.11.

A variation of the tradition which viewed versatility both as a form of cunning and positive flexibility is witnessed in Philo's discussion of Joseph's political career. Joseph's "coat of many colors" represents both the politician's falseness and the true statesman's resourcefulness in peace and war.[88] Philo's discussion shows, as does Maximus of Tyre's defence of versatility, to be discussed below, that two issues come into focus in positive adaptation, namely, the unrestricted association with all in light of human diversity, and psychagogic adaptation in light of different dispositions.

Joseph's "coat of many colors" reminds us of the flatterer in Athenaeus who continually changes his coats as he goes to the marketplace.[89] Philo often evaluates diversity negatively. He contrasts Joseph's leadership style with that of Isaac. Isaac is a leader who leads a noble company and learns from no teacher but himself; he disdains any use of soft and milky food suited to infants and little children and uses only strong nourishment fit for grown men. But Joseph leads a company which "yields and is ready to give in" and is drawn in different directions, caught up in an unceasing cycle of warfare "revolving round the many-sided soul."[90] In sharp contrast to the negative depiction of Joseph in the *Allegorical Interpretation* as a man who is wise in his own deceit, a favorable picture emerges of Joseph's "coat of many colours" in *On Joseph*. Joseph "assumes a coat of varied colors" because "political life is a thing varied and multiple, liable to innumerable changes, brought about by personalities, circumstances, motives, individualities of conduct, differences in occasions and places."[91] The politician is like a pilot who does not confine his guidance of the ship to one method but changes them with the changes of the wind and a physician who does not use a single form of treatment for all his patients, nor even for an individual, but watches all the changes of symptoms and varies his salutary processess, sometimes using one kind and sometimes another. The political man must, like a pilot and physician, be "a man of

---

[88] Philo, *On Dreams* 1.210; *On Joseph* 32.
[89] Athenaeus, *Sophists at Dinner* 236EF.
[90] Philo, *On Dreams* 2.10–16; *On Noah's Work as a Planter* 44; *On the Migration of Abraham* 152–53; *Moses* 2.289. Cf. L. K. K. Day, *The Intermediary World and Patterns of Perfection in Philo and Hebrews* (Missoula, MT, 1975), pp. 131–34; H. W. Attridge, *The Epistle to the Hebrews* (Philadelphia, 1989), p. 37 n. 28.
[91] Philo, *On Joseph* 32–34 (cf. Gen. 37.3), ποικίλον γὰρ πολιτεία καὶ πολύτροπον. Compare Josephus' description of God as ποικίλη τέ ἐστι καὶ πολύτροπος (*Antiquities* 10.8.3.142).

many sides and many forms," different in peace and war, changing as those who venture to oppose him are few or many, and to effect the common good he will outstrip all others in his personal activity.[92]

Philo not only compares the good statesman to a pilot and a physician, but also to a "good guardian" and "affectionate father"; the leadership of such a person has in view only the common good. If speaking in the assembly, the good statesman will

> leave all talk of flattery to others and resort only to such as is salutary and beneficial, reproving, warning, correcting in words studied to show a sober frankness without foolish and frantic arrogance.[93]

His frankness will include harsh discipline, as will the frank speech of parents, guardians, teachers, and all persons in charge. In this the good statesman follows the example of a physician who in his benevolent treatment devotes himself to his patient, "to save him to the best of his ability, even if he must use cautery or surgery."[94] Philo has then compared the political man to a physician in *On Joseph* 32-34 and 75-79. In the former text the analogy is used to accentuate the diversity of conditions, the need for manifold treatment, and the need for the political man, like the pilot, to adapt himself to diverse circumstances; this text displays then a positive evaluation of the diverse conditions and the importance of flexibility for the political leader in light of these conditions. The latter text uses the analogy of physicians to make the point that in cases when the sickness is severe, a more drastic treatment is needed. Even in this case, however, the analogy emphasizes the adaptability of the good statesman, since the method employed is applied in view of, and adapted to, the condition.

When discussing the polytropic nature of the citizen's life, Philo records his view that the wise can indeed put on different robes for different occasions. A "twofold perfection" is witnessed in Moses'

---

[92] Philo, *On Joseph* 33-34. A negative evaluation follows on the servile status of politicians and popular orators. See also *Allegorical Interpretation* 3.179; *The Worse Attacks the Better* 7; *On Sobriety* 14; *On Husbandry* 56; *On the Confusion of Tongues* 71; *On Drunkenness* 35, 82-86. Most of Philo's eulogized attributes of the political person are the same as those of the political person in Plutarch's *Precepts of Statecraft*. See 799C; 800AB; 802EF; 810C; 815B; and 825D-F. See fn. 83, above.

[93] Philo, *On Joseph* 73. Cf. ibid., 67-69 and 75.

[94] Ibid., 76; cf. 74. For Philo's classification of humans, see A. Mendelson, *Secular Education in Philo of Alexandria* (Cincinnati: Hebrew Union College Press, 1982), pp. 47-59.

institution of an external and internal altar and in the two different robes for the high priest as symbols representing the virtues of either kind. The wise man must put on the unadorned robe of truth when he retires from human pursuits to worship "the one," but when he passes to the life of a citizen he must don another robe whose manifold richness is a marvel to the eye. For life is many-sided and requires that the pilot in control of the rudder should be wise with a wisdom of manifold variety. Thus, although Philo's remarks on versatility are often negative, he also values diversity and versatility. He, like Maximus of Tyre below, reflects a Platonic tradition of the positive evaluation of Socratic indirection.

Maximus of Tyre's discourse *That a Philosopher's Discourse Is Adapted to Every Subject* offers a sustained defence of versatility, adaptation, and manifold hortatory practice.[95] Adaptation is needed when associating unreservedly with all and in psychagogy. Maximus asks why dramatic actors do not think it absurd appearing at different times in different *personae* although they are the same person, but when the philosopher conforms the manner of his speaking to the nature of things, some think that he acts in "a polyphonic manner out of tune" like the Homeric Proteus, "naturally multiform and manifold."[96] Maximus argues inductively in defence of polyphony. Human life is not static but in a continual flux. In view of the perpetual changes of life "one reason and one manner of speaking" and the enchantment or ψυχαγωγία of melodies does not suffice. There is need for a "manlier" muse which has many modes. Just as the art of the physician is capable of governing the indigence and satiety of the continually moving body, so the philosophers' discourse is capable of affecting human life, being adapted to the passions, "mitigating sorrowful circumstances, and joining in the celebration of the more joyous ones."[97]

The rest of the discourse focuses on the "contests of the soul," including a critique of sophists who believe philosophy consists of the arts of diction, contentions, and sophisms. True philosophy requires teachers who can elevate the souls of the young, govern their

---

[95] Maximus of Tyre, *Discourse* 1 (1, 5–18, 3 Hobein).
[96] Ibid., 1.1a–c (2.10–15 Hobein), σχηματίζοιτο δὲ τῷ ἤθει τοῦ λόγου πρὸς τὴν φύσιν τῶν πραγμάτων. Πολύφωνος—πολύμορφος.
[97] Ibid., 1.2a (3.1 Hobein, ἐκ μελῶν ψυχαγωγίας); 2b; 2f (3.5–7, 10–13; 4.10–11 Hobein); 1.3a (4.21–22 Hobein; cf. 2, 10–12; Hobein); 1.1b–h (4, 12–19 Hobein) ὁ λόγος τῶν φιλοσόφων ... ξυναρμοζόμενον τοῖς πάθεσιν. See Philo, *On Drunkenness* 170; *Moses* 1.117.

ambition, and measure their inclinations with reference to pleasure and pain and nothing else. The taming practices of a horse breaker are analogous to the discourse of the philosopher, who attempts neither to extinguish the ardour of the colts nor give them a free rein without restraint. As a skillful horseman employs the bridle and the whip to govern the ardour of a colt, the discourse of the philosopher governs the soul of humans in a similar fashion, "mixed with his manners and passions."[98] Those who desire philosophy should choose the person who possesses an appropriate type of discourse, whether old or young, poor or rich. Socrates was indeed poor and the poor man will imitate and derive advantage from him but no one recounts that Socrates betook himself only to the poor. On the contrary, he also betook himself to the rich, the renowned and well-born; he associated both with the strong and weak.[99]

Finally, Maximus discusses different modes of philosophizing and reveals the close tie between a philosopher's σχῆμα and λόγος.[100] The garb of each actor on the social stage should not distract us from his message, although the philosopher's σχῆμα can contribute to his dramatic performance.[101] The philosopher's garb influences his discourse, as is evident in the different forms of exhortation exhibited by different philosophers: Pythagoras, for example, dressed in purple like Aristippus, perplexed or reproved; Socrates, on the other hand, in his garment, confuted; Xenophon, with a corselet and a shield, persuaded; and Diogenes, with a staff and a scrip after the manner of Telephus, reproached. Maximus here reflects a tradition which recognized a special province of speech for different philosophers.[102] In Maximus' defense of versatility he has sounded the theme of association with all and the importance of discrimination of speech in the use of the mixed method in psychagogic guidance.

As Maximus, Epictetus likewise recognizes a special province of speech for different philosophers. Epictetus notes that God had counselled Socrates to take the office of "examining and confuting men," Diogenes the office of "rebuking men in a kingly manner," and Zeno that of "instructing men and laying down doctrines." Here Epictetus

---

[98] Maximus of Tyre, *Discourse* 1.5c, h; 8a, c–e; (8, 16–17; 10, 16–17; 13, 17–20; 14, 10–15, 3 Hobein).
[99] Maximus of Tyre, *Discourse* 1.9a–d (15, 4–17 Hobein).
[100] See my discussion on pp. 20–23, above.
[101] Maximus of Tyre, *Discourse*, 1.10a–f (16, 17–20; 17, 1–4, 7–14, 17–19 Hobein).
[102] Ibid., 1.10e–f (17, 14–21 Hobein).

uses the analogy of the "doctor's office" and the "school of philosophy." In the care of the young, it is not enough to possess the necessary "drugs" which are manifold, including a style of exhortation, refutation, and instruction.[103] Also needed is a knowledge of when or how to apply them. Both Maximus and Epictetus reflect on the professional σχῆμα of a psychagogue in light of the characteristic activity expected from such persons, a σχῆμα involving a variation in the use of λογοί. As philosophers differentiated between the σχῆμα of a philosopher and that of other professions, differences were then also postulated within the profession of the philosophic σχῆμα, contingent on the type of discourse used.[104]

### 1.3.2 *1 Corinthians 9:19–23. A suggestive hypothesis*

An understanding of the debate on how to distinguish flatterers from friends and the question of adaptation, association, freedom, and servility, in the context of patronage, has implications for our understanding of Epicurean practice, to be discussed in chapter three. This debate can also assist us in explicating Paul's self-presentation in 1 Cor 9:19–23 and 10:32–33, to be fully discussed in the final chapter of this book. Issues raised in Maximus of Tyre's and Philo's defences of versatility and others who discuss different types of students also throw light on the matter. The pericope of 9:19–23 reveals a twofold perspective, namely, adaptation in the unreserved association with all in light of human diversity and psychagogic adaptation requiring attentiveness to students of different dispositions. The former is accentuated by Paul in his reference to "Jews," "those under the law" and the "lawless ones," as well as the "many" and "all"; the latter in his reference to the "weak" which accentuates a solicitous concern for the tender ones. Both Philo and Maximus clearly reveal this twofold perspective and show that questions of adaptation center on issues of leadership style.

Adaptation is important in a versatile approach both in association

---

[103] See Epictetus, *Discourse* 3.21.18–24 (cf. 19–20, πρὸς τὸ ἐπιμεληθῆναι νέων); 3.23.27, 30–34. See pp. 1 and 11–12, above. Demetrius also refers to different manners of speaking (*On Style* 296–98). One will deal with his subject in an "Aristippean" fashion by way of exposition and emphatic assertion; another will, like Xenophon, express the same thought in the way of precept. The "Socratic" manner would recast the same in an interrogative form with an entire absence of what is proverbially known as "Gothic bluntness" (cf. 216). On the Cynic manner of speech distinguished by its mordant wit, see ibid., 259–61.

[104] Cf. Dio Chrysostom, *Discourse* 72; Epictetus, *Discourse* 4.8.

with the many and in psychagogy; it is required because of the diversity of humans and variation in the human condition. The form of the pericope in 1 Cor 9:19–23 indicates, then, that Paul draws on a common tradition and expresses a certain mode of leadership. Paul also reflects a tradition where important characteristics of flatterers and obsequious persons combine. In order to recruit others one must be willing to obsequiously associate with different types of people. The theme of association with others, a theme which has wider application and use in 1 Corinthians than recruitment does, asks with whom one does associate and for what purposes: namely, to recruit and/or benefit them, to change their behavior or to make a statement with regard to one's own superiority. In his expression of an affable practice, Paul denies exclusive allegiance to a few influential patrons in Corinth and expresses his wish to associate indiscriminately with all.

Paul's expressed concern for the weak reflects his awareness of the need for different modes of guidance for different types of humans. Paul's affable approach towards the "weak" is one aspect of his guidance of the Corinthians; the other is seen in his stringent guidance of the "wise" in Corinth. The close connection between the philosopher's σχῆμα and λόγος that we have seen, indicates that Paul's reflections on his affable approach do have implications for his use of different types of discourse. Paul's harsh and gentle guidance of the Corinthians includes his use of the mixed method of exhortation, a widely used method which has also already emerged in Plutarch's and Maximus of Tyre's discussion of flatterers and friends and Philo's discussion of the political man.[105] It was especially in his use of both praise and blame that the true friend differed from the flatterer. Adaptability is important in the right use of the mixed method of exhortation; such adaptability is concerned with the well-being of others. In his use of this widespread pedagogical means, Paul's psychagogic adaptation is attentive to different character types and human dispositions.

As versatility and psychagogy converge in Maximus and Philo, so do they in the pericope of 1 Cor 9:19–23. I shall devote my attention to psychagogy before returning again to the issue of versatility and association in 1 Cor 9 in the final chapter of this book. The psychagogic perspective on early Christian texts is necessary if we

---

[105] See pp. 33–36 and 39–41, above.

are fully to appreciate Paul's self-presentation and function as a guide of his converts and the practices he attempts to implement in his communities. However, before discussing psychagogic adaptability in the next chapter, let me pause for a moment and draw attention to the various aspects of ancient discussions of positive adaptability in light of the requirement of the opportune moment.

1.4 *Adaptability Valued by Orators, Philosophers, and Moralists*

Within the above traditions of the politician's and philosopher's resourcefulness a recognition has emerged of the need for manifold hortatory devices to affect others and of the importance of adaptability. In their use of manifold hortatory means to affect others, the truthful friend and the frank counselor, as well as the political person and the philosopher, need to adapt and be discriminating in speech in their guidance of others. Although the charge of hypocrisy was ever present and the similarities to the practice of flatterers inevitable, the frank counselor and politician needed to be versatile in light of the pressing task at hand. As the flatterer had to adapt so also did physicians and orators who must respectively take into account differences of climate and constitution in regulating the diet of the patient, and change their discourse in light of the different needs of their auditors.[106] Such positive adaptability was widely discussed and valued by orators, philosophers, and moralists.

Adaptation was discussed with reference to changes in appearance, customs, convictions, beliefs, and language. Change in outward appearance was a concern of the cultured classes at the time, evident in Ovid's and Apuleius' *Metamorphoses* and in discussions on the philosopher's σχῆμα and the appearances of different vocations.[107] Ample evidence exists of how flatterers conformed to the demands of the situation and how orators and philosophers thought best to adapt to different auditors. Negative evaluation of adaptation is found in discussions of flatterers, demagogues, and the friend of many. A positive evaluation of adaptation, devoid of notions of cunning and

---

[106] See Philodemus, *Rhetoric* v. 2, 74, fr. XII = v. 2, 106, frs. XIII, XIV; v. 2, 115, fr. VI Sudhaus.
[107] Dio Chrysostom, *Discourses* 70 and 71; Maximus of Tyre, *Discourse* 1. See pp. 20–23, 28–30 and 42 above.

deceit, is seen in discussions of the opportune moment by moralists and orators, to be discussed below, and in discussion of the various hortatory means for different types of students, to be discussed in the next chapter. Adapting one's behavior involved a change in one's customary ways of behaving, but adaptation in speech, often discussed under propriety of speech and character portrayal, had to factor in the social status, vocation, age and disposition of the addressees in an attempt to be discriminating.

According to George Kennedy, καιρός as a rhetorical term is largely restricted to the classical period. Kennedy notes, as does Dionysius of Halicarnassus, that one of the reasons why the subject of the opportune moment did not receive great attention was simply that it cannot be reduced to rules. Dionysius complains that no definitive treatise had been written on the καιρός either by a rhetorician or philosopher, "nor did Gorgias of Leontini, who first tried to write on it, write anything worth mentioning."[108] Despite this negative evaluation, Gorgias' focus on the concept of the opportune, with its consideration of time, place, and circumstance, influenced the theory of style.

An orator who sways the emotions of the audience is a ψυχαγωγός, like a poet who leads souls through a kind of incantation. The need to adapt to types of auditors was a requisite for successful persuasion.[109] The manner of address is to be matched by subject matter and the condition of the auditors, their dispositions and psychological conditions. Rhetoricians similarly discussed the need to adapt the style of discourse depending on the cause, audience, speaker, or occasion, when considering propriety of style and character portrayal. Adaptability of speech to character had to take into consideration such contingencies as the time, place, and circumstances of the speech, the character of the speaker and the types of auditors. Such considerations also became a common concern of philosophers and moralists when discussing different types of pupils and the necessary means and methods of dealing with each. Similar concerns surfaced also among early Christians.[110]

---

[108] Dionysius Halicarnassus, *On the Arrangement of Words* 12; Gorgias, *Palamedes* 22; Plato, *Phaedrus* 271A; *Gorgias* 513B; G. Kennedy, *The Art of Persuasion in Greece* (Princeton: Princeton University Press, 1963), pp. 63, 66–67, 92.

[109] Maximus of Tyre's discourse *That a Philosopher's Discourse Is Adapted to Every Subject* (*Discourse* 1; 1, 5–18, 3 Hobein) deals with this subject. See Seneca, *Epistle* 64.8–9.

[110] A. J. Malherbe, *Paul and the Popular Philosophers* (Minneapolis, 1989), pp. 138–43.

Earlier I noted Plato's definition of rhetoric as the art which leads the soul by means of words. Plato shows how important adaptation is for persuasion. Four things must be considered by the rhetor in his attempt to produce conviction. Firstly, he must accurately describe the soul and explain the nature of that to which his words are to be addressed. Secondly, he will say what the soul's "action is and toward what it is directed, or how it is acted upon and by what." Thirdly, "he will classify the speeches and the soul and will adapt each to the other, showing the causes of the effects produced and why one kind of soul is necessarily persuaded by certain classes of speeches, and another is not." This entails offering to the "complex soul elaborate and harmonious discourses, and simple talks to the simple soul."[111] And, fourthly, the opportune moment for speech must be considered. One has gained oratorical ability when one has learned the individual differences among one's auditors, the application of proper speech to them, as well as knowledge of the times for speaking and keeping silent and the favorable occasions for various types of speeches.

Adaptation requires knowledge of the time, place, occasion, subject matter and the auditors. The need for such a practice is captured by Aristotle after his description of the difference between the characters of the young and old, and before describing those in the prime of life, "since all people are willing to agree with speeches that harmonize with their own character and to speakers who resemble them...."[112] The efficacy of the persuasive word depends on the character of the orator, his relationship with his hearers, and his knowledge of his audience. In order to arouse, quench, or modify a passion, or change the disposition of another, the orator must not only consider the age, fortune, character, disposition, moral habits, emotions and passion of his audience, but must also factor in their opinions and beliefs. These are all important when the focus is on the audience and its "transformation."

Subsequent writers did not always follow Plato's psychologizing approach of describing one's auditors in terms of certain dispositions of character or psychological conditions. This is clear from the approach taken by Theon of Alexandria and Quintilian, whose

---
[111] See Plato, *Phaedrus* 270D–271D ποικίλῃ μὲν ποικίλους ψυχῇ καὶ παναρμονίους διδοὺς λόγους, ἁπλοῦς δὲ ἁπλῇ... τέχνη ψυχαγωγία τις διὰ λόγων. See also 261A and 272A.
[112] Aristotle, *Rhetoric* 1390a; 1377b24–27; 1388b32–1389a2.

concerns in many ways coincide, indicating a shared *Zeitgeist* of Quintilian's *Oratorical Institutions* and Theon's *Progymnasmata*. Theon addresses the teacher's practical classroom application of his time and gives evidence of the importance of the teacher's adaptation and of the pupil's implementation of comparable principles. This is most evident in the discussion of character portrayal which is one of the elementary rhetorical exercises addressed in Theon's *Progymnasmata*.[113] The species of panegyric, protreptic and epistolary speeches, fall under this exercise.

Theon defines προσωποποιΐα as "the introduction of a character which sets forth in a non-controversial way words suitable both to the character himself and to the subject."[114] Theon, as does Hermogenes later, describes two types of character portrayal, general and specific. A specified character portrays the words of a known historical or mythical figure, but an unspecified character invents both the character (a "husband," a "wife," a "farmer," a "pretentious person," a "superstitious person") and the words such a person says on a given occasion.[115] When constructing a "character," one should consider the character's age, the occasion, place, status, and the matter at hand. Only then should one try to speak appropriate words.[116] Because of age, some words fit some characters and others fit other characters; the same words do not fit an older and a younger person. Because of gender, different words are appropriate to a woman and a man; because of status, different words are appropriate to a slave and a freeman; because of vocation, different words are appropriate to a soldier and a farmer; on account of disposition, different words are appropriate to one in love and one showing self-control; on account of nationality, some words are characteristic of the Laconian whereas other words are characteristic of the Attic person. We should assign words that are fitting to each subject, aiming at

---

[113] Theon probably wrote at the end of the first century CE, a few years prior to Quintilian. See J. R. Butts, *The Progymnasmata of Theon: A New Text with Translation and Commentary* (Diss., Clarement Graduate School, 1986), pp. 2–5; W. Stegemann, "Theon," PW, RE 5A (1934), cols. 2037–54; S. F. Bonner, *Education in Ancient Rome* (Berkeley, 1977), pp. 267–70.

[114] Theon, *Progymnasmata* 8.1–2 Butts. See the discussion in 8.11–37 Butts ed.

[115] See Hermogenes, *Progymnasmata* 9 (cf. Quintilian, *Oratorical Institutions* 9.2.29–37). On Hermogenes, see H. Rabe, *Hermogenis Opera* (Leipzig: Teubner, 1913; repr. Stuttgart, 1969), pp. 1–27. On Aphthonius, see H. Rabe, *Aphthonii Progymnasmata* (Leipzig: Teubner, 1926).

[116] Theon, *Progymnasmata* 8.9–15, 75–76 Butts.

what is appropriate to the characters, occasion, place, time, and status. Suitable resources are necessary because the "variance of characters and subjects is manifold."[117]

One of the best means of adaptation and persuasion is to lend a person a voice through character portrayal. When we select words appropriate to the portrayed character it produces conviction. Both Quintilian and Seneca agree that character portrayal is well suited for adaptation and that its skillful use can increase one's persuasiveness. Characterization functions as a precept, well suited for individual cases and persons, and especially helpful in guiding the progressing person.[118] For Cicero "imitation of manners and behavior" is a considerable ornament of style, "extremely effective in calming down an audience and often also in exciting it."[119] Character portrayal is effective in amplification, helpful in explaining a statement or for embellishment. Quintilian notes that the imitation of other persons' characteristics is one of several devices which serve to excite the gentler emotions.[120] Character portrayal was thus recognized, although differently, as a helpful tool in persuasion. Much information may be gained from Quintilian's *Oratorical Institutions*, Books 11.1 and 9.2.29–37. The latter discusses personification as a "figure of speech." Here

> we display the inner thoughts of our adversaries as though they were talking with themselves (but we shall only carry conviction if we represent them as uttering what they may reasonably be supposed to have had in their minds); or without sacrifice of credibility we may introduce conversations between ourselves and others, or of others among themselves, and put words of advice, reproach, complaint, praise or pity into the mouths of appropriate persons.[121]

In Book 11.1 personification is discussed under propriety of speech. It is "concerned with persons," and involves the "portrayal of the

---

[117] Ibid., 8.16–29 and 34–42 Butts. Note *ad Herennium* 4.1.63; 4.53.66.
[118] Seneca, *Epistle* 95.66.
[119] Cicero, *The Making of an Orator* 3.204–05.
[120] Quintilian, *Oratorical Institutions* 9.2.58; 9.3.99. When stirring the emotions of others one must first feel these emotions and not counterfeit them by "accommodating our words and looks and make no attempt to adapt our own feelings to the emotions to be expressed." In *ad Her.* 4.53.66, personification is said to be most useful in amplification as well as in an appeal to pity and for Demetrius it is a "figure of thought" which produces "energy of style" (*On Style* 5.265–66). Personification is a "figure" with which the orator should be familiar (Cicero, *The Making of an Orator* 3.205; *The Orator* 25.85).
[121] Quintilian, *Oratorical Institutions* 9.2.30.

emotions of children, women, and nations," and even of voiceless things, all of which need to be represented in character. Such representation requires the assumption of a role which demands knowledge of what best suits each character that one plays. One must take into account fortune, rank, and the achievements of each individual, as well as sex and age, though character will make the chief difference. One must know suitable words for such "roles" as sons, parents, rich men, old men, gentle or harsh of temper, misers, superstitious persons, cowards, and mockers. One must also observe the character of those before whom we speak, whether one is speaking before the emperor, a magistrate, a senator, a private citizen, or merely a free man. A different tone is also demanded by trials in the public courts and in cases submitted to arbitration, and when speaking before the assembly of the senate or the fickle populace. Also, the same style will not be suitable for use before a judge of weighty character and one of a more frivolous disposition, "while a learned judge must not be addressed in the same tone that we should employ before a soldier or a rustic." One should also refrain from insulting whole classes, races, or communities, even though at times "our duty toward our client will force us to say something on the general character of a whole class of people, such as freedmen, soldiers, taxfarmer, or the like."[122]

Although Cicero had only briefly discussed questions relating to the requirements for the delivery of speech in his *The Making of an Orator*, he captured the main point when noting, "One single style of oratory is not suited to every case, not to every audience, nor every speaker, nor every occasion."[123] No single kind of oratory suits every cause, audience, speaker or occasion. Most rules of rhetoric are liable to be altered by the nature of the case, circumstances of time and place, and by different types of auditors. The rules of oratory are then the children of expediency. Propriety of style had to be achieved if the rhetor was to be successful in his adaptation.[124] A mixed style was needed both for aesthetic and emotional purposes, since the audience was not a homogeneous whole, but varied and

---

[122] For references in this paragraph see ibid., 11.1.41–43, 45, 86; 3.8.35, 38, 49–52; 1.9.3.

[123] This is Quintilian's view. Ibid., 11.1.4; 2.13.2; Cicero, *The Making of an Orator* 3.210–12; *The Orator* 21–23.

[124] Aristotle, *Rhetoric* 1408a; Quintilian, *Oratorical Institutions* 11.1.1–2; Theon, *Progymnasmata* 8.34–37 Butts.

mixed with regard to age, sex, social class, and interests and aspirations.[125] It was the καιρός, the rhetorical moment, determined by the rhetorical audience, which was all important.[126] The contingent nature of rhetoric and the requirement of adaptability led some orators to view rhetoric as an "art," like navigation and medicine. Inflexible rules do not suit rhetoric; science has infallible rules, whereas the rules of art alter their nature contingent on the occasion. This is due to different notions of the appropriate, the just and the unjust, the expedient and harmful, the noble or honorable and the disgraceful, as well as virtue and vice.[127]

The requirement of "the opportune moment" is extended even to the gods, both in Clement's *The Pedagogue*, which details God's "manifold ways" of speaking (cf. Heb 1:1), and in Plutarch's *On the Delays of the Divine Vengeance*. In Plutarch, God is like a physician who "administers punishment to each patient as a medicine, a punishment neither given in the same amount in every case nor after the same interval for all."[128] Similarly, Clement's divine word uses manifold hortatory devices in his effort to benefit mankind and adapts "completely to the disposition of each, being strict with one, forgiving another" in his effort to save the erring ones; the divine pedagogue sympathizes from his great philanthropy with the nature of each person.[129] In Clement's case, the pedagogical traditions are utilized to cast light on the nature and activity of the divine pedagogue and make explicit many of the presuppositions of a psychagogic discourse. The ideal psychagogue is he who knows the diversity among humans

---

[125] Or, as Plato said in his *Phaedrus*: a "simple soul" requires a simple style; a mixed audience an elaborate and harmonious discourse (277BC). Contrast Plutarch's *How to Study Poetry* 25D.

[126] Quintilian, *Oratorical Institutions* 3.4.6–16; 3.7.1–28; 3.8.1–70; 2.17.22–25; Anonymus Sequerianus 30–32. Cf. G. M. A. Grube, "Theodorus of Gadara," *AJPh* 80.4 (1958), p. 345. Cf. D. A. Russell & N. G. Wilson, *Menander Rhetor* (Oxford, 1981), p. xix.

[127] Or the domains of different types of rhetoric, namely, forensic, deliberative, and epideictic, which aimed at different types of hearers, namely, judges concerned with past facts or future prospects, and spectators concerned with the present performance of an orator. Quintilian, *Oratorical Institutions* 2.13.2, 16; 2.8; Aristotle, *Rhetoric* 1408ab; 1358b1–7; 1391b21; Philostratus, *On the Hero* 19.3; Hermogenes, *On Stasis* 1; Philodemus, *Rhetoric* vol. 2, 214; col. 30a19 Sudhaus.

[128] Plutarch, *On the Delays of the Divine Vengeance* 549F–550A. Plutarch notes that "the cure of the soul" which goes by the name of chastisement and justice is the greatest of all arts.

[129] Clement, *Ped.* 66.2 and 4–5 (GCS 126, 28–31; 129, 6–17 Stählin-Treu). Compare Plutarch, *On the Delays of the Divine Vengeance* 562D, "But god is surely neither ignorant of the disposition and nature of each individual...."

and adapts himself with perfect knowledge to each individual case. Various traditions thus value diversity of exhortation, adaptability, and the need for special attentiveness to the individual case.

I have emphasized the circumstantial requirements an orator might face in light of the opportune moment in his delivery of a discourse. The basic distinction involves the speaker, subject matter and audience, the coordination of the last two being particularly important in adaptation. Beyond the general requirement of time, occasion, place, and circumstance, the following cover most aspects mentioned with regard to one's auditors: Age, sex, family relations, status (e.g. slave or freeman; distinguished or humble position), vocation (e.g. soldier or farmer), fortune (noble birth, wealth), social position (power or rank), previous experience and achievements, disposition (e.g. in love or showing self-control; harsh or gentle temper), and character types (misers, cowards, mockers, superstitious persons) displaying certain passions, habits, beliefs or opinions. Also, whole classes of people (e.g. freedmen, soldiers, taxfarmers), people of different nationality (Laconian or Attic), different race or different communities have sufficiently many things in common for them to be lent a voice in personification. Finally, the texture of the audience is important, for example whether it consists of a single person or a few, whether it is the senate, the populace of a city, judges, or private individuals. It was thus incumbent on an orator to have access to a pool of hortatory techniques in order to be discriminating in speech in light of the different dispositions of people and in light of the various conditions in which they found themselves. The same was true of the frank counselor or mature guide in their guidance of different types of students.

In the next chapter I shall document a widespread urge among people of the late Republic and the early Empire to seek out the advice of more mature persons. I will pull together some of the more central and recurring features and presuppositions of psychagogy within varied traditions and its relation to pedagogy. I shall focus especially on the basic formal structure of a psychagogic discourse, namely, the mixed method of moral exhortation or harsh and gentle guidance used by the mature guide in his psychagogic guidance and adaptability to students of different dispositions.

CHAPTER TWO

# PSYCHAGOGY AND THE MIXED METHOD OF MORAL EXHORTATION

## 2.1 *The Psychagogic Perspective*

### 2.1.1 *The mature guide*

Ample evidence exists of the social practice of seeking a mature guide or teacher. The classic examples of Justin Martyr and Galen come to mind, both of whom relate their search among the various philosophical "schools" of the day: Stoics, Platonists, the Peripatetics, and Epicureans.[1] At the end of their search, Galen became a sceptic, Justin a Christian. Willingness to look for a mature guide was part of an educational pattern of the day, occurring mainly during the period of adolescence but sometimes lasting into adulthood. It reveals the tendency of the age to look for someone to direct one in a spiritual quest for a lifestyle or in the "art of living."

Seneca's epistolary psychagogy of Lucilius reflects many presuppositions of psychagogy. To Lucilius' indecisiveness Seneca has a predictable solution: "[One] needs a helping hand, and someone to instruct one."[2] No one has sufficient strength to rise above his condition without assistance. Galen's text on curing the passions is also illustrative. He advises anyone who wishes to take proper care of himself to seek the aid of another, not, however, a technician known for his competence and learning, but simply a man of good reputation "whose uncompromising frankness one can have the opportunity of experiencing."[3] Those who allow others to diagnose them make the fewest mistakes, while those who take it for granted that they are good, without allowing others to judge, stumble most seriously

---

[1] Galen, *On the Passions and Errors of the Soul* 8 (Kühn, V, 41–41); Justin Martyr, *Dialogue with Trypho* 2.3–6; R. M. Grant, *Greek Apologists of the Second Century* (Philadelphia, 1988), p. 51.

[2] Seneca, *Epistle* 52.2; 42.1. I have modified the Loeb translation. On Seneca's epistolary psychagogy, see I. Hadot, *Seneca und die griechisch-römische Tradition der Seelenleitung* (Berlin, 1969).

[3] M. Foucault, *The Care of the Self* (New York, 1988), pp. 52–53; Galen, *On the Passions and Errors of the Soul* 1.1; 3.6–10; *On the Doctrines of Hippocrates and Plato* 2.5.3–7.

and most frequently. It is no slight indication of progress when someone does not rejoice in hiding his fault but confesses and feels the need of somebody to admonish him. Those with a hostile attitude toward the ones who take them to task are incurable whereas those who patiently submit to admonition are in less serious plight. Likewise, Asclepius "bestows his [aid] more on those who are eager to have him as their doctor than on those who are not eager."[4]

The social matrix enabling such a relationship to form was already in place. Michel Foucault puts his finger on the right cultural pulse in noting that when one appealed to another in whom one recognized an aptitude for guidance and counseling, "one was exercising a right. And it was a duty that one was performing when one lavished one's assistance on another, or when one gratefully received the lessons the other might give."[5] This penchant of adults to look after their souls and to seek out philosophers who would direct them towards the flourishing life was satirized extensively by Lucian. He makes fun of Hermotimus who had devoted himself to caring for himself for forty years under the direction of a master. Lucian sarcastically requests Hermotimus to: "Act as my crutch, and lead me by the hand."[6]

Such texts are evidence of a widespread social phenomenon; Lucian's satires hardly focus on an obscure practice. Even evidence suggesting the contrary bears witness to the existence of such practice. Such evidence criticizes the prosperous who do not avail themselves of such "services." Dio Chrysostom uses Aesop's fable of the wise owl which attracted birds that came for advice and implies that present day "owls" do "collect a great company" of birds! Reflecting on his return from exile and "conversion" Dio similarly speaks of his activity in Rome where he addressed a great number of people. Dio hopes for an edict bidding young and old regularly to consort with a competent teacher, whether a Greek or a Roman, a Scythian or an Indian, who can heal the maladies of their souls.[7] Again, when Philo of Alexandria complains that those who in their desire for

---

[4] According to Alexander of Aphrodisias, *On Fate* XXXII, 204.25–28, R. W. Sharples ed., *Alexander of Aphrodisias On Fate* (London, 1983), pp. 84–85.

[5] Foucault, *The Care of the Self*, pp. 52–53.

[6] Lucian, *Hermotimus* 1–2. See also Plutarch, *Progress in Virtue* 82A; Isocrates, *Antidosis* 290.

[7] Dio wants to establish another Apollo on the Acropolis and considers himself to be a competent teacher, although not on a par with Socrates and Diogenes (*Discourses* 27.7–10; 72.11–16; 13.9–13).

health commit themselves to physicians are not willing to cast off their sickness of soul by resorting to the wise, he employs a traditional critique.[8] We should track down such persons and exhort them to join us and humanize our bestial life! These examples reveal a socio-cultural norm; some members of society are invested with the function of being moral and psychological guides who have the right to correct others. The "director of souls" has an achieved and recognized authority to command, cajole, admonish, pacify, and console willing recipients under his guidance.

Ilsetraut Hadot has shown that the work of a spiritual guide is considerably aided by authority and friendship.[9] But it is precisely authority in friendship which makes psychagogy ambiguous. The issue is succinctly captured by Menander Rhetor in his discussion of the different types of farewell speeches, which are three in number depending on the relationship of the persons in question. The first type is when a superior is sending off an inferior; the second, when the two are equal; and the third, when the relationship is that of an inferior to a superior. The first emphasizes advice, the second affection, and the third encomium. The first can admit of advice, when a superior is sending off an inferior, for example a teacher his pupil, "because his own position gives him a character which makes advice appropriate."[10] But in the second type, when a friend sees off an equal friend, "even if the speaker in these circumstances is superior to the person who is going away, nevertheless the common title, the fact that both are friends, deprives him of his advisory status."[11] This text emphasizes that advisory status displays a degree of superiority and, secondly, that an advisory status can never be unambiguous in a relationship of equality.

The text from Menander succinctly captures a paradox of

---

[8] Philo, *Every Good Man is Free* 12, 20, 63 and 64. Compare Isocrates, *Antidosis* 289–90; *To Demonicus* 3–5; Epictetus, *Discourse* 3.23.36

[9] I. Hadot's definition of a "spiritual guide" is somewhat broader than the one adopted here ("The Spiritual Guide," in *Classical Mediterranean Spirituality* [ed. A. H. Armstrong; New York, 1986], pp. 436–459). The following are singled out for having assumed the function of "spiritual guides": the educator, musician, and poet (Chiron the Centaur, Phoenix and Orpheus), the legislator, sage, statesman and king, or the spiritual guide of a collective (e.g. Solon), and the philosopher.

[10] *On Farewell Speeches* 395.1–32. For the quote see 395.4–12. References are to *Menander Rhetor*, ed. with transl. and comm. by D. A. Russell and N. G. Wilson (Oxford, 1981), pp. 126–29.

[11] Ibid., 395.12–20. According to Cicero, equality excludes advice and judgment (*On Duties* 3.10.43).

psychagogy in a status-oriented society. A mature status is ambiguous for several reasons. Two are important in psychagogy. The first relates to the location of the participants on different strata in a hierarchical society. It is thus problematic when a person of a mature spiritual status, but of a perceived lower social status, advises another of a higher social status. Thus it is not difficult to imagine that a clash might occur when a freedman or an artisan and a Jew, one of them teaching in Nicopolis (= Epictetus) the other in Corinth/Ephesus (= Paul), exhorts and advises others of a higher social ranking. The second reason has to do with symmetrical and asymmetrical relations. A friend's status in the role of an advisor is never unambiguous, particularly in friendship of equality. In the role of a friend the relationship is symmetrical, but in that of an advisor the relationship is asymmetrical. The presence of both reciprocal and superior/inferior relations can be seen in Paul as a "father" of the Corinthian community and "brother" of its members.

My unqualified discussion of persons of more "advanced status" is not only ambiguous but also positively misleading. It is ambiguous because I have not yet defined in what sense a person is of an advanced status and it is misleading because of the possible identification of such a person with other types of persons of special standing, according to such available criteria of measuring social stratification as power, occupational prestige, income or wealth, education and knowledge, religious and ritual purity, family and ethnic-group position, and local-community status.[12] What I mean by "advanced status" is a sense of being spiritually or morally mature, considered by another to be in a position to give valued advice. Such a position of superiority might be acquired by age, experience, knowledge, or education, or simply by superior personal aptitude or by a sense of divine commissioning and can become more permanent, guaranteeing the psychagogue's attraction and legitimation. The focus here is on psychagogy as a reciprocal relationship of leader and follower in which each engages with the other in the pursuit of a common aim. This recognizes that "we must see power—and leadership—as not things but as relationships" rooted in certain values. This functional definition views leadership as "transformational."[13]

---

[12] Cf. W. A Meeks, *The First Urban Christians* (New Haven, 1983), p. 54.

[13] J. McGregor Burns, *Leadership* (New York, 1978), p. 11; T. J. Sergiovanni & R. J. Starratt, *Supervision. Human Perspectives* (New York, 1988), pp. 198–199, 216–

My interchangeable use of the terms "philosopher," "psychagogue," and "spiritual guide" reflects the fluid state of affairs during our period with regard to the classification of moralists. Many authors who engaged in psychagogy, such as Plutarch, Dio, and Epictetus, for example, attempted to classify themselves as "philosophers," as opposed to "sophists" and "demagogues." Also, "psychagogy" accentuates the activity of guidance and a "psychagogue" is by definition one who participates in such an activity, regardless of philosophical alignment. In this I follow many a moralist, such as for example Dio Chrysostom, who argues from the garb of the person to his profession, such as a sailor, farmer, shepherd, huntsman, or a philosopher, to the characteristic activity expected from each profession. Dio claims to follow a common perception; thus, when

> people see a man in the garb of the philosopher, they reason in his case that it is not for sailing or for farming or for tending sheep that he is thus arrayed, but rather that he has got himself ready to deal with human beings, aiming to admonish them and put them to the test and not to flatter or spare any one of them, but, on the contrary, aiming to reprove them to the best of his ability by his words and to show what sort of persons they are.[14]

The function of a psychagogue was often compared to those of a pilot and a physician whose "guiding" and "steering" of a ship and "healing" and "tending" of a patient were thought to encapsulate the essence of psychagogy. Even if a pilot or a physician were a slave, his word would be heeded.[15] This focus on a certain praxis should prevent the term "psychagogue" from becoming an all-

---

230. For divine commissioning, see Dio Chrysostom (*Discourse* 13), Epictetus (*Discourse* 3.21.17–20), and Paul (1 Cor 15:8–10; 9:1; Acts 26:12–18). See also Isocrates, *Antidosis* 206–08.

[14] Dio Chrysostom, *Discourse* 72.9. The example of the huntsman is found in *Discourse* 70.2 where the same point is made concerning the activity to be expected from a huntsman. Cf. *Discourse* 13.28. See G. R. Stanton, "Sophists and Philosophers: Problems of Classification," *AJP* 94 (1973), pp. 350–64, on how Plutarch, Dio, Epictetus, Aelius Aristides and Marcus Aurelius, classified themselves, and their philosophical alignment. Cf. J. Hall, *Lucian's Satire* (New York, 1981), pp. 189–91. One should not press my point since there is a tendency not to describe oneself as a "philosopher."

[15] As Diogenes of Sinope aptly put it: "To Xeniades who purchased him he said, 'You must obey me, although I am a slave; for, if a physician or a steersman were in slavery, he would be obeyed'." In Diogenes Laertius, *Lives of Eminent Philosophers* 6.30. See also Dio Chrysostom, *Discourses* 13.18; 17.2; 27.7–10; and F. Decleva Caizzi, ed., *Antisthenis fragmenta* (Milan, 1966), fr. 15. Note G. W. Bowersock, *Greek Sophists in the Roman Empire* (Oxford, 1969), pp. 19 and 59–75.

encompassing category or protean sponge with which diverse data can be absorbed.[16] I thus view "psychagogy" as a certain praxis in a relationship between a mature person and others who accept his leadership. It does not depend on any one social context, such as private homes, workshops, wrestling-schools, cloistered walks, public place, or the market place and street corner. Issues centering on the ambiguous status of the psychagogue and his motives are present regardless of the social context. The same holds true whether the advice is sought out, proffered unsolicited, or forced on the audience, and whether the psychagogue is a resident philosopher who does not appear in public at all or a resident philosopher who appears at least in lecture-halls, a touring lecturer, or a transient public speaker who might speak un/invited in more commonly accessible social settings.

### 2.1.2 *Psychagogy and moral instruction*

I have drawn attention to the penchant of adults to look after their souls and to seek out the advice of more mature spiritual persons. This propensity of the age shows that psychagogy falls under the rubric of adult education or, perhaps better, from the period of adolescence and early adulthood, into adulthood. As such, psychagogy can be viewed as a means of moral instruction since the inculcation of a certain view of ourselves and reality is latent in psychagogy. On the highest level of generalization, psychagogy is thus a pedagogical activity where the formation of a certain *paideia* is in view.[17] Here, the pedagogical function of the psychagogue comes to the fore, insofar as we understand *paideia* as inclusive of the endeavor to make a person fit for life, including the formation of a person's moral and religious attitudes. One should thus attempt to elucidate ancient psychagogic theory and practice as a reflection of a certain form of pedagogy. One of the functions of psychagogy is then the perpetuation and transmission of traditional Greek folk morality and popular teaching methods (moral and pedagogical traditions) as well as the

---

[16] Cf. S. K. Stowers, "Social Status, Public Speaking and Private Teaching: The Circumstances of Paul's Preaching Activity," *NovT* 26.1 (1984), pp. 63, 74.

[17] A. Dihle conflates the two in "Ethik," *RAC* VI (Stuttgart, 1966), cols. 659–60. Hadot (*Seneca und die griechisch-römische Tradition der Seelenleitung*, p. 10) suggests that the origin of psychagogy is found within the framework of "allgemeiner Erziehung, sofern man unter Erziehung (παιδεία) die Gesamtheit der Bestrebungen versteht, einem Menschen Lebenstüchtigkei zu verleihen."

creative inculcation of a (new) belief in the formation of the self-definition of the recipients.

During the early Empire, the distinction between paraenesis and protrepsis is blurred. Many a protreptic discourse has a paraenetic function, and, conversely, many a paraenetic discourse has a protreptic function. In spite of this overlap, the distinction between recruitment and psychagogy is fairly uncomplicated.[18] It is more difficult to distinguish psychagogy and instruction, both of which have to do with the process of educating new recruits properly. We can view psychagogy as a "rite of passage" and a form of "enculturation," the structuring of an alternative viewpoint to the one previously held. But the guidance of neophytes at the early stages of liminality is also applicable to the more mature since they can lapse. Psychagogy is thus a process that continues well beyond an initiatory phase, its duration depending upon the aptitude of the student and the skill of the psychagogue.[19] Some students might thus need to be exhorted by precepts like other neophytes whereas precepts are less applicable to others who are advancing faster.[20]

Inculcation is a part of psychagogy since a paraenetic discourse includes a didactic element, even to the extent that we can speak of "paraenetic instruction." Ancient epistolary theorists, such as Ps.-Demetrius, recognized this:

---

[18] Clement of Alexandria calls his protrepsis a Προτρεπτικὸς πρὸς Ἑλληνάς but Pseudo-Justin (third century) calls his protrepsis a *Paraenetic Address to the Greeks*. Clement calls his paraenetic work to the newly baptized Ὁ προτρεπτικὸς εἰς ὑπομονήν, and Ennodius (fifth century) makes his appeals in the manner of a protrepsis in his Παραίνεσις διδασκαλία. A. J. Malherbe, *Moral Exhortation. A Greco-Roman Sourcebook* (LEC 4; Philadelphia, 1986), p. 121. The references to Pseudo-Justin and Ennodius are Malherbe's.

[19] In that sense psychagogy is not an initiatory ritual. W. A. Meeks treats the hortatory and edificational material of the Pauline corpus under the subtitle of "minor rituals" (*The First Urban Christians*, pp. 142–50). See J. M. King, "Patterns of Enculturation in Communal Society," in C. J. Calhoun and J. A. J. Ianni (eds.), *The Anthropological Study of Education* (The Hague and Paris, 1976), pp. 75–104; V. Turner, *The Forest of Symbols* (Ithaca, 1967), pp. 93–111; and L. G. Perdue, "The Social Character of Paraenesis and Paraenetic Literature," *Semeia* 50 (1990), pp. 5–39.

[20] Thus, to take an Epicurean example, some are easily led from the early stages of guidance into a detailed exposition of the workings of the universe through a reading of the thirty-seven volumes of *On Nature*. For others, the smaller epitome and Epicurus' *Principal Doctrines* will suffice. A distinction is made between an advanced type of education that teaches one to unravel obscure writings and the common sense that allows even the illiterate to understand a "letter written by our leaders to private individuals" (PHerc. 1005 cols. 13.3–15; 17.6–9). See Asmis, "Philodemus' Epicureanism," *ANRW* 36.4 (1990), p. 2380.

> For admonition is the instilling of sense in the person who is being admonished, and teaching him what should and should not be done.[21]

In moral exhortation and paraenesis, preceptive aspects are more dominant than dogmatic ones; "[correct] belief" is less important than "[correct] moral behavior" and a certain "attitude" towards life and your teacher. Paraenesis has thus a practical dimension which focuses on beliefs regarding certain "behavior" or a "way of life," teaching what should and should not be done. Inculcation of beliefs is indirectly pursued through behavioral modification. Detailed teaching of beliefs or dogmatic instruction is thus subsidiary in exhortation when compared to situational precepts (which include beliefs) and an appeal to models (which imply beliefs). The imagistic and enactive modes of representation are then more prevalent in psychagogy than is the lexical mode of representation.[22] Here a psychagogue takes on a parental function and that of a friend. These roles are in turn incorporated into the roles of the truthful person and frank counselor, roles antithetical to that of the flatterer.

Moralists who attempted to assist others in their quest for a certain lifestyle can be viewed as proponents of an "art of living" (ἡ περὶ τὸν βίον τέχνη).[23] Although moralists differed as to whether this art of living well could be taught, they all emphasize that certain individuals instinctively do what should be done while others need to be led by more forceful means. Moral instruction features different aptitudes and dispositions and diverse means to effect different types of students. I view psychagogy primarily as moral exhortation where traditional forms of commanding and appealing occur. Through these the psychagogue attempts to influence an individual or group toward the achievement of specific goals.

### 2.1.3 *The diversity of exhortation*[24]

Diversity of exhortation is pertinent for adaptation because of human diversity and different human dispositions. Adaptation under-

---

[21] Ps.-Demetrius, *Epistolary Types* 7 (34, 31–33 Malherbe). Cf. Aristotle, *Politics* 1260b5–7.

[22] M. Horowits, "Modes of Representation of Thought," *JAPA* 20 (1972), pp. 793–819.

[23] Sextus Empiricus suggests (*Outlines of Pyrrhonism* 3.239–40, 249–52) that the Epicureans should be viewed as such. See Plutarch's *Can Virtue be Taught?* 439A–440C. The function of many a "spiritual exercise" was precisely to assist in this "art of living." Cf. P. Hadot, *Exercices Spirituels et Philosophie Antique* (Paris, 1987), pp. 15–29.

[24] On the hortatory tradition see P. Hartlich, *De exhortationum a Graecis Romanisque*

scores the diverse nature of the audience. A mixed audience demands resourcefulness and diverse methods of exhortation, which in turn implies a recognition of the mixed nature of the human disposition; both the audience and the human disposition require a diverse and multiple treatment. A close tie exists thus between the moralist's view of the human condition and his execution of the task at hand. In light of the diversity of human experience and of the human condition, access to a pool of various forms of hortatory terms and practices was pertinent.

An orator needed to be resourceful because of human diversity. Progymnasmatic writers note that some of the elementary exercises are well suited for the epideictic orator, others for training in the assembly, and still others for the court orator.[25] The various exercises are analysed from the vantage point of their persuasiveness in particular settings. The same holds true for Ps.-Libanius' and Ps.-Demetrius' description of epistolary types, many of which are characterized by traditional hortatory terms.[26] Ps.-Demetrius hopes that the various types may offer the young "diverse means of persuasion," as time teaches an older person the same.[27] Also, Theon's resources for argumentation in personification have in view the persuasiveness of a character portrayal in specific settings.[28] Thus, through character portrayal we exhort someone to do that which is possible, easy, noble, fitting, advantageous, just, holy, and pleasant. If we argue the contrary, we will not be persuasive. These resources and

---

*scriptarum historia et indole*. Leipziger Studien zur Classichen philologie 11.2 (Leipzig, 1889), who distinguished betweeen paraenesis and protrepsis, but was refuted by T. C. Burgess, "Epideictic Literature," *Studies in Classical Philology* 3 (1902), pp. 229–33; R. Vetschera, *Zur griechischen Paränese* (Smichow/Prague, 1912); B. Fiore, S. J., *The Function of Personal Example in the Socratic and Pastoral Epistles* (AnBib 105; Rome, 1986), pp. 39–42; M. D. Jordan, "Ancient Philosophic Protreptic and the Problem of Persuasive Genres," *Rhetorica* 4 (1986), pp. 309–333.

[25] T. Burgess, "Epideictic Literature," *Studies in Classical Philology* 3 (1902), pp. 108–09 n. 1.

[26] In his discussion of the handbook of "Demetrius", A. J. Malherbe (*Ancient Epistolary Theorists*. SBLSBS 19. Atlanta, Georgia, 1988, p. 4) notes:

> The manual in its present form is not so much a collection of sample letters as it is a selection of styles appropriate to different circumstances and a guide to the tone in which letters are to be written. The description of the letters, with the examples offered to illustrate the stylistic principles involved, betray a rhetorical interest in defining various types of exhortation.

[27] Letters, as Ps.-Demetrius notes, "can be composed in a great number of styles, but are written in those which always fit the particular circumstance"; *Epistolary Types* (30, 3–4 and 20 Malherbe).

[28] Theon, *Progymnasmata* 8.43–50 Butts.

different forms of persuasion are important contextual tools to be utilized in different settings, maximizing the persuasive effects of a discourse on different characters.

It is not necessary for my purposes to describe the various literary techniques that developed within a psychagogic discourse or the different spiritual exercises used for improvement.[29] The form of the literary context of a psychagogic discourse should not restrict us unduly either, whatever its epistolary and rhetorical context. This is so regardless of the fact that hortatory means influenced the classification of epistolary types,[30] and regardless of the fact that psychagogy occurs mainly within the epideictic and deliberative genres. It is in the latter context, however, and in the mixed method of exhortation of harsh and gentle guidance that the basic structure of a psychagogic discourse emerges. This can be seen most clearly in *The Pedagogue* of Clement of Alexandria where we find the fullest description available of hortatory terms and their psychagogic use, recognizing the need for diversity in moral exhortation.

In Book 1.1, 9 Clement focuses on "blame and dissuasion." Here we find illustrations of at least twelve terms of hortatory blame, namely, admonition, castigation, indignation, rebuke, visitation, censure, cross-examination, instruction, railing, accusation, faultfinding and disparaging blame. To these should be added reproach and threats.[31] The

---

[29] See R. J. Newman, "Cotidie meditare. Theory and Practice of the Meditatio in Imperial Stoicism," *ANRW* 36.3 (1989), pp. 1473–1517.

[30] This is true e.g. of the friendly, blaming, reproachful, consoling, censorious, admonishing, threatening, vituperative, praising, ironic, paraenetic, sympathetic, angry, didactic, reproving, encouraging, advisory, and mixed style. See fn. 26, above.

[31] See *Ped.* 76.1–4 on νουθέτησις (GCS 134, 13–32 Stählin-Treu; cf. 65.2; 94.2); 77.1–2 on ἐπιτίμησις (GCS 134, 33–135, 10); 81.2 on κατανεμέσησις (GCS 137, 20–26); 78.1 on ἐπίπληξις (GCS 135, 21–28; cf. 66.5; 82.2; 94.2); 79.2 on ἐπισκοπή (GCS 136, 20–28); 77.3 on μέμψις (GCS 135, 11–20); 78.2–4 on ἔλεγχος (GCS 135, 29–136, 12; cf. 64.1; 72.1; 82.2; 85.4; 88.1); 79.1 on φρένωσις (GCS 136, 13–19); 80.1 on λοιδορία (GCS 136, 29–32; cf. 66.2); 80.2 on ἔνκλησις (GCS 137, 1–7); 80.3 on μεμψιμοιρία (GCS 137, 8–12) and 81.1 on διάσυρσις (GCS 137, 13–19). I have rearranged Clement's ordering, grouping together similar terms. Thus ἐπίπληξις and κατανεμέσησις follow ἐπιτίμησις, because they are both said to be a variation of it, and ἐπισκοπή, being a variation of ἐπίπληξις, follows it. See 65.1 on ὀνειδισμός (GCS 128, 8–10) and 75.1 on threats (GCS 133, 29–31): σῴζειν ... τοὺς νηπίους, νουθετῶν, ἐπιτιμῶν, ἐπιπλήττων, ἐλέγχων, ἀπειλούμενος, ἰώμενος, ἐπαγγελλόμενος, χαριζόμενος.... Besides Clement, compare Seneca's types of exhortation in his reference to Posidonius' preceptorial division of the hortatory department (suasio, consolatio, dissuasio, adhortatio, objurgatio, laudatio, exhortatio and admonitio, adding causarum inquisita and descriptio, *Epistles* 94.39, 49; 95.34, 65). See also Musonius Rufus, fr. 49 (130, 9–10 Hense), 'Cum philosophus' inquit 'hortatur, monet, saudet, obiurgat aliudve quid disciplinarum disseret'; and Quintilian, *Oratorical Institutions* 9.2.30.

divine pedagogue legitimately uses these harsh means of persuasion in his attempt to "save the children." They are all manifestations of a "philanthropic pedagogy," a versatile and very useful "therapy."[32] Such a pedagogy recognizes the need for both praise and blame, all the above terms being an example of blame and dissuasion, the "harsh" dimension of the pedagogue's method. The economy of dealing stringently with humans is salutary, conducive to repentance and the prevention of sins.[33] What follows in chapter ten, which deals with "praise and persuasion," the "gentleness of the word," is not the same detailed listing of hortatory terms as in chapter nine.[34] Instead, Clement reflects on the threefold nature of advice, that which uses examples from time gone by, that which calls attention to conclusions drawn from present events, and that in which advice is drawn from future events. Clement also discusses encouragement, benediction, exhortation, and forgiveness.[35]

Influenced by a peripatetic distinction, Clement classifies hortatory discourse in light of the threefold schema of habits, actions and passions, focusing on types of discourses utilized when attempting to influence or modify the behavior of others. Habits are the domain of protreptic discourse, actions that of paraenetic discourse, the passions that of consolatory and therapeutic discourse.[36] Hortatory terms are employed in light of the diverse nature of the audience and are expected to have an effect on the recipients! Philosophers debated to what extent these should be used and whether one should apply them

---

[32] Clement, *Ped.* 66.4; 74.3; 75.1, 3; 89.4; 91.1; 97.3 (GCS 129, 7–8; 133, 17–18, 29–31; 134, 11–12; 142, 24–25; 143, 17–18; 148, 2–10 Stählin-Treu). Compare Plato, *Gorgias* 487A.

[33] The title of chapter nine suggests that the purpose of hortatory blame is to "punish justly" and be "beneficent." See *Ped.* 64.4–66.4; 74.2–4; 83.2 (GCS 128, 4–129, 8; 133, 11–25; 138, 21–139, 2).

[34] Ibid., 89.1, 3–4 (GCS 142, 13–14, τὸ ἤπιον τοῦ λόγου); 1.4–2.2 (GCS 90, 16–91, 2 Stählin-Treu).

[35] Ibid., 90.2–93.1 (GCS 143, 2–145, 16 Stählin-Treu). The formal structure of a psychagogic discourse overlaps with the epideictic and deliberative genres, betraying features of both. The συμβουλευτικὸς λόγος includes the προτρεπτικὸν καὶ παρακλητικὸν εἶδος using persuasion and dissuasion (τὸ ἀποτρεπτικός καὶ προτρεπτικός) when arguing for the beneficial (τὸ συμφέρον). The ἐνκωμιαστικὸς λόγος includes λοιδορητικὸν καὶ ὀνειδιστικὸν εἶδος, using praise and blame (τὸ ψεκτικός καὶ τὸ ἐπαινετικός) when arguing for the good (τὸ καλόν). Psychagogy aims at both the good and beneficial as it encourages us on the way to salvation (πρὸς σωτηρίαν), using both blame and dissuasion (τὸ ψεκτικὸν καὶ ἀποτρεπτικὸν εἶδος) and praise and persuasion (τὸ προτρεπτικὸν καὶ ἐπαινετκὸν εἶδος), or harsh and gentle means of persuasion.

[36] *Ped.* 1.1–2, 4; 66.1; 89.1–4 (GCS 89, 25–90, 11, 16–22; 128, 24–26, 142, 10 27 Stählin-Treu); Aristotle, *Nicomachean Ethics* 1103a17–19; *Poetics* 1447a28.

only to the progressing person or also to the "perfect person." Rhetoricians also debated the appropriate use of praise and blame, such as whether it mainly finds its place within the epideictic genre. If we place praise and blame in the "third division," what kind of oratory are we using when

> we complain, console, pacify, excite, terrify, encourage, instruct, explain obscurities, narrate, plead for mercy, thank, congratulate, reproach, abuse, describe, command, retract, express our desires and opinions, to mention no other of the many possibilities?[37]

The question is Quintilian's as he answers those who argued for countless kinds of rhetoric. Quintilian, an "adherent of the older view," as he himself says, accepts the threepart division of rhetoric but registers his view, as does Clement later, of the closeness of the epideictic and deliberative genres when noting that the tasks of oratory must either be concerned with the law-courts or with themes lying outside the law courts. The above examples are evidence of attempts to classify modes of expressions into different divisions of rhetoric; they also reveal a debate about the nature, function and effectiveness of hortatory discourse and the ways in which language could be employed to sway the opinion of others.

It is not my purpose to provide an analysis of paraenetic and protreptic terms in Philodemus or Paul. However, knowledge of attempts to systematize the hortatory department of philosophy is important because of the insight it yields for the psychagogic use and function of such terms, especially when set within the broader historical perspective of the literary techniques considered appropriate to effect moral transformation. Furthermore, discussions of these forms gives us leverage in elucidating the presuppositions of the student-teacher relationship, particularly those which relate to the guide's authority, his conceptualization of the student's psychology and dilemma, and proposed treatment. Precision can be gained from the study of such literary forms and conventions. The real challenge, though, for a more socio-historically oriented approach is how the presence of these forms in a literary context illumine their intended function and thus yield evidence concerning the social context in which they occur. My focus on psychagogic activity through the manifestation of paraenetic and protreptic elements naturally leads

---

[37] Quintilian, *Oratorical Institutions* 3.4.3. Cf. also 3.4.6.

us to the fatherly and brotherly roles since in both of these roles exhortation takes precedence over teaching. This focus not only helps us to illuminate the social context in which the literary conventions of hortatory discourse are employed but also constitutes an attempt to counter the danger of this book possibly having a "scant grip on reality."[38]

### 2.1.4 *The recipients of psychagogic guidance and the need for versatility*

Psychagogy is a relationship between more and less mature persons and implies a differentiation among persons whom the psychagogue directs. A philosopher deals with different types of pupils, of different character, upbringing, and disposition. Present in the psychagogic perspective is also the possibility of growth which, because of the different aptitudes among recipients, cannot be uniform. Those who willingly submit to admonition are thus in a less serious plight, while those with a hostile attitude toward the ones who admonish them are incurable. This view emphasizes differences among the recipients depending on their attitude, which in turn determines the effect of the psychagogic discourse. Here we find an example of different character types based on their dispositions and attitudes, a common theme among moralists.

The need for adaptability surfaces among moralists in their discussion of different students, a discussion which recognizes the diversity of character types and dispositions and the need for the teacher to be attentive in light of that diversity and have at his disposal a versatile and flexible approach. This is clear in Musonius Rufus, who draws attention to different types of pupils in the same breath as he emphasizes the need for the philosopher to recognize the different effects of his arguments on students according to the character, upbringing, and disposition of each. In light of this the philosopher should, instead of rehearsing a multitude of arguments and proofs to his pupils, rather "touch upon each one with just measure, [and] seek to penetrate to the very intellect of his hearer...."[39]

---

[38] This is A. D. Momigliano's phrase in a critique of W. Jaeger's *Paideia*. Cf. Sir M. I. Finley's remarks in his *The Use and Abuse of History* (New York, 1987), p. 78.

[39] Musonius Rufus, *Fragment* 1 (5, 6–7 Hense = 36, 1.1–2 Lutz). Musonius distinguished, as did Xenophon earlier (*Mem.* 4.1.3–4), between those who are gifted and those who are not. He remarks that "it is not an easy thing to persuade soft young men (Τῶν νέων τοὺς μαλακοὺς οὐκ ἔστι προτρέψαι ῥᾴδιον:) ... but the gifted young men (οἱ δ' εὐφυεῖς), even if you try to dissuade them, take hold of reason all the more

CHAPTER TWO

Attentiveness to the needs of each individual secures the teacher's effectiveness. Different methods are needed for different pupils.

Many authors discussed different types of people in light of moral progress. The possibility of progress receives a sharp focus in the medical analogy which viewed the human predicament as a form of sickness.[40] Improvement depended on the severity of the illness, which in turn was contingent on how moralists assessed the severity of "sicknesses" such as lust, greed, avarice, ambition, notoriety, contentiousness, pretentiousness, anger and arrogance. The appropriate treatment depended on the "sickness" in question, defined in view of the human condition. Each sickness needed to be treated with different hortatory means, all of which presuppose the possibility of change. The medical analogy illustrated then the function of philosophy, its content, methods, forms and procedures, and the process of moral exhortation. The therapeutic model, different aptitudes, and different methods, all require a knowledge of the condition of the recipients so that the guide can adapt his methods appropriately in view of the "sickness" in question. The focus here, nevertheless, is on "Seelenleitung" rather than "Seelenheilung," although these two images are related in ancient psychagogy as the analogy of the medical model and moral exhortation indicates.[41]

In Seneca's view those making progress fall into three classes defined relative to their attainment of wisdom and to the "diseases of

---

firmly" (fr. 46 (129, 6–14 Hense = Epictetus, *Discourse* 3.6.9–10)). See also fr. 16 (83, 9–21 Hense) on different types of pupils. Cf. Cicero, *Tusculan Disputations* 4.31–32.

[40] Philosophers found in medical treatment a simile of their own endeavor. See Cicero, *Tusculan Disputations* 4.10.23; 4.11.26; 4.27.58; Dio Chrysostom, *Discourse* 27.7–10; 77/78.43–45; Galen, *On the Doctrines of Hippocrates and Plato* 298.31–34 = SVF 3.471 (120.18–22); M. Frede, *Essays in Ancient Philosophy* (Minneapolis, 1987), pp. 225–242; L. Edelstein, *Ancient Medicine* (Edd. by O. Temkin and C. L. Temkin; Baltimore, 1987), pp. 323, 329, 333, 336–37, 350.

[41] Note the use of ψυχαγωγία in a medical context: LSJ ψυχαγωγία, s.v. III. On the use of the term "Seelenleitung" see I. Hadot, *Seneca und die griechisch-römische Tradition der Seelenleitung* (Berlin, 1969); on "Seelenheilung" see H. G. Ingenkamp, *Plutarchs Schriften über die Heilung der Seele* (Göttingen, 1971). P. Rabbow uses both words in the title of his work *Antike Schriften über Seelenheilung und Seelenleitung auf ihre Quellen Untersucht. I. Die Therapie des Zorns*. Berlin, 1914), but uses *Seelenführung* in his classic work on psychagogy (*Seelenführung, Methodik der Exercitien in der Antike*. München, 1954). Both "Leitung" and "Führung" inadequately characterize the content of Rabbow's later work which focuses on meditational exercises, which are a kind of self-healing device. Spiritual exercises might of course be recommended as valuable in a course of psychagogic guidance but they are not part of the psychagogic process itself as defined here.

the soul," the passions.⁴² First are those who have come close to wisdom but have not put their good into practice. This class is very near perfection but on slippery ground, since they still feel the passions although they have escaped the diseases of the mind. Their assurance has not yet been tested. Those in the second class have laid aside both the greatest ills of the mind and its passions, but yet are not in assured possession of immunity. They can still slip back into their former state. The third class is beyond the reach of many of the great vices but not beyond the reach of all.⁴³

Seneca informs us about Epicurus' classification of students.⁴⁴ Epicurus presumably classified students into three categories, depending on their different aptitudes. The first are those who on their own, without any one's assistance, work their way to the truth. The second are those who need outside help, who will not proceed unless someone leads the way; these will follow the guide faithfully. The third are those who do not need a guide as much as they require someone to encourage and force them along. Such a classification is present in the work of most moralists. Thus, when Epictetus says that his function as a teacher is to "make you independent," he registers his students' dependence on him and his hope that they might advance to the first category described above.⁴⁵ The second and third group of students in Epicurus' classification, in turn, set the stage for variations in the forms of exhortation required; mild forms of exhortation and admonition are applicable to students of

---

⁴² Seneca, *Epistles* 75.8–18; 72.6–11. The three classes of the progressing ones are still "fools." The "basest" and the "wise" fall on each side of the spectrum (75.7–8, 15). Seneca speaks of the difference between the wise and the progressing ones with reference to the irrational and rational. The wise is resolute because his rational part is in complete control. This does not entail his withdrawal from the category of man since he continues to feel pain and "turn pale." The wise stands erect under any load; he knows that he was born to carry burdens. But the progressing person, whose mind sags and bends, and wavers in uncertainty, is "weak" (71.26–27). Seneca defines "disease" as a "persistent perversion of the judgment, so that things which are mildly desirable are thought to be highly desirable" (75.10–12; 72.6). On Stoic views of progress see L. L. Haber, *Prokope: Stoic Views on Moral Progress in the Context of Stoic Developmental Psychology* (Diss., University of California at Berkeley, 1973); Diogenes Laertius, *Lives of Eminent Philosophers* 7.127; Epictetus, *Discourse* 1.4.

⁴³ Seneca, *Epistle* 75.9, 13–14. They have thus, Seneca explains, escaped avarice but still feel anger; they are not longer troubled by lust, but are still troubled by ambition.

⁴⁴ Idem, *Epistle* 52.3–4 = Epicurus, fr. 192 Us. Compare Isocrates, *Antidosis* 208.

⁴⁵ Epictetus, *Discourse* 2.19.29. Cf. 3.2; 4.2; 3.6.9–10 on Epictetus' twofold classification of students.

the second group whereas more stringent types are necessary for members of the third group.

As the moralists discuss different types of pupils and concerns for the tender ones, they also remark on the relationship between the various types and give advice as to the appropriate attitude of each student to the other. Seneca for example advises Lucilius not to despise those who can gain salvation only with the assistance of others and informs us that Epicurus had special praise for those who can work their way to the truth without any one's assistance and said that those who need some assitance should not be despised but rather respected. Epicurus was ready to congratulate this latter class but felt more respect for the third, because "it is a greater credit to have brought about the same result with the more difficult material upon which to work."[46]

Besides the above examples of the common view of different types of humans, one might refer to Plutarch's discussion of various types of young men and the ways in which they listen to admonitions and rebukes.[47] And Quintilian who discusses the mutual duties of teachers and pupils refers to different types of students and the appropriate treatment for each. It is a sign of a good teacher that he be able to "differentiate between the abilities of his respective pupils and to know their natural bent."[48] In Philodemus' *On Frank Criticism* we meet two types of pupils, namely, the recalcitrant ones and those who obediently follow instruction. Similarly, Paul refers to community members as "obedient" and "disobedient." A subtle awareness of differences among humans can also be seen in Paul's characterization of people as "weak" and "strong."[49] Paul urges the "wise" Corinthians not to "destroy" the weak who need special treatment. These classifications show both differences among pupils and their aptitudes and a required sensitivity of the teacher to factor in these differences in his guidance, both in his adaptation and the methods he employs. Understood is that each type of pupil or each type of disposition requires a particular treatment.

According to Iamblichus, it was Pythagoras who had discovered

---

[46] Seneca, *Epistles* 75:15; 52.3–6. Compare Aristotle, *Nicomachean Ethics* 1162a34–1165b36; *Eudemian Ethics* 1242b35–1243a14; *Great Ethics* 1213b18–30.

[47] Plutarch, *On Listening to Lectures* 46C–47E.

[48] See Quintilian, *Oratorical Institutions* 2.8.1; 2.2.1–14; 2.3.10; 2.4.8–12.

[49] See 1 Cor 8:7–11; 9:22; Rom 14:1; 15:1; and pp. 238–39, 274–77, 299–310 and 329–332, below.

the method of communicating to each "the appropriate portion of wisdom according to each one's own nature and ability."⁵⁰ The same method was appreciated, I would maintain, by most philosophers and moralists who engaged in one form or another of a teacher-student relationship.⁵¹ Such a classification of students also set the stage for variations in the forms of exhortation required. Different aptitudes among students and different methods require knowledge of recipients so that one can adapt one's methods appropriately in view of the condition in question. The differences among students required both sensitivity towards the differences and adaptation in one's discourse to accommodate them, as did the various circumstantial requirements noted by orators.

## 2.2 Adaptability and the Mixed Method of Praise and Blame

That adaptability and the use of praise and blame are closely related is evident from Plutarch's detailed exposition of frank speech and the opportune moment.⁵² The considered use of beneficial harshness characterizes a true friend and it is in the candid approach to faults that the friend differs from the flatterer. A flatterer does not oppose his "friends" and is willing to tolerate anything; he adapts to everything, no matter how demeaning. Praise and blame is thus one of the most secure means of distinguishing flatterers from friends but this method raises concerns for adaptability since its use demands attentiveness to the opportune moment. If blame is used indiscriminately or not at the right moment it becomes destructive; instead of saving by effecting a cure or change through shame or fear, it destroys the person:

> There is the greatest difference between admonition and reproach. For the former is gentle and amicable, the latter hard and insolent; the former corrects those who err, the latter merely censures them.⁵³

---

⁵⁰ See *Iamblichus, On the Pythagorean Way of Life* 9.49 and 30.180-83 (Dillon & Hershbell; Atlanta, 1991), pp. 72, 190-92; F. Decleva Caizzi (ed.), *Antisthenis fragmenta* (Milan, 1966), fr. 51. For the importance of the opportune moment for Pythagoras, see C. J. de Vogel, *Pythagoras and Early Pythagoreanism* (Assen, 1966), pp. 113-33.
⁵¹ Cf. A. J. Malherbe, "'Pastoral Care' in the Thessalonian Church," *NTS* 36 (1990), p. 382.
⁵² Plutarch, *How to Tell a Flatterer from a Friend* 59B and 68D-74D.
⁵³ *Gnomologium Byzantinum* 59 (176, Wachsmuth), πλεῖστον διαφέρει τὸ νουθετεῖν τοῦ ὀνειδίζειν· τὸ μὲν γὰρ ἤπιόν τε καὶ φίλον, τὸ δὲ σκληρόν τε καὶ ὑβριστικόν· καὶ τὸ μὲν διορθοῖ

Now censure is a mark of good-will, not of ill-will. For both he who is a friend and he who is not, reproach; but the enemy does so in scorn, the friend in kindness.[54]

... and he who reproaches a friend dissolves friendship.[55]

Complaisance gets us friends, plain speaking hate.[56]

These texts distinguish different forms and functions of blame and place value on admonition as opposed to reproach in the correction of faults; they also note the dangers for friendship in a harsh approach and put forward dispositional criteria to test whether one using harshness is a friend or a foe. One of the topics of friendship was whether and how one should correct the errors of one's friends. While many doubted that friendship could withstand reproach, others defended the use of blame among friends. In his definition of the "admonishing type of letter," Ps.-Demetrius pre-emptively notes: "Do not, then, think that the person who would rebuke sins had neither parents nor a (proper) upbringing, nor, worst of all, that he has no relative or friend."[57] Such a remark would not be called for if it did not reflect a belief to the contrary.

One solution to this dilemma, adopted, for example, by Joseph, according to the *Testament of Joseph*, was simply to advise the concealment of faults and the refraining from reproach for the sake of brotherly unanimity.[58] This, however, was not the preferred course of action among moralists and was, for example, expressly advised against among the friends in the Epicurean schools in Athens and Naples. A strong undercurrent, furthermore, existed in the philosophic-moral tradition which emphasized the value and need of a certain harshness in moral guidance, particularly when accompanied by other more

---

τοὺς ἁμαρτάνοντας, τὸ δὲ μόνον ἐλέγχει. Transl. by A. J. Malherbe, *Paul and the Popular Philosophers* (Minneapolis, 1989), p. 42. I have adjusted the translation.

[54] Clement, *Ped.* 66.1 (GCS 128, 26–29 Stählin-Treu), τὸ ψέγειν ... ἄμφω μὲν γὰρ ὀνειδίζετον. Compare Isocrates, *Concerning Peace* 72.

[55] Sirach 22:20, καὶ ὁ ὀνειδίζων φίλον διαλύσει φιλίαν.

[56] Terence, *Andria* 1.1.41, "Obsequium amicos, veritas odium parit." Cf. Cicero, *On Friendship* 89.

[57] Ps.-Demetrius, *Epistolary Types* 7 (34, 37–39 Malherbe).

[58] *T. Jos.* 17.1–4, "You see, children how great things I endured, that I should not put my brothers to shame. Do you also, therefore, love one another and with patience hide one another's faults; for God delights in the unity of brothers.... (Such was my attitude) also when my brothers came in Egypt, when they learnt that I returned the money to them and did not reproach them but even comforted them...." H. W. Hollander and M. de Jonge, *The Testaments of the Twelve Patriarchs* (Leiden, 1985), pp. 403, 405 Cf. *T. Jos.* 11.2 and *T. Sim.* 4.6. See also Prov 17:9; *Diog.* 9:5; 1 Pet 4:8; Jas 5:10.

soothing measures.[59] At the same time, concerns regarding the destructive nature of harshness were raised. The use of harshness demands that we recognize the degree of blame, its purpose, and whether it is delivered in an untimely fashion or not. Below I document a debate in antiquity centering on the suitability of beneficial blame in the correction of faults. The harshness of some of the Cynics, the successors of blame poetry, contrasts with this type of harshness. In light of the positive use of blame, I discuss the limitations of gentleness and harshness as criteria to distinguish "harsh" and "gentle" philosophers.

### 2.2.1 The "mixed method" proper

"With gentle words at times, at others harsh."[60]

One of the most relevant means by which a moralist adapted to the needs of others and wielded his power as a guide of souls, was the mixture of gentle and harsh elements of persuasion. Although praise and blame were used in various contexts, for example, in discussions of the epideictic genre, they were an especially valuable pedagogical hortatory means in the care of the young. A mild method presupposes that the ailment is easily cured and displays a positive view of the human condition; the more pessimistic the view of the human condition was, the harsher the method employed. This is also true, *mutatis mutandis*, of the use of the mixed method in the care of the young; the harsher the method, the greater the sickness.

Philodemus is, as far as I know, the only author of Greco-Roman antiquity who labels the mixing of praise and blame as the "mixed method."[61] But this way of exhorting in an attempt to influence others was valued by most moralists and was thought to be particularly effective in the guidance of the weak and progressing persons. Below I document its use in Dio Chrysostom, Clement of Alexandria, Sextus Empiricus, Plutarch, Quintilian, Maximus of Tyre, Cicero,

---

[59] Plutarch, *How to Tell a Flatterer from a Friend* 49EF; 55B-E; Epictetus, *Discourse* 3.23.30, "Man, the lecture room of the philosopher is a hospital; you ought not to walk out of it in pleasure, but in pain." Cf. Seneca, *Epistle* 52.12-14 and 75.5, "Our words should aim not to please but to help."

[60] Homer, *Iliad* 12.267, spoken of the chiding of the two Ajaxes to their laggard fellow soldiers.

[61] Philodemus, *On Frank Criticism* fr. 58.7-8, μείκτος τρόπος. Cf. Ps.-Libanius, *Epistolary Styles* 45 (72, 6 Malherbe) on the "mixed" letter type.

and Seneca. In chapter three we will see its use by Philodemus; in chapter six, its use by Paul.

#### 2.2.1.1 *The mixture of harsh and gentle means of exhortation*

The quotation at the beginning of this section occurs in Dio's description of the ideal Cynic:

> But as for himself... [he] will strive to preserve his individuality in seemly fashion... always honoring and promoting virtue and sobriety and trying to lead all men thereto, partly by persuading and exhorting, partly by abusing and reproaching, in the hope that he may thereby rescue somebody from folly... and soft living, taking them aside privately one by one and also admonishing them in groups every time he finds opportunity, 'With gentle words at times, at others harsh.'[62]

Dio claims to be like a physician who, when there is need for surgery or cautery, would not, for example, in the case of his father, mother or children, "cut with a duller knife or cauterize with milder fire, but, on the contrary, he would use the most potent and vigorous treatment possible."[63] The same applies to his fellow citizens, friends, and kinsmen; he increases the "vehemence of his admonition and exhortation for himself and them alike."[64] Dio has here described the mixed method, its purpose of aiding all, and the need for the use of beneficial harshness. "A bad philosopher is," Dio notes, "marked by a lack of severity."[65]

Clement displays a conscientious use of the method, its purpose and rationale. This is evident from his contrast between a "gentle" and a more "stringent" approach in the discussion of hortatory persuasive and dissuasive terms in chapters nine and ten of book one of *The Pedagogue*. Harshness and gentleness are both legitimate and necessary for the successful execution of the divine pedagogue's task. Towards the end of *The Pedagogue* Clement reflects on the mixed nature of the divine psychagogy:

> The philanthropic pedagogue bestows aid on us in manifold ways, now offering advice, now rebuke; he holds up to us the dishonor of those who have sinned and makes clear their deserved punishment, both to guide our souls and to admonish us.[66]

---

[62] Dio Chrysostom, *Discourse* 77/78.38, παρακαλῶν ... λοιδορούμενος καὶ ὀνειδίζων.
[63] Idem, *Discourse* 77/78.43, βοηθεῖν ἅπασιν ... τέμνειν ἢ καίειν.
[64] Ibid., 77/78.42.
[65] Idem, *Discourse* 32.17–19. Compare 32.7–11.
[66] Clement, *Ped.* 3.8; 43.2 (GCS 261, 21–24 Stählin-Treu). On Clement, see also pp. 62–64, above.

The practice of physicians throws light on the method and Clement uses here the common analogy of bodily ailment and psychological frailty: "Just as our body needs a physician when it is sick, so, too, when we are weak, our soul needs the pedagogue to cure its passions."[67] Just as there is a harsh and gentle παρρησία, the savior "applies not only mild remedies" but also "stringent ones"; fear, for example, is bitter, but it confers health.[68] More stringent measures, such as wormwood or hellebore, and in other cases even surgery, are sometimes needed because of the severity of the illness.[69] Clement answers the deduction of those who conclude that the divine pedagogue cannot be good since he uses the rod and threats, becomes angry and inflicts punishment. In Clement's view it is not at all inconsistent that the saving word employs railing or reproach in its care. These are simply medicines which awaken shame for sins:

> If there is need for reproach or blame, then there is also occasion to wound, not to death, but to its salvation, a soul grown callous; in such a way he inflicts a little pain, but spares it eternal death.[70]

---

[67] Clement, *Ped.* 3.3 (GCS 91, 11–13 Stählin-Treu). On Chrysippus' use of this analogy in his work *On the Passions*, see SVF 3.471 (120.18–22); 3.458 (111.8–12); 3.460 (112.1–13). See p. 118 (fn. 69), below.

[68] Clement, *Ped.* 83.2 (GCS 138, 21–139, 2 Stählin-Treu). See also 96.1–2 (GCS 147, 2–14) where Clement quotes the parable of the mustard seed in Matt 13:31, "by the bitterness of the mustard-seed he suggests, too, that the unpleasantness and the purgative nature of correction are all to our advantage."

[69] Epictetus prays that he should never have for a friend a "wise fool" (σοφὸν μωρόν) for there is nothing harder to handle (*Discourse* 2.15.14). Epictetus registers his view that the worse condition requires a harsher treatment: "'I have decided,' he says! Why yes, and so have madmen; but the firmer their decision is about what is false, the more hellebore they need." According to Seneca, Aristo, following Chrysippus, used an analogy of mental and physical disease, equating the false opinions with insanity and madness, which should be treated by a hellebore, namely, the doctrines of philosophy and not precepts only (*Epistle* 94.17). Cf. also Ps.-Socrates, *Epistle* 8.14–16 (ed. Malherbe), "when you have drunk the hellebore, it will benefit you, for it is much stronger than the wine of Dionysius. The one produces great madness and the other cures it." Cf. Menander 708K "If you on giving help do chide the recipient, then you are besprinkling Attic honey with wormwood." Lucretius and Quintilian use the simile to express their views of their respective projects. Quintilian, quoting Lucretius, expresses anxiety that he might in his work have had too little honey and too much wormwood, and "that though the student may find it a healthy draught, it will be far from agreeable" (*Oratorical Institutions* 3.1.4). Lucretius, *On the Nature of Things* 4.11, "And as physicians when they seek to give | A draught of bitter wormwood to a child, | First smear along the edge that rims the cup | The liquid sweets of honey, gulden-hued."

[70] Clement, *Ped.* 74.2–3 (GCS 133, 11–18 Stählin-Treu τοῦ σωτηρίου λόγου κηδεμονικῶς λοιδορεῖσθαι) Ibid., 62.1; 64.3 (GCS 126, 22–26; 127, 34128, 4). Ὀνειδισμός is a φαρμακεία and the use of ἔλεγχος is like a "surgery performed on the passions

The "art of censure" inflicts benevolent pain which is a mark of good-will, not hate. Blame, however, must be followed by more soothing measures. The pedagogue first artfully slides into censure by reviling as though to arouse by the whip of sharp words minds become sluggish; then he encourages the same persons. Those whom praise does not stimulate are spurred on by blame, and those whom blame does not stir up to seek salvation are by denunciation raised towards the truth. The condition of those exhorted determines the degree of harshness; more stringent method is needed for the more severely ill and those difficult to cure. "Some," Clement notes, "are hard to cure"; these are "forged as iron is with fire, hammer and anvil, that is, by threats, censure and punishment"; others adhere to faith as "selftaught and as acting of their own free will, grow by praise."[71] Similarly, in the moral domain, those who suffer from a disease difficult to cure, such as self-conceit, need a harsher form of treatment. But those who instinctively do the correct thing need not be admonished; praise is only an incentive for them to continue what they are already doing. Severe measures would simply destroy these "self-taught" persons. To these categories of those difficult to cure and those doing well other moralists added those who are incurable.[72]

Some hold that only the perfect person is worthy of praise and the bad one of blame, others that all men are bad and that "the form of education making use of rebuke and censure" is suitable for men and not for God who alone is wise and perfect. It is however because of different types of recipients and different disposition of those guided that praise and blame are remedies more necessary for men than any other sort. Different modes of persuasion are appropriate for each type of progressing person. Finally, Clement underlines that "the word adapts himself completely to the disposition of each, being strict with one, forgiving another," and that the more stringent measures aim at the salvation of sinners.[73] The above brings

---

of the soul" which need to be "removed by the surgeon's knife" (64.4–65.1; GCS 128, 6–11).

[71] Clement, *Ped.* 93.2–94.1 (145, 16–32 Stählin-Treu). Clement attributes to the Epicureans a view which holds that blame only is suitable for humans, not praise (cf. Epicurus, Us. fr. 71, 3).

[72] Plato, *Gorgias* 525BC ("it is through bitter throes of pain that they receive their benefit"); *Protagoras* 325AB; Philo, *The Worse Attacks the Better* 178. On those who can be cured, see Plutarch, *On the Delays of the Divine Vengeance* 551E; Dio Chrysostom, *Discourse* 32.17–20, 30, 33.

[73] Clement, *Ped.* 66.1–5 (GCS 128, 26–29, 31–129, 2; 129, 4–6, 14–17 Stählin-

to the fore the need for praise and blame, for recognizing resourcefulness in exhortation, for the beneficial use of harshness and for the need to adapt to whatever is most suitable to each individual.

Sextus Empiricus describes the mixed method when polemicizing against the dogmatists. Sextus also uses a medical analogy; the use of a stringent method is dictated by the severity of the sickness. Physicians who cure bodily ailments have "remedies which differ in strength, and apply the severe ones to those whose ailments are severe and the milder to those mildly affected."[74] Similarly, the sceptic propounds arguments which differ in strength, employing those which are weighty and capable by their stringency of disposing of the dogmatists' ailment, self-conceit, in cases where the mischief is due to a severe attack of rashness. But "in the case of those whose ailment of conceit is superficial and easy to cure, and whom it is possible to restore to health by milder methods of persuasion," he employs "the milder arguments."[75] At one time the sceptic uses arguments that are weighty in their persuasiveness and at another time such as appear less impressive since these frequently suffice. The philanthropic sceptic thus recognizes, like the most "philanthropic physician" in Maximus, the need for a more stringent method in severe cases although a milder one is often sufficient.[76]

Plutarch underlines the effectiveness of the mixed method when dealing with a troubled spirit which cannot put up with unmixed admonition;[77] a light admixture of praise which mitigates the peremptory tone of the censure is most helpful. The Ps.-Plutarchean tract *On the Education of Children* similarly emphasizes that children should be led to honorable practices by means of encouragement and reasoning, and not by blows or ill-treatment which are fit for slaves rather than freeborns.[78] This does not mean that blame should not

---

Treu, τὸ δὲ εἶδος τοῦτο τέχνη ἐστι ψεκτική....). See Plato, *Gorgias* 477A.

[74] Sextus Empiricus, *Outlines of Pyrrhonism* 3.32, 280. Cf. also 1.20, 164 and 177.

[75] Ibid., 3.281. LSJ s.v., εὐίατος. Aristotle, *Nicomachean Ethics* 1121a20; 1146a34; Theophrastus, *Hist. Pl.* 5.4.5; Porphyry, *On Abstinence* 1.56; Clement, *Ped.* 94.1 (145, 27–32 Stählin-Treu).

[76] Maximus of Tyre, *Discourse* 14.4 (174, 15–16 Hobein).

[77] Plutarch, *How to Tell a Flatterer from a Friend* 72B–D, νουθεσίαν ἄκρατον. As examples Plutarch notes e.g. Homer, *Iliad* 13.116; 5.171, and Euripides, *Phoenecian Women* 1688.

[78] Ps.-Plutarch, *On the Education of Children* 8F–9A. Biting is a form of reproach used on slaves. Galen, *On the Passions*, reports that his mother used to bite her slaves when she lost her temper. See R. B. Branham, *Unruly Eloquence* (Cambridge, Mass., 1989), pp. 266–67.

be used on freeborns. In fact, praise and blame are more helpful for the freeborn than any sort of ill-usage; praise incites them towards the honourable and blame keeps them from the disgraceful. Rebuke and praise should furthermore be used alternately and in a variety of ways. It is well to shame children by rebuke when they are full of confidence and then to cheer them up by praise, to imitate nurses who offer their babies the breast for comfort after they have made them cry. The practice of fathers and physicians also throws light on the manner of exhortation. Plutarch has no regard for fathers who are harsh in their manners; but

> as physicians, by mixing bitter drugs with sweet syrups, have found that the agreeable taste gains access for what is beneficial, so fathers should combine the abruptness of their rebukes with mildness, and at one time grant some licence to the desires of their children, and slacken the reins a little, and then at another time draw them tight again.[79]

Careful supervision and different approaches are needed depending on the age and disposition of the young. Hope of reward and fear of punishment are important to restrain their impulses. Wise fathers ought to be vigilant and to bring the young to reason by instruction, by threats and by putting forward good examples.

Quintilian's discussion of the aptitude of pupils and their treatment is pertinent. Quintilian disapproves of flogging, although it is the regular custom. But the teacher must adopt a parental attitude and be able to govern the behavior of his pupils by the strictness of his discipline. The teacher should be strict but not austere; the more he admonishes, the less he will have to punish. He must avoid sarcasm and abuse. In order to avoid the charge of corruption, and because of the special attention required by the weak, Quintilian does not approve of boys sitting with young men and thinks it desirable to keep the weaker members separate from the more mature. One must avoid a dull and uninteresting teacher, even as we avoid a dry and arid soil for plants that are still young and tender, for with such a teacher the growth of boys is stunted. Because of their weakness, the teacher must not be unduly severe in correcting faults. As the farmer's pruning-hook should not be applied while the leaves are yet

---

[79] Ps.-Plutarch, *On the Education of Children* 13D, τὴν τῶν ἐπιτιμημάτων ἀποτομίαν τῇ πραότητι μιγνύναι. See ibid., 11E; 12B–D, and Plutarch, *On Moral Virtue* 452D; *Precepts of Statecraft* 810C. Compare Maximus of Tyre, *Discourse* 1.8c–e (14, 10–15, 3 Hobein); Seneca *On Anger* 2.21.1–7; and Dio Chrysostom *Discourse* 32.25–28.

young (for they are unable as yet to endure a scar), so the instructor should be as kind as possible at this stage; remedies, which are harsh by nature, must be applied with a gentle hand.[80]

In *On Anger* Seneca uses physicians as an example and employs the analogy of the curb and the spur in the guidance of the young. One should set a young man "right both by admonition and by force, by measures both gentle and harsh ... stinting, not our reproof, but our anger. For what physician will show anger toward a patient?"[81] Apparently, Seneca's interlocutor had thought otherwise: "'What then?' you say; 'is not correction (castigatio) sometimes necessary?'" Yes, "but with discretion, not with anger. For it will not hurt, but will heal under the guise of hurting." If milder measures fail to bring relief, physicians will progress to a harsher treatment. Similarly,

> it becomes a guardian of the law, the ruler of the state, to heal human nature by the use of words, and these of the milder sort, as long as he can, to the end that he may persuade someone to do what he ought to do.... Let him pass next to harsher language, in which he will still aim at admonition and reproof. Lastly, let him resort to punishment, yet still making it light and not irrevocable. Extreme punishment let him appoint only to extreme crime, so that no man will lose his life unless it is to the benefit even of the loser to lose it.[82]

No treatment seems harsh if its result is salutary; "counsel, conversation, encouragement, comfort, and sometimes even reproof flourish best in friendships."[83] But reproof one should use, as cautery and amputation, rarely and reluctantly and only if unavoidable and if no other remedy is available; "we may apply a mild reproof, so combined, however, with earnestness, that, while severity is shown, offensive language is avoided. Nay more, we must show clearly that even that very harshness which goes with our reproof is designed for the good of the person reproved."[84]

---

[80] Quintilian, *Oratorical Institutions* 1.3.13–14; 2.2.4, 7, 14; 2.4.8–12. Cf. also 11.1.90.
[81] Seneca, *On Anger* 1.15.1 (et molliter et aspere); 2.21.1–3, "By freedom the spirit grows, by servitude it is crushed; if it is commended... it mounts up, but these same measures breed insolence... therefore we must guide the child between the two extremes, using now the curb, now the spur."
[82] Seneca, *On Anger* 1.6.3. Cf. 1.6.1–2.
[83] Cicero, *On Duties* 1.56, 58.
[84] Ibid., 1.136–37, genus castigandi. Cf. Lucian, *Apology* 2, τεμνόμενον ... ἐπὶ σωτηρίᾳ.

### 2.2.2 *Destructive harshness and the weak and tender students*

We have seen examples of the classification of different types of students and the use of the mixed method in the reformatory ethic of moralists and the use of salutary harshness. It was particularly in the use of harsher means of persuasion that concerns were raised as to its possible adverse impact on the insecure students. Inconsiderate harshness might destroy their interest in philosophy instead of saving whatever inkling of interest they might have. Moralists often refer to these insecure students as "weak," accentuating their psychological disposition.

The term "weakness" is used variously in Greco-Roman antiquity. It can be used of physical frailty, disease or sickness, or the lack of physical strength. The term can also be used for being weak in social power, poor, or socially humble, or even for a weak discourse or argument. Plutarch can thus speak of a "poor speaker" and the fact that one can weaken the force of one's words by one's actions.[85] Οἱ ἀσθενεῖς, like οἱ πολλοί, are often referred to as a recognized category, in contrast to the "strong." In such contexts the "weak" often refer to the socially humble.[86] It is not difficult to find reference to a woman being powerless because of the weakness of her nature, although a frequently met saying is simply "the weakness of human nature."[87]

The terminology of weakness presents itself naturally in the moral sphere in light of the common analogy of bodily health and sickness to moral health or sickness. In such a context moralists often advise against a destructive approach for the weak or progressing person and use the dichotomy of salvation and destruction to drive home their point. Such texts provide evidence of the common use of the term σῴζω and ἀπόλλυμι in a moral context; instead of "destroying" (ἀπόλλυμι) the weak students, i.e. deterring his/her progress, one

---

[85] Plutarch, *On Brotherly Love* 401A; *On Having Many Friends* 88F; Epictetus, *Discourse* 3.22.101; Philo, *On Abraham* 26; Hippocrates, *The Art* 6.1–3; Demetrius, *On Style* 240; Athenaeus, *Sophists at Dinner* 162B. LSJ s.v. οἱ ἀσθενεῖς.

[86] Dio Chrysostom notes that "enmity can not only expose and humiliate the weak... but also annoy those who are prosperous" (*Discourse* 40.20). Cf. Musonius Rufus (fr. 2, 36.16–33 Hense).

[87] Epicurus, *Vatican Sentences* 37; Philodemus, *On Frank Criticism* col. 22b1; Maximus of Tyre, *Discourse* 2.2; 4.5a (20, 5; 45, 13 Hobein); Dio Chrysostom, *Discourse* 40.21; Plutarch, *On the Control of Anger* 463D; Aristotle, *Great Ethics* 1213b2–18. For reference to women's weakness, see Philodemus, *On Frank Criticism* col. 22b; P. Lond. 971, 4; Cicero, *On Friendship* 46; 1 Esdras 4.32–34; *1 Clem.* 6.2.

should "save" (σῴζω) them, i.e., aid or benefit the progressing one.[88] The moralists' concern for the weak and insecure students is inherent in the ancient reformatory ethic and sets the stage for psychagogic adaptability and instructions with regard to different types of students.

Dio Chrysostom notes that there are two systems for the diagnosis and therapy of vice, just as there are for maladies in general, namely, purgative and surgical. The former treatment is the proper function of those who have the power through persuasion and reason to calm and soften the soul. "These indeed are saviors and guardians of all who can be saved...."[89] Both types of practitioners are required by the state, but the type found in public office should be much the milder of the two,

> for in administering punishment one should be sparing, but not so in imparting instruction; and a good prince is marked by compassion, a bad philosopher by lack of severity. For while the harshness of the one in punishing destroys, the other's severity of speech is by nature salutary.[90]

This quotation contrasts destructive punishment with salutary harshness. Concerns focusing on the negative effects of harsh speech surface in Plutarch's *On Listening to Lectures*. Here we encounter a discussion of three different types of young men, their respective dispositions, and the appropriate way of exhorting each one of them. The theme of the essay is the proper behavior of pupils in the lecture-room and the stress is on the improvement and upbuilding of character. After having dealt with the young who are "dead to all modesty because of an habitual and continued acquaintance with wrongdoing," Plutarch turns his attention to "young men of the opposite disposition."[91] These run away without looking back and try to desert philosophy if they ever hear a single word directed against themselves; and,

---

[88] "Medicine," as Apuleius said, "is sought out not for the purpose of destroying men but rather for that of saving them" (*Metamorphoses* 10.11). See Clement, *Ped.* 3.3 (GCS 91, 11–13 Stählin-Treu); Philo, *On the Migration of Abraham* 124; *On Abraham* 176–77. For the use of διαφθείρω, "to ruin," see Dio Chrysostom, *Discourse* 43.10 (διαφθείρειν τοὺς νέους); 77/78.45; Diodorus Siculus, *Library of History* 16.54.4 (διέφθειρε τὰ ἤθη τῶν ἀνθρώπων); Isocrates, *To Demonicus* 22.

[89] Dio Chrysostom, *Discourse* 32.17–20, 30, 33.

[90] Ibid., 32.18, τὸ μὲν γὰρ τῆς τιμωρίας σκληρὸν ἀπόλλυσι τὸ δὲ τοῦ λόγου πικρὸν σῴζειν πέφυκε. Compare Isocrates, *To Antipater* 6, διὰ δὲ τοὺς ἐπὶ τῷ βελτίστῳ παρρησιαζομένους πολλὰ σῴζεσθαι καὶ τῶν ἐπιδόξων διαφθαρήσεσθαι πραγμάτων. Plato, *Laws* 909A, "and they shall company with them to minister to their souls' salvation by admonition" (ἐπὶ νουθετήσει τε καὶ τῇ τῆς ψυχῆς σωτηρίᾳ ὁμιλοῦντες·). See also Clement, *Ped.* 75.1 (GCS 133, 29–91 Stählin-Treu) and *Ep. Diog.* 29.1–29 (Malherbe).

[91] Plutarch, *On Listening to Lectures* 46DE.

although the sense of modesty which nature had bestowed upon them is an admirable beginning for salvation, they lose it through effeminacy and weakness, since they display no firmness under reproof, nor do they accept corrections with the proper spirit. . . .[92]

Here we find the concepts of weakness and strength, and those of salvation and destruction. The destruction comes about because the young cannot bear the reproof and correction administered. The young experience dejecting influences as a "result of weakness" and also experience a "weakening of purpose" by the sober advice of friends and the bitter criticisms of the unfriendly. Plutarch speaks of untrained temperaments, unsteady and fluctuating, owing to "weakness of will." He also speaks of anger, an outburst of passion, which is caused by ἀσθένεια. All these hinder the progress of the young. For "present salvation" it is important to have either good friends or ardent enemies.[93] Reason and law must obtain a suitable and salutary grip on the emotions of the young and efficaciously set them upon the right path.[94]

Epictetus does not often use σῴζω in a moral context. Two texts, however, show that he was acquainted with such a use. At the end of his *To the Man Who had Become Shameless*, Epictetus reverts back to his usual theme of the need for self scrutiny.[95] One should not give in too easily but learn from how the gymnastic trainer of boys acts. The boy he is training is thrown; "get up," he says, "and wrestle again, till you get strong." React, Epictetus advises, in some such way yourself, for I would have you know that there is nothing more easily prevailed upon than a human soul:

> You have but to will a thing and it has happened, the reform has been made . . . For it is within you that both destruction and deliverance lie.—But what good do I get after all that?— . . . Instead of shameless, you will be self-respecting . . . instead of dissolute, self-controlled. If you are looking for anything else greater than these things, go ahead and do what you are doing; not even a god can any longer save you.[96]

---

[92] Ibid., 46E, ἀρχὴν πρὸς τὸ σωθῆναι; ἀπολλύουσι διὰ τρυφὴν καὶ μαλακίαν.

[93] Idem, *How to Tell a Flatterer from a Friend* 74C; *Progress in Virtue* 78B; 82A; *On the Control of Anger* 453DE = Musonius Rufus, fr. 36 ed. Hense (δεῖ ἀεὶ θεραπευομένους βιοῦν τοὺς σῴζεσθαι μέλλοντας).

[94] Plutarch, *On Moral Virtue* 452D (ἐμμελῆ καὶ σωτήριον ἁφὴν ἁπτόμενος. . . .); *How to Profit by One's Enemies* 89B; 90C; *On Tranquility of Mind* 456F; 457B.

[95] Epictetus, *Discourse* 4.9.13–18, "And now, therefore, are you not willing to come to your own rescue?" (νῦν οὖν οὐ θέλεις σαυτῷ βοηθῆσαι;).

[96] Ibid., 4.9.16–18, ἔσωθεν γάρ ἐστι καὶ ἀπώλεια καὶ βοήθεια . . . οὐδὲ θεῶν σέ τις ἔτι

Towards the end of the *Encheiridion*, Epictetus asks, "What sort of a teacher, then, do you still wait for, that you should put off reforming yourself until he arrives? You are no longer a lad, but already a fullgrown man." If someone puts off paying attention to himself, he will make no progress but will continue to be a layman:

> Make up your mind... that the fitting thing for you to do is to live as a mature man who is making progress... remember that now is the contest... and that it is impossible to delay any longer, and that it depends on a single day and a single action, whether progress is lost or saved.[97]

Epictetus sometimes equates the uneducated with the weak; every faculty, he says, acquired by "the uneducated and the weak" is dangerous for them, as being apt to make them conceited. Adults look like children when they are uneducated in life. Such a person is "all conceited and puffed up" because he will not listen to reason, "much less submitting if any one by way of reproof reminds him of what he lacks and wherein he has gone astray."[98] An irresolute person is weak in character with a "sick soul" (ἀσθενὴς ψυχή). The starting point in philosophy is when there is "a consciousness of man's own weakness" and one realizes that the "governing principle is weak."[99] In Epictetus the salvation-destruction dichotomy occurs in a discussion on progress using the contrast between a young lad and full grown man which is a variation of the common child/mature person contrast. The dichotomy is related to progress which cannot be hindered except by the individual himself; it thus requires strenuous self-effort. Plutarch and Dio, on the other hand, emphasize the effect of exhortation on the young which can either destroy or save them, i.e., thwart or aid their progress.

*2.2.3 The appropriateness of praise and blame for the progressing person*
Just as unrelieved blame can be destructive so can indiscriminate praise.[100] Despite such dangers, both praise and blame are needed in the care of the young; one to spur on to action, the other to correct

---

σῶσαι δύναται. Compare Plato, *Republic* 492A, ἐὰν μή τις αὐτῇ βοηθήσας θεῶν τύχῃ.
[97] Epictetus, *Encheiridion* 51.2, ἀπόλλυται προκοπὴ καὶ σῴζεται. See also *Discourse* 1.18.8.
[98] Idem, *Discourse* 1.15.29; 1.8.8; 3.19.6.
[99] Idem, *Discourse* 1.26.16; 2.11; 2.15.20; 4.5.34.
[100] See Plutarch, *How to Tell a Flatterer from a Friend* 56B; Maximus of Tyre, *Discourse* 25.4f–6d (303, 4–304, 13).

and deter. The use of praise and blame was problematic on two fronts. Firstly, in order to effect a change through blame, the correct time and degree of harshness in the corrective process had to be determined in order to mitigate its adverse effects. Secondly, the question of the efficacy of the persuasive word was problematic in light of fate and perfection. If fate is believed in, it renders null and void the legitimate use of praise and blame, since both assign responsibility to the recipient. Also, if someone has already achieved the desired goal of perfection, there is no need for correction. But if humans are culpable, they need to be both praised and blamed.

The incompatibility of praise and blame with determinism became a standard anti-determinist argument, possibly popularized by Carneades. If we postulate the existence of wrong and right actions, virtue and vice must of necessity exist, and the noble or praiseworthy, and the base or blameworthy. Also, since praise and blame affect its recipients, one must know which objects are subject to change. Since praise and blame are connected with responsible action, one does not blame someone for non-acquired characteristics or for what happens of necessity.[101] Epicureans used such anti-deterministic arguments, emphasizing the use of the admonitory, reformatory, and retaliatory mode of discourse.[102] The use of different hortatory means shows that something depends on us. A reformatory ethic lays emphasis on human responsibility in correctional psychagogy. On the basis of soft-determinism, Stoics insisted that punishment and reward were compatible with determinism and recognized the legitimate use of praise and blame for the progressing person.[103]

In *Epistles* 94–95 Seneca shows how exhortation relates to the progressing person in certain forms of Stoicism. *Epistle* 94 asks whether doctrines of philosophy without precepts are sufficient to achieve the

---

[101] Philodemus, *Rhetoric* v. 4, col. 32a6–8 Sudhaus. See also Epictetus, *Discourse* 2.16.6–7; 2.17.1–2 and 10; Aristotle, *Nicomachean Ethics* 1109b31; 1113b23–25; *Eudemian Ethics* 1223a10; *Great Ethics* 1187a19–21; *Rhetoric* 1359a.

[102] Diogenes of Oenoanda notes, "if fate is believed in, that is the end of all censure and admonition, and even the wicked <will not be open to blame>" (Fr. 32 Chilton). Epicurus, *Letter to Menoeceus* 133; *On Nature* [34.25] 21–34; D. Sedley, "Epicurus' Refutation of Determinism," Συζήτησις: *Studi sull' epicureismo greco e romano offerti a Marcello Gigante* (Naples, 1983), vol. 1, p. 24 n. 18; Long & Sedley, *The Hellenistic Philosophers*, 1.103 and 106; 2.105–109, 112.

[103] SVF 2.1000 (293.34–41; 294.30–34); R. W. Sharples, *Alexander of Aphrodisias On Fate* (London, 1983), pp. 150, 100, 216; *On Fate* XXXIV 206.25–30; XXXV 207.5–7, 12–22; XXXVI 210.8–10.

happy life; *Epistle* 95 whether precepts without dogmas will suffice. Seneca concludes that these are complementary. The difference between the two is that precepts are "appropriate to the individual person," not "framed for mankind at large"; both are a form of advice (94.1, 31). Aristo the Stoic claimed that precepts were of slight importance; one should instead proceed deductively from a definition of the supreme good, from which one can deduce a precept for each individual occasion. Aristo rejects precepts because of the difficulty in individualizing doctrines and giving rules for each individual case. On Aristo's theory, even consolation, paraenesis, exhortation, and praise and blame, are superfluous. Seneca concedes that precepts alone are not effective in eradicating mistaken beliefs but they are beneficial in refreshing the memory and giving a greater specificity to the matter at hand. Individual differences and the demands of particular situations also require precepts or specific advice. Hortatory means are helpful; they give a sense of shame, assist suggestion by reason and add the motive for doing a given thing. Finally, admonition is necessary, since it teaches conduct which is important for virtue.[104]

In *Epistle* 71 Seneca draws up some contrasting characteristics of the wise and progressing person in relation to the supreme good and error. The progressing one has difficulty in acting out his beliefs and doctrines have not thoroughly permeated his soul. He needs to be exhorted by another who has advanced further.[105] In *Epistle* 94.48–52 Seneca reflects on the importance of exhortation as instrumental for the progressing person. This—the fact that one is not yet perfect but is still progressing—is Seneca's most significant evidence for the importance of preceptual guidance. In this, Seneca questions the definition postulated for the "perfect man" and bridges the great divide between the improving person and the wise person of the old Stoic position. The one who has understood what he should do is not wise until his mind is metamorphosed into the shape of that which he has learned. Neither precepts nor consolation, exhortation, persuasion or proofs are superfluous when it comes to the perfecting of virtue. These hortatory means require a sound state of mind and are helpful in producing one. Both precepts and doctrines are necessary because of

---

[104] Seneca, *Epistle* 94.2, 5–17, 21, 30, 32, 39, 42, and 44–45. In Aristo's view, paraenesis and exhortation are the business of nurses and pedagogues. See Sextus Empiricus, *Against the Dogmatics* 1.12.
[105] Seneca, *Epistle* 71.19–20, 26, 29–30.

the different aptitude of individuals and applied in accordance with the individual's progress:

> But the approach to these qualities is slow, and in the meantime, in practical matters, the path should be pointed out for the benefit of one who is still short of perfection, but is making progress. Wisdom by her own agency may perhaps show herself this path without the help of admonition; for she has brought the soul to a stage where it can be impelled in the right direction. Weaker characters, however, need someone to precede them, to say: 'Avoid this,' or 'do that.'[106]

Seneca focuses here on the need for assistance because of our depraved condition, reminiscing about the golden age when plain vice could be treated by plain cures; "in order to root out a deep-seated belief in wrong ideas, conduct must [now] be regulated by doctrines."[107] Dogmas are also necessary for attaining a fixed standard of judgment and for proofs and reasonings. But in order for doctrines to be effective, they must be mixed with precepts. Precepts are familiar even to the uninitiated before they are admitted to the sacred rites and the hidden truths of philosophy are revealed to them.[108] Certain persons have indeed made great progress towards virtue by obeying bare precepts alone, something which is ordinarily a matter of time and teaching. But a sluggish person, hampered by his evil habits, must have this soul-rust incessantly rubbed off. Precepts are of no avail unless we first remove the conditions—for example, the cause of a mistaken belief—that are likely to stand in the way of precepts. The soul of a weak person must first be set free by the accepted principles of philosophy in order to benefit from precepts.

After remarking on the importance of precepts for the weak, Seneca approvingly notes Posidonius' view that precepts, persuasion, consolation, and encouragement—as well as aetiology and personification—are all necessary hortatory means. Seneca thus recognizes the need for manifold hortatory devices to assist the immature. He also adds that the function of character portrayal is equivalent to that of precepts. Both precepts and character portrayal—the gentler forms of persuasion—are important for the progressing one since they can easily be adapted to his condition.[109] These gentle means of

---

[106] Idem, *Epistle* 94.51. Compare Cicero, *On Friendship* 7–10 and 21.
[107] Seneca, *Epistle* 95.4–6, 10–17, 29, 31, 34, 55, 72; Plutarch, *On the Control of Anger* 463D.
[108] Seneca, *Epistle* 95.64; cf. 95.36–37; 90.5–7. See Clement, *Ped.* 94.1 (145, 30–32 Stählin-Treu).
[109] Seneca, *Epistle* 95.65–66. Precepts are well suited for the uninitiated, weak, or

persuasion are contrasted to the harshness of dogmatic guidance. Besides recognizing the legitimacy of preceptorial guidance, Seneca also emphasizes the need for a harsher method which is needed because of a present depraved condition.

Plutarch's criticism of the Stoics also shows that praise and blame were especially applied to the progressing person.[110] Plutarch notes that his opponents often incite young men with praise and chastise them with admonitions; in the first case, pleasure is the consequence, in the second, pain: "Admonition and blame engender repentance and shame, to the first of which pain belongs in kind, to the second fear."[111] Admonition produces repentance through grief; blame shame through fear. Both are used to effect a change in another human being. Plutarch evidently agreed. Part of the function of blame was for reason to obtain a "suitable and salutary grip" on the emotions of young men, whether on shame, desire, repentance, pleasure, pain or grief, or ambition. This would set the young upon the right path. Blame or admonition, and the concomitant fear and pain, were thus important instrumental means in the care of the young. Stoics thus continued to use harsh and gentle forms of persuasion in their attempt to influence others; they had the right and duty to censure others.[112]

*2.2.4 The philotropeic method and the beneficial use of harshness*

We have seen examples from authors who recognize the beneficial use of harshness. A correct kind of caring does not shun exposing and censuring faults; it is a caring which might indeed hurt on occasion. Such beneficial pain, however, leads to true pleasure. These

---

the less mature, or as Maximus of Tyre said of fables, "For a fable is a more elegant interpreter of things which are not clearly seen because of the weakness of human nature" (*Discourse* 4.5a; 45, 12–14 Hobein). On Posidonius, see A. Dihle, "Posidonius' System of Moral Philosophy," *JHS* 93 (1973), pp. 50–57, and I. G. Kidd, *Posidonius II. The Commentary* (Cambridge University Press, 1988), pp. 646–51.

[110] Plutarch is arguing in defense of the Platonist-Peripatetic position against Chrysippus and uses Stoic practice as evidence against their theoretical stance on ἀπάθεια. See J. M. Dillon, "Metriopatheia and Apatheia: Some Reflections on a Controversy in Later Greek Ethics," in J. P. Anthon and A. Preus (eds.), *Essays in Ancient Greek Philosophy* (Albany, 1983), vol. 2, pp. 511–12.

[111] Plutarch, *On Moral Virtue* 452C. For Stoic views on grief and fear, which constituted two of the four classes of the passions, see SVF 3.407–20 and Diogenes Laertius *Lives of Eminent Philosophers* 7.111–14.

[112] Plutarch, *On Moral Virtue* 452C–D. Note Plutarch's statement, "these methods they use especially towards correction or improvement." Epictetus says that the philosopher's consciousness of his commission to reform others affords him the right (ἐξουσία) to censure them (*Discourse* 3.22.94).

issues surface in discussions of how to distinguish flatterers from friends and how to treat different types of people, and are clearly seen in Isocrates' discourses on moral education.[113] The widely used pedagogical mixed method of exhortation is in essence a variation of the admonitory kind of education advocated by the Elean Stranger in Plato's *The Sophist*, the method of fathers, who sometimes show anger at the errors of their sons and sometimes more gently exhort them.[114] Most aspects of this tradition coalesce, as we shall see in the next chapter, in the communal psychagogy witnessed in Philodemus' *On Frank Criticism*.

I take my clue from Philodemus' *On Frank Criticism* and label the method used to set the young on course and recognizing the need to adapt to each disposition and character, the "philotropeic method." This method recognizes the diverse nature and condition of people. The execution of this method depends on the student's condition and character. The frank counselor will "become attached to the person's character; if he attaches himself to those of a noble character," Philodemus asks, "why not also to those of a wicked character?"[115] In this he is like Alcibiades, the greatest flatterer, who could associate with good and bad alike. The frank counselor will, though, unlike the flatterer, become φιλότροπος. He will dedicate himself to the character of each person, to the noble "because of mirth," and to the wicked "because of sympathy," because sympathy is the cause of his own relief.[116] In his classification of persons as "noble" or

---

[113] Isocrates, *Letter to Philip* 1.1,22; *To Nicocles* 2, 28, 42–43, 48–53; *To Demonicus* 3–6, 22, 30–31, 45–46; *Concerning Peace* 72. Note the eulogized attributes of Diodotus in *To Antipater* 3–6; cf. *Antidosis* 206–14; 288–90. See also Plato, *Protagoras* 325AB; *Sophist* 229E–230A; *Gorgias* 525A–C; Aristotle, *Nicomachean Ethics* 1180a6–14; and Xenophon, *On Household Management* 13.6–12; 14.8.

[114] Plato, *Sophist* 229E–230A τὸ νουθετητικὸν εἶδος τῆς παιδείας. Plato contrasts the method of cross-examining (ἔλεγχος) with admonitory education (230B–231B) and discusses i) ἡ κολαστικὴ τέχνη; ii) ἡ διδασκαλικὴ τέχνη; iii) ἡ σοφιστικὴ τέχνη. The mixed method of praise and blame, or the use of pleasure and pain in psychagogy, is the same method of nurturing advocated by Plato in the case of infants (*Laws* 791D–793A). The formal structure of a psychagogic discourse reflected in Clement's *Pedagogue* (see pp. 62–63) builds thus on a well established tradition of harsh and gentle guidance, reflected in the common contrast between purgative and surgical methods and the analogy of slackening and tightening of the rein or the use of the curb and the spur. Cf. fns. 79 and 81, above.

[115] Philodemus, *On Frank Criticism* fr. 43.1–4, γενησόμενον φιλότροπον· εἰ δὲ ἀγαθῶν, πῶς οὐχὶ καὶ τῶν κακῶν; in the papyri φιλότροπον is preserved as ΦΙΛΟ. ΤΡΟΠΟΝ. A TLG search has not yielded another instance of this word in Greek literature. Cf. also ibid., cols. 4a1–6a8.

[116] Philodemus, *On Frank Criticism* fr. 43.4–8, ὡς γὰρ ἕνεκεν εὐφροσύνη[ς] ἐκείνων,

"wicked," Philodemus follows a common practice of classifying humans in psychological and ethical terms. The need of the psychagogue to "attach" himself to the character of his recipients, be they "base" or "noble," reminds us of Alcibiades' willingness to associate with all; Paul's statement in 1 Cor 9:19–23 is imbued with similar concerns.

The terms σωτηρία, as well as θεραπεία, βοήθεια and κηδεμονία, were all used to characterize the activity of moralists who saw their task as that of benefiting people.[117] Παρρησία which is a form of "solicitude" (κηδεμονία) and "relief" (βοήθεια) is characterized by Philodemus as ποικίλος; frank speech is "varied" both in the sense of being discriminating in light of a mixed audience and because it legitimately applies both praise and blame. Whatever means are available, including harshness, should then be used in an attempt to benefit others. It was commonplace that harshness should be used in a beneficial way. This is reflected in a gnomic saying of Menander, "The harshest man, admonishing a son, in his words is bitter, but in his action is a father."[118] The "venerable method of our fathers" thus includes harshness; this way of treating your sons, Plato notes, would most properly be called an "admonitory kind of education."[119] Paul's use of fatherly admonition and threats of even more severe measures lodges him securely within this tradition (1 Cor 4:14–21; 2 Cor 13:1–4). Moralists recognized certain professions as legitimate wielders of harshness. Fathers and mothers, as well as nurses and physicians, were the one's most commonly mentioned. Other legitimate wielders of harshness were guardians, teachers, and seniors, or all persons in charge, as, for example, rulers or statesmen.[120]

As Cicero, Plutarch, Seneca, Quintilian, Dio Chrysostom, Seneca,

---

οὕτω καὶ τούτων προσήκει συνπαθίας χάριν, δι' ἥν βοηθούμεθα.... Cf. Plutarch, *Alcibiades* 23.4.

[117] LSJ s.v. Cf Sextus Empiricus, *Outlines of Pyrrhonism* 3.32.280; *Ep. Diog.* 29.14–26 (Malherbe).

[118] Menander, 662K. Note again Dio Chrysostom, *Discourse* 32.17–19, 26, who contrasts the harshness which destroys and the severity of speech which is salutary (cf. 77/78.40), and Clement, *Ped.* 75.1 (GCS 133, 29–31 Stählin-Treu). Beneficial harshness is, however, applied, to "remediable offences" (ἰάσιμα ἁμαρτήματα), not "incurable crimes" (cf. Plato, *Gorgias* 525BC).

[119] Plato, *Sophist* 230A; 229E. See fn. 114, above.

[120] Philo mentions parents, guardians, teachers, physicians, and statesmen (*On Joseph* 73–79; *On the Migration of Abraham* 110–11; 118). Maximus of Tyre mentions philosophers, physicians, fathers, pilots, teachers, mothers, and nurses (*Discourse* 1). Plutarch refers to statesmen, counsellors, rulers, fathers, and physicians. See his *Precepts of Statecraft* 802F (παρρησία πατρικῆς); 815B; 825D–F.

Maximus of Tyre, and Philodemus recognize the importance of harsh and gentle means of persuasion, so does Paul. The mixture of praise and blame in 1 Corinthians squarely lodges Paul within this tradition. The gentle or affable approach is evident when the weak are in view and is succinctly stated both in 1 Cor 9:19-23 and 10:32-33. The harsh approach is apparent when disobedient members are in view and is represented by Paul's imagery of the rod in 1 Cor 4:20-21 and by his use of threats in the same passage as well as in 2 Cor 13:1-4.[121] In his use of such contrasting means of persuasion, Paul shares attributes of character types widely discussed during his time. He is like the obsequious person who is affable in his approach, ready to accommodate the many, but whose affable approach does not exclude causing pain.[122] He is also like the simple, forthright, and truthful persons who all openly criticize their friends. Paul's standing as a "father" and a "brother/friend" of the Corinthians aligns him with other recognized wielders of harshness. Paul's harshness is used when dealing with recalcitrant students and is an example of a friend's frank speech towards his friends which recognizes the salutary effects of harshness.

Agreement is not found, however, on the proper degree and nature of harshness in the reformatory ethic. Some, for example Philo and Clement, would go so far as to claim that even abuse and curses can be morally good if the intention is right. In a text discussing Deut 23:5 where God is said to have turned Balaam's curses into a blessing, Philo claims that one can be intent on conveying a blessing although one seems to be reviling and accusing with the voice. This is the custom of proctors, home tutors, schoolmasters, parents, seniors, magistrates, and laws; "all of these, by reproaches, and sometimes by punishments, effect improvement in the souls of those whom they are educating"; and, "not one of them is an enemy to a single person, but all are friends of them all: and the business of friends inspired by genuine and unfeigned goodwill is to use plain language without any spite whatever."[123] Each treatment, whether marked by prayer and a blessing or by abuse and a curse, should not be judged by the way it finds expression in speech. Rather, the speaker's inten-

---

[121] Cf. Clement, *Ped.* 82.1 (138, 4-7 Stählin-Treu); Prov 23:13-14.

[122] Cf. Aristotle, *Nicomachean Ethics* 1127a3-6.

[123] Philo, *On the Migration of Abraham* 110-11, 115-118. See Isocrates, *Concerning Peace* 72.

tion should be considered when evaluating the spoken word. This recognition of the legitimate use of harshness in moral exhortation, even to the point of a curse, abuse, or disparaging blame, and the recognition that the harshness of a ruler is not determined by his natural disposition but by the character of those whom he rules,[124] complicates issues relating to the classification of philosophers as "harsh" or "gentle," a classification which has been used to characterize two "types" of Cynics in Greco-Roman antiquity. What degree of harshness is required for a philosopher to be classified as a "harsh philosopher"?

## 2.3 "Harsh" and "Gentle" Philosophers

Scholars generally recognize two types of Cynics: an austere, rigorous one, and a milder, hedonistic strain.[125] From the perspective of moral exhortation, the rigorous type was harsh, the mild type gentle. Below I draw attention to some of the limitations in the use of "harsh" and "gentle" means of persuasion as classificatory tools for different "types" of philosophers. Also, I want to emphasize that the contrast of harshness and gentleness was very common and not solely used in order to differentiate between different types of Cynics, although the contrast can be seen with greater clarity among Cynics than among many other philosophers. But, in the final analysis, "harsh" and "gentle" means of exhortation cannot be used as criteria to distinguish between "harsh" and "gentle" philosophers.

To begin with, much of the material using the contrasting poles of harshness and gentleness is traditional, found in different contexts. It could, for example, be applied to political rule and to masters. The use of the contrasting poles of harshness and gentleness to characterize political rule is clear for example in Isocrates, Cicero, Philo,

---

[124] See Isocrates, *Nicocles or the Cyprians* 55: "Do not think that it is their natural dispositions alone which make rulers harsh or gentle, but the character of the citizens as well; for many before now have been compelled by the depravity of their subjects to rule more harshly than they wished."

[125] See G. A. Gerhard, *Phoinix von Kolophon* (Leipzig, 1909), pp. 64–72, 165–68; idem, "Zur Legende vom Kyniker Diogenes," *ARW* 15 (1912), pp. 388–408; B. Fiore, S. J., *The Function of Personal Example in the Socratic and Pastoral Epistles*, pp. 101–126; A. J. Malherbe, *Paul and the Popular Philosophers*, pp. 13–19; and E. Norden, "Beiträge zur Geschichte der griechischen Philosophie," *Jahrbücher für classische Philologie*, Supplementband 19, 2 (1893), pp. 392–410.

Plutarch, and Dio Chrysostom.¹²⁶ Dio contrasts two types of rule as he explains the nature of the *demos*. One includes real guardians and good leaders who deal out hardships among their subjects rarely and only as necessity demands. Others are harsh and savage tyrants who cannot listen to words of fairness; with them flattery and deception prevail. In like manner, democracy is of two kinds. The more prevalent kind is both bold and arrogant, difficult to please in anything, a multifarious and dreadful beast indeed. But the other "is reasonable and gentle and truly mild, disposed to accept frankness of speech and not to care to be pampered in everything, fair, magnanimous, showing respect for good men and good advice, grateful to those who admonish and instruct...."¹²⁷ A democracy of this sort is directed just as a "noble steed," namely, with "gentleness by means of simple reins, since it does not need the curb," although it recognizes the need to sometimes dispense harshness.

The above authors all use harshness and gentleness to draw attention to the desirable mode of political rule and execution of power. One should also note that the discussion of gentleness and harshness was a standard one among philosophers, as can, for example, be witnessed from Aristotle's discussion in his *Nicomachean Ethics* and the *Eudemian Ethics*.¹²⁸ Harshness, like the proverbial bluntness of the Scythians, was generally deplored, and the emphasis on mildness was common among philosophic moralists of the Early Empire. The contrasting poles of harshness and gentleness were commonly used to draw up a contrast between desirable and undesirable human relations in different social contexts.¹²⁹

---

¹²⁶ Isocrates, *To Philip* 116–17; *Nicocles or the Cyprians* 55–57; *To Antipater* 5–6; Plutarch, *Precepts of Statecraft* 808D–809B; Cicero, *On Duties* 1.88. Slaves should accept the authority of their masters with all deference, "not only those who are kind and gentle but also those who are harsh" (1 Pet 2:18).

¹²⁷ Dio Chrysostom, *Discourse* 32.25–28; cf. 3.32–39; 40.35–6. On the two kinds of δῆμος see Hoïstad, *Cynic Hero and Cynic King*, pp. 161–64, 184–86. A statesman recognizes the value of the mixed method; indeed, it is Plutarch in his *Precepts of Statecraft* who gives us one of the most succinct description of the method: "For blame which is mingled with praise and contains nothing insulting but merely frank speech (ὁ γὰρ μεμιγμένος ἐπαίνῳ ψόγος οὐκ ἔχων ὕβριν ἀλλὰ παρρησίαν), and arouses not anger but a pricking of the conscience and repentance, appears both kindly and healing; but abusive speech (λοιδορίαι) is not at all fitting for statesmen" (810C).

¹²⁸ Aristotle, *Nicomachean Ethics* 1125b26–1126b10; *Eudemian Ethics* 1221b10–16. Note Zeno's view of the "rough man" in Diogenes Laertius, *Lives of Eminent Philosophers* 7.117. Stoics held that the wise man could be harsh in the same way as wine is said to be harsh when employed for medical purposes. This differs from the harshness of the "bad man" (ὁ φαῦλος; Epictetus, *Discourse* 2.22.36).

¹²⁹ This is witnessed in early Indo-European society and the archaic Greek com-

Besides this general point, one must recognize the ambivalent nature of the Cynic evidence itself. The Cynic epistles reflect a debate within the Cynic tradition and it is here that the clash between two types of Cynics receives its hard edge. The harsh, austere Cynics include Peregrinus and Oenomaus; their views are reflected in the letters of Crates, Diogenes, Heraclitus, and Hippocrates. They tended to be wandering Cynics, who modeled their life after Heracles. The views of the mild, gentle, or hedonistic Cynics are reflected in writings of such Stoic authors as Musonius Rufus, Epictetus, and Dio Chrysostom, as well as in the letters of the Socratics. These tended to be resident Cynics, whose model, oddly, was Odysseus. The Socratic epistles are valuable evidence of an attempt to bring rigoristic and hedonistic Cynicism into harmony.[130] The epistles reflecting the views of the harsher Cynics are couched in a debate as to who the father of Cynicism was and the original inventor of the Cynic garb, namely, Diogenes or Odysseus. Diogenes became the paradigm of the superior and rigoristic Cynics; Odysseus, particularly as seen through the lenses of Antisthenes, that of the moderate Cynics. The evidence reflects two "types" of behavioral pattern in light of the view held with regard to the human condition, what means should be used to benefit others, and how and with whom one should associate.

The Cynic evidence shows some incongruous results. One can, for example, draw attention to a tradition which eulogizes the adaptability of Diogenes, who in the Cynic epistles of Crates and Diogenes is the paradigm of the consistent and rigorous Cynic. Some authors stress the harshness of Antisthenes who represents the adaptable and affable paradigm of the milder Cynics. Diogenes Laertius relates some of Antisthenes' responses to questions addressed to him: "To the question why he had but few disciples he replied, 'Because I use a silver rod to eject them.' When he was asked why he was so bitter in reproving his pupils he replied, 'Physicians are just the same with their patients.'"[131] The fact that harshness and gentleness was used in various domains of human affairs and the ambivalent nature of the Cynic evidence should alert us to the fact that "harshness" and "gentleness" are classificatory tools only. The contrasting poles have

---

munity in the practice of counterbalancing praise and blame. Cf. G. Nagy, *The Best of the Achaeans* (Baltimore, 1979), p. 222. See Anacharsis, *Epistle* 9.50.5–11, ἔλεγε δὲ οὐ τὴν ἄντικρυς. οὐ γὰρ ἦν Σκύθης.

[130] A. J. Malherbe, *Cynic Epistles* (1986), p. 29; idem, *Paul and the Popular Philosophers*, pp. 13–15.

[131] Diogenes Laertius, *Lives of Eminent Philosophers* 6.4, 22; Horace, *Epistle* 18.1–16.

been used heuristically by scholars to contrast two modes of behavior.

In the Cynic tradition this contrast has received its sharpest edge; Cynics were taken to epitomize harshness, and the κυνικὸς τρόπος and their biting (δακνεῖν) and barking (ὑλακτεῖν) became legendary.[132] As A. J. Malherbe notes, "in Imperial times reviling, berating Cynics were such a common sight that the legendary figure Timon the misanthrope was remembered as a Cynic."[133] Although Malherbe has expressed his views of the similarity between Paul and the Cynics by means of the contrast of harshness and gentleness in moral exhortation, he relates harshness and gentleness to a whole "syndrome" of traditions and characteristics attributed to the Cynics.

However, Dio's description of the ideal Cynic position is interestingly no different, at least with regard to issues of harshness and gentleness, from that of the many authors noted above.[134] Dio's fourth type of philosopher, for example, is a harsh Cynic who does speak with παρρησία, and who, on the basis of his freedom, strives to lay bare the shortcomings of his audience as the first step in improving them. According to Dio, the fault of such a Cynic is that he displays boldness sparingly, and confuses λοιδορία with παρρησία. Both Philodemus and Plutarch also criticize those philosophers who confuse λοιδορία with παρρησία.[135] Furthermore, it is apparent in light of *Discourse* 77/78.38 that Dio recognizes the legitimate use of λοιδορία and ὀνειδισμός for the genuine philosopher. In this he is like the fourth type of philosopher in *Discourse* 32, namely, the harsh Cynic who also employs λοιδορία. And, in this he is different from Paul in 1 Thess 2, although Paul recognizes the place for harsher speech elsewhere, as, for example, in 1 Cor 4:14–21 and 2 Cor 10–13. Dio represents the view that the philosopher should not consistently be harsh, but should on occasion be gentle as a nurse. Paul, on the other hand, says that although he could have been demanding of the Thessalonians, he was gentle as a nurse. The discrepancy here between Paul and Dio is that Paul emphasizes his gentleness, Dio his use of harshness.

---

[132] Plutarch, *Brutus* 34; *How to Tell a Flatterer from a Friend* 69CD; 70B.

[133] Malherbe, *Paul and the Popular Philosophers*, p. 40; F. Bertram, *Die Timonlegende. Eine Entwicklungsgeschichte des Misanthropentypus in der antiken Literatur* (1906), pp. 33, 38, 40–42.

[134] Dio Chrysostom, *Discourse* 32.11–12. See pp. 71–77, above.

[135] Plutarch *How to Tell a Flatterer from a Friend* 66A; Philodemus, *On Frank Criticism* fr. 60.

Dio Chrysostom's description of the ideal Cynic in *Discourse* 77/78.38 uses traditional material also found in Philodemus, Plutarch, Sextus Empiricus, Maximus of Tyre, and Clement. On the analogy of the "harsh" and "gentle" Cynics classification based in part on Dio's description, we could maintain that in Plutarch we find a conflict between an "ideal mild Platonist" as opposed to a rigoristic one, and in Philodemus an "ideal mild Epicurean" as opposed to a "harsh Epicurean." If then a philosopher conscientiously uses the mixed method of praise and blame, should he be called both a "harsh" and a "gentle" philosopher, or perhaps a "mixed philosopher"! The divine word in Clement's *The Pedagogue* employs blasphemy, railing, and reviling, besides threats, i.e., the harshest forms of blame possible. Clement, however, is at pains to argue for the legitimate, beneficial, and considerate use of these harsh forms of blame. Should the divine word be classified as "harsh?" Some of the Cynics who allegedly used these harsher forms of blame have been labelled "harsh" by scholars.

But "harsh" and "gentle" philosophers cannot be distinguished on the basis of the degree of harshness. Thus, with regard to the nature of the hortatory means employed, the difference between the "harsh" and "gentle" Cynic, lay not so much in the degree of harshness—according to Dio both use λοιδορία—but rather in its purpose and manner and the view of the human condition it reflects. In this, Dio follows the same kind of logic as Philo, Clement, and others, who, when evaluating the use of harshness, emphasize the intention of the one using it. The harsh Cynic of *Discourse* 32.11 makes a hurried exit; his hit and run tactic does not include a didactic element. The ideal philosopher of *Discourse* 77/78.38 abuses and reproaches in the hope that he may thereby rescue somebody from folly. These two then used their harshness for different purposes. The harsh Cynics, as Malherbe notes, made "a profession of abusiveness, considering shamelessness to be freedom. Their frankness was a cover for their cowardice and benefited no one"; also, the "harshness of some Cynics resulted from a pessimistic view of mankind. They saw no way of improving man except by the most abusive scolding. It was especially these men who were accused of misanthropy."[136] Malherbe notes

---

[136] Malherbe, *Paul and the Popular Philosophers*, p. 41. See Ps.-Heraclitus, *Epistles* 2.4–5, 7, Ps.-Diogenes, *Epistle* 27.18; and Ps. Hippocrates, *Epistle* 17.28, 43. I do not wish to enter into a debate as to whether the harsh Cynics wanted to improve

that as early as with Crates a reaction surfaced against the stress on harshness and suggests that the stress on gentleness of Musonius, Dio, and Demonax, should be seen against this background.[137]

Now against what background should we then view the stress on gentleness, for example in Maximus of Tyre, Sextus Empiricus, Clement of Alexandria, Plutarch, Philodemus, and Paul? Is their harshness a negative foil which they want to discourage? Each of these authors represents a non-Cynic tradition, a Platonic, Pyrrhonic, Pythagorean, Peripatetic, Epicurean, and an early Christian tradition. The debate as to the appropriate manner in which psychagogic guidance should be conducted was then widespread, although Cynics, as polemically described, gave the sharpest edge to the discussion. If it is true that the above debate was widespread we can, consequently, align Paul's self-reflective remarks on harshness and gentleness with any author who utilizes the practice of a nurse or a father as analogues to that of a psychagogue and say that Paul is tapping into a common tradition. We could say, in addition, that the only common feature characterizing these authors of various philosophical persuasions was the belief that occasional harshness could benefit others, at least when delivered εὐκαίρως. This is then perhaps the criterion to be employed to distinguish a harsh philosopher from a gentle one, and can be used "across the board."[138] It is then not the degree of harshness which is the distinguishing criterion but whether λοιδορία, for example, was delivered ἀκαίρως or εὐκαίρως,[139]

---

humankind or not. Even though Malherbe allows here for the possibility that the harsh Cynics wanted to improve man through their abusive scolding, his previous statement that their harshness benefited no one militates against that view. See J. L. Moles, "'Honestius Quam Ambitiosius?'—an Exploration of the Cynic's Attitude to Moral Corruption in his Fellow Men," *JHS* 103 (1983), pp. 103–23, and further below.

[137] Malherbe, *Paul and the Popular Philosophers*, p. 42; Gerhard, *Phoinix von Kolophon*, pp. 39–41; 170–71; Hoïstad, *Cynic Hero and Cynic King*, pp. 127–29. See Plutarch, *Table Talk* 632E; and Julian, *Oration* 6.201B: Crates "used to reprove them not harshly but with a charming manner (ἐπετίμα δὲ οὐ μετὰ πικρίας, ἀλλὰ μετὰ χάριτος) and not so as to seem to persecute those he wanted to reform, but as though he wished to be of use both to them and to the bystanders." However, Julian continues, "this was not the chief end and aim of those Cynics, but as I said their main concern was how they might themselves attain to happiness...." Julian eulogizes both Crates and Diogenes (ibid., 6.201A).

[138] This presupposes that the "harsh Cynics" did not wish to benefit others. See next two footnotes.

[139] This would also seem to be Malherbe's position when he identifies the attitude behind the oxymoron, εὐκαίρως ἀκαίρως, of 2 Tim 4:2, as that of the pessimistic Cynic "who flays his deluded audience." Timothy is then urged to preach irrespective

and whether it was executed in the hope that it might be beneficial for the recipients.[140]

Did the ideal Cynic wish to benefit mankind? Epictetus has no doubts. In his view the Cynic has made all mankind his children; "in that spirit he approaches them all and cares for them all. Or do you fancy that it is in the spirit of idle impertinence he reviles those he meets?"[141] Apparently the interlocutor thought just that. The Cynic is one who "reviles tactlessly—ἀκαίρως—the people he meets."[142] This text reflects a debate as to the mode of execution of harshness among Cynics. In Epictetus' view, the ideal Cynic reviles "as a father, as a brother, and as a servant of Zeus, who is father of us all." He has the courage to speak freely to his own brothers, to his children and kinsmen. In this he provides a greater service to mankind than others who bear their own children.[143] He has the right to "meddle in" other people's affairs, although that will bring forth the charge that he is a "busybody" and a "meddler." But "meddling in other people's affairs" is his proper concern, and, interestingly, he will use λοιδορία in order to benefit others.[144]

I do not wish to enter the debate on whether or not the indis-

---

of the condition of the listeners. But, the listeners here are, according to Malherbe, the heretics in particular, who are "beyond the hope of cure anyway." This last sentence forms the conclusion of the article. It, however, raises a Pandora's box of problematic issues, beyond the purview of this book, namely, why preach to those beyond the hope of cure? It seems to suggest that the common requirement of εὐκαίρως was not sacrificed in light of the pressing news, since the heretics were incurable. Why not just follow the reported practice of Demonax who, according to Lucian, "held aloof only from those who seemed to him to be involved in sin beyond hope of cure" (Lucian, *Demonax* 10). See further below.

[140] Malherbe has now emphasized "radical individualism" rather than "philanthropic" concerns as the motif of the harsh Cynics. Their comments on themselves are made "when they lambaste the multitude who are beyond the hope of cure, or when they compare themselves with the Cynics of milder mien who hold out some hope for society, whom they accuse of pandering to the crowd. What we meet here is not philanthropy or altruism; rather, the concern with the multitudes serves to highlight the superiority of the Cynic who has committed himself without reservation to the life of Diogenes." Idem, *Paul and the Popular Philosophers*, pp. 18–19, 40 n. 33.

[141] Epictetus, *Discourse* 3.22.81–82, 93, . . . λοιδορεῖσθαι τοῖς ἀπαντῶσιν.

[142] Ibid., 3.22.50, τοῖς ἀπαντῶσι λοιδορεῖσθαι ἀκαίρως.

[143] Ibid., 3.22.77, 82. For the Cynic is a "friend and servant to the gods" see 3.22.95.

[144] Ibid., 3.22.96–97. This is interesting for at least two reasons. First, in this Epictetus agrees with my "across the board" criterion to distinguish harsh and gentle philosophers. He rejects the "tactless reviling" (λοιδορεῖσθαι ἀκαίρως) of all which, in his interlocutor's view, was seen as typical of the Cynics. Secondly, Epictetus' Stoicized version of the Ideal Cynic cannot represent that of the austere Cynic. Epictetus' "gentle" type of Cynic represents then a tradition which recognizes both the ideal

criminate and tactless reviling of the harsher type of Cynics was well intended or not. Instead, I want to emphasize two implicit presuppositions present when the focus is on the different forms and degrees of moral persuasion. The first has to do with the issue of association with others and the second with the related view of the effect of persuasion. If a moralist felt that the condition of his recipients was unredeemable, beyond the hope of cure, he withdrew his care and felt no need to associate with such persons. Moralists might disagree as to precisely what constituted an incurable state, and whether there were any incurable ones, but if the disease was seen as well advanced, three options were generally available. Firstly, one might opt for surgery or such medication as hellebore or wormwood, namely, a harsh form of moral exhoration in order to effect a cure. Secondly, one might stay with the patient and reclaim him when the sickness went into remission.[145] Or, thirdly, one might simply, after a diagnosis, come to the conclusion that the sickness was truly at the point of no return.

All these options were maintained by different moralists. In the next chapter we shall see examples of all three in Philodemus, who flatly rejects the last one. These approaches reflect different views of the human condition and the degree of harshness needed in order to effect a cure. There is a close tie between the moralist's view of the human condition and his execution of the task at hand.[146] The more pessimistic the view of the human condition is, the harsher the method employed, and vice versa. Maximus of Tyre criticizes those who think that the philosopher should not omit any opportunity of philosophising and says that the "herd of men is naturally mild," but is, because of diminished rational capacity, persuaded with difficulty. All the same, that herd of men does "require a musical shepherd who does not punish its disobedience with the whip or the spur."[147] In light of the human condition, Maximus emphasizes a gentle approach in a context which contains an oblique critique of the practice of those philosophers who indiscriminately use whatever means they think appropriate in whatever situation.

---

of benefitting others and the use of "an opportune" λοιδορία in that endeavor. Compare Epictetus' view of the moral condition of "the multitude" (οἱ πολλοί) in *Discourse* 2.18, *That We Ought Not to be Angry With the Erring* (cf. 2.18.2–4) and *Discourse* 3.13.22–23. Cf. Plutarch, *Precepts of Statecraft* 800B, "... for it is a difficult task to change the multitude," and 810C. See below.

[145] For this approach see Philodemus' *On Frank Criticism* frs. 65–66.
[146] Malherbe, *Paul and the Popular Philosophers*, pp. 16–20, 40, and 130–32.
[147] Maximus of Tyre, *Discourse* 1.3bc; 3e–f (4, 22–5, 10; 5, 17–6, 9 Hobein).

Similar points were brought home in Seneca's discussion of the need for dogmas.[148] Even though man is naturally the "gentlest class of being" who can be guided by gentle persuasion, there is need for a harsher method in view of the present depraved condition. The same holds true with regard to the condition of those under the moralist's care. A more advanced state of sickness demanded a more stringent method. This debate about the degree of persuasion included the question of association: with whom was it worthwhile to associate? Demonax was said to be everybody's friend and could associate with all, except those beyond the hope of cure![149] This stricture is important because it shows that even the mildest of Cynics could agree with harsher Cynics that some were incurable. Paul's willingness to associate with all and sundry in order to benefit them (1 Cor 9:19–22) indicates then a very positive view of the human condition and a belief that his λόγος could benefit all.

Other factors than the degree of persuasion affect the classification of "harsh" and "gentle" Cynics, such as adaptation and rigorism, the view of the philosopher's garb and his weapons, softness and courage, as well as the association with the base. It also holds true that the debate about harshness and gentleness is seen with greater clarity among Cynics than among many other philosophers, particularly in their debate over who the founder of the Cynic way of life was (Antisthenes or Diogenes) and who the paradigmatic figure should be (Odysseus or Heracles). However, as Eduard Norden has pointed out, although ἁπλοῦς and ἁπλότης were catchwords popular among Cynics to the extent that Antisthenes was called a "simple hound," the same words were common also among the Stoics and neo-Platonists, and we might, of course, add, among some early Christians. We should also note that Odysseus and Heracles as paradigms of the virtuous life were not used exclusively by Cynics. Stoics made claims to both paradigms, and, with regard to Odysseus, both Epicureans of late Republican times and Plutarch can use him both positively and negatively.[150] And although the analogy between biting

---

[148] Seneca, *Epistle* 95.17, 29–32, and 34. See p. 84, above.

[149] Lucian, *Demonax* 10, He "held aloof only from those who seemed to him to be involved in sin beyond hope of cure" (μόνοις ἐξιστάμενος... ὑπὲρ τὴν τῆς θεραπείας ἐλπίδα διαμαρτάνειν).

[150] Diogenes Laertius, *Lives of Eminent Philosophers* 6.13; J. Amstutz, ΑΠΛΟΤΗΣ: *Eine begriffsgeschichtliche Studie zum jüdisch-christlichen Griechisch* (Bonn, 1968); Philodemus, *Rhetoric* v. 2, fr. IV, p. 77 Sudhaus = Odysseus and Adrastus "were the most eloquent of

and the language of blame poetry is traditional, as well as that of the biting of the Cynic dogs, the successors of blame poetry, the equation of biting with various forms of blame was common quite apart from the Cynic connection.[151] All these factors extend the issues beyond the confines of the Cynics.

In conclusion, the degree or mode of persuasion cannot then be used to distinguish "harsh" and "gentle" philosophers. Now, because of the tendentiousness of the criterion of "harshness" and "gentleness," two courses are open to me. Firstly, I could continue to focus on other aspects of the contrast between gentleness and harshness in moral guidance, particularly those which relate to the view to the human condition implicit in its use, as I have already done in this chapter. Or secondly, I could introduce moralists other than Cynics as comparative material to Paul. This is what I do in the next chapter, as I focus on the psychagogic practices of the Epicureans.

---

heroes," but in *On Flattery* (PHerc. 223 fr. 3, p. 128 Gigante-Indelli), Odysseus is seen as a parasite; Plutarch uses Odysseus as a negative example but later as a positive example of one who applies a moderate form of παρρησία. Cf. *How to Tell a Flatterer from a Friend* 52C, 53B, 66F–67A, and 74B. Epictetus, *Discourse* 2.24.26; 3.24.12–14; Origin, *Against Celsus* 3.66. See Norden, "Beiträge zur Geschichte der griechischen Philosophie," pp. 394–95 and 403.

[151] See pp. 114–24, below, on "harsh Epicureans." Cf. Philodemus, *On Anger* cols. 12.18; 37.19; 38.7; 41.8 Indelli. See Branham, *Unruly Eloquence*, pp. 266–67 n. 34; Demetrius, *On Style* 261 ("every variety of Cynic speech reminds you of a dog that is ready to bite even as it fawns"); Diogenes, *Fragment* 35 Mullach; Plutarch, *On Tranquility of Mind* 468A ("By this gentle and philosophic argument he showed the Cynic's abuse to be idle yapping"); *How to Tell a Flatterer from a Friend* 59C, 68A–70D, 72A. Epictetus equates "biting" with "reviling" (*Discourse* 2.22.28, τὸ δάκνειν ἀλλήλους ἢ λοιδορεῖσθαι). The comparison of blame and bite occurs already in Pindar, *Pythian Odes* 2.52–53 (cf. Nagy, *The Best of Acheans*, pp. 224–25). In a context discussing harshness, truth, pleasure, and deception, Athenaeus notes: "Most philosophers have a natural tendency to be more abusive than the comic poets...." (*Sophists at Dinner* 220A). Examples follow of the abusive manners of Aescines and Antisthenes, Socrates' disciples. Cf. also Ps.-Libanius, *Epistolary Styles* 92 (80, 40–41 Malherbe), "... for it is not fitting that philosophers engage in slander."

# PART TWO
# EPICUREAN PSYCHAGOGY

CHAPTER THREE

EPICUREAN COMMUNAL PSYCHAGOGY

Philodemus' *On Frank Criticism* contains evidence of a debate among Epicureans similar to the debate between the milder and more rigoristic Cynics, which also centered on the appropriateness of harsh treatment and the adaptation of speech to different recipients. As such, the Epicureans were sharers in this ubiquitous tradition on which I have focused. Below I shall continue to focus on the implicit presuppositions of the use of the mixed method, especially as it relates to the classification of students and the social relations highlighted in the use of that method. The Philodemean material presents a promising comparison to Paul because of its communal setting and because of member participation in the psychagogic process. Although Epicureans and Paul shared with other moralists a positive view of the effectiveness of the mixed method of praise and blame, the common use of hortatory practices which included harsh and gentle dimensions, the composition of the constituents of these respective communities, and the participatory and rotational forms of these practices set them apart from others who shared in this common tradition.

By the middle of the first century BCE a flourishing Epicurean community existed in Naples under the leadership of the Greek teacher Siro. At nearby Herculaneum the Syrian Epicurean, Philodemus of Gadara, the house-philosopher of the influential patron Calpurnius Piso, father-in-law of Julius Caesar, was attracting a wide circle of students. Epicureanism also had its contemporary exponents in Latin— Catius Insuber, Rabirius, and C. Amafinius, whose prose tracts enjoyed popularity in Rome and in various Italian towns, and the poet Lucretius. The relationship between the various Epicurean groups in Italy is not clear but apparently Siro's group in Naples and that of Philodemus at Herculaneum had an open exchange of views.[1] Both

---

[1] We know that the poets of Siro's group, L. Varius Rufus and Quintilius Varus, and possibly Virgil and Plotius Tucca, associated with Philodemus as well, and that the discussion between Philodemus and his fellow Epicureans at Naples extended also to philosophical matters (PHerc. 312). See A. Körte, "Augusteer bei Philodem," *RhM* 45 (1890), pp. 172–77; H. Jones, *The Epicurean Tradition* (New York, 1989),

Philodemus and Siro were former pupils of Zeno of Sidon, the scholarch of the Epicurean school in Athens, and one would expect a certain co-ordination in their efforts in promoting Epicurean views in southern Italy. Both groups cultivated interest in literary and philosophical study, thus escaping the charge traditionally levelled at Epicureans that they maintained a deliberate disregard for general learning; Cicero, for example, refers to both Siro and Philodemus as the "excellent and learned friends" of Torquatus.[2]

Philodemus' scholarly interest is evident from the number of papyrus rolls recovered from Piso's suburban villa at Herculaneum. These include both Philodemus' transcripts of the lecture notes he took at Zeno's classes in Athens—for example, his book *On Frank Criticism*, which I will discuss below—and also Philodemus' own compositions, including writings on historical matters, on scientific method, on rhetoric, music, and poetry, theological writings, including the works *On Piety* and *On the Gods*, and, finally, works on ethics.[3] The ethical writings include an introduction to ethics, a work in several books *On Death*, and a work in ten books *On Vices and the Opposing Virtues*, which includes one book *On Household Management*, one *On Arrogance*, and probably three books *On Flattery*.[4] Finally, Philodemus wrote an *Epitome on Conduct and Character, from the Lectures of Zeno*, which includes a work *On Anger* and the above mentioned *On Frank Criticism*.[5]

---

pp. 65–69; H. M. Howe, "Amafinius, Lucretius, and Cicero," *AJPh* 77 (1951), pp. 57–62; D. P. Fowler, "Lucretius and Politics," in M. Griffin and J. Barnes (eds.), *Philosophia Togata. Essays on Philosophy and Roman Society* (Oxford, 1989), pp. 120–50; Cicero, *Letters to His Friends* 15.16.1; 15.19.2; *Academica* 1.5; *Tusculan Disputations* 4.7.

[2] The Epicurean spokesman in Cicero's *On Ends*. See 2.119.

[3] See E. Asmis, "Philodemus' Epicureanism," *ANRW* 36.4 (Berlin/New York, 1990), pp. 2369–2406. Historical works: PHerc. 1018, *Index Stoicorum*; PHerc. 164 and 1021, *Index Academicorum*; PHerc. 155 and 339, *On the Stoics*; PHerc. 1232 and 1289, *On Epicurus*; PHerc. 1418 and 310, *Works on the Records of Epicurus and Some Others*; PHerc. 1005, *To Friends of the School*. Work on scientific method: *On Phenomena and Inferences* = PHerc. 1065. On which see P. H. de Lacy and E. A. de Lacy, *Philodemus: On Methods of Inference* (2nd ed. Naples, 1978). Works on rhetoric, music, and poetry: *On Rhetoric* and *On Poems* are preserved in numerous papyri; PHerc. 1497, *On Music*; PHerc. 1507, *On the Good King according to Homer*. Theological writings: PHerc. 1428, *On Piety*; PHerc. 26, *On the Gods*; PHerc. 152 and 157, *On the Way of Life of the Gods*.

[4] The untitled introduction to ethics (PHerc. 1251) is known as *Comparetti Ethics* in honor of its first editor; PHerc. 1050, *On Death*; PHerc. 1424, *On Household Management*; PHerc. 1008, *On Arrogance*; PHerc. 222, 223, 1082, 1089, 1457, and 1675, *On Flattery*. See also PHerc. 346 edited by M. Capasso, *Trattato etico epicureo* (Naples, 1982).

[5] PHerc. 182, *On Anger*; PHerc. 1471, *On Frank Criticism*. Philodemus' work *On Anger* was edited by C. Wilke, *Philodemi de ira liber*, Leipzig, 1914, and has been re-

At the end of his work *On Household Management*, Philodemus discusses sources of income for the philosopher, concluding that the best way to make money is to share philosophical discourses with receptive men, next, to be a gentleman farmer, and, finally, to manage a reputable business.[6] These occupations are worthwhile because they allow, as Philodemus explains, the "leisurely retreat with friends" to enjoy the Epicurean way of life. This hierarchy of occupations undoubtedly reflects Philodemus' own position and that of his patron Piso. As house-philosopher or "friend" of a wealthy patron, Philodemus not only had the leisure to indulge his scholarly interests but also to participate in the instruction and formation of recruits who attached themselves to the Epicurean group at Herculaneum; Philodemus has correctly been characterized as "a typical teacher of Epicureanism, spreading his school's gospel at the intersection of the Greek and Roman worlds."[7]

Although Cicero's claim that the Epicureans "took Italy by storm" is an exaggeration, it reflects an awareness of a growing Epicurean presence during the last years of the Roman republic.[8] The Epicurean school in Naples and the circle of Philodemus in nearby Herculaneum were important intellectual centers at this time.[9] The Epicureans were not closed within the confines of a private club; a new evaluation of φιλοδοξία and public engagement emerged; "live unknown" was not strictly followed.[10] Their influence on well known literary figures such as Virgil, Horace, Tibullus, Catullus, Seneca, and others, has been

---

edited, with a translation and commentary by G. Indelli, *Filodemo, L'Ira* (La scuola di Epicuro 5; Naples, 1988).

[6] *On Household Management* col. 23.22–36; on this see Asmis, "Philodemus' Epicureanism," p. 2388.

[7] D. Sedley, "Philosophical Allegiance in the Greco-Roman World," *Philosophia Togata*, p. 103.

[8] Cicero, *Tusculan Disputations* 4.3.7. See C. J. Castner, *Prosopography of the Roman Epicureans from the Second Century B.C. to the Second Century A.D.* [Frankfurt a. M.] 1988. Cf. also A. Momigliano's review of B. Farrington, *Science and Politics in the Ancient World* in *JRS* 31 (1941), pp. 149–57. For the view that the Latin contributors to the spread of Epicureanism were more successful than their Greek counterparts, see pp. 170–75, below.

[9] For an account of Philodemus' life and literary activity, see R. Philippson, "Philodemos," *RE* 19.2 (1938), cols. 2444–2482; M. Gigante, *La Bibliothèque de Philodème et l'Épicurisme Romain*. Paris, 1987; de Lacy and de Lacy, *Philodemus: On Methods of Inference*, pp. 145–52; Asmis, "Philodemus' Epicureanism," pp. 2369–2406.

[10] T. Gargiulo, "PHerc. 222: Filodemo sull' adulazione," *CErc* 11 (1981), p. 105. Plutarch claims that Epicurus' practice contradicts his precepts: "you are telling . . . Epicurus . . . not to write to your friends in Asia, not to enlist recruits from Egypt, not to cultivate the youth of Lampsacus, not to circulate books to every man and

documented.[11] But in spite of these encounters, the Epicurean communities were separate entities from society at large, perhaps even "alternative communities,"[12] as references to "members of the household" (οἱ οἰκεῖοι) over against "outsiders" (οἱ ἔξωθεν), and "intimate fellows" (οἱ συνήθεις) as opposed to "those outside the intimate fellowship" (οἱ ἔξω τῆς συνηθείας) suggest.[13]

## 3.1 The Nature of Παρρησία. The Debate

### 3.1.1 The present focus

The above contrast between insiders and outsiders is also seen in the use of the term παρρησία among Epicureans. In Philodemus' view, παρρησία has two perspectives, one directed "towards all men" and another directed "towards one's intimate associates."[14] For the former the best available example is Lucian, who in his *Alexander the False Prophet* assumes the role of the rational Epicurean who, together with the Christians, attempts to deflate the false prophet Alexander of Abonouteichos and his claims of special standing with the divine.[15]

---

every woman in which you advertise your wisdom" (*Is 'Live Unknown' a Wise Precept?* 1128F-1129A; cf. frs. 106-07 Us. and *Epicurea* 87, 23-28).

[11] C. Jensen, "Die Bibliothek von Herculaneum," *Bonner Jahrbücher* 135 (1930), pp. 56-59; J. I. M. Tait, *Philodemus' Influence on the Latin Poets* (Diss., Bryn Mawr, 1941), pp. 1-4.

[12] See B. Frischer's description of the Epicurean community as a surrogate family in *The Sculpted Word. Epicureanism and Philosophical Recruitment in Ancient Greece* (Berkeley: University of California Press, 1982), pp. 206-07. Fr. 3.8-10 of *On Frank Criticism* speaks of ill repute in the eyes of the "public" (οἱ πολλοί) and of separation from one's family members. In col. 7a2-3, Philodemus speaks of the teacher in the same breath as a father and an elder, and in fr. 44.7 he says that the teacher feels [family] affection (στέργειν) for his students (cf. also fr. 54.1; col. 8b2; and App. Tab. III H).

[13] *On Epicurus* PHerc. 1232, fr. 8, col. 1.6-12, "[But Epicurus says] that he invites these very people to join in a feast, just as he invites others—all those who are members of his household and he asks them to exclude none of the 'outsiders' who are well disposed both to him and to his friends" (transl. by D. Clay, "The Cults of Epicurus," *CErc* 16 (1986), pp. 13-14); *On Frank Criticism* col. 14a10-11, "For he also despises outsiders"; App. Tab. III F ("difficulties caused by outsiders"); *On Anger* col. 26.24-25 Indelli (οἰκείους τε καὶ τῶν ἔξωθεν ἀνθρώπους); PHerc. 1457, fr. 16.3-5; cf. E. Kondo, ("Per l'interpretazione del pensiero filodemeo sulla adulazione nel PHerc. 1457," *CErc* 4 (1974), p. 48); *On Vices* cols. 2.32-35; 8.28-30 (καὶ τὸ πρὸ[ς τοὺς φίλους ἐν τοῖς ἔξωθεν ἴσον εἶναι τῶν ἄλλων ἐπι[τρ]ε[χ]όντων . . .). See C. Jensen, *Ein neuer Brief Epikurs* (Berlin, 1933), pp. 17, 27, 44.

[14] PHerc. 1082, col. 2.1-3, πρὸς ἅπαντας ἀνθρώπους versus πρὸς τοὺς συνήθεις.

[15] Lucian, *Alexander* 17, 25, 61; Epicurus, *Vatican Sentences* 29; D. Clay, "A Lost

Frank speech is thus an integral part of Epicurean anti-oracular activity and their agenda of enlightening persons about the workings of the universe and the nature of the gods, i.e. to combat the fear of death and of the gods as well as fear of other humans.

Later I shall argue that Paul's "apology" in 1 Corinthians 9 is comparable to Philodemus' defence of his "friendship" with his patron Piso.[16] An additional area of congruence is evident in Philodemus' recognition of the twofold aspect of frank speech relating to intimate associates and towards all men. Although the contrast between "insiders" and "outsiders" becomes more pronounced in early Christian groups subsequent to Paul, the Pauline corpus shows an inchoate view of inside-outside boundaries.[17] In his first use of the term παρρησία, Paul applies it to his preaching of the gospel and also uses the term to describe his manner of speaking to the Corinthians.[18] This view of frank speech as both a centripetal and a centrifugal force links Paul and the Epicureans closely together. Epicurus is said to have spoken with frankness to all, and later Epicureans attempted to disseminate the doctrines of their master far and wide. Similarly, everything we know from Paul's work suggests a rigorous recruitment effort and the founding of communities.

The point is not that there is a perfect match between Paul's practices and those of Philodemus, nor that the practices of these two are unique when compared to other moralists. Rather, there are certain distinct features common to the Epicurean communities and those of Paul. One of these is this inside-outside mentality recognizing a twofold perspective of frank speech; other features—which I will discuss in the next chapters and which are important for the respective views of psychagogy—include a shared view of the importance of the friendship with many and a community wide use of frank speech in the practice of exhortation, edification, and correction.

The word παρρησία was originally used in the political sphere to express the right of the free-born Athenian but is from Isocrates

---

Epicurean Community," *GRBS* 30.2 (1989), pp. 325–35; R. B. Branham, *Unruly Eloquence* (Cambridge, 1989), pp. 179–210.

[16] Defamed by Cicero in 55 BCE in a bitter speech against Piso (*Against Piso* 70–71).

[17] 1 Thess 4:12; Gal 6:11; 1 Cor 5:12. Cf. 1 Cor 14:23–24; Gal 6:10; and Eph 2:19. See W. C. van Unnik, "Die Rücksicht auf die Reaktion der Nicht-Christen als Motiv in der altchristlichen Paränese," in *Judentum-Urchristentum—Kirche, Festschrift für Joachim Jeremias* (Berlin, 1964), pp. 221–34.

[18] 2 Cor 7:4; 1 Thess 2:2. Compare Acts 4:29, 31; 9:27–28; 14:3; 18:26; 19·8; 28:31.

onward an integral part of friendship. The authors I discussed in chapter two emphasized the importance of frank speech in friendship. Philo shows that Hellenized Jews recognized frank speech as a constituent part of friendship; a "man of worth" has παρρησία to reproach boldly. The audacity of rashness belongs to the presumptuous, but the audacity of courage to a friend; "frank speech is," then, "akin to friendship."[19] Also, the use of reproaches by those who improve the soul of those being educated, shows that

> not one of them is an enemy to a single person, but all are friends of them all: and the business of friends inspired by genuine and unfeigned goodwill is to use plain language without any spite whatever.[20]

Plutarch's remark on frank speech as the "language of friendship" and as the "most potent medicine in friendship," needing all care to find the right occasion, shows the close connection of frank speech with friendship and the difficulties in its use.[21] Both of these aspects of παρρησία surface in *On Frank Criticism* where Philodemus discusses frank speech under the topic of how and when frankly to reprimand your friends' failings. The topic of frank speech is thus a part of the theme of moral education, or the correction of faults among friends in the improvement of character, discussed earlier by Plato, Aristotle, Xenophon, and Isocrates.[22] It is especially in Isocrates that we find the change in connotation of the word παρρησία that was originally used in the political sphere of the right of the free-born Athenian to express his views unhindered. From then on, the word παρρησία was seen as a sign of goodwill towards one's friends and close in meaning to ἐλέγχω and νουθετέω.[23] The pinnacle of this development is

---

[19] Philo, *Who is the Heir* 19 and 21, παρρησία δὲ φιλίας συγγενές.

[20] Philo, *On the Migration of Abraham* 116–17, φίλοι δὲ πᾶσι πάντες·—ἔργον ἐλευθεροστομεῖν ἄνευ τοῦ κακονοεῖν.

[21] Plutarch, *How to Tell a Flatterer from a Friend* 74D. Note *Sirach* 22:22, "But abuse (ὀνειδισμοῦ), scorn, a secret betrayed, a stab in the back—these will make any friend keep his distance" (NEB).

[22] Plato, *Protagoras* 325AB; *Gorgias* 525B; Aristotle, *Nicomachean Ethics* 1171a21–1172a15; 1180a6–14; *Eudemian Ethics* 1242b35–1243a14; 1243b15–40; *Great Ethics* 1213b18–30. The young thus need friendship to keep them from error, as the old need it for someone to care for them and support the actions that fail because of weakness, and those in their prime in order to do fine actions (*Nicomachean Ethics* 1155a12–16). Xenophon, *On Household Management* 13.6–9; Isocrates, *To Demonicus* 1–6, 11–12, 20, 22, 24–26, 29–31, 45–46; *To Nicocles* 2, 12, 28, 42–43, 45–49; *Antidosis* 206–14, 289–90. See also *Nicocles or the Cyprians* 55, 57; *Concerning Peace* 14–15, 70, 72; and *To Antipater* 3–4, 7, 9.

[23] E. Peterson, "Zur Bedeutungsgeschichte von Παρρησία," in *Reinhold-Seeberg*

seen in *The Pedagogue* of Clement of Alexandria, who discusses the use of hortatory blame in the divine word's use of frank speech in psychagogy.[24] Philodemus' *On Frank Criticism* is a valuable example of this tradition.

3.1.2 *The nature of* παρρησία *in Philodemus'* Περὶ παρρησίας
Philodemus of Gadara's handbook Περὶ παρρησίας, the only known work of antiquity with that title, is of great importance for the social history of Epicureanism.[25] It gives evidence for methods of instruction among Epicureans and contains hypothetical questions and answers on psychagogic theory as well as reflections on psychagogic practice. A thorough discussion of the treatise is not possible since the complete work is not extant, but a fairly comprehensive picture may be gained of late Epicurean psychagogy and communal pedagogy.[26] This may be achieved by focusing on questions which the treatise itself raises, questions faced by any practitioner of the "art of moral guidance."[27] Also, we will better understand the

---

*Festschrift* (Leipzig, 1929), pp. 285–86; G. Bohnenblust, *Beiträge zum Topos* ΠΕΡΙ ΦΙΛΙΑΣ (Berlin, 1905), pp. 35–36; G. Scarpat, *Parrhesia. Storia del termine e delle sue traduzioni in latino* (Brescia, 1964). Related terms include ἐξουσία, ἐλευθεροστομέω, θαρρέω, εὐτολμία, and ἀλήθεια. The change in meaning of παρρησία is clear where Isocrates remarks that things which contribute to the education of men in private life include "παρρησία and the privilege which is openly granted to friends to rebuke and to enemies to attack each other's faults" (*To Nicocles* 3; cf. *To Philip* 72; *To Demonicus* 20–31). Παρρησία is a σημεῖον τῆς εὐνοίας τῆς πρὸς τοὺς φίλους (see Bohnenblust, ibid., p. 35). From a later period, see the *Epistle of Aristeas* 125 for the close connection of παρρησία and φιλία in the relationship between "friends" and counselors of kings (APOT 2:107).
[24] See pp. 62–64 and 72–75, above.
[25] *De libertate dicendi* (PHerc. 1471). A. Olivieri (ed.), *Philodemi* ΠΕΡΙ ΠΑΡΡΗΣΙΑΣ (Leipzig: Teubner, 1914). D. Clay, *Lucretius and Epicurus* (Ithaca/London, 1983), p. 173; and "Individual and Community in the First Generation of the Epicurean School," Συζήτησις: *Studi sull'epicureismo greco e romano offerti a Marcello Gigante* (Biblioteca della Parola del Passato 16; Naples, 1983), vol. 1, p. 270.
[26] M. Gigante, *Ricerche Filodemee. Seconda edizione riveduta e accresciuta* (Naples, 1983), pp. 55–113. See also N. W. de Witt, "Organization and Procedure in Epicurean Groups," *CPh* 31 (1936), pp. 205–211; idem, "Epicurean Contubernium," *TAPA* 57 (1936), pp. 55–63.
[27] Cf. de Lacy & de Lacy, *Philodemus: On Methods of Inference*, p. 201 n. 64. There are series of problems raised throughout the treatise, including, "Will the wise man candidly refer his own affairs to his friends?" (fr. 81) "Why do people resent frank criticism from those that they recognize as more clever and, indeed, as leaders?" (col. 20a1–5); "Why do women resent frank criticism more than men?" (col. 21b12–14); "Why do famous people resent it more than others?" (col. 23a–b) "Why are old people more resentful?" (col. 24a7–9). See Asmis, "Philodemus' Epicureanism," p. 2394.

psychagogy exemplified by focusing on the analogy of conjectural art and medical practice. The medical analogy highlights characteristics of the methods, forms, and procedures of the "moral physician," and reveals latent presuppositions concerning the pupils' sickness. Finally, we will understand better the view of moral guidance by a topical analysis of the fragments, for example, by focusing on the common use of various terms of moral exhortation which often reveal the nature of the guidance in question.

The many variations of hortatory blame and the frequency of such terms as error and correction are thus significant in a work entitled Περὶ παρρησίας.[28] It shows that παρρησία is a form of blame or frank criticism of error. The most appropriate translation of Περὶ παρρησίας is thus *On Frank Criticism*. The preponderance of terms associated with the ethic of friendship in the extant fragments demand that we view these practices as an extension of the ethic of friendship. Members admonish and censure each other in friendship.[29] Also, a forthcoming attitude toward others is the ideal. Or, as fragment 28 puts it,

> while many fine things come out of friendship, none of them is as great as having someone with whom one may discuss what is in one's heart, and to whom one can listen when he does the same. For nature intensely desires to disclose what one thinks to others.

*On Frank Criticism*,[30] "an epitome from the lectures of Zeno,"[31] appears

---

[28] See the index of Olivieri's edition for the use of ἐξ-/ἁμαρτάνω, ἁμάρτ-ημα/ία, ἁμαρτωλός, διαμαρτ-άνω/ία, διά-/παράπτωσις, διαπίπτω, παραλογίζεσθαι, διορθ-εύω/ωσις and μετάθεσις. Terms of blame and dissuasion include ἀποτρέπω, ἐλέγχω, νουθεσία, νουθέτησις, νουθετέω, ἐπιτίμησις, ὀνειδίζεσθαι, λοιδορία/-εῖν and διασυρτικός. Cf. also κατυβρίζω, κακολογέω, καταβαλλέω, καταβλητικός, πομπεύω, χλευάζω, βλασφημέω and ἀνακρίνω.

[29] Περὶ παρρησίας is then a περὶ φιλίας τόπος. Friendship terms, scattered throughout the fragments, include φιλία, φιλέω, φίλησις, φίλος, φιλικός, ἀγαπάω, ἀγάπη, ἀγάπησις, ἐράω, στέργω, στοργή, and φιλοπαρρησιαστής. See tab. V extr. fragm. (App.), βού[λεται μὲν δ]ιὰ φ[ιλίας νουθετεῖν, "for he wants to admonish through friendship." Ἐπιτίμησις, an example of παρρησία, is united with φιλέω in *On Anger* col. 35.19 Indelli, διὰ τὸ ψ[ιλεῖν] ἐπιτίμησις. ...

[30] Cited as the περὶ παρρησίας λόγος, in *On Anger* col. 36.24–25 Indelli. See the reference to περὶ παρρησίας πραγματεία in PHerc. 1082 col. 1.1–7 (W. Crönert, *Kolotes und Menedemos* (Amsterdam, 1965), p. 127 n. 534) and τὸ τάγμα τῆς παρρησίας in *On Frank Criticism* col. 13b4 and *Rhetoric* v. 2, p. 1 Sudhaus. See Gigante, *Ricerche Filodemee*, p. 60. Wilke proposed in his edition (p. vii) that *On Anger* belonged to the same epitome of Zeno's work as Περὶ παρρησίας.

[31] The subscript of the papyrus PHerc. 1471 is: Φιλοδήμου τῶν κατ' ἐπιτομὴν ἐπειργασμένων περὶ ἠθῶν καὶ βίων ἐκ τῶν Ζήνωνο[ς σχο]λῶν ... ὅ ἐστι περὶ παρρ[η]σίας. We also find a reference to ἐκ τῶν Ζηνωνος σχολῶν in PHerc. 1389. See Kondo, "Per l'interpretazione del pensiero filodemeo sulla adulazione nel PHerc. 1457," p. 45.

together with *On Anger* in a larger work *On Conduct and Character*. Based on the title of the work in which it appears, παρρησία should be seen as a behavior or a way of life.³² T. Gargiulo has elaborated this thesis by arguing that the virtue Philodemus contrasts with flattery is not frank speech but friendship.³³ Philodemus' discussion of flattery and friendship is influenced by Aristotle's classification of virtue as a medium between two vices where friendship is viewed as the mean between flattery and enmity.³⁴ Just as frank speech is a *sine qua non* of friendship, so are assent, speaking in order to please, and praise, characteristics of flattery. PHerc. 1082 is pertinent:

> Let us make it clear to them that the goods of friendship are very durable and that flattery is the antagonist of friendship; let us also consider well the goods that rise from frank speech, both (the frank speech) directed towards one's intimate associates, and (the frank speech) directed towards all men, and let us avoid as vain the company of adulators, and still more let us not mix with them but seek cohabitation with those who speak candidly.³⁵

Gargiulo recognizes that one can read "the goods of discussion" in line one, i.e., δ[ιὰ ὁμι]λίας ... ἀγαθά instead of δ[ιὰ φι]λίας ... ἀγαθά, but thinks that the exaltation of those goods as "the most constant goods" makes it probable that φιλία is the correct word. But the admonition encouraging readers to seek to live with those who talk freely and avoid those who flatter continues the contrast of flattery and conversation at the beginning of the pericope. For the Epicureans conversations and reasoning together are indispensable.³⁶ Παρρησία is then a type of ὁμιλία. In any case, the contrast between παρρησία and κολακεία is indisputable.³⁷ Frank speech is intricately connected

---

³² And not, as maintained by R. Philippson ("Philodemus," cols. 2460, 2467–74), as a virtue opposed to the vice of κολακεία. So Gigante, *Ricerche Filodemee*, pp. 59–62.

³³ Gargiulo, "PHerc. 222: Filodemo Sull' adulazione," pp. 104–5. See also E. A. Méndez, "PHerc. 1089: Filodemo 'Sobre la Adulación,'" *CErc* 13 (1983), pp. 122–24.

³⁴ Illustrated by PHerc. 1082 which deals with flattery (cf. col. 2.1–4, φιλία ... ἧς ἀντ[ί]παλός ἐστιν ἡ κολακεία). See F. Longo Auricchio, "Sulla Concezione Filodemea dell'Adulazione," *CErc* 16 (1986), p. 82, and Aristotle, *Great Ethics* 1193a20–22; *Eudemian Ethics* 1233b30ff.

³⁵ PHerc. 1082, col. 2.1–14. My translation. The virtue which is the opposite (ἀρετὴ ἀντικειμένη) of flattery (κολακεία) is thus not frank speech (παρρησία) but friendship (φιλία). Cf. Gargiulo, "PHerc. 222: Filodemo Sull' adulazione," p. 104.

³⁶ I.e., ὁμιλία, κοινολογίαι, συλλογίζεσθαι, and συζήτησις. For συζητητικὸς τρόπος as a pedagogical technique, see *Vatican Sentences* 74 and Philodemus, *On Anger* 19.25–26 Indelli; *On Frank Criticism* fr. 53.2. Cf. F. Amoroso, "Filodemo sulla Conversazione," *CErc* 5 (1975), pp. 63–76.

³⁷ In *On Household Management* col. 23.22–36, Philodemus contrasts non-combative

with friendship but is neither an art nor a virtue; rather, it is a stochastic method used by friends in the art of therapeutic healing of souls, comparable to the methods used by physicians in the art of healing and by pilots in the art of navigation.

Philodemus' fragmentary works *On Flattery*, which display traditionally noted features of flattery, are an important link in the discussion of servility to the great and how to distinguish flatterers from friends. These works are important because, except for Plutarch's and later Maximus of Tyre's treatises on this topic, there are few texts extant subsequent to Theophrastus' *Characters*.[38] Here we gain insight into Philodemus' views on flattery, particularly as it relates to friendship, frank speech, and patronage. Philodemus defends the right of the wise man to associate with a patron and discusses the relationship between a flatterer and a friend as well as advancing a positive form of obsequiousness. Philodemus contrasts flattery with friendship and reveals apparent similarities between flatterers and friends as he attempts to account for the practice of the wise man in his service to a patron which might be compared to that of the flatterer. Interestingly, what emerges is not only that traditional characteristics of flattery are negatively valued but also a positive evaluation of a right form of obsequiousness among one's philosophical friends. Philodemus advocates an obliging approach among the friends of the Epicurean community.

Six Herculanean papyri have been attributed to Philodemus' work *On Flattery*. Content and paleographical evidence confirms the existence of (at least) three books on flattery (PHerc. 222, 1457, 1675), belonging to Philodemus' large work *On Vices and the Opposing Virtues*.[39] Philodemus' works *On Flattery* are influenced by Aristotle's classification

---

philosophical discourses, shared with receptive men, and sophistic and contentious discourses. For "outspoken persons" vs. flatterers see PHerc. 1457 fr. 12.5–6; col. 1.23–24; Plutarch, *On Tranquility of Mind* 472F.

[38] In his fundamental study on flattery (*Kolax*, Leipzig, 1883) O. Ribbeck did not consider the Herculanean papyri, both because his interest lay in literary texts of Greek and Latin comedy, and because at that time Philodemus' texts on flattery had not yet been published in critical editions. Note Longo Auricchio, "Sulla Concezione Filodemea dell' Adulazione," pp. 79, 81–82, and 91.

[39] Περὶ κακιῶν καὶ τῶν ἀντικειμένων ἀρετῶν. Pace Longo Auricchio, "Sulla concezione Filodemea dell'adulazione," pp. 79–82. PHerc. 222, 223, 1082, 1089, 1457 and 1675 probably belonged to Philodemus' *On Flattery*: The subscriptio of PHerc. 222 confirms that it was the 7th book of *On Vices*. Auricchio conjectures that PHerc. 1457 could be the 8th book; Gargiulo ("PHerc. 222: Filodemo sull' Adulazione," p. 103) that PHerc. 1675 was the 6th book.

of virtue as a mean between two vices.[40] Friendship is the mean between flattery and enmity. The first book on flattery (PHerc. 1675) examines both the flatterer's view and disposition towards the flattered ones and the relationship between Alexander and persons next to him, in this case Anaxarchus and Callisthenes. Philodemus is critical towards the flattered one, his servants and relatives.[41] Philodemus' second book on flattery (PHerc. 222) contrasts flattery and friendship, and offers a new Epicurean evaluation of the love of fame and glory (φιλοδοξία). Two other papyri, namely, PHerc. 1082 and 1089, also contrast flattery and friendship; additionally, PHerc. 1089 gives a dispositional analysis of the flatterer and the friend.[42] Finally, the third book on flattery (PHerc. 1457) concentrates, after a classificatory excursus on vices akin to flattery, on obsequiousness. Here Philodemus quotes in its entirety the fifth *Character* of Theophrastus and gives evidence for the tradition that combined the definitions of the obsequious person and the flatterer.[43]

The importance of the issue of flattery among Epicureans has been explained variously. Firstly, one should not forget the importance of flattery in ancient ethics; from the fifth century onwards flatterers, just like slaves, were a recognized component of society and the vice they personified assumes an elevated importance in subsequent ethical and rhetorical treatises. Secondly, given the importance of friendship in Epicureanism, its opposite vice was bound to have been worthy of consideration; thirdly, Philodemus' works on flattery probably aimed at correcting the behavior of the Epicurean wise man, who, like Horace a generation later, was charged with servility towards the rich and powerful. This was incumbent on Philodemus both because of his relationship with Piso and because flattery was part of charges of servility in anti-Epicurean polemic. Epicurus is said to have flattered Mithras and Idomeneus for his own pleasure, and Epicurus' symposia were seen as assemblies of flatterers, excessively praising each other. Finally, Cicero's unflattering account of Piso's and Philodemus' relationship is well known.[44]

---

[40] Aristotle, *Great Ethics* 1193a20–22; *Eudemian Ethics* 1233b30–32.
[41] V. de Falco, "Appunti sul περὶ κολακείας di Filodemo. pap. erc. 1675," *RIGI* 10 (1926), pp. 15–26.
[42] Méndez, "PHerc. 1089: Filodemo 'Sobre la Adulación'," pp. 121–138.
[43] See pp. 24–25, above, and E. Kondo, "I 'Caratteri' de Teofrasto nei Papiri Ercolanesi," *CErc* 1 (1971), pp. 73–87; idem, "Per l'Interpretazione del Pensiero Filodemeo sulla Adulazione nel PHerc. 1457," pp. 43–56.
[44] Athenaeus, *Sophists at Dinner* 182A; 279F; Diogenes Laertius, *Lives of Eminent*

Although one would expect that most of the Epicureans at Herculaneum saw no problem with Philodemus' relationship with Piso, other Epicureans apparently saw things differently. This is evident from Philodemus' defensive mode in his works on flattery which reveals a dispute among Epicureans. Philodemus defends the right of the wise man—presented in the *persona* of Epicurus—to associate with a patron. He discusses the relationship between a "flatterer" and a "friend" and advances a positive form of obsequiousness.[45] Philodemus contrasts flattery with friendship and reveals apparent similarities between flatterers and friends as he attempts to account for the practice of the wise man in his service to a patron, which might be compared to that of the flatterer. Philodemus thus recognizes, as does Horace a generation later, the apparent similarities between flatterers and friends in their service to a patron.

Philodemus' defence gives evidence for the overlapping of the issues of association, obsequiousness, and adaptation. Philodemus, consciously and with semantic acuteness, makes the distinction between pleasing the multitude and being obliging towards one's friends. Thus, although an ingratiating and assenting conversation has affinities with sycophantic discourses, it also forms part of the ideal of fellowship among the Epicureans. Although Philodemus claims that the wise man is free from the vice of flattery, he defensively recognizes some of the apparent similarities between flatterers and friends. The wise man thus talks so wonderfully that he fascinates the soul of his audience, "bewitching the mind like the fabulous siren," and has particular prestige among his friends.[46] Philodemus warns of the dangers of obsequiousness in the circle of friends, recognizing at the same

---

*Philosophers* 10.4–5. Cicero calls Philodemus a "flatterer" (*Against Piso* 68–71; cf. 70). See P. H. de Lacy, "The Patrons of Philosophers," *CP* 34 (1939), pp. 59–65; M. Gigante, "La biblioteca de Filodemo," *CErc* 15 (1985), p. 24; Longo Auricchio, "Sulla concezione Filodemea dell'adulazione," p. 82; R. L. Hunter, "Horace on Friendship and Free Speech (Epistles 1.18 and Satires 1.4)," *Hermes* 113 (1985), pp. 480–490; Gargiulo ("PHerc. 222: Filodemo Sull'adulazione," pp. 103, 105) suggests that the apologetic tone of PHerc. 222 where the behavior of the wise man is contrasted to that of the flatterer should be interpreted in light of Cicero's invective. See Gigante, *Ricerche Filodemee* (Naples, 1983), pp. 32–40.

[45] PHerc. 222, cols. 2 and 4. See Gargiulo, "PHerc. 222: Filodemo Sull'adulazione," pp. 105–06; Longo Auricchio, "Sulla concezione Filodemea dell'adulazione," p. 80; and Méndez, "PHerc. 1089: Filodemo 'Sobre la Adulación'," pp. 121–138. Cf. Plutarch, *How to Tell a Flatterer from a Friend* 49B.

[46] PHerc. 1457, cols. 10.17–19; 8.1–3; col. 11.10–15; PHerc. 222, cols. 2.1–12, 20–21; col. 4; Gargiulo, "PHerc. 222: Filodemo sull' Adulazione," pp. 105–06. See PHerc. 1089, cols. 3.1–2; 5.2.

time that continuous proximity often leads to hypocrisy and bragging and an attempt to please others. It is possible, however, to remain free from the sly and persuasive vice of obsequiousness with the help of philosophy and the company of friends. Also, there are many people who like to tell and do pleasant things, never committing an evil or unfair deed, because, as Philodemus explains, we have to treat many people with regard.[47]

In the context Philodemus distinguishes between the verbs ἀνδάνειν and ἀρέσκειν as he criticizes Nicasicrates who saw "delighting your neighbours as a dangerous pleasure" (τὸ τοῖς πέλας ἀνδάνειν ὡς [ζ]η[μ]ιο[ῦσαν] τὴν ἀρέσκειαν; col. 10.11–13). If we take οἱ πολλοί in col. 11.16 as referring to "the multitude," as the common comparison of flatterers with demagogues suggests, we have a contrast here between "neighbours" (οἱ πέλας) and the "multitude" (οἱ πολλοί), which is, I submit, analogous to Philodemus' contrast elsewhere between "insiders", namely fellow Epicureans, and "outsiders", those who do not belong to the Epicurean group. This understanding of "neighbours" as fellow students and disciples in the Epicurean community indicates that pleasing your fellow students (τὸ τοῖς πέλας ἀνδάνειν) is not a damaging complaisance as pleasing the multitude is (τοῖς πολλοῖς ἀρέσκειν).[48]

Philodemus' discussion in *On Frank Criticism* is also in a defensive mode, revealing a dispute over methods of correcting disciples within the Epicurean school, focusing both on the problem of obsequiousness and that of harshness in the frank correction of one's friends. Philodemus rejects both sycophantic techniques and the indiscriminate and unrelieved use of harshness. His remarks are, though, in a

---

[47] PHerc. 1457, col. 11.16–25, οἱ πολλοὶ πεφύκασιν χα[ρί]ζεσθαι ... μηδὲν [αἰ]σχρὸν ἢ ἄδικον ἐπιτηδεύοντας ὑπὲρ οὗ προσδεόμεθα τοὺς πολλοὺς ἀπ[ο]θεραπεύειν.

[48] This understanding of "neighbours" as fellow disciples is confirmed by *On Frank Criticism*, where Philodemus speaks of the way in which the teacher admonishes his disciples "in a way not understandable to τοῖς πέλας" (fr. 61). My interpretation of PHerc. 1457 is in line with that of Kondo, "Per L'Interpretazione del Pensiero Filodemeo sulla Adulazione nel PHerc. 1457," pp. 54–56. Compare fr. 187 Us., "I [sc. Epicurus] never tried to please the multitude because I do not know what they like and what I know they do not understand," with *Vatican Sentences* 64 and 67. Philodemus' *Rhetoric* contains some disparaging remarks on pleasing the multitude as well as discussing different means of persuasion which either please or displease the multitude (See v. 1, col. 8, p. 237; col. 94, p. 373; v. 2, fr. XVII, p. 157; col. 23, p. 17; col. 24, pp. 18–19; cols. 15–18, pp. 219–223 Sudhaus). For the "insider/outsider" contrast in Philodemus and Paul, see pp. 103–105, above, and 195–98 and 260–64, below.

defensive mode since both obsequiousness and harshness coincide to a certain extent with a legitimate aspect of true frankness of speech; furthermore, these remarks reveal a debate with other Epicureans on the appropriate mode of exhortation in the curing of moral ills.[49] The concerns with real and counterfeit frankness surface in columns 1–2. Here, Philodemus uses a dispositional analysis to distinguish the one who correctly wields frank speech and the one who does so incorrectly. The one who pretends to use frankness is an ἀλαζών and the person of a roguish character is compared to the flatterer.[50] Philodemus rejects their pretentiousness, sycophantic techniques, and reviling, but applauds the frank speech of the person of a refined character actuated by goodwill, steadfast in principle, immune

> from any tendency to demagogy, free from envy, saying only what fits the occasion, and is not likely to be carried away so as to revile, abuse, bully, or hurt, by using insolence and sycophantic techniques.[51]

Such a person is neither prone to blame others, nor easily provoked nor bickersome; and, contrary to the person of a depraved disposition, he is not harsh or bitter.[52] Different character types thus use different forms of persuasion. Philodemus contrasts two types of persuasion in

---

[49] See Clarence E. Glad, "Frank Speech, Flattery, and Friendship in Philodemus," in John T. Fitzgerald (ed.), *Friendship, Flattery, and Frankness of Speech* (SupNovT; Leiden: E. J. Brill, forthcoming). Philodemus also contrasts two methods of exhortation, distinguishable by harshness, in *On Anger* (cols. 1.8–27; 19.12–27; 27.19–39; 35.18–39.7; 44.15–27). See cols. 27.19–21 (τῆι ἀνεπιεικεῖ καὶ ἀνημέρωι καὶ τραχείαι διαθέσει), 38.1–3; and 42.30–31 (ἀνήμρος διάθεσις).

[50] *On Frank Criticism* col. 1a1–4, "How shall we distinguish between the one whose frank criticism arises from a cultivated disposition, and the one whose frank criticism arises from a boorish disposition" (διάθεσις ἀστείας vs. διάθεσις φαύλης/μοχθηρᾶς). The discussion runs from col. 1 stating the problem to col. 2b. Cf. 3a1–3 "Enough, then, has been said on this topic." Philodemus also uses a dispositional analysis in his *On Anger* in order to distinguish different types of exhortation (*On Anger* col. 24.1 Indelli). Ἀστεῖος is opposite to the ἄγροικος and ἀηδής, the ill-bred man (Cf. Theophrastus, *Character* 20). Philo also contrasts ὁ ἀστεῖος and ὁ φαῦλος in his discussion of παρρησία (*Who is the Heir* 19; *On Abraham* 20 and 22). Pretentiousness among the students is also a concern in the fragments (col. 16b2–9). Fr. 88 asks, "how shall we recognize the one who has borne frank criticism correctly and the one who only pretends to have done so?" (See Epicurus, *Vatican Sentences* 54 = fr. 220 Us.).

[51] Philodemus, *On Frank Criticism* col. 1b5–13. In fr. 85.7–9, the teacher (ὁ καθηγούμενος) is characterized as being of a "cheerful, loving and gentle disposition" (διάθεσις εὐήμερος καὶ φιλόφιλος καὶ ἤπιος). For the use of κολακευτικαὶ τέχναι in col. 1b13 compare *Rhetoric* 2, XLI 35–XLII 1 Longo Auricchio, φανερὸν γὰ[ρ δ᾽ ὅ]τι καὶ τεχ[ν]ίτην ... κ[αὶ] κόλακα, and PHerc. 1089, col. 7.5–6, κολακικῶς ὁμιλῆσ[ι; cf. Amoroso, "Filodemo sulla conversazione," pp. 63–4. See O. Ribbeck, *Kolax* (Leipzig, 1883), pp. 65–67.

[52] *On Frank Criticism* col. 2a1–9, ... μηδὲ τραχὺς μηδὲ πικρός.

order to suggest how to use frank speech correctly in psychagogic guidance. Such a contrast also serves as a guideline as to how a pretentious person in the community may be detected.

Epicureanism was not a monolithic movement. At the time of Philodemus a lively debate existed among Epicureans. Cicero suggests that Epicureans held three different theories of friendship and gave different solutions to the question of how to prove the supreme good, and differed as to the relationship of the virtues to pleasure. We also hear of "dissident" Epicureans who should be thought of "immediately as enemies," and others who had "withdrawn themselves" from the community.[53] These dissident Epicureans surface in particular in Philodemus' *On Rhetoric*, which contains divergent views on the nature of art and rhetoric, and PHerc. 1005, on the problem of canonization. To these works we should add PHerc. 831, *On Anger*, and *On Frank Criticism*, all of which yield evidence of a debate among Epicureans on questions of harshness and gentleness. Some are reluctant to recognize an "intra-mural" debate among Epicureans, maintaining that a heterodoxy within one group would undermine the foundation on which it stood.[54] A more nuanced interpretation is in order.

*To Friends of the School* gives evidence of a debate among Epicureans on canonization.[55] Philodemus attacks those who "call themselves Epicureans" but are not "true" Epicureans for their unorthodox views with regard to the writings of the Epicurean leaders, for deviating from these writings and circulating and attributing their own writings to Epicurus and his associates. Philodemus disagrees with the type of research conducted and information gathered from and highlighted in these writings.[56]

Philodemus' *On Rhetoric* gives evidence of a debate between Epicureans

---

[53] Cicero, *On Ends* 1.66–70; 2. 25, 30–31; cf. PHerc. 1005, cols. 14–15, pp. 179–80 Angeli. See F. Longo Auricchio & A. T. Guerra, "Aspetti e problemi della dissidenza epicurea," *CErc* 11 (1981), pp. 25–40; cf. p. 29; and Asmis, "Philodemus' Epicureanism," pp. 2377–80; 2400–02.

[54] T. Maslowski ("Cicero, Philodemus, Lucretius," *Eos* (1978), p. 216) is influenced by an uncritical acceptance of de Witt's description of the social structure of Epicurean groups. See p. 153, below.

[55] A. Angeli, in the latest edition of PHerc. 1005 (*Filodemo, Agli Amici di Scuola (PHerc. 1005)* [Naples, 1988], p. 75), suggests that the title of the work should read Πρὸς τοὺς [ἑταίρους] or Πρὸς τοὺς [συνήθεις], in the sense of "To Friends of the School."

[56] Those who emphasize the love affairs of Epicurus' friends, for example, are castigated (PHerc. 1418, col. 15.3–13; cf. col. 2.6–15 and PHerc. 1005, col. 8). See Asmis, "Philodemus' Epicureanism," p. 2379.

of the Rhodian school and the school in Athens-Naples, this time on the nature of rhetoric and the definition of art. Some claimed that rhetoric does not change since "art does not vary with locality and does not adapt itself to different peoples," whereas others defended rhetoric's adaptability. The various camps manipulated their common tradition, each quoting and paraphrasing authoritative texts from Epicurus. Philodemus questions the claim of sophists that only they know how to praise or blame and condemns sophistic rhetoric since it has often been "a lying and pernicious discipline."[57] Epideictic oratory requires insight into the nature of virtue and vice and praise and blame. Philodemus implies, referring to his own non-extant book *On Praise*, that only philosophers have such knowledge: "If Peithos is rightly thought a goddess," he writes, "this is due to philosophy; unlike rhetorical persuasion, philosophical persuasion does not harm."[58] Philosophical discourses are non-combative, full of tranquillity, producing peace of mind, contrary to the destructive nature of the discourses of sophists, demagogues, and sycophants.[59] The same contrast surfaces in *On Frank Criticism* (cols. 1–2), which rejects sycophantic techniques that destroy, instead of contributing to, the tranquil life. This contrast between two character types and their respective modes of persuasion reflects a debate among Epicureans about the nature of moral exhortation.

Marcello Gigante contends that the above contrast, comparable to Seneca's contrast between philosophy and philology, refers to the Epicurean sage of a refined disposition and to false pedagogues, full of arrogance, grandiloquent, and finicky, outside the Epicurean school, but this is problematic.[60] To begin with, the critique focuses on the mode of exhortation, irrespective of locality. The commonplace contrast between philology and philosophy gives no evidence for the

---

[57] Philodemus, *Rhetoric* v. 1, pp. 216–224; v. 2, pp. 256–263; v. 2, 127, fr. XII; v. 2, 74, fr. XII = 2, 106, frs. XIII and XIV Sudhaus; H. M. Hubbell, "The *Rhetorica* of Philodemus," *TCAAS* 23 (1920), p. 288. Diogenes Laertius is aware of divisions among Epicureans (*Lives of Eminent Philosophers* 10.26): Longo Auricchio & Guerra, "Aspetti e problemi della dissidenza epicurea," p. 26.

[58] *Rhetoric* v. 1, col. 32.2–10, p. 269; col. 32.32–37, p. 270; col. 38a24–25, p. 219, ἐν τ[ῷ π]ερὶ ἐπαίνου λόγωι; v. 4, col. 30a19–32a8 Sudhaus. See Asmis, "Philodemus' Epicureanism," p. 2402.

[59] Philodemus, *On Household Management* col. 23.22–36; Asmis, "Philodemus' Epicureanism," 2388.

[60] M. Gigante, "Philodème: Sur la liberté de parole," ACGB (Paris: Société d'Édition <Les Belles Lettres>, 1969), pp. 215–17; Philodemus, *On Frank Criticism* cols. 2a7–8; 1a.

locality of these scholars. Philodemus criticizes these scholars' manner of exhortation, which presupposes that they are exhorting in the community rather than teaching grammar.[61] Philodemus' critique is then similar to that of Seneca, who uses the contrasts to criticize both advisers who teach, not how to live, but how to debate and pupils who come to their teachers to develop, not their souls, but their wits.[62] The contention that these scholars must have been outside the Epicurean school is complicated by several further factors. Being fond of philosophical argument as part of the common search for wisdom was valued by Epicureans. Also, the term φιλόλογος was used for being "fond of philosophical argument," or "fond of learning and literature," or simply for a "scholar," without negative connotations.[63] Philodemus can even apply it to himself![64] If Philodemus thought these scholars were outside the community, he would have stated so more clearly since he otherwise made clear distinctions between "insiders" and "outsiders."[65]

Philodemus uses the approach of these literary scholars to discredit harshness and sycophancy in persuasion. Athenaeus' *Sophists at Dinner* also yields evidence of "harsh" Epicureans. In an anecdote preceding the author's statement of intent, namely, to scrutinize all self-professed philosophers, Athenaeus quotes a saying of Agathon, "If I speak the truth, I shall not cheer you up; but if I in any way cheer you up, I shall not speak the truth," showing that his concerns center on harshness, truth, pleasure, and deception.[66] Masurius tells of a symposium at the palace of Alexander the son of Antiochus Epiphanes,

---

[61] Philodemus, *On Frank Criticism* col. 10a1–5, ". . . but if a philosopher or scholar . . . criticizes him frankly as described, he will not be angry. . . ." See also col. 8a8–9 and fr. 37.

[62] Seneca, *Epistle* 108.23, "Thus the study of wisdom has become the study of words." A φιλόλογος is one ὁ φιλῶν λόγους καὶ σπουδάζων περὶ παιδείαν (Phrynichus, IId; 371).

[63] LSJ, s.v. See A. Dihle, "Philosophe—Fachwissenschaft—Allgemeinbildung," *Ent. Fond. Hardt* 32 (Geneva, 1986), pp. 200–08. Ὁ φιλόσοφος and ὁ φιλόλογος are close in Plato's *Republic* 582E.

[64] Asmis ("Philodemus' Epicureanism," 2392) wishes to include a reference to Philodemus as a "lover of discourse" or φιλόλογος in *On Death* cols. 25.37–39; 33.23–24; 38.8. Philodemus uses φιλολογία in *On Anger* col. 2.21 and φιλόλογος in *On Frank Criticism* fr. 37.4; cols. 8a9; 10a2. Epicurus' *Vatican Sentences* 74 refers to a philosophical discussion (ἐν φιλολόγῳ συζητήσει). See fn. 36, above. People do not progress if they do "not share in the good of joint inquiry" (Philodemus, *On Anger* col. 19.25–27 Indelli μήτε [τ]οῦ διὰ συζητήσεως μετέχειν ἀγαθοῦ·).

[65] See PHerc. 1082 col. 2.1–4; PHerc. 1457 fr. 16.3–5. Refer to pp. 103–104, above.

[66] Athenaeus, *Sophists at Dinner* 211A–215C; 220A.

which an Epicurean philosopher, Diogenes, attended. Diogenes used to be welcome at the court although the king delighted in the doctrines of the Stoics. Alexander regarded Diogenes highly, in spite of the fact that the latter lived a depraved life and had a slanderous and bitter tongue. At the symposium Diogenes incessantly praised an actress. These two aspects of Diogenes' behavior, namely, a bitter tongue and incessant praise, are characteristic of flatterers. Masurius concentrates on harshness and says that Antiochus VI Epiphanes, who succeeded to the kingdom, did not tolerate the abusive manners of Diogenes and ordered his throat to be cut. Such a decisive act was ordered by one who was "gentle in all circumstances" and, yes, a φιλόλογος![67] Athenaeus thus gives an anecdote of contrasting behaviors—harsh vs. gentle—in his work when carefully scrutinizing those who profess to be philosophers, and the example given of a harsh type of philosopher is identified as an Epicurean.[68]

Evidence from the first century BCE lends credibility to this tradition. PHerc. 831 recommends philosophy for curing fickleness. The work is a paraenesis that admonishes the reader to avoid this evil. The Epicurean author who stood to the addressee in the relation of teacher to pupil follows a common form of arrangement, namely, diagnosis, defining the nature of the moral error, followed by a prescribed cure.[69] The author rejects harshness in curing fickleness, "but to rail at the aforementioned abnormality is out of place; on the contrary, it is necessary to cure it."[70] Philodemus agrees in his *On Anger*, conceding to his opponent that an older Epicurean is correct

---

[67] Ibid., 211D.

[68] According to Diogenes Laertius (*Lives of Eminent Philosophers* 10.24–25), Apollodorus was known as the "tyrant of the garden" (Κηποτύραννος) but Polyaenus was "a just and kindly man, as Philodemus and his pupils affirm" (ἐπιεικὴς καὶ φιλικός, ὡς οἱ περὶ Φιλόδημόν φασι).

[69] This is probably a treatise by Demetrius the Laconian. See R. Philippson, "Papyrus Herculanensis 831," *Studien zu Epikur und den Epikureern* (Hildesheim, 1983), pp. 284–98. Chrysippus' method in his work on the emotions was prescriptive and is found in numerous popular treatises on vices and passions, for example, in Cicero (*Tusculan Disputations*, Books 3–4), and in Seneca's, Plutarch's, and Philodemus' works on anger. See ibid., p. 285; idem, *Hermes* 67 (1932), pp. 245–94; idem, "Philodems Buch über den Zorn," *Rh. Mus.* 71 (1916), pp. 425–60. Chrysippus' *On the Passions* was in four books, the first three defining the nature of the different passions and the fourth—called the τὸ περὶ παθῶν θεραπευτικός—their cure. See SVF 3.458 (111.8–12); 3.460 (112.1–13); Diogenes Laertius, *Lives of Eminent Philosophers* 7.111; and pp. 72–73, above. Note also Plutarch, *How to Tell a Flatterer from a Friend* 74A ἡ θεραπευτικὴ παρρησία.

[70] PHerc. 831, col. 5.9–11, ἄτοπον] δὲ λοιδορεῖν τὸ πρ[οειρημέ]νον παράλλαγμα, ἀλλ[ὰ δεῖ θερ]απεύειν. My translation. See Philippson, "Papyrus Herculanensis 831," p. 286.

when he disapproves of the mere censure of an angry man. The mere censure of the emotions, advocated by Bion and Chrysippus, is ineffectual.[71] One should rather visualize the illness; when the shameful consequences of such a vice are put before the eyes of those suffering, they become intent on a cure.[72] This debate concerns the degree of harshness used in the cure of moral ills. Demetrius' and Philodemus' rejection of the censure of fickleness and anger is not a foil used in order to advocate a gentler approach but reflects rather a contrary view held by other Epicureans.

The same debate is seen in *On Frank Criticism* where Philodemus rejects the use of harshness in moral exhortation in view of the different dispositions and conditions of the pupils. Evidence for this occurs in contexts discussing how to treat the weak, those difficult to cure, the incurable, and those who have apostasized from philosophy, and how to retain and reclaim students who might have disobeyed and been disassociated, psychologically or physically, from the community. Fragment 59 notes two among many reasons why some abandon philosophy: "For they are either weak or incurable by frankness."[73] Fragment 60.1–7 continues:

> And some maintained that one should apply frank speech towards people like this, others, on the other hand, that one should use a bitter form of frankness similar to reproach, even as those who revile from malevolence.

The contention concerns the appropriate treatment of the "weak" and "incurable" ones. Both agreed that these should not be shunned but disagreed on the cure. Some thought παρρησία would suffice; others that λοιδορία was necessary. The following lines speak of charmers who "with their deceitful and manifold pleasantries turn many away by seizing the intensity of the emotions and subduing

---

[71] Philodemus, *On Anger* col. 1.7–20 Indelli, εἰ μὲν οὖν ἐπετίμα τοῖς ψέγουσι μ[ό]νον ... ὡς Βίων ἐν τῶι Περὶ τῆς ὀργῆς καὶ Χρύσιππος ἐν τ[ῶ]ι Πε[ρ]ὶ παθῶν θεραπευ[τι]κῶι, κἂν μετρίως ἵστατο (M. Gigante & G. Indelli, "Bione e l'Epicureismo," *CErc* 8 (1978), pp. 125–26).

[72] Philodemus, *On Anger* cols. 1.21–27; 3.13; 4.15–16 Indelli, κακὰ τιθέναι πρὸ ὀμμάτων. Cf. *On Frank Criticism* fr. 26.3–4.

[73] Idem, *On Frank Criticism* fr. 59.9–11 and 1–2, "and sometimes he will even abandon philosophy." Recent converts experience dejecting influences which, as the result of weakness, affect them; these include the sober advice of friends and bitter criticism of the unfriendly, which "have even made some persons renounce philosophy altogether" (Plutarch, *Progress in Virtue* 78AB). On deserting philosophy see also *On Listening to Lectures* 46E and pp. 78–81, above.

them by enchantment" (fr. 60.8–12). As Philodemus rejects the "psychagogy" of those of an unrefined disposition, so he rejects that of these charmers because of its detrimental effect on friends of the community. Philodemus rejects both the reviling of the "incurable ones" and the "weak," and the bitter frankness of the young who use "biting frankness," approximating λοιδορία. The young err in their excessive and intemperate use of παρρησία, characterized as a tumor that needs a drastic operation (col. 17a). But Philodemus rejects λοιδορία, as did Dio Chrysostom in his description of the ideal Cynic and Plutarch as he lamented the great dearth of those friends who do not confuse λοιδορία and ψόγος with παρρησία.[74] One should not revile or treat the erring one spitefully; instead, mistakes should be considered with sympathy. The use of inconsiderate harshness severs the social relations between friends of the community.

Right and wrong psychagogy is seen in the contrast between an admonition actuated by the concern for the good of others and an admonition which is altogether biting with moderate irony.[75] The "cheerful admonishing" (νουθετεῖν ἱλαρῶς) as opposed to νουθετεῖν ἀγνώστως (fr. 61), echoes the joyous use of the philotropeic method (fr. 43, εὐφροσύνη). Fragments 57 to 70 highlight, with the help of the medical analogy, the correct mode of admonition, asking whether the mature can fail in their use of frank speech and answering in the affirmative. These fragments recognize the legitimate use of harsh speech, as does column 2b, which notes that the psychagogue can use bitter methods comparable to wormwood. This puts Philodemus on the defensive since the method he advocates has apparent similarities, not only to the practice of the ironic and pretentious man, but also to the methods used by flatterers and obsequious persons. Philodemus defends both a legitimate use of harshness and an appropriate form of obsequiousness among the friends in the community (cf. pp. 112–14, above).

Now pretentiousness accentuates a certain relationship. In Aristotle, truthfulness in social life is the mean between pretentiousness and

---

[74] Dio Chrysostom, *Discourse* 32.11–13; Plutarch, *How to Tell a Flatterer from a Friend* 66A; *Precepts of Statecraft* 810C; Philodemus, *On Frank Criticism* fr. 79.8–12. See pp. 92–94, above.

[75] Ibid., fr. 26.4–7, κηδεμονικὴ νουθέτησις. Cf. also fr. 42.6, and col. 13b12; cf. Plutarch, *How to Tell a Flatterer from a Friend* 55B, παρρησία κηδεμονική; Epictetus, *Gnom.*, 63, κηδεμονικὸς ἀνήρ. Clement was later to define νουθέτησις as "benevolent blame" (ψόγος κηδεμονικός, *Ped.* 76.1) and recognized also a benevolent use of λοιδορία (*Ped.* 74.2). See pp. 72–75, above.

self-deprecation. The truth-telling in question concerns claims made about oneself. The definition in the *Eudemian Ethics* of the person between the dissembler and the charlatan—called truthful, sincere or "downright"—is broadened in that he is a lover of truth contrasted to a lover of falsehood.[76] Here we see the inchoate steps towards further expansion where these concepts come to be eulogized attributes in interpersonal relations. Philodemus' description in *On Vices* of the εἴρων, combined with the ἀλαζών, gives evidence for the ironic and pretentious person's behavior towards others:

> Usually he praises the man he will censure, but always minimizes and blames himself and those like himself, thereby perverting what he wants to say. He is, however, well aware of his own cleverness to deceive and give a trustworthy impression.[77]

"He," furthermore, "never calls anybody by his bare name, but 'the beautiful Phaedrus' and 'the wise Lysias', and uses ambiguous epithets like worthy, pleasant, simple, noble, manly." And, at a dinner party, he "listens with open mouth to a man who will prove something, then mocks him covertly by nodding to others...."[78] These aspects of the ironic person remind us of the flatterer. Socrates both praises the person he censures, deprecates himself, is clever in his own deceptiveness, and is flattering at parties. Philodemus' reference to the ἀλαζών reveals then an Epicurean critique of Socrates.[79] It is also paramount for Philodemus to undermine the activity of the pretentious person for a more subtle reason: the Epicurean psychagogue is like the Socratic εἴρων and ἀλαζών who both praises and admonishes the same people! The wise Epicurean is then not in every respect the reversal of Socrates.[80] Socratic indirection indeed

---

[76] Aristotle, *Eudemian Ethics* 1221a1-3; 1233b38-1234a3; *Nicomachean Ethics* 1108a9-10, 19-21; 1127a13-b33; *Great Ethics* 1193a28-35.

[77] Philodemus, *On Vices* col. 21.37-23.37. Cf. col. 21.37-38.

[78] Ibid., cols. 22.2-4; 22.27-32; 23.23-26. Translated by K. Kleve, "Scurra Atticus: The Epicurean View of Socrates," Συζήτησις, vol. 1, pp. 246-47. Ἀλαζών is close in meaning to ψευδής: Theophrastus, *Characters* 23.1; Plato, *Republic* 560C; *Gorgias* 525A; Aristophanes, *Clouds* 102.

[79] Plutarch, *Reply to Colotes* 1117D, Socrates' arguments were ἀλαζόνες or charlatans. M. T. Riley, "The Epicurean Criticism of Socrates," *Phoenix* 34 (1980), pp. 55-68; Kleve, "Scurra Atticus: The Epicurean View of Socrates," Συζήτησις, vol. 1, pp. 227-53; A. A. Long, "Socrates in Hellenistic Philosophy," *The Classical Quarterly* n.s. Vol. 38.1 (1988), pp. 150-71; S. K. Stowers, "Paul on the Use and Abuse of Reason," in *Greeks, Romans, and Christians* (1990), pp. 272-74.

[80] Contra K. Kleve, "Scurra Atticus: The Epicurean View of Socrates," Συζήτησις, vol. 1, p. 248.

appeared inimical to Epicurean frankness, but one of the more effective means of persuasion advocated in *On Frank Criticism* is the subtle approach of mixing praise and blame. Hence, it was important for Philodemus to give advice as to how to detect a pretentious person among the friends of the community.

Obsequiousness, deception, and chatter, are constituent parts of the flatterer's "psychagogy."[81] But Philodemus describes the method of charmers who pretend to be on friendly terms with those they flatter in similar terms to the method of the moral corrector. Charmers divert and charm many people with "deceitful and manifold pleasantries" and psychagogues "tame men with perseverance to friendship with themselves even as physicians through manifold aids succour persons without passion."[82] The physicians' "manifold aids" remind us not only of the "varied and good method" of the Epicurean teachers, but also of the "manifold pleasantries" of imposters (frs. 60.11–12; 68.1–2; 10.1). Terms such as τιθασεύω, "to tame or domesticate," and compounds of τρέχω, used to describe both the teachers and flatterers, reinforce their apparent closeness. The term ὑποτρέχω is close in meaning to κολακεύω, as is clear when Philodemus presents the Peripatetic position on anger.[83] Philodemus' neologism προστροχαστής shows the semantic closeness of compounds of τρέχω with flattery and Philodemus' attempt to highlight the special imprint of Epicurean practice. The latter is clear from a practice rejected in *On Frank Criticism*: "and we do not run to (our) teachers so that we may appear to bear goodwill towards them."[84]

The similarities between flatterers and psychagogues were conspicuous enough for Philodemus to explain them, just as he emphasizes the differences between the pretentious person and psychagogues in light of their similarities and defends an appropriate form of obsequi-

---

[81] PHerc. 336/1150, col. 18.2–4, p. 118 Indelli. For commentary see ibid., pp. 171–72. See p. 18, above.

[82] *On Frank Criticism* fr. 86.2 7. Cf. 60.8–12. The close semantic range of "charmers" (γόητες) and "flatterers" is well established: Longo Auricchio, "Sulla Concezione Filodemea dell'Adulazione," p. 89.

[83] Philodemus, *On Anger* cols. 31–32 (cf. 31.28, 31–32). See J. Annas, "Epicurean Emotions," *GRBS* 30.2 (1989), pp. 145–64. Cf. *On Frank Criticism* fr. 82. Τρεχέδειπνος, "the one who runs to dinner," is one of the commonest epithets of the parasite (see Ribbeck, *Kolax*, pp. 15–16).

[84] *On Frank Criticism* fr. 52.6–9 (cf. Gigante, *Ricerche Filodemee*, p. 100). And the former from PHerc. 1457 where "the one who runs up to" is said to behave like the one who "speaks in order to please." Cf. Longo Auricchio, "Sulla Concezione Filodemea dell'Adulazione," pp. 90–91.

ousness. *On Flattery* concedes that there are certain similarities between flatterers and the wise, as when the wise man talks so wonderfully that he fascinates the soul of his audience, "bewitching the mind like the fabulous siren."[85] The Epicurean teacher is a dealer in proverbs or apophthegms, just as Metrodorus speaks to Polyaenus, often giving an insinuating and pleasant discourse.[86] PHerc. 1457 draws a line between the "intimate fellows" and "those outside the intimate fellowship"; the latter are to be treated with respect; the former are treated with honor and respect and worthy to be flattered![87] Flatterers and the wise are then like in their praise, obsequiousness, and flattery, but different in their use of blame. If flatterers blame at all, they do so inconsiderately and harshly.[88] Unrelieved harshness is rejected in the art of psychagogy, although it can be harsh; this art is varied like the "manifold aid" of physicians, "bountifully mixed with praise and exhortation to do those things which belong to the good."[89] It teaches, gives advice, and spurs on to proper action. The "order of frankness" belongs thus to deliberative rhetoric. A mixed method should be applied to the erring ones; and they should be exhorted frequently. Blame should be followed by more soothing measures. So, Philodemus clearly sides with those who recognized the need for praise and blame for progressing persons.[90]

The identity of those Epicureans advocating harshness eludes us. But we should remember that *On Frank Criticism* derives from Zeno's lecture notes and discussions in the school in Athens, and these discussions continued in Naples and Herculaneum. I have introduced

---

[85] PHerc. 222, cols. 2.4–7, 20–21; Gargiulo, "PHerc. 222: Filodemo sull' Adulazione," pp. 105–06.

[86] Philodemus, *On Frank Criticism* col. 6a8–15. See δελεάζω in fr. 26.11 in the meaning of "seduce." For the pleasant discourse of the wise see fr. 87.1–3 (the teacher throws out the false opinions of students by singing) and fr. 74.1–2, "being lifted up/exalted by hymns/chants."

[87] Kondo, "Per l'interpretazione del pensiero filodemeo sulla adulazione nel PHerc. 1457," p. 48.

[88] PHerc. 1675, col. 11, pp. 20–21 de Falco; Longo Auricchio, "Sulla Concezione Filodemea dell'Adulazione," pp. 85–86.

[89] Philodemus, *On Frank Criticism* frs. 68.1–7; 10.1–2; 86.5–7.

[90] Praise and blame are both bountifully represented in the hortatory terms in *On Frank Criticism* (see p. 108, fn. 28, above). Terms of praise and exhortation include ἐπαινέω, ἔπαινος, αἴνεσις, προτρέπω, παραινέω, παραίνεσις, παρακαλέω, ἐπιτείνω, and διακελεύομαι. See also σώζω, κηδεμονία, θεραπεύω, κουφίζεσθαι, κομίζεσθαι, and βοηθεία. Cf. *On Frank Criticism* col. 13b3–6, "since it makes the order of frankness into a deliberative speech"; col. 13b13; and fr. 58.6–9, where the teacher is said to use frank speech "often in a mixed manner when an error has occurred."

evidence for a tradition of harsh Epicureans and of a debate among Epicureans on the correct mode of exhortation which rejected flattery and harsh censure of the emotions. All this lends credence to the view that the two contrasting approaches to moral exhortation and psychagogic guidance were held by opposing Epicureans. This puts the burden of proof on the shoulders of those who would maintain that the contrasting position discouraged is simply a foil, i.e., non-existent, or a critique of pedagogical practices in vogue outside the Epicurean community.

This dispute over methods of correcting disciples within the Epicurean school is a variation of the debate among non-Epicureans on the appropriate means of persuasion in moral reformation that I documented in chapter two. As we shall see in some detail below, this debate centers on the question of the appropriate treatment for students of different dispositions. Philodemus' *On Frank Criticism* allows us not only to gauge in detail the nature of the above debate, but reveals also an intriguing rotational form of psychagogy which expects the active participation of all members of the community in the correction of each other. The disciples of the school are urged to be forthcoming and reveal their shortcomings to their fellow-students and leaders for correction.

## 3.2 *Epicurean Communal Psychagogy: Philodemus'* On Frank Criticism

### 3.2.1 *Mutual participation in edification, admonition, and correction. Openness and concealment; confession and reporting; trust and distrust*

The first fragment of *On Frank Criticism* draws attention to the participatory nature of Epicurean psychagogy: "On the occasion when someone fails in perceiving errors together or in discerning that which is useful, he/she arouses distrust" (1.1–4). Error is no solitary affair; neither is its correction. The Epicurean ideal of fellowship expected participation of members in the evaluation and correction of each other. Besides the issue of openness—members are encouraged to be forthcoming with regard to their faults—*On Frank Criticism* is also concerned with the contrary practice of concealment. The friends of the community are encouraged not to conceal their faults, but to confess them to others. "Confessional practice" is somewhat anachronistic but describes such an activity well. Some of the fragments refer to reporting and spying as well as the reluctance of some to be forthcoming. Member evaluation also included "patting on the back" for a thing well done. Although outsiders in their critique focused on this latter aspect, *On Frank Criticism* is mainly concerned with frank criticism of faults.[91]

Two attendant factors emerge. Firstly, if anyone does not adhere to established communal norms among the friends, he/she arouses distrust. Secondly, a practice of confession and reporting encountered a strong psychological hindrance, succinctly captured by Menander, "Don't tell your secret to your friend and you will not fear him when he turns into an enemy."[92] Frank speech serves the truth and is not afraid to censure a friend; the truth, however, might be difficult to bear.[93] Both of these factors surface in *On Frank Criticism*. Other moralists discuss how forthcoming one should be towards others and whether and to what extent one should trust another. In light of the propensity of humans to harm each other, Dio Chrysostom advises caution in trusting people. One should be equally on one's guard towards all, and not be more trustful even towards a friend, a close acquaintance or a blood-relative.[94] Dio recounts the saying of a Spartan who, to the offer of a guarantee (πίστις) of friendship from certain persons, replied that there was only one guarantee, namely, "their inability to do harm even if they wished."[95] Any guarantee that "consists in phrases, in acquaintanceship, in oaths, in kinship" is laughable, foolish and utterly weak. From Lucian's *Toxaris*, which deals with the question of faithful friends, we know the Scythians had adopted one of these "laughable and foolish" guarantees, namely, blood-oaths.[96] Lucian's discussion shows, as well as that of Dio in the above discourse—and *Discourse 73, On Trust*—that questions of trust

---

[91] Athenaeus (*Sophists at Dinner* 182A = Fr. 56 Usener) says that Epicurus' *Symposium* consists of a crowd of flatterers praising one another. Clement of Alexandria, on the other hand, notes the Epicurean emphasis on blame and correction (*Ped.* 93.1; 145, 14 Stählin-Treu). See p. 74, fn. 71, above.

[92] Frs. 695K; 545K.

[93] The words regularly used in this connection are ἀνέχεσθαι and ὑπο-φέρω/μένω. See Philodemus, *On Frank Criticism* frs. 2.6; 80.5; cols. 10a10; 10b8; 12b8; and 13b11; Epictetus, *Discourse* 3.4.12; 3.21.5; *Encheiridion* 30; Dio Chrysostom, *Discourse* 32.8; Josephus, *Antiquities* 7.372; 17.342; Heb 13:13; Epicurus, *Vatican Sentences* 34, 39, 56–57; Diogenes Laertius, *Lives of Eminent Philosophers* 7.12. For Paul's use of this motif see pp. 321–23, below.

[94] Dio Chrysostom, *On Distrust, Discourse* 74.1. Cf. also *Nicomachean Ethics* 1124b28–30.

[95] Dio Chrysostom, *Discourse* 74.11–12; Epicurus, *Principal Doctrines* 31–35; Lucretius, *On the Nature of Things* 5.1020.

[96] Lucian, *Toxaris* 37. See further pp. 166–69, below.

and distrust, sincerity and deception, between members of society were of concern to authors of the early Empire.

The same concerns surface in Plutarch's *Concerning Talkativeness* and *On Curiosity*, as well as in Epictetus' *To Those Who Lightly Talk About Their Own Affairs*.[97] The last work warns of the dangers of openness: if you think that every person you meet is a friend you are just a "babbler." We should only divulge our secrets to faithful, respectful, and dependable persons. It is true that nobody would despise a friendly and faithful counselor; nobody would reject a person who is ready "to share his difficulties, as he would share a burden with him, and to make them light for him by the very fact of his sharing in them."[98] The suggestion of the treatise is, however, that there is a great dearth of such reliable persons. In the case of the Epicureans these issues were particularly pressing in light of their communal psychagogy. Intimate acquaintanceship, a constitutive part of the Epicurean ideal of fellowship, constituted the guarantee and basis of their friendly relations and allowed members to be forthright with each other in spite of attendant dangers. Diogenes succinct statement—εἰ δ' ἀπίστων οὐδὲ φίλων—even though noting Epicurus' disagreement with the Pythagorean maxim κοινὰ τὰ φίλων—captures the importance of trust in Epicurean friendship which did involve mutual mental support and relief.[99]

Philodemus' *On Anger* reveals that the community of friends has two aims: reform of character and theoretical inquiry. Anger thwarts the progress of people both because they do not share in the good of joint inquiry and because they cannot stand the rebukes of corrections of teachers and fellow students. Reform of character requires thus an emotional change and active participation of all.[100] In Epicurean psychagogy the correction of errors is important, part of the project of reform of character, described as "turning the reason around"; amendment of errors, which is achieved through mutual

---

[97] Plutarch, 502B–515A and 515B–523B, and Epictetus, *Discourse* 4.13, respectively. See Epictetus, *Discourse* 2.22.24, 30, 34; 3.14.18, and 3.16 *That One should Enter Cautiously into Social Intercourse*; Plutarch, *How to Tell a Flatterer from a Friend* 70F; *On the Control of Anger* 463B–D. See also *Is 'Live Unknown' a Wise Precept?* 1128D–E.

[98] Epictetus, *Discourse* 4.13.16 and 23, οἱ ἀπόρρητοι λόγοι πίστεως χρείαν ἔχουσι....

[99] According to Diogenes Laertius, the reason why Epicurus did not think that property should be held in common was that "such practice... implied mistrust" (*Lives of Eminent Philosophers* 10.11).

[100] Philodemus, *On Anger* col. 19.14–27 Indelli, ἀπροβάτους... τῶι μήτε καθηγητὰς ἀνέχεσθαι μήτε συσχολάζοντας, ἂν ἐπιτιμῶσι καὶ διορθῶσιν....

correction and encouragement, is requisite for progress in wisdom.[101] Through confession, errors are brought out into the open for critique and correction. In such a practice we witness also the Epicurean critique of Stoic pedagogy which, so the charge went, was indirect instead of plainly speaking the truth.[102] Indirection, instead of disclosing the truth, closed it up even further. In order to gain legitimacy for a confessional practice, Philodemus focuses on Heracleides' "confession" which, as he notes, was praised by Epicurus. Heracleides was forthcoming

> because he thought the censures he would receive on account of what he revealed were less important than their benefits; and so he disclosed his errors to Epicurus.[103]

This fragment subtly brings home the concerns we saw in Dio and Menander above. To reveal one's shortcomings might generate the censure of others. The basic fear was that the student's openness would bring on an even sharper critique than if he would conceal his faults. In light of the perceived tendency of the age to speak ill of others and expose their shortcomings, these concerns are understandable.[104] How far should one go in revealing one's secrets? This question is put forward in light of a basic vulnerability and distrust of others. It was feared that the information disclosed might prove disgraceful. The flatterer also successfully uses openness; in an attempt to strengthen "fellow feeling," he brings out into the open even innermost secrets.[105] If he, for example, knows that the flattered one is unfortunate in his marriage or suspicious towards his house-

---

[101] Philodemus, *On Frank Criticism* frs. 13.7-8; 22; col. 14b9-11; *On the Stoics* 17.23 (ed. Crönert, *Kolotes und Menedemos*, p. 57). On προκοπή see *On Frank Criticism* frs. 10.10; 33.3; *On Death* 17.33; 23.8; PHerc. 1414, col. 16.9; Epicurus, fr. 521 Us.; Diogenes Laertius, *Lives of Eminent Philosophers* 10.120. Compare ibid., 7.127.

[102] See Riley, "The Epicurean Criticism of Socrates," pp. 67-8, on the rejection of Socrates' philosophical style. For Epicurean practice, see P. Rabbow, *Seelenführung. Methodik der Exerzitien in der Antike* (München, 1954), pp. 260-79. In his discussion of forcible diction, Demetrius contrasts cross-examination with plain teaching (*On Style* 279, σαφῶς διδάσκοντι ἐῴκει καὶ οὐκ ἐλέγχοντι).

[103] Philodemus, *On Frank Criticism* fr. 49.2-7. For Epicurean confessional practice see S. Sudhaus, "Epikur als Beichtvater," *ARW* 14 (1911), pp. 647-48; W. Schmid, "Contritio und 'ultima linea rerum' in neuen Epikureischen Texten," *Rh. Mus.* N. F. 100 (1957), pp. 301-14. See also idem, "Epikur," *RAC* 5 (1962), cols. 741-43.

[104] Cf. Plutarch, *On Being a Busybody* 521E; Athenaeus, *Sophists at Dinner* 220A; Epictetus, *Discourse* 1.18.10. See also Isocrates, *To Nicocles* 47; *Antidosis* 147-48.

[105] Plutarch, *How to Tell a Flatterer from a Friend* 53F-54A. For ἀπόρρητα ("innermost secrets"), see PHerc. 1089, col. 5.6-7, in Méndez, "PHerc. 1089: Filodemo

hold, he divulges secret faults of his in similar matters. This makes their fellow-feeling stronger, which leads the flattered one to disclose some of his own secrets. Then he is afraid to abandon the confidential relation.

But the handbook encourages students, in spite of attendant dangers, not to hold back but to reveal their faults and innermost secrets to others. Concealment is discouraged; openness encouraged. One should bring errors into the open, so that they no longer remain hidden and can be corrected.[106] The benefits of such an openness outweigh any conceivable setback. Fr. 49 uses the word μηνύω for the "confession" of Heracleides. "To reveal" or "disclose what is secret" is also used in fr. 42.1–7:

> And many of the intimate associates will spontaneously disclose what is secret, without the teacher examining closely with concern and in detail.

The young are advised not to hide their errors, but to entrust them to the teacher. If they confess their mistakes, the teacher will give them an attentive ear.[107] Also "to act in secret is doubtless most unfriendly; the one who does not bring everything out into the open will be hiding these from the most excellent of friends."[108] Fragment 42 relates that "most" of the intimate associates disclose things relating to themselves "willingly." At the same time, this also subtly brings home the point that not all do. Consequently, the teacher has to "investigate" or "examine closely" the one who is reluctant to disclose his errors or be otherwise forthcoming. But the teacher is not the only one in a position to examine others who find it difficult to disclose their faults. Some are thus therapeutically treated, gently and with ease, and without the teacher's knowledge, by those who have shared their experience (8.4–11). Also, the teacher's success when

---

'Sobre la Adulación'," p. 134. Cf. *On Anger* p. 54 W; Stobaeus, *Anthology* 3.41; and Isocrates, *To Demonicus* 22 and 24.

[106] Cf. Epicurus, fr. 522 Us. "... initium est salutis notitia peccati." See Seneca, *Epistle* 97.15–16 = fr. 531 Us. See also Plutarch, *Progress in Virtue* 82AB.

[107] *On Frank Criticism* frs. 28; 51.1 (ἀκ[ού]σει μᾶλλον) and fr. 79.9 Herc. Olivieri did not include six frs. in his edition of *On Frank Criticism* which are found in the first edition: *Herculanensium Voluminum quae supersunt*, vol. 5, part 2 (Naples, 1843), frs. 77, 79, 84, 87, 91 and 93. I identify these frs. with "Herc." See M. Gigante, "Motive Paideutici Nell' Opera Filodemea Sulla Liberta' De Parola," *CErc* 4 (1974), pp. 37–42.

[108] Ibid., fr. 41.2–8. The "most excellent of friends" is the wise teacher. See the reference to Epicurus in PHerc. 1232 fr. 9, col. 1.8–9, ed. Vogliano p. 72: ἐ]ξοχώτατον λαμβά[νειν τοῦτ]ο τἀνδρός. See Longo Auricchio, "La Scuola di Epicuro," p. 24.

admonishing might escape his notice, but it is apparent to others (61.6-12). Other members are sometimes in a better position to discover their fellow students' mistakes. Then they should either correct them or report them to the teachers, just like Polyaenus, who reported Apollonides' status to Epicurus when the student was losing his ardor in his pursuit of Epicureanism (49.7-10).

It is not difficult to imagine that such a reporting of misdemeanors might be looked on unfavorably by the erring one and that students might refrain from engaging in such a practice: "Most people restrain themselves from accusing, so that they themselves not be slandered, who criticize others who think badly" (fr. 51.5-10). Because of this reluctance Philodemus has to explain preemptively (fr. 50.3-10):

> For if a person desires his friend to attain correction, he [sc. Epicurus] will not consider him a slanderer, when he is not this sort of person, but one who loves his friend: for he knows the difference well between these two sorts of people.

The fragment continues by noting that one who does not report the errors of his fellow students is mean to his friend and a lover of evil! This contrasts sharply with the description of the teacher as cheerful and gentle, one who loves his friend.[109] But reporting of errors should not go too far: "And we do not run to the teachers in order to appear to show them goodwill, by reporting what one said or did against them, and against one's intimate fellows."[110] The pupils should rather behave with loyalty towards their fellow students and not run to the teachers as adulators and slanderers. The students refuse to be brutal toward those who do not confess their mistakes, giving "measure for measure" (fr. 52.1-3); instead of accusing and being brutal with fellow students, we should rather, Philodemus advises, "become accusers of ourselves, if we err in any respect" (fr. 51.2-5).

Philodemus, similarly to Diogenes of Oenoanda's description of the purpose of his colonnade two centuries later, speaks of the reciprocal practice of benefiting each other in salvific terms. In this he follows the common parlance of moralists of the period. The students mutually perceive their sins in order to gain salvation; they

---

[109] Frs. 50.10-12 (κακόφιλον καὶ φιλόκακον) and 85.7-9, ὁ καθηγούμενος εὐημέρωι καὶ φιλοψίλωι καὶ ἡπίωι. . . .
[110] Ibid., fr. 52.6-12. See Gigante, *Ricerche Filodemee*, pp. 99-100, 107.

"support" and "save each other."¹¹¹ They can accomplish this because they have the "strength to bear easily and have as support a grand good-will" (36.2–4). Frankness also "strengthens the reciprocal goodwill of those in preparation."¹¹² One of the means then to attain progress, besides self-correction (52.2–5), is reciprocal and consists in benevolent help both from the leaders and fellow students: "that he himself may be able to be therapeutically treated, either by us or by another of the fellow students" (79.1–4).

The question whether the wise will also change each other with frank speech receives an affirmative answer. As the wise remind the students of correct behavior, so they also remind each other: "If, then, the wise men know each other, they will be reminded gladly by one another in the ways we have described, as [they are reminded] by themselves, and will feel the most gentle sting and will be grateful" (cols. 8b6–13). The wise remind each other when they reason fraudulently because of great weakness or because of the unpleasantness of the toils that have befallen them. The wise heighten the awareness they have of each other's presence and progress and increase the cohesiveness of their relationship by mutual correction and confession of faults (cols. 9a1–8). The wise should strive after the same in their relation with those in preparation with them. The τόπος itself, "Whether the wise man will frankly refer his own affairs to his friends?" is significant, since it signals, if a negative response is given, a practice contrary to the one advocated (frs. 81.1–4; 54.2–6; 55). One could sharpen the question by asking, should the mature continue to participate in the communal practice of openness? The answer is yes, and it is important for our conceptualization of the relationships advocated as part of the Epicurean fellowship. Mature members should not disassociate themselves from others less mature. On

---

¹¹¹ See Epicurus, fr. 522 Us., on gaining salvation. Philodemus, *On Frank Criticism* frs. 1; 36.1–2, καὶ τὸ δ[ι' ἀλ]λήλων σώ(ι)ζεσθαι. For other instances of σώζειν see frs. 34.3; 78.6 and col. 6b3 which speaks of a person who has been "saved" by frank criticism. For σωτήρ see fr. 40.8 and for σωτηρία see fr. 4.9; App. Tab. II D2 (App.). See Diogenes, frs. 1 and 2, "... I wished by making use of this colonnade to set forth in public the remedies which bring salvation, remedies of which I would say in a word that all kinds have been revealed" (fr. 2, V–VI; τὰ τῆς σωτηρίας φάρμακα; Chilton).

¹¹² *On Frank Criticism* frs. 79.2–4 Herc. and 25.3–8. Cf. Gigante, *Ricerche Filodemee*, pp. 101–02. Philodemus' treatise *On Gratitude* (PHerc. 1414; cf. cols. 10 and 16) reveals that goodwill, and gratitude for benevolent help, is basic to the Philodemean ideal of mutual psychagogy and friendship. See A. T. Guerra, "Filodemo sulla Gratitudine," *CErc* 7 (1977), pp. 96–113.

the contrary, the wise are advised to be forthcoming to those in preparation "for the sake of their restoration" (55.5–6).

The participatory nature of late Epicurean psychagogy is evident throughout the fragments. Fragment 45.1–6 says: "We will admonish others with great confidence, both now and when they have become prominent, the offshoots of our teachers." The "we," probably leaders in the school, admonish "others" as well as those who have gained a visible position in the community. The "others" also emerge in fragment 61:

> [The guide] causes grief to the admonished one in a way unintelligible to his comrades . . . [the pupil], however, does not feel the pain of [the teacher's] words if admonished by someone in a cheerful way. Sometimes the teacher does not realize that his success is fictitious, while it has often become obvious to the others.[113]

The reference to the πέλας, ἄλλοι, and ἔνιοι is significant. The admonition delivered is no private affair. The presence of others is not only assumed but explicitly stated. The teacher may grieve the admonished one "in an unintelligible way to others near him" (ἀγνώστως τοῖς πέλας). Οἱ πέλας are fellow students who do not understand the reason for the teacher's admonition. On occasion, Philodemus rejects the harshness of "some" of the students (cols. 7b1; 17ab); here the ἔνιοι, on the other hand, know how to admonish correctly. The admonished one does not suffer destructive pain if admonished by someone in a calm and cheerful way. The following lines draw a contrast between the καθηγούμενος and the ἄλλοι, confirming that the ἄλλοι are identical to the πέλας and ἔνιοι. These are the "studyfellows" or "intimate fellows" who assist in the teacher's correction. That the "young" assist in the admonitory practices of the confraternity is clear also from col. 17a: the young—who have a disposition to err—have a tendency to use bitter frankness when they admonish (cf. also col. 16a6–12). Such harshness needs to be corrected and can only be healed by a surgical operation, i.e., by a scalpel. Here the young fail and need to be corrected. In fragment 61, however, it is the teacher who fails. "Others" who are present evaluate whether the teacher is successful; and they alleviate the distress caused by the teacher by attending to and correctly admonishing the one who was

---

[113] *On Frank Criticism* fr. 61.1–10. I follow here the textual emendation of Gigante for line 4: .α. καὶ μεδ(ὲν) ἂν ἱλαρῶς ἐνίοις. Cf. *Ricerche Filodemee*, pp. 81–83.

inconsiderately admonished. The teacher's success should not be "wrapped by doubt." It is authentic only if it is obvious to others too; other members are an integral part of the process.

We have seen four dimensions of Epicurean correctional practice; one involving self-correction, another when a correction is administered by "others," thirdly, when members report errors to the teachers for them to correct, and finally, when the wise correct each other. We have witnessed a network of social relations in which active participation of friends is presupposed in mutual edification, admonition, and correction. All are progressing, only some have matured more than others. Philodemus has a very positive view of the human condition and the possibility of progress. He rejects an inconsiderate and harsh approach to moral ills and advocates a gentle approach.[114] He has no sympathy for those who claim to be beyond mistake; such a view is absurd.[115] Occasionally, Philodemus speaks of the wise as "perfect" in contrast to one who fails to understand, is senseless, or ignorant. But the wise man should not hate the one who commits pardonable mistakes, "remembering that he is not perfect himself and that all men are accustomed to err."[116]

The wise are, therefore, not perfect in the sense that they are faultless; they can progress in their use of frankness and in their attitude towards others (fr. 2.1–7). Some fragments thus focus on the attitude of those who correct others since they can become presumptuous. I shall look at these and the nature of the correctional practice advocated when I discuss different types of students and approaches present in the handbook. But first I discuss the medical imagery which emphasizes the means and methods of correct diagnosis and prognosis, the legitimate use of harshness, the stochastic nature of Epicurean psychagogy, and the possibility of the mature person's failure in his care of others.

---

[114] Therapy should be done with a "moderate discourse" or "moderate censure" (frs. 6.7–8; 20.1–2) and one should "rebuke gently and agreeably" (col. 16a8). See also frs. 26.8; 38; 52.2; 85.9; and cols. 4b8–9; 8b12 (cf. *On Anger* 19.19; 28.39; 44.27 Indelli).

[115] Philodemus, *On Frank Criticism* cols. 18b13–14; 19b7–9. See pp. 299–310, below, on Paul's critique of the supposedly "wise" in Corinth.

[116] Philodemus, *On Frank Criticism* frs. 46.5–11; 55.8; cols. 8a2–9; 10a8–10; 9a7–8. Note fr. 74.5–9, which refers to a person who has "shed some faults" but "does not achieve perfection in everything."

### 3.2.2 Medical imagery and the stochastic method[117]

Just as it is impossible to obtain bodily health without resorting to physicians, so must the pupil place himself in the hands of the teachers and entrust them with the care of his soul.[118] Philodemus uses medical imagery to throw light on the process of moral exhortation and to emphasize the need for perseverance in difficult cases, patient care on the part of the doctor, and the legitimate use of harshness in case of recalcitrant students. The medical model also underlines the conjectural nature of the treatment in which issues of adaptability crystallize. The psychagogue's method is conjectural in the same way as is the art of a physician, a rhetor, or a pilot, namely, no general rules can be generated which are valid for all instances. Each situation creates its own rules to which a physician, rhetor, or pilot must adapt. The art in question is thus subservient to the situation, namely, the patient, the audience, or the weather at sea.

The therapeutic model was common during Hellenistic times; philosophy was seen as the means by which to cure human ills.[119] The medical model was also valued by Epicureans.[120] In *On Frank Criticism* this analogy presents a coherent pedagogical vision of frank

---

[117] The obsolete word "stochastic" means "pertaining to chance or conjecture," and refers to the psychagogue's method in the assessment and correction of moral faults. See further below.

[118] Philodemus, *On Frank Criticism* fr. 39. Cf. the textual emendation in lines 4–5 of Gigante, *Ricerche Filodemee*, p. 77 n. 110, [ἑαυτοὺς] ο[ἷ]ον ἐπι⟨ρ⟩ρίπτειν.

[119] For the therapeutic model among the Stoics see A.-J. Voelke, "La fonction thérapeutique du Logos selon Chrysippe," *Études de Lettres* 4 (1981) 57–71; G. B. Kerford, "Two Problems Concerning Impulses," *On Stoic and Peripatetic Ethics: The Work of Arius Didymus* (ed. W. W. Fortenbaugh; New Brunswick, NJ, 1983), pp. 87–93; and I. G. Kidd, "Euemptosia-Proneness to Disease," in ibid., pp. 107–117. For the therapeutic model in ancient scepticism, see D. E. Hahm, "The Diaeretic Method and the Purpose of Arius' Doxography," in ibid., pp. 15–37.

[120] Epicurus, fr. 221 Us. = Porphyry, *Ad Marc.* 31; *Letter to Menoeceus* 122; *Vatican Sentences* 64. For the therapeutic model in Epicureanism see J. F. Duvernoy, "Le modèle médical de l'éthique dans l'épicurisme," *Justifications de l'éthique. XIXe Congrès de l'Association de Societés de philosophie de langue française*, Bruxelles-Louvain la Neuve, 6–9 Septembre 1982 (Brussels, 1984), pp. 171–77; idem, "Guérir par la philosophie (sur le modèle médical de l'éthique dans l'épicurisme)," *Revue de l'Enseignemente philosophique* 34/5, 1984; A.-J. Voelke, "Santé de l'âme et bonheur de la raison. La function thérapeutique de la philosophie dans l'épicurisme," *Études de Lettres* 3 (1986), pp. 67–87; idem, "Opinions vides et troubles de l'âme: La medication Epicurienne," *Jeux et Contre-Jeux. Mélanges offerts à Pierre-André Stucki pour son 50ème anniversaire.* Éd. par Pierre Bühler (Neuchâtel, 1986), pp. 8–16; M. Nussbaum, "Therapeutic Arguments: Epicurus and Aristotle," *Norms of Nature. Studies in Hellenistic Ethics* (ed. M. Schofield and G. Striker; Cambridge, 1986), pp. 31–74; and M. Gigante, "'Philosophia Medicans' in Filodemo," *CErc* 5 (1975), pp. 53–61.

speech as a technique whose chief aim is to remedy mistakes or the passions for the recovery and salvation of consenting pupils. On the basis of the medical imagery, M. Gigante has shown that the therapy in Philodemus is of two kinds, namely, medicinal and surgical, curing the disease either by drugs or the scalpel, thus conforming to a Hippocratic norm. Pharmacy is mixed in nature; it can apply both sweet and bitter medicine. Other drugs besides purgatives include wormwood and hellebore.[121] These, as well as the surgical method, parallel the sharpness which is a legitimate aspect of frank speech. The medical analogy emphasizes the mixed nature of exhortation and is thus evidence for good contextual judgment as promulgated and practiced by Epicurean spiritual directors. The comparison with physicians also underlines the conjectural nature of the method, which displays in unequivocal terms the principle of adaptation to the particular case. The medical analogy thus emphasizes the conjectural nature of Epicurean psychagogy, the means and methods of correct diagnosis, as well as the legitimate use of harshness.

The conjectural method was based on empirical observation and probable arguments from symptoms or signs.[122] Although the term τέχνη does not appear in the extant fragments of *On Frank Criticism*, the treatise contains language appropriate to the arts and is a kind of handbook which identifies and resolves questions that would be faced by a practitioner of the art.[123] The very first fragment draws a distinction between certainty and conjecture, a distinction which was common in discussions about the nature of "art" (τέχνη) as opposed to that of "science" (ἐπιστήμη):

> Generally, the sage and the philosopher use frank speech unrigidly by reasonable conjecture with the help of probable arguments.[124]

---

[121] Gigante, *Ricerche Filodemee*, p. 75. Cf. Euripides, fr. 403, 6 N (2); Plato, *Statesman* 298C; *Republic* 406D; 407D. On the divisions of medicine in Plato, the first two species of five are "pharmacy" and "surgery." The other three are dietetics, prescription of remedies, and diagnosis. See Diogenes Laertius, *Lives of Eminent Philosophers* 3.85.

[122] Plato, *Gorgias* 464C; *Philebus* 55E–56B; M. Frede, *Essays in Ancient Philosophy* (Minneapolis, 1987), pp. 243–60; L. Edelstein, *Ancient Medicine* (Baltimore/London, 1987), pp. 195–203.

[123] So P. H. de Lacy and E. A. de Lacy, *Philodemus: On Methods of Inference* (2nd ed. Naples, 1978), p. 201.

[124] Philodemus, *On Frank Criticism* fr. 1.5–9. Note Gigante's emendation, παγίως ο[ὐδέν instead of Olivieri's παγίως (*Ricerche Filodemee*, 63); *Rhetoric* v. 1, p. 247, 11–12 Sudhaus.

The emphasis on conjecture is a recurring theme in the fragments, particularly where the corrector of moral faults is compared to a physician. Frank speech is thus a conjectural method used in the art of therapeutic healing of souls, comparable to the methods used by physicians in the art of healing and pilots in the art of navigation. The end result of all three is uncertain and all face recurring mistakes.[125] As a physician and a navigator, the moral director can make mistakes in the execution of his art. He is like a physician who accidentally kills his patient and a captain who sometimes loses his ship. All three may occasionally, in spite of the best of intentions, fail.

As Philodemus compares the psychagogue to a doctor, he asks "whether it appears that we who are more advanced do err with regard to perfect reasoning?" (56.1–3). In general the sage does not err with regard to perfect reasoning and prudence but does so in his use of frank speech, "in so far as one does not happen to attain the end and to pass beyond the human person who cannot constantly be on his guard" (56.8–13). The following fragments highlight the stochastic nature of the psychagogue's task and suggest that perfect success is not always achieved. The wise can reason falsely and apply frank speech out of place. The discussion revolves around the correct and incorrect use of frank speech for different character types or dispositions, namely, the weak, the incurable, and the recalcitrant, all of which require individualized and different treatment. The sage will not cease to exert his method until he purifies the young under his care (cf. 16.3–5). That process can be long and arduous since the diagnosis is often uncertain. But the sage must diagnose the sickness albeit by means of probable signs.[126] Such a diagnosis cannot be certain since it is based on probable signs—an angry man frowns, a modest one blushes, at least in most cases!

It is then necessary to acknowledge that "probable conjecture cannot always turn out to be correct as one had hoped, even if plausibility consists in the highest degree in probable elements . . ." (fr. 57.5–11).

---

[125] *On Frank Criticism* frs. 1, 39–40, 57, 63–65, 69; and col. 17a. Philodemus' views on the nature of art are complex. Philodemus responds to the critique that art must always produce beneficial results: "But the captain sometimes loses his ship, the physician kills his patient. We must either deny that navigation and medicine are arts, or abandon the demand that all arts must always be beneficial" (Transl. Hubbell, p. 268 = Sudh. v. 1, 19, col. 1 = Supp. 11). See Sedley, "Philosophical Allegiance," *Philosophia Togata*, pp. 107–17; Asmis, "Philodemus' Epicureanism," pp. 2400–02.

[126] *On Frank Criticism* frs. 69.4–10; 63.6–7; 57.4–5; *Rhetoric* v. 1 pp. 369, 373 Sudhaus; Gigante, *Ricerche Filodemee*, p. 76.

The doctor must, however, interpret the signs of an illness and might, for example, suppose that the patient needs a purging. If the diagnosis happens to be incorrect, the physician does not at another date refuse to give a purging if it is needed. If the psychagogue gives up, it would be

> similar to a physician supposing by means of probable signs that someone needs a purgation, but then he errs with regard to the probable signs and will never again purge another sickness in this way (63.3–11).[127]

Philodemus compares these procedures of physicians with the corrector of moral faults when he attends the recalcitrant student who does not "obey" the frank criticism of his teacher (64.2–5): "For even a physician who is not successful in treating a sickness with a clyster, gives an enema again for the same illness" (64.5–8). The teacher must, in light of his failure, modify his approach; "and because of this he will apply his frank speech again, because he was not effective before, and he will apply it again and again, in order to succeed, if not now, then later" (64.8–12). Philodemus applies this general lesson to the way in which a psychagogue should deal with a recalcitrant student. He should not give up but continue to criticize frankly the recalcitrant ones. He might not be successful on the first or even the second day, but might attain his goal on the third (65.9–11).

In his effort to reclaim the recalcitrant one, the psychagogue must then stick with the patient. Sometimes he is not successful except when using more drastic measures. The medical analogy emphasizes thus both the conjectural nature of the therapeutic task and the legitimate and beneficial aspects of harshness. "Biting" was a common metaphor for harsh censure. Philodemus uses the phrase τὸ δηκτικὸν τῆς παρρησίας, recognizing a legitimate use of harshness. "Everyone," he says, "admits that stirring up will be salutary" and describes the admonition of the "excellent physician" as a dissection.[128] Besides surgery, Philodemus refers to two bitter drugs, namely, wormwood and hellebore. We have only a short reference to the latter, but the former surfaces both in *On Frank Criticism* and in *On Anger*.[129] Ariston

---

[127] For this meaning of κένωμα, see Dioscorides, *De mat. med.* 5.11; Plutarch, *Isis and Osiris* 381C; Gigante, "'Philosophia Medicans' in Filodemo," p. 57.

[128] See Philodemus, *On Frank Criticism* frs. 32.7–9; 16.2–3; 26.9; cols. 8b11–12; 21b7–8; 22a7; App. Tab. IV I. For τὸ δηκτικὸν τῆς παρρησίας see col. 17a4–10. See *On Anger* cols. 12.18; 37.19; 38.7; 41.8 Indelli, and Plutarch, *How to Tell a Flatterer from a Friend* 55B.

[129] *On Frank Criticism* App. Tab. XII ib. 1–2; Plutarch, *On the Control of Anger* 453D,

of Chios had compared the harshness of wormwood with παρρησία: "The bitterness of wormwood cuts similarly to frank speech."[130] Philodemus agrees that the use of wormwood can be necessary.[131] There are cases when a person of refined disposition uses bitter methods comparable to wormwood. The wise man is also susceptible to anger and will even punish, but he does not go

> for punishing [the other person] as something enjoyable—for nothing pleasant is offered—but as something most necessary, and what results is most unpleasant, as with drinking wormwood, and surgery.[132]

The analogy with hellebore, wormwood, and surgery emphasizes the legitimate use of harshness in moral exhortation. Significantly, the most sustained use of the medical analogy (frs. 63–69) occurs as Philodemus focuses on the recalcitrant students. Their "sickness" is of such a nature that it requires more drastic measures. But the obedient student needs only a gentle treatment. It is thus the pupils' condition that determines the nature of the remedy or exhortation applied.

### 3.2.3 *Types of students and approaches*

As Philodemus debates issues of harshness with other Epicureans he focuses on the use of harsh exhortation on different types of students. Two types of students or dispositions surface throughout the fragments, namely, the "weak" and obedient ones and the "strong" or disobedient ones.[133] The former are also referred to as those who are insecure in their new philosophic way of life or have apostasized from philosophy. The latter are referred to as stubborn or recalcitrant pupils, those who find it difficult to stand the frank criticism of others or violently resist frank speech, and the irascible and incurable ones. Each of these types of students needs a unique treatment. Philodemus often refers to these types collectively as the "young" or

---

"For I do not think that reason should be used in one's cure as we use hellebore, and be washed out of the body together with the disease, but it must remain in the soul and keep watch and ward over the judgments."

[130] SVF 1.383 (88.4–5).

[131] In *On Frank Criticism* col. 2 b3–7, Philodemus says that the wise person bestows praise gladly, but endures frank criticism as something which is unpleasant, and just like wormwood.

[132] Idem, *On Anger* col. 44.9–22 Indelli. Transl. by Annas, "Epicurean Emotions," p. 159.

[133] Philodemus refers to the former as ἁπαλοί and the latter as ἰσχυροί (fr. 7.1 5). See frs. 36.4–9; 45.7–11; 65.9–11; col. 13a12–13; and D. Clay, "Individual and community in the first generation of the Epicurean school," Συζήτησις, vol. 1, p. 270.

"those in preparation." We have here then a variation of the theme of care of the young (ἐπιμέλεια τῶν νέων). The "young" are recent converts or beginning students of philosophy, irrespective of their age, not solely a temporal category but also a modal and qualitative one.[134] The different types of students are referred to not only as the young, but also as those in (co-) preparation,[135] fellow students,[136] one's neighbours,[137] pupils,[138] laymen,[139] children,[140] intimate fellows[141] or friends.[142] Sometimes, the pupils are simply referred to as "some" (of the friends).[143]

Besides discussing different types of pupils, Philodemus also asks questions concerning the application of frank speech to persons of different professions, sex, and age. Those particularly resentful of frank criticism include politicians (col. 18a–b), famous people,[144] women,[145] and old people.[146] In the case of politicians, this is so because of their ambition and desire for renown. Reminiscent of Clement of Alexandria two centuries later and his discussion of reasons why salvation is difficult for a rich man, Philodemus remarks that students are "not difficult to save," except if they feel the need to show

---

[134] Philodemus, *On Frank Criticism* frs. 31.2; 36.5; 52.4; 71.8; 83.8; cols. 6a6; 16a10; *Rhetoric* v. 1, col. 30.34–36, p. 267 Sudhaus. Cf. Plato, *Laws* 659E; 951DE; *Herm. Vis.* 3.5.4, Νέοι εἰσὶν ἐν τῇ πίστει . . . ; and *Vis.* 3.13.4. See M. P. Nilsson, *Die Hellenistische Schule* (München, 1955), pp. 34–42 and 77.

[135] Or (συν)κατασκευαζόμενοι: *On Frank Criticism* frs. 2.3; 25.6; 53.4, 7; 55.3; 71.2; 76.3; col. 12b7.

[136] Or οἱ συσχολάζοντες, -όντοι. Cf. ibid., frs. 75.4–5; 79.2–3.

[137] Or οἱ πέλας. Cf. ibid., fr. 61.2; *SV* 67; and PHerc. 1457 col. 10.

[138] Or μαθηταί. Cf. *On Frank Criticism* fr. 87.1–4.

[139] Or ἰδιώτης. Cf. ibid., col. 11b1. See also PHerc. 222, col. 4.6–7; *On Household Management* col. 9.14–16; *On Death* cols. 23.9; 31.12; 35.28; *Index Stoicorum* cols. 17.10, 57; Diogenes of Oenoanda fr. 20, II 4–5; Plato, *Sophist* 221C–D; Aristotle, *Politics* 1266a31. See Gargiulo, "PHerc. 222: Filodemo Sull' Adulazione," pp. 107, 117.

[140] *On Frank Criticism* fr. 18.1; col. 24b10; *On Vices* col. 8.15 Jensen, *Ein neuer Brief Epikurs*, p. 29.

[141] Or οἱ συνήθεις. Cf. *On Frank Criticism* frs. 42.2; 52.12; 54.11.

[142] Ibid., frs. 8.10; 41.7; 50.7; 55.7; 70.3; 81.3, 8; 84.2; col. 13a10.

[143] Ibid., frs. 61; 70.8, cols. 19a11, 19b10–11, 13a10 ἄλλοι φίλοι.

[144] Ibid., col. 22b10–13, "Why, all other things being equal, do wealthy and famous people resent frank criticism more than others?" In col. 7a7–10, Philodemus explains that both those who are superior and the common people must be admonished as the individual case demands.

[145] Ibid., col. 21b12–14, "Why do women resent frank criticism?" Philodemus emphasizes that as the teachers in the community differ, so do the students: "just as a boy differs from a woman, and at the same time old men will differ from young men" (col. 6a4–8).

[146] Ibid., col. 24a7–9, "Why are old people more resentful?" Cf. cols. 24b1–12 and a4–8; 7a1–2.

off before crowds.[147] In the case of women, part of the problem is that there is greater psychological insecurity involved.[148] In the case of famous people and old men, part of the problem is that they think they are criticized from impure motives and because they believe they are wiser than others.[149] As Philodemus focuses on the effect frank speech has on people of different professions, sex, and age, he also asks what effect frank speech has on pupils of different dispositions. Here different types of students emerge, namely, those violently resisting frankness, those irascible, those who cannot tolerate frank criticism, and, finally, those of a lesser intellectual ability.[150] The capacity of the young of different dispositions to bear the frank speech of the sage is a major concern of the handbook.

The fact that Epicureans distinguished between different types of pupils based on their disposition or aptitude was well known in antiquity. I have referred to Seneca's testimony that Epicurus classified students into three categories.[151] The first type, i.e., those who on their own are able to work their way to the truth, is a common type often referred to by moralists. Epicureans valued such "self taught" students; Epicurus himself had claimed to be self-taught.[152] The second and third types both needed assistance; the former will not proceed unless someone leads the way but will follow the guide faithfully; the latter do not need a guide so much as someone to encourage them and force them along. This last type figures prominently in *On*

---

[147] Ibid., fr. 34.3–8. See Clement, *Who Is the Rich Person Who Will Be Saved?* 2.

[148] Women are more sensitive than others when frankly criticized, more distressed by disgrace and more wont to suspect evil motives on the part of those who admonish them; *On Frank Criticism* col. 22a–b.

[149] Famous people think that they are rebuked out of envy and that they see their sins more clearly than the wise (col. 23a–b). Old men think that people criticize them out of disdain and that they are wiser because of their age (col. 24a–b).

[150] See fr. 5.4–8, "It is possible to see from what has been said also how one ought to be frank with the one who violently resists frankness"; 31.1–8, some of the young become very irritated when rebuked: "they receive whatever is said in frankness annoyingly"; 67.9–11, "whether he should also speak frankly toward those who cannot endure it and toward an irascible person?"; 70.5–7 "how will he deal with those who become angry with him on account of his frankness?" and col. 20a1–5, "Why do people resent frank speech from those whom they recognize as more clever, and, indeed, as leaders?"

[151] Seneca, *Epistle* 52.3–4 = Fr. 192 Us. See pp. 67–68, above.

[152] A.-J. Festugière, *Epicurus and His Gods* (Oxford, 1955), p. 34; A. J. Malherbe, *Paul and the Thessalonians* (Philadelphia, 1987), p. 105. See Cicero *On Ends* 1.71–72; Seneca, *Epistles* 95.36; 71.19–20; Clement, *Ped.* 94.1 (145, 30–32 Stählin-Treu). Philodemus contrasts a person who has needed frank speech very little in order to mature with a person who has been "saved" by it (col. 6b1–3).

*Frank Criticism*. He, viewed by some as "incurable," is the recalcitrant one who is easily irritated and resists frank criticism. He needs to be forced along with more stringent measures, but those who follow the guide faithfully are led by gentler means.

Besides this two-type distinction of recalcitrant and obedient students, Philodemus also distinguishes between an advanced type of education that teaches one to unravel obscure writings and an illiterate common sense that allows even slaves to understand a "letter written by our leaders to private individuals."[153] Here Philodemus follows his master who spoke of two types of students dependent on their aptitude in unraveling different types of writings. So the purpose of the *Letter to Herodotus* is twofold, namely, to summarize succinctly for memorization the physical theory for those unable to study carefully the thirty seven books *On Nature* and to aid the advanced students to memorize and fix in their minds an outline of the whole subject.[154] The aim is to aid in memorization both novices and mature students. Epicureans are then on par with other moralists who make distinctions between persons based on their aptitudes and dispositions. The nature of the aid rendered to the various types differed.[155]

In his work *On Anger*, Philodemus identifies anger as hindrance to progress. Because of it, students will not be able to bear the criticism of either their leaders or fellow students. Anger can also thwart the teacher's success:

---

[153] PHerc. 1005, col. 13.3–15; Asmis, "Philodemus' Epicureanism," p. 2380.

[154] Diogenes Laertius, *Lives of Eminent Philosophers* 10.35–36, 83, 135. The *Letter to Menoeceus* is to be memorized or "exercised" day and night, by oneself or someone like oneself. See I. Hadot, "Épicure et l'enseignement philosophique hellénistique et romain," *ACGB* 1968 (Paris, 1969), pp. 347–54; and Clay, *Lucretius and Epicurus*, pp. 173–75.

[155] Philodemus explains that the nature of frank speech will differ depending on whether it is spoken toward a student who has become upset, or toward one who has relapsed, or toward one who is agitated, or toward one who is bashful, or, finally, toward one who is very obstinate (col. 4a1–8). That Philodemus was interested in classifying humans in psychological and ethical terms is clear from his works *On Flattery*, *On Frank Criticism*, *On Anger*, and from a section at the end of his work *On Vices*, which contains a letter of the Peripatetic Ariston of Ceos (*On the Relieving of Arrogance*. Philodemus, *De vitiis* (ed. C. Jensen, Leipzig, Teubner, 1911), col. 10.10–16.28, Περὶ τοῦ κουφίζειν ὑπερηφανίας ἐπιστολήν) who continued the Theophrastean tradition of writing Χαρακτῆρες (OCD 112). After this letter, Philodemus draws on Ariston's analysis of character types, discussing the stubborn person (col. 16.29–17.17), the blunt person (17.17–19.2), the all knower (20.3–37), the haughty person (21.1–37), the ironic person (21.37–23.37) and the belittler (24.1–21). See C. Jensen, "Ariston von Keos bei Philodem," *Hermes* 46 (1911), pp. 393–406; and W. Knögel, *Der Peripatetiker Ariston von Keos bei Philodem*. Leipzig, 1933.

But the sage is not [to be] angrily disposed towards those in preparation. For if he does not advance in this, how will each one of them be able altogether boldly to withstand frank criticism? (fr. 2.1–7)

It is difficult for students to put up with an angrily administered frankness. The sage is to modify his approach in light of its negative effects. A gentle treatment is important both in light of the condition of the students and in view of the negative effects of harshness. Some are too weak to benefit from frank criticism. If the teacher does not speak discretely, "some, being swiftly deprived of their conscience, will not benefit (others) greatly" (53.10–13). Because of their weakness, the pupils cannot bear the frank speech of the sage angrily administered. The sage should change his approach because of the tenderness of the pupils. A gentle approach does, though, not exclude admonition or rebuke for other pupils of another disposition. But the rebuke should be moderate, similar to the way in which Epicurus addressed Pythocles (6.7–8).[156]

When discussing the practice of communal confessions above, we saw that when members are not forthcoming with regard to errors the teacher might have to "investigate" them closely. If we view fr. 43 as thematically close to fr. 42, it is particularly in such an investigation that the philotropeic method should be adhered to:

> He will become attached to a person's character. And, if he attaches himself to those of a noble character, why not also to those of a wicked character? For just as (we adapt ourselves) to the noble because of cheerfulness, it is also proper (to adapt) to the wicked because of sympathy, on account of which we (ourselves) receive aid (fr. 43.1–8).

Philodemus rejects an abusive and disparaging approach. One should not revile or treat the erring one spitefully; rather, "errors should be taken up in sympathy, not ridicule."[157] The "natural weakness" of the erring should rather be pitied and forgiven, not derided or "bespattered with mud."[158] If the young are ridiculed or inopportunely reproved, they become downcast and accept criticism badly:

---

[156] The words of the one who uses frank speech without becoming angry but devotes himself to the erring one with goodwill, give little pain but heal greatly. See *On Frank Criticism*, fr. 38.1–6 and Plutarch, *How to Tell a Flatterer from a Friend* 73D–E.

[157] *On Frank Criticism*, fr. 79.9–12; App. Tab. III G; IV J; fr. 37.5–9, "... nor to frankly criticize in a haughty and harsh way, nor to say any insolent and abusive thing, or sarcastic things...."

[158] Ibid., frs. 16.5–11; 20.5–6. Cf. col. 22b2–4, μὴ προπηλακίζεσθαι (LSJ, s.v.). See also App. Tab. IV J ("not haughtily ridiculing their weaknesses") and fr. 23.1–5.

"Therefore some of them, mocked, cannot endure to listen to the teacher with goodwill" (31.9–12). The sage should calm his angry students just as Heracles calmed the Stymphacian birds.[159] He should apply frank speech opportunely and cheerfully in order to increase the goodwill between him and those in preparation (25.3–8). If he fails, the young, because of the chastisement, might become irritated and "hate everyone in the world" (26.2–4). But the young need to be reproved when they are envious or scornful or when they are inconsiderately harsh themselves (fr. 62.1–4; col. 17a). The duty of the teachers and fellow-students is to amend and to correct; such a correction will entail reproof or ἐπιτίμησις which is a type of παρρησία (fr. 75). In degree, it is harsher than νουθεσία but should also be delivered with goodwill and opportunely. In *On Moral Virtue* Plutarch emphasizes that the passions should not be extirpated; instead, they need a therapy and an education. Admonition and censure engender repentance and shame, of which the first is a kind of pain or grief, the second a kind of fear. Philodemus agrees. Admonition should inflict grief which engenders repentance; the teacher, however, should be careful so the erring one is not overcome by grief.[160]

Philodemus distinguishes two types of frank speech. For some who have erred παρρησία suffices, but others require a more bitter dose. After noting that Epicurus addressed Pythocles with moderate censure, Philodemus draws attention to the stubborn pupils who, although rebuked and "shouted at," will hardly change. The only hope to change them is through harsh frankness.[161] Sharpness is then recognized as legitimate and necessary; its degree depends on the perceived ailment. As the wise try to sway the young men's inclination and liberate them from mistakes, some of the pupils become stiff; whatever means available should then be used to attempt to change their false thoughts and behaviors. One fragment, where we overhear the voice of the student, graphically depicts such harsh measure as a "beating":

---

[159] Ibid., fr. 87.1–4, "as Heracles singing and throwing out the opinions of herds of winged students." Cf. fr. 74.1–2, "lifted up by odes."

[160] Hence the need to determine the proper occasion for frank criticism. Cf. Philodemus, *On Frank Criticism* frs. 25; 84; 86.7–8; cols. 4a7–8; 5b4–6; 6a1–8; 17b1–6. On shame, see ibid., frs. 71.1–6; 85.1–4; and col. 13a7–9; cf. fr. 50.1. See also Plutarch, *On Moral Virtue* 451C; 452C; *Precepts of Statecraft* 810C; SVF 3.411 (99.22–29); and pp. 35–36 and 69–81, above.

[161] *On Frank Criticism* frs. 6.1–8; 7.5–11, τῶι σκληρῶι χρήσεται τῆς παρρησίας εἴδει.

I did not sin then, but now he will deem me deserving of frank criticism if he catches me ... For I declare that I did not even sin before, but I fell of my own will into the ignorance of youth; and on account of that he had to give me a beating.[162]

The frank speech wielded by the Epicurean psychagogue is varied in nature. Both relief (βοήθεια) and therapy (θεραπεία) are described as varied:

> Seeing that the good method as we have characterized it is varied and that it is mixed with bountiful praises, and exhorts [them] to do those things which follow the good attributes they possess.... (68.1-7; cf. 86.6-7; 10.1-7)

This method exhorts the young to do good, thus conforming to Epicurus' definition of τέχνη: "Art is the method which produces what is useful in life."[163] The sage continues to work with the young until he can purify those under his care; although some cases require the sole use of bitterness, he does not use bitter techniques only but mixes praise and blame: "But he will be regained in that manner, namely, when the sting of censure is followed by praise."[164] With the word διαφιλοτεχνεῖν Philodemus emphasizes one way in which the wise will use his art. He will "often use his varied and excellent art in this fashion. But," Philodemus continues, "he sometimes exercises his frankness 'simply,' thinking that one must sometimes take a risk, if they will not listen otherwise" (fr. 10.1-7). The mode of execution referred to as the "simple use of frank speech," I take to be simple as opposed to mixed in the sense that blame is solely involved. Philodemus' suggestion that only harshness should be used is contrary to the method he regularly advocates, highlighted in his description of φιλοτεχνία as ποικίλη and in his reference to the μεικτὸς τρόπος in fr. 58.7-9.[165]

---

[162] Ibid., fr. 83.7-10. Μαστιγόω is probably used here metaphorically for harsh criticism or castigation. See pp. 277-80, below.

[163] Epicurus, fr. 227b Us. Contrast the definition of κακοτεχνία in fr. 51 Us. See Gigante, *Ricerche Filodemee*, p. 73.

[164] *On Frank Criticism* App. Tab. IV I.

[165] In this I find myself in agreement with de Witt who sees "ethical correction" as either "simple (ἁπλῆ, 10.4; 35.8), that is straightforward and direct, or mixed (μικτή, 58.7-8), that is, compounded of reproof, generous praise and exhortation (68.3-7)" ("Organization and Procedure in Epicurean Groups," p. 209). In this I am at variance with Gigante's position ("Philodème: Sur la liberté de parole," pp. 208-09). Gigante correctly points out that the other occurrence of ἁπλῶς in fr. 35.8-9 does not support de Witt's position; it occurs in a completely different context,

In order to explicate the meaning of the "simple method" in fr. 10, it is paramount to look at the context. The matter addressed, I suggest, is a continuation of the one sounded in fr. 5.4–8: "It is possible to see from what has been said also how one ought to be frank with the one who violently resists frank speech." I have noted a variation of the same theme in frs. 67 and 70, and col. 20a. In these fragments students of different dispositions surface, namely, those who violently resist frankness, those who are irascible, those who cannot bear or tolerate frank criticism, and finally, those of a lesser intellectual capacity. The reason why the young have difficulty in putting up with the frank speech of the sage differs, depending on the disposition described. Part of the answer in col. 20a is that the students admit the leaders' superiority in theoretical inquiry but think themselves much superior in the affairs of life.[166] In this context (cf. cols. 15a–21b) the above question is answered by reference to the pretentious person who does not recognize his own faults but thinks he is perfect. Frs. 67 and 70 answer the question by reference to the motif of the recalcitrant student and by emphasizing the need of the moral director to imitate the manifold method of physicians who use both harsh and more soothing medicines.

Those who violently resist frank speech and become easily irritated when criticized are like the "incurable ones" who are irredeemable because of their hostile attitude.[167] Philodemus, however, has a positive view of the human condition, a view which led moralists to advocate a gentle approach. This is also why Philodemus rejects the

---

referring to someone who is "simply completely accused" because of a transgression. In my view, the other three fragments, namely, frs. 10, 58 and 68, support de Witt's position. In Gigante's view fr. 58.7–8,—κατὰ μεικτὸν τρόπον διαπτώσεως γενομένης—refers to the complexity of ways in which the sage can fail; he translates, "selon le genre mixte de l'erreur qui s'est produite." I, on the other hand, take the whole clause—οὐκ ὀλι⟨γ⟩άκις δὲ κατὰ μεικτὸν τρόπον διαπτ[ώ]σεως γενομέ[ν]ης—as dependent on παρρησιάσασθαι (πρὸς αὐτούς) in lines 5–6, and translate, "to speak frankly towards them, not seldom, but in a mixed manner when failure has occurred." I take διαπτ[ώ]σεως γενομέ[ν]ης then as a genitive absolute. Such a reading, as well as frs. 68 and 10, support the contrast between a mixed and simple method of moral exhortation. Fr. 68 both refers to the varied nature of the good method (ποικίλης τε φ[ιλοτ]εχνίας οὔσης), and to the fact that it is "mixed with bountiful praises" and exhortation. Fr. 10 refers to the "simple" application of frankness in case of the recalcitrant student. Gigante, however, takes it to refer to the conjectural nature of frankness and translates: "Cependant, il exercera parfois la liberté de parole sans 'art' (ἁ[πλ]ῶς). . . ."

[166] Ibid., col. 20a5–12. Cf. Asmis, "Philodemus' Epicureanism," p. 2394.
[167] *On Frank Criticism* fr. 5; Plutarch, *Progress in Virtue* 82A.

view of the "some" in fr. 60 who maintained that those who are difficult to heal with frank speech as well as the weak should be addressed with reviling. In Philodemus' view, there are no incurable ones, no faults which cannot be redeemed, although anger and ambition thwart one's progress. "Those making no progress" (ἀπρόβατοι) are unable to advance because "they refrain from participating in the common search of the good."[168] Without the assistance of others the young remain "unexamined"; until a prognosis is made which could be a plausible means of correcting one's faults, they remain untreated.[169] Although one might think on the basis of probable signs that a sick person will not be cured, the psychagogue will imitate physicians and exhort on the basis of these reasonable, although uncertain, signs (69.4–10). Angry persons do not make progress also because they are "unable to put up with the teacher or their fellow students who reprove and correct them."[170] The reason why they cannot bear the reproving is explained by a medical analogy: "Just as malignant ulcers cannot bear the use of soothing drugs."[171] A stronger dose of medicine is required. This is the backdrop against which to view frs. 5–10 of *On Frank Criticism*.

In my view, when Philodemus in fr. 10 refers to the "simple" use of frank speech he still has the "strong" or "stubborn" pupils in mind, referred to in frs. 7.2–3 and 6 as ἰσχυροί, and those introduced in fr. 6 who might need to be corrected with a harsher form of frank speech. This I infer from the reference again to the ἰσχυροί in fr. 10.9, as well as from the information given in fr. 10.7 that the simple form of frank speech is used in the case of those who are not otherwise obedient. The issue is then what form of persuasion is appropriate for a recalcitrant and stubborn student. That the focus is on the mode of the admonitory and correctional treatment is clear from the contrast in fr. 6.1–4 between frank speech and a more bitter approach, from the reference in fr. 6.7–8 to "moderate censure," from the reference in fr. 7.9–11 to a "harsh form of frankness," and, finally, from the reference to "simple frankness" in fr. 10.4–5. There

---

[168] *On Anger* col. 19.25–27, μήτε [τ]οῦ διὰ συζητήσεως μετέχειν ἀγαθοῦ. See p. 126, fn. 100, above.
[169] *On Frank Criticism* fr. 84.8–14, ἀθεράπευτοι. Cf. Gigante, *Ricerche Filodemee*, p. 72.
[170] *On Anger* col. 19.12–17 Indelli.
[171] Ibid., col. 19.17–21. For ἤπια φάρμακα see Homer, *Iliad* 4.218; 11.515. Philodemus compares angry people with epileptics (*On Anger* 9.21. See also Plutarch, *On the Control of Anger* 453E; 455C; and Seneca, *On Anger* 3.10.3). Cf. Gigante, *Ricerche Filodemee*, pp. 100–01.

is also a similar contrast in column 2b between the legitimate use of harshness, referred to by the analogy of wormwood, and the mixed use of frank speech.[172] Philodemus has then in frs. 6–10 successively introduced the need for the use of the harsh approach in moral exhortation. The simple or plain use of frankness is equivalent to "harsh frankness," i.e., when it is not mixed with praise or gentler means of persuasion. The mixed or subtle use is when the erring one is addressed with both praise and blame. Sometimes such an approach yields to a more forthright approach, as, for example, in the case of those who are "exceedingly stubborn"; one must sometimes "take a risk in the case of those who will not listen otherwise."[173] The risk consists in the blunt approach which might become destructive. Or, when the passions are at their height, it might be ineffectual. But it is needed because of the condition of the recalcitrants.

Philodemus uses animal analogies to throw further light on the guidance of the recalcitrant ones. In the analogy between the young and animals that struggle to shake the yoke from their necks, he focuses on the disobedient students (cf. ἀπαυχενίζω in fr. 71). In fr. 87 Herc. the teacher tames the restlessness and impatience of the young, as if they were foals. He bears with their undisciplined nature and intermittently slackens and pulls the reins.[174] Philodemus depends here on Xenophon's *On Household Management* where Ischomachus explains to Socrates the way in which to mould a good superintendent: creatures learn obedience in two ways, being punished when they disobey or rewarded when eager to serve. An analogy with a horsebreaker taming a foal by slackening and tightening the rein and the way in which lapdogs learn to obey reveals that obedience will be rewarded, disobedience punished.[175] Such a "beastly education"

---

[172] See also col. 19a1–3 which contrasts "to censure" with "common frank speech": μ[έμφεσθ[αι], καὶ οὐχὶ τῆι παρρησία[ι] κοινῶς·

[173] Ibid., fr. 10.5–9, τοὺς [ὑπε]ρβαλλόντως ἰσχυροὺς.... The above reading of the "simple method" in fr. 10 is supported by Philodemus' *On Gratitude*, col. 15.14, ἁπλῷ λόγῳ.

[174] *On Frank Criticism* fr. 87. Herc., τοὺς νέους πωλοδαμνᾶσθαι. See p. 128, fn. 107, above. For the analogy of the taming practices of a horse breaker and the slackening and tightening of the rein, see Ps.-Plutarch, *On the Education of Children* 13F; Maximus of Tyre, *Discourse* 1.3b; 3e–f; 8c–e (4, 22–5, 8; 5, 17–6, 9; 14, 10–15, 3 Hobein), and pp. 76–77 and 85–86, above. For Paul's use of this motif, see pp. 304 and 326–29, below.

[175] This is evident from the contrast between ἀνθρωποδαμνική and πωλοδαμνική

(θηριώδης παιδεία) is well suited for slaves and can also be used when moulding a good superintendent.

Philodemus, however, rejects this type of education in the guidance of the young, not because it includes punishment but rather because of the nature of the punishment; it is too harsh and unacceptable within the confraternity.[176] The pupils thus refuse to be "brutal" towards those who do not confess their mistakes.[177] Instead, one should induce a riotous and disobedient pupil to reasoning obedience by seasoning his disposition, "turning his reason around" or attempt to change his inclination.[178] Some of the fragments which focus on the disobedient students emphasize not the legitimate use of harshness but rather the patient exercise of the psychagogue's care. Because of the severity of the sickness the teacher should thus remain with the sick and not prematurely stop rendering aid. The desirable outcome of the patient exercise of the teacher's admonition is to reclaim the disobedient to obedience. Fragments 65–66 underline the patient exercise of the teacher's παρρησία in the form of νουθέτησις as well as the progressive deliverance of the passion of arrogance of the disobedient one:

> [The pupil] first despises [the admonition] as an alien insult, but later he will give up and obey the admonition. When he has been relieved of the passions that made him arrogant or in general thwarted [his progress], he will listen.[179]

The teacher's admonition leads the pupil gradually to lay down the perverting passions which make the young haughty and hinder their search for peace of mind. The pupil will obey the teacher and admit his mistakes after having "opposed an opinion with an opinion" and the catharsis is complete, namely, when relieved of the passions. The teacher must stay with the recalcitrant student, for "if he turns away too quickly from assisting the erring one," he might lose him.[180] But

---

τέχνη. See Xenophon, *On Household Management* 13.6–9 and Gigante, *Ricerche Filodemee*, pp. 104–08.

[176] Philodemus, *On Household Management* 7.10–26. Punishment is recognized as appropriate for the sage in *On Anger* col. 44.9–22. See Annas, "Epicurean Emotions," pp. 155–59.

[177] *On Frank Criticism* fr. 52.2–3. See also fr. 19.1–5, which opposes the immobile and insensible educator of the young. Cf. Gigante, *Ricerche Filodemee*, pp. 99–101.

[178] *On Frank Criticism* frs. 13.7–8; 91 Herc., and Gigante, *Ricerche Filodemee*, pp. 108–09.

[179] *On Frank Criticism* fr. 66.2–10. See Gigante, *Ricerche Filodemee*, pp. 79–80.

[180] *On Frank Criticism* frs. 67.5–9; 66.13; 86.2–4. For a discussion of the "relieving of arrogance" see Philodemus, *On Vices* col. 10.11–13, Jensen. See fn. 155, above.

if he stays with him he might, if not on the first or second day, achieve his purpose on the third day:

> Thus the young man, in the full exuberance of sickness, disobeys; but now, while the sickness is in remission, he will be reclaimed [to obedience].[181]

When the passions are at their height it is difficult to reason with the recalcitrant ones. Admonitions "applied to the passions when they are at their height and swollen, can scarcely accomplish anything at all, and that with difficulty."[182] The teacher should thus not prematurely leave the disobedient since he might then not be present when the sickness is in remission. Besides emphasizing the need of patient care, Philodemus thus underlines the importance of good contextual judgment.

We have now seen the use of the conjectural method in psychagogy. I have emphasized three points. Firstly, good contextual judgment and adaptation is integral to this method. Secondly, patient care is paramount in severe cases. And, thirdly, more severe measures are needed because of the condition of the recalcitrant who can only be brought to obedience through harsh forms of persuasion. A gentler approach suffices in the case of the tender, the weak, and the obedient. In the early part of this section I drew attention to one of the concerns of the treatise, namely, the capacity of the pupils to bear frank criticism, contingent both on its mode of execution and on their condition. A gentle treatment is advocated in light of the condition of the students and in view of the negative effects wrongly delivered frank speech has on the pupils.

Philodemus is acquainted with different uses of terms for weakness and strength. In *On Anger*, for example, he answers critics who had attempted to subvert the Epicurean view of anger by appealing to *Principal Doctrine* 1, which maintains that God is not subject to anger or favoritism. Such attitudes belong only to a "weak" nature. The critics claimed that Epicureans made the strongest person weak by assigning anger to him. In reply, Philodemus maintains that one must distinguish kinds of strengths and weaknesses: all human beings are subject to the weakness of anger and favoritism. But this type of

---

[181] Philodemus, *On Frank Criticism* fr. 65.8–11. Plato suggested that the disobedient and incorrigible (ἀνίατοι) should be cast out of the state; *Protagoras* 325AB; *Gorgias* 526B; *Republic* 410A; Aristotle, *Nicomachean Ethics* 1180a6–14; Seneca, *On Anger* 1.15.1; 1.16.3. See James 5:19 and Plutarch, *How to Tell a Flatterer from a Friend* 70E.

[182] As Plutarch said in the *On the Control of Anger* 453E.

weakness does not diminish political or physical strength, for example. There are thus different types of weaknesses and strengths to be reckoned with, one of these being the strength of the stubborn pupils and the weakness of the tender ones.[183] The theme of strength and weakness and the theme of contempt are brought together in columns 22a–b and 24a. The latter relates weakness to older men as it asks why old people are more resentful of frank criticism than others. In the former the strong are advised not to look with contempt on the weak. Judging from the question asked, "why do women resent frank speech?" the weak would appear to refer to women and the strong to men. However, both the women and the old are part of the community and thus among the pupils.[184] Also, Philodemus refers to different types of students of different dispositions with terms of weakness and strength, referring to the strong and stubborn pupils as ἰσχυροί and the weak and tender ones as ἁπαλοί.[185] The one who is insecure and falling away from the philosophic way of life is called the "weak one" in fr. 58.9–10; one of the reasons why some "apostasize" from philosophy is because of their weakness.

Weakness and weak students also surface in fragment 93 Herc. and col. 9a. The latter refers to the mutual assistance of the wise when they due to "great weakness" reckon fraudulently. The wise not only assist each other, they also assist the young when they are weak. If the young want to continue to live together with others they must accept the norms of the common life. When they are weak the wise take them in/on their arms and remind and reproach them with moderate censure.[186] If censure is used at all for the weak, it becomes disastrous if not followed by praise; the "sting of censure" should be relieved by subsequent praise (App. Tab. IV I). Also, one should not reprove the weak in the presence of others.[187] Fragment 58.5–9 refers to the mixed method used on those who have erred

---

[183] Philodemus, *On Anger* col. 43.14–41. For this see Asmis, "Philodemus' Epicureanism," p. 2399.

[184] This is clear from cols. 6a1–8 and 22a of *On Frank Criticism*.

[185] Ibid., fr. 7.1–6. See fr. 10.9; col. 22b5 and App. Tab. III G. See Plato, *Phaedrus* 245A; *Sentences of Ps.-Phocylides* 150, "Do not apply your hand violently to tender children" (213–14, van der Horst ed.).

[186] *On Frank Criticism* fr. 93.4–6 Herc. Ἐὰν δ[ὲ τὴν ἀσ]θένειαν... ἀναλήψεται... τ[ὸν νέ]ον ἐπ[ιτιμ]ῶν μετρίαις ὑπ[ο]μνήσεσιν (Gigante, *Ricerche Filodemee*, pp. 109–10); col. 8b8; and Epicurus fr. 152 Us.

[187] The one who does not use frankness correctly "will submit even the weak to a cross examination in the presence of many or all" (*On Frank Criticism* App. Tab. III G).

and also advises that one ought to consider whether the student is able to improve when he has gotten worse over a long period of time. Fragment 59 continues the saga, noting that when a person falls away from philosophy, either because he is weak or incurable by frank speech, he will perhaps quickly hate the sage; some, however, will tolerate his frank speech, whereas others cannot be helped unless they have received some benefit before.

In Philodemus' view harsh censure (ἐπιτίμησις) can be applied, and then only moderately, when the sickness in question demands it, as in the case of the recalcitrant students who violently resist frank criticism. Benevolent care can then include blame, the severity of which is contingent on the nature of the illness in question. The teachers use harsh remedies as wise doctors do when they correct the inappropriate use of the "biting frankness" of the young. The retaliatory nature of the young must then be harshly corrected.[188] But there is no discrepancy between frs. 59–60 which reject bitter frankness in the form of λοιδορία for the weak or those who might be thought to be "incurable," and frs. 6–10 which allow the use of ἐπιτίμησις, a harsher form of frank speech.[189] In the latter instance, the focus is on the recalcitrant students who violently resist frankness; in the former, on those whose commitments in the philosophic way of life are in danger of being undermined, because they either are weak or have not been able to benefit from the frank criticism of the sage. A bitter frank speech in the form of λοιδορία would simply destroy them.

A certain typology emerges of Philodemus' critics who wanted to use a more forceful approach in the treatment of the weak and incurable ones. These critics, who are, in fact, the recalcitrant students, are compared to pretentious persons who do not recognize their own faults. With these Philodemus debates issues of harshness in moral exhortation. Interestingly, the description given of these students reveals that they themselves are like the "incurable ones"! Among the erring ones, the incurable have a hostile attitude and show a hot temper towards those who take them to task. They are contrasted with those who "patiently submit to admonition and wel-

---

[188] *On Frank Criticism* col. 17a. See Gigante, *Ricerche Filodemee*, p. 86 n. 158. Philodemus also rejects a retaliatory approach in his work on anger. Cf. Annas, "Epicurean Emotions," pp. 155–56.

[189] Λοιδορία might even be necessary in some instances. See pp. 72–75, above, and Philodemus, *On Anger* col. 35.18–36.6; cf. 35.22–23, πολλάκις δὲ καὶ λοιδορητικὴ ψυχῆς εὐκινησίαι.

come it" and disclose their depravity and do not "rejoice in hiding their faults or take satisfaction in its not being known, but confess it, and feel the need of somebody to take them in hand and admonish them;" but the one who "does not regret his error is incurable!"[190] They do not submit to or welcome admonition and resist when some of their fellow students or teachers criticize them; and, they are not remorseful or grieved by their error, as they should be, and are not forthcoming with regard to their faults.[191]

The obstinacy of these students and the fact that they do not recognize their own sins obstructs the task of correctional psychagogy in the community. When rebuked, they think that they have not sinned or that their sins will not be detected. These pupils thus hide their sins and are not forthcoming, contrary to the ideal of openness expounded throughout the fragments. When rebuked they are irritated and their sinful disposition and pretentiousness is exposed.[192] However, because of their desire for popularity, they do not benefit from frank criticism (cols. 17b6-9; 18b2-10). Because they think they are perfect they are more willing to engage in frank criticism of others than to receive it. They even resent being frankly criticized by those whom they recognize as more knowledgeable and as leaders. They thus claim to be wise and mature enough to correct others, since "those who admonish others are called 'more knowledgeable' and 'wise'"![193] But those who think they need no correction, Philodemus charges, suffer from self-deception; they are "foolish" and not perfect at all, contrary to what they claim.[194] Harsh means are appropriate for these pretentious and recalcitrant students who do not repent or recognize their need for correction. This debate on leadership qualification and

---

[190] Aristotle, *Nicomachean Ethics* 1150a23; 1137a29; 1165b18-23; Plutarch, *Progress in Virtue* 82A. See Maximus' description of Critias' incurable and all-various disease, at the end of his *Discourse 7, Which are the more Noxious Diseases, those of the Body or those of the Soul?*

[191] *On Frank Criticism*, cols. 15a-21b; cf. 15a8-10; 16a10-12.

[192] Ibid., frs. 41.4-10; 65.11-13; 66.13-15; cols. 15b7-14; 16b1-2, 6-7; 17a2-3, 8-13; 18b7-10, 13-14; 19b8-9.

[193] Ibid., col. 21b5-7. The reason why these students are more willing to engage in frank criticism than to receive it is that "they think that they are wiser than others" and "that the task of frank criticism belongs to them"; they, therefore, "reprove others who are slower" (col. 19a5-8). These students thus resent being frankly criticized even by those whom they acknowledge as more clever because they think that they are far superior in their understanding of what is best for the conduct of life, although these teachers are more clever in putting "questions into words" (col. 20a5-10).

[194] Ibid., col. 10a6-10, τῶν ἀφρ[όνω]ν καὶ μ[ὴ] τελείων.

style among the Epicureans is comparable to the debate we shall later witness between Paul and the self-styled "wise" in Corinth.

We have come to the end of our survey of the psychagogic practices among Epicureans. Both symmetrical and asymmetrical forms of social relationships are evident in these practices. The asymmetrical relationship is accentuated when viewing the disobedient pupil whom a psychagogue attempts to change to an obedient follower of authority, but it starts to fade when the friendly relationship between the corrector and the corrected one is accentuated, and when the emphasis falls on the mistakes of the wise and the friendly cooperation of all. One might argue that in light of the medical model, Philodemus emphasizes an asymmetrical social relationship between the friends. However, as I have argued, the purpose of the medical imagery is not to underline the asymmetry between members of the confraternity but to emphasize the conjectural nature of psychagogy, the need for adaptation to the particular case, the legitimate use of harshness, as well as the importance of openness for correct diagnosis. Below I shall enlarge on the social relationship of the friends of the Epicurean community in light of the psychagogic practices documented above.

### 3.2.4 *Symmetry and/or asymmetry? Authority and obedience*

M. Nussbaum has argued that the therapeutic argument within an Epicurean ambit is non-mutual and asymmetrical: "The medical model creates a sharp distinction of roles: doctor and patient, active and passive, authority and obedient follower of authority."[195] The pupil is encouraged to follow the example of medicine and put himself entirely in the power of the doctor. He must "give (himself) over to" and "put (himself) into the hands of the teacher." He must, says Philodemus, "throw (himself), so to speak, into the hand of the leaders and depend on them alone" (fr. 39.2–4):

> The pupil must show him his failings without concealment and tell his defects in the open. For if he considers him the one guide of correct speech and deed, the one whom he calls the only savior and to whom, saying 'with him at my side', he gives himself over to be therapeuti-

---

[195] M. C. Nussbaum, "Therapeutic Arguments: Epicurus and Aristotle," in M. Schofield and G. Striker (eds.), *The Norms of Nature. Studies in Hellenistic Ethics* (Cambridge, 1986), pp. 46–47.

cally treated, then how could he not show the things in which he requires therapeutic treatment, and receive his criticism?[196]

Such openness is required in order to bring the symptoms out into the open for diagnosis and is needed before the doctor can give a correct prognosis of the sickness. The medical model is thus used to emphasize the means by which a correct diagnosis can be made. Nussbaum thus correctly emphasizes a presupposition of the medical analogy itself but has drawn unwarranted social conclusions on the basis of its use. It is both theoretically and textually problematic to assume a direct correlation between the medical analogy and the social situation of which the text is supposed to be a part.[197]

M. Nussbaum's emphasis on asymmetry is similar to that of de Witt who argued for a structured nature of the social organization of the Epicurean community, hierarchically descending from the wise to "those in preparation" with several distinct social groups in between: σοφός—φιλόσοφοι—φιλόλογοι—καθηγηταί—συνήθεις—and κατασκευαζόμενοι. There are three grades of teachers, namely, the φιλόλογος or "junior," corresponding to an assistant professor, the φιλόσοφος, corresponding to an associate professor, and the σοφός, a full professor. The last two were closely related. The same is true of the συνήθεις and κατασκευαζόμενοι, although the former are more advanced in wisdom than the majority. They are "the ranking members of the group," regularly denoted by "we" in the fragments. The latter, on the other hand, are the "youngest recruits . . . subject to reproof and admonition from all members of the group, even from one another." These de Witt seems to equate with the "young"; the φιλόλογος was responsible for their early guidance.[198]

M. Gigante has questioned de Witt's explication. From Gigante's exposition of the nature of the fellowship, it is clear that he prefers a two-level approach instead of de Witt's six hierarchical levels.[199]

---

[196] *On Frank Criticism* fr. 40. Transl. by Nussbaum, ibid., p. 49. See *On Anger* col. 4.4–23 Indelli. M. Gigante had also recognized the connection between the need for openness and correct prognosis ("'Philosophia Medicans' in Filodemo," pp. 52, 57). Note de Witt's remark: "Lastly, the leaders were genuine psychiatrists, engaged in purifying men of their faults just as the physician purified their bodies of disease" ("Organization and Procedure in Epicurean Groups," p. 211).

[197] See R. L. Rohrbaugh, "'Social Location of Thought' as a Heuristic Construct in New Testament Study," *JSNT* 30 (1987), pp. 103–19. Cf. p. 310, below.

[198] de Witt, "Organization and Procedure in Epicurean Groups," pp. 205–211; cf. 207–08; idem, "Epicurean Contubernium," pp. 55–63.

[199] The συνδιαγωγή or *felix contuberninum*. Gigante, "Philodème: Sur la liberté de

He holds that the φιλόλογοι are common pedagogues outside the Epicurean community and the σοφοί, φιλόσοφοι, and καθηγηταί, are the wise teachers, not distinguishable according to grades. Frs. 41 and 44 do not differentiate between the sages contingent on their wisdom but simply affirm that the sage is superior and that he is the most excellent of friends. Frs. 1 and 35 neither establish such a differentiation since here the learned Epicurean is called both ὁ σοφός and ὁ φιλόσοφος ἀνήρ. And the "we" throughout the fragments does not refer to a class inferior to that of the "philosopher," but to the teachers who are wise but can err. They can fall into a momentary error which can be annulled by a sincere collaboration of the teacher and the one aspiring to wisdom, through their common desire for reciprocal salvation drawn from the doctrine of their "savior" Epicurus. The συνήθεις and κατασκευαζόμενοι are the young of the community who live in close familiarity with the teacher.[200] Gigante also calls these the "uninitiated" and equates them with the συσχολάζοντες who collaborated with the teachers. Gigante emphasizes then the free and open coexistence of masters and disciples who together search for the way to free themselves from error, relying on goodwill, friendship, and gratitude.

As we have seen, the fragments allow us to gauge in some detail the collaborative nature of Epicurean psychagogy. Fellow students collaborated not only with the wise but also with each other. Although de Witt claims to have discovered the social structure of the community, he also states that the wise is "not sustained in his position by any *rigid scheme of offices*"; members "differed from one another only in the varying degrees of their advancement toward wisdom, and none attained so near to perfection as to be immune from error."[201] On this score de Witt was on the right track, although he

---

parole," pp. 196–217. Συνδιαγωγή (Diogenes Laertius, *Lives of Eminent philosophers* 10.6) was rendered by "contubernium" under the Empire (de Witt, "Epicurean Contubernium," pp. 55–63). See Seneca, *Epistle* 6.6, "It was not the class-room of Epicurus, but living together under the same roof (non schola Epicuri sed contubernium), that made great men of Metrodorus, Hermarchus, and Polyaenus."

[200] Gigante, *Ricerche Filodemee*, pp. 97, 110. For the equation of the "study follows" and "those in preparation" with the "young" see idem "Philodème: Sur la liberté de parole," pp. 206 and 216.

[201] de Witt, "Organization and Procedure in Epicurean Groups," p. 206. My emphasis. The reference to the culpability of all in fr. 45 "diminishes the interval between the head of the school and his associates" (ibid., p. 208). de Witt also notes: "The prime requisite was a willingness to submit oneself to the voluntary discipline of the brotherhood, the bond of union being mutual affect, φιλία.... The

was unsuccessfull in deducing some of the more significant implications of his position. Also, de Witt's emphasis falls more on the psychagogic "procedure" in Epicurean groups than on its "organization." de Witt draws attention to a basic asymmetry between members which is not predicated on the function of a certain role or office but on the varying degrees of advancement toward wisdom. Gigante's emphasis on the collaborative nature of Epicurean psychagogy, on the other hand, draws attention to a basic symmetry present in the relationship between the sages and the fellow students. This de Witt recognized also in his emphasis on the culpability of all and on good-will, voluntary co-operation, and friendship. Both Gigante and de Witt have correctly gauged the similar situation of leaders and fellow-disciples.

I suggest that we attempt to account for both the symmetrical and asymmetrical elements of Epicurean psychagogy and recognize the non-rigid nature of the roles in question, especially the role of the one who provides care. We must emphasize that the medical model is not used to highlight asymmetrical social relations between the doctor and the patient; nor does it say anything about the status of the "doctor". It is rather used to characterize the state of the pupils and the means, methods, and procedures of the doctor, and to draw attention to the conjectural nature of psychagogy, the need for adaptation and the legitimate use of harshness. The function of the medical model is thus not to emphasize the asymmetrical relationship between the corrector and the one corrected. Philodemus is at pains to point out that the doctor can fail like everybody else. This is clear from his use of the medical term κάθαρσις. A "purification" is achieved by means of the purgative method or refutation.[202] Philodemus uses the analogy of purgatives in frs. 63 and 64 to accentuate not the purification of the sick but the possible wrong diagnosis of the moral physician. He too might need a κάθαρσις.

Similarly in fr. 46 the emphasis is not on the purification of the young pupils but on the "purification of the mistakes" of the wise:

---

expectation was that the initiate would gain a new disposition, διάθεσις, amenable to correction by leaders and fellow-disciples." Idem, "Epicurean Contubernium," p. 57.

[202] *On Frank Criticism* fr. 46.4–5. Cf. Gigante, *Ricerche Filodemee*, p. 78. Plato had already compared "the purificators of souls" and the "physicians of the body," noting that refutation is the principal form of purification (*The Sophist* 230C–D). Philodemus thus combines the methods of cross-examination and "admonitory education." See pp. 42–43, 86, and 127 (fn. 102), above.

"For how will he," Philodemus asks, "hate the one who commits pardonable mistakes, since he knows that he is not perfect and recalls that all men are accustomed to err" (46.5–11).[203] The emphasis is on the common lot of both teachers and pupils. If we then focus solely on the idea that the doctor's function is that of dispensing aid we find it is not only the teachers but also the fellow students in general who render therapeutic aid. Because of this it is misleading to presuppose a sharp asymmetrical relationship between the doctor(s) and patient(s) within the community based on the use of medical imagery. The appellations of "doctor" and "patient" are not, therefore, rigid social categories. One who is a doctor in the morning might be a patient in the evening. This Nussbaum does not recognize.

The medical model cannot be used to support a rigid asymmetrical relationship between members of the community. The culpability of all, including the doctor, is presupposed. The participatory nature of the common psychagogy shows that the teachers are not the sole dispensors of aid. In some cases the process begins with the fellow students who can either report back to the teachers or punish other students (frs. 8.9–11; 49; 51–52; and 61). When a fellow student censures another, the relationship between them is analogous to that between a doctor and a patient. The reciprocal nature of the activity of benefiting each other accentuates the symmetrical relationship between members. We have then witnessed both symmetrical and asymmetrical relations in the communal psychagogy of the Epicurean fellowship. Both aspects are seen in the reference to the teacher as the "most excellent of friends." Fr. 42 with its emphasis on the teacher examining the intimate fellows sharpens the contrast between the two, and it is, of course, true that "disorderliness" and "disobedience," which call for censure and correction, accentuate the asymmetry of Epicurean psychagogy. However, the teachers are also among the κατασκευαζόμενοι, at least in the sense that they are not immune from errors and recognize a greater authority, namely, that of Epicurus. All of the above factors underline the fluid nature of this participatory psychagogy with instances of both symmetrical and asymmetrical relations between the friends of the community.

Fr. 44.6–9 speaks of the one who is pure, who loves, who is morally superior, and knows how to heal. The following fragment continues by noting that "we" will admonish others with great confidence, both

---

[203] Cf. Menander, fr. 432 K.-T., ἄνθρωπος ὢν ἥμαρτον· οὐ θαυμαστέον.

now and when they have "become prominent, the offshoots of our teachers." The one who admonishes is "wise" and "clever" (cols. 20a1–5; 21b4–7); his authority is predicated on his intellectual capacity, not on an "office" or attributed status. His superiority is predicated on a functional capacity, namely, the ability to heal. The doctor can purify the patient because he himself has been cleansed. It is his capacity that is accentuated; he has achieved his status because he is capable of assisting others. He is still one of the friends, albeit the "most excellent of friends" (fr. 41). His authority does not depend on the socially attributed status of an office but on a function or acquired status, as is also clear when Philodemus emphasizes that those in an eminent position, politicians, or famous people are not excluded from admonition. In addition, the sole authority of the one who admonishes and the admonished one, of the doctor and the patient, is Epicurus. He is the purifier of all, also the wise: "The basic and most important [principle] is," then, "that we,"—i.e., those who have admonished others in a position of authority—"will obey Epicurus, according to whom we have chosen to live."[204]

There is thus a built-in hierarchy within the fellowship with Epicurus as the sole authority at the top. The authority of others within the confraternity is predicated on their function or ability to heal and admonish others. The fragments clearly reveal the tensions present because of such a diastratic solidarity which allows even those of an inferior character and social position to admonish others.[205] This would, finally, not be such an anomaly for the Epicurean friends of unequal

---

[204] *On Frank Criticism* fr. 45.7–11. Transl. by Asmis, "Philodemus' Epicureanism," p. 2394. Epicurus is referred to as an object of veneration in fr. 55.

[205] Fr. 36.4–9 says that one should even at times "obey [the admonitions] of those of an inferior disposition," and accept such an admonition in the right spirit. In fr. 75.1–8, "fellow-students" are said to offer themselves to carry out the task of correction in cases when the rebuke is not administered by the teachers. That tensions are inevitable in such a practice is clear: col. 12b6–9 says that those in preparation frankly criticise others who accept it grudgingly or not at all, and col. 14a3–10 advises that one who exhorts others should "remember who he is and to whom he gives exhortation," be they those who are inferior or "the great man who is coming to philosophy," which is probably a reference to Piso. See also cols. 7a7–10; 20a8–12; and frs. 52.4–5; 86.1. If I am correct in stating that those of a lesser moral standing could (sometimes) frankly criticize others in the community, such a practice would run counter to the requirement of self-scrutiny necessary for the ideal psychagogue. See also Ps.-Plutarch, *On the Education of Children* 14A–B, "If the life they [sc. fathers] lead is wholly bad, they are not free to frankly censure [παρρησίαν...ἐπιτιμᾶν] even their slaves, let alone their sons." I have adjusted the Loeb translation.

power and status, since frank speech was associated predominantly with the topic of unequal friendship in Greco-Roman antiquity.[206]

I have detailed the importance of obedience among the pupils of the Epicurean confraternity.[207] But both teachers and fellow students recognized a higher authority, namely Epicurus, the "most excellent man"[208] and their "only savior."[209] Epicurean devotion to the authority of Epicurus was well known to Seneca, but evidence shows that there was wide divergence of opinion as to how such obedience should be manifested.[210] Such a debate, however, should not deflect our attention from the unquestioned position of Epicurus. F. Longo Auricchio has demonstrated the veneration later Epicureans had, not only for the founder of the Garden, but also for his closest associates, particularly Metrodorus, Hermarchus, and Polyainos.[211] These leaders provide a standard in life and doctrine for subsequent Epicureans. Both Epicurus and Metrodoros are used as an example in *On*

---

[206] See D. Konstan, "Frankness, Flattery and Friendship," in John T. Fitzgerald (ed.), *Friendship, Flattery, and Frankness of Speech* (SupNovT; Leiden: E. J. Brill, forthcoming).

[207] The vice of disobedience is recurringly advised against in the fragments. Submissiveness and fear are paramount for successful correction—at least in the case of slaves: "For confidence breeds carelessness, slackness, disobedience: fear makes men more attentive, more obedient, more amenable to discipline" (Xenophon, *Memorabilia* 3.5.5).

[208] Although the "most excellent of friends" in fr. 41.7–8 and the "only savior and guide" of fr. 40.5–9 have, by way of transfer terminology, been applied to the Epicuran teachers, it is clear that Epicurus himself is the person most properly described by such terminology. The teachers have, then, assumed the cloak of Epicurus, perhaps as an embodiment of the Epicurean tradition. It is as such that they are a model to be emulated (fr. 45.9–11; cols. 5a7–10; 13a12–13).

[209] My identification of the "only savior" (fr. 40.8) as Epicurus is at variance with the views of de Witt, Gigante, Riley ("The Epicurean Criticism of Socrates," p. 65), and Nussbaum ("Therapeutic Arguments," pp. 46–47, 49), who all simply reiterate what the text says, namely, that the pupil acknowledges the teacher, master or guide as the "only savior", the "one guide of correct speech and deed." In de Witt's view, this is the "head of the school" ("Organization and Procedure in the Epicurean Groups," p. 206); in Gigante's view, the "master-guide" ("Philodème: Sur la liberté de parole," p. 211). In my view, only one person could receive such an appellation among the Epicureans, namely Epicurus himself. C. Jensen agrees with the identification of the "only savior" as Epicurus (*Ein neuer Brief Epikurs*, p. 81 n. 2). Cf. Longo Auricchio, "La scuola di Epicuro," p. 24, Epicurus = τοῦ καθηγεμόνος καὶ σωτῆρος. On "Epicurus as Savior," see Frischer, *The Sculpted Word*, pp. 231–240. Clay says ("A Lost Epicurean Community," p. 325 n. 41) that the beginning of the concept of Epicurus as σωτήρ is PHerc. 346 (fr. 3 iv.b.7; cf. also vii.24; iv.24–28 Capasso).

[210] Seneca, *Epistle* 25.4–5 (Sic fac, inquit, omnia tamquam spectet Epicurus); 33.4; 82.11. Cf. Clay, "Individual and Community," pp. 256–57, 264–66. See p. 115, above.

[211] Longo Auricchio, "La Scuola di Epicuro," pp. 21–31.

*Frank Criticism* of how the wise man employs frank speech towards his friends, and one of the fragments refers to the "enthusiastic frank voices of the (Epicurean) masters."²¹²

Finally, one should be mindful of the informal nature of pedagogical practices at this time. The term Philodemus regularly employs for the Epicurean teacher, namely καθηγητής, is thus used during this time as the title of a private tutor, most often in charge of a small group of tutorial students.²¹³ The term καθηγηταί, then, did not have the official connotations it later came to have. Plutarch calls Ammonius "our teacher" and a "philosopher" and describes his fellow-students as γνώριμοι and συνήθεις.²¹⁴ Plutarch records a conversation at Ammonius' house at a party to which he had invited all the "successful teachers," many other "men of letters" (φιλόλογοι), and his circle of friends. Plutarch's reference to οἱ καθηγηταὶ ἡμῶν shows that his friends also had their own καθηγηταί as Plutarch had his.²¹⁵ J. Glucker concludes that when Plutarch speaks of Ammonius and of his fellow students under Ammonius, he is using well-defined terms which clearly refer to private education.²¹⁶

The informal nature of καθηγηταί can also be seen from Philodemus' reference to the teacher in the same breath as an elder and a father.²¹⁷ His status as a teacher is comparable to that of an elder or a father; his advice is valued because of an acquired expertise, similar to that an elder or a father has achieved. The teacher was likely in charge of small groups of students. By the same token, the συνήθεις of the Epicurean community are not ranking members of the group but are, like the students of Ammonius, "merely the private 'tutorial students' of the καθηγητής."²¹⁸ As συνήθεις, οἱ

---

²¹² Philodemus, *On Frank Criticism* frs. 5.1-4; 6.7-8; 15.6-10. The first Epicureans are referred to as οἱ ἄνδρες. See Longo Auricchio, "La Scuola di Epicuro," p. 22.

²¹³ J. Glucker, *Antiochus and the Late Academy* (Göttingen, 1978), pp. 103, 132. Philodemus does have a very special use for terms of the καθηγ-root: *On Frank Criticism*, frs. 31.11; 39.2; 42.5; 45.5; 46.3; 52.6; 70.4; 75.3; 76.1; 80.2; 85.7; cols. 5a9; 5b1-2; 7a2; and 20a3-4.

²¹⁴ Plutarch *How to Tell a Flatterer from a Friend* 70E, ὁ ἡμέτερος καθηγητής; *The Obsolescence of Oracles* 410F; *Themistius* 32.4 ὁ φιλόσοφος; *Table Talk* 736D.

²¹⁵ Plutarch, *Table Talk* 719F.

²¹⁶ J. Glucker claims that "private tutors, καθηγηταί, were an extremely common species of teachers in the Hellenistic-Roman world. The term is already in use as early as the second century B.C.—if not a century earlier—and by the time of Cicero, it has become a common and accepted phenomenon in places as far apart as Egypt and Italy" (*Antiochus and the Late Academy*, pp. 125-26, 133-34).

²¹⁷ *On Frank Criticism* col. 7a1-3, πρεσβύτερος ἢ καθηγητὴς ἢ πατὴ]ρ....

²¹⁸ J. Glucker registers his agreement with de Witt's position that the various

συσχολάζοντες was also a common term for fellow-students; it surfaces both in *On Anger* and *On Frank Criticism*. These texts include reference to exhortational and correctional activity as well as a reference to the καθηγηταί. Apparently the συσχολάζοντες, like the συνήθεις, also participated closely with the καθηγηταί. It would therefore seem best to imagine a social matrix where members of the Epicurean community met in group-sessions of "fellow-students" and "intimate associates" at which the teacher, one or more, presided as the more experienced and mature member(s), but at which the active participation of all was a desideratum.[219]

The above psychagogic practices presuppose, therefore, intellectual, spiritual, and moral distinctions between members of the fellowship, which in turn indicate different aptitudes and the possibility of growth and relapse. The mature have a recognized responsibility to care for and, if need be, correct the less mature. Such responsibility comes about precisely in light of their having progressed further. They are in a position to evaluate the immature with regard to the perceived norms of the community. The emphasis on the culpability of all, however, reduces the asymmetrical emphasis in such a system. And, if we predicate the differences between members on their spiritual or moral progress and not on some fixed social roles, we are well on our way to perceiving the fluid nature of this practice and might be willing to see these "roles" as functional. Furthermore, in predicating the differences on spiritual and moral progress, we are bound to recognize that as the doctor might be a doctor in the morning and a patient in the afternoon, so might the "one in preparation" advance to another level or slide to a lower level, if we wish to retain a hierarchical-structural terminology. But what is accentuated in this fluid system of rotational psychagogy is its collaborative nature. The friends of the fellowship, be they teachers or fellow-students, participate in mutual edification, admonition, and correction. Philodemus presents this practice as an instantiation of the ethic of friendship.

---

epithets of καθηγ- apply to "teachers in charge of small groups" (*Antiochus and the Late Academy*, p. 132).

[219] Philodemus, *On Anger* cols. 19.11, 15–16, 19; *On Frank Criticism* frs. 75.4–5; 79.2–3. Plutarch, *How to Tell a Flatterer from a Friend* 47E, refers to the more apt fellow students of Cleanthes and Xenocrates. See Diogenes Laertius, *Lives of Eminent Philosophers* 4.24; 10.16–21. Refer back to p. 12 for Foucault's characterization of the Epicurean communities.

CHAPTER FOUR

PSYCHAGOGY AND FRIENDSHIP

4.1 *Psychagogy and Friendship among Epicureans*

I have argued that the care of souls among Epicureans was communal, not restricted to a few members invested with distinguished authority. The role of a "psychagogue" was thus transient and functional. A rotational psychagogy was a constituent part of the fellowship. It aided in character formation and countered mental disturbances and the fear of other people. Such fear, like the fear of the gods, the unpredictable universe and death, was among the mental fears destroying human happiness.[1] The Epicurean fellowship was thus concerned both with physical and spiritual well-being.[2] Although few works were purportedly written by Epicureans on friendship, we know that they valued friendship highly. Also the psychagogy in *On Frank Criticism* is viewed as a sign of friendship; the περὶ παρρησίας and περὶ φιλίας topoi converge.[3] But since *On Frank Criticism* deals mainly with practical aspects of the fellowship, we should not expect to find information here concerning systemic views of friendship.

Two aspects of friendship can, though, be extrapolated in light of Epicurean psychagogy. First, the forthcoming attitude and confessional practice we have seen are part of the Epicurean ideal of friendship. A second more subtle aspect can be abstracted from the correctional practices and open-ended nature of the fellowship. These practices gain significance in light of ancient discussions on having many friends and the importance of testing a person's character before friendship is proffered. The reason for these correctional practices—

---

[1] Epicurus, *Principal Doctrines* 11 and 13. Cf. J. M. Rist, "Epicurus on Friendship," *CP* 75.2 (1980), pp. 121–29.
[2] Philodemus, *On Household Management*, cols. 26.1–14, 18–28; 27.6–9. See pp. 162 (fn. 4) and 172 (fn. 50), below.
[3] See pp. 105–108, above. See Diogenes Laertius, *Lives of Eminent Philosophers* 10.24–25; 27–28. Cf. J. Bollack, "Les Maximes de l'Amitié," *ACGB* 1968 (Paris, 1969), pp. 221–236; and A. Tuilier, "La notion de φιλία dans ses rapports avec certains fondements sociaux de l'épicurisme," *ACGB* 1968 (Paris, 1969), pp. 318–29.

and the reason for the very existence of a work like *On Frank Criticism*—is, in my view, the unregulated recruitment criterion among Epicureans. Before individuals could join the family of friends they did not need to pass a nobility or character test; such a "screening process" started only after they became members of the community of friends.

### 4.1.1 *Friendship, openness, and trust*

In his discussion of reputable occupations in *On Household Management*, Philodemus not only advocates occupations which secure the leisure to be in a company of friends and enjoy the Epicurean way of life, but also underscores the importance of friendship. Sharing one's income with friends is essential to its acquisition and preservation; caring for friends and others is more profitable than caring for one's fields, and, friends are "the safest treasures with respect to fortune." People should gratify both themselves and their friends in prosperity, but in times of need people should even put the needs of their friends above their own. In both prosperity and adversity one should consult with one's friends before reaching a decision. Friends are so important that one must make sure that they will be provided for upon one's death, just as one's own children are.[4] Such remarks underscore the physical benefits accruing from friendship; but Epicurean friends were also concerned with each other's spiritual well-being. Besides the frank and friendly correction of faults, *On Frank Criticism* reflects an ideal of non-concealment among friends of the community which accords well with some of Epicurus' sayings on friendship and justice. The forthcoming attitude advocated is also said to be one of the finest things coming out of friendship:

> while many fine things come out of friendship, none of them is as great as having someone with whom one may discuss what is in one's heart, and to whom one can listen when he does the same. For nature intensely desires to disclose what one thinks to others (fr. 28.1–10).

According to Cicero, three views on friendship were in vogue among Epicureans. The first underscores the importance of pleasure in friendship but recognizes also an altruistic element; the second emphasizes pleasure as the original impulse towards friendship which grows into

---

[4] Philodemus, *On Household Management* cols. 24.19–25.4; 26.1–14, 18–28; 27.6–9. Cf. E. Asmis, "Philodemus' Epicureanism," *ANRW* 2.36.4 (Berlin/New York, 1990), pp. 2389–90. *On Frank Criticism* fr. 4.4–10, also gives evidence for a physical support system among the Epicureans.

intimacy and love for the friend's own sake; and the third holds that men have made a sort of compact to love their friends no less than themselves.[5] The above quoted fragment 28 emphasizes the intimacy of friendship without accentuating the security resulting from it. But such openness is instrumental for correct diagnosis and shows the intricate connection of friendship with its attendant benefits. Friendship is then valued both as the means to an end and as an end in itself.[6] Among the three views mentioned by Cicero, fragment 28 best belongs to the view which, although recognizing the utility of friendship, valued it for itself.[7] Some scholars have seen a tension between those sayings of Epicurus which claim that only one's own pleasure is desirable for itself and those which suggest an altruistic concern for others' interests. This apparent tension is not evident in Philodemus; what we find here is rather a tension due to the spatial and psychological closeness of friends in mutual psychagogy, manifest in bursts of anger and partiality towards others.[8]

Some of Epicurus' sayings on friendship and justice can be seen as a precipitating cause for later Epicurean emphasis on openness.[9] These sayings emphasize the negative aspect of concealment, the mutual pledge of not harming, mutual noninterference, compacts of mutual help, as well as the ἀσφάλεια and πίστις of friendship and the attendant mental relief.[10] Although fear of other humans is not encapsulated in "the fourfold remedy"—"God presents no fears, death no worries. And while good is readily attainable, evil is readily endurable"—such fear is, alongside fear of the gods and death, considered

---

[5] Cicero, *On Ends* 1.66–70. See also 1.78–85.
[6] Plato, *Republic* 2.357. Cf. A. A. Long, "Pleasure and Social Utility—The Virtues of Being Epicurean," *Ent. Fond. Hardt* 32 (Geneva, 1986), pp. 305–06 n. 22.
[7] The identification of the second view with that held by Siro and Philodemus was made by Hirzel 1, 170ff. Cf. W. Brinckmann, *Der Begriff der Freundschaft in Senecas Briefen* (1963), p. 17.
[8] This is countered through a recurrent warning against anger and contempt in *On Frank Criticism*. Cf. Epicurus, *Principal Doctrines* 1; *Vatican Sentences* 1. For the above tension see ibid., 23, Cicero, *On Ends* 1.68 and P. Mitsis, *Epicurus' Ethical Theory* (Ithaca, 1988), pp. 100–01. For a critique see D. K. O'Connor, "The Invulnerable Pleasures of Epicurean Friendship," *GRBS* 30.2 (1989), pp. 182–84.
[9] Mitsis speculates (*Epicurus' Ethical Theory*, pp. 109–10 n. 22) that ambiguities of *amicitia* might have facilitated a later conflation of Epicurus' theories of justice and friendship; R. Philippson, "Die Rechtsphilosophie der Epikureer," *Archiv für Geschichte der Philosophie* 23 (1910), pp. 433–46.
[10] Epicurus, *Vatican Sentences* 7, 23, 34, 61, 66, 70; *Principal Doctrines* 6, 7, 13, 14, 17, 27–29, 31–35, 38–40; Lucretius, *On the Nature of Things* 2.16–19; 3.37–39; 5.1020–26; Cicero, *On Ends* 1.68.

a threat against human security to be combated as other fears are.[11] Fear of other humans was attacked by a preemptive strike, so to speak, by maintaining an open attitude designed to deflate any signs of hostility. *On Frank Criticism* is our prime evidence for such an activity. Frank speech was necessary, then, both when combating fear of death and the gods and fear of other humans.

One should try by any means whatsoever to procure security from threats posed by others. Becoming renowned is the wrong way to obtain such security; a more secure route is a quiet life withdrawn from the multitude in the company of friends. One can never attain such security if one is still alarmed by unexplained natural phenomena.[12] Some of Epicurus' sayings emphasizing the need for a communal pledge not to harm others do accentuate threats of physical damage, but it would be a mistake to empty such security of all psychological significance. The Epicurean fellowship also aims at the alleviation of mental disturbances. *Vatican Sentences* 34 and 61 emphasize this psychological security. What really helps us when we are assisted by our friends is not so much our friends' help but rather "the confidence of their help."[13] Help is to be expected from friendship; indeed, all friendship, although "choiceworthy for itself, has its beginning in utility."[14] Epicureans were confident that they could depend on each other for assistance. Human trust remained an ideal; openness was a virtue, concealment a sin. If a friend does not participate in communal correction, he arouses distrust; and if someone proves unfaithful, the lives of his friends will be confounded.[15]

Some of Epicurus' sayings also draw attention to the intimacy of fellowship. According to *Vatican Sentences* 61, "the most beautiful too is the sight of those near and dear to us, when our original kinship makes us of one mind; for such sight is a great incitement to this

---

[11] Philodemus, *Adversus Sophistas*, ed. F. Sbordone (Napoli, 1947), col. 4.10–14. See F. Sbordone, "Il Quadrifarmaco Epicureo," *CErc* 13 (1983), pp. 117–19; A.-J. Festugière, *Epicurus and his Gods* (Oxford, 1955), pp. 27–50. For ordinary fear, the object of which is clearly apprehended and which represents a real threat to safety, contrasted with "unexplained" fear with respect to something vague, resulting in a sense of alarm, see D. Konstan, *Some Aspects of Epicurean Psychology* (Leiden, 1973), pp. 16–18.

[12] Epicurus, *Principal Doctrines* 14, ἡ ἐκ τῆς ἡσυχίας καὶ ἐκχωρήσεως τῶν πολλῶν ἀσφάλεια. On the company of friends in retreat, see *On Household Management* col. 23.11–18.

[13] Epicurus, *Vatican Sentences* 34, πίστεως τῆς περὶ τῆς χρείας.

[14] Ibid., 23 Πᾶσα φιλία δι' ἑαυτὴν αἱρετή· ἀρχὴν δ' εἴληφεν ἀπὸ τῆς ὠφελείας.

[15] Philodemus, *On Frank Criticism* fr. 1; Epicurus, *Vatican Sentences* 56–57 and 39.

end."[16] The closeness between friends required by the practice of openness is then congruent with an ideal voiced by Epicurus. The *Letter to Menoeceus* concludes with an exhortation to study its contents "night and day by yourself and with someone like you"; conversations and mutual contemplation are also central elements of divine friendship according to Philodemus.[17] Such evidence not only confirms a group study approach—also clearly indicated by the communal practices I have documented—but accentuates the form and content of the friends' likeness. A φίλος ὅμοιος is one who participates in shared pursuits; his likeness is not predicated on his character traits but on a shared activity and a common way of life, in likeness of pursuits (ὁμοιότης ἐπιτηδευμάτων).

4.1.2 *Frank criticism and the friendship of many*
The apparent ease with which recruits joined the Epicurean groups of friends has implications for the view of friendship valued.[18] An associational type of friendship is less strict in the screening process than a contractual type which might give more formal expressions to the mutual obligations of friendship. Later Epicurean willingness to accept new friends flies in the face of Epicurus' own stricture against such a practice.[19] The fault, however, lies in the open-ended nature of the fellowship, which, because its obligations were not primarily to the *polis*, could admit both slaves and women.[20] Also, the willingness to accept friends without a screening process should be seen as

---

[16] See also ibid., 18 "Remove sight, association and contact, and the passion of love is at an end."

[17] A. A. Long and D. N. Sedley, *The Hellenistic Philosophers* (Cambridge, 1987), vol. 1, p. 144; Philodemus, *On the Gods* 3, fr. 84, col. 13, 36–9, 36 Diels. Such sentiments were ascribed by Zeller to Epicurus' "effeminacy" and the need for Epicurean friends to ground the truth of their convictions in mutual approval (*Die Philosophie der Griechen* v. iii (Leipzig, 1903), p. 467; cf. Mitsis, *Epicurus' Ethical Theory*, p. 123 n. 49). See Diogenes Laertius, *Lives of Eminent Philosophers* 10.135 and 5.

[18] B. Frischer has argued for passive Epicurean recruitment (*The Sculpted Word. Epicureanism and Philosophical Recruitment in Ancient Greece*. Berkeley, 1982). For a critique, see D. D. Obbink, "POxy. 215 and Epicurean Religious Theôria," *Atti del XVII Congresso Internaz. di Papirologia*, Vol. II (1984), pp. 607–19. Compare Epictetus, *Discourse* 3.23.27.

[19] Epicurus, *Vatican Sentences* 28, "We must not approve either those who are always ready for friendship, or those who hang back, but for friendship's sake we must even run risks."

[20] See Festugière, *Epicurus and his Gods*, pp. 29–30; J. M. Rist, "Epicurus on Friendship," p. 127; D. Clay, "The cults of Epicurus," *CErc* 16 (1986) p. 24 n. 15. See pp. 170–75, below.

an expansion of the concept of "friendship of many." Virtue is not, as it is in Cicero, Plutarch, and Aristotle, the *sine qua non* of friendship. No character or nobility test had to be passed before individuals could join the community of friends.

Friendship of many faced the same critique as flattery, namely, that of insincerity and the deliberate change of character. Such "negative" features should be confronted by a period of testing. A man of many friends resembles promiscuous women whose friendship had been split up into a multitude of loyalties. Such contingencies of life as time, or rather the lack of it, to form friendship on the basis of permanency of character and likeness of virtue, precluded the possibility of having many friends.[21] The importance of testing a person's character before friendship was proffered was a recurring theme among writers on friendship who often noted the Theophrastean maxim— οὐ φιλοῦντα δεῖ κρίνειν, ἀλλὰ κρίναντα φιλεῖν.[22] A similar maxim was that of Cleitarchus, "Do not be rash to make friends and, when once they are made, do not drop them."[23] A nobility test is emphasized by those who valued friendship of character. Such "perfect friendship" is based on similarity of character, found among noble and virtuous males.[24]

Fidelity and loyal friends are treated at length in Lucian's *Toxaris*, which recounts a conversation between Toxaris, a Scythian, and Mnesippus, a Greek. Orestes and Pylades, the paradigmatic model of loyal friendship among the Greeks, were also so valued by the Scythians. But the Greeks are, Toxaris charges, better in praising than practising friendship. Toxaris attributes the strength of Scythian friendships to the way in which they make friends, which included a screening

---

[21] Lucian *Toxaris* 37; Plutarch, *On Having Many Friends* 93C; *How to Tell a Flatterer from a Friend* 59F; Athenaeus, *Sophists at Dinner* 255C, flattery is "a short-lived profession"; Maximus of Tyre, *Discourse* 14.6, "Friendship is increased, flattery confuted, by time" (177, 19–22 Hobein).

[22] Fr. 74, p. 181, ed. Wimmer, 1862. Cicero, *On Friendship* 85; Seneca, *Epistle* 3.2; 9.6; *On Beneficence* 2.2.1; Plutarch, *On Brotherly Love* 482B; *How to Tell a Flatterer from a Friend* 49D; *On Having Many Friends* 94B; Maximus of Tyre, *Discourse* 20.3; Themistius, *Orations* 327D; Stobaeus, *Anthology* 4.659, ed. Hense; G. Heylbut, *De Theophrasti libris Περὶ φιλίας* (1876), pp. 22–24; G. Bohnenblust, *Beiträge zum Topos ΠΕΡΙ ΦΙΛΙΑΣ* (1905), pp. 32–34; Brinckmann, *Der Begriff der Freundscahft in Senecas Briefen*, pp. 23–24, 34. Cf. *Sirach* 6:7–17.

[23] This is referred to as a saying of Solon in Diogenes Laertius, *Lives of Eminent Philosophers* 1.60; cf. *Clitarchi sent.* 88–89 (ed. Elter), μὴ ταχέως τοὺς φίλους κτῶ. οὓς ἂν κτήσῃ φίλους τήρει.

[24] Stobaeus, *Anthology* 2.33.7, ὅτι ἡ ὁμοιότης τῶν τρόπων φιλίαν ἀπεργάζεται. See Diogenes Laertius, *Lives of Eminent Philosophers* 7.124, noting Zeno's views.

process, formal compacts, solemn oaths, and "blood brotherhood." Scythians were permitted at most to enter into three such compacts.[25] This was to establish lasting friendships in which friends are willing to live and die for each other. With the exception of oaths, Mnesippus could agree with the Scythian practice of procuring friends. A period of testing and difficulties in the friendship of many are frequently noted by Greek theoreticians in their discussions of steadfast friends.

According to Aristotle, the proper number of friends needed for the happy life depends on the type of friendship in question.[26] With friends for utility, it is good to have neither no friends nor many, since it is hard to return many people's services and life is too short for it! A few friends for pleasure are enough, too. In friendship of good people, the limit is set by the requirement of "living together," and meeting and enjoying each other.[27] Also, it is not possible to be a close friend to many, as it is impossible to be passionately in love with many.[28] One must become accustomed to the beloved. But it is possible "to please many people when the friendship is for utility or pleasure, since many people can be pleased in these ways, and the services take little time."[29] Experience confirms this. Friendship of companions is thus not found in groups of many people, and the friendship celebrated in song is always between two people. By contrast,

> those who have many friends and treat everyone as close to them seem to be friends of no one, except in a fellow-citizen's way. These people are regarded as ingratiating. Certainly it is possible to be a friend of many in a fellow-citizen's way, and still to be a truly decent person, not ingratiating; but it is impossible to be many people's friend for their virtue and for themselves.[30]

The discussion in the *Eudemian Ethics* and the *Great Ethics* corroborates

---

[25] Lucian, *Toxaris* 37. On "blood-brotherhood" see Herodotus, *Histories* 4.70.

[26] Aristotle comes back to the friendship of many after treating complete friendship, i.e., character friendship, and incomplete friendship, i.e., friendship for utility and pleasure. All of these can be either a friendship of equality or superiority/inferiority (*Nicomachean Ethics* 1155a28–30; 1170b20–1171a20).

[27] Ibid., 1158a1–10. The requirement of "living together" should not be restricted to its physical dimension. Cf. A. Price, *Love and Friendship in Plato and Aristotle* (Oxford, 1989), p. 118.

[28] Aristotle, *Nicomachean Ethics* 1171a7–13. Aristotle makes the same point when discussing perfect friendship in *Eudemian Ethics* 1238a8–10.

[29] Idem, *Nicomachean Ethics* 1158a10–16 διὰ τὸ χρήσιμον δὲ καὶ τὸ ἡδὺ πολλοῖς ἀρέσκειν ἐνδέχεται.

[30] Ibid., 1171a15–20; cf. a13–15, οὐ γίνονται γὰρ φίλοι πολλοὶ κατὰ τὴν ἑταιρικὴν φιλίαν.

the above. The former raises the problem of testing many in light of the requirement of "living together" and suggests that an "active community of perception" must of necessity be "in a smaller circle."[31] The latter emphasizes that friendship between good men is the firmest and most noble type of friendship, based on unchangeable virtue. But advantage and pleasure, and the friendship based on them, are always changing. The friendship "of the multitude is based on the advantageous, and the friendship based on pleasure is found between coarse and commonplace persons."[32] The friendship between good men is the friendship of likeness but the friendship of the multitude and commonplace persons is the friendship of unlikeness, for the ignorant are friends of the knowledgeable and the poor of the wealthy. Equality and similarity, above all the similarity of virtue, constitute true friendship; Aristotle thus emphasizes love of attributes or virtuous human character in ideal friendship.[33]

The above points become the underpinning of Plutarch's *On Having Many Friends*, which emphasizes likeness of unchangeable virtue and character screening for enduring friendship. Plutarch incidentally remarks on the value of having many friends;[34] his concern, though, is difficulties in the "friendship of many." The adaptable friend of many throws into sharpest relief notions of unlikeness and change. Plutarch refers to eulogized pairs of steadfast friends and has no praise for the practices of the day "by which many get the name of friend by drinking a single glass together, or by playing ball or gambling together, or by spending a night under the same roof, and so pick up a friendship from inn, gymnasium, or market place," a friendship of cattle and crows that flock and herd together.[35] Plutarch

---

[31] *Eudemian Ethics* 1245b20–26 ἐν ἐλάττοσιν ἀνάγκη τὴν ἐνέργειαν τῆς συναισθήσεως εἶναι. "Primary friendship" is stable because it is not quickly formed and does not exist among base people (φαῦλοι). Those who become friends without the test of time are not real friends. Ibid., 1237b8–1238a3; *Great Ethics* 1213b2–18. Compare Isocrates, *To Demonicus* 1.

[32] *Great Ethics* 1209b11–19; "multitude" = οἱ πολλοί.

[33] *Great Ethics* 1210a7–16; *Nicomachean Ethics* 1159b12–15; 1159b2–4, ἡ δ' ἰσότης καὶ ὁμοιότης φιλότης, καὶ μάλιστα μὲν ἡ τῶν κατ' ἀρετὴν ὁμοιότης· In Plato's view, things most alike must be filled with contention and hatred, but things most unalike with friendship, "since the poor man must needs be friendly to the rich, and the weak to the strong, for the sake of their assistance, and also the sick man to the doctor; and every ignorant person has to value the well-informed" (*Lysis* 215DE).

[34] Plutarch, *How to Tell a Flatterer from a Friend* 65A. Cf. also *On Brotherly Love* 490E.

[35] Plutarch, *On Having Many Friends* 94ABEF; 93CDEF; 95AB. Plutarch refers to the friendship of Theseus and Peirithous, Achilles and Patroclus, Orestes and Pylades,

assumes that the many friends do not live together in a community but reside at different places and life settings. We ought not to accept chance acquaintances but only adopt persons as friends after spending a long time in evaluating them. Daily companionship is a great incentive to intimacy and goodwill; having many friends procures the opposite result.

The greatest obstacle to having many friends is that friendship comes into being through likeness. The all-adaptable person derides the advice of Theognis to Cyrnus because the changes of a cuttlefish have no depth. The flatterer and the friend of many cannot commit themselves fully to their "friends." Linguistic usage sharpens the contrast. Ἐξομοιόω describes the assimilation of the cuttlefish; συνεξομοιόω that of a friend. Two friends should jointly assimilate to each other; friendship seeks to effect a thorough-going likeness in characters, feelings, language, pursuits, and dispositions. Unchangeable aristocratic virtue and character are valued. Individual differences are overridden and "likeness" becomes a quasi-metaphysical construct of personal attributes and dispositional characteristics. Versatility is an example of a conniving character, an impediment to a permanent relationship.[36]

The criteria Plutarch and Maximus of Tyre use to distinguish flatterers from friends reveal their views on simplicity and versatility, and their bias towards certain types of friendship. The friendship advocated is one of equality, brought to the fore by a theory of likeness and equality. Both value character friendship built on an upright moral character. In Plutarch's view, a friend should be like-minded; there should be likeness of pursuits and characters. Change is detested, constancy applauded. Plutarch, then, eulogizes one aspect of aristocratic friendship, namely, permanency of taste, interest, and, especially, character.[37] Maximus claims that "friendship is equality of manners."[38] Flattery and obsequiousness accentuate the inequality of a relationship. If friendship is equality of manners, the good will be a friend to the good, but the flatterer cannot be the friend of a

---

Phintias and Damon, and Epameinondas and Polopidas. Approval through judgment is the most important thing in friendship.

[36] Plutarch, *On Having Many Friends* 97ABE; 96ACDF ... ὅτι τῇ φιλίᾳ γένεσις δι' ὁμοιότητός ἐστιν; Stobaeus, *Anthology* 2.33.7.

[37] Idem, *How to Tell a Flatterer from a Friend* 51A–C; 52A–53B.

[38] Maximus of Tyre *Discourse* 14.7 (178, 15–179, 6 Hobein), ἡ φιλία ἰσότης τρόπου; 14.6 (176, 20–177, 22; 178, 2–3 Hobein); Plutarch *How to Tell a Flatterer from a Friend* 52A, φιλίας ὁμοιοτρόπου καὶ συνηθείας ἐραστῇ προσήκει.

good man, for flattery cannot endure equality of condition.³⁹

This emphasis on aristocratic virtue appears also in Cicero's *On Friendship* in his critique of Epicureans.⁴⁰ Although Cicero sides with the middle Stoic position that no one has ever become "wise" and adapts the word "virtue" to the standards of everyday life, his views still fall within the ideal of true friendship among aristocratic males, equal in virtue and aspiration. Affectionate bonds unite two persons only, or, at most, a few good men.⁴¹ Cicero thus eulogizes traditional pairs of friends, to which he adds Scipio and Laelius. Self-sufficiency and virtue are requisite for friendship; these are the qualities which one is attracted to in the beloved. Although the term "friendship" can be applied to a relationship between the many, such as fellow countrymen or relatives, such relationships are inconstant and not destroyed although we eliminate goodwill from them, something which is unthinkable in true friendship. Cicero argues against the Cyrenaic view of expediency as the basis of friendship and affirms that friendship has its origin not in need and weakness but in nature and virtue. Here Cicero defensively notes that virtue is not unfeeling, unwilling to serve, or proudly exclusive. In spite of Cicero's apologetic remarks, the watered-down friendship of many is clearly less preferable than character friendship.⁴² Cicero's critique of the Epicureans also displays some truth:

> Some of these men teach that too much intimacy in friendship should be avoided, lest it be necessary for one man to be full of anxiety for

---

³⁹ Maximus of Tyre, *Discourse* 14.7 (178, 15–179, 6 Hobein); Plutarch, *How to Tell a Flatterer from a Friend* 54C.

⁴⁰ T. Maslowski, "The Chronology of Cicero's anti-Epicureanism," *Eos* (1974), pp. 55–78.

⁴¹ Cicero, *On Friendship* 15 and 18–23; *On Duties* 3.45 and *On Ends* 2.79. See also *On Duties* 1.53 (= Panaetius) and Seneca, *Epistles* 48.3; 9.17. Although Cicero (or Panaetius) discusses "ordinary or vulgar friendships" (*On Friendship* 76–100) and lightens the rigorism of the older Stoics (Brinckmann, *Der Begriff der Freundschaft in Senecas Briefen*, pp. 21, 26), the qualification in the text is needed. Women, although influential in Roman society, were classed with the weak and unfortunate (see *On Friendship* 46). Cf. J. P. V. D. Balsdon, *Roman Women: their history and habits* (Oxford, 1974).

⁴² Cicero loved Africanus "because of a certain admiration for his virtue"; *On Friendship* 19, 28, 30, 32, 48–51, 61. Cicero uses the traditional motif of "friendship is likeness" (50). For the views of Aristippus of Cyrene see Diogenes Laertius, *Lives of Eminent Philosophers* 2.91–93 (cf. also 7.124). It is somewhat of a cliché that for a Stoic the terms "friend" and "human" are coextensive; a Stoic is a friend of everybody (Seneca, *Epistles* 48.1–4; 47.1, 15–19). In practice, however, and in light of their emphasis on aristocratic friendship, Stoics did not value the friendship of many as critiqued by Plutarch's *On Having Many Friends*, in spite of evidence to the contrary (SVF 3.631; 161.15–19).

many; that each one of us has business of his own, enough and to spare; that it is annoying to be too much involved in the affairs of other people ... for, they say, an essential of a happy life is freedom from care, and this the soul cannot enjoy if one man is, as it were, in travail for many.[43]

Cicero's remark reflects how an Epicurean would attempt to find a viable solution to the tension between the ideal of ἀταραξία and πολυφιλία. The friendship Cicero attacks emphasizes mutual aid over and above intimacy as the basis of friendship. Those least endowed with firmness of character and strength of body have the greatest longing for friendship; and "helpless women more than men, seek its shelter, the poor more than the rich, and the unfortunate more than those who are accounted fortunate."[44] Cicero's disgust with this "noble philosophy" could not be clearer. We ought to choose men who are firm and constant and put the disposition of prospective friends "as we do those of horses, to a preliminary test."[45] Such a test is needed in order to establish whether a person is really like-minded. One should love one's friend after having appraised him and not appraise him after having begun to love him.

Perhaps we should allow Cicero's intuition when he contrasts Epicurean practice with their tenets to be the guide to our reconstruction. Cicero's emphasis on Epicurean practice would seem to be in tune with known Epicurean recruitment practices. Cicero also implies that Epicureans valued the common friendship of the many when he contrasts their friendship with the friendship between eulogized pairs of friends and when he lambasts the Epicurean and Cyraenaic friendship based on weakness and need.[46] Although it can

---

[43] Cicero, *On Friendship* 45. Compare Aristotle's "unemotional friendship" on pp. 37-38, above.
[44] Cicero, *On Friendship* 46-47 and 52.
[45] Ibid., 62-63. Cf. also 65 and 85
[46] Cicero, *On Friendship* 45-47 and 51-52. After having referred to legends of pairs of friends, Cicero says: "Yet Epicurus in a single house and that a small one maintained a whole company of friends, united by the closest sympathy and affection; and this still goes on in the Epicuruan school" (*On Ends* 1.65; cf. Seneca, *Epistle* 6.6). Later Cicero, again after a reference to eulogized pairs of steadfast friends (Phintias and Damon, and Pylades and Orestes), charges that Epicurean tenets on expediency and pleasure undermine the very foundations of friendship, and to the interlocutor's remarks—'But Epicurus himself had many friends' and 'But he won many disciples'—replies that the witness of the crowd does not carry much weight and "the fact that Epicurus himself was a good man and that many Epicureans both have been and today are loyal to their friends ... enforce the value of moral goodness and diminish that of pleasure ... these people's deeds ... seem to be better

be demonstrated that the Latin-speaking contributors to the spread of Epicureanism in Italy were more successful than their Greek counterparts and that they largely recruited members from the lower classes—Cicero at least criticizes the "unsophisticated" audience of the former[47]—*On Frank Criticism* reflects the presence of individuals of different social status and power.[48]

Philodemus also shows that he, in spite of his relationship with Piso, has faith in ordinary and common people. He emphasizes the commonality of all, recognizing that all humans are subject to the weakness of anger and favoritism and that all are accustomed to err and in need of correction; also, when correcting others one should without distinction attach oneself to the person's character, be he noble or base.[49] Philodemus places all humans on the same level in his work *On Death*; all inhabit a city that is unfortified against death; everyone is ephemeral, like vessels of glass and clay that will not remain unbroken. Philodemus makes clear, although he cites illustrious examples, that the same values belong to the humble. Some ordinary people bear the yoke of an unjust condemnation no less courageously than some famous men; there are even many ordinary people who have friends that care about them. Epicureans thus form a mutual support group in case of death.[50]

We can explicate the correctional aspects of Epicurean psychagogy

---

than their words" (*On Ends* 1.80–82). The interlocutor's objection is only meaningful if he and those he represents valued the friendship of many. Cicero's reference to the "multitude" and Epicurean practice suggests the same. See Philodemus, *Rhetoric* vol. 1, col. 30.34–36, p. 267 Sudhaus, νέους ὠφε[λοῦσι] καὶ π[ολ]λοῖς πολλὰς [π]αρέχο[ντ]αι χρείας καὶ [φί]λους ἔχουσι πολλούς τε [κ]αὶ γενναίους ("they assist the young and offer many people many services and have many and noble friends").

[47] Cicero, *Academica* 1.5; *Tusculan Disputations* 4.7; *Letters to His Friends* 15.19.2.

[48] One of the questions asked in the fragments is why eminent persons are more resentful of criticism than others (col. 22b10–24a6). Col. 7a8–10 notes that eminent men and common people must be admonished differently. The "great man who is coming to philosophy" in col. 14a6–10 is probably Piso. It is clear from col. 22a–b that women are part of the community and are, in this context, classified with the weak students. Women are also referred to in col. 6a which lists different types of students. Col. 12a5–6 refers to slaves. On the tensions present because of diastratic solidarity, or the participation of individuals of different moral character and social status, see frs. 36.4–9; 43; 44.6–9; 46 and cols. 12b6–9 and 14a, and pp. 152–60, above. Women were also part of the Epicurean community in Athens. See C. J. Castner, "Epicurean Hetairai as Dedicants to Healing Divinities," *GRBS* 22 (1982), pp. 51–57.

[49] Philodemus, *On Anger* col. 43.14–41; *On Frank Criticism* frs. 43 and 46.

[50] Philodemus, *On Death*, cols. 23.2–15; 35.24–34; 37.23–25, 27–29; 39.1–25. For these references see Asmis, "Philodemus' Epicureanism," pp. 2392–93.

in light of discussions of the friendship of many. Aristotle said that if it is possible to live with and share the perceptions of many at once, it is desirable that they be the largest number possible; but, as that is very difficult, active community of perception must of necessity be in a smaller circle. Such community of perception is expanded in Epicurean psychagogy where errors were communally perceived.[51] The friends of the community, including women and slaves, openly confessed and corrected each other's shortcomings. Such correction is subsequent to the establishment of friendship, not antecedent as required by the Theophrastean maxim. No nobility test had to be passed before friendship was proffered. Epicureans were willing to befriend both the noble and the base and were, like Alcibiades, willing to associate with good and bad alike.[52]

The reasons why the Theophrastean maxim is not adhered to are two; firstly, a non-rigid recruitment criterion; secondly, common and indiscriminate or "vulgar" friendship with the many, including slaves and women, weak and poor, is valued.[53] The friendship of many entails that individuals of different characters and social statuses could join the different Epicurean groups of friends. In general, it holds true for most writers on friendship—regardless of Plato's intricacies in his *Lysis*—that friendship of unlikeness is the kind whose basis is profit. Friendship of likeness is friendship of the good, reliable, and morally upright; the friendship of unlikeness with its basis in profit, on the other hand, is the friendship of the pliant flatterer and friend of many and that of the base. Thus, although it is indeed true that virtue is not unimportant in Epicurean philosophy, the emphasis on the advantageous as the basis or initial impulse towards friendship and the social realities of the Epicurean movement in the first century

---

[51] Philodemus, *On Frank Criticism* fr. 1.2–3, συναισθάνεσθαι τὰς ἁμαρτίας. Contra LSJ s.v. III, which translates συναισθάνεσθαι in fr. 1 as *to be aware of in oneself*, τὰς ἁμαρτίας. Compare Aristotle, *Eudemian Ethics* 1245b20–26, ἐνέργειαν τῆς συναισθήσεως.

[52] *On Frank Criticism* fr. 43; Plutarch, *Alcibiades* 23.4. This squares well with the view that members of the Epicurean movement were at this time largely recruited from the lower classes of Rome and Italy. Cf. Maslowski, "The Chronology of Cicero's anti-Epicureanism," pp. 75–76; H. Jones, *The Epicurean Tradition* (New York, 1989), pp. 69–70. *On Frank Criticism* fr. 8.9–11, says that in some cases the teacher will tell some of the student's friends to speak with him, i.e., instead of doing it himself. And fr. 70.1–4 indicates that one can come for advice either to the teachers or to one's friends who are, in this instance, not among the teachers. And col. 13a7–11 relates that in some cases the student will, because of shame, avoid the wise man, but will retain regard for the opinion of the *other* friends.

[53] Cf. Plutarch, *On Having Many Friends* 96A, Πολύκοινος καὶ πάνδημος φιλία.

BCE are more congruous with friendship of pleasure and utility than that of character.

An underlying issue in the friendship of many is the question of association and what criteria should be established as boundary markers of association. What are the criteria adhered to in selecting a friend? Epicureans of late Republican times rejected virtue as a requisite before friendship could be established. They were instead willing to admit indiscriminately to the community of friends individuals, men and women, slaves and free men, from all walks of life, thus establishing a community of friends which cut across other recognized forms of individual and group boundaries. The similarities of such a practice with the behavior of flatterers and the friends of many is apparent. It is no coincidence that the flatterer is introduced after Cicero's discussion of the Theophrastean precept and his discussion of steadfast friendship, or that Plutarch contrasts the polypic character of the friend of many with the reliable friend.[54] The flatterer and the friend of many display the abhorred features of the versatile, pliant, and readily changeable person, which a period of testing should eradicate. The behavior of the flatterer and the friend of many militated against the loyalty and reliability required in true friendship. What secured these was the screening process of the prospective friend in advance of proffering friendship. No evidence exists of such a character test being applied before one could join the friends of the Epicurean community. Character formation became an intramural affair among the Epicureans in Athens and Naples.

This positive view of the friendship of many and the correctional aspects of Epicurean psychagogy does then have implication for their recruitment practices. In this instance we must proceed by hypothesis, since no theory of recruitment is preserved in the extant Epicurean writings.[55] The more time-consuming process of educating new recruits properly belongs under the heading of psychagogy rather than recruitment. Although we can speak of "recruiting activities within the organization"[56] which are in most instances limited to reception and initial orientation of new recruits in their new-found faith, it is best simply to recognize that recruitment and psychagogy form part

---

[54] Cicero, *On Friendship* 85–86 and 88–95/100, respectively; Plutarch, *On Having Many Friends* 96–97.

[55] Cf. B. Frischer, *The Sculpted Word*, pp. 67–71.

[56] As does Frischer, ibid., p. 68.

of a continuum, since the concept of a "novice" is not a temporal category and the length of the process of enculturation varies from one member to another. Clear cut distinctions are then not available since the period of "liminality"—when the destructuring of the recruit's sense of personal and social identity in preparation for its restructuring in an alternative culture takes place—differs from one individual to another. One can only assume that after their reception and initial orientation, recruits became participants in a communal psychagogy which involved an active attempt to influence the moral character of all, including the new recruits. Such psychagogic practices reflect the tensions felt by the psychologically alienated recruits.[57]

4.2 *The Individual and the Community*

It is well known that Epicurus was concerned with the nurture of his groups of followers, his "fellow philosophers" as he calls them in his last will and testament.[58] His letters were written with nurture in mind.[59] These letters were meant both for the friend to whom it was written and the circle of his friends.[60] The philosophical letter had in view the education of Epicureans spread around the Mediterranean sea and attempted to secure unity among groups of Epicurus' followers in diverse settings.[61] Such letters were probably read aloud at a communal gathering.[62] As such, the letters aimed at attaining

---

[57] See A. J. Malherbe's treatment of the condition of new converts in *Paul and the Thessalonians* (Fortress Press, 1987), pp. 36–46.
[58] Preserved in Diogenes Laertius, *Lives of Eminent Philosophers* 10.16–21. Cf. D. Clay, *Lucretius and Epicurus* (Ithaca and London, 1983), pp. 54–81.
[59] Philodemus' *Works on the Records of Epicurus and Some Others* (PHerc. 1418 and 310) deals with the early history of the Epicurean school and contains numerous excerpts of letters by Epicurus and his friends (L. Spina, "Il trattato di Filodemo su Epicuro e altri (PHerc. 1418)," *CErc* 7 (1977), pp. 43–83). PHerc. 176 also contains excerpts from letters by Epicurus and others.
[60] Arrighetti, *Epicuro* (2) [59], 3. Cf. Clay, *Lucretius and Epicurus*, p. 58; C. Jensen, *Ein neuer Brief Epikurs, Wiederhergestellt und erklärt* (Berlin, 1933), p. 54. See Epicurus, fr. 138 Us.; Seneca, *Epistle* 7.11.
[61] Clay, *Lucretius and Epicurus*, p. 173. Epicurus states in a letter to Idomeneus that he wrote letters both to individuals and to groups (Arrighetti, *Epicuro* (2) [59], 3–4). The Letter of Epicurus to Herodotus was known to Pythocles (cf. *Letter to Pythocles* 85). This habit of the communal letter is attested by Diogenes of Oenoanda, fr. 51 Col. III.7–8 Chilton. I obtained these references from D. Clay, ibid., p. 326. See also Us. frs. 131–164; esp. frs. 135–36.
[62] Cf. fr. 143 Us. "Lord and healer, my dear Leontion, what a loud applause you drew from us when we read aloud your dear letter."

communal unity and securing the integral connection between the individual and the community ethos. Communal epistolary psychagogy thus represents an example of how the friendship topos "to be of one soul and mind" is attained in a communal setting. It also demonstrates how individuals of different social and ethnic-cultural value systems accommodate themselves to a shared communal ideal. Similarly, the correspondence of Philodemus displays *Lebensformen* intended to construe, in the Epicurean school, a faithful and concrete image of the individual as part of a larger community.[63] In such epistolary psychagogy, a spiritual guide attempts to lead faithful followers. Such epistolary psychagogy is most clearly seen, in its individualized version, in Seneca's letters to Lucilius; the comparable communal version of such epistolary psychagogy is witnessed in Paul's letters to the proto-Christian communities.[64]

Diskin Clay has drawn our attention to the "hero cult" features of the Epicurean communities, where members strengthened their bonds of "fellow-feeling" by and in their emulation, commemoration, and imitation of Epicurus and his first collaborators.[65] The cult included annual sacrificial offerings to the members of Epicurus' family; the annual celebration of Epicurus' birthday on the 10th of Gamelion; the festivals held on the 20th of each month in honor of Epicurus and Metrodorus, as well as other festivals and common meals. These practices of the first generation Epicureans in Athens tended to blur individual features and a "distinct physiognomy begins to emerge for the group itself."[66] The evidence brought forth by Diskin Clay illustrates in many details the character of the festivals devoted to the memory of the Epicurean dead. Taken together, these aspects give us a picture of the religious foundation of Epicurean society and a

---

[63] Noted by M. Gigante, "La Biblioteca di Filodemo," *CErc* 15 (1985), p. 15. Cf. W. Liebich, *Aufbau, Absicht und Form der Pragmateiai Philodems* (Berlin, 1960).

[64] For an extensive discussion of hortatory letters and letters by philosophers, see S. K. Stowers, *Letter Writing in Greco-Roman Antiquity* (LEC 5. Philadelphia, 1986).

[65] See Clay, "The Cults of Epicurus," pp. 11–28, on the memorial character of Epicurean festivals. See also idem, "Individual and Community in the First Generation of the Epicurean School," Συζήτησις: *Studi sull' epicureismo greco e romano offerti a Marcello Gigante* (Biblioteca della Parola del Passato 16; Naples, 1983), vol. 1, pp. 262–70, and *Lucretius and Epicurus*, pp. 169–191. Note also de Witt's remark, "Epicureanism was primarily a cult of the founder and his way of life and only secondarily a system of thought" ("Organization and Procedure in Epicurean Groups," *CPh* 31 (1936), p. 205).

[66] Clay, "Individual and Community in the First Generation of the Epicurean School," Συζήτησις (Naples, 1983), vol. 1, p. 291.

"fuller appreciation of the religious praxis of the Epicureans from the time of the founding of the hero cults of Epicurus until the age of Pliny and Plutarch."[67]

The benefits of the private cults Epicurus established for his community, of the commemorative festivals and meals, which survived in Italy in the first century BCE, were not only to give members of the community a model in the lives and deaths of the philosophers who had come before them to show them the way, but also to make for a sense of group identity and belonging, thereby giving coherence and social identity to the diverse members of the community. The cult,

> had as its effects, and likely as its purpose, to unite a group of 'friends' which included non Athenians, women, a slave, and children. That is, those private cults which assured and renewed the solidarity of the family made for a new kind of social solidarity. None of the dead honored by these cults could have benefited from these offerings, but they formed a bridge which made it possible for a new member of the group of 'fellow philosophers' to cross over from the family and civic cults with which he was familiar into a new religious society with very different conceptions of death, the gods and the meaning of prayer and sacrifice.[68]

I have argued for member participation in evaluation, admonition, and correction in the Epicurean fellowship. We can now add that the "cult of Epicurus" had other solidarity mechanisms than those elaborated by D. Clay. Openness and participation in mutual psychagogy also strengthen social cohesion and the intensity of fellow feeling among the friends. This social network is thus an important means in the effort to achieve unity of spirit in a common pursuit.[69] Openness and participation in edification and reformation are then important aspects of the principle of adaptability in a communal setting and in the effort to implement the social practice of unified thinking.

---

[67] Idem, "The Cults of Epicurus," pp. 12, 24, 27–28.
[68] Ibid., p. 24 n. 15.
[69] This sought after unity became a well known aspect of the Epicurean communites; Eusebius, *Praep. Ev.* 14.5: "The school of Epicurus resembles a true commonwealth, altogether free of factionalism, sharing one mind and one disposition, of which there were and are and, it appears, will be willing followers." Cf. Cicero, *On Ends* 1.65; Seneca, *Epistle* 6.6; Epicurus, *Vatican Sentences* 78; Diogenes Laertius, *Lives of Eminent Philosophers* 10.120b. Likeness of purpose led to a "community of like feeling": Clay, "Individual and Community in the First Generation of the Epicurean School," Συζήτησις, v. 1, pp. 262–64; Plato, *Republic* 462A–B; 464D; Plutarch, *How to Tell a Flatterer from a Friend* 51B; Acts 14:15.

Openness, reciprocal exhortation, and mutual correction of faults, are all evidence of a symbiosis or fusion of horizons between individual and communal interests. Character development is an anomaly when devoid of communal dimensions since it forms an integral part of the ideal of community. Epicurean participatory psychagogy then throws into bold relief the integral connection between the individual and the community.

In my introduction I suggested that the religious aspects of the Epicurean groups, their commemorative festivals and common meals, their submission to the authority of Epicurus, their "only savior," the diversity and debate among later Epicureans with regard to canonization and the attempt to establish the authoritative words of Epicurus, as well as their practice of epistolary psychagogy, are a great incentive for comparison with the proto-Christian communities. I also advanced the hypothesis that a special congruity existed between the early Pauline communities and the Epicureans, particularly as it relates to the widespread communal pattern of mutual participation of members in exhortation, edification, and correction. We have now seen evidence for this psychagogy among the Epicureans, and I have explicated this practice in light of Epicurean views on friendship, arguing that the correctional aspects of their psychagogy implies that Epicureans valued the friendship of many.

As we shall see in the final two chapters of this book, evidence exists for a communal psychagogy in the Pauline communities similar to that found among the Epicureans. The function of Pauline psychagogy can also be explained within the friendship topos. There is no evidence that a nobility test was required before individuals could join the Pauline communities. As character formation became an intramural affair among the Epicureans, so, as is clear from 1 Cor 5:9–13, for example, the formation of good moral conduct became an intracommunal affair in the Pauline communities. As with the Epicureans, there is a redefinition in Paul of Aristotle's concept of "living together" and "active community of perception."[70]

The correctional dimension of Pauline communal psychagogy can also be explained in light of the friendship topic of having many friends. Later I shall argue that one of several reasons why Paul refused to associate solely with some of his Corinthian patrons was

---

[70] Note G. Fuchs, *Die Aussagen über die Freundschaft im Neuen Testament, verglichen mit denen des Aristoteles (Nic. Eth. 8/9)* (Borna-Leipzig, 1914), p. 34.

that he challenged the very premise of that relationship, thereby also implying a positive view of the friendship of many. Instead of an exclusive friendship with some of these patrons, Paul's adaptable and all-obliging approach (1 Cor 9:19–23; 10:32–33) represents views close to those of people who valued indiscriminate or "vulgar" friendship with the many. Just as Philodemus advocated an obliging approach among the Epicurean friends, so does Paul when he calls on the Corinthians to imitate his all-obliging approach not only towards the multitude but also members of the "church of God" (1 Cor 10:32–11:1; 8:11).

Some of the criteria used to distinguish flatterers and friends become void in the communal context of the Epicurean and Pauline communities where the "softer" and "feminine" values now take precedence over harder values of a stringent set of male-dominated character traits.[71] The versatile approach of the frank counselor to his many friends is not only valued but necessitated by the communal context in which he functions. His flexibility of conduct and speech came close to the commonly noted characteristics of the friend of many, the flatterer, and the obsequious person. One should be willing to please and delight the many. Such a friendship forcefully clashes with friendship between social and moral equals, which values primarily the other person's virtuous attributes. Those who valued versatility more than the constancy of certain virtuous attributes had to counter the strong undercurrent manifest in Plutarch's analysis and succinctly captured in Aristotle's *Eudemian Ethics*, "for the good is simple, whereas the bad is multiform."[72] The expressed willingness in both Paul and Philodemus to associate with and please all, noble or base, has distinct similarities to Aristotle's so-called "unemotional friendship" as well as traits associated with the obsequious person and with the frank counselor who, contrary to the flatterer, is willing to cause beneficial pain as he corrects his friend's faults.[73]

In Philodemus the versatile and friendly spiritual guide attaches himself to the characters of his philosophical friends, whether base

---

[71] Obsequiousness was considered a "soft value," linked to women, children, and the weak and powerless. See Philodemus, PHerc. 1457, col. 8.19–21. See pp. 112–13 and 120–24, above.

[72] Aristotle continues, "the good man is always alike and does not change in character, whereas the wicked... are quite different in the evening from what they are in the morning" (*Eudemian Ethics* 1239b11–12).

[73] See pp. 36–38 and 170–71, above.

or noble, as did Alcibiades in his attempt to influence the many. This approach I have labelled "philotropeic," a solicitous attachment to a friend's character, regardless of the nature of his attributes. Paul's affable approach also expresses values which, if acted out, have affinities with the behavior of the flatterer and the friend of many. We could, of course, spotlight the manner in which the friend of many and the flatterer are described and underscore their insincerity and deliberate change of character in their accommodation to the many.[74] Plutarch draws a sharp contrast between a steadfast friend, who is rare and hard to find, and the pliant and readily changeable friend of many, and uses the protean person to underscore that versatility is one of several hurdles to enduring friendship. This requirement of likeness and constancy in a friend proceeds from a positive evaluation of Aristotle's perfect friendship and friendship of equality. As such, it is restricted to friendship between social and moral equals in terms of aristocratic character.

This is, however, not emphasized by Paul. It is of course likely that Paul's patrons valued such character friendship since in most cases they were probably Paul's social superiors. Here hospitality, equality, recommendation, intimacy, reciprocity, obligation, sponsorship, giving and receiving, and the antithetical relationship of enmity played a role. As such, patronal friendship is the best social context in which to view Paul's relations with his patrons.[75] Paul deliberately entrusts himself to people who are his social equals or superiors, seeking their assistance in his recruitment efforts. But Paul's willingness to associate with all and please the multitude and act to its advantage, emphasize both the usefulness and inequality of the relationship and an obsequious servility. Paul's friendship relation with his converts or recipients of his guidance comes closer then to paternal and fraternal friendship and that of the useful kind, and friendship of inequality. Paul's dictum of adaptability in 1 Cor 9:19–23 emphasizes exactly the benefits accrued from such a relationship both in the association with the many and in psychagogy. Also, the context in which this dictum is set forth is precisely a context in which Paul rejects demands made on him on the basis of patronal friendship. Finally, it

---

[74] This is crucial for P. Marshall who inferentially assimilates Paul's view of friendship with Aristotle's "perfect friendship" and "friendship of (aristocratic) equality" (*Enmity in Corinth* (Tübingen, 1987), pp. 70–71, 229–30). So also H. D. Betz in *Galatians* (1979), pp. 220–37 (on Gal 4:12–20). See pp. 15–17, above, and 264–72, below.

[75] Marshall, *Enmity in Corinth*, pp. 133–164.

must be emphasized that most theorists of friendship in antiquity emphasized that "perfect friendship" was limited ideally to one and a couple at most. But friendship for utility or pleasure had a greater flexibility in this regard.

In the final chapters of this book, I focus on Pauline psychagogy which expected, as did Epicurean psychagogy, community wide participation of members of different moral standing and spiritual aptitude in the edification and correction of each others. Pauline psychagogy is as well an extension of the ethic of friendship in which different types of friends correct, nurture, and guide each other.

PART THREE

PAULINE PSYCHAGOGY

CHAPTER FIVE

PAULINE PSYCHAGOGY

I have claimed that there are demonstrable similarities in the practice of the "household of Epicurus" and the "household of faith."[1] This is evident in a shared epistolary psychagogy, a positive view of the friendship of many, and participatory psychagogy. Such psychagogy has affinities with the ingratiating and "soft" approach of flatterers. There is a similar merging of the individual and the community among both and a contrast between insiders and outsiders. Although not full fledged, one does find a fairly consistent distinction in Paul between insiders and outsiders. The Jesus tradition has preserved the command to love one's enemies; in proto-Christianity one finds, though, "une tendance à limiter l'amour à l'espace interne de la communauté."[2] Within this internal communal space of the Pauline communities we find a participatory psychagogy commensurable with the psychagogy witnessed in Philodemus' *On Frank Criticism*.

Before turning my attention in the final chapter of this book to the Corinthian community, I shall in this chapter address the broader issues of the communal dimensions of Pauline psychagogy witnessed both in the Corinthian correspondence and elsewhere in his letters and which provide the general context for the particular concerns addressed in 1 Corinthians. The hypothesis pursued here is that in the communities Paul founded, he envisaged the participation of members in the evaluation and correction of each other through mutual edification, admonition, and correction, similar to the practices witnessed among Epicureans in Athens and Naples eighty years earlier. In spite of the ubiquitous nature of this participation, it was particularly the function of the more mature members to evaluate

---

[1] Gal 6:10; Eph 2:19. It is not intrinsically unlikely that Paul was acquainted with Epicurean practice. Luke records that Paul debated in Athens with both Epicurean and Stoic philosophers (Acts 17:18). See also the reference to God's help in Paul's speech before Agrippa, where Luke uses a term commonly used for Epicurus' succor of mankind (i.e. ἐπικουρία, a hap. leg. in the NT: Acts 26:22).

[2] G. Theissen, "Vers une théorie de l'histoire sociale du christianisme primitif," *ETR* 63 (1988.2), p. 208. See 1 Thess 4:12; Gal 6:11; 1 Cor 5:12; 14:23–24.

and pass judgment on the immature. From such an activity, three things follow: Firstly, a basic asymmetry between members contingent on their different spiritual and moral aptitudes; secondly, spiritual and/or moral formation and progress or maturation; and, thirdly, the presence in the community of members of different psychological dispositions.

## 5.1 *Paul, the Psychagogue, and Pauline Psychagogy*

It is not important that we be able to classify Paul as a "psychagogue"[3] but rather that we recognize his participation in a widespread "psychagogic" activity. In Paul's moral exhortation and letter writing we witness methods of psychagogic guidance similar to those of other contemporary moralists. Such a practice reflects Paul's leadership. Some scholars, however, have argued that there is no theory of leadership in Paul and draw attention to the lack of conventional terms of leadership in Paul's letters.[4] But the absence of certain terms is inconsequential for our question; everything we know of Paul's activities shows a person in a position to give advice, whether solicited or not, and as such Paul is in a leadership position. We might disagree as to the nature of Paul's leadership, whether it should be viewed in "charismatic" or institutional terms or a combination of these, or whether Paul's status as a mature guide is achieved or attributed.[5] Although scholars have customarily associated spiritual guidance with later Christian groups, Paul's psychagogic leadership concerns the spiritual growth of his communities, described as the "care daily required of me," the "anxious concern for all the communities," and a willingness to "spend himself to the limit on account of their souls."[6]

---

[3] As others have argued, for example, with the concept of the "divine man" (D. Georgi, *The Opponents of Paul in Second Corinthians* (Philadelphia, 1986) and "sophist." According to E. A. Judge, Paul was a sophist who fits into the class of touring lecturers like Aelius Aristides and Dio Chrysostom ("The Early Christians as a Scholastic Community: Part II," *JRH* 1 (1960), pp. 125–37.

[4] E. A. Judge, "St. Paul as a Radical Critic of Society," *Interchange* 16 (1974), pp. 196–97.

[5] R. Bendix, "Umbildungen des Persönlichen Charismas. Eine Anwendung von Max Webers Charismabegriff auf des Frühchristentum," in W. Schlüchter, ed., *Max Webers Sicht des antiken Christentums* (Frankfurt, 1985), pp. 404–43; Meeks, *The First Urban Christians*, pp. 131–39.

[6] 2 Cor 11:28; 12:15. Cf. Seneca, *On Providence* 5; Philodemus, *On Frank Criticism* fr. 7.

Paul spotlights his psychagogic nurture of the proto-Christian communities by the imagery he applies to himself and his activity. The image of a "builder" and the allied imagery of agriculture are both connected to the activity of nourishing.[7] Paul never explicitly uses such terms as a "shepherd," an "overseer," a "laborer," or that of a "teacher" to characterize his psychagogic activity,[8] and he rarely uses the terms "apostle," "ambassador," "servant of Christ," "steward of the mysteries of God," and "helper," and does not appeal to these in argumentation or to reinforce what he says. Other more frequent models are paternalistic, drawn from familial concepts of the ancient household, that of a father as well as a brother.[9] He also uses maternal imagery[10] and that of a "nurse."[11] The images of a slave and a servant are frequent.[12] Paul thus resorts mainly to terms drawn from the language of servitude and the ancient household to describe his relationship with members of his communities. This emphasis on "servitude" does not, however, exclude an ideal of leaderhip; it simply underscores the mode of such a leadership. The presence of both paternal and fraternal imagery in Paul's nurturing paternity of the Corinthians is significant.

One could view such "roles" as "a collection of reciprocally typified actions" performed by a kind of actor on the social stage.[13] Works

---

[7] For the building metaphor, see 1 Thess 5:11; 1 Cor 3:9–17; 14:3–5, 12, 26; 2 Cor 10:8; 12:19; 13:10; Rom 14:19; 15:2; Ph. Vielhauer, *Oikodome. Das Bild vom Bau in der christlichen Literatur vom Neuen Testament bis Clemens Alexandrinus* (Munich, 1979). For agricultural imagery, see Gal 6:7–9; 1 Cor 3:6–9; 2 Cor 9:6–14; H. D. Betz, *2 Corinthians 8 and 9* (Philadelphia, 1985), pp. 98–100.

[8] See though Gal 6:6 for a reference to a "teacher" and Eph 4:11 for a "shepherd".

[9] 1 Cor 1:1; 4:15, 17; 5:11; 16:12; 2 Cor 1:1; Gal 6:1; 1 Thess 4:9; 2 Thess 3:15; Rom 8:29; 12:10; Phm 16 ("a beloved brother"). For Paul's spiritual "paternity," see P. Gutierrez, *La paternité spirituelle selon Saint Paul* (Paris, 1968), pp. 87–223.

[10] Only in Gal 4:19 where Paul says that he endures birth pangs until Christ is "morphosed" in/among the Galatians. B. R. Gaventa, "The Maternity of Paul: An Exegetical Study of Galatians 4:19," in R. T. Fortna and B. R. Gaventa (eds.), *The Conversation Continues. Studies in Paul & John in Honor of J. Louis Martyn* (Nashville, 1990), pp. 189–201. Curiously, Gaventa contrasts Paul's nurturing maternity with the patriarchal authority manifest in his paternity, as if nurture was absent from the latter metaphor (ibid., 198). Paul uses also the metaphor of feeding the Corinthians with milk in 1 Cor 3:1–3 and 4:15, and Phlm 10 alludes to the concept of "begetting."

[11] 1 Thess 2:7. See Malherbe, *Paul and the Popular Philosophers*, pp. 35–48, and B. R. Gaventa, "Apostles as Babes and Nurses in 1 Thessalonians 2:7," in J. T. Carroll, C. H. Cosgrove, and E. E. Johnson (eds.), *Faith and History: Essays in Honor of Paul W. Meyer* (Atlanta, 1991), pp. 193–207.

[12] Cf. 1 Cor 3:5; 9:19; 2 Cor 4:5; 6:3–4; 8:4, 19, 20; 11:8. See D. B. Martin, *Slavery as Salvation. The Metaphor of Slavery in Pauline Christianity* (New Haven, 1990).

[13] P. Berger and T. Luckmann, *The Social Construction of Reality* (New York, 1966),

on flattery and friendship in Greco-Roman antiquity tap into culturally predicated notions of typical actions manifested in the social roles of certain character types and discuss what constitutes appropriate actions for each type. How a friend should treat another friend spotlights actions considered appropriate for that role. Paul radiates often contradictory messages as an actor on the social stage who adapts many roles, a "construction worker," "farmer," "slave," "freeman," "father," "brother" or a "friend." All these roles have latent presuppositions implying different things contingent on their social evaluation.

In psychagogy this is seen on two interrelated levels; the first relates to authority and submission, the second to the status implications of the roles. The parental role, for example, implies both the nurture of a child and the submission of the child to parental authority.[14] And Paul's use of agricultural imagery in 1 Corinthians had probably more negative than positive implications for many in Corinth, at least at the upper end of the social spectrum. More relevant than the particular circumstances in Corinth are general views and class views of such roles, e.g., urban deprecation of agricultural laborers. We know that Corinth was a center of crafts and commerce; it was of great commercial importance and its handicrafts were widely known in antiquity. Agriculture around Corinth, on the other hand, seems to have been very poor. This militates against Paul in his use of agricultural imagery, although the situation is different, for example, in Philippi, which was primarily a center of agriculture rather than commerce.[15] Different expectations towards the vocational terms used invite social tensions.

There is then a basic ambiguity in Paul's leadership authority, predicated on the different roles he adopts, both because of the different social expectations toward these roles and because of their often contrary functions, as is, for example, the case with Paul's use of fictive kinship terms. When, for example, Paul uses both paternal and fraternal roles and speaks of the Corinthians as "children" and "brothers," he is using roles which constitute two different metaphorical fields, one primarily exemplifying a superior-inferior relationship and

---

pp. 56, 74–79. Cf. also E. Best, *Paul and his Converts* (Edinburgh, 1988), pp. 17, 133.

[14] Paul refers to members as "children of God" and his children. See 1 Thess 2:11; Gal 3:26; 4:19; 1 Cor 4:14–17; 2 Cor 6:13; 12:14; Phil 2:15, 22; Rom 8:16, 21; 9:8.

[15] D. Engels, *Roman Corinth* (Chicago and London, 1990), pp. 51, 67, 73, 213 n. 64; Meeks, *The First Urban Christians*, pp. 46, 48.

another a reciprocal relationship. The roles of a "father" and a "brother" generate different and sometimes conflicing messages with regard to Paul's relationship with his converts. The two somewhat dissimilar paternal and fraternal roles can, however, be explicated in light of Paul's psychagogic leadership. The role accentuated depends on the condition of those guided. Recalcitrant members need the forceful guidance of a stern father; obedient ones that of a considerate friend or brother. Both aspects of Paul's leadership style surface in his guidance of the Corinthians. Thus, although one must be attentive to the particular dimension of the role of family members emphasized in any given context, this twofold standing of the spiritual guide as a father and a friend, when seen as representative of types of leadership, displays a contrasting relationship of symmetry and asymmetry. Such a twofold approach reflects Paul's use of different modes of guidance appropriate for different types of students.

Paul's psychagogic leadership thus factors in the condition of those whom he guides and presupposes different types of people. Paul's manner of classifying people is on a par with other moralists' distinction between different types of students. Such a distinction is found in Paul's reference to persons as "weak" and "strong," "obedient" and "disobedient," and in his remarks on maturity and perfection.[16] Paul's discourse presupposes people in different states and stages of moral-spiritual maturity, as well as education. Inherent in the building and agricultural metaphor is a growth model. The parental role also implies the nurture and formation of a child. That the word "children" was used metaphorically for the relation of teacher and pupils simply reinforces the presence of a didactic element. Paul's view of human existence is not static; expressions about the "metamorphosis" of the mind and the "language of progress" imply the same. Paul envisages a change in the "minds" and behavior of others, in "faith" or "love," or in "love" towards others. All these can improve or deteriorate and stipulate the desirability of good moral conduct. The same is true of Paul's directives that one consider things approved by society as morally good.[17]

Two dimensions of Pauline psychagogy are apparent; firstly, facilitating growth and strengthening others; secondly, correction of faults.

---

[16] Gal 6:1–3; Phil 3:14–16; 1 Cor 2:6–3:3; 4:14–21; 8:7–10; 9:22; Rom 14:1; 15:1.
[17] Phil 1:8–9; 1 Thess 3:10, 12; 4:1, 10; 2 Cor 3:18; 4:16–18; 5:17; 10:15; 13:5–11; Rom 12:1–2. Paul speaks of the προκοπή of the gospel, the Philippians, and his own (Phil 1:12, 25; 3:12–18, 21).

In his thanksgiving in 1 Corinthians, Paul remarks that his readers "possess full knowledge" and "can give full expression to it; there is indeed, no single gift you lack."[18] This remark is interesting in light of Paul's castigations later in the same letter and in light of Paul's comments elsewhere that one of the reasons why he or his proxies anticipate coming to a community is to remedy what is "lacking" among them.[19] Whether 1 Cor 1:7 is sarcastic or not, the claim of lacking in nothing implies a claim of completeness. Paul's use of τὰ ὑστερήματα and καταρτίζω suggests both "lack" and the need to remedy the detriment. Although "lack" is not present in Rom 1:11, Paul's desire to bring his readers some "spiritual gift" is the desire to impart something of benefit to them and to strengthen them.[20]

In Paul's nurture an intricate balance is evident between divine and human agency. When Paul reflects on the growth of those who had appropriated his message, he does so from three perspectives: a divine one, his own, and the person's own. Paul, though, makes his instrumental function clear in no uncertain terms. Thus, when agonizing over his pending death, he emphasizes his assistance in the development of the gospel and in the progress of the Philippians' "faith."[21] Paul's focus, however, is not on individual character development but on the development of the individual as part of a community. Communal edification is qualitatively better than self-edification (1 Cor 10:33; 14:1–6). Paul's guidance attempts thus to facilitate the growth of the individual as part of a larger whole and correct deviant behavior in light of a communal norm. Nurture and correction are two interrelated aspects of Pauline psychagogy.

## 5.2 *Pauline Communal Psychagogy*

### 5.2.1 *Pauline psychagogy?*

Paul's letters show that community members could assume a psychagogic function. It is important to examine the evidence for this

---

[18] 1 Cor 1:7, μὴ ὑστερεῖσθαι ἐν μηδενὶ χαρίσματι. NEB translation.
[19] See 1 Thess 3:10; 2 Cor 13:9; Gal 6:1; cf. also 2 Cor 8:14 and 1 Cor 1:10 and 16:17–18.
[20] In 12:6 the χαρίσματα are said to be allotted by God's grace. For strengthening see 1 Thess 3:2; 2 Thess 2:17; Acts 14:22, which all use both παρακαλέω and στηρίζω.
[21] Phil 1:12, 25. For the divine perspective see Phil 1:6; 2:13. For the responsibility of individuals, see Phil 2:12b and 1 Cor 9:24–27. Cf. 1 Thess 2:13; Gal 2:8; 1 Cor 1:8; 15:58; 16:10–11; 2 Cor 3:5.

communal psychagogy since, as with Paul himself, such activity has in the past been associated only with later developments among Christian groups.[22] I will also attempt to relate the evidence for such psychagogy to the enumeration of the various tasks that members of the community could assume, listed in 1 Cor 12:8–10, 28–30, and Rom 12:3–8, all of which appear where the metaphor of the body is used as an image for the community which is unified, despite having different members, each with his/her own function. It is not necessary for my purpose to discuss these texts in detail; others have done so adequately.[23] But I will try to be clear about the relation of psychagogy to the functions and leadership roles referred to in these texts.[24]

Rom 12:6–8 lists the following leadership roles and their mode of manifestation: prophecy, done in proportion to the faith of the one prophesying; service, manifested in service; he who teaches uses his gift in teaching; he who exhorts in his exhortation; he who gives in liberality; he who gives aid does so with zeal; and he who consoles does so with cheerfulness. 1 Cor 12:4–7 refers to varieties of gifts, services, and workings, given to each for the common good. Examples given in 1 Cor 12:8–10 of the individually varied "manifestation of the spirit" are: utterance of wisdom, utterance of knowledge, faith, gifts of healing, miraculous powers, prophecy, the ability to distinguish true spirits from false, ecstatic utterance, and its interpretation. Finally, 1 Cor 12:28 speaks of God putting in the churches, in hierarchical order, apostles, prophets, teachers, (miraculous) powers, gifts

---

[22] The adoption by Christians of the practice of spiritual guidance is thus normally seen in fourth century monasticism (P. Hadot, *Exercices Spirituels et Philosophie Antique*. Paris, 1987 (2), pp. 59–74) and in the *Exercitia spiritualia* of Ignatius Loyola (P. Rabbow, *Seelenführung. Methodik der Exerzitien in der Antike* (München, 1954), pp. 151–59, 189–214). See though R. Valantasis, *Spiritual Guides of the Third Century* (Minneapolis, 1991) and T. Bonhoeffer, *Ursprung und Wesen der christlichen Seelsorge* (BEvT 95; Munich, 1985). See P. Brown, *The Body and Society* (New York, 1988), pp. 227–29, on the monks of Egypt opening up their hearts to their spiritual fathers and to each others, and on the importance in such a practice of the gift of discernment. See also C. A. Volz, *Pastoral Life and Practice in the early Church* (Minneapolis, 1990), pp. 139–79; and T. C. Oden, *Care of Souls in the Classic Tradition* (Philadelphia, 1984). See also La Bonnardière, A.-M., "Portez les fardeaux les uns des autres: éxègese augustinienne de Gal 6:2," *Didaskalia* I (1971), pp. 201–15.

[23] See W. A. Meeks, *The First Urban Christians* (New Haven, 1983), pp. 134–36; E. Käsemann, *Commentary on Romans* (Grand Rapids, 1980), pp. 331–42; B. Holmberg, *Paul and Power. The Structure of Authority in the Primitive Church as Reflected in the Pauline Epistles* (Philadelphia, 1980), pp. 95–201; J. H. Schütz, *Paul and the Anatomy of Apostolic Authority* (Cambridge, 1975), pp. 149–80.

[24] I have here partially adopted the terminology of W. Meeks, who speaks of "leaders and functions" in connection with these texts (*The First Urban Christians*, p. 135).

of healing, assistances or gifts of support, guidances or gifts of direction, and ecstatic utterance.

In 1 Cor 12:29–30, Paul adds "interpreters," but omits from his list in verse 28 assistances and guidances. This omission is perhaps insignificant, but a possible implication should not be overlooked. Paul had in 12:4–7 emphasized that each member of the community receives a certain manifestation of the spirit for the common good, but in 12:29–30 he emphasizes the distribution of these manifestations as opposed to concentration on any one or several of these manifestations. Paul asks: Are all apostles? Are all prophets? Are all teachers? Are all able to work miracles? Do all have gifts of healing? Do all speak in tongues of ecstasy? Can all interpret them? The clear implication is that Paul expects a negative answer for each of these questions.

I suggest that the reason why Paul omitted "the ability to help others or power to guide them"[25] is because every member could potentially assume such a function. This omission suggests then a wide-ranging dispersion of the two gifts left out of the list in verses 29 and 30. All these lists, which are different and make their own statements each within its own intertextuality, accentuate functions which are more limited in nature. Most of the psychagogic terms that I document below do not appear here precisely because they feature functions which are more widely distributed and form a part of the activity of mutual support in vogue in the Pauline communities. Other texts in the Pauline corpus not only suggest this wider distribution of psychagogic responsibilities, but also give explicit evidence of such a dispersion.

### 5.2.2 *Member participation in communal psychagogy*

I have suggested that Paul envisages a community where individuals participate in a common psychagogy. I am not concerned with Paul's well known call for reciprocal love or his wish that members seek to

---

[25] This is the NEB translation of ἀντιλήμψεις, κυβερνήσεις, omitted by Paul in verse 30, but included by him in verse 28. C. K. Barrett's translation of ἀντιλήμψεις as "gifts of support" and κυβερνήσεις as "gifts of direction" is reflected in the body of my text. Barrett speculates that *support* may foreshadow the work of deacons (διάκονοι) and *direction* that of bishops (ἐπίσκοποι). See *A Commentary on the First Epistle to the Corinthians* (New York, 1968), pp. 295–96. As I have noted the function of κυβερνήτης and ἰατρός was compared to the psychagogue's role. Note the "gifts of healing" in 1 Cor 12:9, 28. See 12:31, 14:6 and 26, and note Eph 4:11. Cf. Philo, *On Joseph* 34.

do good to each other or his appeal to members to pledge not to harm or even envy or challenge each other![26] Compliance with such a call leads indeed to active member participation and a community-wide dispersion of activity concerned with the well-being of others. Such behavior would indeed be relevant to psychagogy; it not only accentuates the appropriate context for psychagogic activity but also its mode of expression. My concern here is rather those texts that envisage an active participation in edification, admonition, and correction, where members have an influence over the fate of another member, for example, in judgment, but also, more generally, in correction, comfort, consolation, encouragement, exhortation, and edification. Evidence for such practice is fourfold; firstly, texts that suggest reciprocated benefits from an engagement in a common endeavor; secondly, those texts that show Paul's practice of sending his fellow-workers as his representatives and envoys; thirdly, texts that reflect an actual practice of resident members of the community commented on by Paul, and fourthly, Paul's own directives to members of a local community to participate in such a practice.

### 5.2.2.1 *Reciprocal benefits from a common endeavor*
We have several statements referring to reciprocal benefits from a common quest. I have noted the importance attached to Paul as a psychagogue who imparts benefits to others (Rom 1:11). But such an activity is not a one-way street. The reason why Paul wanted to see the Romans was "to be among you to be myself encouraged by your faith as well as you by mine" (Rom 1:12). In 1 Cor 16:18 Paul refers to his relief of mind and that of the Corinthians by the arrival of Stephanas, Fortunatus, and Achaicus.[27] Paul is not simply saying that he was relieved by their safe arrival, but through the use of an epistolographic formula he notes that he and the Corinthians were refreshed in spirit through a letter brought to them. This spotlights the mutual benefits accrued from an epistolary psychagogy. Paul

---

[26] 1 Thess 3:12; 4:9–10; 5:15, 26; Gal 5:13–15, 26; 6:10; 1 Cor 14:1.
[27] Cf. A. J. Malherbe, "Did the Thessalonians write to Paul?" in R. T. Fortna and B. R. Gaventa (eds.) *The Conversation Continues* (Nashville, 1990), p. 254. For a similar use of ἀναπαύω, see 2 Cor 7:13 where Titus' mind is set at rest by the Corinthians and Phm 7 where "the hearts of the saints" are "refreshed" through Philemon. For the "fellowship of a common faith" deepening the understanding, and of Philemon's love delighting and encouraging Paul, see Phm 6–7 and 20. Phil 2:19 speaks of Paul hoping to be cheered up by hearing news of the Philippians (LSJ s.v. εὐψυχέω; J. AJ 2.6.9; BGU 1097.15 (i A.D.); Poll. 3.135). See also Rom 15:32, "... and be refreshed in your company."

succinctly describes a mutual non-epistolary psychagogy in 1 Thess 5:11–15. The Thessalonians form a mutual support group; they should encourage one another, build one another up, admonish the idlers, encourage the fainthearted, help the weak, and always seek to do good to one another and to all. These reciprocal activities benefit individuals as part of a community, facilitating their goal of being "blameless" at the return of their Lord.[28]

These activities are apparently fused with a divine element (1 Thess 5:23–24). The same is true of the mutual psychagogy practiced among the Corinthians, as seen in Paul's reflections on encouragement, comfort, and consolation, both in 1 Corinthians 14 and the early part of 2 Corinthians (1:3–7; 2:7; 7:4–13): Predictably, however, God encourages and comforts through a human agent. It is God, Paul notes, who comforts the downcast, who has "comforted us by the arrival of Titus" (7:6). The high concentration here of such terms as "sufferings," "distress," and "grief," is significant.[29] We should view the stress placed here on mutual comfort and encouragement in light of the emphasis on common suffering requiring mutual relief.[30]

2 Cor 1 also draws attention to the foundation of all comfort in the suffering of God and Christ, whose act of comforting becomes the source of peoples' comfort and the source of the benefits accrued in turn through their subsequent care of others: "He [sc. God] comforts us in all our troubles, so that we in turn may be able to comfort others in any trouble of theirs and to share with them the consolation we ourselves receive from God" (1:4); also, "if distress be our lot, it is the price we pay for your consolation, for your salvation. If our lot be consolation, it is to help us bring you comfort, and strength to face with fortitude the same sufferings we now endure" (1:6). These texts draw attention to the presence of a divine element in human suffering and consolation, and the interactive and other regarding aspects of both. They, together with the phrase "the place you have in our heart is such that we live together and die together"

---

[28] 1 Thess 5:23, 8–10 (cf. διό in v. 11).

[29] For τὰ παθήματα see 2 Cor 1:5, 6, 7; 4:8–9; for θλῖψις see 2 Cor 1:4, 6, 8; 2:4; 4:17; 7:4: 8:2, 13; for λυπέω and λύπη see 2 Cor 2:1, 2, 3, 4, 5, 7; 6:10; 7:5, 8, 9, 10, 11. Also, two peristasis catalogues occur in these early chapters. 2 Cor 4:8–9 and 6:3–10; Cf. also 2 Cor 11:23–29 and 1 Cor 4:9–13. See J. T. Fitzgerald, *Cracks in an Earthen Vessel* (Atlanta, Georgia, 1988).

[30] For παράκλησις, see 2 Cor 1:3, 4, 5, 6, 7; 2:7; 7:4, 6, 7, and 13, all of which occur in the "Letter of Reconciliation" if we follow partition theories of 2 Corinthians (1:1–2:13; 7:5–16; 13:11–13).

(2 Cor 7:3), capture the reciprocal benefits which accrue from both negative and positive life experiences the Corinthians face. The benefits resulting from mutual exhortation and consolation are properly termed "psychagogic."

### 5.2.2.2 *The psychagogic "proxy"*

The second piece of evidence concerns Paul's practice of sending fellow-workers as his envoys. In 1 Thessalonians Paul expresses his hope to be able to see his readers again and to be able to "mend [their] faith where it falls short."[31] In the meantime, however, Timothy is sent with the purpose of "making them firm and encourage them on account of their faith" (3:2). Timothy, as Paul's proxy, assumes a similar psychagogic function to Paul and acts as his representative. The same text also reveals the close connection between human and divine agency in the case of Paul's envoys, as in his own case. Timothy's visit and the letter he brings to the Thessalonians should "make their hearts firm"; but divine agency is not forgotten and Paul expresses his hope that the Lord may "make your hearts firm."[32] Although the terms Paul uses here, namely καταρτίζω and ὑστηρέω, are epistolographic clichés expressing a writer's desire to fill a correspondent's need by means of a letter, both terms have a wider usage in Paul as is clear from the use of καρταρτίζω in Gal 6:1, 1 Cor 1:10 and 2 Cor 13:11, and from the use of ὑστηρέω and περισσεύω in Phil 2:12 and 1 Cor 8:8 (cf. 1:7). The Thessalonians are solidified in their faith both by Timothy's presence and encouragement and through the letter of which he is the bearer.

### 5.2.2.3 *Participatory communal psychagogy*

The third piece of evidence comes from texts which reflect a psychagogic practice of stationary members. Such a practice is seen in the text from 1 Thessalonians already referred to (5:11–15) and is also evident throughout the Corinthian correspondence in texts which refer to intracommunal care and correction. As Paul reflects on this mutual psychagogy in 1 Cor 14 he focuses on different forms of

---

[31] 1 Thess 3:10. Timothy was probably a bearer of a letter from Paul to the Thessalonians. Cf. Malherbe, "Did the Thessalonians write to Paul?" *The Conversation Continues*, pp. 252–53. See also M. M. Mitchell, "New Testament Envoys in the Context of Greco-Roman Diplomatic and Epistolary Conventions: The Example of Timothy and Titus," *JBL* 111.4 (1992), pp. 641–62.

[32] 1 Cor 4:17 mentions Paul having sent Timothy to the Corinthians "to remind you of the way of life in Christ which I follow, and which I teach everywhere in all our congregations." Cf. 1 Cor 16:10–11.

"speech", namely, ecstatic utterances, prophecy, revelation, prayers, songs, thanksgiving, words of knowledge, interpretation and teaching (14:2–4, 6, 13–15, 19, 31), and their effect on the individual and others, both inside and outside the community. Paul contrasts ecstatic speech and prophecy, individual and collective edification, and rational and non-rational spiritual exercises. A person who "speaks in tongues" does not "speak to men but God" but the one who prophesizes "speaks to men for their upbuilding, encouragement and consolation" (vv. 2–3). The former builds up himself, the latter the church (v. 4). Ecstatic speech, like prayers, songs, and thanksgiving (cf. vv. 14–17), is an appropriate individual spiritual exercise for personal edification; prophecy, on the other hand, has primarily a communal psychagogic function for collective edification.

Of importance are Paul's remarks on the different functions and effects ecstatic speech and prophecy have on people of different spiritual status inside the community and on "outsiders". To begin with, one should not lose sight of the psychagogic effect or edificatory function of psalms, hymns, and spiritual odes. All these came to have an admonitory and didactic function in the Pauline school.[33] Paul also recognized the rational-cognitive, as well as the inspirational, function of hymns and prayers, both for the individual and the community.[34] These have different effects on people of different levels of maturity. They have an inspirational value for self-edification but their rational-cognitive aspect edifies novices (vv. 16–17; ὁ ἰδιώτης) who perhaps do not have the gift of ecstatic speech or interpretation. Apparently, such an "upbuilding" of novices is to be expected from these spiritual odes and prayers.

After his remarks on the different effects of spiritual odes and prayers, Paul urges his readers not to be children in understanding but rather to be infants in evil and adults in thinking (v. 20). Paul then expands on the implications of his discussion of individual and collective spiritual exercises indicating that although they have value primarily for members of the community, both can have a recruitment function. Paul claims that ecstatic utterances are a "sign" not for believers but for "unbelievers" (v. 22). Although it is not immedi-

---

[33] Col 3:16 "... teach and admonish one another in all wisdom, and sing psalms and hymns and spiritual songs with thankfulness in your hearts to God." See Meeks, *The First Urban Christians*, pp. 144–50.

[34] 1 Cor 14:15 ψαλῶ τῷ πνεύματι, ψαλῶ δὲ καὶ τῷ νοΐ. Cf. 14:26; Phil 2:6–11; Eph 5:18–20.

ately clear how individual spiritual exercises for personal edification are a "sign for unbelievers", I suggest that a clue to a socio-culturally sensitive understanding of this phenomena is to recognize both the competitive element of Greco-Roman society and the widespread use of various forms of spiritual exercises for self-edification. These "unbelievers", whose presense is assumed on the fringes of the Corinthian community, were well acquinted with such spiritual exercies and recognized, with a touch of envy, the effectiveness of ecstatic speech, spiritual odes and prayers among the Corinthians. This effectiveness increased their possible use and success in recruitment!

Next Paul contextualizes the phenomena of ecstatic speech and prophecy in communal worship (vv. 23–25) envisaging two social scenarios: one when "all speak in tongues" and another when "all prophesy". In the former instance, if a "novice and/or an unbeliever enters" they will conclude that the Corinthians are mad. Although "tongues" as individual spiritual exercises can effect "unbelievers" positively, they apparently have a reverse effect if used indiscriminately in a communal gathering. But when "all prophesy" and an "unbeliever and/or a novice" enters it does not cause confusion but persuades the unbeliever of the truth of the Corinthian belief (vv. 24–25). I think we must assume that Paul reflects here on the proper communal expression of prophecy which he expands on in vv. 26–33. Thus, although prophecy has primarily an intracommunal function for communal edification (v. 3) and as such is not a sign for "unbelievers" (v. 22), it is precisely when prophecy, with its multifarious character, directed to the church, is done properly, that "recruitment" ensues. This shows that, so far as the congregation is concerned, psychagogy and recruitment are not separable. 1 Cor 14 reveals then, as do 1 Cor 5 and 8–9 (to be discussed in chapter six), the intricate connection between psychagogy and recruitment and the blurred communal boundaries of early Christian groups; both unbelievers (οἱ ἄπιστοι) and novices are effected by the psychagogic practices of the community.[35]

Paul attempts to deflate the value of individual spiritual exercises and emphasizes those which are also intelligible to others. It is thus the rational interactive function of prophetic utterance which is valued more highly than ecstatic utterance which can have individual but might not have communal benefits. The person who utters a

---

[35] See pp. 255–64, below.

prophetic word is thus "worth more" than the "man of ecstatic speech—unless indeed he can explain its meaning and so help build up the community" (1 Cor 14:5). The utterances should be publicly sharable and thus in ordinary language and understandable terms; the ultimate evaluating criterion is the communally constructive nature of the act. The value of the prophetic word is thus its edificatory, admonitory, and didactic or cognitive psychagogic effects. Many can indeed prophesy, but they must do it one by one, "so that all may learn and all be encouraged."[36] And it is precisely because of these rational-cognitive functions that the prophetic word not only requires but also generates order and can have the effect on the ἰδιῶται and ἄπιστοι that it does, namely, it convicts and judges them, ἐλέγχεται ὑπὸ πάντων, ἀνακρίνεται ὑπὸ πάντων (14:24).

The word ἀνακρίνω, used here, together with ἐλέγχω, to note the effect of the prophetic word on novices [laymen] and non-believers, is also used earlier in 1 Corinthians where a comparable function is envisaged with regard to the immature (2:15; 4:3–5). Here we have evidence for participation, not only in communal edification but also in communal correction. Whatever else Paul is concerned with in the early part of 1 Corinthians, issues of evaluation and judgement of members of the community form part of his concerns. The issue of judgment is particularly clear in chapters five and six, the one in light of a committed fault, and the other in settling issues of dispute among community members and the need for a spiritually mature person in the community to settle the issues. The precise nature of the issues does not concern us here, but rather some of its presuppositions and its participatory nature.[37]

1 Cor 6:1–7 gives evidence, as does 1 Cor 2:15, of a mature person presiding as a judge. The latter text gives a vague statement of such a practice; the former a concrete example. The former envisages a mature person, a σοφός (ἀνήρ), settling a dispute between members of the community so that they need not take the issue into a pagan law-court. The dismaying exclamation, "can it be that there is not a single wise man among you able to give a decision in a brother's

---

[36] 1 Cor 14:31, ἵνα πάντες μανθάνωσιν καὶ πάντες παρακαλῶνται. Those who prophesy "speak to other people for their upbuilding and encouragement and consolation" (ἀνθρώποις λαλεῖ οἰκοδομὴν καὶ παράκλησιν καὶ παραμυθίαν; 14.3). Cf. 1 Cor 14:4–6, 10, 12, 17, 19, 24, 26.

[37] For ἀνακρίνω see 1 Cor 2:15; 4:3; 9:3; 10:25, 27. See further pp. 291 and 301–310, below.

cause!" (6:5b) brings into sharp relief Paul's expectation that some should assume such a function. Paul laments the Corinthians' lack of maturity, an immaturity which results in a faulty judgement with regard to their standing, a failure to "distinguish the body" with regard to the Lord's Supper, and an inability to settle issues relating to intra-communal affairs (11:27–34). Although Paul's use of σοφός in 6:5b is probably ironic,[38] his statement is made in light of the claim of some in Corinth that they were "wise" and thus competent judges of others. Paul's ironic statement does not suggest, then, that he did not expect mature persons in the community to settle disputes between members of the community.[39]

Paul advocates that members participate in the correction of others, also implying that such mutual correction was already being practiced in the community. As a part of judgement Paul advices a shunning of the one at fault and draws a general lesson from an incident of sexual immorality to include any "so-called brother" who "leads a loose life, or is grasping, or idolatrous, a slanderer, a drunkard, or a swindler. You should not even eat with any such person" (1 Cor 5:9, 11). All within the fellowship are advised to implement such a practice. A similar corrective procedure of distancing by others in the Pauline school from a "disobedient" member shows that the goal of such shunning is a shaming into repentance.[40] That such a corrective treatment by the community could be traumatic can be clearly seen from 2 Cor 2:5–11. The punishment inflicted by the majority of the community had in Paul's view already served its intended function: "The man's sorrow must not be made so severe as to overwhelm him." It was now time to "forgive the offender and put heart into him."[41] Paul thus warns the Corinthians not to be too harsh in their punishment and advises that the corrective treatment should end on an edificatory and encouraging note. Such texts envisage a scenario where community members preside as "judges" over others.

---

[38] As Paul's use of the term elsewhere in 1 Corinthians suggests (cf. 1:19, 20, 25, 26, 27; 3:10, 18, 19, 20).
[39] See A. C. Mitchell, "Rich and Poor in the Courts of Corinth: Litigiousness and status in 1 Corinthians 6.1–11," *NTS* 39 (1993), pp. 562–586.
[40] 2 Thess 3:6 and 14–15, on which see pp. 207–208, below.
[41] 2 Cor 2:7. This text does not refer to the same "fault" as 1 Cor 5:1–13. Cf. C. K. Barrett, *Essays on Paul* (Philadelphia, 1982), pp. 108–17. See pp. 119–20 and 129–32, above, on Philodemus' views on forgiveness and concerns for the destructive nature of punishment.

### 5.2.2.4 *Paul's call for participatory psychagogy*

The above practice has been abstracted from both indirect and direct evidence which reflects and assumes such a social practice of mutual psychagogy. Our final piece of evidence is found in Paul's actual call for member participation in psychagogy. I have discussed the practice of mutual consolation, edification, and correction among the Corinthians. In earlier correspondence Paul had attempted to implement such participatory practices of edification and correction. He urged the Thessalonians to "comfort" or "encourage each other," adding that they should also "build up each other, person to person."[42] Paul also exhorts the Thessalonians to "admonish the disorderly, encourage the fainthearted, support and care for the weak, and be patient with them all" (5:14). The function of admonishing is the responsibility of all members, since the injunction in 5:14 is addressed to the ἀδελφοί in general.

Νουθεσία is a form of hortatory blame used in the correction of error, which aims at the repentance of the erring one. Paul attempts thus to implement a psychagogy of mutual edification in the community which includes a dimension of blame or a psychagogy of a harsher sort.[43] We have seen texts which refer to the "mending" of certain aspects of the life of community members, and the "judgement" by one member of another.[44] All these terms, i.e., νουθετέω, καταρτίζω, and ἀνακρίνω, draw attention to and presuppose a practice of mutual evaluation and correction. Gal 6:1 is particularly significant:

> Brethren, if a man is overtaken in any trespass, you who are spiritual should restore him in a spirit of gentleness. Look to yourself, lest you too be tempted.

---

[42] 1 Thess 4:18, παρακαλεῖτε ἀλλήλους; 5:11, οἰκοδομεῖτε εἰς τὸν ἕνα. For the phrase εἰς τὸν ἕνα see A. J. Malherbe, "'Pastoral Care' in the Thessalonian Church," *NTS* 36 (1990), pp. 388–89. Malherbe argues (ibid., 375–91) that 1 Thess 5.14 should be understood in the context of discussions of the theory and practice of appropriate speech in ancient psychagogy. Discussing the consoling type, Ps.-Demetrius 5 advices: "Bear then, what has happened as lightly as you can, and exhort yourself just as you would exhort someone else" (καθὼς ἄλλῳ παρῄνεσας, σαυτῷ παραίνεσον; Malherbe 34, 17–19). Cf. also the 2nd cent. CE papyrus from Oxyrhynchus, ("Therefore, comfort one another"—παρηγορεῖτε οὖν ἑαυτούς. Grenfell and Hunt (2), Fig. 31. Ἑαυτούς is equivalent to ἀλλήλους (A. Deissmann, *Light from the Ancient East*, 1927, p. 176).

[43] Compare 2 Thess 3:14–15. If 2 Thessalonians was written by Paul, such a practice is not only implicit in some of Paul's more cryptic remarks but quite explicit.

[44] 1 Thess 3:10; 2 Cor 13:9, 11; Eph 4:12; 1 Cor 2:15. See also 6:5.

This text also addresses the ἀδελφοί of the Galatian community. It uses the term καταρτίζω, employed in 1 Thess 3:10 of the mending of that which is lacking in the faith of the Thessalonians, in 1 Cor 1:10 in an appeal to the Corinthians to be "firmly joined" in unity of mind and thought, in 2 Cor 13:9 and 11 as an injunction to the Corinthians that they mend their ways, and in Eph 4:12 for one of the functions of leaders in the Pauline school. Gal 6:2 adds the term βαστάζω, later to be used in Rom 15:1 of the responsibility of the strong towards the weak;[45] and, finally, 6:1 identifies those who do the correcting or mending of the fault in question as πνευματικοί, the same appellation Paul later uses in 1 Cor 2:15 of the one who can judge the worth of everything, including his fellow-humans.

Apparently, no one is exempt from failure and the need for correction. The indeterminate ἄνθρωπος suggests that it might include any of the ἀδελφοί. Also, Gal 6:1 allows for the possibility that the one who "detects" the erring one is not the one who corrects him, thus opening the door for a possible social matrix of reporting of errors similar to the practice reflected in Philodemus' *On Frank Criticism*.[46] The text stipulates that the "spiritual ones" should amend and restore in gentleness (ἐν πνεύματι πραΰτητος) the erring one(s). The nature of the fault is not at issue. We should not exclude the possibility that everyone might assume the function of a "corrector," but the phrase ὑμεῖς οἱ πνευματικοὶ καταρτίζετε τὸν τοιοῦτον draws attention to distinctions within the community where the spiritual ones correct others. That readers are expected to recognize such persons is clear from the casual nature of Paul's train of thought, which does not feel the need to identify these spiritual persons, the criteria by which they are selected for this role, or any of their recognized characteristics.

This text then implies a functional hierarchy, namely, every member can assume the function of a corrector, although not at the same time or under the same circumstances. And, when they do, an hierarchical relationship exists between them and those they correct, but only temporarily. But the context also emphasizes the common lot

---

[45] But used here to emphasize the responsibility of both ('Ἀλλήλων τὰ βάρη βαστάζετε. . . .).

[46] Compare the *hapax legomenon* προλαμβάνω (BAGD s.v. 2b, *detect, overtake, surprise* τινά *someone* pass.) in Gal 6:1 with its use in Philodemus' *On Frank Criticism* fr. 56.1–3, where other community members (probably some of the "wise") might "discover" ("whether it appears. . . .") that the more advanced err with regard to perfect reasoning. See pp. 128–29, 132, and 135, above.

and responsibility of all, and the reciprocal nature of the practice. And, Paul is concerned with the inherent dangers of such a practice. The function of a corrector, dependent on his spiritual maturity, might thus open the door for a conceited attitude towards the immature. Paul accentuates, therefore, the responsibility of the mature and emphasizes that those who correct others must be gentle and not attach any further significance to their standing beyond its purpose of mending the ways of those at fault.[47]

This ends our survey of the evidence for Pauline psychagogy. We are now in a position to define more closely "psychagogic activity" in contradistinction to the leadership roles of 1 Cor 12:8–10, 28–30 and Rom 12:6–8. The texts I have identified contain the following words: παρακαλέω (παράκλησις),[48] νουθετέω (νουθεσία),[49] ἀνα/διακρίνω,[50] καταρτίζω,[51] οἰκοδομέω,[52] ἀναπαύω,[53] στηρίζω,[54] παραμυθέομαι,[55] βαστάζω,[56] ἀναπληρόω,[57] συμπαρακαλέω,[58] εὐψυχέω,[59] and

---

[47] Hence the warning in Gal 6:1b and 3 against self-deception. Paul also emphasizes his own meekness as he assumes the role of a corrective father in 2 Cor 10:1. See pp. 323–24, below.

[48] For παρακαλέω, see 1 Thess 2:12; 3:2, 7; 4:1, 18; 5:11, 14; 2 Thess 2:7, 17; 3:12; Phil 4:2; 1 Cor 1:10; 4:16; 14:31; 16:15–16; 2 Cor 1:4, 6; 2:7, 8; 5:20; 6:1; 7:6, 7, 13; 8:6; 10:1; 13:11; Rom 12:1, 8; 15:30; 16:17; Tit 1:9; Col 4:8; Phm 10. For παράκλησις, see 1 Thess 2:3; 2 Thess 2:16; Phil 2:1; 1 Cor 14:3; 2 Cor 1:3, 4, 5, 6, 7; 2:7; 7:4, 6, 7, 13; 8:4, 17; Rom 15:4, 5; Phm 7. See C. J. Bjerkelund, *Parakalô: Form, Funktion und Sinn der parakalô-Sätze in den paulinischen Briefen* (Oslo), 1967; Schmitz-Stählin, "παρακαλέω παράκλησις," *TDNT* 5 (1967), pp. 773–99.

[49] Νουθετέω, 1 Thess 5:12, 14; 2 Thess 3:15; 1 Cor 4:14; Rom 15:14; Col 1:28; 3:16. See also Acts 20:31. Νουθεσία, 1 Cor 10:11; Eph 6:4; Tit 3:10. J. Behm, "νουθετέω, νουθεσία," *TDNT* 4 (1967), pp. 1019–22.

[50] Ἀνακρίνω, 1 Cor 4:7; 11:31; 14:24. Διακρίνω, 1 Cor 2:14–15; 4:3–4; 6:5; 9:3; 10:25, 27; 11:29, 31, 32. Cf. also 1 Cor 4:7; 14:29; and Rom 4:20; 14:23. See also the use of διάκρισις in 1 Cor 12:10 and Rom 14:1, and my discussion on pp. 222–23, below.

[51] 1 Thess 3:10; Gal 6:1; 2 Cor 13:9, 11. G. Delling, "ἄρτιος, κτλ," *TDNT* 1 (1964), pp. 475–76.

[52] 1 Thess 5:11; 1 Cor 10:23b; 14:3, 4, 5, 12, 17, 21; 2 Cor 10:8; 12:19; 13:10; Rom 14:19; 15:2.

[53] 1 Cor 16:17–18; 2 Cor 2:13; 7:13; Phm 7 and 20. For συναναπαύομαι, see Rom 15:32.

[54] 1 Thess 3:2, 13; 2 Thess 2:17; Rom 1:11; 1 Pet 5:10, God will καταρτίσει, στηρίξει, σθενώσει, θεμελιώσει; Luke 22:32; Acts 14:22; G. Harder, "στηρίζω, κτλ," *TDNT* 37 (1971), pp. 653–57.

[55] 1 Thess 2:12; 5:14; 1 Cor 14:3. G. Stählin, "παραμυθέομαι, κτλ," *TDNT* 5 (1967), pp. 816–18.

[56] Gal 6:2; Rom 15:1. See Deissmann, *Bible Studies*, pp. 102–104, 257.

[57] Phil 3:30; 1 Cor 16:17. See G. Delling, "ἀναπληρόω," *TDNT* 6 (1968), pp. 305–06.

[58] Rom 1:12.

[59] Phil 2:19.

ἀντέχεσθαι,⁶⁰ as well as ἀντίλημψις and κυβέρνησις.⁶¹ To these one should add ἐλέγχειν in 1 Cor 14:24 and the word σῴζειν to be discussed in chapter six.⁶² These terms are scattered throughout the Pauline corpus with the highest concentration in 1 Thessalonians, Romans and the Corinthian correspondence.⁶³

Interestingly, when compared to the hortatory terms in Philodemus' *On Frank Criticism* and Clement's *Pedagogue*,⁶⁴ hortatory blaming terms in the Pauline corpus are few in number. The psychagogy Paul attempts to implement in his communities is then not of the harsher sort. Paul specifically rejects the severity of the Corinthians' use of ἐπιτιμία, which probably included harsh rebuke or censure, and suggests that the Corinthians avoid a community member who continues to be a λοίδορος.⁶⁵ He also rejects a psychagogy which destroys the weak (Rom 14:15; 1 Cor 8). But Paul, as we shall later see, expects members to use νουθεσία (Rom 15:14; 1 Thess 5:14) and correction of a harsher type in their psychagogy and does so himself throughout 1 and 2 Corinthians.

None of the above terms occur in the lists of 1 Cor 12:8-10, 28-30 or 14:6. But 1 Cor 14:26 mentions ψαλμός, the psychagogic effect of which I noted, and Rom 12:8 refers to ὁ παρακαλῶν and ὁ ἐλεῶν

---

⁶⁰ 1 Thess 5:14. See *On Frank Criticism*, fr. 5.7.
⁶¹ 1 Cor 12:28. Cf. also Acts 20:35, δεῖ ἀντιλαμβάνεσθαι τῶν ἀσθενούντων. Ἀντίλημψις is functionally equivalent to ἀντέχεσθαι (1 Thess 5:14) and βοήθεια. See *On Frank Criticism*, frs. 18.5; 43.7; 67.8-9; and 86.7.
⁶² For σῴζειν, see 1 Cor 5:5; 7:16a; 9:22b; and 10:33; Rom 11:14; 1 Tim 4:16; Js 5:20. For ἐλέγχειν, see Tit 1:9, 13, and p. 198, above.
⁶³ Eleven of these terms occur in the Corinthian correspondence (i.e., παρακαλέω, νουθετέω, νουθεσία, ἀνακρίνω, διακρίνω, οἰκοδομέω, παραμυθέομαι, ἀναπληρόω, ἐλέγχειν, ἀντίλημψις, and κυβερνήσεις in 1 Cor, and παρακαλέω, παράκλησις, καταρτίζω, οἰκοδομέω, ἀναπαύω, and in 2 Cor), nine in Romans (i.e., νουθετέω, ἀνακρίνω, διακρίσις, οἰκοδομέω, στηρίζω, βαστάζω, συμπαρακαλέω, παρακαλῶν, ἐλεῶν), seven in the Thessalonian correspondence (i.e., νουθετέω, παρακαλέω, καταρτίζω, οἰκοδομέω, στηρίζω, παραμυθέομαι, and ἀντέχεσθαι in 1 Thess, and νουθετέω and στηρίζω in 2 Thess). Two of these terms occur in Gal (i.e., καταρτίζω, βαστάζω), two in Phil (ἀναπληρόω, εὐψυχέω), and three in Phm (i.e., παρακαλέω, παράκλησις, ἀναπαύω). Most of these terms occur also in texts from the Pauline school, for example Eph, Col, Tit, and 1 and 2 Tim, as well as Heb.
⁶⁴ See p. 108 (fn. 28), above, on hortatory dissuasive terms in Philodemus and p. 123 (fn. 90) for hortatory persuasive terms. See p. 62 (fn. 31) above, on Clement of Alexandria.
⁶⁵ See 2 Cor 2:6; 1 Cor 5:11; 6:10. That a slanderous person is referred to in a vice list does not preempt Paul's statement of all significance with regard to the actual situation he is countering.

whose functions coincide with that of παρακαλέω and παραμυθέομαι.⁶⁶ I suggest that the reason why most of the psychagogic terms are not included in these lists is because Paul thought that every member should participate in a communal psychagogy. Or, alternatively, that the psychagogic functions had a wider dispersion in the community than those singled out in the above lists. This does not mean that all members had the same abilities with regard to psychagogy or were at the same level, having developed the same skills. Neither does it entail that "teaching," "prophecy," or "service," for example, excluded a "psychagogic function." The point is rather that the functions Paul singles out in the more stylized lists are examples of more limiting individual appropriations. The focus is thus not on how many members of the community ought to exercise any one particular function but rather on the variety of options available. The implication is (and this is explicitly stated in 1 Cor 12:29–30) that not all can assume any of the functions identified, at least, at any one given time. Both ἀντιλήμψεις and κυβερνήσεις are therefore left out of the repeated list in 1 Cor 12:29–30.

In light of the fourfold evidence discussed above, there is clear indication of a communal practice of mutual edification and correction, where the emphasis falls not on the person but the function of the charisma.⁶⁷ Pauline psychagogy then squares well with the functional nature of late Epicurean psychagogy. In both communities there is a wide dispersion of the mutual activity of edification, exhortation, and correction, which in the Pauline case probably demanded an openness similar to that which I documented among the Epicureans. Although we have not witnessed in Paul a practice of mutual confession of sins, Pauline correctional psychagogy more likely than not did benefit from such forthrightness. But we find in nascent form comparable practices and do not have to wait long before openness and the confession of sins becomes a valued aspect of the participatory psychagogy among some early Christian groups, as, for example, in the community practice reflected in James 5:14–20.⁶⁸

---

⁶⁶ Compare Rom 12.8 (ὁ ἐλεῶν ἐν ἱλαρότητι) with *On Frank Criticism*, fr. 43.4 (εὐφροσύνη).
⁶⁷ For "personal charisma" contrasted to "functional charisma," see W. Schlüchter, "Max Webers Analyse des antiken Christentums," in W. Schlüchter, ed., *Max Webers Sicht des antiken Christentums* (Frankfurt, 1985), pp. 11–71; and fn. 5, p. 186, above.
⁶⁸ On Js 5:14–20, see M. Dibelius, *James. A Commentary on the Epistle of James* (1975), 252–60. Such openness is envisaged among the "presbyters" in 1 Tim 5:19–20. See

As in Philodemus, these early Christian communities were also interested in not thwarting the progress of members as well as "bringing back" those who had "fallen" or "wandered away."[69] It now remains to explore some implications of the social relationships involved in such a practice, a relationship that both implies a certain authority and obedience, and concomitantly a twofold relationship of symmetry and asymmetry. In this, too, Pauline psychagogy squares well with that reflected in Philodemus' *On Frank Criticism*.

### 5.2.3 *Authority and obedience in Pauline psychagogy*

Authority is inherent both in nurture and correction; the guide's authority is particularly evident in corrective psychagogy but also needed in edificatory psychagogy. Interestingly, in 2 Corinthians, in a context in which at least part of the debate is over Paul's leadership qualifications, Paul claims that the aim of his authority is not severely to judge and punish but to build up. Paul's authorial voice speaks with force as he claims for himself power to destroy strongholds and arguments, being ready to punish every disobedience. He clinches his claim concerning his authority (ἐξουσία), stating, contrary to what one perhaps might expect, that it was given him "for building you up and not for destroying you."[70] There is a touch of accusation in Paul's remark since, as we shall later see, this is precisely

---

[*Did.* 4.14 ("You shall confess your failings in the assembly...."); 15.3 (Ἐλέγχετε δὲ ἀλλήλους); *Barn.* 19.12; 21.4. See also Clement's description of the services of loving friends: "One is able to beg your life from God, another to hearten you when sick, another to weep and lament in sympathy on your behalf before the Lord of all, another to teach some part of what is useful for salvation, another to give outspoken warning (ὁ δὲ νουθετῆσαι μετὰ παρρησίας), another friendly counsel, and all to love you truly, without guile... flattery or pretence" (*Who Is the Rich Person Who Will Be Saved?* 35).

[69] Philodemus, *On Frank Criticism*, frs. 58–60, 65. See Polycarp, *Phil.* 6.1, Presbyters should "bring back those who have wandered, caring for all the weak (ἐπισκεπτόμενοι πάντας ἀσθενεῖς), neglecting not the widow, orphan, or the poor"; 11.4 erring presbyters should be called back "as fallible and straying members, that you may make whole the body of you all. For in doing this you edify yourselves"; *1 Clem.* 59.4; *2 Clem.* 15.1; 19;1; 17.2, "Let us then help one another, and bring back those that are weak in goodness (τοὺς ἀσθενοῦντας ἀνάγειν περὶ τὸν ἀγαθόν), that we may all be saved, and convert and exhort one another." See also *Herm. Vis.* 1.3.1–2; *Man.* 8.10. For this and the next two sections below, see pp. 119–20 and 152–60, above.

[70] 2 Cor 10:3–6, 8, εἰς οἰκοδομὴν, καὶ οὐκ εἰς καθαίρεσιν ὑμῶν. Paul repeats the same in 2 Cor 13:9–10 and 12:19. The combination of "building up" and "destroying" is frequent in the OT (Isa 49.17; Jer 24.6; 31.28; 42.10; 45.41; Ezek 36.36; Psalms 28.5) descriptive both of God's dealing with his people and the prophets (J. Dupont, *Gnosis* (Paris, 1949), pp. 239–41). See pp. 315–24, below.

what he accuses the wise of in 1 Cor 8, namely, that their use of ἐξουσία in an attempt to reform the weak destroyed rather than built them up. In spite of the tense situation and clear threats on Paul's part that he might have to use even more severe measures, Paul emphasizes not his corrective authority but edificatory authority. Correction and edification are intertwined; authority is needed for both. A certain asymmetry is thus built into psychagogy which receives its sharpest focus in its corrective aspects but is present also in its edificatory aspects.

That Paul expects obedience from members to his authority is clear; not as clear, though, is that he expects members to acknowledge authority mutually among each other. Such authority, however, can be established from the practice of communal correction I drew attention to above. Two texts are explicit in their call for subordination of some members to others in the community, namely, 1 Thess 5:12-13 and 1 Cor 16:15-16.[71] The latter exhorts readers to "be subject to" such men as those of the household of Stephanas who had devoted themselves to the service of the saints, as well as to every fellow worker and laborer! The former text calls on members to respect "those who labor among you and guide you in the Lord and admonish you" and to esteem them very highly in love because of their work. The function of those in authority is of interest. Four (at least) are specified, namely, service, labor, guidance, and admonition. For my purposes, admonishing is most important.

Above I suggested that 1 Thess 5:14, with its exhortation to admonish the disorderly, gives evidence for the practice of mutual correction. That admonition is not solely the function of the προϊστάμενοι referred to in 5:12 is clear, since Paul's injunction in v. 14 is addressed to the ἀδελφοί in general, as it was also in Gal 6:1. Paul

---

[71] Similarly, the Philippians are urged to "honor" men like Epaphroditus, presumably because of his "risking his life to render me the service you could not give." Phil 2:29-30; cf. 1 Cor 16.17. For προϊστάμενος see Rom 12:8; Acts 20:35. On the possible connotations of προϊστάμενοι, see P. Millett, "Patronage and its avoidance in classical Athens," in *Patronage in Ancient Society*, ed. by A. Wallace-Hadrill (London/New York, 1990), pp. 33-35; W. Meeks, *The First Urban Christians* (1983), pp. 134, 58, 60, 79, 82. In 1 Pet 5:5 elders are exhorted to "tend the flock of God" and not to "lord over those in their charge" (1:14, 17, 22; 2:13, 18; 3:1). See Eph 5:21, "Be subject to one another out of reverence for Christ" (for the inclusive lists of addressees here, see 5:22-6:9) and Col 3:18-4:1. The injunction in *1 Clem.* 38.1-2, "let each be subject to his neighbour, according to the position granted to him," is followed by, "Let the strong care for the weak and let the weak reverence the strong."

urges the Thessalonians to "respect" those who admonish others. Admonition necessitates authority and submission; it implies an authoritative status. The one who admonishes has the right and duty to draw attention to and mend the fault of another. Such authority is also inherent in the process of "mending" and "judging" which, together with "admonishing," I identified as part of correctional psychagogy. The word παρακαλέω also implies the use of authority and such exhortation is one of the charisms community members could assume.[72] If correctional authority was exercised with severity, it could become destructive and lead to conditions of enmity or to the wounding of the one reprimanded by causing excessive grief (2 Cor 2:5-9).

2 Thessalonians, by contrast, reflects a fairly consistent Pauline tradition or a picture of the way in which it should ideally have operated.[73] Part of corrective psychagogy is to shame erring members into repentance through disassociation. Paul urges his readers to admonish the disorderly both in 1 and 2 Thessalonians. In 2 Thessalonians Paul recommends a certain distancing procedure from those who do not follow the received tradition and fall into "disorderly habits," similar to his injunction to the Corinthians with regard to "immoral men" in the community and to the Romans with regard to "those who stir up quarrel and lead others astray" and "seduce the mind of innocent people with smooth and specious words."[74] A little further on in the text (the) Paul (inist) becomes more explicit with regard to the procedure to be taken, its desired result, and mode of operation:

> 14) If anyone disobeys our instruction given by letter, mark him well, and have no dealings with him so that he may be ashamed. 15) Do not regard him as an enemy, but admonish him like a brother.[75]

---

[72] Rom 12:1, 8; 15:30; 16:17. See Dunn, *Word Biblical Commentary Romans 9-16*, p. 730.
[73] If 2 Thessalonians was written by Paul, as I suspect, my argument gains additional force. Cf R. Jewett, *The Thessalonian Correspondence* (Philadelphia, 1986), p. 17.
[74] 2 Thess 3:6 ("keep away from any brother who is living in idleness and not in accord with the tradition that you received from us)"; Rom 16:17; 1 Cor 5:9. See also 2 Tim 3:5.
[75] 2 Thess 3:14-15 ... τοῦτον σημειοῦσθε μὴ συναναμίγνυσθαι αὐτῷ, ἵνα ἐντραπῇ. καὶ μὴ ἐχθρὸν ἡγεῖσθε, ἀλλὰ νουθετεῖτε ὡς ἀδελφόν. Polycarp advises that erring presbyters should not be regarded as enemies but should be called back as fallible and straying members (*Phil.* 11.4). See also Tit 3:10-11, "After a first and second admonition have nothing more to do with anyone who causes divisions...." and note *Did.* 15.3, "Let none speak with any who has done a wrong to his neighbour, nor let him hear a word from you until he repents."

The Thessalonians are instructed to take special notice of or "mark well" the disobedient one. The term Paul uses here, namely, σημειόω, is the same used in *On Frank Criticism* fr. 57.4–5, for the diagnosis of the "sickness" of the young. Philodemus uses here the analogy of the work of a physician on severe cases and the Epicurean psychagogue's treatment of racalcitrant students! Paul similarly suggests that the disobedient one should be "diagnosed" correctly. After such a diagnosis a prognosis ensues, which in this instance includes a process of shunning. The brother is also to be admonished in a friendly fashion. The disobedient one should not be treated as an enemy but as a brother. Such treatment entails admonition and shunning which aims at shaming the disobedient brother into repentance.[76] This implies a twofold relationship of symmetry and asymmetry; the former is spotlighted by the fraternal imagery and the latter by the enforcement procedures used to secure obedience.

### 5.2.4 *Symmetry and/or asymmetry in Pauline psychagogy?*

I have emphasized that an advisory status requires a degree of superiority or asymmetrical relationship; also, in a relationship of equality, an advisory status is never unambiguous since the symmetrical aspect of the relationship clashes with the authority required by the advisory status.[77] Among members of the Pauline communities, and in Paul's own relationship with them, both types of relationships are present in edificatory and corrective psychagogy. Which relationship is accentuated depends on the use of authority; when the slumbering authority is activated, particularly in corrective psychagogy, a symmetrical relationship becomes asymmetrical. Paul as a "father" and a "brother"/"friend", displays this twofold structural relation I am postulating for him as well as for other members of the community in a psychagogic context.

I thus deduce a twofold structure in Pauline psychagogy, namely,

---

[76] The aim of Pauline correctional psychagogy is to shame erring members into repentance through blame and disassociation. The purpose of Paul's "severe letter" sent to the Corinthians was "to wound [them] into repentance" (2 Cor 7:8–13). See pp. 315–17, below. See further my discussion on 1 Cor 5:9 and 11, on the purpose of association and disassociation in Pauline psychagogy (pp. 260–62) and on Paul's stringent approach in 2 Cor (cf. 2:9; 7:15; 10:5–6; pp. 315–24).

[77] This is succinctly captured by Simone Weil: "When anyone wishes to put himself under a human being or consents to be subordinated to him, there is no trace of friendship. Racine's Pylades is not the friend of Orestes. There is no friendship where there is inequality...." in E. Welty and R. A. Sharp (eds.), *The Norton Book of Friendship* (New York/London, 1991), p. 526.

a symmetrical structural axis, upon which members are differentiated as brothers or sisters, or friends, and an asymmetrical axis between the father of the community and its members and between mature and immature ones. Sibling relations are then not devoid of an hierarchical axis.[78] Thus when a "brother" corrects and admonishes another "brother," their egalitarian relationship recedes into the background and a hierarchical relationship comes into the foreground. This is true even in the case when equals criticize and correct each other as equals, knowing that their positions can always be reversed.[79] Which relationship is accentuated depends on the function any one assumes on a given occasion. Sometimes a member is in a position to admonish others; on another occasion the same individual is admonished by others. Such a rotational practice is, I submit, the reason why some second century Gnostics justifiably found affinity with Paul in their emphasis on the rotation of responsibilities.[80]

Although my study is not concerned with social status, it is important not to lose sight of the possible ramifications of social stratification for our study.[81] We have seen some of the tensions in psychagogy centering around the ambiguous status of the mature guide. A clash might easily occur when a psychagogue of a lower social status attempts to guide another of a higher social status. It is not difficult to imagine that Paul's directives to participate in common exhortation and correction could easily become a source of tension in a status-conscious community, despite its probable intended function

---

[78] Despite claims to the contrary. Cf. N. Peterson, *Rediscovering Paul: Philemon and the Sociology of Paul's Narrative World* (Philadelphia, 1985), p. 158.

[79] As was the case in Philodemus' *On Frank Criticism* cols. 8b–9a, where the wise benefited from reciprocal criticism. See pp. 130–31, above.

[80] See E. H. Pagels, *The Gnostic Gospels* (New York, 1989), pp. 33–43; idem, *The Gnostic Paul. Gnostic Exegesis of the Pauline Letters* (Philadelphia, 1975), pp. 53–94, 111. For communal authority and "spiritual power" and the development from diversified forms of church leadership to a more unified hierarchy of church office in early Christianity, see H. von Campenhausen, *Kirchliches Amt und Geistliche Vollmacht in den ersten drei Jahrhunderten* (Tübingen: J. C. B. Mohr (Paul Siebeck), 1963), pp. 32–134. For such "rotational psychagogy" in Philodemus, refer to pp. 124–32, above. Plutarch gives a succinct description of such a practice, advising that it is "better to bear patiently with a friend who affects to offer admonition; for if later he errs himself, and requires admonition, this very fact, in a certain way, gives our frank speaking a chance to speak frankly" (*How to Tell a Flatterer from a Friend* 72F; 74E). Compare Isocrates, *Nicocles or the Cyprians* 57; *Antidosis* 289–90; and *1 Clem.* 38.1–2. Cf. 1 Pet 4:10, "... serve one another with whatever gift each of you has received."

[81] Gerd Theissen has demonstrated that issues of social status exacerbated the tensions among the Corinthians (*The Social Setting of Pauline Christianity. Essays on Corinth* (Philadelphia, 1982).

of encouraging greater social integration. This would have been so if that directive cut across the lines of existing social status, for example, when a slave or a freedman or a person from the merchant class felt he was entitled to admonish another member of a higher status, e.g., a Gaius, a Crispus, a Stephanas, an Erastus, or a Prisca and Aquila, all of whom we know to have been of a relatively high social status.[82] More likely, Paul's directives did not cut across existing social barriers.[83] Neither possibility can, however, be positively supported by the internal evidence.

But this should not deter us from postulating a scenario based on a reasonably informed speculation with regard to possible tensions in Pauline psychagogy. Firstly, there was probably tension inherent simply in the fact that it included active participation of members of such diverse status as masters and slaves, free and unfree, men and women.[84] Secondly, a source of tension appears in the classification of different types of people contingent on different aptitudes or dispositions. This classification, thirdly, spotlights the tensions inherent in psychagogy particularly when issues of superiority and inferiority and those of equality and inequality are involved.

Plutarch's essay *On Brotherly Love* reveals a similar asymmetrical axis in a symmetrical social structure. Honor and power due to nature, fortune, age, and even sex, introduce an hierarchical axis into an egalitarian relationship. Plutarch works from *de facto* distinctions between biological brothers and/or sisters, and describes the various mechanisms which can beneficially reduce tensions between the two. Plutarch advises the superior to take his brothers as partners in those respects in which he is considered to be superior and adopt them into his friendship; secondly, he should

> make manifest to them neither haughtiness nor disdain, but rather, by deferring to them and conforming his character to theirs, to make his superiority secure from envy and to equalize, so far as this is attainable, the disparity of his fortune by his moderation of spirit.[85]

Plutarch identifies the emotions displayed by the older and the younger

---

[82] Theissen, ibid., 94–95; Meeks, *The First Urban Christians*, pp. 55–63.

[83] See *Barn.* 19.4 ("You shall not respect persons when reproving the faults of someone") and 1 Tim 5:1 ("Don't rebuke an elder, but exhort [him]"—πρεσβυτέρῳ μὴ ἐπιπλήξῃς ἀλλὰ παρακάλει).

[84] See A. C. Wire, *The Corinthian Women Prophets* (Minneapolis, 1990), p. 270, for bibliography on women in the Pauline churches. Cf. *Patrologia graeca* 21:644B.

[85] Plutarch, *On Brotherly Love* 484D. See 480F, 484C–486A and 492D.

brother, arrogance and neglect among the former, contempt, envy and jealousy, among the latter.[86] The older should be solicitous and admonish the younger as a comrade. Among the many honors which it is fitting that the young render to their elders, obedience is most highly esteemed! In light of the various social occasions where invidious comparisons can be made, it is of no slight importance to resist the spirit of contentiousness, practising the art of mutual concession.[87]

Both Plutarch and Paul take a functional approach to existing inequalities, the former using the analogy of different functions of unequal fingers and the latter that of the different functions of parts of the same body. The terminology of weakness and strength suggests itself in such a context;[88] some "parts" of the Corinthian "body" are thus "weaker" than others (1 Cor 12:22). Paul not only uses the terminology of the "weak" and the "strong" (or "wise" and "powerful") to characterize members of his communities but also such terms as a "child" and a "perfect (or full-grown) person."[89] Such characterizations underline differences between people based on their maturity and draw attention to a basic asymmetrical axis in their social relationships. The point of both the finger and body analogy is, though, that inequality does not entail inferiority-superiority.[90] Weakness in one area does not necessarily mean inferiority as a person or weakness in other areas. The "weak" and "strong" remain different but proportionally equal; acceptance and accommodation is the norm.

"Proportional friendship" in which unequals, such as two brothers or a father and a son, might in friendship become equals proportionally,

---

[86] These are the reasons for quarrels between brothers. Ibid., 486B–491C. See also 484F and 485B–C.

[87] Ibid., 487A–C; 488A. For a similar reasoning as in Plutarch see *1 Clem.* 37.1–38.2.

[88] See Athenaeus description of the body of a polyp: "though the other parts are very strong, the neck is weak" (*Sophists at Dinner* 317D).

[89] 1 Cor 3:1–3. See fn. 16 on p. 189, above.

[90] Plutarch, *On Brotherly Love* 486A. Plutarch describes the same social scenario as Theissen's "love-patriarchalism" in the proto-Christian communities, namely, an equalization in light of *de facto* social inequality. Social asymmetry prevailed and social institutions remained intact but inequities were ameliorated by the transfusion of a spirit of concern, respect, and personal solicitude. Theissen warns us, however, that Paul's "revaluation of all norms of social rank and dominance" had no revolutionizing consequences in the social realm (*The Social Setting of Pauline Christianity. Essays on Corinth*, pp. 138–39, 290–94). E. A. Judge is inclined to deduce the contrary: "St. Paul as a Radical Critic of Society," *Interchange* 16 (1974), p. 197. See M. I. Finley, *Ancient Slavery and Modern Ideology* (Penguin Books, 1980), pp. 120–122; G. E. M. de Ste. Croix, *The Class Struggle in the Ancient Greek World, from the Archaic Age to the Arab Conquests* (Ithaca, 1981), pp. 107–08, 419–21.

without stepping out of their otherwise fixed social roles, also postulates an hierarchical and egalitarian axis in the same relationship.[91] The same is true in participatory psychagogy among friends. The asymmetry evidenced between the mature guide and those whom he guides, is alleviated, not obliterated, in Paul's insistence on reciprocity. But such a symmetry fades in light of admonition and correction and the lack of emphasis on hierarchy in Paul clashes with the basic asymmetry of psychagogy. Thus both symmetrical and asymmetrical relations are intact in the community and the relation in evidence at any given time is contingent on such functional factors as admonition and praise.

When Paul, or any member of the community, assumes the cloak of a "corrector," an attendant factor is the asymmetrical aspect of the relationship. But when Paul assumes the cloak of an encouraging and comforting fellow-worker and brother, who through his fraternal imagery attempts to implement and inculcate a degree of comradery, the symmetrical relationship is emphasised. There is then a twofold relationship of symmetry and asymmetry present in the psychagogic practices of mutual edification, exhortation, and correction.

The practices discussed above presuppose, then, as did those witnessed in Philodemus' *On Frank Criticism*, intellectual, spiritual, and moral distinctions among people, which in turn indicate different aptitudes and the possibility of growth and relapse. The mature are to care for, succor, and, if need be, correct the immature. They evaluate the behavior and beliefs of the immature with regard to the norms of the community. With such a function comes the possibility of self conceit and humiliation of those of lesser standing, precisely the issue Paul warns against in Gal 6:1–3. Presupposed in Paul's discussion are both a basic asymmetry in light of judgment and evaluation, and concerns for the caricature of such a practice. Such an account would best seem to fit the fluid nature of Pauline and Philodemean psychagogy.

---

[91] See Aristotle's discussion of friendship between unequals in his *Nicomachean Ethics* 1158b11–1159b24. Cf. 1158b23–28; 1159a33–1159b2; 1163b11–12; and *Eudemian Ethics* 1241b25–1243b39. There are, Aristotle explains, two sorts of equality, numerical and proportional. Examples of proportional friendship, which emphasizes that love should be proportional, corresponding to the friend's worth, are aristocratic and royal partnerships, and the friendship of a father and a son. Examples of numerical equality is the partnership of democracy and the friendship of comrades and brothers.

## A Modified Hypothesis

The first part of the hypothesis is substantiated by the evidence: Paul did envisage an active "participation of members in the evaluation and correction of each other through mutual edification, admonition and correction" (See pp. 185-86, above). The second part of the hypothesis—it was particularly the function of the more mature members to evaluate and pass judgement on the immature—must be somewhat modified. Some texts do substantiate this second part (Gal 6:1-5; 1 Cor 2:15). But in light of texts that emphasize the mutuality of admonition, we must deduce that the activity of evaluation was not appropriate exclusively for advanced members, if by that we understand some recognized social role among limited members of the community. We must instead recognize that every member could theoretically assume such a role. The asymmetry implicit in such an activity is functional, non-permanent, and non-institutional. This follows because of the twofold foci of asymmetry and symmetry and because of the two-level relationship between members, namely, an egalitarian and hierarchical one, and also because of the attendant recognition that every member may err and thus need correction and admonition. As among the Epicureans, the authority latent in psychagogy and the status of a "psychagogue" is in lieu of the "office" itself. The authority in question is not attributed or ascribed to an office but is achieved or acquired.[92] The achieved authority is then both personal and functional![93]

### 5.3 *Pauline Communal Psychagogy and the Function of Romans 14:1–15:14*

I have demonstrated the presence of an asymmetrical relationship among people in the Pauline communities, evident above all in the

---

[92] J. Pitt-Rivers, "Honour and Social Status," in *Honour and Shame: The Values of Mediterranean Society* (ed. J. G. Peristiay; Chicago, 1966), pp. 21-23; and B. J. Malina, *The New Testament World. Insights from Cultural Anthropology* (Atlanta, Georgia, 1981), pp. 29-30.
[93] For authority and obedience in Epicurean rotational psychagogy, see pp. 152-60, above. My thesis of the demonstrative similarities between the Epicurean and the Pauline communities is at variance with G. Theissen's claim that among the cults of the ancient world only early Christians and Jews formed a "diastratic solidarity" and "diasporal cohesion," displaying a structure that cuts across social strata or classes and geographical regions (*Social Reality and the Early Christians* [Minneapolis,

practice of mutual correction and judgement. Here emphasis falls on human distinctions; some are more mature than others. Paul, however, attempts to alleviate the possible tensions of such an asymmetry (cf. Gal 6:1–3) and emphasizes the responsibility of the mature. It is my contention that the above social practice of communal psychagogy is presupposed in Paul's discussion in Romans 14–15. Participatory admonitory psychagogy is the substructure of Paul's discourse. An asymmetrical relationship between the "weak" and "powerful" is assumed but Paul emphasizes the responsibility of the latter and the need of accommodation for both. Paul's major concern is to correct the strong who thwart the progress of the weak and destroy them (14:15). In and through his own psychagogic guidance Paul indirectly guides and attempts to teach members of his communities to implement a certain form of mutual psychagogy. This psychagogic metatext is the best perspective from which to view Rom 14:1–15:14 and 1 Cor 8:1–11:1, to be discussed in the final chapter of this book.[94] Before dicussing the former text, I shall reflect on its larger literary context and introduce my hypothesis of its function and that of 1 Cor 8:1–11:1.

Both texts yield evidence of matters relating to psychagogic practice in ancient reformatory ethics. In such contexts the terms "weakness" and "strength" are used to underline different levels of maturity among people. Paul is critical of the mature's grieving and "destruction" of the tender and immature "students". What Paul reacts to, I submit, in both texts is the "forceful" or misguided leading of the mature which instead of "saving" the "weak", excessively grieved and "destroyed" them (Rom 14:15; 1 Cor 8:11); the mature should rather care for and save the insecure and carry their weaknesses. Both the "wise" in Corinth and the "powerful" in Rome had attempted to rationally persuade the weak of the untenability of their position or educate them on the basis of their rational stance towards religion and morality. The mature not only disagreed with the inferences drawn by the weak on the basis of their common faith in one God but actively attempted to persuade them of the "illogicality"

---

1992], pp. 213–19). My thesis is also at variance with Judge's claim that Paul is promoting a *"new* kind of community education for adults" (my emphasis). See p. 12 (fn. 24), above, and p. 336, below.

[94] Literary theorists use the word "metatext" in order to describe the believable cultural context one construes for any given text. See R. Scholes, *Protocols of Reading* (New Haven, 1989), pp. 1–49.

of their position or to sway their opinions. Such a reading suggests a moral and non-apocalyptic understanding of the terms "salvation" and "destruction" used by Paul in these contexts.

Although there are distinct differences between Romans 14:1–15:14 and 1 Cor 8:1–11:1, such as the nature of the issues addressed, I maintain that there are not only clear similarities between the two but that Paul's concern is the same in both, namely, to prevent the undermining of an immature person's commitment to his faith. The differences between these texts should not be pressed too hard either, since both address problems relating to the rational worship of one God in contradistinction to idol worship in which those more rationally oriented attempt to correct the irrational beliefs of the weak; in the Roman text these matters are discussed in a general way relating to questions of "profane" food and whether one day is different from another, but in 1 Corinthians 8 the specific issue relates to "idol-sacrificed food."[95] Both texts reveal different implications of a belief in one God among people of different psychological dispositions or debate between two types of people regarding what constitutes divinely sanctioned behavior. The weak, unlike the wise and powerful, believed that the eating of food, especially meat offered to idols, had negative consequences for their standing before God. Paul attempts to alleviate possible tensions in light of an apparent asymmetry because of different levels of maturity and emphasizes especially the responsibility of the mature who should be considerate towards the immature.

In the larger literary context of both texts, Paul presents ethical guidelines for communal psychagogy based on the principle of adaptability. Paul contextualizes the psychagogic practices of both communities in an ethic of adaptability using the metaphor of members as parts of a body each having different abilities to help others. Considerateness and affable behavior is not only advocated towards people of the same community but also towards those outside the community. This twofold perspective is evident in the larger context of 1 Cor 5:1–11:1, as well as that of Rom 12–15. The miscellaneous

---

[95] The problem of idol worship and food offered to idols is clearly present in 1 Cor 8 and 10. Idol worship is also present in the larger context of Rom 14:1–15:14 which addresses the correct form of worship (cf. 12:1) in a gentile community in contradistinction to the ungodly and unacceptable worship of idols (Rom 1). Cf. Stanley K. Stowers, *A Rereading of Romans. Justice, Jews, & Gentiles* (New Haven: Yale University Press, 1994), pp. 317–18.

exhortations in 12:9–21 do fit the ethic of adaptability, especially those which relate to the topic of friendship and those which urge the readers to meet other people on their level by sharing in the emotional experiences of others rather than being haughty. Adaptation is here also related to the questions of associating with outsiders, whether they are the socially humble, "enemies" or the ruling authorities.[96]

In his psychagogic directives, Paul urges the mature to aid the weak instead of pleasing themselves. The command to love one's neighbor sums up the ethic of adaptability, an ethic which is, in Paul's view, simply an extension of Christ's all-accommodating behavior. Paul thus urges his readers to imitate Christ, for "Christ did not please himself."[97] In both contexts Paul discourages the mature's concern with self-mastery and moral achievement, both their own and that of others, and advocates behavior based on an ethic of adaptability which should accommodate the (conflicting) views of people of different levels of maturity. Below I discuss the above issues further as they appear in the Roman text also providing suggestive remarks and a proleptic reading of 1 Cor 8:1–11:1, to be fully discussed in chapter six.

We begin with two points. Firstly, when Paul says in Romans 14:13a, "Therefore, cease judging one another," is he suggesting that an earlier instituted activity of mutual judgment among the Thessalonians, Galatians, and Corinthians (cf. 1 Thess 5:12–14; Gal 6:1–5; 1 Cor 2:14–16; 5:1–13; 6:1–7; and 2 Cor 2:5–10) should not be practiced among members of the Roman community? Our query is: Does Paul suggest that he wants an earlier instituted activity of mutual evaluation and correction to cease? Or, to put it differently, did he wish to abrogate the hierarchical, asymmetrical axis of the relationship between members in light of divine adjudication? Secondly, if

---

[96] See Rom 12:9–10, 13–15, 16, 17–21, and 13:1–7. In a context emphasizing issues both of adaptability and association, Paul underscores the importance of associating with the socially humble. See Rom 12:16, "Do not be haughty but readily associate with the humble." In Rom 16:17–19, Paul gives advice regarding the way in which community members should behave towards those who destroy the moral fabric of the community. This topic, as we shall see, is a major concern of Paul in 1 Corinthians 5:1–11:1. See pp. 247–49, 254–64, and 268–72, below.

[97] Rom 13:8–10; 15:1–3, 7–8; 1 Cor 9:21–22; 10:33–11:1; 13. Christ has adapted himself to the condition of others, thus being the prime example of affable and obliging behavior. This Paul emphasizes on several occasions (cf. Phil 2:5–11; Gal 4:3–5, and pp. 254, 257–58, and 294, below) and does so also in these contexts (cf. 1 Cor 10:32–11:1; Rom 15:3 and 8, Χριστὸν διάκονον γεγενῆσθαι περιτομῆς...).

νουθετέω (Rom 15:14) means "to put in the mind, instruct or instill sense,"[98] we should not be reluctant to see a pedagogical agenda in Paul's advice nor exclude all "strengthening of the weak" in the sense of growth in understanding and belief.

In Paul's view mature members should evaluate their erring co-members. His exhortation, "therefore cease judging one another" (Rom 14:13a), does not aim at abrogating that practice but attempts rather to rectify a social praxis gone awry. This is done by giving it a metaphysical underpinning by referring to God's impartiality and final judgment. Judgment among members should continue but in a way that guards against mutual caricature and arrogance. In light of Paul's remark in Rom 14:13a, we must rather ask the question, "What kind or type of judgment is excluded?" The section where Paul's admonition occurs is clearly framed by two parallel imperatives (14:1, "Welcome those who are weak with respect to faith"; 15:7, "welcome, therefore, one another"). Many view 15:8–13 as a natural continuation of 14:1–15:7 and see a clear break between 15:13 and 14.[99] I suggest that we include verse fourteen in this larger unit and interpret Paul's statement there ("You are able to admonish one another") in light of his discussion of the weak and the powerful. This larger unit is then a concrete example of how Paul envisages the praxis of νουθεσία.[100]

This allows us to connect Rom 14:1–15:14 with my discussion of the admonitory practices above. But νουθετέω is not the only resonance between this text and the communal psychagogy I have discussed. Rom 14:19 and 15:2 treat edification, and Rom 15:1 recalls Gal 6:1–3. Both use the verb βαστάζω and contrast two "types" of

---

[98] For the etymology of "admonition" see Clement, *Ped.* 94.2 (146, 5–6 Stählin-Treu), τὸ δὲ ἐτυμολογεῖται, ἡ νουθέτησις, νοῦ ἐνθεματισμός. . . .

[99] A few examples will suffice: W. A. Meeks, "Judgment and the Brother: Romans 14.1–15.13," in G. F. Hawthorne with O. Betz (eds.), *Tradition and Interpretation in the New Testament. Essays in Honor of E. Earle Ellis* (W. B. Eerdmans, 1987), pp. 290–300; L. E. Keck, "Christology, Soteriology, and the Praise of God (Romans 15.7–13)," in R. T. Fortna and B. R. Gaventa (eds.), *The Conversation Continues. Studies in Paul & John in Honor of J. Louis Martyn* (Nashville, 1990), pp. 85–97; J. D. G. Dunn, *Romans 9–16. Word Biblical Commentary. Vol. 38B.* (Dallas, TX, 1988), pp. 853–54; C. E. B. Cranfield, *A Critical and Exegetical Commentary on the Epistle to the Romans* (Edinburgh, 1979), 2.699, 748–49.

[100] After the above statement Paul reflects on his rather bold reminder in the letter (15:15a, "I have written you rather boldly. . . .) and on the reasons for his delay of coming to Rome (15:15b–22). This section continues Paul's introductory remarks in 1:8–15.

persons: "the spiritual one" and the "erring one," on the one hand, and "the strong" and "the powerless," on the other hand. Rom 15:1 accentuates the obligation of the strong, with whom Paul identifies, "We, the powerful, ought to carry the weaknesses of the powerless." The injunction in Gal 6:2, "Bear one another's burdens," is more general but follows the example given of the spiritual ones correcting the erring one. These resonances, together with the recurrent use of words on the κριν- root, show that this section in Romans relates to correctional psychagogy and presupposes the social practice of communal psychagogy which I documented in the previous section.[101]

I have noted the two parallel imperatives of Rom 14:1 and 15:7 ("Welcome those who are weak with respect to faith"; "welcome, therefore, one another") which frame Paul's argumentation in this section. The latter reveals that the discussion in 14:1–15:6 has implication for all of Paul's readers; the former that Paul's injunction is addressed to those he calls "the powerful" in 15:1. Although Paul, as we shall see, gives specific guidelines for both character types (14:3–13a), namely the "weak" and "powerful," and urges both to accept each other as he begins the closing remarks of this section (15:7), his main concern is the obligations of the "powerful" in light of the problem of the insecure (14:13b–15:6; cf. 14:1–2, 22–23, 13b–21): "We, the powerful, ought to carry the weaknesses of those who are without strength" (15:1).

The exhortation in Rom 15:1 immediately follows Paul's argument in chapter 14, framed by an *inclusio* in 14:1–2 and 22–23:

v. 1  Τὸν δὲ ἀσθενοῦντα τῇ πίστει προσλαμβάνεσθε,
       μὴ εἰς διακρίσεις διαλογισμῶν.
v. 2  ὃς μὲν πιστεύει φαγεῖν πάντα, ὁ δὲ ἀσθενῶν λάχανα ἐσθίει.
v. 22 σὺ πίστιν [ἣν] ἔχεις κατὰ σεαυτὸν ἔχε ἐνώπιον τοῦ θεοῦ.
       μακάριος ὁ μὴ κρίνων ἑαυτὸν ἐν ᾧ δοκιμάζει·
v. 23 ὁ δὲ διακρινόμενος ἐὰν φάγῃ κατακέκριται, ὅτι οὐκ ἐκ πίστεως·
       πᾶν δὲ ὃ οὐκ ἐκ πίστεως ἁμαρτία ἐστίν.

---

[101] For terms of the κριν- root, see 14:1, 3, 5, 10, 13, 22, 23 (cf. δοκιμ- in 14:18, 22). Admonition (15:14) is a form of judgment which requires evaluation (compare Rom 14:23 and Tit 3:10–11, αὐτοκατάκριτος). I have spoken of Pauline psychagogy as "correctional" and "edificational." The former draws attention to the evaluative and corrective aspects of psychagogy, the latter to nurture and relief. The edificatory and corrective aspects are two interrelated dimensions of ancient "psychagogy."

The *inclusio* gives poignancy to Paul's prodding in chapter 14 and has implication for our understanding of what is enclosed. Here we find a closely knit argumentation focusing on two character types and their relationship in view of different interpretations of the divine sanction of human behavior.[102] The *inclusio* shows that Paul is concerned mainly with the one "who is weak in faith" (v. 1), called "the one who doubts" in v. 23. This "weak one" eats only vegetables (v. 2) and is "condemned" if he eats [meat] because it is not "of faith" (v. 22). Such a person fails and stands condemned since he is not convinced of the validity of such behavior.[103] The one who does not condemn himself by what he approves is on the other hand happy (v. 22b). Although such a one "has faith to eat everything" (v. 2) he should keep to himself the "faith he has" before God (v. 22a). Such persons should accept the "weak in faith" and not attempt to persuade him of his ill founded reasonings (v. 1).

In Rom 14:1 Paul urges the strong "to welcome those who are weak in faith, not for judgments about reasonings." That the encoded readers are the "strong" is clear from the description of those the readers are urged to accept as "weak in belief" and the activity advised against, "not for judgments about reasonings."[104] The weak person eats (only) vegetables as opposed to someone who believes he may eat "everything." The contrast is continued in vv. 3–4, identifying the attitude of both, with a specific injunction given to each, "those who eat should not despise those who abstain" and "those who abstain should not pass judgment on those who eat."

After these injunctions, Paul focuses on the weak one in verse 4, "You—who are you (to be) judging someone else's house slave?" The addressee is the encoded weak, the person who only eats vegetables, as is clear from verse ten where the address is repeated, first with an addressee in view who judges a brother, then with an addressee in view who despises a brother. The two are distinguished by their

---

[102] That the main question is a certain eating practice can be seen from Paul's argumentation in chapter 14. The *inclusio* refers to the question of eating and not eating (vv. 2, 23a) and is in focus as Paul addresses the problem that the acting out of one's strongly held beliefs might have on another (vv. 15–21; cf. also vv. 3, 6b). Whether one day is different from another is referred to in vv. 5–6a.

[103] Interpreting πᾶν δὲ ὃ οὐκ ἐκ πίστεως ἁμαρτία ἐστίν in v. 23b in light of Paul's remark in v. 22b, μακάριος ὁ μὴ κρίνων ἑαυτὸν ἐν ᾧ δοκιμάζει. For the same approach in 1 Cor 8:7–11, see pp. 284–89, below.

[104] See pp. 222–23 below on Rom 14:1b.

attitude towards the other.[105] Verse ten speaks then against the facile equations of the respective attitudes identified in verse three.[106] Paul has in 14:1–4 identified two types of persons, one characterized as "weak with respect to belief" (v. 1), the other later identified as the "powerful" (15:1). Paul has also identified their attitude towards each other which in both cases should be modified; the strong should not despise the weak and the weak should not pass judgement on the strong.[107] With the imperatives in 14:3 Paul condemns both attitudes but goes on in v. 4 to concentrate on the judgmental.

After having urged both types of persons to abandon their respective attitudes, Paul refers to another issue which divides the two: "Someone judges one day to be more important than another, someone else judges every day to be alike" (v. 5a). Paul does not dwell on this matter except to stress that "each has to be fully convinced in his own mind" (v. 5b) and if one does have a preference for one day over another it should be for one's master (v. 6a). The same applies to the matter of eating which Paul returns to in v. 6b.[108] Before addressing both persons in v. 10 and identifying their respective attitudes again, Paul underlines their responsibility towards each other (v. 7) and accountability towards their common master (vv. 8–9). Paul repeats the latter again after his identification of the two, now with scriptural support (v. 11) and an inferential connective (ἄρα [οὖν])

---

[105] Both in v. 3 (ὁ ἐσθίων τὸν μὴ ἐσθίοντα μὴ ἐξουθενείτω, ὁ δὲ μὴ ἐσθίων τὸν ἐσθίοντα μὴ κρινέτω) and v. 10 (σὺ δὲ τί κρίνεις τὸν ἀδελφόν σου; ἢ καὶ σὺ τί ἐξουθενεῖς τὸν ἀδελφόν σου;).

[106] Contra Meeks who finds the identification of the addressee in v. 4 as the encoded weak unlikely for two reasons. Firstly, "the next sentence (v. 5) uses κρίνει on both sides of the antithesis." Secondly, the "two verbs in v. 3, ἐξουθενεῖν and κρίνειν, are equivalent, though the nuances are appropriate to the two sides, and they are taken up again in the second apostrophe, v. 10, which balances v. 4." I address Meek's first reason in the text. Meeks' second reason does not hold much weight, since, even though Paul uses the verb κρίνω to characterize the view of two antithetical positions in verse 5, the verb is not used to describe the "attitude" of the two types of persons as is the case in verse 3 and 10. Κρίνω is also the most natural verb to use in an expression like the one in verse five, and has no significance in determining the semantic closeness of the verbs ἐξουθενέω and κρίνω. Throughout this section Paul plays on the different meanings of verbs of the κριν- root (vs. 5, 13a, b). The translation of verse 4 is Meeks' ("Judgment and the Brother: Romans 14:1–15:13," p. 295).

[107] Paul's terminology reminds us of 2 Cor 10:10 where both ἐξουθενημένος and ἀσθενής occur. The "wise" at Corinth described Paul's speech as "contemptible" and his bodily presence, which includes a manifestation of his speech, as "weak." See also 1 Cor 2:2–4; 1:28; 6:4; 16:11; Gal 4:14.

[108] The one who eats and the one who does not eat does so "to/for the Lord, [for he] [and] gives thanks to God" (Rom 14:6b).

which provides added weight to Paul's reasoning: "We shall all stand before the judgment seat of God" and "each of us will, therefore, [have to] give an account of himself to God" (vv. 10b, 12).

Paul thus attempts to effect a change in the judgmental attitude of both persons by referring to God's impartiality and final judgement. Paul also uses a divine precedent for the same purpose. Christ is said to have accepted "you" (plural; 15:7b); both the weak and the powerful should, likewise, accept each other (15:7a). The weak should accept the one who eats everything because God has done so (14:3); and those who eat everything should accept those who are "weak in faith" (14:1) and should please their neighbour "for Christ too did not please himself" (15:3). After the emphasis on the common standing of both as slaves of the same master Paul gives the injunction, "let us, therefore, cease judging one another" (14:13a, Μηκέτι οὖν ἀλλήλους κρίνωμεν).

One might suggest that this injunction is only applicable to the weak, advising them not to assume the cloak of a corrector. The idea here is perhaps that each slave has a job to be determined by the master (cf. 14:3b–4). If the master makes one a judge and the other something else, the weaker one who is not a judge should not take on a role that the master has only given to another. It is not his function to judge the slave of another or undermine his standing before his master; his own master will adjudicate the issue. This is the sense in which a Paulinist has picked up Paul's point, "Therefore do not let anyone condemn you in matters of food and drink or of observing festivals, new moons, or sabbaths" (Col 2:16). He also uses the motif of disqualification, precisely the point of Paul's critique in Rom 14:3b–4.[109] The judgement which should cease among the weak is one that is exclusionary; a judgment which disqualifies others as partners in a common endeavor on the basis of their behavior and beliefs.[110] The judgmental attitude of the weak proceeds from a self-condemnatory act which expands individually appropriated criteria for behavior to include others (cf. v. 23).

---

[109] Col 2:16. The author uses the motif of disqualification in 2:18, καταβραβεύω. LSJ, s.v. "*give judgment against* one *as* βραβεύς, and so, *deprive* one *of the prize, deprive* one *of one's right.*"
[110] The judgmental attitude of the weak evaluated negatively the standing of the strong before their common master. I infer this from Paul's emphasis in v. 4 that it is the master who adjudicates the issues of "standing" and "falling" (out of favor) of the house slave who "has faith to eat everything."

Although one could claim that Paul's injunction in Rom 14:13a is more appropriate for the weak than the strong, other matters preclude such an inference. In 14:13a Paul draws the conclusion (οὖν) from his emphasis on the accountability of both towards God (cf. ἕκαστος, vv. 5, 12), indicating that he addresses both the vegetarians and those who value one day above another, and those who eat "everything" and value all days equally (cf. ἀλλήλων). With the hortatory subjunctive in the first persons plural, Paul involves himself closely in the issue addressed. The phrase "not for judgments about reasonings" in 14:1b shows that Paul has already in this section spoken of a judgmental activity among the strong as well as the weak. As in v. 5, κρίνω in 13a is then appropriate for both persons and is not at all incongruent with the different meanings of ἐξουθενέω and κρίνω in 14:3. If Paul is addressing both persons in v. 13a, is he advising the strong to cease an activity he previously said was appropriately theirs? He is not, since the issue as it relates to the strong is also a certain form of judging encapsulated in v. 1b. Paul thus urges both to cease a certain judging: Those who abstain should not "disqualify" the "strong" because of what they eat and the "strong" should accept the "weak" [but] "not for judgment about reasonings."[111]

What type of judgment precisely should the strong cease? In order to answer this quesion we must look more closely at the phrase διάκρισις διαλογισμῶν in 14:1. What exactly does μὴ εἰς διακρίσεις διαλογισμῶν signify? The term διάκρισις is used of the differentiation of good and evil which requires a critical examination and a certain expertise and, yes, maturity.[112] In 1 Cor 12:10 Paul had used the

---

[111] If one should attach any significance to the fact that Paul uses the first person plural hortatory subjunctive in v. 13a and not the plural imperative here as he does in vv. 1 and 13b, it could be seen as evidence for the fact that these imperatives are specifically addressed to the "powerful" collectively but the hortatory subjunctive is used because Paul has both the "weak" and the "powerful" in mind. Despite the use of the first person plural form in a hortatory subjunctive, the speaker does not necessarily include him- or herself among the participants. Cf. Stanley E. Porter, *Idioms of the Greek New Testament* (2nd ed. Sheffield: JSOT Press, 1994), p. 58. When Paul addresses either those who eat or those who abstain or individuals of either conviction (ἕκαστος), he uses the singular imperative (vv. 3, 5, 15, 16, 20, 22; 15:2). Paul also uses a hortatory subjunctive in v. 19 in an exhortation applicable to both types of persons, although the focus is on the responsibilty of the powerful in that context. Both are also clearly in view in 15:7 (ἀλλήλους) although Paul uses the plural imperative as in 14:1. As in Rom 14, Paul uses the 1st and 2nd person plural throughout in Rom 6 (cf. 6:1, ἐπιμένωμεν τῇ ἁμαρτίᾳ; 6:13, 15) speaking with, to and about his Roman gentile audience.

[112] See Heb 5:14 "solid food is for the mature . . . whose faculties have been

term διάκρισις when discussing the different "spiritual gifts." One of the gifts is the ability to "discriminate" between [different types] of spirits (διακρίσεις πνευμάτων). I suggest that Paul's use of the term in Rom 14:1b is in tune with its common meaning of *discrimination* which squares well with his own use of the term elsewhere.[113] Paul has also used διαλογισμοί before in its basic meaning of *thought, opinion* or *reasoning*. In Rom 1:21 he refers to the Gentiles who "became futile in their thinking" and in 1 Cor 3:20 he quotes Psalm 93:11: "The Lord knows the thoughts of the wise, that they are futile." If we understand διάκρισις in the metaphorical sense of [judicial] decision, we can translate 14:1b, "[but] not for judgments about reasonings."[114]

Judgment is based on evaluation and is the result of discrimination between different forms of reasoning, good and bad. Making distinctions between types of reasoning leads to distinctions among persons; better and worse forms of reasoning become the criterion of distinction between persons. Although διάκρισις applies to the "discriminating" between types of "reasoning" and not to the separation of people, we are warranted in recognizing the connotation of "separation" for διάκρισις as in the use of the word in James 2:4 where the author uses both διακρίνω and διαλογισμοί together. James gives examples of partiality, such as pampering a man with gold rings in fine clothing and being disrespectful towards another man in shabby clothing, arguing that partiality is a manifestation of evil διαλογισμοί which makes improper distinctions between people.[115] After a rational analysis of the beliefs of the weak the strong concluded that the weak did not measure up to their rational standards; they are faulty in their reasoning concerning what is permissible and forbidden.

---

trained by practice to distinguish good from evil" (τελείων ... διὰ τὴν ἕξιν τὰ αἰσθητήρια γεγυμνασμένα ἐχόντων πρὸς διάκρισιν καλοῦ τε καὶ κακοῦ). See also *1 Clem.* 48.5 (σοφὸς ἐν διακρίσει λόγων).

[113] Besides 1 Cor 12:10, note 1 Cor 4:7, τίς σε διακρίνει; who concedes you any superiority?

[114] Rom 14:1 thus describes how the strong should not accept the weak in faith. Εἰς is used for the purpose of an action and the genitive of διαλογισμοί is one of quality, definition or description. One could also translate 14:1b " ... but not for [the purpose of] discriminations of reasonings" or even " ... but not for rational discrimination/judgment" (Cf. Stanley E. Porter, *Idioms of the Greek New Testament*, pp. 92–93, 152). LSJ s.v. takes Rom 14:1 to be a metaphorical sense of *judicial decision* or *judgment*, but BAA as *quarrel*. But the two references to the latter meaning, namely, Polyb. 18.28.3 and Dio Chrys. 21 [38].21, hardly suffice to resolve the matter for Rom 14:1.

[115] Jas 2:4, οὐ διεκρίθητε ἐν ἑαυτοῖς καὶ ἐγένεσθε κριταὶ διαλογισμῶν πονηρῶν; Cf. 2:9.

Paul's injunction is given in light of the negative impact such discrimination has on the weak, an impact suggested by προσλαμβάνω used to signal the theme of this section. This term accentuates the intimacy of the relationship advocated and its closeness to familial and friendship imagery.[116] Paul urges the strong not to cause a rift in their relationship with the weak on account of certain forms of reasoning but to accept them into their friendship:[117] "Take into friendship those who are weak in faith but not for judgments about reasonings." Such an acceptance is needed in spite of the fact that they already are members of the same community! Paul sounds the same in 15:7, now including both persons. Προσλαμβάνω is also used in 14:3 and 15:7b to encourage acceptance and mutual aid in light of divine acceptance. As God and Christ had accepted all types of gentile persons into friendship, so should the weak and strong accept each other into their circle of friends instead of rejecting each other.

We overhear a debate on variance in beliefs and practices which has caused the strained relations Paul attempts to rectify. The judgmental and contemptuous attitudes of the powerful and weak towards each others' behavior evaluated negatively the standing of the other before their common master. The strong believed that food or drink do not win divine favor nor provoke divine wrath. The weak disagreed and a viable solution had to be mapped out. Although Paul's reflections betray a "rationalistic" bent (cf. 14:5b, 14, 22–23) and he had earlier urged his readers to participate in rational worship (12:1), Paul disapproves of the way the powerful attempt rationally to persuade the weak of the "irrationality" of their position.

In relation to the question whether Paul encourages the weak and strong to cease judging each other, W. Meeks states: "In anticipation of God's eventual judgment, the Christian is advised to judge his own behavior, but not to judge fellow Christians."[118] Such a reading

---

[116] See BAA, s.v. 2b, *in seine Gemeinschaft* (Häuslichkeit u.ä.) *aufnehmen* τινά jmdn. Cf. BAG, s.v. 2b, *receive or accept in one's society, in(to) one's home or circle of acquaintances.* LSJ s.v. I, 3, Sophocles, *Oedipus Coloneus* 378; Diodorus Siculus, *Library of History* 10.4.6: Dionysius urged Phintias and Damon to "include [himself] ... in their friendship" (εἰς τὴν φιλίαν προσλαβέσθαι). Plato, *Laws* 951D–E, refers to a synod (cf. 908A; 909A) which shall be a mixed body of young men and old (νέων καὶ πρεσβυτέρων μεμιγμένος): "None of these members shall go alone, but each of them shall bring with him a companion—a young man, selected by himself, between thirty and forty years old" (ἕκαστος ... ἴτω μετὰ νέου ... τὸν ἀρέσκοντα αὐτῷ προσλαμβάνων).

[117] Similar to Plutarch's advice that the superior brother accepts the inferior brother into his friendship. See *On Brotherly Love* 484D (συνεισποιοῦντα ταῖς φιλίαις).

[118] Meeks, "Judgment and the Brother: Romans 14:1–15:13," p. 293.

gives undue weight to the motif of divine impartiality present in this text, or rather misapplies this theme by supposing that Paul uses it to eliminate all judging of others or to redirect all evaluation and criticism solely to oneself. The function of the motif of divine impartiality is rather to show that the strong and the weak are on an equal footing in their standing before God, and neither can pass judgment on the other as it relates to that standing. The master himself decides the fate of his own house slaves, not other fellow slaves who have no jurisdiction here.[119]

Meeks draws the following implication from the "theological axiom" of divine impartiality: "It is the just, impartial judgment of the one God, therefore, that eliminates the distinction (or separation, διαστολή) between Jew and Gentile within the community of faith" and "renders human distinctions invalid"; Meeks then urges Christians to cease judging one another and to reach out to Jews and every human being.[120] It is, I grant, tempting to read Romans 14 in a way that supports admirable ecumenical concerns, but ultimately such an exegesis is inadequate and introduces anachronistic considerations. With such a present day agenda in sight, Meeks has not "seen" aspects of the text more in tune with the social realities of the proto-Christian communities, a reality which he himself has helped us understand more fully.

Since the injunction in Rom 14:13a could imply that the strong should cease an activity that was appropriately theirs, Paul directs his attention after 13a to the "strong" and spells out their obligations in terms reminiscent of the obligations of the "spiritual ones" in Gal 6:1–3. The change from 1st pers. pl. in Rom 14:13a to 2nd pers. pl. in 14:13b, and the use of οὖν in 14:13a and ἀλλά in 14:13b, as well as the shift in meaning of κρίνω from 14:13a to b, all indicate a narrowing of focus in 14:13b. That the strong and their responsibilities are primarily in view in Rom 14:13b–15:1, is clear both from the focus on the detrimental behavior of those who eat on those who abstain and in light of the similarities between this section and 1 Cor 8:1–13, where the "wise" and their obligations towards the "weak" are in view.[121]

---

[119] Rom 14:4b. This is perceptively seen by Meeks as implied by the context ("Judgment and the Brother: Romans 14:1–15:13," p. 295).

[120] Meeks, "Judgment and the Brother: Romans 14:1–15:13," pp. 296–98. Cf. J. M. Bassler, *Divine Impartiality: Paul and a Theological Axiom* (Chico, 1982), pp. 162–64.

[121] Rom 14:13b, "Decide rather not to put an offense or downfall in the brother's

Instead of evaluating the beliefs of the weak, the powerful should rather "decide" (κρίνατε) not to put an offense in front of "a brother" (13b).[122] Paul's remarks are directed towards a social situation in which the insecure, contrary to their conviction, do imitate the strong and eat meat or drink wine (vv. 15–16, 20–21, 23). Paul both assumes that the strong act out their firmly held beliefs and that the weak emulate the strong and also eat meat which "grieves" and "destroys" them. This implies the strong did not only attempt to rationally evaluate the false beliefs of the weak but tried also to teach them by way of example. When the weak one imitates the strong and eats meat he stands condemned because it is contrary to his conviction. I think we should yield to the temptation to see here an echo of Paul's reasoning in 1 Cor 8, to be discussed in detail in the next chapter. The strong cause the ruin of the weak by their reasoned arguments when the weak follow their example and exhortation to also eat food.

Paul begins by registering his agreement with the position of the strong with regard to the question of whether food is profane or not (v. 14)[123] and then in v. 15 directs his attention to a specific matter when "on account of food" a brother is "grieved." In such a case the strong is not "walking in love." Paul urges the strong not to let his food "ruin" his brother, concluding: "so do not let your good be spoken of as evil" (v. 16, οὖν). The "good" (ἀγαθός) in question refers to the knowledge "in Lord Jesus" that "nothing is profane in itself" (v. 14). This "good" comes into ill repute if it grieves and ruins a brother for whom Christ died. After a warning on the negative consequences "food" can have, Paul's reflection on the "kingdom of God"

---

way"; 14:15, "If your brother is being injured (λυπεῖται) by what you eat, you are no longer walking in love. Do not let what you eat cause the ruin (ἀπόλλυε) of one for whom Christ died." Cf. also 14:20–21. Note the use of πρόσκομμα in 1 Cor 8:9, σκανδαλίζειν in 8:13, and ἀπόλλυμι in 8:11.

[122] Paul's use of fraternal imagery in this section is pronounced (cf. 14:13b, a brother; 15, your brother; and 21, your brother (cf. also v. 15b, that one). For πρόσκομμα and σκάνδαλον (-λίζω), see e.g. K. Müller, *Anstoss und Gericht: Eine Studie zum jüdischen Hintergrund des paulinischen Skandalon-Begriffs* (Munich, 1969); J. Dupont, *Gnosis*, pp. 268–79; and J. Lindblom, "Zur Begriff 'Anstoss' im Neuen Testament," *Strena Philologica Upsaliensis* (1922), pp. 1–6.

[123] Cf. Cranfield, *A Critical and Exegetical Commentary on the Epistle to the Romans*, 2.711–12. Rom 14:14, "I know and am persuaded in the Lord Jesus that nothing is unclean in itself; but it is unclean for anyone who thinks it is unclean." Paul continues to grant that the convictions of the strong are in line with his own views (Cf. 14:20, "all things are clean"—πάντα μὲν καθαρά; 22b) and identifies himself finally with the position of the "powerful" (15:1).

as consisting not in "eating and drinking but righteousness, peace, and joy in the holy spirit" (v. 17) could not have been more appropriate. For he who serves Christ "in this" is not only "pleasing to God" but also "approved among men" (v. 18). Here Paul continues (cf. v. 16) his reflections on the praiseworthy behavior of those who, in spite of their own rational convictions, do not cause the ruin of their brother by acting out these convictions. With an inferential connective (ἄρα οὖν) Paul provides added emphasis to his exhortation after these reflections: "Let us then pursue what makes for peace and what makes for the edification of one another" (v. 19).

After this exhortation Paul again specifically addresses a strong person, urging him again not to "for the sake of food tear down the work of God" (v. 20a). The same sequence of thought as in vv. 14–16 follows in vv. 20b–21 where Paul reflects, now with the terms καλός and κακός, on the standards of appropriate behavior. "All things are clean," Paul grants, "but it is wicked for the person who eats with offense."[124] Although one cannot syntactically determine whether "the person" refers to the strong or the weak, I would maintain that it signifies the latter thus contrasting the differences between the position of the weak and that of the strong in v. 20a. Paul is then referring to the fact that the weak actually stumbles by following the example of the strong. He stumbles because he "eats with offense" or a "bad conscience" and contrary to his own conviction (v. 23). In light of the negative impact such emulation has on the weak, Paul lays the responsibility on the shoulders of the strong and claims it to be "fine" (καλός; cf. v. 16) not to eat meat or drink wine "nor anything by which your brother stumbles." With the verb προσκόπτω, Paul concludes the argument begun in 13b indicating that his main concern is the negative consequences the behavior of the strong has on the insecure.[125]

Paul now closes the chapter (vv. 22–23). In line with his argument in vv. 13b–21, Paul advises the strong to refrain from doing anything by which "a brother stumbles," and urges those with conviction to eat everything to keep their faith for themselves "in front of God" (v. 22a) instead of actively attempting to cure the weak rationally and by means of an example. A person who does not condemn

---

[124] 14:20b, πάντα μὲν καθαρά, ἀλλὰ κακὸν τῷ ἀνθρώπῳ τῷ διὰ προσκόμματος ἐσθίοντι.
[125] This is underlined by τιθέναι πρόσκομμα / σκάνδαλον in vv. 13 and 20, προσκόπτω in v. 21, καταλύω in v. 20a, ἀπόλλυμι and λυπεῖν in v. 15.

himself by what he approves is indeed happy (v. 22b), but the "doubting one" is condemned if he eats because "he does not act from faith." Paul harks back to language used earlier to describe the behavior of Abraham who "did not weaken in faith... No distrust made him waver... but he grew strong in his faith...." (Rom 4:19–20).[126] Not everyone, apparently, is like Abraham; competing views as to what constitutes divinely approved behavior leads to negative evaluation and judgment of a contrary practice.

At the beginning of chapter 14 Paul advised the strong to take the weak into their friendship and do so without evaluating their opinions concerning food and days. Now he urges the strong "to carry the weaknesses of the powerless" (15:1, τὰ ἀσθενήματα τῶν ἀδυνάτων βαστάζειν). The term βαστάζω was common in medical contexts, as was the term ἀσθένημα, and close in meaning to θεραπεύω. Lars Rydbeck who argued that the language of the New Testament is the written language of the educated people, not that of the vulgar papyri, and compared it to the "technical prose" found in writings on astronomy, mathematics, pharmacology, and philology, has shown that βαστάζω is close in meaning to αἴρω, "to take away," and that an older meaning of βαστάζω, still in use at this time, is "to take on oneself, to carry, to bear."[127]

Βαστάζω is used with both therapeutic and non-therapeutic connotations.[128] We could then underline either the meaning "to carry" or "to take away" in Rom 15:1 and Paul would be saying something different in each case. The former highlights the responsibility of the strong. But the meaning "to take away" emphasizes an active engagement on the part of the strong to remedy the frailty or "ailment"

---

[126] Rom 14:22–23a, "... happy is the one who does not condemn himself by what he approves. But the one who doubts is condemned, if he eats, because he does not act from faith..."; 4:19–20, καὶ μὴ ἀσθενήσας τῇ πίστει... ἀλλ' ἐνεδυναμώθη τῇ πίστει.... Διακρίνεσθαι is only used in these two texts by Paul in the sense of to "waver" or "doubt" Compare Js 1:6–8.

[127] See L. Rydbeck, *Fachprosa, Vermeintliche Volkssprache und Neues Testament* (Lund, 1967), pp. 154–66. Rydbeck also investigated medical writings in the *Corpus Hippocraticum*. See Galen, *De compositione medicamentorum per genera* 2.14, ψώρας τε θεραπεύει καὶ ὑπώπια βαστάζει, "he heals the itching disease and takes away the weal/bruise." Cf. Matt 8:16–17. For the use of this imagery in a therapeutic context, see 1 *Clem.* 16.4–5, "He it is who beareth our sins (ἁμαρτίας... φέρει)... with his bruises were we healed (τῷ μώλωπι αὐτοῦ ἡμεῖς ἰάθημεν)." Cf. also Ignatius, *Eph.* 7.1–2; 20.2; 21.1.

[128] Ignatius, *Pol.* 1.2–3, "Help (βάσταζε) all men, as the Lord also helps you... Bear (βάσταζε) the sicknesses of all as a perfect athlete." In *Diogn.* 10.5–6, the phrase ἀναδέχεται βάρος is used to characterize someone's wish to help a (weak) neighbour. Note Epictetus, *Discourse* 2.9.22.

(ἀσθένημα) of the weak. This latter meaning is unlikely since it would contradict Paul's argument in Rom 14:1. Both βαστάζω and ἀσθένημα show, though, that Paul's discussion is from the point of view of the strong; as in Corinth, Paul attempts to modify an approach taken to the weak and uses terms dear to those he criticizes.

The strong are to help the weak by taking the weight of the burden they carry. Lightening a load by sharing a burden, particularly in times of adversity, was a common motif in the friendship tradition. It was at those times, as Ennius noted, that a faithful friend might be recognised.[129] Being open towards your friends was sometimes described with the imagery of lightening a load by sharing a burden.[130] A terminology of weakness easily suggests itself in the use of such imagery. In *On Grief*, Dio contrasts a person strong in spirit who more easily carries life's troubles than one weak in spirit; because of their capacity, the strong can help the weak carry their load.[131]

Paul's use of λύπη in Rom 14:15 suggests that the load in question relates to the importance of certain eating habits as a criterion of divine approval. With regard to meat-eating the weak are insecure; vegetarianism is the solution. The strong lighten the load of the weak by listening to their trepidations with regard to food and days and by not behaving in such a manner as to grieve the weak. As friends, they should lighten, not increase, their λύπη by sharing it. If they act out their beliefs they do not walk in love and they undermine the weaks' commitment by causing a destructive λύπη, which instead of "saving" the weak, "destroys" them.[132] The "destruction" entails the undermining of new commitment and the severing of relations among individuals by the attendant shunning of others. It is

---

[129] Quoted by Cicero in *On Friendship* 64; cf. ibid., 22; Xenophon, *Memorabilia* 2.7.1–14; Menander, 534K.

[130] Many authors of early Imperial society focused on the negative aspects of entrusting things concerning yourself to others. See pp. 125–26, above, and note Epictetus, *Discourse* 4.13.16; Aristotle, *Nicomachean Ethics* 1155a12–16.

[131] Dio Chrysostom, *Discourse* 16:11; 39.3, "To whom are afflictions lighter than to those who bear them together, like a heavy load?" Contrast Teles, Περὶ αὐταρκείας: ἀσθενὴς πάλιν· μὴ ζήτει τὰ τοῦ ἰσχυροῦ [φορτία βαστάζειν καὶ διατραχηλίζεσθαι] (10, 7 Hense).

[132] Aristotle, *Eudemian Ethics* 1240a33–35, "we shall reckon it affection (ἀγαπᾶν) to grieve with one who grieves not for some ulterior motive." Cf. ibid., 1244a24–25; 1240a39–1240b1; 1245b26–1246a25, and *Nicomachean Ethics* 1171a29; 1171a21–b27. In a friendship of pleasure one wishes to share the friend's grief and joy. Compare Rom 12:15. Alcibiades is said to have changed his manners when they grieved others (Plutarch, *Alcibiades* 23.5).

of significance that moralists were concerned with addressing the issue of not thwarting the progress of a weak person, insecure in the philosophic way of life. Paul's concerns are the same.[133]

One of the reasons why scholars are unwilling to accept such a mundane reading is because of an anachronistic theological reading of the terms "destruction" and "salvation" (Rom 14:15; 1 Cor 8:11; 9:22). Paul's argumentation is indeed lodged in a world view within which the divine sanctions or disapproves certain behavior revealing an intricate connection between religion and morality or between a social reality and an interpretative dimension of the divine with which the social reality is imbued. Divine "destruction" or "salvation" play out in a social context anchored in a view of reality which includes the divine as a significant factor. Here different views emerge concerning what beliefs and behavior constitute a legitimate criterion for divine approval.[134] A metaphysical dimension is used to disqualify others. Paul insists that it is the common master of the different house slaves, namely God, who gives the final verdict with regard to both types of persons.

No one doubts that the terms "salvation" and "destruction" have metaphysical connotations in Paul's vocabulary. Paul uses the pair to characterise a social practice as divinely acceptable or not and urges the strong to cease an activity which "destroys" the weak and legitimizes such an injunction with a reference to God's own acceptance of the weak. Paul also uses these terms to refer to God's activity in the past or the future to deter action in the present and as distinctive modes relative to divine approval and disapproval.[135] Finally, it can be demonstrated that "salvation" and "destruction" were interpreted "apocalyptically" by some later Christians, who almost abstracted the terms from their social implications. Such a development can, for example, be seen in James 4:11–12.[136] This text does

---

[133] Rom 14:15; 1 Cor 8:11. The terms ἀπόλλυμι, λυπέω and τύπτω, express these concerns. Note *Sirach* 30:23, πολλοὺς γὰρ ἀπώλεσεν ἡ λύπη. See pp. 78–81, above.

[134] In both Romans and 1 Cor this is expressed by the use of the verb παρίστημι (Cf. 1 Cor 8:8; Rom 14:4 (ἴστημι), 10, 22; BAGD s.v.). Compare Ps 109:31 (LXX).

[135] 1 Cor 1:18, 26–28; 3:15–18; 10:9–12; 11:27–34; Jude 5–7.

[136] Js 4:11–12, "There is one ... judge, he who is able to save and to destroy. But who are you that you judge your neighbor?" See 5:13–19 and *Herm. Man.* 12.6.3; Heb 10:39; Pol. *Phil.* 6.1–2; 2 *Clem.* 15.1. Some texts from the 2nd cent. C. E. reveal a debate as to whether a human being, and not only God, can exert an influence over humans described by the terms "salvation" and "destruction." This is true of 2 *Clem.* 17.1–2 and *Herm. Sim.* 9.23.4 (μνησικακεῖ ὡς δυνάμενος ἀπολέσαι ἢ σῶσαι αὐτόν). The former emphasises the duty of humans to save each other from

indeed support Meeks' interpretation above. Judgmental activity should cease in light of divine adjudication. But that is James, not Romans!

It does not require a great deal of reading in Paul's contemporary moralists to find these terms used of the detrimental and positive influence one has over another person. If it is true that the discussion in Rom 14–15 concerns communal psychagogy we should look to the way that other texts on psychagogy employ the terms which occur here and not to apocalyptic texts. I think we must then defamiliarize these terms and allow other nuances of meaning, more congruent with the social realities of the time and the context of Rom 14–15, as well as 1 Cor 8, to infiltrate our understanding.[137]

Although my construal above remains hypothetical, we should, nevertheless, not shy away from it. If we postulate that members of the Pauline communities met, like members of the Epicurean communities in Athens, Naples, and Herculaneum, in small groups of friends, whether in a household setting or not, the social reality of the practice of exclusion would be real. But I am not concerned here with this hypothetical social possibility but rather with some possible systemic implications of such a practice. A dispute over acceptable beliefs and behavior should not sever the relationship between members or constitute the precise criterion for divine approval or wrath. Paul renounces judgement which has become a criterion for continual friendship, similar to the way in which the judgment of another preceded the proffering of friendship among those who used a nobility test for friendship. A judgment which excludes and "disqualifies" another from the circle of friends because of his faulty reasoning should cease; modification of the false beliefs and reasonings of the weak is not a requisite for friendship. The weak should cease a judgement which severs the relationship with a "strong" person because his beliefs and behavior are considered unacceptable. Both forms of judgement sever a relationship of friendship.

The reason why Paul devalues judgment is because it has become

---

destruction but the latter draws attention to God as a model to be imitated in not destroying others. Even within an apocalyptic framework, "destruction" is explained in ethical and psychological terms (*Herm. Sim.* 6.2.1–4).

[137] Apparently, if Dunn is correct, "all recent commentators" are in need of such a defamiliarization: "As all recent commentators agree, what is in view in ἀπόλλυμι [in Rom 14:15] is final eschatological ruin, the opposite of the final judgment of acquittal" (*Romans 9–16*, p. 821). See Clement, *Ped.* 66.2; Xenophon, *Memorabilia* 1.2.32, 35, and Epicurus, *Vatican Sentences* 37 (σώζεται-διαλύεται). For my non-apocalyptic reading of 1 Cor 8, see pp. 275–90, below.

an evaluative criterion for continued membership or friendship. The rational evaluation of the beliefs of the weak had drastic consequences in spite of having been intended to cure them. Paul attempts to alert both the strong and the weak to this; the weak should desist from judging and the strong should cease their contempt and activity which grieves the weak. Paul emphasizes the responsibilities of the mature persons and attempts to mend their evaluative process which, he says, destroys and thwarts the progress of the insecure instead of saving them. Paul seeks to prevent members from judging in a way that would exclude others and destroy the fabric of the community. Without the acceptance of both the strong and the weak of each other, they not only threaten to sever their communal ties but put their common worship in jeopardy. Paul's argumentation proceeds towards this final point.[138]

Now in light of Paul's insistence on the responsibilities of the strong, his remark at the end of this section in Romans—"I am confident ... that you are able to admonish one another" (15:14)—is striking. It squares well, however, with the social practice of rotational psychagogy that I have postulated for the Pauline communities. The emphasis falls on the responsibility of the mature but the immature are not excluded.[139] Thus, in spite of their maturity the strong are not immune from failure, and if they err the weak can attempt to put some sense into them.[140] Before noting the mutuality of admonition in Rom 15:14, Paul remarks that both the strong and the weak are full of goodness, "filled with all knowledge,"[141] and thus qualified to admonish others.

In light of the close association of νουθεσία and παιδεία, we can appropriately say that Paul is here, in spite of his critique, advocating an "admonitory kind of education," or a type of education which makes use of rebuke and censure. Such a pedagogy has a strong

---

[138] See Rom 15:5–6; cf. 12:16. The threat against unity in 15:6–8 and the "glorification of God" in verses 7 and 9a tie together Rom 14:1 15:6 and 15:8 13. For the conjunction of the motives of "glory of God" and "unity", see *1 Clem.* 34.5–7 and John 17:21–23.

[139] In Gal 6:1–3 Paul also first underlines the responsibility of the mature and then the responsibility of both the immature and the mature (cf. v. 3, ἀλλήλων τὰ βάρη βαστάζετε). Cf. *Diog.* 10:6.

[140] The same is true of the wise Epicurean in *On Frank Criticism* frs. 45; 55–56. See pp. 129–32, above.

[141] Rom 15:14, πεπληρωμένοι πάσης [τῆς] γνώσεως. Compare 1 Cor 1:5, "... that in every way you were enriched in him with all speech and all knowledge" (ὅτι ἐν παντὶ ἐπλουτίσθητε ἐν αὐτῷ, ἐν παντὶ λόγῳ καὶ πάσῃ γνώσει).

didactic element, focusing on behavior modification and attitude change through admonition and blame in the reformation of others. Apparently, early Christian appropriation of certain elements of Greek παιδεία took place much earlier than Werner Jaeger and others ever suspected![142] In chapter six we shall see Paul's use of admonitory pedagogy in 1 Corinthians where issues of destructive guidance and psychagogy as a pedagogy aiming at a certain παιδεία come to the fore.

Stanley K. Stowers has put forth an ingenious hypothesis which might explain the debate between Paul and the "wise" in Corinth, suggesting that we can make sense of the puzzling evidence by recognizing that some Corinthians had adopted a "therapeutic model of Christianity" with its "assumptions about the role of reason." Paul opposes this view of reason's function in texts such as Rom 14 and 1 Cor 8 which describe "reason's functioning in a therapeutic situation of the more rational and the weak."[143] The "weak" properly belong within the context of therapeutic models of the Hellenistic philosophies. Instead of ignoring the weak, the strong wanted actively to attempt to educate them from the vantage point of their firmly held beliefs regarding food and days. Such an activity entailed an attempt to dispel the false beliefs and false reasoning of the weak by means of more rational arguments. Stowers has correctly seen the significance of Rom 14:1b as a shorthand reference by Paul to such an activity among the strong.[144]

Two things are important to note. Firstly, Paul does not say that

---

[142] See W. Jaeger, *Early Christianity and Greek Paideia* (Cambridge, Mass., 1961), cf. pp. 105–06. As I noted on p. 58, above, psychagogy is, on the highest level of generalization, a pedagogical activity where the formation of a certain *paideia* is in view (note I. Hadot, *Seneca und die griechisch-römische Tradition der Seelenleitung*, p. 10; idem, *Arts Libéraux et Philosophie dans la Pensée Antique* (Paris, 1984)), chp. 1. On the admonitory type of education see Plato, *The Sophist* 230A (τὸ νουθετητικὸν εἶδος τῆς παιδείας) and p. .86, above. For the view that the language of the Jesus traditions and their patterns of persuasion bring a new ethos to expression and thus create a new type of paideia, see B. L. Mack & V. K. Robbins, *Patterns of Persuasion in the Gospels* (Sonoma, California, 1989), pp. 203–08.

[143] Stanley K. Stowers, "Paul on the Use and Abuse of Reason," in D. L. Balch, E. Ferguson and W. A. Meeks (eds.), *Greeks, Romans, and Christians. Essays in Honor of Abraham J. Malherbe* (Minneapolis, 1990), pp. 283 and 286. 2 Cor 10 is also seen as evidence for this hypothesis. Stowers does not focus on the obligations of the strong as I have done.

[144] In ancient therapeutic practice the alternative to ignoring the weak, either because they are too far gone or because their illness is not taken seriously, is actively to attempt a cure. In Stowers' view, the latter is the case in Rom 14:1; the former in 1 Cor 8.

the strong, instead of actively attempting to cure the weak, should ignore them. On the contrary, as we have seen he spells out their obligations towards the weak in no uncertain terms. Secondly, it is the nature of the attempted cure and its consequences of which Paul disapproves. Stowers argues convincingly that Paul does not elevate reason as the dominant criterion of community interaction as the therapeutic model does. Paul does not, like the wise Corinthians, use reason as a principle of social hierarchy. On this score, Paul and the wise disagreed, just as they disagreed as to the approach to be taken towards the weak.

Now if we emphasize the discrepancy between Paul's views and those he criticizes and minimize possible agreements, we tend to sidestep Paul's positive use of some terms. Both Paul and his critics were, I maintain, of one mind with regard to the designation of some people as "weak." Both before and after his experience in Corinth, Paul uses the "weak" (ἀσθενής) and "spiritual ones" ((οἱ) πνευματικοί) in therapeutic contexts and there is no indication that he wants to discard any of these terms when writing 1 Corinthians.[145] Thus, with regard to the designation of some as "weak," Paul shows no reluctance in using the term in Rom 14 or any trepidation because of the possible implications of his language. The evidence suggests then that it is Paul himself who used the designation of some as "weak," a designation with which the Corinthian wise agreed.[146] If it is correct that Paul utilizes terms dear to his critics, 1 Corinthians is an extended discussion with these critics and reveals Paul's adaptability towards the wise. Paul seizes the ground he shares with his critics and attempts to lay bare his own interpretation. Accommodation, however, always entails some influence.

But when Paul uses the designation of some as "weak" and uses therapeutic terms such as βαστάζω (Rom 15:1; Gal 6:2) and καταρτίζω (Gal 6:1), he does so not to emphasize the predicament of the weak but rather the responsibility of the mature towards those whose commitment is still uncertain.[147] Paul does not emphasize the "sickness"

---

[145] 1 Cor 2:15; 8:7, 9, 10, 11, 12; 9:22; 1 Thess 5:14; Gal 6:1.

[146] Before writing 1 Cor, Paul had used ἀσθενής and πνευματικοί in "psychagogic" contexts (1 Thess 5:14; Gal 6:1-3). If Gal is later than 1 Cor, we would have to note that, independently of the tensions in Corinth, Paul values the term πνευματικοί as a designation for the mature who correct others. For the dating of Paul's letters, see for example G. Lüdemann, *Paul, Apostle to the Gentiles* (Philadelphia, 1984).

[147] The concept of "novice" is not temporal, since the length of the process of

of the weak or the ways to effect a cure but the responsibilities of the mature in light of the predicament of the weak. The use of therapeutic terms in exemplifying the status of some does not, then, necessarily entail a therapeutic model of the human predicament. Instead of ignoring the weak, the strong wanted actively to attempt to educate them from the vantage point of their firmly held beliefs. Such an activity entailed an attempt to dispel the false beliefs of the weak by means of rational arguments. This holds true, contrary to what Stowers maintains, for the Corinthian situation also. In neither Rom 14:1–15:14 nor 1 Cor 8:1–11:1 had the mature written off the weak; in both they had attempted to cure them. It is the nature of the attempted cure and its consequences of which Paul disapproves in both instances; instead of ruining the weak, the mature should care for and support the insecure.[148]

It now remains to study Paul's own psychagogic guidance in the Corinthian correspondence where the above issues come to the fore. As among the Epicureans, Paul's psychagogic guidance recognizes different approaches for different types of student. When the focus is on the weak and insecure, Paul's approach is mild; an attempt is made to alleviate the asymmetrical aspects of the relationship and Paul rejects a harsh and inconsiderate approach towards the weak. But when it is a question of a recalcitrant student, Paul's approach is more stringent and the asymmetry of the relationship is accentuated by threats and calls for obedience. In the final chapter of this book, I look at Paul's psychagogic guidance of the weak and tender students and that of the recalcitrant ones of the Corinthian community.

---

enculturation varies from one member to another. See pp. 174–75, above. Καταρτίζω (BAGD, s.v. 1a, *restore to its former condition, put to rights* τὶ *someth.*) was commonly used as a surgical term of setting a bone or joint: Wettstein on Matt 4:21; J. B. Lightfoot, *The Epistle of St. Paul to the Galatians* (Grand Rapids, 1976), p. 215. See 1 Thess 3:10; 2 Cor 13:9, 11. Psychagogic responsibility is underscored with the *hap leg* προλαμβάνω in Gal 6:1 (cf. BAGD s.v., 2b). See *On Frank Criticism* fr. 56.1–3 and fn. 46 on p. 201, above.

[148] To use Paul's language in 1 Thess 5:14, ἀντέχεσθε τῶν ἀσθενῶν LSJ, s.v. III 2b, c.

CHAPTER SIX

# PAUL'S PSYCHAGOGIC ADAPTABILITY AND THE WEAK AND RECALCITRANT MEMBERS OF THE CORINTHIAN COMMUNITY

It is now commonly accepted—albeit difficult to demonstrate critically—that Paul is coaxing the Corinthians along by using their own language, which in due course he attempts to modify. Paul uses antithetical contrasts in his discussion with the Corinthians. Some of these contrasts have been used in attempts to construe a believable picture of the Corinthian ideology.[1] It has been more difficult to associate these contrasts with the opposition of 2 Corinthians, the "false apostles," "Hebrews," the "Israelites," and the "servants of Christ" (2 Cor 11:13, 22, and 23). Many thus opt to see the "opponents" of 2 Corinthians as different from those of 1 Corinthians.

It is not my purpose to reconstruct the self-designation of some of the Corinthians.[2] I am rather concerned with the pedagogical traditions Paul uses, the information Paul's method yields of his critics,

---

[1] See 1 Cor 1:25–27; 2:6, 14–15; 3:1, 18; 4:8–10; 15:12: πνευματικός (sc. ἄνθρωπος)—ψυχικός ἄνθρωπος; οἱ πνευματικοί versus σάρκινοι and νήπιοι ἐν Χριστῷ; οἱ τέλειοι/νήπιοι; τὰ μωρὰ τοῦ κόσμου—τὰ μωρὰ τοῦ θεοῦ; σοφός—μωρός; heavenly and earthly; weakness versus strength, disgrace and honor, those on their way to salvation or destruction, besides such key concepts as σοφία and γνῶσις. See W. Lütgert, *Freiheitspredigt und Schwarmgeister in Korinth* (Gütersloh, 1908); J. Weiss, *Der erste Korintherbrief* (MeyerK 5; 9th ed.; Göttingen, 1910), pp. xviii–xix; 73–75; R. Reitzenstein, *Die hellenistischen Mysterienreligionen* (Teubner, 1927), pp. 338–39; J. Dupont, *Gnosis. La Connaissance religieuse dans les épîtres de saint Paul* (Paris, 1949); N. Hugedé, *La Métaphore du Miroir dans les Épîtres de Saint Paul aux Corinthiens* (Neuchatel, 1958), pp. 177–84; P. J. du Plessis, *ΤΕΛΕΙΟΣ. The Idea of Perfection in the New Testament* (Kampen, 1959); U. Wilckens, *Weisheit und Torheit* (Tübingen, 1959); B. A. Pearson, *The Pneumatikos Psychikos Terminology in 1 Corinthians* (Missoula, Montana, 1973); M. Winter, *Pneumatiker und Psychiker in Korinth* (Marburg, 1975); R. A. Horsley, "Wisdom of Word and Words of Wisdom in Corinth," *CBQ* 39.2 (1977), pp. 224–39; idem, "'How can some of you say that there is no Resurrection of the Dead?' Spiritual Elitism in Corinth," *NovT* 20.3 (1978), pp. 203–31.

[2] For a systematic analysis of such a reconstruction, see D. Georgi (*The Opponents of Paul in Second Corinthians*. Philadelphia, 1986). See also J. C. Hurd, Jr., *The Origin of I Corinthians* (New York, 1965), pp. 61, 96–113; H. D. Betz, *2 Corinthians 8 and 9* (Philadelphia, 1985), pp. 3–36, and J. L. Summey, *Identifying Paul's Opponents* (Scheffield, 1990).

and Paul's reactions to the charges levelled against him.³ In this I extrapolate evidence from both 1 and 2 Corinthians. Heuristically, my approach views the problems addressed by the various letters as commensurable. The problems are commensurable since they are viewed from the same perspective, i.e., Paul's own, and the focus throughout remains on the detrimental effect the behavior of some has on the community as a whole.⁴

Significantly, the attitude Paul counters centers on the attitude of the "wise" in Corinth towards others in the community, not against himself. This is seen in Paul's focus on arrogance apparent in his use of καύχημα, καυχάομαι, φυσίωσις and φυσιόω.⁵ The γνῶσις valued by some in Corinth is said to "puff up," contrary to ἀγάπη which "builds up"; this "love" is also negatively described as οὐ φυσιοῦται (1 Cor 8:1; 13:4). The detrimental conduct of the φρόνιμοι in Corinth⁶ remains the same in 1 and 2 Corinthians. Thus, when Paul reflects on his upcoming third visit to Corinth, he is afraid of finding discord,

---

³ Such an approach must, of course, be ever attentive to the dangers of "mirror reading." Cf. G. Lyons, *Pauline Autobiography. Toward a New Understanding* (Atlanta: Scholars Press, 1985), pp. 79–121.

⁴ From both partition and unity theory perspectives, information from the various sections of 2 Cor is valuable, both retrospective of Paul's treatment of the Corinthians and their (mis)understanding and charges, and as evidence for Paul's continual guidance. I assume that 2 Cor is composed of two letters and that chps. 10–13 was sent subsequent to 1–9. See Furnish, *2 Corinthians*, pp. 29–54, 129–30, 141, 218, 475–79; Betz, *2 Corinthians 8 and 9*, pp. 12–13, 21–22, 141–44; and S. K. Stowers, "Peri men gar and the integrity of 2 Cor 8 and 9," *NovT* 32.4 (1990), pp. 340–48. W. Schmithals sees Paul's opponents the same in 1 and 2 Cor, namely, Gnostics (*Die Gnosis in Korinth* (Göttingen, 1969 (3); cf. J. Munck, *Paul and the Salvation of Mankind* (Atlanta: John Knox Press, 1977), pp. 186–88. For Georgi, 2 Cor 10–13 necessitates a truly new situation (*The Opponents of Paul in Second Corinthians*, pp. 1–9, 14–21). In Murphy-O'Connor's view, the πνευματικοί remain the focus of opposition in 2 Cor too and welcomed the Judaizing intruders. The clearest sign of their presence is that the same criticism surfaces in 2 Cor as in 1 Cor See "Pneumatikoi and Judaizers in 2 Cor 2:14–4:6," *ABR* 34 (1986), pp. 42–58; idem, "Philo and 2 Cor 6:14–7:1," *RB* 95.1 (1988), pp. 55–69; idem, "'Being at home in the body we are in exile from the Lord' (2 Cor 5.6b)," *RB* 93.2 (1986), pp. 214–21; idem, "Pneumatikoi in 2 Corinthians," *PIBA* 11 (1988), pp. 59–66; idem, "Another Jesus (2 Cor 11:4)," *RB* 97.2 (1990), pp. 238–51.

⁵ All the NT occurrences of φυσιόω, except one (Col 2:18), are in 1 Cor (8:1; 4:6, 18, 19; 5:2; 13:4); φυσίωσις occurs only in 2 Cor 12:20. For other occurrences of arrogance, see 1 Cor 1:17, 26, 31; 2:4–5; 3:1, 18, 21; 5:6; 6:9; 8:11; 2 Cor 5:12; 10:5, 7, 15; 11:20; 12:7, 10, 14, 20 (Rom 12:16).

⁶ And/or possibly the ψυχικοί (and οἱ σαρκικοί) who, in Jude 17–19, are those who cause division in the community. The author of James, like Paul, ties jealousy and quarrels to the activity of the ψυχικοί (Jas 3:13–18; 1 Cor 3:3, 15). Cf. 1 *Clem.* 13.1; 14.1; 38.2; 39.1. Paul labels the Corinthians φρόνιμοι in 1 Cor 10:15 and 2 Cor 11:19 (cf. Rom 11:25). Contrast 1 Cor 4:10.

jealousy, explosive tempers, cases of self-seeking, slanders, gossiping, cases of arrogance and general disorder among them. He also notes that he may have to shed tears over those who have continued in their former sinning and have not repented of the impurity, sexual immorality, and licentiousness they practiced.[7]

Strife, jealousy, arrogance, pride, and general disorder, are among the recurring aspects of the community life in Corinth that Paul addressed. Paul integrates his characterization of these vices in terms of psychological and ethical traits into a pattern of his hortatory style.[8] No one claims that the puffed-up "wise" are identical to the "super-apostles (2 Cor 11:5), the "false apostles", the "deceitful workmen", and those who were masquerading as apostles of Christ (2 Cor 11:13), but it is difficult not to see that Paul's focus throughout is the detrimental effect the actions of some have on others, a behavior which ran counter to the principle of adaptability in destroying rather than fostering communal unity.

We can assemble a typology of the Corinthian critics on the basis of Paul's description of them. The "wise" in Corinth, like the "wise" at Herculaneum, display traits characteristic of arrogant and recalcitrant persons who cannot tolerate frank criticism. That Paul was familiar with character portrayals of the pretentious and arrogant person is evident from Rom 2:1–5.[9] A recurring vice moralists addressed among people was a contemptuous attitude towards others. Paul warns the "strong" of the same in Rom 14 and deplores the overweening attitude of the "wise" in Corinth, charging them with arrogance and pride and, yes, harshness.[10] With these Paul debates pedagogical issues, centering on questions of leadership qualification and style or the appropriate mode of spiritual guidance; both issues feature questions of maturity and immaturity. The matter of leadership qualification surfaces in the early chapters of 1 Corinthians. At issue was who could legitimately evaluate others or was mature enough

---

[7] 2 Cor 12:20–21. See V. P. Furnish, *2 Corinthians* (AB 32A; Garden City, NY, 1984), pp. 561–62.

[8] On ἔρις see 1 Cor 1:11; 3:3; on ζῆλος 1 Cor 3:3; on arrogance, haughtiness, and pride, see fn. 5, above; on ἀκαταστασίαι, see Paul's discussion throughout 1 Cor 5–14.

[9] S. K. Stowers, *The Diatribe and Paul's Letter to the Romans* (Chico, 1981), pp. 93–6, 110–12. Philodemus, *On Frank Criticism* cols. 15b–21a. See pp. 150–52, above.

[10] 1 Cor 4:6, 10; 8:11–13; 10:15; 2 Cor 11:17–19. Arrogance and "harshness" were often closely related. See Isocrates, *To Demonicus* 30–31; and *To Philip* 116; Theophrastus, *Characters* 24; Philodemus, *On Vices* col. 10.11–13 Jensen.

to be both exempt from blame and in a rightful position to guide others, thus featuring the intricate relationship between maturity and leadership qualification. Evidence of the question of leadership style which centered on the legitimate use of harshness in moral exhortation became a central bone of contention between Paul and the "wise" and is found throughout the Corinthian correspondence. In this debate a certain typology emerges not only of the "wise" as recalcitrant students but also of the "weak" who display traits of tender and insecure students who need a gentle guidance.

We can appreciate the issue of leadership style by focusing on Paul's imagery of harshness which can be explicated in light of ancient Greek educational theory. Evidence for the dispute on harshness is fourfold. Firstly, we have direct evidence that some in Corinth had charged Paul with being unduly harsh both in his letters and a visit to them. Paul's reflections on "grief" where some in Corinth complain of the excessive λύπη Paul caused show that questions concerning excessive harshness in moral exhortation were debated by Paul and some in Corinth.[11] Secondly, we have indirect evidence for this debate in the terms ἀνέχεσθαι and καταναρκᾶν.[12] Here Paul, reverting back to imagery of ancient Greek educational theory, asks the disobedient to submit as obedient students to his discipline, which he as their father can rightly exert. Thirdly, that the issue is one of harshness and appropriate mode of guidance is seen in Paul's oblique threats of harsh discipline. Through subtle threats Paul attempts both to exert his authority over the Corinthians and to shame them into repentance. The phrase πνεῦμα πραΰτητος suggests that the issue is one of corrective discipline by a more mature person and his methods of guidance.[13] Finally, Paul deplores the inconsiderate harshness of the wise in their attempt to reform the weak through rational arguments and by means of a forceful example and criticizes the wise for their harshness when correcting others; on the other hand, he justifies his own harshness in view of its end result, namely, it grieved the Corinthians into repentance.[14] This dispute on harshness also centers on questions of flexible and versatile guidance.

---

[11] Cf. 2 Cor 1:24; 10:9–10; 12:14–16. Note 2 Cor 2:1, τὸ μὴ πάλιν ἐν λύπῃ πρὸς ὑμᾶς ἐλθεῖν.
[12] 2 Cor 11:1, 4, 9, 19, 20; 12:13, 14.
[13] 1 Cor 4:14–21; 2 Cor 10:6; 12:21; 13:1–2, 10. For the phrase πνεῦμα πραΰτητος see, 1 Cor 4:21; cf. 2 Cor 10:1; Gal 6:1. See Plutarch, *On Tranquility of Mind* 476F.
[14] 1 Cor 8; 2 Cor 2; 7:9.

In chapter one I discussed the blurred line between beguilement and truthful guidance, between adaptation which is concerned either with personal gain or the well being of others. Such tendentiousness also inheres in Paul's remarks on his own flexible behavior. Throughout the early chapters of this book I advanced a suggestive hypothesis regarding the function of 1 Cor 9:19–23, claiming that the flexible approach articulated in this pericope relates to the motives of association with all in recruitment and to an affable approach in psychagogy.[15] The affable approach needed for the weak and tender is one side of the mixed method I discussed in chapter two. The harsh dimension of the mixed method, needed because of the disposition of the recalcitrant students, is also evident throughout the Corinthian correspondence. Paul's flexible approach requires an accommodation in an attempt to benefit as many as possible, both those who belong to the community and others. Such emphasis is evident throughout the larger literary context of 1 Cor 5:1–11:1 where Paul concerns himself with issues of adaptability, versatility, and the association of different types of people.

Contrary to the "wise" in Corinth, Paul subscribes to an affable and versatile leadership model both in "recruitment" and "psychagogy". Paul's flexible recruitment practice which included association with different character types, including the immoral, was seen as reprehensible and somewhat askew to his earlier recommendation to the Corinthians. Some in Corinth also questioned Paul's affable psychagogy, wishing instead to be more forthright in their guidance of the weak (1 Cor 8). Before discussing the form and function of 1 Cor 9:19–23 and the motifs of adaptation, versatility and association, evident both in this pericope and its larger literary context, a few general remarks on Paul's flexible life and adaptability in the epistolary and hortatory context of 1 Corinthians are in order.

### 6.1 *Paul's Adaptability in Conduct and Speech*

Paul's life was indeed multi-faceted, spanning various demographic and cultural dimensions. Ethnically a Jew, Paul wrote in Greek and was a Roman citizen.[16] Paul, the Jew, had an agenda which included

---

[15] Refer to pp. 1–4, 15–17, 43–45, 87–88, 104–105 and 178–81, above.
[16] For the value of a "Greek," like Paul the Jew, possessing Roman citizenship in

non-Jews. As an active "itinerant recruiter" and "community organizer,"[17] Paul was both exposed to different customs around the Mediterranean basin and faced the task of integrating the various viewpoints presented by his converts. Common expectations towards transient public speakers and psychagogic nurture were present in the cities where Paul founded communities. In order to be persuasive Paul needed to understand the customs of the recipients and the acceptable ways and means of presenting oneself (favorably) to one's audience. Here Paul availed himself of common ways and means of conceptualizing his activity.[18] Charges leveled against Paul do have a familiar ring from the public arena where religious and philosophical recruiters encountered the charge of being a charlatan or fraud as others scrutinized their motives.[19] Regardless of the precise social matrix of Paul's activity, we confidently maintain that Paul functioned in a commonly recognized role associated with the transient propagandist of the eastern Mediterranean world,[20] a role which Jews (probably) also assumed.[21]

---

the early Principate see G. E. M. de Ste. Croix, *The Class Struggle in the Ancient Greek World From the Archaic Age to the Arab Conquests* (Ithaca, New York, 1981), pp. 455–56.

[17] Contrast G. Theissen's "community organizer" versus "itinerant charismatic" in *The Social Setting of Pauline Christianity. Essays on Corinth* (Philadelphia, 1982), pp. 27–67.

[18] See A. J. Malherbe, *Paul and the Popular Philosophers* (Minneapolis, 1989), pp. 76–77. This can be seen also on the literary level in the use of various literary forms and metaphors with classical echoes. See R. Renehan, "Classical Greek Quotations in the New Testament," in D. Neiman and M. Schatkin (eds.), *The Heritage of the Early Church* (OCA 195; Rome, 1973), pp. 17–46.

[19] L. Friedländer, *Darstellungen aus der Sittengeschichte Roms, in der Zeit von August bis Ausgang der Antonine* (9th and 10th ed. by G. Wissowa; 4 vols. Leipzig, 1919–21), vol. 4, pp. 301–308. See Dio Chrysostom, *Discourses* 13.14, 31; 32.8, and pp. 53–58, above.

[20] U. Kahrstedt, *Kulturgeschichte der römischen Kaiserzeit* (Bern, 1958), pp. 306–13, 353–54; S. Dill, *Roman Society from Nero to Marcus Aurelius* (London, 1904), pp. 334–83; W. L. Liefeld, "The Wandering Preacher as a Social Figure in the Roman Empire," (Diss., Columbia University, 1967); P. Bowers, "Paul and Religious Propaganda in the First Century," *NovT* 22.4 (1980), pp. 316–23. R. F. Hock argues for the workshop as the social matrix of Paul's activity (*The Social Context of Paul's Ministry* [1980], pp. 37–42); S. K. Stowers argues for the household ("Social Status, Public Speaking and Private Teaching: The Circumstances of Paul's Preaching Activity," *NovT* 26 [1984], pp. 59–82).

[21] D. Georgi, *The Opponents of Paul in Second Corinthians*, pp. 83–228. The evidence for Jewish propagandistic endeavor is scant. See S. McKnight, *A Light among the Gentiles. Jewish Missionary Activity in the Second Temple Period* (Minneapolis, 1990), S. J. D. Cohen, "Adolph Harnack's 'The Mission and Expansion of Judaism': Christianity Succeeds Where Judaism Fails," *The Future of Early Christianity. Essays in honor of Helmut Koester* (ed. B. A. Pearson; Minneapolis, 1991), pp. 166–69.

This "Hellenistic" context required a flexible approach on Paul's part. Although there was a certain measure of uniformity around the Mediterranean basin due to Roman rule, Paul's travels throughout Palestine, Arabia, Syria, Asia Minor, Greece and Italy gave him ample opportunity to experience the differences in mentality and customs among these various regions. The same applies to differences among such urban centres as Jerusalem, Caesarea, Tarsus, the Syrian and Pisidian Antioch, Iconium, Lystra (and Derbe), Troas, Philippi, Thessalonica, Beroea, Corinth, Ephesus, Athens, and Rome, many of which Paul, according to the author of Acts at least, visited more than once,[22] and the small provincial towns of the rural areas encountered throughout his travels. That Paul's travels made a lasting impact on his self-image is not to be doubted. Working on this soil thus paved the way for, indeed, necessitated, Paul's adaptability. Such a flexibility probably did not appeal much to the Romans whom Paul encountered.[23] Paul, however, wanted to accommodate himself, without restriction, to all those he met in order to be the most effective in his role as God's herald. "I have become everything in turn to men of every sort" (1 Cor 9:22b) would then be an expression of both a fact and a desire. Paul could say, like Tennyson's Ulysses, "I am a part of all that I have met...."[24]

Paul's view of the circumstances of his life have found their expression in the peristasis catalogues which often note the adverse nature of these circumstances, thus requiring adaptation and resourcefulness in order to survive.[25] These catalogues and the various physical circumstances Paul encountered do not tell us much as to the ways in which he might have had to adapt in light of different customs or the vocation or disposition of those he met. 2 Cor 11:23–29 with its reference to "labors," "imprisonments," "shipwrecks," and "frequent journeys," is somewhat more detailed than the other catalogues (1 Cor 4:9–13, "we wander from place to place"; 2 Cor 4:8–9; 6:3–10), but much is left to the imagination. We only have some of the circumstantial contexts within which Paul needed to adapt in his more transient role and its necessity.

---

[22] See J. C. Hurd, Jr., *The Origin of 1 Corinthians*, p. 29.

[23] W. B. Stanford, *The Ulysses Theme* (New York, 1968), pp. 129, 148, notes the tendency among Romans to regard the Greeks as fickle opportunists.

[24] Cf. W. D. Davies, *Invitation to the New Testament* (London, 1967), p. 241.

[25] Cf. 2 Cor 11:26–27. See J. T. Fitzgerald, *Cracks in an Earthen Vessel: An Examination of the Catalogues of Hardships in the Corinthian Correspondence* (Atlanta, 1988), p. 37.

Many of Paul's experiences would have resonance with the experience of other transient speakers, such as Dio Chrysostom when he began roaming about everywhere and put on a humble attire. Dio's identity was not clear to those he met; they sometimes called him a tramp, a beggar, and even a philosopher. In his "frequent journeys," documented by the author of Acts, Paul's affinity with the "much-turned" and "much-travelled" Odysseus and the "roaming" Dio Chrysostom is all too clear.[26] Paul had probably, as Diogenes of Sinope and Aristippus, "discovered the means of adapting himself to circumstances" and was "capable of adapting himself to place, time and person, and playing his part appropriately under whatever circumstances."[27] But acknowledging that Paul in his transient role is comparable to Odysseus and Dio, for example, only gives us the context of our question and the reasons for its necessity, but does not begin to explicate the extent, nature, and possible forms of such an adaptation.

We can begin to concretize Paul's adaptation by studying how he cast his activity in different guises and uses manifold imagery to conceptualize his activity.[28] Evidence for Paul's adaptability is found in reflections on his activity, in the practice he attempts to implement in his communities, and in his own approach in his letters. The last gives evidence for Paul's verbal adaptability and shows us how he implemented his own theory of adaptation. The letter to the Romans, as does Gal 4:12, takes us to the center of Paul's self-presentation as a Jewish anomaly who adapts and identifies with the Gentiles and their particular justification in Christ.[29] It is probably correct that more cultural diversity requires more behavioral accommodation. The "rambunctious Corinthian church" with its multifarious constituents presents itself then as an ideal case study of Paul's

---

[26] Dio Chrysostom, *Discourse* 13.11; Paul, 1 Cor 4:11; 2 Cor 11:26; Phil 4:11–14.

[27] Diogenes Laertius, *Lives of Eminent Philosophers* 6.22; 2.66. Horace contrasts the conduct of the Cyrenaic Aristippus, who could adapt to any circumstance, with the less sensible behavior of Diogenes, the Cynic, who courted the common people (*Epistle* 1.17.13–32).

[28] For example as a nurturing spiritual father and considerate friend or brother. See pp. 186–90, above.

[29] Gal 4:12, Γίνεσθε ὡς ἐγώ, ὅτι κἀγὼ ὡς ὑμεῖς, ἀδελφοί, δέομαι ὑμῶν. In H. D. Betz' view, this verse presupposes a "strange 'missionary doctrine'" exemplified by Paul's becoming a Christian outside the Torah in order to save the Galatians (*Galatians. A Commentary on Paul's Letter to the Churches in Galatia* [Hermeneia; Philadelphia, 1979], pp. 220–37). Betz misses the force of Paul's Jewish anomaly when he says that Paul lived among the Galatians as a Christian, neither as a Jew nor as a pagan.

adaptation.³⁰ The Corinthian correspondence gives us much information for Paul's flexible approach, both in Paul's succinct reference to his own affable practice in 1 Cor 9:19–23 and 10:32–33, and throughout the letter where Paul adapts, in his use of hortatory terms and techniques, for example, to the different constituents of the Corinthian community.

Paul's letters were written at a time when the hortatory tradition was in a state of flux and attempts at systematization were in their infancy. His letters form a continuum with the hortatory tradition in antiquity and hortatory techniques are prominent throughout his letters.³¹ The terms παρακαλέω, παράκλησις, νουθετέω, νουθεσία, ἀναμιμνῄσκω, παραγγέλλω, as well as (ἢ) οὐκ οἴδατε ὅτι, and the setting forth of a model to be imitated, bring the hortatory nature of 1 Corinthians into relief. Besides noticeable affinities with hortatory blaming letters, this letter shares features of the letter of friendship.³² Many philophronetic features of ancient letters are present in 1 Corinthians, such as reference to common correspondence, the metaphorical use of "brother" and "sister," language expressing concern for the well-being of the recipients, statements of intent of upcoming visits, and the use of τί οὖν ἐστιν, ἀδελφοί, ἀλλὰ ἐρεῖ τις·, and τί οὖν φημι; all indicating a friendly diatribal exchange with an imaginary interlocutor. And, at the beginning of his paraenesis in 1:10, Paul employs one of the proverbial expressions of friendship. The common presence-absence motif of the friendly letter also occurs. The letter is a substitute for the author's actual presence by which the pain of separation is mediated, and an executor of its author's will. In light of these features it is best to see 1 Corinthians as a friendly hortatory blaming letter.³³

---

³⁰ D. Engels, *Roman Corinth. An Alternative Model for the Classical City* (Chicago, 1990), p. 93.

³¹ As, for example, in 1 Thessalonians. See Malherbe, *Paul and the Popular Philosophers*, pp. 49–66.

³² For παρακαλέω see 1 Cor 1:10; 4:13, 16; 14:31; and 16:15–16; for παράκλησις see 14:3; for νουθετέω see 4:14; for νουθεσία see 11:10; for ἀναμιμνῄσκω see 4:17; for παραγγέλλω see 7:10; 9:14; and 11:17; for (ἢ) οὐκ οἴδατε ὅτι, see 3:16; 5:6; 6:2, 3, 9, 15, 16, 19; 9:13, 24 (cf. also (οὐ) θέλω δὲ ὑμᾶς γίνεσθαι / εἰδέναι ὅτι in 10:20 and 11:3; and οἴδατε ... ὅτι in 16:15). On the call for imitation see 4:16 and 11:1 (μιμηταί μου γίνεσθε). Cf. Ps.-Demetrius 1 (32, 1–17 Malherbe); H. Koskenniemi, *Studien zur Idee und Phraeseologie des griechischen Briefes bis 400 n. Chr.* (Helsinki, 1956), pp. 115–27. On hortatory blaming letters, see S. K. Stowers, *Letter Writing in Greco-Roman Antiquity* (Philadelphia, 1986), pp. 125–141.

³³ For the above noted features, see 1 Cor 1:10, "I appeal to you ... that you be

It is important to recognize both the hortatory practices of the participatory psychagogy in vogue in Paul's communities and the hortatory features of Paul's own psychagogic guidance.[34] Paul shows not only an awareness of different hortatory terms and techniques but also a keen recognition of varying degrees of harshness in their use and their effects on others. From a psychagogic perspective it is somewhat fallacious to classify hortatory terms and their function in either the epideictic or advisory genres of rhetoric since characteristics of both genres are inherent in a psychagogic discourse. 1 Corinthians betrays the basic pattern of such a discourse. The formal epistolary nature of this letter gives example of Paul's guidance in the role of a frank and friendly counselor who mixes praise and blame as he presents the honorable and the shameful, the expedient and useful, and the choiceworthy and what should be rejected. This mixture of praise and blame, evident throughout in the letter, shows Paul's concern with adaptation and for the impact his hortatory means do have on the recipients of the letter.[35]

Issues of adaptation are evident within the larger literary context of 1 Cor 9:19–23, as is clear from Paul's mixture of praise and blame. An affable approach is also evident in Paul's use of the terms σύμφορος (5:12; 7:35; 10:23; 12:7), εὐσχήμων (7:35; cf. 7:36; 13:5), and καλός (7:1, 8, 26, 37, 38; cf. 5:6), which underline the consequences of his directives. These terms are so-called "common topics" which relate to the aim of a discourse, including the expedient, the honorable

---

united in the same mind and the same judgment" (cf. 2 Cor 13:11); 1:1; 4:18–21; 5:9, 11; 6:12–20; 7:1, 15, 25; 8:1; 9:5; 10:19, 23–11:1; 11:2, 32; 12:1; 14:26; 15:35; 16:1, 5–7, 12; M. Bünker, *Briefformular* (Göttingen, 1984), pp. 22–34; and Koskenniemi, *Studien zur Idee und Phraseologie des griechischen Briefes bis 400 n. Chr.*, pp. 64–66, 147, 170–71. For the presence/absence motif in 1 Cor 5:3; 11:34, see K. Thraede, *Grundzüge griechisch-römischer Brieftopik* (Munich, 1970) and pp. 324–25, below. See also D. Lührmann, "Freundschaftsbrief trotz Spannungen. Zu Gattung und Aufbau des Ersten Korintherbriefes," *Studien zum Text and zur Ethik des Neuen Testaments* (ed. W. Schrage; Berlin, 1986), pp. 298–314.

[34] See pp. 62, 64–65 and 202–204, above.

[35] In Chapter Two, we saw the need for adaptability in psychagogic guidance in the use of the mixed method of praise and blame. The common use of praise and blame in psychagogic guidance intertwines the formal aspects of both the epideictic and deliberative genres. Although psychagogy highlights rather the epideictic features of the letter, it is not my purpose to contest Margaret M. Mitchell's hypothesis that 1 Corinthians is a compositional unity containing a deliberative argument urging concord in the Corinthian community (*Paul and the Rhetoric of Reconciliation: An Exegetical Investigation of the Language and Composition of 1 Corinthians*; HUT 28. Tübingen: Mohr-Siebeck, 1991).

and just, the possible, greatness, and their contraries.³⁶ An orator must have at his fingertips propositions on these topics and prove that the course to which he exhorts is just, lawful, expedient, honorable, pleasant and practical. Common topics are situational and take seriously the contingencies of the addressees' life and add to the persuasiveness of the appeal. The concern with the beneficial, edifying, decent, and good, in an epistolary context which combines dissuasion and persuasion with praise and blame, underscores the consequentialist nature of the endeavor and Paul's concern with adaptation.

Paul's appeals are couched in specific and general advice, with praise for choiceworthy action and sometimes harsh blame for the opposite.³⁷ All of this is done in a friendly and "brotherly" fashion. Paul appeals to the tradition he and the Corinthians share, to his own judgment on issues, and to the teaching of nature as well as to the capacity of his readers to deliberate and come to a reasonable conclusion.³⁸ Paul's response in 1 Cor 7 shows his non-rigid approach, emphasizing individually different appropriations of a common tradition. After the remarks on marriage and the expression of his wish that all people be like himself, Paul notes that each has his own gift from God. The word ἕκαστος draws attention to individual differences and the religious impact of such differences; each should live according to the gift the Lord has apportioned him.³⁹ This is, Paul notes, how he orders in all the churches.

Paul also spotlights different ethical authorities and their relative importance. He contrasts saying something by way of concession, not of command, and draws attention to his own opinions, claiming to have the spirit of God.⁴⁰ Sometimes Paul concedes not having any

---

³⁶ Aristotle, *Rhetoric* 1358b23; 1362a18; 1359a38; 1365b; Anaximenes, *Rhet. ad Alexandrum* 1421b 23–26; 1427b39–41; 1428a1–2; H. Lausberg, *Handbuch der literarischen Rhetorik* (Münich, 1973), 1.51–61 # 53–65. Later rhetoricians recognize advantage as the aim of the deliberative genre, adding worth or honor as a desideratum. The same holds true for epideictic oratory. See Cicero, *The Making of an Orator* 2.82, *de Invent.* 2.155–58; [Cicero] *ad Her.* 3.2.3; 3.3.8; Theon, *Progymnasmata* 8.43–50 (ed. Butts); Quintilian, *Oratorical Institutions* 3.8.22–25; 3.4.16; 3.7.28; 11.1.8–9, 14.

³⁷ In his use of harshness, a friend aims at that which is noble and beneficial (πρὸς τὸ καλὸν καὶ συμφέρον; Plutarch, *How to Tell a Flatterer from a Friend* 55D).

³⁸ Cf. S. K. Stowers, "Paul on the Use and Abuse of Reason," in D. L. Balch, E. Ferguson and W. A. Meeks (eds.), *Greeks, Romans, and Christians. Essays in Honor of Abraham J. Malherbe* (Minneapolis, 1990), pp. 262–66.

³⁹ 1 Cor 7:17. See also Rom 12:3, 6 and 14:22, and my discussion on pp. 219–28, above.

⁴⁰ 1 Cor 7:6, 40. Contrast 1 Cor 2:16 and see my discussion on pp. 301–304, below.

command from the Lord and contrasts his opinion and the Lord's. As to the married, it is not his command but the Lord's that they should remain married. Paul claims not to have any command from the Lord with regard to the virgins but still gives his own opinion. In his opinion it is "well" (καλός) for the unmarried and the widows to remain as they are. As an exception, however, under certain conditions, "they should marry" (7:8-12).

In a casuistic manner, Paul gives an instance when the "good" may be modified; when the unmarried and the widows do not live continently they should marry. By this Paul has underscored the "good" as a behavioral standard and particularizes an exception to the good by a reference to an emotional state of mind which overrides the good. Paul also uses the term καλός to underline the desirability of action—"It is a good thing for a man to stay as he is" (7:26). Paul's overall concern is the welfare of the Corinthians, for what is expedient and beneficial as well as for what is "decent" or "seemly." His aim is to "promote undistracted propriety and devotion toward God" (7:35). Paul's adaptation is then necessitated by his concern for the community united in a common worship. This is also clear from Paul's use of a common topic in chapter eleven where he appeals to the Corinthians' understanding, the "teaching of nature," what is "fitting" and the "habit" of not being contentious (1 Cor 11:13-16).

The larger context within which the dictum of adaptability occurs, namely 1 Cor 5:1-11:1, forms a thematic unity of freedom and rights, as well as that of association of different types of people, inside and outside the community.[41] Throughout, Paul's rhetorical audience is seen in terms of a twofold solution to the human predicament, namely, ascetic and conceptual-intellectual, analogous to a therapeutic model recommended by Plutarch.[42] The ascetic solution is evident in 1 Cor 7; the conceptual-intellectual one in 6:12-20 and 8:1-11:1. Both are

---

[41] This is evident from 1 Cor 6:12-20 with its focus on moral freedom and from the recurrence of key terms in 6:12-11:1: Ἔξεστιν is used twice in 6:12 and in 10:23; ἐλεύθερος occurs in 7:21, 22, 39; 9:1, 10; ἐλευθερία in 10:29; ἐξουσία in 7:37; 8:9; 9:4, 5, 6, 12, 18; and ἐξουσιάζω in 6:12 and 7:4. See S. K. Stowers, "A 'Debate' over Freedom: I Corinthians 6:12-20," *Christian Teaching: Studies in Honor of LeMoine G. Lewis* (ed. Everett Ferguson; Abilene, TX, 1981), pp. 59-71.

[42] I.e., ἄσκησις and ἐπιλογισμοί, succinctly stated in Plutarch's *On Compliancy* 532D. These "solutions" correspond to what scholars have labelled "libertine" and "ascetic" (Weiss, *Korintherbrief*, p. 169). Paul assumes the presence of both these "tendencies" within the community.

248                      CHAPTER SIX

means to achieve self-mastery. Interestingly, Paul is stringent when he attempts to modify the intellectual position but flexible when it comes to the ascetic position. He also partially uses the ascetic dimension in order to counter the intellectual self-mastery of the wise by showing them a correct kind of (ascetic) self-mastery (9:24–10:13), one which goes to the extreme to benefit others and not only oneself.

In 1 Cor 7 Paul discusses the rights of husbands and wives, widows, the unmarried, and slaves. Freedom and the eating of meat sacrificed to idols and the way to reform others is the topic in chapter 8. In chapter 9 Paul uses himself as an example of voluntarily restricting one's freedom for the good of others. After a dire warning and emphasis on self-discipline in 10:1–13 (cf. 9:24–27), and a discussion of the dangers of participation in sacrificial meals (10:14–22), Paul returns in 10:23 to the slogan of 6:12, arguing that individual freedom must be restricted by communal advantage. As Paul is critical of the wise in this context so also in 6:12–20 where Paul in no uncertain terms affirms what the wise deny. The well-attested version of the Stoic paradox "only the wise man is truly free,"—"all things are permitted for me"—is stated and modified twice; freedom of action should be beneficial to the actor and not lead to the loss of freedom. Two further slogans are advanced for the libertine position, "food is meant for the stomach and the stomach for food and God will destroy both one and the other" and "every sin which a man commits is apart from the body."[43] The body is morally irrelevant. Paul counters with an exhortation, "flee immorality" and "glorify God in your body" (1 Cor 6:18a; 20b; cf. 10:14).

In his criticism of the "wise" Paul calls for imitation of his conduct as he has imitated that of Christ (11:1). Just before his call for imitation, Paul gives the wise two criteria of conduct, as he relativizes their behavior situationally. Firstly, "whatever you do, do everything for the glory of God." Secondly,

> give no offense to Jews or to Greeks or to the church of God, just as I try to please everyone in everything I do (πάντα πᾶσιν ἀρέσκω), not seeking my own advantage, but that of many, so that they may be saved (1 Cor 10:32–33).

---

[43] 1 Cor 6:13ab, 18b. That these are the parameters of the slogans and reflect the Corinthian position is shown by J. Murphy-O'Connor, "Corinthian Slogans in 1 Cor 6:12–20," *CBQ* 40.3 (1978) 391–96. Cf. W. L. Willis, *Idol Meat in Corinth. The Pauline Argument in 1 Corinthians 8 and 10* (SBLDS 68; Chico, California, 1985), pp. 123–222.

These criteria are the driving force of Paul's vocation. Paul wishes to benefit all and seek the advantage of many, to "please everyone in everything." Paul does "all things" for the gospel and urges his readers to do everything for the glory of God. By emphasizing what benefits others over against self-benefit, Paul counters Epictetus' saying that "every living thing is to nothing so devoted as to its own interest."[44] This emphasis, together with the reference to the "groups" and "disposition" in 1 Cor 9:19–23 and 10:32–33, and οἱ πολλοί in the latter text, expands the horizon of Paul's readers from the individual to the many, from self-advantage to the advantage of others, and is our clue to Paul's purpose in the overall context of his dictum of adaptation.[45] The emphasis on recruitment and psychagogy evident in the form of 1 Cor 9:19–23 is also present in 10:32–33 with its reference both to the "church of God" and also to "Jews" and "Greeks." One must adapt to and associate with different types of people both within and outside the community in order to please and benefit as many as possible.

*6.2 The Form and Function of 1 Corinthians 9:19–23: Adaptability in the Unreserved Association with All and in Psychagogy*

The classic statement on Paul's affable approach is found in 1 Cor 9:19–23. This pericope reveals a distinct form which should guide our understanding of its function:

19 Ἐλεύθερος γὰρ ὢν ἐκ πάντων πᾶσιν ἐμαυτὸν ἐδούλωσα,
    ἵνα τοὺς πλείονας κερδήσω.
20 καὶ ἐγενόμην
  (1) τοῖς Ἰουδαίοις ὡς Ἰουδαῖος,
    ἵνα Ἰουδαίους κερδήσω.
  (2) τοῖς ὑπὸ νόμον ὡς ὑπὸ νόμον, μὴ ὢν αὐτὸς ὑπὸ νόμον,
    ἵνα τοὺς ὑπὸ νόμον κερδήσω.
21 (3) τοῖς ἀνόμοις ὡς ἄνομος, μὴ ὢν ἄνομος θεοῦ ἀλλ' ἔννομος Χριστοῦ,
    ἵνα κερδάνω τοὺς ἀνόμους.

---

[44] 1 Cor 10:33, 24. See 1 *Clem.* 48.6. Compare Epictetus, *Discourse* 2.22.15–16, 26–27.

[45] Οἱ πολλοί is a standard way of referring to the "multitude" (LSJ s.v.); Epictetus, *Discourse* 3.4.12; Isocrates, *Letter to Philip* 1.22; *To Demonicus* 17; *To Nicocles* 45; 50.

22a ἐγενόμην
 *(4)* τοῖς ἀσθενέσιν ἀσθενής,
        ἵνα τοὺς ἀσθενεῖς <u>κερδήσω</u>.
22b τοῖς πᾶσιν **γέγονα** πάντα,
        ἵνα πάντως τινὰς <u>σώσω</u>.
23 πάντα δὲ ποιῶ διὰ τὸ εὐαγγέλιον,
        ἵνα συγκοινωνὸς αὐτοῦ γένωμαι.

19 For though I am free with respect to all, I have made myself a slave to all,
    so that I might win more of them.
20 *(1)* To the Jews *I became* as a Jew,
    in order to win Jews.
 *(2)* To those under the law I became as one under the law
  (though I myself am not under the law)
    so that I might win those under the law.
21 *(3)* To the lawless ones I became as a lawless one
 (though I am not free from God's law but am under Christ's law)
    so that I might win the lawless ones.
22a *(4)* To the weak *I became* weak,
    so that I might win the weak.
22b Indeed, *I have become* everything in turn to men of every sort,
    so that in one way or another I may save some.
23 I do it all for the sake of the gospel,
    so that I may share in its blessings.[46]

This pericope begins and rounds off with a general claim of wide applicability: Paul has made himself a slave to all [people] (πᾶσιν ἐμαυτὸν ἐδούλωσα, v. 19) and has become all things to all (τοῖς πᾶσιν γέγονα πάντα, v. 22b) those [people] mentioned in vv. 20–22a, namely, "Jews," "those under the law," "the lawless ones," and "the weak."[47] Paul's affable approach has a specific goal in mind, expressed in a

---

[46] I have adjusted the translation of NRSV using the "lawless ones" instead of "those outside the law." I use the NEB translation of verse 22b. J. Weiss saw in this pericope formally a chiastic correspondence, B (v. 20a) C (v. 20b) C' (v. 21a) B' (v. 22b) in vv. 20–22, but in content a *parallelismus membrorum*, BC B'C'. See "Beiträge zur Paulinischen Rhetorik," *Theologische Studien, Bernhard Weiss zu seinem 70. Geburtstag dargebracht* (Göttingen, 1897), pp. 194–95. N. W. Lund identified the chiastic structure of 9:19–22 with A (v. 19) B (v. 20a) C (v. 20b) C' (v. 21) B' (v. 22a) A' (v. 22b). See *Chiasmus in the New Testament. A Study in the Form and Function of Chiastic Structures*. Peabody, MA: Hendrickson Pub., 1992 (org. publ. 1942), pp. 147–48.

[47] C. K. Barrett notes that the definite article (τοῖς πᾶσιν) "groups together all the

sequence of five identical purpose clauses (ἵνα κερδήσω, ἵνα κερδήσω, ἵνα κερδήσω, ἵνα κερδάνω, ἵνα κερδήσω; vv. 19, 20, 21, 22a), one ἵνα σώσω clause (v. 22b; 10:33, ἵνα σωθῶσιν) and a general purpose clause (v. 23). The purpose of Paul's voluntary slavery and adaptation is to "gain" or "win" all these people or as many as possible (ἵνα τοὺς πλείονας κερδήσω),⁴⁸ saving or benefitting some in one way or another (ἵνα παντῶς τινὰς σώσω; v. 22b). Paul rounds off this pericope by stating that he does this all for the sake of the gospel so that he may share in its benefits (or "be a fellow-participant in the gospel," ἵνα συγκοινωνὸς αὐτοῦ (sc. τοῦ εὐαγγελίου) γένωμαι; v. 23).

The words σῴζω and κερδαίνω used in the purpose clauses express Paul's concern. Σῴζω is a common term among moralists used to connote their concern to benefit others; κερδαίνω, on the other hand, often denotes personal profit.⁴⁹ These two terms are sometimes used together, bringing the above contrast to the foreground, as, for example, in two speeches in which Antisthenes contrasts Ajax and Odysseus in defence of the latter. In the former speech Ajax accuses Odysseus of acting secretively, willing to suffer ill treatment, if he might thereby gain (κερδαίνω) something. In the latter speech Odysseus replies, referring to the analogy of steersmen who night and day look out how to save the sailors, claiming, "so do I myself and I save both you and all the other men."⁵⁰ This contrast is also seen in the Cynic *Epistle of Diogenes*. Dionysius is encouraged to accept the guidance of a pedagogue who "carries a very painful whip" so that he may be "saved." The urgency of the proposal is seen in Dionysius' association with people who corrupt and destroy him; the latter are not looking out for any good they might do him, but rather "searching for whatever personal gain they might make."⁵¹ Similarly, Dio Chrysostom finds it shocking if some who come in a guise of philosopher chant verses of their own composition and do that with a

---

examples" given (*A Commentary on The First Epistle to the Corinthians* (New York: Harper & Row, 1968, p. 215).

⁴⁸ Or "the majority" (οἱ πλείονες); cf. 1 Cor 10:5; 15:6.

⁴⁹ LSJ s.v. Cf. Jas 4:13; Matt 25:16; Titus 1:11. See Philodemus, *On Frank Criticism* frs. 34.3–4; 36.1–2. Col. 6b1–3 contrasts a person who, in order to mature, has needed frank speech very little with a person who has been "saved" by it (ὁ δὲ διὰ ταύτης σεσωσμένος). Cf. pp. 78–80, above.

⁵⁰ F. Decleva Caizzi (ed.), *Antisthenis fragmenta* (Milan, 1966), frs. 14 (Ajax) and 15 (Odysseus).

⁵¹ *Ep. Diog.* 29.1–3 (126, 1–28 Malherbe), παιδαγωγῶν ... σκῦτος δὲ ἀλγεινότατον φέροντα ... σωθήσῃ ... διαφθείροιεν ... ὅ τι κερδανοῦσι ζητοῦσιν. ...

view to their own profit and reputation, and not to improve others. This is "as if a physician when visiting patients would disregard their treatment and restoration of health."[52]

The term κερδαίνω is integral to Paul's self-identity as God's instrument in benefiting humans.[53] Paul's enslavement to all in order to be a participant in the gospel has resonance with his "counting everything as loss," even his achievements as a Jew. In view of the distinction between personal profit and advantage of other, Paul's adaptation apparently benefits both others and himself (9:23b)! However, we should not attempt to distinguish too sharply the meaning of the terms κερδαίνω and σῴζω, since Paul uses both to describe the end goal of his adaptation.[54] The purpose of Paul's voluntary slavery and unmitigated adaptation to all is to win over and benefit as many as he possibly can for the sake of the good news of which he is a herald. This requires not only good-will but strenuous effort, self-discipline and perseverence as the following pericope emphasizes (9:24–27).

1 Cor 9:19–23 is still ambivalent, firstly, because the nature of Paul's adaptation is not specified; secondly, because the identification of the groups is not clear; and thirdly, because it aligns Paul's practice to the all-conforming flatterer. Paul accentuates his adaptation in the "language of becoming," by repeating γίνομαι in verse 20 before the listing of the people and in verse 22a when referring to the weak and in his claim to have become all things to all in v. 22b. The chiastic structure of the pericope shows the inclusive nature of Paul's adaptation: Paul has "made himself a slave to all" and has "become everything in turn to men of every sort" (vv. 19, 22b).[55]

Paul's "language of becoming" in this text has baffled scholars. C. K. Barrett, for example, notes that Paul differs from all "non-Christian Pharisees" in that he was ready to cease to be a Jew: "But

---

[52] *Discourse* 32.10, κέρδους ἕνεκεν ... σωτηρίας αὐτῶν καὶ τῆς θεραπείας ἀμελήσειε.

[53] Note Phil 3:7–9; 1:21. Cf. 1 Pet 3:1. D. Daube explains κερδαίνω as a "rabbinic missionary term." See *The New Testament and Rabbinic Judaism* (London, 1956), pp. 352–61.

[54] Paul uses σῴζω to describe the purpose of his recruitment and the effect his message has (See fns. 59–60, below). Cf. Clement's use of κερδαίνω in *Ped.* 74.2 (GCS 133, 17 Stählin-Treu) in the sense of sparing a soul's eternal death by the use of salutary harshness.

[55] Paul uses a similar motif in his repetition of γίνομαι where he urges his readers to change in order to "become" something else than what they "are" (see 1 Cor 3:18; 7:20–24; and 14:20 (cf. 4:15) as well as the use of ὡς μὴ in 7:29–31).

Paul (as he himself affirms elsewhere, notably 2 Cor xi.22; Phil iii.5) was a Jew. He could *become* a Jew only if, having been a Jew, he had ceased to be one and become something else. His Judaism was no longer of his very being, but a guise he could adopt or discard at will."[56] H. Conzelmann finds a way out of this dilemma by claiming that the ὡς in verse 20, "to the Jews I became *as* a Jew" is superfluous. The same holds true for the ὡς in verse 22, "to the weak I became *as* weak," witnessed in MSS C D F G and other authorities. The latter is introduced secondarily in order to remove the offense of the suggestion that Paul should be said to have been weak. As to the former, the ὡς is superfluous because "[Paul] *is* a Jew." The ὡς in verses 20b and 21 is on the other hand perfectly appropriate since "to the Gentiles [Paul] must *become* a Gentile."[57]

An answer to the above dilemma is provided by several different clues. Our first clue to an understanding of the dictum of adaptation in 1 Cor 9:19–23 is found in discussions of the flatterer, the friend of many, the political man and also in defences of versatility. Here, the idea of association with different kinds of people is important as is also the social matrix of patronage and the question of what changes in adaptation. Our second clue comes from the close connection between the philosopher's σχῆμα and λόγος, and our third from ancient discussions of character portrayals.[58] Finally, the form of this pericope is significant for its function within the larger literary context.

With his reference to the "weak" Paul underlines his practice of adaptation in psychagogic nurture and with his reference to the "groups" of people his flexible approach in the transient role of itinerant recruiter. Successful psychagogy and recruitment both require adaptation to different types of ethical characters, i.e., the good and lawless, and to persons of different psychological disposition. The distinction between recruitment and psychagogy or formation within

---

[56] C. K. Barrett, *A Commentary on the First Epistle to the Corinthians*, p. 211; See also B. Hall: "The oddity of v. 20d ("not being myself under law"), indeed of the whole verse, is that Paul *is* a Jew." In "All Things to All People: A Study of 1 Corinthians 9:19–23," in R. T. Fortna and B. R. Gaventa (eds.), *The Conversation Continues. Studies in Paul & John. In Honor of J. Louis Martyn* (Nashville, 1990), pp. 139–40. P. W. Gooch resolves the above dilemma by claiming that Paul had ". . . a new identity 'in Christ'. He is really a Jew no longer—but no more is he a Gentile. . . ." ("The ethics of accommodation: A study in Paul," *Tyndale Bulletin* 29 (1978), p. 111). Gooch's solution is similar to Betz's in his discussion of Gal 4:12.
[57] H. Conzelmann, *1 Corinthians* (Philadelphia, 1975), pp. 159 n. 5, 161 n. 20.
[58] See pp. 20–23, 42–43, and 48–49, above.

the community is heuristic more than a reflection of an actual condition since these form part of a continuum. Both novices and nonbelievers could be affected by the word of prophetic utterance in Corinthian worship, showing the fluid state of affairs regarding communal boundaries among early Christian groups, also seen from Paul's use of identical words to describe the effect on both.[59] The purpose of associating with "outsiders" is to benefit them, to recruit or "save" them; this is also the reason why one can associate in marriage with an "unbeliever." The purpose of harsh correction of the immoral and an affable approach towards the psychologically weak is also to save or benefit them.[60]

The reference to the various "groups" of people to which Paul adapts and the inclusive nature of Paul's voluntary slavery and adaptation, suggests the motif of unrestricted association with all, also accentuated by the reference to "the many" in 1 Cor 9:19, 22 and 10:33, and by the contrast between personal and communal advantage present in the larger context. In order to interpret the function of this pericope what is significant is not the identity of the groups as such but rather this reference to "the many" and to the "weak" at the end of the pericope, distinguished from the groups by the repetition of ἐγενόμην and by the omission of the ὡς before the "weak."[61]

This emphasis on adaptation in light of human diversity and psychagogic adaptation in light of the human disposition displays a distinct structure representing a common tradition which is clearly

---

[59] This is true both of the words that occur in 1 Cor 14:24, namely, ἐλέγχειν and ἀνακρίνειν (4:5; 10:25, 27), and the words σῴζειν and ἀπόλλυμι (1 Cor 1:18; 3:15; 8:10; 9:22b; 10:9, 33). See W. Meeks, "'Since Then You Would Need To Go Out Of The World': Group Boundaries in Pauline Christianity," in *Critical History and Biblical Faith: New Testament Perspectives* (ed. T. J. Ryan; Villanova, Pa.: College Theology Society, 1979), pp. 4–29, and pp. 174–75 and 195–98, above.

[60] Paul is concerned with recruitment throughout the letter (cf. 1 Cor 1:18–21; 9:19–27; 10:28–31; 15:1–3). "Recruitment" is highlighted by the words κηρύσσω (1:23; 9:27; 15:11, 12; cf. also 2 Cor 1:19; 11:4), κήρυγμα (1:21; 2:4; 15:14), εὐαγγελίζω (1:17; 9:16, 18; 15:1–2), and τὸ εὐαγγέλιον (4:15; 9:12, 14, 18, 23). See also the reference to the "word of the cross" in 1:18 where Paul uses the contrast between "those who are saved or lost." See 1 Cor 1:21 (ὁ θεὸς ... σῶσαι τοὺς πιστεύοντας·); 5:5 (ἵνα τὸ πνεῦμα σωθῇ ἐν τῇ ἡμέρᾳ τοῦ κυρίου); 7:16 (τί γὰρ οἶδας, γύναι, εἰ τὸν ἄνδρα σώσεις; ἢ τί οἶδας, ἄνερ, εἰ τὴν γυναῖκα σώσεις); 9:22b (τοῖς πᾶσιν γέγονα πάντα, ἵνα πάντως τινὰς σώσω); 10:33b (μὴ ζητῶν ἐμαυτοῦ σύμφορον ἀλλὰ τὸ τῶν πολλῶν, ἵνα σωθῶσιν); and 15:2 (δι' οὗ καὶ σῴζεσθε). See also 3:15.

[61] Introduced later in C D G and R. Paul uses ὡς before Ἰουδαῖος, ὑπὸ νόμον and ἄνομος.

articulated in Philo's description of the political man and Maximus of Tyre's defense of versatility.[62] The good statesman is like a pilot and physician who need to adapt in light of diverse circumstances and conditions. To bring home the latter point, Philo notes the use of stringent measures by physicians, guardians, affectionate fathers, and all persons in charge. Philo and Maximus both emphasize a flexible approach in light of human diversity and the importance of adapting in view of the human disposition. This same twofold perspective is evident in Paul's emphasis on accommodation in the unrestricted association with all or the "multitude" and the importance of psychagogic adaptation in the care of the weak.

Paul refers in 1 Cor 9:20-22a to four distinct "groups" of people, namely, "Jews" (οἱ Ἰουδαῖοι), "those under the law" (οἱ ὑπο νόμον), "the lawless ones" (οἱ ἄνομοι), and the "weak" (οἱ ἀσθενεῖς). Paul's Jewish identity is evident from the fact that he distinguishes himself from people of the second and third group by specific qualifications ("though I myself am not under the law" / "though I am not free from God's law but am under Christ's law"). By these qualifications and by mentioning two distinct groups of people after having referred to the Jews without qualification, Paul indicates that people of the second and third group are others than Jews or what is significant is not their ethnicity as such.

One might claim that Paul's listing of "Jews", "Greeks", and "the church of God" at the end of his discussion of this section (10:32-33) gives suggestive evidence for the fact that Paul is indeed referring to "Gentiles" in the second and third instance in 1 Cor 9:20-21. However, if Paul wanted to say that he adapted himself to "Gentiles" after having claimed to have adapted himself to the Jews, one would have expected him to have used Ἕλληνες (or even ἔθνη) or ἄπιστοι as he does throughout this letter and elsewhere.[63] This shows that what is significant for Paul as he refers to people of the second and third group here is not their ethnicity as such. By diverting from his regular way of speaking which is to refer to "Jews and Gentiles", Paul indicates that he wants to say something specific

---

[62] See pp. 38-45, above.
[63] Besides 1 Cor 10:32, Paul uses the phrase Ἰουδαῖοι καὶ Ἕλληνες in 1 Cor 1:24; 12:13; Rom 1:16; 2:9-10; 3:9; 10:12; and Gal 3:28 (cf. Col. 3:11). For other instances of Ἕλλην, see 1 Cor 1:22 and Gal 2:3. For ἄπιστοι, see 1 Cor 6:6; 7:12-15; 14:22-24 (cf. also 2 Cor 4:4; 6:14-15). For (τὰ) ἔθνη, see 1 Cor 1:23; Rom 16:4; and Gal 2.12, 14.

about people other than Jews, namely, the "lawless ones" and those "under the law." In 10:32 Paul reverts back to his normal way of speaking, referring collectively to "Greeks" when denoting people other than Jews.

Although we can understand the function of this pericope without an identification of the people of the second and third group, I am not suggesting that their identity is insignificant or that such a knowledge might not be illuminating for Paul's social practice. Absolute certainty is simply not attainable. My reading, however, does have implications for our understanding of the function of this pericope within its rhetorical context as well as for the identity of those Paul refers to. My reading, in particular, raises the likelihood that the word οἱ ἄνομοι has a moral connotation and shows that οἱ ἀσθενεῖς refers to those who are psychologically weak. Such connotations gain support from understanding the function of this pericope in view of the larger context with its theme of association with different types of people of different dispositions.

The identity of people of the second group ("those under the law") is not clear. Paul uses οἱ ὑπὸ νόμον only in 1 Cor 9:20 and Gal 4:5.[64] These people were possibly "God-fearers" who wanted to follow some aspects of the Jewish law and thereby gain self-mastery, an issue with which Paul was concerned on other occasions, as we know.[65] Certain forms of self-mastery are also clearly present in the larger epistolary context. I have claimed that Paul uses the pericope of 9:24–27 to emphasize a correct kind of self-mastery, namely, one which is concerned for the well-being of others and not simply self-edification. Individual spiritual exercises are also clearly subsumed under collective edification in chapter 14. The emphasis on self-mastery is evident in the claim of the wise to be totally in charge of their own destiny, being able to evaluate their own spiritual growth and that of

---

[64] Gal 4:5, ἵνα τοὺς ὑπὸ νόμον ἐξαγοράσῃ ("in order that he might redeem those under the law"). Paul explains that this purpose is achieved through Jesus' adaptability ("God sent his son, γενόμενον ἐκ γυναικός, γενόμενον ὑπὸ νόμον, ἵνα. . . ."). See also Paul's reflections on Christ's affable behavior in 2 Cor 5:20–21; 8:9; Rom 8:3; Gal 3:13; and Phil 2:5–11. See p. 216 (fn. 97), above.

[65] These people are referred to in Acts 17:4 as οἱ σεβόμενοι Ἕλληνες. For Paul's concern with such issues, see Stanley K. Stowers, *A Rereading of Romans*, pp. 42–82. Πλεονέκτης (and πλεονεξία; cf. 1 Cor 5:9) is clearly connected with the discourse on self-mastery as is ἐγκράτεια (9:25) and ἀσθένεια (cf. 8:7–10; 9:22b) showing that Paul describes the practical issues in Corinth in psychological and ethical terms. See pp. 276–90, below.

others, especially the weak. "Weakness" as we shall see below also formed part of the discourse of self-mastery. I am not claiming that all these people are being referred to when Paul says he adapted himself to those "under the law". I am simply drawing attention to the presence of issues relating to self-mastery in the letter, thus raising the likelihood that "those under the law" were indeed concerned with such matters.

The identity of people of the third group is not clear either but the larger rhetorical context and function of this pericope would seem to suggest that, contrary to a widespread view, Paul is not referring here to "Gentiles" as such or those who do not possess or have some particular law but rather to lawless and immoral people. The claim that ὁ ἄνομος and οἱ ἄνομοι were common terms for gentiles or technical expressions for gentiles is not supported by the evidence. Ἄνομος and cognates usually mean "evil", "wicked", or "sinful" in Jewish literature before 70 CE and the vast majority of examples refer to Jews or to the wicked in general and not to gentiles. "Outside the law" is then not its most natural translation but rather "transgressor", "lawless men", "lawlessness", "evildoer" and "wickedness".[66]

Paul does not use οἱ ἄνομοι or ἄνομος elsewhere, but uses the adv. ἀνόμως in Rom 2:12 (together with the adv. ἐννόμως, a hapax, as is ἔννομος in 1 Cor 9:21), and ἀνομία in Rom 4:7 (= Ps 32:1), 6:19, and 2 Cor 6:14. The opposition of ἄνομος to ἔννομον in v. 21 in the phrase μὴ ὢν ἄνομος θεοῦ ἀλλ' ἔννομος Χριστοῦ (RSV = "not being without law toward God but under the law of Christ") need not indicate that the contrast implies the states of having and not having the law or that "without (or outside) the law" and "under the law" are the most plausible translations. This is clear from a text from Heliodorus' *Ethiopian Story* (8.8.57) which also uses the opposition of ὁ ἔννομος ὑπερόπτης ("a loyal contemner" or "one who lawfully despises") with ἄνομον βουλευμάτων ("disloyal designs" or "lawless intrigues").

Regardless of exactly how one translates the phrase ἔννομος Χριστοῦ, it can, in light of the above contrast and Paul's use of ὁ νόμος τοῦ Χριστοῦ *(hapax)* in Gal 6:2, be construed as Paul's way of emphasizing that although his adaptation towards the immoral could be seen as ungodly it is in complete accord with "Christ's law" and affable

---

[66] For this, see Stanley K. Stowers, *A Rereading of Romans*, pp. 134–38.

behavior.⁶⁷ Indeed, it is Christ's behavior that forms the examplary pattern of Paul's own affable conduct (1 Cor 11:1). Ἄνομοι is sometimes used in connection with ἄδικοι, increasing the likelihood of a moral reading of the former term. Paul can then indirectly be referring to the ἄδικοι (cf. 6:9) when he says he adapted himself to οἱ ἄνομοι. I have adopted the translation of "the lawless ones" in order to draw attention to the moral connotations present in the word ἄνομοι.⁶⁸

In his effort to benefit others, Paul was then willing to associate with people of different moral standing. Although the identity of the "groups" referred to in 9:20–22 is not crucial for our understanding of the function of this pericope, a moral connotation of οἱ ἄνομοι gains support from the above suggested function of the pericope. The offensiveness of such a blatantly circular argument can be somewhat lessened when we realize that Paul is concerned with the association of people of different moral standing in the larger literary context of the pericope. Reverberations of the issues hinted at in 1 Cor 9:19–23 are found in its wider context in Paul's concern with a right and wrong form of association between different types of people both within and outside the community. Guidelines concerning intramural behavior are given in chapters 8–14 where Paul discusses, among others things, the relative importance of individual and collective spiritual exercises, the association of rich and poor in the community, and the approach to be taken towards the weak. Discussions on matters relating to the association with outsiders and the immoral occur in chapters 5–7, 9–10, and 14.

With whom one should associate relates to cultural norms regarding acceptable behavior, centering on the habits, customs, and manners which separate people.⁶⁹ Such matters are for instance at issue in Gal 2:11–14. The bone of contention between Peter, Paul, and

---

⁶⁷ See also Rom 3:27, νόμος πίστεως, and 8:2, νόμος τοῦ πνεύματος τῆς ζωῆς ἐν Χριστῷ Ἰησοῦ.

⁶⁸ *1 Clem.* 16.13; 56.11 (Job 5:22); 18.13; 35.9, 5; 45.4 (ἄνομοι opposed to δίκαιοι). *Herm. Vis.* 3.6.1, 4; *Sim.* 5.5.3; 9.9.1; *Diogn.* 9.3–6; Heliodorus, *Ethiopian Story* 8.8.57. In *Who Is the Rich Person Who Will Be Saved?* 20, Clement describes a rich man as ἔννομος ἄνθρωπος or law-abiding or upright and uses the phrase "law of Christ" in 23 (Χριστοῦ νόμος) in an ethical sense, contrasted with wrongdoing (ἀδικία).

⁶⁹ We have seen that such issues were widely discussed during Paul's time. Association with many was thought to ruin good moral behavior. Besides the works referred to on pp. 125–26, above, see Seneca, *Epistles* 103 (*On the Dangers of Association with Our Fellow-Men*) and 7 (*On Crowds*).

James was the question of association with the undesirable, in this instance the gentiles.⁷⁰ When reflecting on his affable approach in 1 Corinthians, Paul had already experienced the repercussions of an accommodating practice; in Galatia, however, he is the stringent one, Peter the flexible one. Peter used to eat with gentile "sinners" until pressured by James; then he kept himself separate for fear of the circumcision faction.⁷¹ The issue of "becoming" concerns a change in certain practices involving association, for example, one's presence at a dinner party with a member of society previously shunned. Such a practice reminds us of flatterers and the friend of many, and the common animal analogies used to characterize them. The cunning of the polyp became proverbial. Thus, when the author of *Barnabas* explains a Jewish food law which forbade the consumption of a lamprey, a polyp or a cuttlefish, he notes that this is advice not to "consort with or become like such men who are utterly ungodly and who are already condemned to death, just as these fish alone are accursed."⁷²

Paul's willingness to associate with all encountered a strong countertendency among those who emphasized the separation from the "immoral." But the incentive for Paul's behavior was strong, found in the message of which he was the herald. The self-abasement and change in Christ's "appearance" to that of a slave, shows that in his willingness to take on different σχήματα, Paul is imitating Christ, as he himself says (1 Cor 11:1). A willingness to change or hide one's status for the benefit of others is also seen in Joseph's deliberate act of self-disguise for the good of his brothers, in Theseus sharing in Peirithous' imprisonment, in Demetrius' self-disguise in order to benefit his wrongfully imprisoned slave Antiphilus, and in Odysseus' voluntary suffering and self-abasement.⁷³ Paul's dictum is imbued with

---

⁷⁰ So argued by E. P. Sanders, "Jewish Association with Gentiles in Galatians 2:11–14," in R. T. Fortna and B. R. Gaventa (eds.), *The Conversation Continues*, pp. 170–188.

⁷¹ Gal 2:12–13, μετὰ τῶν ἐθνῶν συνήσθιεν· Note the reference to Peter's ὑπόκρισις. Perhaps Paul learned something from Peter here. Peter is charged with "living like a Gentile" and "forcing Gentiles to live like Jews" (2:14).

⁷² *Barn.* 10.5; Lev 11:10. Τέλος εἰσὶν ἀσεβεῖς is used with a moral connotation in this context.

⁷³ *T. Jos.* 3–9; Plutarch, *On Having Many Friends* 96A–D; Lucian, *Toxaris* 29–34. Cf. Josephus, *Antiquities* 10.11, on a king who exchanges his kingly robes for sackcloth and takes on a σχῆμα ταπεινόν. See Diodorus Siculus, *Library of History* 10.4.6, and pp. 38–40, above. Paul spoke of changes in σχῆμα and adopting a guise, both in reference to Christ's becoming a slave and to the duplicitous behavior of his

similar concerns; one should employ whatever means necessary in order to benefit others.

Paul's advice concerning "outsiders" and "insiders" in 1 Cor 5 is congruent with his remarks in 9:19–23 which shows the need for associating with immoral persons—ἄνομοι—*outside* the community in order to recruit or benefit them. That such behavior was seen as "lawless" by some goes without saying. But Paul emphasizes that such a conduct is upright and law-abiding, congruent with the "law of Christ" and explains the need for associating with different types of people in light of recruitment.[74] Paul's recruitment involved acceptance of such claims as "Christ died and lived again, that he might be Lord both of the dead and of the living."[75] Paul works out the behavioral consequences of the acceptance of such claims by attempting to have the immoral cease their immoral behavior, now that they have joined the community. Their presense, however, reflects the result, and success, of Paul's recruitment efforts; he has associated with different kinds of people and attracted diverse individuals to the community. The question as to with whom one should associate became a way of demarcating the blurred boundary between "the insiders" (οἱ ἔσω) and "the outsiders" (οἱ ἔξω), thus qualifying the nature of the community morally both as to who could join it and who should leave it.

From 1 Cor 5 and 6 it is clear that "immoral" people continued to be a part—although an undesirable one—of the community. As in his previous letter to the Corinthians, the vice Paul focuses on now is sexual immorality (or πορνεία; 5:1–5, 9; 6:12–20). The Corinthians had understood Paul's advice that they stop associating with οἱ πόρνοι to mean οἱ πόρνοι "of this world" or the πλεονέκται, εἰδωλολάτραι, and ἅρπαγες. Not so! What Paul meant was for the Corinthians to stop associating with any "so-called brother" who is a πόρνος, πλεονέκτης, εἰδωλολάτρης, ἅρπαξ, μέθυσος, and λοίδορος (5:9–11). The list of those in the community the Corinthians are advised not to mingle with, has obvious resonance with the problematic issues dealt with in the letter, especially the reference to the πόρνος,

---

counter psychagogues in Corinth (Phil 2:5–11 (σχῆμα and μορφή); 2 Cor 11:13–15). See fn. 64, above, on Gal 4:4–5, and p. 294, below.

[74] Cf. 1 Cor 9:22b; 10:33b. A pagan husband/wife and a Christian wife/husband should continue to live together (or associate with one another) since they might "save" each other (7:12–16).

[75] Rom 14:9. See also 1 Cor 8:6; 14:25; 1 Thess 1:9; and Gal 4:8–10.

πλεονέκτης, and εἰδωλολάτρης. Some had apparently displayed many vices before joining the community; they should now go through a reformation of character. Moral betterment is needed because οἱ ἄδικοι will not "inherit the kingdom of God."[76] The list of the "unjust" in 6:9–10 repeats πόρνοι, πλεονέκται, εἰδωλολάτραι, ἅρπαγες, μέθυσοι and λοίδοροι, from the list in 5:9–11, but becomes more detailed in adding μοιχοί, μαλακοί, ἀρσενοκοῖται, and κλέπται.

1 Cor 5:9–13 concerns behavior seen to be grossly damaging and ungodly, and not beliefs. Others should not condone such vices but should shun such persons. The Corinthians can associate with the "immoral" of this world but not with those in the community who continue to live immorally. In such a case, others should (eventually) have nothing to do with them; they "should not even eat with any such person" (v. 11). What is advised for the betterment of such vice-ridden persons is withdrawal; the purpose of shunning them is to reform their character by shaming them into repentance.[77] This harsh measure is needed because of a depraved condition. Members should influence each others' moral behavior. Paul, then, expects behavior modification in order to achieve the goal of good moral conduct. This shows an active attempt in both Epicurean and Pauline communities to influence the moral character of new recruits.[78]

The main thrust of Paul's argument in chapters 5–6 is to urge

---

[76] 1 Cor 6:9, ἢ οὐκ οἴδατε ὅτι ἄδικοι θεοῦ βασιλείαν οὐ κληρονομήσουσιν; See 1 Cor 5:8; 6:11 (καὶ ταῦτά τινες ἦτε), and 19–20.

[77] The reason why one should disassociate from the immoral and adapt to the weak is then the same, namely, to secure continual membership in the community of friends. On such a reading, 5:9–13 explains the procedure of expelling someone from the community; the "offender" is not expelled forthwith; one should first attempt to shame him into repentance. Part of Pauline correctional psychagogy is, as we have seen, to shame into repentance erring members through disassociation and the practice of shunning (see pp. 207–208, above). This practice is seen in 2 Thess 3:14–15 with regard to one who disobeys communal instruction, in 2 Thess 3:6 with regard to one who lives in idleness, in Tit 3:10–11 with regard to one who causes divisions, and in 1 Cor 5:9–13 with regard to the "immoral." As in 2 Thess 3:14–15, Paul uses the term συναναμίγνυμι also in 1 Cor 5:9, 11 (abs. w. dat of the pers.), "to mix up together"; pass. "to mingle or associate with." For Paul's warning in Rom 16:17 against those who seduce with smooth and specious words, compare Philodemus' discussion of the same problem in *On Frank Criticism* fr. 26.11; col. 1b5–13; and PHerc. 1082 col. 2.1–14. Note Epictetus' remark on the association of characters of different moral standing: "But different characters do not mix in this fashion; you cannot act the part of Thersites and that of Agamemnon too" (*Discourse* 4.2.8–10). Paul's quote from Menander's lost comedy *Thais* in 1 Cor 15:34, "Bad company ruins good morals," had more likely than not implications for relationships in the community.

[78] See pp. 170–75, above, on the presence of people of different moral standing

moral betterment and to define the extent of one's association with "the immoral." The readers are advised not to associate with people in the community who continue to behave immorally although they can continue to associate with the immoral outside the community. In light of this leeway, Paul must define further one's association with the immoral of this world. Paul is quite explicit that members settle disputes intramurally and not bring law-suits against a brother to the "unjust" (6:1, οἱ ἄδικοι) or "unbelievers" (6:6, οἱ ἄπιστοι). Neither should one associate with prostitutes (6:12–20).[79]

Later in the letter (10:1–22) Paul returns to the question of association with "outsiders" and defines the limits of one's association with the world (How far can one possibly go? 10:23, "Everything is permissible, but . . ."). Paul is mainly concerned with the danger of idolatry in 10:1–13 as is clear from the conclusion of his argument in 10:14, "Therefore, flee idolatry!" This danger is dealt with from a psychological viewpoint. The readers are warned against "putting their desires on evil things," an attitude which will surely bring destruction.[80] Paul holds up to the readers as symbols for admonition and warning the experience of the wilderness generation (10:6, 11). He then deals with the problem of idolatry in 10:14–22. The reference to pagan meals is not focal but is used to indicate the social occasion which can lead one to idolatry. Although Paul, as we shall see, grants that one can eat meat offered to idols, he warns his readers not to participate in idol worship.

Although there are limits to one's association with "unbelievers" or "outsiders", Paul does recognize continual social interaction with these people. "Unbelievers" might thus attend a Corinthian service (14:22–24) or associate with "insiders" in marriage (7:12–16). These "unbelievers" witness both the individual and collective spiritual exercises practiced by the Corinthians and might be recruited because of them.[81] "Insiders" can also continue to dine with these people regardless of their moral attributes (10:27) although they are forbidden to dine with a "believer" who continues to behave immorally

---

in the Epicurean groups in Athens and Naples, on pp. 136–37 and 142–48, above, on Epicurean correctional psychagogy.

[79] 1 Cor 6:18, φεύγετε τὴν πορνείαν·

[80] 1 Cor 10:6, εἰς τὸ μὴ εἶναι ἡμᾶς ἐπιθυμητὰς κακῶν; This is contextualized in four warnings against idolatry, fornication, testing the Lord, and grumbling (10:7–10). See Rom 1:23–24; 7:7–8; 13:8–10; Gal 5:16–24; and W. L. Willis, *Idol Meat in Corinth*, pp. 143–53.

[81] See pp. 195–98, above.

(5:11). Paul delineates, then, obligations towards people within and outside the community by reference to their moral attributes and makes clear the purpose both of association and disassociation with the immoral and unbelievers. The purpose of association is recruitment; that of disassociation reformation of character.

Although Paul is explicit as to behavior one puts up with in οἱ ἔξω and what one does not accept in an ἀδελφός, or οἱ ἔσω, differences should, as we have seen, be allowed to exist among the "brethren" about things indifferent, such as beliefs about food and days which have different behavioral ramifications. Diverse beliefs and behaviors on these matters are recognized. Modification of such beliefs and attendant behavior should cease if it becomes destructive.[82] In this sense a non-rigid recruitment criterion should not be followed by a stringent criterion of unified beliefs on all matters or a unified code of behavior be adhered to in order to secure continual membership. An unconditional admission criterion and Paul's positive view of the friendship of many entails that individuals of different moral standards could join the circle of friends in the Pauline groups without having to adhere to a stringent set of beliefs or pass a litmus test for a certain code of behavior. The lack of such a nobility test does not necessarily suggest that Paul advocates that all behaviors be accepted although he does emphasize the importance of not disassociating oneself from the immoral.

Paul's self-reflective remarks on his accommodating behavior in 1 Cor 9:19–23 occur then within a larger literary context in which Paul's flexible approach is evident. I have shown how the theme of adaptation is integrated into Paul's concern with the association of different types of people both within and outside the community in recruitment and psychagogy. Before discussing how the motif of adaptation relates to Pauline psychagogy and his guidance of the weak in 1 Cor 8, I shall pursue one final aspect of the theme of association of different character types. I have claimed that two perspectives are evident in this pericope, namely, those of psychagogy and recruitment. A third more subtle perspective of this pericope, related to the issue of association and also brought to the fore by reference to "the many," underlines a critical function of 1 Cor 9. Here Paul rejects an exclusive allegiance to a few patrons in Corinth and advocates an allegiance to the many, underscoring his willingness

---

[82] See my discussion of Rom 14:1–15:14 on pp. 222–31, above.

to associate with all and please the many. I shall pursue the hypothesis that authors who discussed issues of versatility and servility to the powerful in the social matrix of patronage yield evidence which we can bring to bear on Paul's concern in 1 Cor 9.

### 6.2.1 *The social grid of patronage and Paul's dictum of adaptability*

Authors critical of the social practice of patronage can be used to explicate further the theme of "association of different character types" in Paul. Some of the same concerns emerge in the analogous relationship of Philodemus and Piso and that of Paul's relationship with his patrons in Corinth.[83] Paul's emphasis on adaptation in the solicitous concern for all values positively an unassuming and affable approach. Here the issues of adaptation, association, and obsequiousness overlap. In 1 Cor 9 Paul raises in a defensive mode issues of liberty, the rights of a free man, servility and adaptability. The apparent similarities between Paul's conduct and the behavior of flatterers and obsequious persons who were alike in their adaptation and avidity to be obliging gain significance in the social matrix of patronage.

In chapter 8 Paul discusses a behavior of the wise which has a disastrous impact on the weak and urges his readers to desist in such a practice. Paul puts himself forward as an example of one who is willing to abridge his freedom and change his behavior by "never again" eating meat offered to idols if that causes another to stumble (8:13). What follows is a presentation of Paul as an example of one who does not insist on his own right, unlike the wise in chapter 8, but is willing to curtail any behavior which affects others negatively, working strenuously in order to benefit others.[84]

After Paul's claim that he will never again eat meat if that causes another brother to stumble, he asks: "Am I not free? Am I not an apostle? Have I not seen Jesus our Lord? Are you not my work in the Lord?"[85] All these questions expect a positive answer and raise issues relating to Paul's qualifications and function as the spiritual founder of the Corinthian community. Although Paul's standing as

---

[83] See pp. 103–105, 111–13, 122–23, and 177–81, above.

[84] A. J. Malherbe has demonstrated the close connection of Paul's argument in 1 Cor 8 and 9. "Determinism and Free Will in Paul: The Argument of 1 Corinthians 8 and 9," in *Paul in His Hellenistic Context* (ed. Troels Engberg-Pedersen; Edinburgh: T. & T. Clark, 1994), pp. 231–55.

[85] 1 Cor 9:1. Compare Epictetus, *Discourse* 3.22.48, ". . . Am I not free from fear? Am I not free?"

an apostle and founder of the community should be secure, the behavior he presents for emulation needs to be accounted for (9:3, ἀπολογία).⁸⁶ Paul goes on to ask a series of questions repeating the crucial term ἐξουσία which he had used in 8:9 of the "right" of the wise to eat meat offered to idols: "Do we not have the right to our food and drink?" (9:4) "Do we not have the right to be accompanied by a believing wife, as do the other apostles and the brothers of the Lord and Cephas?" Or is it only Barnabas and I who have no right to refrain from working for a living?" (9:5)

A series of arguments combined with further rhetorical questions ensues, emphasizing that Paul did have the right to demand financial support (vv. 3-12). In vss. 11-12 Paul advances his own practice as an example of foregoing one's right. Paul's presentation of himself as an example consists in not insisting on his right to financial support. Neither would the Corinthians insist on their right to eat meat. The parallell between the two cases is not self-evidently clear but we can begin to explicate the matter by asking the nature and purpose of not making use of one's right. In the former instance the wise have the right to eat meat offered to idols but are asked not to do so in order not to destroy the weak. In the latter instance Paul has the right to financial support but decides not to insist on that right in order, as he says himself, "not to put an impediment in the way of the gospel of Christ" (v. 12)

Regardless of the uncertainties surrounding the meaning of v. 12a,⁸⁷ it is clear that the right to eat sacrificed meat and to financial support are in focus in the context. It is also clear that the conduct Paul presents for emulation is that of refraining from making use of a right to financial support in order not to be an impediment to the gospel; he is thus able to offer himself as a model for the advice given in chapter 8. When discussing the rightful remuneration for services, Paul thus claims to have waived his right to support for preaching the gospel.⁸⁸ His "pay" consists not in financial remunerations for serviced rendered but in his own offering of the gospel "free

---

⁸⁶ For the problems of viewing 1 Cor 9 either as a prospective or retrospective apology, see Margaret M. Mitchell, *Paul and the Rhetoric of Reconciliation*, pp. 243-50. See p. 15, above.

⁸⁷ εἰ ἄλλοι τῆς ὑμῶν ἐξουσίας μετέχουσιν, οὐ μᾶλλον ἡμεῖς; could be translated "If others share in your exousia, do not we the more?" or "If others share in exousia over you, do not we the more?" A. J. Malherbe, "Determinism and Free Will in Paul: The Argument of 1 Corinthians 8 and 9," p. 241 (n. 17).

⁸⁸ See vss. 12b, ἀλλ' οὐκ ἐχρησάμεθα τῇ ἐξουσίᾳ ταύτῃ . . .; 15α, Ἐγὼ δὲ οὐ κέχρημαι οὐδενὶ τούτων; 18b, εἰς τὸ μὴ καταχρήσασθαι τῇ ἐξουσίᾳ μου ἐν τῷ εὐαγγελίῳ.

of charge" to all.[89] This refraining from financial support is a matter of "boast" to Paul (v. 15); it sets him apart from other preachers (cf. 2 Cor 11:10–12) and aligns Paul with the Cynics: "As their humble attire was disdained by the masses and set them apart, so Paul's manual labor, which enable him to forego financial support, was also esteemed low in his society and set him apart."[90]

The first reference to financial support in 1 Corinthians occurs in this context and raises the question why Paul uses the right to support in his self-presentation. Why not simply take an example which is closer to the matter at hand, namely, the right to eat food offered to idols? Paul could have claimed to have such a right and refrained from using it in order not to destroy the weak. To this question there are at least two (interrelated) answers. Either such an example would not be pertinent since Paul probably ate sacrificed meat himself and the wise in Corinth knew it; or Paul uses an example the Corinthians know best and which conveys his message most forcefully. On such a reading, Paul's reflections are triggered by his behavior towards his patron(s) in Corinth;[91] his self-reflective thoughts on his rights to reject remuneration make sense if he had received and refused a financial offer, or at least if we view these remarks in the context of a debate between Paul and the Corinthian patrons.

The practice then which exemplifies Paul's freedom in this context is his refusal to accept financial support. Malherbe has shown that Paul, in a Stoic manner, emphasizes his freedom as the basis of his right to receive or refuse financial remuneration for services rendered (9:1–5, 12b and 15). Paul willingly does what necessity has laid upon him, thus exercizing his freedom. His freedom did not compel him to insist on his right, but allowed him to forego it.[92] By doing so he was free from all men which at the same time made it possible for

---

[89] 9:18a, ἵνα εὐαγγελιζόμενος ἀδάπανον θήσω τὸ εὐαγγέλιον . . .; cf. also v. 12b. Note the verbal affinities here with Paul's claim in 2 Cor 12:15. See p. 186, above.

[90] A. J. Malherbe, "Determinism and Free Will in Paul: The Argument of 1 Corinthians 8 and 9," p. 249. Although Malherbe does not accept the hypothesis of Paul's rejection of financial support from the Corinthian patrons to explain 1 Cor 9, he all the same states again and again what the text says, namely, that Paul refrained from accepting financial support (cf. ibid., pp. 241, 242, 249, and 250–51).

[91] Pace P. Marshall, *Enmity in Corinth* (Tübingen: Mohr (Siebeck), 1987), p. 174. Although the first rhetorical question in 9:4 ("Do we not have the right to our food and drink?") clearly relates to the discussion of sacrificed meat in chapter 8," the latter rhetorical questions do not and thus require a special explanation.

[92] A. J. Malherbe, "Determinism and Free Will in Paul: The Argument of 1 Corinthians 8 and 9," pp. 241–42, 249, 250–51 and 255.

him to become the slave of all (vss. 18–19). As Paul had distinguished himself from the second and third groups referred to in the pericope of 9:19–22 by his qualifications in vv. 20b and 21, so does he distinguish himself from demagogues by his qualification in v. 19.[93] All the same, a dyadic picture emerges in this chapter of Paul as both free and a slave.

How could one be free and a slave at the same time? This conundrum had at least two dimensions; first, extracted from its social context and with the focus on the passions, a (wise) person could be free even though a slave, or a slave, even though free.[94] The other dimension, more in tune with the social realities of the time, is discussed by Dio Chrysostom.[95] A free man addresses a dilemma raised by a slave: "I do not see how I am to become a slave when, in fact, I am free; but as for you, it is not impossible that you have become free by your master's having emancipated you. But what do you mean by saying that I might become a slave?" The slave points to a socially well known function, "I mean that great numbers of men, we may suppose, who are free-born sell themselves, so that they are slaves by contract, sometimes on no easy terms but the most severe imaginable." Similarly, Davus, Horace' slave, charges his master that he is no better off than himself, since in fact his master is a mere puppet on Maecenas' strings.[96] Dio and Horace refer here to the common practice of offering your services for pay to wealthy patrons.[97] Those who did so were, during the terms of the contract, both free and slaves. Such "slaves" could be viewed as either "flatterers" or "friends" of the patron.

In patronage, "flatterers" and "friends" thus shared many traits

---

[93] 1 Cor 9:19, Ἐλεύθερος γὰρ ὢν ἐκ πάντων πᾶσιν ἐμαυτὸν ἐδούλωσα.... (cf. 9:1). For the qualifications in vv. 20b and 21, see p. 255, above.

[94] This problem was especially addressed by the Stoics. See Epictetus, *Discourse* 4.1; Dio Chrysostom, *Discourses* 14 and 15; Philo, *Every Good Man is Free*; Cicero's *Stoic Paradoxes*, and Horace, *Satires* 2.7.

[95] Dio Chrysostom, *Discourse* 15.21–23. Cf. also *Discourse* 77/78.35, and Athenaeus, *Sophists at Dinner* 260D.

[96] Horace, *Satires* 2.7.81–82. The charge precedes the general discussion of the Stoic paradox.

[97] The term "pay" is misleading since in most instances the remuneration was in the form of sporadic and modest gifts which could not be regarded as a regular income. A certain measure of financial independence was thus required. In spite of this, friends of the rich might anticipate certain definite benefits. See P. White, "Amicitia and the Profession of Poetry," 86–92. R. Saller questions White's attempt to play down the material aspect of the exchange between a poet and his patron (*Personal Patronage under the Early Empire*, p. 28).

and the boundary between the two had become rather hazy. This is the impetus for Lucian's satirical wit when, in his *On Salaried Posts in Great Houses*, he calls friendship another name for slavery and flattery. Lucian wonders if friendship may be applied to the "slavery" of those who hold salaried posts in great houses, such as students of philosophy, grammarians, and rhetoricians, and all who think fit to serve for hire as educators. These Lucian wants to bring back to freedom. But it is not worthwhile to try to turn away flatterers from such positions, for they are not too good for it. Lucian proceeds to investigate the motives for such a way of life in order to, as he says, "do away with in advance" their "defence and the primary object of such a voluntary slavery."[98] Later, when in an administrative position in the civil service in Egypt, Lucian had to defend himself from the above attack. Lucian recognizes that his change of heart could draw forth criticism of inconsistency, hypocrisy and flattery but points to the difference between entering a rich man's private house as "a hireling, where one is a slave" and entering public service where one administers public affairs and makes oneself "of service to states and whole provinces" and is paid by the Emperor for doing so.[99]

Demagogues and flatterers are akin and each has the strongest influence with the respective ruling power, flatterers with tyrants and demagogues with the multitude.[100] Flatterers do not, unlike demagogues, attend upon poor or unimportant persons. By claiming to be the slave of all, willing to associate with the many and not simply with the powerful and morally upright, Paul's obligations include the "multitude". With his language of servility Paul rejects his role as the exclusive "friend," "flatterer" or "servant" of his patrons and takes on that of the "demagogue" of the many. Paul's rejection and defence of his behavior in 1 Cor 9 has formal parallels with that of Lucian, who, in his *Apology for 'On Salaried Posts in Great Houses'* drew a distinction between those whose "slavery" was limited to the pri-

---

[98] Lucian, *On Salaried Posts in Great Houses* 1, 4–6, 19–20. Lucian satirizes the dictum Πάντα ἡμῖν κοινὰ ἔσται, which the prospective hireling takes to indicate that his salary will be bountiful. When it comes to settling the stipend, the lord of the house calls on one of his "friends" who suggests a stipend far less than expected and remarks: "many distinguished men, even if they had to pay for it, would like ... to associate with this gentleman and be seen about him in the guise of companions and friends." *The Parasite* 22 calls φιλία the first step of "the parasitic art."

[99] Lucian, *Apology for the 'On Salaried Posts in Great Houses'* 9 and 11–12.

[100] Aristotle, *Politics* 1292a22–24; Plutarch, *How to Tell a Flatterer from a Friend* 49C; *Precepts of Statecraft* 800B; 802E; 807A; Horace, *Epistle* 1.17.

vate house of a rich man and those, like himself, whose "public service" was to "states and whole nations." In both cases we have a reworking of the notion of obligation and its sphere of activity.

We have seen Paul's emphasis on having waived his right to financial support in 1 Cor 9:3-12. Through the rest of the chapter Paul focuses on recruitment which he introduces in v. 12 as he explains why he has decided not to insist on his right to support, namely, in order "not to put an impediment in the way of the gospel of Christ." Paul claims that he wants to offer the gospel free of charge to all (9:18a), but stating the motive for rejecting financial support does not explain why accepting support is an impediment to the fulfillment of that motive. Why would the acceptance of financial assistance be an impediment to the gospel? In point of fact, Paul rejects support because it derives from the house of a socially powerful patron; its acceptance would have put an undue burden on him regardless of its precise social ramification.[101]

An excessively limited service to a patron would have underminded Paul's whole undertaking. A patron might have felt he was entitled to more of Paul's time, for example, than others in the community were, limiting Paul's sphere of activity and making the gospel not equally accessible to all. In light of such demands Paul claims to be free "from all men"; and it is precisely such a freedom which allows him to become the enslaved leader of "all," to "please everyone," and to offer his services "free of charge" equally to all (1 Cor 9:1, 18a, 19). Paul emphasizes the practical side of his rejection; he associates unreservedly with all and concerns himself with the plight of those who are of a "weak" disposition, psychologically uncertain in their new way of life. That Paul's attempt to "please everyone" was

---

[101] For some of the obligations of clients see White, "Amicitia and the Profession of Poetry," p. 78. That Paul did accept maintenance on other occasions (Phil 4:10-20; 2 Cor 11:7-12) might be because no such demands were present as in Corinth. I interpret Paul's later refusal (2 Cor 3:1-3; 4:2; 5:12; 12:11) to submit additional letters of recommendation from the same perspective, namely, they required the recounting of aristocratic virtues, in this case forceful and authoritative guidance and oratorical eloquence. By a standard definition, "patronal relationships" are asymmetrical, i.e., between parties of different social statuses which offer different kinds of goods and services in the exchange. Besides, patronage is a reciprocal social relationship, involving exchange of services which are personal as opposed to commercial. This is Sallers's definition in *Personal Patronage under the Early Empire* (p. 1) and followed by most contributors in Wallace-Hadrill (ed.), *Patronage in Ancient Society* (pp. 3-4).

displeasing to the wise in Corinth goes without saying; indeed, "to please the multitude is to displease the wise."[102]

If we explain Paul's rejection of support in light of demands contingent on the institution of patronal friendship, we are in a position to define even more closely a further implication of Paul's decision within ancient discussions on friendship. Although patronal friendship is a relationship between social unequals, it demanded that the client display some aristocratic virtue or practical skill that would benefit the patron. Paul's refusal challenges that premise; aristocratic virtue is too exclusive a criterion. This qualification of patronal friendship shows Paul's willingness to associate with all, noble or base, and implies a positive view of obsequiousness and a type of friendship relation which the Greeks called πολυφιλία or the friendship of the many which made relationships possible between persons of different moral and social standing.

As is clear from his amicable relationship with the household of Stephanas, Paul does not reject patronal friendship as such but rather exclusive demands made by some of his patrons.[103] These demands limited Paul's sphere of activity by requiring an allegiance to the few at the expense of an allegiance to the many. One can not only construe Paul's rejection in view of its "practical" consequences but also as a positive affirmation of the friendship of many and willingness to associate unreservedly with all. This reason is systemic in nature and, as such, it need not have been entertained analytically by Paul but is rather a way in which we can interpret Paul's decision in light of the premise of the first reason. This second reason can also be interpreted in light of the basic premise of patronal friendship, viz., that it was based on character. That premise is rejected by Paul, both as a defining aspect of the relation between community members and as a criterion to be met before joining the community.

---

[102] Ps.-Plutarch, *On the Education of Children* 6B; Epictetus, *Discourse* 4.13.10; Plato, *Republic* 492A–B. Compare Philodemus' positive view of obsequiousness on pp. 112–14 and 120–23, above.

[103] 1 Cor 16:15–16. The rift in the relationship between Paul and some Corinthian patrons was then not because Paul rejects "patronal friendship" but rather because of demands made on the basis of such friendship. Other issues complicated the relationship between Paul and these patrons, such as their dispute over leadership style and qualification. Who these patrons were remains an educated guess. Gaius remains a possibility. Cf. E. A. Judge, "Cultural Conformity and Innovation in Paul: Some Clues from Contemporary Documents," *TynBul* 35 (1984), pp. 12–17, 23–24; J. K. Chow, *Patronage and Power. A Study of Social Networks in Corinth* (JSNTSS 75; Sheffield, 1992).

The impetus of Paul's rejection of an exclusive allegiance to a few patrons is his willingness to associate with and benefit all, regardless of their moral attributes. The friendship most in tune with Paul's affable approach is not character friendship but is more akin to friendship for utility or pleasure.[104] Paul endorses a friendship which is offered to all, not solely to moral equals. In this we should see Paul's unique contribution to the contemporary debate on servility to the great.[105] Finally, Paul avoids becoming attached to the house of a powerful patron, thus following his previous advice to freedmen of the community in Corinth.[106]

Authors who discussed questions of versatility in the context of patronage present, then, evidence which we can bring to bear on Paul's concern in 1 Cor 9. Paul argues from his own behavior and gives an example of himself for the wise in Corinth to emulate, calling on them to restrict their freedom and stop eating meat offered to

---

[104] Since it is, as Aristotle explains, possible to please or benefit many people in such a friendship (*Nichomachean Ethics* 1158a16).

[105] This subtle use of the friendship tradition, extrapolated in light of the function of 1 Cor 9, is also supported by the psychagogic practices of the Pauline communities. Perhaps we have here discovered an answer to the conundrum of why Paul avoids terms of the φιλ-root, preferring the term ἀγαπάω (Φιλέω occurs only once in the Pauline corpus in 1 Cor 16:22, φιλαδελφία only twice, namely, 1 Thess 4:9 and Rom 12:10. Φίλημα occurs in 1 Cor 16:20; 2 Cor 13:12 and Rom 16:16. On Paul's use of the friendship topos, see H. D. Betz, *Galatians*, pp. 221–233). Some have suggested that the reason why Paul avoided terms of the φιλ-root is because these were terms of status and discrimination (E. A. Judge, "St. Paul as a Radical Critic of Society," *Interchange* 16 (1974), pp. 196–97; Marshall, *Enmity in Corinth*, pp. 133–34, 146 n. 77). Others suggest that Paul's avoidance is because of the anthropocentric connotations of these terms. Paul wanted to emphasize the theocentric grounding of the relationship between people (J. N. Sevenster, "Waarom spreekt Paulus nooit van vrienden en vriendschap?" NTT 9 (1954/55), pp. 356–363; idem, *Paul and Seneca* (NovTSup 4; Leiden, 1961), pp. 174–80; A. J. Malherbe, *Paul and the Thessalonians*, pp. 104–05; idem, *Paul and the Popular Philosophers*, pp. 62–63). But the friendship term Paul uses (ἀγαπᾶν) is even more anthropocentric than the one he avoids, used in the sense of valuing something for the benefits it yields and to denote concern for another person's well-being (Plato, *Lysis* 215A; Aristotle, *Nicomachean Ethics* 1156a13; *Eudemian Ethics* 1240a33–35; Plutarch, *That a Philosopher Ought to Converse Especially with Men in Power* 777E). Terms of the φιλ-root highlight an "affectionate" aspect of a relationship that ἀγαπ- does not (Philo uses φιλέω of courtesans, parasites, flatterers, and harlots, when he refers to their practice as the hurtful outgrowths of the tree of friendship; *Concerning Noah's Work as a Planter* 105–106). For the pre-Christian use of ἀγαπ-, see R. Joly, *Le vocabulaire chrétien de l'amour est-il original? Φιλεῖν et Ἀγαπᾶν dans le grec antique* (Bruxelles, 1968), pp. 10–47.

[106] S. S. Bartchy (*First-Century Slavery and the Interpretation of 1 Corinthians 7.21* [Chico, 1973], pp. 46–48, 181) suggests that Paul was acquainted with "time-limited self-sale into slavery" and that Paul's prohibition in 7:23 ("Therefore do not sell yourselves into slavery") has such a slavery in view.

idols since this ruins the weak. Paul is willing to waive his right to financial support and associate unreservedly with all, noble or base, being affable and obliging to the multitude and members of the Corinthian community. The rejection of an exclusive allegience to a few patrons is explained in light of the need to associate with the many in order to recruit or benefit them. Here different views have emerged relating to the question of with whom one should associate. Paul seems to treat the wealthy patrons and the "wise" who probably belonged to the entourage of these patrons as community leaders with whom he debates issues of leadership. In the context of 1 Cor 8–9 this debate concerns not only questions of versatility and the association of different character types but also matters of psychagogic guidance to which we now turn.

### 6.2.2 *The psychagogic dimension of 1 Corinthians 9:19–23*

In my introduction I noted the apparent similarities between Antisthenes' defence of Odysseus and Paul's description of himself in the context of 1 Cor 9:19–23.[107] Odysseus' ambiguous standing and the fact that others also, such as Aristippus and Hippias of Elis, could be used as positive models of versatility, should, however, warn us against aligning Paul too closely with the Antisthenic tradition.[108] Antisthenes' attempt to absolve his hero of charges of duplicity, however, is an example of the speech-behavior aspect of adaptation. Antisthenes interpreted πολύτροπος to refer to Odysseus' verbal adaptation rather than understanding it in the pejorative ethical sense of often changing one's character.[109]

---

[107] A. J. Malherbe writes (*Paul and the Popular Philosophers*, pp. 118–19):

> We return to the question why Paul uses the Antisthenic tradition. His opponents may have described him in terms reminiscent of the unflattering depiction of Odysseus, to which Paul responded by applying the tradition in his own way. The similarities between the criticism made of Antisthenes and Paul are obvious.... If Hermann Funke is correct (cf. "Antisthenes bei Paulus," *Hermes* 98 (1970), pp. 459–71), Paul had already in 1 Corinthians 9:24–27 made use of Antisthenic tradition to describe his ministry. And we have seen that in the immediately preceding verses he describes himself in a manner that echoes Antisthenes' Odysseus. It is therefore likely that it is Paul who in some respect thought of himself along the lines of the Antisthenic ideal. Having once introduced the tradition in the discussion with Corinth, he now (i.e., in 2 Cor 10:3–6) also uses it to defend himself.

[108] Cynics were divided over the value of Odysseus' example. So were also the Epicureans and Plutarch. Dio Chrysostom mentions Odysseus, along with Hippias of Elis, as examples of versatility (*Discourse* 71) but there is an implicit critique of the two in his description of how the philosopher should excel. Horace refers to Aristippus (*Epistle* 1.18.1–16). See pp. 97–98 (fn. 150), above.

[109] Cf. Stanford, *The Ulysses Theme*, pp. 96–100.

By Paul's time versatility and charges of cunning focused both on behavior and speech; one could adapt both by conforming to different manners as well as being discriminating in speech. Discrimination in speech is already seen in Pythagoras' practice of teaching his disciples to speak to children in childlike terms, to women in womenlike terms, to governors in governmental terms and to ephebes in ephebic terms.[110] Such concerns are also present in the moralists' focus on different types of students and by rhetoricans in their discussion of character portrayal. Because of this, and in light of the intricate connection between the philosopher's σχῆμα and λόγος, we should be careful not to focus solely on adaptation in behavior when explicating Paul's statements on adaptability.

I have shown that the form of 1 Cor 9:19–23 viewed against discussions of the flatterer, the friend of many, the political man, and defences of versatility in the social matrix of patronage, throws light on its function. I have also claimed that the intricate connection between the philosopher's "appearance" and "word" as well as character portrayal form two of our clues to the understanding of this pericope. Besides Paul's adaptation to different types of people, this text also refers to his adaptation to people of different disposition. This Paul does by construing the person of the "weak" and adapts to his condition by lending that type of person a voice. Psychagogic adaptation occurs in the domain of speech and can be profitably pursued through character portrayal which functions like a precept, indirectly guiding immature students.[111]

Character portrayal was discussed by some rhetoricans as a "figure of thought." When Demetrius gives an example of personification, he asks his readers to "imagine that your ancestors, or Hellas, or your native land, assuming a woman's form (σχῆμα), should address such and such reproaches to you."[112] Similarly, when Paul says he became weak, he assumes the σχῆμα of the weak through character portrayal. The example Paul has left us in this epistolary context is a presentation of the character of those who are "weak in conscience" as well as the character of the "wise" as they react as

---

[110] Decleva Caizzi (ed.), *Antisthenis fragmenta*, fr. 51.
[111] See pp. 47–50 and 84–85, above. Ancient readers understood that Paul is using προσωποποιία in 1 Cor 9:22. According to Rufinus, Origen thus referred to 1 Cor 9:22 in order to explain Paul's character portrayal in Rom 7 (*Com. Rm.* 6.9 [1086A]). See S. K. Stowers, *A Rereading of Romans*, p. 267.
[112] Demetrius, *On Style* 265 ("figure of thought" = σχῆμα διανοίας).

imaginary interlocutors to Paul's instructions (cf. on 10:25–29, below). Character portrayal is used not only to reproach the wise in Corinth but to guide the weak as well as the wise, because both, owing to their immaturity, needed to be "shown" the truth.

Paul's discussion of the "weak" reflects comparable concern of moralists for the immature students or recent converts who are insecure in their new way of life. These concerns set the stage for Paul's discussion of psychagogic adaptability and instructions with regard to the weak. Although we need not identity the groups in 1 Cor 9:19–23 in order to understand the function of this pericope, it is paramount for an understanding of its psychagogic perspective that we perceive the significance of the "weak." I have shown that Maximus of Tyre and Philo discuss issues of versatility by referring to human diversity and the human disposition and have claimed that Paul's pericope and its larger context also reflects this twofold perspective. Although Philo gives examples of stringent measures needed because of disobedience and Paul refers to the affable approach needed because of the tenderness of the weak, the similarities of Paul and Philo are unmistakable. In both the human disposition is the criterion which determines the mode of guidance. Later we shall see evidence in 1 Corinthians for Paul's use of more stringent measures in the case of the recalcitrant ones.

Paul, like other Hellenized Jews, uses various compounds of the word "weakness." He uses the substantives ἀσθένεια and ἀσθένημα, the verbal form ἀσθενέω, and the adjectival form ἀσθενής.[113] In light of the diverse meanings of these words, the precise meaning of "weakness" in any one Pauline text must be determined intertextually in light of its context and by other Pauline usages as well as from the cogency of the parallels adduced. The criteria to determine the meaning of the word "weak" in 1 Cor 9:22 and 8:7–12 are three: firstly, and most important, are the contextual constraints of the passages; secondly, the cogency of the parallels adduced in order

---

[113] For ἀσθένεια see Gal 4:13; 1 Cor 2:3; 15:43; 2 Cor 11:30; 12:5, 9–10; 13:4; Rom 6:19; 8:26. For ἀσθένημα see Rom 15:1. For ἀσθενέω see Phil 2:26–27; 1 Cor 8:11–12; 2 Cor 11:21, 29; 12:10; 13:3; Rom 4:19; 8:3; 14:1, 2, 21. For ἀσθενής see 1 Thess 5:14; Gal 4:9; 1 Cor 1:25; 4:10; 8:7, 9, 10; 9:22; 11:30; 12:22; 2 Cor 10:10; Rom 5:6. See D. A. Black, *Paul, Apostle of Weakness. Astheneia and its Cognates in the Pauline Literature* (New York, 1984). The oppressed and needy are referred to as "weak," e.g., in Ps 6:2; Jdt 9:11; *T. Job.* 25.10; *T. Jos.* 1.6; cf. H. W. Hollander, *Joseph as an Ethical Model in the Testaments of the Twelve Patriarchs* (Leiden, 1981), pp. 72–3, 130–31.

to illuminate Paul's usage; and, thirdly, an awareness of the various possible components of meaning of the words "weak" and "weakness."

In light of the many "components of meaning" in the word "weakness," we must guard against two fallacies. Firstly, we must not commit what James Barr has called "the illegitimate totality transfer," and, we must, secondly, avoid what linguists call "the etymological fallacy." Instead of committing these two fallacies, we must subscribe to what has been called the "semantic axiom number one." We commit the illegitimate totality transfer when the "'meaning' of a word (understood as the total series of relations in which it is used in the literature), is read into a particular case as its sense and implication".[114] The etymological fallacy occurs when we postulate some core meaning of a word as its true meaning, which may then be abstracted from a hypothetical original meaning from which all other meanings of the word are derived. Instead of doing this, we must reckon with synchronic meaning when determining the diachronic meaning of a word. This in effect recognizes the semantic axiom number one, which emphasizes the importance of context in determining the signification and primary meaning of words. This means that only one of many components of meanings of a particular word is accentuated in a specific context.[115]

Any reading which sidesteps the contextual constraints of the meaning of "weak" is inadequate. Paul's identification with the weak is, as we have seen, accentuated by the omission of ὡς before the weak; he "became weak" himself. Οἱ ἀσθενεῖς are mentioned last in 9:22 for climactic purposes and with obvious resonance with the general context of this pericope. It would indeed be curious if Paul had not had those "weak in conscience" in 8:7–12 in mind when claiming in 9:22 to have become weak to the weak in order to benefit them. Our major clue as to the meaning of the "weak" in both texts should be taken from Paul's overall concern for the weak in these chapters. An incentive for seeing Paul's concern here as the

---

[114] J. Barr, *The Semantics of Biblical Language* (Oxford, 1961), pp. 218; 231–33; J. Lyons, *Language and Linguistics* (Cambridge, 1981), p. 55; M. Joos, "Semantic Axiom Number One," *Language* 47 (1972), pp. 258–265; F. de Saussure, *Course in General Linguistics* (Fontana/Collins, 1974).
[115] For componential analysis of meaning see W. H. Goodenough, "Componential Analysis and the Study of Meaning," *Language* 32 (1956), pp. 195–216; E. A. Nida, J. P. Louw & R. B. Smith, "Semantic Domains and Componential Analysis of Meaning," in *Current Issues in Linguistic Theory* (ed. R. W. Cole; Bloomington & London, 1977), pp. 139–167.

same as that of moralists who describe their students as "weak" is found in the contrast between ἀπόλλυμι and σῴζω. Paul makes a specific point: The wise in Corinth "destroy" the weak by their behavior but Paul wishes to "save them" (1 Cor 8:11; 9:22a).[116]

The term "weakness" (ἀσθένεια) is inherent in the moralists' reformatory ethic often occurring in conjunction with the terms "salvation" and "destruction." The primary signification of the word "weak" in such contexts refers to the psychological disposition of the weak. These authors give evidence for the common use of the term σῴζω in a moral context, emphasizing the need to aid or benefit the progressing one; the negative effects of progress are often highlighted by the term ἀπόλλυμι.[117] This, as we have seen, was common parlance among moralists when discussing the insecure students, emphasizing that great care should be exercised when dealing with them; inconsiderate harshness might destroy their interest in philosophy instead of saving whatever inkling of interest they might have. Paul's use of the dichotomy of salvation and destruction when discussing "the weak", as well as the conjunction of weakness with "knowledge" (γνῶσις) and "conscience" (συνείδησις; 8:1, 7, 10–12), to be discussed below, confirms that Paul is following a standard way of speaking of some as psychologically weak or insecure. This establishes the psychagogic dimension of 1 Cor 9:19–23, suggesting that Paul is concerned with

---

[116] 1 Cor 8:11, "So by your knowledge those weak believers for whom Christ died are destroyed (ἀπόλλυται γὰρ ὁ ἀσθενῶν). But when you thus sin against members of your family, and wound their conscience when it is weak, you sin against Christ" (cf. Rom 14:15, "If your brother is being injured by what you eat, you are no longer walking in love. Do not let what you eat cause the ruin of one for whom Christ died").

[117] Moralists who discuss moral reformation and the closely related topic of self-mastery, use the term ἀσθένεια to describe those who are insecure and feeble and need the assistance of others. See pp. 78–81, 129–30, 148–51, and 228–30, above. Besides the texts referred to in fns. 59–60, above, see Paul's use of σῴζω to accentuate his benefiting the Corinthians in 2 Cor 1:6. In 1 Cor 11:27–34 the theme of salvation and destruction is related of therapeutic harshness or severe discipline. The same contrast is expressed by the words to "build up" and its antithesis, to "ruin" (1 Cor 8:1; 2 Cor 10:8; 13:10; J. Dupont, *Gnosis. La Connaissance religieuse dans les Épîtres de Saint Paul*, pp. 239–41). The terms σῴζω and βοηθέω, as well as ῥύομαι and σκεπάζω, are used among Hellenistic Jews to express an action of "saving." *T.Benj.* 3.4–5; Ex 12:27; 1 Sam 26:24 LXX; Jdt 8:15; Ps 17:7–8; 27:5; 64:1–2; Sir 51:2–3; 3 Macc 6:6–8 (Hollander, *Joseph as an Ethical Model in the Testaments of the Twelve Patriarchs*, p. 128 n. 27). See Clement, *Who Is the Rich Person Who Will Be Saved?* 16, When the wealth of passion is destroyed, it brings salvation (ἀπολόμενος δὲ σωτήριος). Cf. *Ped.* 66.2 (GCS 128, 30 Stählin-Treu).

not deterring the progress of the weak and expresses these concerns in identical terms to contemporary moralists.

The destruction and salvation of the "weak" is couched in a contrast imbued with religious significance in Paul. Similarly, the tension between the weak and those more rationally oriented reflects a debate as to what constitutes divinely approved behavior. The importance of weakness and strength in the Corinthian correspondence has an implication beyond Paul's concern for the weak in 1 Cor 8.[118] However, the above noted usage of the salvation-destruction dichotomy alerts us to Paul's concern and supports a non-apocalyptic reading of its use in this context (1 Cor 8:11; 9:22).[119] I have argued for a comparable reading of Rom 14:1–15:14. Moralists emphasize the effect of exhortation on the young which can either destroy or save them, i.e., thwart or aid their progress. Paul expresses the same when he rejects the harsh approach taken by the Corinthian wise towards the weak, an approach which strikes and fills their wavering minds with bad feelings. Because of their previous habituation the weak feel insecure when questions concerning the consumption of meat offered to idols surface. They, in spite of their confession of "one God, the Father" and "one Lord, Jesus Christ," and their rejection of the existence of idols, still felt that meat offered to idols was invested with curious power. Paul's vocabulary conforms to a standard practice of referring to students of philosophy as weak, witnessed among moralists of the period, such as Epictetus, Dio, Plutarch, Seneca, and Philodemus.

*6.3 Psychagogic Adaptability and the Weak and Tender Students (1 Cor 8:1–13; 10:24–11:1)*

The concern of not thwarting the progress of the insecure is seen in 1 Corinthians 8. With the verb τύπτω (8:12) Paul underscores the end result of the behavior of the wise, namely, their eating in a temple meat offered to idols strikes or wounds the conscience of the weak. By this, Paul seems to suggest, the wise attempted to educate the weak by their example. Apparently, this manner of guidance

---

[118] Cf. 1 Cor 1:18 and 2 Cor 2:15 and 4:3.
[119] Paul is quite capable of combining philosophical argument with apocalyptic threat (1 Cor 6:18).

became destructive; instead of building the weak up it destroyed them. In light of the end result of their activity, the manner of the wise persons' attempt to build up the conscience of the weak can be characterized as "harsh." Paul does not question the right of the wise to guide the weak but rejects their pedagogy and mode of spiritual guidance. Paul disapproves not only of the attitude of the "wise" but also the way in which they attempt to reform the weak.

My hypothesis of the function of 1 Cor 9:22b in relation to chapter 8 does not square well with widely held views on these texts. Firstly, it rejects the common eschatological emphasis of the salvation-destruction dichotomy. Secondly, it most emphatically rejects the scholarly consensus that because of the contemptuous attitude of the wise they could not have attempted to actively educate the weak. Thirdly, the primary significance of the "weak" both in 8:7–12 and 9:22b is psychological (or dispositional), not social as is commonly thought.[120]

In order to establish the possibility of the above reading, attentiveness to different semantic connotations of words is important. We must remember that the word τύπτω had a close semantic range with such words as μαστιγόω, παίω and πληγή.[121] All were used metaphorically for the strikes and blows received in moral discipline, to describe the "whip of sharp words" or harsh censure of a recalcitrant student of a sluggish mind or the eradication of the mistaken beliefs of the weak.[122] Such a usage suggested itself naturally to moralists of

---

[120] It has become popular of late to speak of social status in Corinthian studies at the expense of a psychological viewpoint; this is also the case with the "weak" and the "strong." See G. Theissen, "The Strong and the Weak in Corinth: A Sociological Analysis of a Theological Quarrel," *The Social Setting of Pauline Christianity. Essays on Corinth* (Philadelphia, 1982), pp. 121–43.

[121] LSJ s.v. See Aristophanes, *Clouds* 968, τυπτόμενος πολλάς, schol. adds πληγὰς δηλονότι; cf. BAGD s.v. δέρω (2 Cor 11:20) and *Herm. Sim.* 6.2.5, 7; 6.3.1–4. Clement says of the guidance of the divine word: "scourging (μαστιγῶν), pitying, striking (τύπτων), healing, in compassion and discipline (παιδεία)" (*Ped.* 81.3; GCS 137, 30–138, 1 Stählin-Treu). Cf. *Ped.* 66.3 and 82.2 (GCS 138, 8–11 Stählin-Treu): "For reproof and rebuke ("Ελεγχος γὰρ καὶ ἐπίπληξις), as also the original term implies, are the stripes of the soul (πληγαὶ ψυχῆς εἰσι), chastizing sins...." These terms were also used by Hellenistic Jews of God's discipline of the Hebrew nation (cf. Sir. 21:2–3; 22:6–8, 22). When dealing with discipline and exhortation, the author of Hebrews uses the terms παράκλησις, παιδεία (έω), ἐλέγχω and μαστιγόω (12:5–6 = Prov 3:11–12; cf. Acts 23:2, 3b).

[122] Philodemus, *On Frank Criticism* fr. 83; *On Anger* col. 13.23–30, Indelli, οὐδενὸς παιδάριόν [τι] λαλῆσαι ἢ γινόμενον ἐμποδὼν καὶ τύπτειν καὶ λακτίζειν ... ὁ [δὲ] νουθετεῖν περὶ ἁπάντων ἤδη; col. 13.5–11 Indelli, τὸν] μὲν τυπτόμενον ἥκιστα βλάπτουσιν, αὐτοὶ δ' ἑαυτοὺς λυμαίνονται παντοδαπῶς; Maximus of Tyre, *Discourse* 3e–f (5, 17–6, 9 Hobein);

the Republic and early Principate in light of the introduction of beating for the great mass of humble citizens,[123] and in light of the harshness of Greek as well as Roman educational theory and practice.[124] Although all these words are also regularly used of the physical blows of whipping or flogging,[125] it is the metaphorical sense (of verbal reproofs) which is applicable here.[126] A text from Dio Chrysostom's *On Slavery and Freedom II* brings me to the point I wish to make. Well into the debate between two interlocutors, one of them notes: "I know that you are being kept by your master, dance attendance upon him, and do whatever he commands; or else you take a beating." The other responds:

> According to that, you can make out that sons also are slaves of their fathers; for they dance attendance upon their fathers ... and they without exception are supported by their fathers and frequently are beaten by them, and they obey any orders their fathers give them. And yet, so far as obeying and being thrashed are concerned, you can go on and assert that the boys who take lessons of schoolmasters are likewise their servants and that the gymnastic trainers are slavemasters of their pupils, or those who teach anything else; for they give orders to their pupils and trounce them when they are disobedient.[127]

---

25.5, ψυχῆς ἠσκημένης καὶ μεμαστιγωμένης; and Clement, *Ped.* 66.2 (GCS 128, 30–34 Stählin-Treu), "It is then not from hatred that the lord reviles men (λοιδορεῖται), for instead of destroying him (ἀπολέσαι) because of his faults, he has suffered for us. Because he is the good educator, he very skillfully slips into blame through reproach (διὰ τῆς λοιδορίας ὑποδύεται τὸν ψόγον), as though to arouse by the whip of sharp words (μάστιγι τῇ βλασφημίᾳ) a mind become sluggish...." Clement then quotes Sir 22:6–7, μάστιγες γὰρ καὶ παιδεία ἐν παντὶ καιρῷ σοφίας....

[123] G. E. M. de Ste. Croix deplores the fact that this development has not received due attention among scholars who have rather focused on legal exemptions to flogging. Ste. Croix claims that even though it is not possible to decide precisely how long before the end of the second century C. E. the flogging of humble citizens became fully "institutionalised", "no one can deny that well before the end of the second century, citizens belonging to the lower classes could legally and properly be flogged for a wide variety of reasons, while their superiors were given legal exemption" (*The Class Struggle in the Ancient World From the Archaic Age to the Arab Conquests*, pp. 458–59).

[124] A. D. Booth, "Punishment, Discipline and Riot in the Schools of Antiquity," *EMC* 17 (1973), pp. 107–114. Learning and whipping become almost synonymous. Cf. *Menandri Sententiae*, ed. Jaekel 573, ὁ μὴ δαρεὶς ἄνθρωπος οὐ παιδεύεται, "The man who is not flogged is not educated."

[125] See for example Paul, 2 Cor 11:23; *Barn.* 5.14; Ps.-Plutarch, *On the Education of Children* 8F–9A.

[126] *1 Clem.* 56.10 (καὶ ἀπὸ μάστιγος γλώσσης σε κρύψει); *Herm. Vis.* 4.2.6; Clement, *Ped.* 66.2 (GCS 128, 33 Stählin Treu); Pi.P.4.219, μάστιξ Πειθοῦς (s.v. LSJ).

[127] Dio Chrysostom, *Discourse* 15.18–19 ... καὶ τύπτουσι μὴ πειθομένους.

Although physical flogging is part of Dio's concern, two deductions are legitimate. Firstly, τύπτω, like πληγή and παίω, is employed to characterize a "harsh act of discipline" by a person in authority towards another of a lesser standing. Τύπτω is close in meaning to λοιδορέω, as πληγή is to ἐπίπληξις.[128] Secondly, not only does such discipline proceed from an authority, recognized as a legitimate wielder of harshness, but is executed in light of disobedience.[129] Plutarch's remark that obedience is one of the most highly esteemed honors that the young render their elders is *a propos*.[130] In light of the common use of τύπτω and related words for the result of harsh exhortation, I think then that we are warranted in recognizing an additional connotation of τύπτω in 1 Cor 8:12 which emphasizes, not only the end result of a certain activity, but also the activity itself, which in this case is a forceful attempt to educate the weak. The wise felt that they, because of their knowledge, had the authority and right to reform the immature. Here we should not forget the close relationship of ἐξουσία and παρρησία, or the right frankly to criticize others.

Although Paul does not tell us the intention of the wise in eating idol meat, most commentators are confident that they can with clarity know the state of mind of the wise. We are thus told, and rightly so in my view, that the heart of the problem was caused by the self-assertive Corinthians and their insistence on their cognitive superiority. But when commentators additonally claim that they can deduce from the often contemptuous attitude of the wise towards the weak that they had no concern for their progress, they have become sidetracked. Cognitive superiority does not necessarily entail a thoroughly negative evaluation of others. It can thus be used to legitimise an

---

[128] Epictetus, *Encheiridion*, 20, Μέμνησο, ὅτι οὐχ ὁ λοιδορῶν ἢ ὁ τύπτων ὑβρίζει...; 30, ἀνέχεσθαι λοιδοροῦντος, παίοντος; Musonius Rufus, fr. 10 (52, 9–53, 13 Hense). Philo remarks that parents, guardians, teachers, and all persons in charge, sometimes reprimand and even beat (τύπτειν) their own children, orphans, wards or pupils. Such a treatment should not be thought of as "evil-speaking or outrage instead of friendliness and benevolence" (*On Joseph* 74). Such treatment, then, recognizes the beneficial use of harshness I have emphasized. Philo has just noted that the statesman when speaking in the assembly "will leave all talk of flattery to others and resort only to such as is salutary and beneficial, reproving, warning, correcting in words studied to shew a sober frankness without foolish and frantic arrogance." Philo's focus on verbal reproof suggests that the metaphorical sense of τύπτω as harsh censure is in view.

[129] Maximus of Tyre (*Discourse* 3e–f (5.17–6, 9 Hobein)), notes that although people are persuaded with difficulty, their disobedience should not be punished with the whip or the spur.

[130] Plutarch, *On Brotherly Love* 487C.

authoritative status and the right and duty to correct and guide others. The apparent discrepancy between the negative attitude of the wise towards others and their reform of the weak is misleading both for modern commentators and ancient critics.[131] Such inconsistency is precisely what the Stoics were criticized for. In spite of their deterministic view of things and often condescending attitude towards others, Stoics shared the common concern of moralists to reform others and continued to use both praise and blame in their attempt to influence others. They continued to use admonition and censure for correction and improvement and the philosopher's consciousness of his commission to reform others affords him the right to censure them. I am postulating this same contradictory stance for the wise in Corinth, whose Stoic bent has been proven by scholars.[132]

The social matrix of such a practice would indeed be similar to that reflected in Philodemus' *On Frank Criticism*, where we repeatedly found warnings against a contemptuous attitude towards others in the practice of mutual psychagogy.[133] The self-assertive wise in Corinth claim then to have the right to eat meat offered to idols, not simply because of their enlightened attitude towards religion and morality but also because of their right to educate the weak from the vantage point of their firmly held beliefs.[134] Then again, although Paul does not tell us the intention of the wise in eating idol meat, he notes that

---

[131] It is a common cliché that the emphasis on spiritual perfection led not only to an arrogant and condescending attitude towards others in the community, but also to indifference. Cf. R. A. Horsley, "'How can some of you say that there is no resurrection of the dead?'" *NovT* 20 (1978), pp. 216–23; idem, "PNEUMATIKOS vs. PSYCHIKOS: Distinctions of Spiritual Status Among the Corinthians," *HTR* 69 (1976), pp. 278. 287; P. Marshall, *Enmity in Corinth*, pp. 182–94; and D. W. Kuck, *Judgment and Community Conflict* (NovTSup 66; Leiden: E. J. Brill, 1992), pp. 190, 214, 218.

[132] See pp. 81–85, above. Plutarch, *On Moral Virtue* 452C-D; *How to Tell a Flatterer From a Friend* 71E; Epictetus, *Discourse* 3.22.94; 2.22.36; Musonius Rufus, fr. 9 (49, 10–12 Hense). The wise could also appeal to the tradition reflected in Thucydides' account of the Corinthians who thought that they had the right to censure their neighbours (*Histories* 1.70.1; cf. νομίζομεν ἄξιοι εἶναι τοῖς πέλας ψόγον ἐπενεγκεῖν.). Paul uses ἐξουσιάζω in 1 Cor 7:4 in the meaning to exercise authority over.

[133] See *On Frank Criticism* frs. 2; 20; 21; 37; 46; 52; 66; 79; cols. 22b; 24a.

[134] This might seem to contradict the demonstrable Stoic bent of the wise in Corinth, but as we have seen, Stoics continued to reform others. The wise had thus not written off the weak. Contra Stowers, "Paul on the Use and Abuse of Reason," *Greeks, Romans, and Christians*, pp. 266–76, 282. My hypothesis squares well, though, with Stowers' hypothesis of the approach taken by the strong in Rom 14:1 and the rational stance of the wise in Corinth towards religion and morality. See pp. 233–34, above.

their pedagogy took the form of an example. The wise ate sacrificed meat in a temple where the weak might see them, and so encouraged them through their example also to eat food sacrificed to idols.[135] Guidance through example, which is equivalent to guidance through precepts, is appropriate for the weak, although Paul rejects it here, presumably because of its negative effects.

Now, one might deduce from Paul's ironic tone that he is not reflecting on an actual practice in Corinth. The contrary deduction is, in my view, more likely. Paul's ironic remarks caricature an actual practice. This is true, for example, of Paul's use of the term οἰκοδομηθήσεται in 1 Cor 8:10, "For if someone sees you who possess knowledge, eating in the temple of an idol, will not this man, since he is weak, (falsely) regard himself as strengthened to eat idol food?" Οἰκοδομέω is a *terminus technicus* for the edification of community members[136] who should build each other up in love.[137] I think that G. Heinrici and Johannes Weiss are correct in suggesting that Paul is ironically repeating a term from the Corinthians' letter. The wise described their attempt to edify the weak with the same term as Paul himself used for the edification of others.[138] They might even have asked Paul in their letter whether they should not build up the conscience of the weak, namely, whether they should not try to make the beliefs of the weak about the non-existence and impotence of idols so strong that they could eat idol-meat without being bothered or harmed.[139] Paul's ironic use of the term, the negative consequences of which are explained in verse 11,[140] shows then that he is taking

---

[135] 1 Cor 8:10, "For if any one sees you, a man of knowledge, at table in an idol's temple, might he not be encouraged ... to eat food offered to idols?"

[136] Cf. Ph. Vielhauer, *Oikodome. Das Bild vom Bau in der christlichen Literatur vom Neuen Testament bis Clemens Alexandrinus* (TBü 65; Münich, 1979), pp. 1–168.

[137] Cf. 1 Cor 8:1b, ἡ ἀγάπη οἰκοδομεῖ. The term ἀγαπᾶν is used in the sense of valuing something for the benefits it yields (see fn. 105, above). This is clear from Philodemus' use of ἀγαπᾶν in *On Frank Criticism* fr. 18.3–5, "But if they do not love him, although they have obtained every kind of [...] nurture and relief...." Cf. tr. 80.7–11, "For they received benefit without disguise because of [their] love [for us]...." In col. 13a3, Philodemus appears also to connect ἀγάπη with the benefits accrued from frank criticism of faults.

[138] C. F. G. Heinrici, *Der erste Brief an die Korinthier* (MeyerK 5; 8th ed.; Göttingen, 1896), pp. 263–64; J. Weiss, *Der erste Korintherbrief*, p. 230; J. Murphy-O'Connor, "Freedom or the Ghetto (I Cor, VIII, 1–13; X, 23–XI, 1)," *RB* 85.4 (1978), p. 548.

[139] R. Jewett, *Paul's Anthropological Terms. A Study of their Use in Conflict Settings* (Leiden, 1971), pp. 402–430; Murphy-O'Connor, "Freedom or the Ghetto," p. 548 n. 20.

[140] γάρ, Blass-Debrunner # 452 (2): "to be sure, just so"; Conzelmann, *1 Corinthians*, p. 149.

issue with a particular form of edification among the wise. Paul's use of τύπτω was perhaps suggested by the wise's claim to be a τύπος or model for the weak. The term οἰκοδομηθήσεται is thus another indication, besides the word τύπτω, that Paul is reacting to a psychagogic guidance by the "wise" which destroys the weak.

A closer look at the text reveals the nature of the psychagogy of the wise. The reference to the slogans at the beginning of 1 Cor 8 shows that the wise also attempted, similarly to the strong in Rom 14:1, rationally to persuade the weak of the untenability of their position. This would indeed suggest a more forceful attempt to sway the opinions of the weak. In 8:4, Paul narrows the focus of the main topic from "now concerning food sacrificed to idols" (8:1) to "concerning the eating of food offered to idols." With οἴδαμεν Paul identifies with the viewpoint of the slogans in verses 1 and 4,[141] "All of us possess knowledge," "no idol in the world really exists," and "there is no God but one." The weak as well as the wise subscribed to these slogans and the confessional formulas in 8:5-6.[142] But beliefs, albeit expressed in identical terms, can lead to different behaviors, due to different inferences of those shared beliefs. Some ate food offered to idols while others refrained from doing so. Although both those who ate and those who abstained subscribed to the slogans in verses one and four, only the former subscribed to the slogan of 8:8, "food will not bring us before (the judgment seat of) God. We are no worse off if we do not eat, and no better off if we do."[143] That the weak believed the contrary is clear from the similar viewpoint of the weak in Romans 14, and from Paul's introduction of the τινές in 8:7 before the slogan in verse eight and after the slogans in verses one and four.

The wise had claimed that πάντες γνῶσιν ἔχομεν (8:1). In light of Paul's qualification, Ἀλλ' οὐκ ἐν πᾶσιν ἡ γνῶσις (8:7), it is clear that the slogan in 8:1 was not meant to be exclusive. The wise assumed

---

[141] When Paul came to write Romans, he says "I know" (14:14), not "we know" (BAGD s.v. 1e), when identifying the position of the strong.

[142] On 1 Cor 8:5-6 as a possible citation see Murphy O'Connor, "I Cor, VIII, 6: Cosmology or Soteriology?" *RB* 85.2 (1978), pp. 253-67. See also R. A. Horsley, "The Background of the Confessional Formula in 1 Cor 8.6," *ZNW* 69.1/2 (1978), pp. 130-35; E. Norden, *Agnostos Theos* (Darmstadt, 1956), pp. 240-50; E. Peterson, *EIS THEOS* (Göttingen, 1926), pp. 251-56; and J. C. Hurd, Jr. *The Origin of 1 Corinthians*, p. 68.

[143] Murphy O'Connor, "Food and Spiritual Gifts in 1 Cor 8:8," *CBQ* 41.2 (1979), pp. 292-98.

that all members of the community possessed the type of γνῶσις under discussion. The inference that this "knowledge," basic to "Christian" belief and shared by all members of the community, must have been the conviction of monotheism, is to the point.[144] When Paul then claims in verse seven that "not everyone has this knowledge," he cannot be referring to the slogans in the previous verses but to the one in verse eight: food is morally and religiously irrelevant, in the view of the wise and of Paul.[145] The "some" in v. 7 do subscribe, as do the wise, to the slogans of v. 4 and the confessional formula of vv. 5–6. However, they are so accustomed to their former idolatry that they think that eating food offered to idols is detrimental to their standing before God, contrary to what is stated in v. 8.

The "some" who lack the knowledge of the slogan in 1 Cor 8:8 are said to "have become so accustomed to idols until now, [that] they still think of the food they eat as food offered to an idol"; and their "conscience" being weak is polluted.[146] This connection of "weakness" with "conscience" (συνείδησις), "knowledge" (γνῶσις), and "habit" (συνήθεια), shows that Paul discusses the problem of the "weak" in vv. 7–12 from a cognitive viewpoint. The term "weakness" was inherent both in the discourse of self-mastery and that of reformatory ethics. The discourse of self-mastery is evident in Paul's characterization of the "weak" as those who lack self-mastery, in the view of the "wise" concerned with self-mastery and moral achievement which emerges and, as I have noted, in Paul's emphasis on self-discipline in 9:24–27. The reformatory ethic emerges also on the basis of the terminology used and from the active attempt of the wise to better the weak, to help them break the fetters of their old habits and make their beliefs and behavior compatible.

Apparently, the weak had deliberated with regard to the content of their beliefs, but had, because of their habits and "weak conscience", abandoned the result of their deliberation. In this the "some" display

---

[144] The knowledge (γνῶσις) referred to in 8.1 is thus not the same as the knowledge referred to in 8.7 ("However, not all possess this knowledge") and 10 ("For if any one sees you, a man of knowledge (ἐάν γάρ τις ἴδῃ σὲ τὸν ἔχοντα γνῶσιν), at table in an idols' temple....").

[145] Compare Rom 14:17. See Weiss, *Der erste Korintherbrief*, pp. 227–28.

[146] 1 Cor 8:7, τινὲς δὲ τῇ συνηθείᾳ ἕως ἄρτι τοῦ εἰδώλου ὡς εἰδωλόθυτον ἐσθίουσιν, ἡ συνείδησις αὐτῶν ἀσθενὴς οὖσα μολύνεται. See *Sirach* 21:28, Μολύνει τὴν ἑαυτοῦ ψυχὴν ὁ ψιθυρίζων. H. A. W. Meyer notes the meaning of "ethical defilement" for the word μολύειν in verse 7. See *Der erste Brief an die Korinther*. KEK 5; 3rd ed. (Göttingen, 1856), pp. 181, 184.

aspects of Aristotle's characterization of those who lack self-mastery and Cicero's description of a person "sick in mind." Aristotle notes that there are two types of incontinence (ἀκρασία), one is impetuosity (προπέτεια), and another weakness (ἀσθένεια). He descibes the respective persons in the following manner:

> For the weak person deliberates, but then his feeling makes him abandon the result of his deliberation; but the impetuous person is led on by his feelings because he has not deliberated.[147]

The knowledge in question had not filtered down to the same level of behavior for the weak as for the wise.[148] From the standpoint of the wise the beliefs of the weak are uninformed. They, in effect, still believe in idols when they think food offered to idols is imbued with special power. Aversion to sacrified food ensues. Cicero, in the context of discussing the meaning of "sickness of soul" and the therapeutic model among the Stoics, says that the product of aversion is defined as "an intense belief, persistent and deeply rooted, which regards a thing that need not be shunned as though it ought to be shunned"; this sort of belief is an "act of judging that one has knowledge where one has none."[149] On this view, the inferential beliefs of the weak do not truly reflect knowledge; their aversion is the result, not of knowledge but of an uninformed and sick mind. J. Jeremias has perceptively seen that the slogans in chapter 8:1, 4, and 8, form a successive argument to justify the eating of idol meat:[150]

*Premise 1*: "All of us possess knowledge" (1 Cor 8:1).
*Premise 2a*: "No idol in the world really exists" (1 Cor 8:4).
*Premise 2b*: "There is no God but one" (1 Cor 8:4).

---

[147] Aristotle, *Nicomachean Ethics* 1150b19–22. The incontinent person (ἀκρατής) is curable (ἰατός) as opposed to the intemperate person (ἀκόλαστος) who is incurable (ἀνίατος; ibid., 1150b29–35; a21–23; 1151a12–15; 1146a10–17, 34–35). See pp. 65–69, on different types of students.

[148] Murphy-O'Connor appropriately speaks of the "time-lag between intellectual and emotional acceptance of monotheism" on the part of the weak ("Freedom or the Ghetto," pp. 545, 554).

[149] Cicero, *Tusculan Disputations* 4.26. For Stoic discussion on weakness and aversion to certain things and the connection of "weakness" with false judgments and beliefs, habits, knowledge, and conscience, see Cicero, Ibid., 4.15; 4.29.42; *On Ends* 5.43; SVF 1.67; 3.177; Seneca, *Epistles* 50.9; 75.10–12; 4 Macc 15:5; Epictetus, *Discourse* 2.15.20, and Lucian, *Slander* 19.

[150] J. Jeremias, "Zur Gedankenführung in den paulinischen Briefen," in *Studia Paulina in honorem Johannis de Zwaan* (Haarlem, 1953), pp. 151–52. The comparison in the text with Aristotle is mine.

*Confessional formula*: "But for us there is one God, the Father, from whom come all things and to whom our own being leads, and one Lord Jesus Christ, through whom all things, including ourselves, come into being" (1 Cor 8:6).

*Inferential belief*: "Food will not bring us before (the judgment seat of) God. We are no worse off if we do not eat, and no better off if we do" (1 Cor 8:8).

This type of argument resembles what Aristotle described in his *Topica* as "dialectical reasoning," where the truth of an argument is established with premises which reflect reputable and acceptable beliefs of most people or at least of the wise.[151] The inferential belief in verse eight is the logical deduction from the content of the agreed upon slogans in verses one and four, and expressed in the confessional formula of verse six. If idols have no "real" existence, food offered to such idols are not invested with magical powers. But the weak had not drawn the same inference as the wise. The practical consequences of the same beliefs and teachings were thus quite different. Both the wise and the weak believed in the non-existence of idols; the eating of food offered to idols defiled the conscience of the latter only and so they refrained.

In 1 Cor 2:6–3:4 Paul agrees with a typology of humans predicated on the wisdom possessed, namely, the mature who can gauge the mysteries of God and the immature who cannot. Although the wise did not feel they needed to level out the differences between themselves and the weak with regard to understanding the mysteries of God, things were apparently different with regard to the basic teachings and beliefs by which they were both constituted. But one must also, Paul claims, postulate a typology predicated on the knowledge of the basic teachings and beliefs of the "Christian" life (1 Thess 1:9; Gal 4:8–10). Here differences also exist, both on a behavioral level and in inferential beliefs (1 Cor 8:8). Only the weak thought that eating of food offered to idols affected their standing with the divine. Paul encourages the wise to respect these differences and be careful not to destroy the weak by attempting to persuade them of their ill-founded deductions. Paul does not debate the validity of the true beliefs and reasonings of the wise or the correctness of their inferential beliefs; instead, he challenges them not to let their "right"

---

[151] Aristotle, *Topica* 100b21.

to eat food offered to idols become an "offense" or "hindrance" to the weak.[152]

Paul's argument in 1 Cor 8:1–8 reveals, then, that the wise did not simply disagree with the inferences drawn by the weak, but attempted as well to persuade the weak of their "illogical" position. In their attempt to cure the weak of their irrational false beliefs and passions (i.e., fears) about the pagan gods and meat offered to such gods, the "wise" follow a procedure recommended by Seneca in the case of the weak who because of habituation cannot set themselves free.[153] In order for a weak person to benefit from precepts, his false beliefs must first be eradicated. Guidance through precepts or examples follows after the eradication of mistaken beliefs. The wise first persuade the weak rationally, then show them how to behave by their example. By eating in the temple of an idol, the wise encourage the weak to do the same. But instead of reforming the weak, this procedure apparently destroyed them.

Although one would suspect that the "weak" normally did not eat sacrificed meat, Paul assumes such social reality in this instance,[154] I suggest, because of the prodding of the wise. Verse 7 introduces the terms "conscience" (συνείδησις) and "weakness," both of which are crucial for any understanding of the text. Instead of rehearsing the various views of the meaning of συνείδησις which have found scholarly support, I accept P. W. Gooch's views on "conscience" in 1 Cor 8 and 10.[155] Gooch abstracts three senses of συνείδησις: firstly, a

---

[152] 1 Cor 8:9, ἡ ἐξουσία ὑμῶν αὕτη πρόσκομμα γένηται τοῖς ἀσθενέσιν. See A. J. Malherbe, "Determinism and Free Will in Paul: The Argument of 1 Corinthians 8 and 9," p. 238.

[153] Seneca, *Epistle* 95.36–37.

[154] The οὐχί in v. 10 expects a positive answer and reflects the same social reality as v. 7, namely, the "weak" did, contrary to their conviction, eat sacrificed meat. That is also a prerequisite for the problem addressed by Paul in chapter 8.

[155] See the cogent arguments presented by P. W. Gooch in "'Conscience' in 1 Corinthians 8 and 10," *NTS* 33 (1987), pp. 244–54. For other views on "conscience" in Paul, see C. A. Pierce, *Conscience in the New Testament* (London, 1955); J. Stelzenberger, *Syneidesis im Neuen Testament*. Paderborn, 1961; J. Dupont, "Syneidesis aux origines de la notion chrétienne de conscience morale," *Studia Hellenistica* 5 (1948), pp. 119–53; C. Spicq, "La conscience dans le Nouveau Testament," *RB* 47 (1938) 50–80; M. Thrall, "The Pauline Use of συνείδησις," *NTS* 14 (1967–68), pp. 118–25; Jewett, *Paul's Anthropological Terms*, pp. 402–46; R. A. Horsley, "Consciousness and Freedom among the Corinthians: I Corinthians 8–10," *CBQ* (1978), pp. 574–89; H.-J. Eckstein, *Der Begriff Syneidesis bei Paulus* (Tübingen, 1983); W. D. Davies, "Conscience and Its Use in the New Testament," *Jewish and Pauline Studies* (London, 1984), pp 243–56. Scholars debate whether or not the term had the meaning of regulative principle in Paul.

"minimal" sense of self-awareness, a conscious knowledge of the self under some description or other; secondly, an internal witness of "bad feeling" or the pain of recognizing that one has done something wrong; and, thirdly, the morally robust idea of conscience as internal lawgiver. In this last sense of moral conscience, conscience becomes the repository of moral beliefs and principles; it sets down rules, and passes judgment to convict or acquit.

Gooch argues that the "minimal" sense fits well in 1 Cor 8:7–10 and that of an awareness of "bad feeling" in 1 Cor 10. In neither context does the sense of "moral conscience" fit. In all three occurrences of συνείδησις in 8:7–12 it is said to be "weak." In addition, those whose "conscience is weak" are called "weak" twice (8:9, 11). The term συνείδησις refers to "an understanding or perception of the self, an understanding which is said to be 'weak.'"[156] This does not imply a weak as opposed to a robust faculty but a sense of the self as weak, as is confirmed by Paul's description of the person as weak in verse 10: ". . . by your knowledge this weak man is destroyed." Gooch suggests then translations which predicate weakness of the subject rather than his or her συνείδησις.

Paul accentuates the psychological condition of the weak and their weak understanding. These persons are so accustomed to their former idolatry that they "feel themselves polluted," or experience themselves as tainted by the idol associated with the meat; they, literally, "eat as though it were [still] idol food" (8:7). The subjective force is also present in the case of the "wounding" of the conscience in verse twelve; what is wounded are the weak person's feelings and self-estimation. As eating meat causes polluted feelings, so it also brings upon the weak a painful wound.

The minimal sense of subjective awareness also fits well in the third instance of conscience in verse ten. Paul is concerned with the dangers of the weak in imitating the behavior of the wise: "Since he is weak will not his συνείδησις be built up to eat idol food?" (8:10b). The ironic connotation of οἰκοδομηθήσεται indicates that if a weak person imitates the wise, he would think that he was edified when he is not. The reason why his "edification" is only a sham is simply because it is uninformed; even though he eats, the weak one still believes in the existence of idols and so-called gods. As such he would feel himself "polluted" and be "destroyed."[157]

---

[156] Gooch, "'Conscience' in 1 Corinthians 8 and 10," pp. 249–250.

[157] An "upbuilding" Calvin appropriately characterized as *ruinosa aedificatio*. Cf.

Such a feeling would not only destroy the weak person's commitments in his newly found faith, but also sever the social relations between the friends. As in Rom 14, we also witness in 1 Cor 8 a tension between the wise and the weak as to the question of divine approval.[158] What constitutes a divinely acceptable behavior? For the weak the eating of meat offered to idols meant the recognition of the existence of idols and a rejection of the "one God, the Father" and "one Lord, Jesus Christ." They felt that the eating of idol-food would jeopardize their standing before God. From the perspective of the strong things were different. Their recognition of "one God, the Father" and "one Lord, Jesus Christ," divested the food offered to idols of all its power. Food is inconsequential for divine approval or disapproval. By attempting to persuade the weak of the same and educate them by having them imitate their behavior, the wise undermined the commitments of the weak. For the weak to imitate the wise meant to consume food still invested with curious powers; it meant a reversal of their turning to God from idols (1 Thess 1:9). This is their "destruction."[159]

Paul, as we have seen, presents himself as an example in 1 Cor 9 where he argues for the importance of not insisting on one's rights. Instead one should devote one's energies to benefiting others. Associating with people of diverse moral standing is legitimate in that endeavor. Some limits though should be set on one's association with others. Although "all things are permissible" one should not go so far as to associate with a prostitute (6:12–18) or "share" in idol worship

---

Tertullian, *De praescr.* 3, "Aedificari in ruinam"; Heinrici, *Der erste Brief an die Korinther*, p. 263. For μολύνω as "ethical defilement" see *Sirach* 21:28; Porphyry, *On Abstinence* 1, 42; Synesius, *Epistle* 5.

[158] Rom 14:4, 10; 1 Cor 8:8. "Divine judgment" is a semantic component of the term παρίστημι (Murphy-O'Connor, "Food and Spiritual Gifts in 1 Cor 8:8," p. 297). For the περισσεύω-ὑστερέω contrast see 1 Cor 1:7; Phil 4:12, 18; Heinrici, *Der erste Brief an die Korinther*, pp. 262–63.

[159] Commenting on 1 Cor 8:11, H. Conzelmann says: "In Paul, however, ἀπολλύναι must not be taken in a weakened sense as moral ruin; here as elsewhere it means eternal damnation (so also in Rom. 14.15)" (*1 Corinthians*, p. 149 n. 38). See pp. 230–31 (fn. 137), above. Cf. also Cranfield, *A Critical and Exegetical Commentary on the Epistle to the Romans*, 2.715; D. W. Kuck, *Judgment and Community Conflict*, p. 183 (n. 176). H. A. W. Meyer qualifies his statement that ἀπόλλυται is "von der ewigen ἀπώλεια gemeint" with "wenn man aus dem Glaubensleben in das sündliche der Gewissenswidrigkeit geräht." See *Der erste Brief an die Korinther*, pp. 184, 181. W. M. L. de Wette is uncommitted but is inclined towards a psychological interpretation of ἀπόλλυται: *Kurze Erklärung der Briefe an die Korinther* (Leipzig, 1841), pp. 70–71. See Philodemus, *On Frank Criticism* frs. 59–60; Plutarch, *On Listening to Lectures* 46E; *Progress in Virtue* 78AB.

(10:1–22). Against the intellectual self-mastery of the wise who displayed an honorable harmony between their beliefs and behavior, Paul forwards a correct kind of ascetic self-mastery. Self-discipline is indeed needed, not for purposes of self-edification, but in order to withstand the temptations of idol-worship and in one's effort to benefit others.[160] This matter of the correct kind of self-mastery and its purpose, ties together Paul's concerns in 1 Cor 8–10, and brings Paul naturally back to the issue of food offered to idols, discussed in chapter 8.

Like a skilled casuist, Paul gives three instances in 1 Cor 10:25–28 where questions concerning conscience might arise with regard to the appropriateness of eating food offered to idols. Here Paul lends voice to the position both of the wise and the weak. The key phrase, "without raising any questions on the ground of conscience" (μηδὲν ἀνακρίνοντες διὰ τὴν συνείδησιν) occurs twice (10:25, 27). Here συνείδησις connotes the "bad feelings" of the weak, a somewhat stronger sense than "self-awareness" suggested for 8:7–12.[161] Two instances are envisaged where the behavior of the wise should not be modified; one where it should. As such this section takes off from 1 Cor 8 where Paul had attempted to modify the behavior of the wise. There Paul had taken a stringent attitude, suggesting he himself would abstain from eating food "forever" if it would cause his brother to stumble. In 1 Cor 10:25–28 Paul recognizes other possible social settings than a temple dining hall and detracts from his stringent position, allowing for the eating of idol meat in a pagan home except when a weaker person objects to it.[162]

The first instance is given in verse 25, "Everything sold in the

---

[160] 1 Cor 9:24–10:13. See pp. 247–49 and 256–64, above.

[161] Convincingly demonstrated by Gooch, "'Conscience' in 1 Corinthians 8 and 10," p. 251. See Philodemus, *Rhet.* vol. 5, fr. 11.4–6, διὰ τὴν τοῦ τοιούτου βίου συνείδησιν. Here Philodemus criticizes orators who on account of their familiar conscience and professional legal life destroy those who come to them. M. Coune compares Philodemus' expression with Paul's phrase μηδὲν ἀνακρίνοντες διὰ τὴν συνείδησιν and suggests the additional nuance of "because of the weak's religious conviction," namely, on account of the knowledge the weak had acquired of the will of God ("Le problème des idolothytes et l'éducation de la syneidêsis," *RSR* 51 (1963), p. 529).

[162] The temple dining hall is probably the context for both 1 Cor 8:10 and 10:14, 21. See R. E. Oster, "Use, Misuse and Neglect of Archaeological Evidence in Some Modern Works on 1 Corinthians (1 Cor 7, 1–5; 8, 10; 11, 2–16; 12, 14–26)," *ZNW* 83.1/2 (1992), pp. 64–67. The archaeological remains of the Corinthian temple of Asclepius and the temple of Demeter and Kore show that both of these temple areas contained numerous dining halls. These were used for ceremonies other than

market you may eat without investigation on account of the bad feelings (of the weak)."¹⁶³ The second in verse 27, "If some nonbeliever invites you to a meal and you want to go, eat everything set out for you without examining it because of (the weak's) bad feelings." And the third in verse 28-29a:

> But if someone says to you, "This is idol food", don't eat for the sake of the person who discloses this, that is, his bad feelings. And I mean his bad feelings, not yours.¹⁶⁴

This last instance shows that Paul's concerns are primarily to ameliorate the detrimental effects one member's behavior has on another. In this his concerns are the same as in chapter eight. In this instance both the weak and the wise are dining in a pagan home. Paul's use of the word ὁ μηνύσας in 10:28 ("the man who informed you") helps in the identification of the "informant" and underscores the psychagogic nature of this pericope.

As in the social practice of mutual psychagogy among the Epicureans in Athens and Naples, Paul uses the word μηνύσας for a person who adheres to an ideal of openness and is forthcoming with regard to his feelings towards others.¹⁶⁵ 1 Cor 10:25-28 does not reveal institutionalized confessional practice in the Corinthian community,¹⁶⁶ but two deductions are legitimate in light of the comparative material. Firstly, in the first two scenarios envisaged by Paul in

---

the official cultus of the deity (e.g. meals, birthday parties, et al.), allowing the apparent contradiction in Paul's advice in chapters 8 and 10 to become understandable. The dining facilities in Corinth thus "provide architectural evidence for a situation in which 'monotheistic' believers (1 Cor 8:4) could attend and participate in activities indigenous to their religio-cultural matrix but which did not require overt participation in the central *cultus* and sacrifices of the religion itself" (ibid., 66-67).

¹⁶³ 1 Cor 10:25. See H. J. Cadbury, "The Macellum of Corinth," *JBL* 53 (1934), pp. 134-41.

¹⁶⁴ I have adopted Gooch's translation ("'Conscience' in 1 Corinthians 8 and 10," p. 252).

¹⁶⁵ The terms ἀνακρίνω and μην-ύσας/ύω occur in both fr. 42 of *On Frank Criticism* and in 1 Cor 10:25-28. Paul uses the word ἀνακρίνω in the phrase "without investigation on account of the bad feelings" in 10:25 and 27 and in 1 Cor 2:15 which highlight the function of the mature in evaluating others (see also 4:3-4; 9:3, and 14:24). The subject of ἀνακρίνω is a mature person who has the right to evaluate the immature. Philodemus also uses the term ἀνακρίνω to connote the mature's evaluation of the immature. The teacher has to "examine closely" the one reluctant to disclose his errors or be otherwise forthcoming towards his associates (frs. 42 and 49). See pp. 128-29 and 141, above.

¹⁶⁶ Note though the "official" connotation of the word μηνύω in 3 Macc 3:11-13; 3:28; and Pap. Par. 10. Discussed by G. Adolf Deissmann in *Bible Studies* (Peabody, MA, 1988), pp. 341-45.

1 Cor 10:25–28 the perspective taken is that of the wise; in the third the perspective is that of the weak. Secondly, the "informant" is not a pagan but a fellow member of the community, whose previous views with regard to the nature of idols linger on.[167] The content of the information given, "this is sacrificial meat," is not as important as the impact of that information on the weak and the conclusion reached by Paul. Paul's overall concern here is an attempt to modify the behavior of the wise that was undermining the commitment of others in the community. It is precisely because of the negative impact their behavior has on the weak that Paul urges the wise to refrain.

In 8:12 Paul graphically depicts that impact as "destruction." The weak saw the wise eat in a temple of an idol without indicating any uneasiness and even imitated the wise. This led to his destruction because his understanding was weak and uninformed. The wise are charged with "sinning" against Christ and their weaker brothers. This charge becomes significant if we postulate, as I did above, an active engagement on the part of the wise who attempted to educate the weak from the vantage point of their firmly held beliefs. If they did not, Paul's charge is somewhat misdirected.

In 1 Cor 10:28 the weak man does not attempt to imitate the wise. Instead he openly confesses his reservations with regard to the behavior of the wise. In 1 Cor 8:10–13 and 10:28 Paul wants the wise not only to change the way in which they wanted to educate the weak, but also to restrict their freedom. Both were necessary for the well-being of the weak. Paul's attempted fairness could not be clearer. The wise are not asked to change their firmly held inferential beliefs (1 Cor 8:8); they are only asked to modify their behavior and pedagogy; and their behavior should only be modified if a person weak in belief brings its ruinous nature to their attention and if their attempt to reform the weak becomes destructive.

That the above stricture might however be objected to by the wise becomes clear from two rhetorical questions of 10:29b–30. Here Paul again lends voice to the position of the strong. The content of the rhetorical questions is appropriate to the disposition and general state of mind of the informed Corinthians. The referent is sufficiently clear. Μου and ἐγώ refer to the informed person whose freedom has

---

[167] That the "informant" is a pagan is maintained by H. Conzelmann and others (cf. *1 Corinthians*, pp. 177–78). See also Murphy-O'Connor, "Freedom or the Ghetto," p. 570 n. 79.

been restricted in the previous verse. The wise responds in light of that restriction:

(1) Why should *my* freedom be subject to the strictures of someone else's bad feelings?
(2) If *I* partake with thankfulness, why should *I* be denounced because of that for which *I* give thanks?

These are legitimate questions from the standpoint of the wise.[168] Although Paul does not here answer the second question directly, his similar remark in Romans 14:16 suggests the direction such an answer might take.[169] The "good" in question is the knowledge of the strong that nothing is profane in and of itself. This "good" might be denounced by the weak and by Paul if the strong grieve the weak by their behavior. Although Paul does not specify a social setting in Rom 14:14–16 where the knowledge of the strong is acted out as it is in 1 Cor 10:25–28, the sequence of events is similar. If the conviction of the strong results in a certain behavior, it destroys or grieves the weak. The answer to the second rhetorical question is thus the same as that given to the first. The stricture in question, however, applies to the liberty or "freedom" (ἐλευθερία) of the wise, not their "right" (ἐξουσία).

The nature and reasons for these strictures are made clear, informed

---

[168] In a fine account of these rhetorical questions D. F. Watson summarily raises and rejects that they qualify as impersonation "because they are not provided with a specific referent ... they would need to be identified as the question of the strong in a manner such as this: 'I can hear you saying....'" ("1 Corinthians 10.23–11.1 in the Light of Greco-Roman Rhetoric," *JBL* 108.2 (1989), p. 313 n. 54). I find no reference to Theon of Alexandria here and this stricture is unneccessary in light of Theon's discussion of character portrayal (see pp. 48–49, above). A personified position does not have to be introduced with a specific referent. It suffices to be in tune with the subject matter and the person's age, status, or disposition. Here, the content of the rhetorical questions is appropriate for the general state of mind of the wise as has been explicated in chapters 8 and 10. The referent is also clear. It is difficult to see how one might possibly argue that the referent in ἡ ἐλευθερία μου is any other than the very person whose freedom to eat has just been restricted in the previous verse. In Rom 14–15 Paul has further personified the characters by labeling them both, one as "powerful" the other as "weak." In this Paul avails himself of an excellent means of adaptation, namely, character portrayal through which he lends the concerns of both the wise and the weak a voice, agreeing with both Theon and Nicolaus who emphasize that character portrayal could be valuably used in letter writing as well as in epideictic and deliberative speeches (Theon, *Progymnasmata* 8.9–10 Butts ed. 442 n. 4; Nicolaus, 66–67 Felten). Personification is consequentialist in nature, highlighting adaptation to the particular case.

[169] Rom 14:15b–16, "Do not let what you eat cause the ruin of one for whom Christ died. So do not let your good be spoken of as evil."

by the general statements bracketing the particular instances given (10:23–24, 31–11:1). Paul agrees with and repeats in a shorter form the slogan of 6:12, πάντα ἔξεστιν, with the same qualification, οὐ πάντα συμφέρει, adding a second one, οὐ πάντα οἰκοδομεῖ, thus criticising self-edification at the expense of a communal good. The correlation between personal advantage and that of many might be skewed. The stricture imposed on the wise indicates that Paul is thinking along similar lines, namely, from a preoccupation with personal advantage to a consideration of others of the same community. This is evident from 10:32–11:1 where Paul presents himself as an example of the behavior advocated. Instead of benefiting the weak, the behavior of the wise ruins them. Whatever behavior has detrimental effects on the insecure should be modified. He urges the wise to restrict their freedom and thus imitate him in his affable behavior as he has imitated Christ.[170] Paul can legitimately present himself as an example since this is precisely what he has done in not making use of his right to financial remuneration.[171]

Paul's flexible approach enunciated in the pericope of 1 Cor 9:19–23 is seen in its wider literary context. I have demonstrated the presence of matters of versatility, adaptability, and psychagogy throughout 1 Cor 5:1–11:1 and claimed that Paul debated these issues with the "wise" and some patrons in Corinth. Paul and his critics did not see eye to eye on matters of spiritual guidance. Evidence for this debate on pedagogical matters is reflected throughout the Corinthian

---

[170] In his accommodating behavior, Paul apparently found a model in Christ's adaptability to which he refers in Phil 2:5–11 and Gal 4:4–5 (See pp. 256 (fn. 64) and 259–60 (fn. 73), above).

[171] 1 Cor 11:1; 9:12, 18. As he rounds off the discussion in 5:1–11:1, Paul urges his readers to emulate his accommodating behavior so that they can be most effective in whatever situation they may find themselves in (cf. 10:32, "whatever you do, do everything. . . ."). Paul's call for imitation does not attempt to elicit some concrete conduct or specific behavioral response as such but is general. Paul's identification with the weak follows the same kind of logic as his extension of patronal friendship. It is a reversal of the natural theory of justice advocated by Callicles in Plato's *Gorgias*. According to this theory, nature subjects the weaker to the stronger, but in the golden age the government was under the jurisdiction of the wise, protecting the weaker from the strong. According to Seneca, Posidonius proposed an overturn of the natural theory of justice and a return to the principles of the golden age (*Epistle* 90.4–5). Paul's aspirations, reflected in his critique of the practice of the wise in Corinth and powerful in Rome and in the guidelines he gives for the relations of the strong and the weak, are reminiscent of the principles of the golden age. Callicles' theory is refuted by Socrates when discussing rhetoric, flattery, and pleasure, versus the beneficial and frank "tester of souls" (Plato, *Gorgias* 482C–486D; 488B). Contrast Plato, *Laws* 777DE.

correspondence and supports our non-apocalyptic and pedagogical reading of 1 Cor 8. Here we have witnessed Paul's advocation of a gentle approach in psychagogic guidance and his critical stance towards the wise who wanted to be more forthright in their guidance of the weak.

The leadership model Paul's sets forth in 1 Cor 9:19–23 and 10:32–11:1 has, then, implications for Paul's own guidance of the Corinthians, reflected in his willingness to associate with people of different moral status and in his considerate approach towards the weak. The leadership model which the wise are to emulate is presented in a context in which Paul is critical of the appraoch the wise have taken towards the weak. In the final section of this book I shall explore an important and contiguous aspect of the above pedagogical debate, namely, Paul's own stringent approach towards the recalcitrant Corinthians, necessary because of their deceptive view of themselves. Evidence for this surfaces throughout 1 Corinthians as well as 2 Corinthians where we find retrospective evidence revealing the repercussions of Paul's critique of the wise and the mounting tensions between Paul and his recalcitrant critics due to their differing view of the use of harsness in psychagogic guidance.

## 6.4 *Paul's Psychagogic Approach Towards the Recalcitrant Corinthians*

Reverberations of the debate between Paul and the "wise" are found in the early parts of 1 Corinthians. In Paul's own approach towards the wise we find evidence for his own stringent approach where a certain characterization of the "wise" as recalcitrant students in need of more forceful guidance emerges. In Paul's view the "wise" needed, because of their self-deceptive view of their status, a forceful corrective. Paul prepares the way for such a corrective in 1 Cor 1–4 before turning his attention in chapters 5–15 to practical issues among the Corinthians which needed to be addressed. Paul's argumentation, his use of the child-mature person contrast and the characterization of "wise" which emerges, yield evidence of the above debate and bring to relief issues of leadership qualification and style, maturity and immaturity, and psychagogic guidance.

In the thanksgiving period Paul compliments the Corinthians for their maturity, only shortly thereafter to lament the immaturity seen in their bickerings. Paul's critique of the very things he praises the

Corinthians for suggests that we already have mock praise in Paul's compliment; and, if so, its purpose is to shame, notwithstanding Paul's explicit denial (4:14). 1 Cor 1:10 and 4:16 form an *inclusio*, making the whole intervening section a παρακαλῶ-period.[172] The preceding verses give the setting and introduce Paul's purpose; the subsequent verses establish the vantage point of Paul's psychagogic guidance as a spiritual father.[173] Although Paul focuses on God's grace and faithfulness and the "riches" the Corinthians have received, it is difficult to remove all ironic nuances from 1:1–9. When Paul describes the Corinthians' "wealth," he ironically focuses on those aspects which they value and Paul later criticizes.[174] As such the thanksgiving, with its close connection to the παρακαλῶ-period of 1:10, sets the stage for Paul's mixture of praise and blame.

Paul mixes the direct and the indirect approach, his purpose becoming clearer and clearer, culminating in an explicit statement of purpose, namely, to admonish the Corinthians as his "beloved children."[175] Paul also makes it clear that his readers' reception of his correctives determines the nature of his approach. As such, we already have an implicit threat and a call to obedience. Paul's authorial voice speaks with force when he perceives the nature of the information conveyed as detrimental to his work. When countering

---

[172] C. J. Bjerkelund, *Parakalô: Form, Funktion und Sinn der parakalô-Sätze in den paulinischen Briefen* (Oslo, 1967), pp. 141–46; F. Lang, *Die Briefe an die Korinther* (NTD 7; Göttingen, 1986), pp. 27–59. See Bünker, *Briefformular*, pp. 51–59, on the rhetorical structure of 1 Cor 1:10–4:21 and J. T. Fitzgerald, *Cracks in an Earthen Vessel*, pp. 117–28, on its hortatory nature.

[173] Namely 1:1–9 and 4:17–21. See P. Gutierrez, *La Paternité Spirituelle selon Saint Paul* (Paris, 1968), pp. 119–97.

[174] Compare 1 Cor 4:8, ἤδη ἐπλουτήσατε with 1:5, ὅτι ἐν παντὶ ἐπλουτίσθητε ἐν αὐτῷ, ἐν παντὶ λόγῳ καὶ πάσῃ γνώσει. Cf. 1 Cor 8:1–3; 12:8; 13:1–2, 8–9; 2 Cor 8:7; 11:6. See C. F. G. Heinrici, *Der erste Brief an die Korinther*, p. 45, and P. T. O'Brien, *Introductory Thanksgivings in the Letters of Paul* (Leiden, 1977), pp. 113–15.

[175] 1 Cor 4:14, ὡς τέκνα μου ἀγαπητὰ νουθετῶ[v]; cf. 10:14; 15:58. According to *Ad Herennium*, there are two kinds of *exordia*, namely, a direct opening and a subtle approach (1.4.6). B. Fiore has demonstrated Paul's use of the oblique approach in 1 Cor 4:6 in the λογὸς εὐσχηματισμένος motif ("'Covert Allusion' in 1 Corinthians 1–4," *CBQ* 47.1 (1985) 85–112). For Demetrius paraenesis, censure, and improvement are the aims of an oblique speech (*On Style* 292–98). In light of the close relation of irony to covert allusions, perhaps it is more correct to say that Paul's remarks are an "ambiguous way of speaking (τὸ ... εἶδος ἀμφίβολον), although not irony, yet has a suggestion of irony" (*On Style* 191; cf. Quintilian, *Oratorical Institutions* 9.2.65; Dion. Hal. *Rhet.* 9.323.1 U). Note Ps.-Libanius' definition of the ironic style (9 (68,17–19 Malherbe)): "The ironic style is that in which we feign praise of someone at the beginning, but at the end display our real aim, inasmuch as we had made our earlier statements in pretense."

an overweening attitude, Paul's response is bound to be more overbearing. Here a patriarchal attitude becomes more pronounced and the asymmetry of his relationship is evident. But in a more conciliatory response, a symmetrical relationship is more evident. These dimensions are two aspects of Paul's pedagogical approach.[176] In the mixture of epideictic and deliberative aspects, Paul has closely interwoven praise and blame with his argumentation, showing that these early chapters are an integral part of the rest of the letter also revealing a distinct hortatory pattern.[177]

6.4.1 *Paul's characterization of the recalcitrant ones*
Paul engages the Corinthians with terminology pertinent both to their views and his, agreeing with the "wise" in Corinth: there are more or less mature persons in the community.[178] Paul, however, disagrees with some of the inferences drawn by the wise relating to perfection and spiritual guidance; for Paul, a mature or "perfect person" (ἀνὴρ τέλειος) is not perfect in the sense of being incapable of error or faultless; he still can progress and fall into momentary error in need of correction.[179] This, I suggest, the "wise" disputed. Paul questions the maturity of the "wise" and their claim to "perfection," of having advanced beyond the need of advice and correction; the "wise" are like children whom Paul, as their spiritual father, has the right to lead and correct.[180] The immaturity of the "wise" is seen in their faulty judgment relating to their status and function; they do not

---

[176] This is, in my view, a more likely explanation than that offered by J. C. Hurd who argues that Paul's sympathetic tone is evident when dealing with written information as opposed to a more censorious approach when addressing information gained through oral reports (*The Origin of 1 Corinthians*, pp. 62, 74–93). The oral reports (1:11; 5:1; 11:17) had reached Paul either from "Chloe's people" or from Stephanas, Fortunatus, and Achaicus. Paul responds to oral reports in 1:10–4:21; 5:1–8, 13b; and 11:17–34. As we have seen, the reporting of misdemeanors to community leaders was part of the ideal of openness valued by the Epicureans at Athens and Herculaneum. On the problem of taking περὶ δέ in 7:1, 25; 8:1; 12:1; 16:1 and 12 as evidence for Paul's respond to written request, see M. M. Mitchell, "Concerning ΠΕΡΙ ΔΕ in 1 Corinthians", *NovT* 31 (1989), pp. 229–56.
[177] Cicero, *De Inventione* 97; Aristotle, *Rhetoric* 1451a.
[178] Contra P. J. du Plessis who sees τέλειοι as referring to "all Christians" (*Teleios*, pp. 179–80).
[179] 1 Cor 2:6; 3:1–2; Phil 3:12–16; E.-B. Allo, *Saint Paul: Première Épître aux Corinthiens* (Paris, 1956), p. 40. The Corinthians' immaturity is seen in their strife and jealousy; they "walk according to a human standard" (1 Cor 3:3; 2 Cor 1:17; 11:18; 10:2–3); Philodemus, *On Frank Criticism* frs. 46; 56; Seneca, *Epistles* 71.29; 94.51; Cicero, *On Friendship* 7–10.
[180] Cf. P. Gutierrez, *La Paternité Spirituelle selon Saint Paul*, pp. 172–75.

realize the interacting effects of knowledge and language; their claim to perfection reveals their immaturity. Paul criticizes the "wise" then for their faulty judgment with regard to their own maturity, their attitude towards the immature, and their claim to be exempt from judgment by others.

It has long been recognized that rhetoric was part of the debate in Corinth between Paul and the "wise" who were concerned with the standards of the art of persuasive speech and evaluated Paul as inferior on account of his unimpressive speech and weak appearance.[181] H. D. Betz has demonstrated that Paul's use of the formula λόγος καὶ γνῶσις in 1 Cor 1:5 where he commends the Corinthians for their abundance in "every form of eloquence and every form of knowledge" was not fortuitous but a calculated move on Paul's part. The formula "eloquence and knowledge" forms part of a tradition going back to Isocrates reflecting an ideal Hellenic education.[182] Paul's use of this formula lodges him squarely within a tradition which relates issues of eloquence and pedagogy and has implications for our understanding of Paul's criticism of the "wise." Paul deflects here, as he did in 1 Cor 8, the value of dialectic reasoning and suggests a different kind of rhetoric, the rhetoric of demonstration in psychagogic guidance.

The formula in 1 Cor 1:5 provides the basic assumption of Paul's arguments in the letter; the formula both states the Corinthians' justified self-praise and contains Paul's critique and clue to his argument. Betz examines the Corinthians' excessive claim in light of the problems connected with self-praise which was thought to breed self-delusion and lead to a disastrous end for the boaster. By the time of Paul there existed a broad cultural consensus saying that only philosophical and religious frauds could in their vanity claim to know everything. What Paul finds lacking among the Corinthians concerns their maturity, not in "eloquence and knowledge" as such but in

---

[181] Cf. T. H. Lim, "'Not in Persuasive Words of Wisdom, but in the Demonstration of the Spirit and Power,'" *NovT* 29.2 (1987), pp. 137–49; cf. 139–40. Paul stands outside the profession of formal speech but claims to have knowledge. Cf. 2 Cor 11:6a, εἰ δὲ καὶ ἰδιώτης τῷ λόγῳ, ἀλλ' οὐ τῇ γνώσει). Ἰδιώτης was often employed to distinguish the amateur from the professional speaker (Dio Chrysostom, *Discourse* 12.17; 42.3; 54.1; Plato, *Ion* 532CD).

[182] Or παιδεία. For Isocrates the formula reads "thinking together with eloquence" (cf. *Antidosis* 293–94, φρόνησις καὶ λόγος). H. D. Betz, "The Problem of Rhetoric and Theology according to the Apostle Paul," in *L'Apôtre Paul* (ed. A. Vanhoye, Leuven University Press, 1986), pp. 32–39.

practical conduct. If any claim to perfection such as the Corinthians evidently make (2:6; 3:1-3, 18; 4:8) is to be sustained, there should be a synthesis of eloquence, knowledge, and practice. In 1 Cor 5-15 Paul tries to facilitate a growth in Corinthian "practice" (ἔργον).

Paul proceeds in 1 Cor 1:18-3:23 to analyze the words "speech" (λόγος), "wisdom" (σοφία), and "knowledge" (γνῶσις). In 1:18-31 Paul focuses on the word λόγος or "speech as the outward verbalization of some kind of content called 'knowledge', which is claimed to represent or reveal wisdom."[183] For Paul, λόγος is "the word of the cross" (1:18) or the kerygma (1:21), the content of which is: "Christ crucified" (1:23). This word cannot be identified with wisdom, because the hearers of the kerygma consist of the lost and the saved; for the former the kerygma is the opposite of wisdom, namely foolishness (1:18). There are thus two kinds of wisdom, namely, the wisdom of God (1:21, 24, 30) and of the world (1:20).

In 1 Cor 2:1-16 rhetoric comes to the fore. Paul claims that he presented his kerygma not "in [or: by] persuasive words of wisdom but in [or: by] a demonstration of spirit and power."[184] Two kinds of rhetoric emerge here, namely, the rhetoric of persuasion and that of demonstration. The persuasiveness of Paul's speech does not come from human reason but divine power; what brings this power to the fore is not dialectic but demonstration or direct display.[185] The kerygma proclaims "the mystery of God" (2:1)—its speech must be revelatory, not superficially persuasive. The "wisdom of God in mystery" can only be revealed; it cannot be taught and learned as a technique is taught and mastered by craftsmen like the rhetoricians of persuasion (2:7-13). This mystery is revealed through the spirit and talked about only by those who are initiates of the mystery to "spiritual people." Only these "pneumatics" are equipped to interpret spiritual things in spiritual terms. In the context of mystery religions, the rhetoric of persuasion is out of place; "another rhetoric is needed which can give expression to inspiration, epiphany, and the showing and viewing of symbols."[186] The word-picture of "Christ crucified" (1:23; cf. 2:2; Gal 3:1) makes its impact not by dialectic reasoning but by a non-lexical mode of persuasion, by the peculiar force expanded by

---

[183] Ibid., p. 34. Compare 1 Cor 12:8.
[184] 1 Cor 2:4, οὐκ ἐν πειθοῖ[ς] σοφίας [λόγοις] ἀλλ' ἐν ἀποδείξει πνεύματος καὶ δυνάμεως.
[185] Or ἀπόδειξις; Betz, "The Problem of Rhetoric and Theology according to the Apostle Paul," p. 37.
[186] Ibid. Cf. 1 Cor 2:6, 10, 15 and 13b (πνευματικοῖς πνευματικὰ συγκρίνοντς).

symbols. It is like a precept profitable for the immature and weak.[187]

Although the term γνῶσις does not occur in 1 Cor 3:1–21, Paul does here examine the concept of "knowledge." A claim to knowledge might be false boasting if not eschatologically rooted (3:18–21a; cf. 3:16, "Do you not know...."). The challenge is to achieve through a rhetoric of self-examination an equilibrium between eloquence, knowledge, and practice. Only such a synthesis can be rightly called "wisdom" and even "wisdom of God" (σοφία τοῦ θεοῦ) and support the claim of the "wise" to be mature. From the above and from the characterization of the "wise" which emerges it is clear that this context yields evidence for matters of pedagogy and spiritual aptitude.

We can gauge the significance of Paul's portrayal of the "wise" by comparing it to material found in Philo whose discussion on progress in wisdom has both formal and substantial affinities to Paul's discussion. The "wise" in Corinth may even have been influenced, perhaps through Apollos, by a type of [Stoic] wisdom speculation such as we find in Philo. Their viewpoint can be explicated in light of the contrast between the perfect person and child, and solid food versus milk, compared to Philo's use of these concepts.[188] One can also point to Philo's negative evaluation of diversity and the importance of correspondence between deeds and words for the "perfect person."[189] The dichotomy of a "mature person" and "child" was part of a common parlance in different contexts, not surprisingly,

---

[187] Mystery terminology is used irrespective of contexts to emphasize levels of maturity and to explicate different pedagogical functions of precepts and dogmas. See for example Seneca, *Ep.* 95.64.

[188] My concern is not whether the wise had been influenced by the sapiential tradition, accentuating the importance of mediating upon Torah, the wisdom of God, in order to progress towards perfection. For the contrast between the mature person and child, see Hugedé, *La Métaphore du Miroir dans les Epîtres de Saint Paul aux Corinthiens*, pp. 177–84. Epictetus equates the "uneducated" with children (*Discourse* 3.19.6) and the "weak" (*Discourse* 1.8.8). Cf. also *Encheiridion* 51.1–3.

[189] See Philo, *On the Posterity and Exile of Cain* 88; *On Noah's Work as a Planter* 44, the "earthy man" is πολύτροπος; *On the Migration of Abraham* 152–53, the "soul of the bad man is mixed"; *On Dreams* 2.10–14; *Moses* 2.289. If the wise in Corinth shared these negative views on diversity, Paul's polyphony did not appeal much to them. The πευματικός-ψυχικός distinction which contrasts "two different levels of religious-ethical ability and achievement," is not found in Philo, but is parallel to the "perfect versus child" contrast found both in Paul and Philo. So R. A. Horsley, "Pneumatikos vs. Psychikos Distinctions of Spiritual Status among the Corinthians," *HTR* 69:3–4 (1976), pp. 269–88. Dupont argued that the πευματικός-ψυχικός contrast in 1 Cor 2:13–14 and 15:44–46, developed within Hellenistic-Jewish exegesis of Gen 2:7 (*Gnosis*, pp. 151–80). See also Pearson, *The Pneumatikos-Psychikos Terminology in 1 Corinthians* (Missoula, 1973).

since the analogy of human growth naturally presents itself where maturation is presupposed. I am then not interested in the source of the terminology but the ethical and religious position it reveals, especially as it relates to the theme of maturation, perfection, and spiritual guidance.

Philo contrasts the "wise" and "perfect person" with the one making progress towards wisdom and conforms to a standard way of conceptualizing persons relative to their achievement in wisdom.[190] Mature persons are already perfect, in need of no further instruction. They have direct contact with the divine and have no need for a human guide. They are leaders like Isaac, who leads a noble company and learns from no teacher but himself. Such a leader disdains making any use of soft and milky food suited to infants and little children; instead, he only uses strong nourishment fit for grown men. Children, as minors, can only consume milk and are dependent on the mature. The wise take God for their guide and teacher, the "less perfect" the wise.[191] Because of their understanding and wisdom, some in Corinth thought they were perfect, wise, strong and nobly born; others were children, fools, weak and disgraced. The wise are "taught by the spirit," and had, like the "self-learnt" person in Philo, intuitively learnt the mysteries of God. As such they were in a rightful position to guide others having achieved the capability of εὐλογία and παρρησία.[192] Such issues are part of Paul's concern also, revolving around the question: "Who can legitimately speak with παρρησία or frankly criticize, evaluate, and admonish others?"

As we saw in my chapter five, correctional psychagogy is evident in 1 Cor 5 and 6. Paul, however, has throughout the first four chapters

---

[190] The wise are regularly contrasted with the μωρός, the μανθάνων, and the σοφιστής. Philo, *On the Sacrifices of Abel and Cain* 7, 8, 11, 43, 65, 121; *Allegorical Interpretation* 1.45, 94, 108; 3.25, 100, 131, 140, 144, 147, 159, 207; *On the Migration of Abraham* 29, 38; *On Sobriety* 9–10; *On the Cherubim* 75; *Who is the Heir* 19, 313–314; *On Dreams* 2.9–10; *On Noah's Work as a Planter* 168; *On Husbandry* 9; Epictetus, *Discourse* 1.4.4; Seneca, *Epistles* 4.2; 124.10; Stobaeus, *Anthology* 2.198. See Hugedé, *La Métaphore du Miroir dans les Epîtres de saint Paul aux Corinthiens*, pp. 179–81. See also A. Mendelson, *Secular Education in Philo of Alexandria* (Cincinnati, 1982), pp. 47–58.

[191] Philo, *Who is the Heir* 19; *On Dreams* 2.10. See Clement, *Ped.* 94.1 (GCS 145, 26–30 Stählin-Treu); 1 Pet 2:2; and Heb 6:1 (ἐπὶ τὴν τελειότητα φερώμεθα).

[192] 1 Cor 4:8, 10. The "self-learnt" person is endowed with a simple nature and with a self which is both a teacher and a learner. See Philo, *On Abraham* 16, 26, 52; *On the Preliminary Studies* 36; *Every Good Man is Free* 95–96, 99, 126; *On the Migration of Abraham* 70–85, 168–170; *Who is the Heir* 14–21; *On Dreams* 1.102–114; *On the Posterity and Exile of Cain* 132. The τέλειος is healthy, but the νήπιος is weak or ill (ἀσθηνής; *On Husbandry* 8–9 and 165; *Allegorical Interpretation* 3.159).

of the letter concerned himself with issues of judgment and evaluation.[193] 1 Cor 2:15 is particularly succinct:

> A man gifted with the spirit can judge the worth of everything, but is not himself subject to judgment by his fellow-men (NEB)—ὁ δὲ πνευματικὸς ἀνακρίνει [τὰ] πάντα, αὐτὸς δὲ ὑπ' οὐδενὸς ἀνακρίνεται.

This text postulates distinctions between people and reveals the responsibility of the mature to evaluate the immature. Here, as in Gal 6:1–3, the mature are called (οἱ) πνευματικοί. Most commentators view 2:15 as integral, not to Paul's own thinking, but that of his critics. Paul, in my view, both agrees and disagrees with the basic presupposition of distinction among people. He does not question the contrast between the τέλειοι and the νήπιοι as such; it is even analogous to the contrast between the "weak" and the "wise" and "strong." In the context of 1 Cor 2:15, Paul distinguishes between persons as to their spiritual aptitude with the terminology of ψυχικός/σάρκινος versus πνευματικός, and νήπιοι and the implied adult (ἀνήρ). The contrast between πνευματικός and ψυχικός occurs in 2:14–16 and that of πνευματικός and νήπιος ἐν Χριστῷ in 3:1–4. It is likely that οἱ τέλειοι of 2:6 are identical to οἱ πνευματικοί in 3:1 and that we have an additional contrast between τέλειοι-νήπιοι in this context.

Issues of maturity and its implication for spiritual guidance are present in 1 Cor 2:13–15. The phrase ἃ καὶ λαλοῦμεν ... ἐν διδακτοῖς πνεύματος indicates that some in Corinth had claimed to be "taught by the spirit." This phrase has an equivalent function to the term θεοδίδακτοι used by Paul in 1 Thess 4:9, and the term αὐτοδίδακτοι, not used by Paul but common in discussions on moral and spiritual growth.[194] A person who claims to be taught by the spirit rejects the need for guidance by another. Psychagogues are redundant when someone claims to be taught by God, taught by the spirit, or to be self-taught. The "self-taught" are themselves in a position of authority, without the need of admonition and assistance. A self-taught person has intuitively learnt things not of this world and commonly not perceived by others; he, without assistance, can gauge the mysteries of God.[195]

---

[193] See D. W. Kuck, *Judgment and Community Conflict* (NovTSup 66; Leiden, 1992).

[194] A. J. Malherbe suggests (*Paul and the Popular Philosophers*, p. 63) that θεοδίδακτοι is a Pauline coinage. See C. R. Roetzel, "Theodidaktoi and Handwork in Philo and 1 Thessalonians," *L'Apôtre Paul* (ed. A. Vanhoye; Louvain, 1986), pp. 324–31.

[195] Some in Corinth had claimed to be in no need of assistance from Paul. See

The quotation from Isaiah 40:13 in 1 Cor 2:16, "For who has known the mind of the Lord so as to instruct him?" and Paul's statement in the same verse—"We, however, possess the mind of Christ"— implies that the question here concerns both perception of "spiritual things" and the function of the mature as "judges" and "advisors" of the immature. Most likely, the "wise" claimed to be competent guides since they had gauged the mysteries of God. Later in the letter Paul counters that he also has "the spirit of God," able to give valued advice, and claims to be excluded from consideration in any human court, at least that of those Corinthians who want to "examine" him. By this over-confident statement Paul both complicates the situation and implies that he is one of the "spiritual ones," to be judged solely by God. Paul, similarly to Rom 14:13a, advises his readers not to pass premature judgment.[196]

1 Cor 2:15 says that the "spiritual one," or a man gifted with the spirit, can judge or "discern all things," but, and this latter phrase is more important for my purposes, "is not himself subject to judgment by any of his fellow-humans." Those who have intuitively learnt the mysteries of God allow of no (human) master. A mature person can "judge the worth of everything," including evaluations of his own standing and that of the less mature. Not so with the immature. Although the parallel from Seneca—"Virtue passes judgment on everything, but nothing passes judgment on virtue"—deals with the wisdom and virtue of the wise, his unwavering spirit and perfect condition of mind, and difference from the progressing person, it says the same thing, because when the wise have matured, they are

---

1 Cor 2:15–16; 2:1, 7, 13; 4:1, 3–5, 8 ("without us you have become kings"); 13:2; 14:2; and 15:51. See Clement's discussion of 1 Thess 4:9 and his exposition of Paul's use of νήπιοι and Gnostic deductions of variations in spiritual maturity (*Ped.* 25.1–52.3; GCS 104, 25–121, 21 Stählin-Treu; cf. 94.1; GCS 145, 30–32). Maximus of Tyre's discussion of the self-taught person clearly shows the related issues of supervision and the connection of being self-taught with knowledge of the gods (*Discourse* 10.5; 118, 6–119, 10 Hobein). Isocrates notes (*To Nicocles* 4) that from the time tyrants are placed in authority, they live without admonition. See *Antidosis* 208, "But when people succeed in making progress through their own diligence alone, how can they fail to improve in a much greater degree ... if they put themselves under a master who is mature...." Cf. Philo, *Who is the Heir* 10; Seneca, *Epistle* 95.36; 71.19–20.

[196] Compare 1 Cor 4:3–5 with Plutarch, *How to Tell a Flatterer from a Friend* 72AB. This text uses, as does 1 Cor 2:15 and 9:3, the verb ἀνακρίνω. Paul's defensive use of ἀνακρίνω in 4:3–4 and 9:3 shows that the "wise" themselves wished to "evaluate" Paul. Compare Paul's remark in 2:16b, "But we have the mind of Christ" with his claim in 1 Cor 7:40, "And I think that I have the spirit of God."

in a position to evaluate others.¹⁹⁷ Seneca thus draws implications from his discussion of the wise with regard to hortatory practices as they relate to the progressing persons who still need to be exhorted by the wise. But the wise who do not have the same difficulty in acting out their beliefs are in no need of exhortation or guidance from others.¹⁹⁸

### 6.4.2 *Paul's stringent guidance of the recalcitrant students*

Earlier I remarked briefly on the hortatory features of the early chapters of 1 Corinthians noting the presence of the mixed method of praise and blame. Here Paul slides into more forceful guidance by his use of dissuasive hortatory means and sets the stage for a more overt blame by his use of the paternal role in which Paul as a father disciplines his children. That transition occurs in a pericope which contains Paul's reflections on the nature of his treatment of the arrogant ones. The second παρακαλῶ-exhortation occurs here (1 Cor 4:16–21). Since Paul focuses on the puffed-up wise, he does not refer to the "brethren" here as he does in 1:10. Consequently, the asymmetry between a father and a disobedient child figures prominently. Paul casts his reflections of his correction of the "puffed up" against his upcoming visit to Corinth:

> But some of you, thinking that I am not coming to you, have become arrogant. But I will come to you soon, if the Lord wills, and I will find out not the talk of these arrogant people but their power. For the kingdom of God depends not on talk but on power. What would you prefer? Am I to come to you with a stick, or with love in a spirit of gentleness?¹⁹⁹

Paul's point is best recast by accentuating the rod imagery in which Paul contemplates shaming the Corinthians when he visits Corinth or to use even harsher methods than he has previously employed. Paul threatens the arrogant with the use of harsh discipline. The rod was commonly used to underline severe discipline through harsh blame and to highlight one dimension of the mixed method of exhortation.

We should be willing to allow a third century interpreter of Paul

---

¹⁹⁷ Seneca, *Epistle* 71.19–20, "Haec de omnibus rebus iudicat, de hac nulla." Cf. also 71.26. Dupont argues that 1 Cor 2:15 cannot have an equivalent function to Seneca's remark (*Gnosis*, pp. 321–27).
¹⁹⁸ Seneca, *Epistle* 94.48–52; 71.29–30. See pp. 82–84, above.
¹⁹⁹ 1 Cor 4:18–21, NRSV. Paul also reflects on his upcoming visit in 1 Cor 11:34 and 16:5–7.

who is thoroughly acquainted with the hortatory tradition to be our guide here. Clement of Alexandria connects Paul's "stringent language" with the harsh dimension of παρρησία and although he takes Galatians 4:16 and 20 as his example, he discusses the use of the rod in *Proverbs* and the etymology of ἔλεγχος and ἐπίπληξις in the same context.[200] Paul's claim that he is writing not to shame but to admonish the Corinthians (1 Cor 4:14), shows his knowledge of the hortatory tradition and awareness of the different types of hortatory blame. Admonition is a form of blame, albeit softer than many other forms of blame; it didactically instills sense in those admonished. Although νουθεσία has been described as the mildest form of blame, its affinities with more stringent forms of blame, such as ἐπίπληξις, should not be lost sight of.[201]

Paul's remarks that he says something to shame the Corinthians shows that he has decided not to wait until his visit to blame the Corinthians outright and thus attempt to effect a change in their behavior through shame. This reveals Paul's conscientious use of harsh blame closer to ἐπιτίμησις or ἐπίπληξις or even διάσυρσις.[202] It was a common cliché in antiquity that fear drives slaves and the "multitude" to repentance but shame free men. Shame was important in both rebuke (ἐπιτίμησις) and reproach (ὀνειδισμός) and was associated with harsher forms of blame.[203] This indicates that 1 Corinthians has affinities also with the letter of rebuke[204] and shows that Paul

---

[200] *Ped.* 81.3–83.2 (GCS 137, 27–139, 2 Stählin-Treu).
[201] See Clement, *Ped.* 94.2 (GCS 146, 5–7 Stählin-Treu), "Rebuking (τὸ ἐπιπλήσσειν) is also called admonishing; and the etymology of admonishing is putting understanding into one; so that rebuking is bringing one to one's senses." See also *Ped.* 76.1 (GCS 134, 13–14 Stählin-Treu). See also Aristotle, *Nicomachean Ethics* 1102b33–1103a2. For the claim that admonition is the mildest form of blame, see Stowers, *Letter Writing in Greco-Roman Antiquity*, p. 125.
[202] See 1 Cor 6:5 and 15:34, πρὸς ἐντροπὴν ὑμῖν λέγω/λαλῶ. Clement defines διάσυρσις or "ridicule" as "disparaging blame." Clement's comment is *a propos*, particularly since πορνεία is one of the issues Paul criticises: "With consummate art, after applying to the virgin the opprobrious name of whoredom (πορνεία), he thereupon calls her back to an honorable life by filling her with shame" (ἐντρέπων μετακαλεῖται; *Ped.* 81.1, GCS 137, 13–19 Stählin-Treu). Clement defines ἐπιτίμησις or "censure" as "blame because of what is shameful (ψόγος ἐπ' αἰσχροῖς), reconciling (the person) to what is noble" (*Ped.* 77.1, GCS 134, 33–34 Stählin-Treu), and ἐπίπληξις or "rebuke" as "reproachful censure, or chiding blame" (*Ped.* 78.1, GCS 135, 21 Stählin-Treu, ἐπιτίμησις ἐπιπληκτικὴ ἢ ψόγος πληκτικός).
[203] Aristotle, *Nicomachean Ethics* 1179b11–15, "For the many (οἱ πολλοί) naturally obey fear, not shame." Cf. also 1180a1–5 and Stowers, *Letter Writing in Greco-Roman Antiquity*, p. 128.
[204] "The censorious type is that written with rebukes on account of errors that

uses admonitory education, instead of cross-examination, to criticize the conceited Corinthians.²⁰⁵

Although Paul later disapproves of the Corinthians' use of ἐπιτιμία,²⁰⁶ he can and does use a psychagogy of a harsher sort, albeit rarely describing it as such or using hortatory terms that are customarily associated with harsh exhortation.²⁰⁷ Paul also claims that the weak and the strong at Rome are able to admonish each other and encourages the Thessalonians to do the same.²⁰⁸ And, in 1 Cor 4:14 Paul admonishes the Corinthians and uses a scriptural *exemplum* in 10:11 as an admonition in his attempt to put some sense into the "wise" in Corinth. The sarcastic reference to the Corinthians as φρόνιμοί in 10:15 would not be lost on those who were acquainted with the etymology of νουθεσία. Paul uses a narrative of the wilderness generation in order to remind the Corinthians that their self-deception can, as it did for the Hebrew nation, cause their ruin. Advice is given in light of a narrative which functions as an admonition attempting to effect a change in the attitude of the "wise."²⁰⁹

Although Paul explicitly denies that he intended to shame the Corinthians, he has set the stage in the early chapters of the letter

---

have already been committed." Ps.-Demetrius, *Epistolary Types* 6 (34, 20–30 Malherbe); Cf. Ps.-Libanius, *Epistolary Styles* 34 and 81 (70, 24 and 80, 1–3 Malherbe); Plutarch, *How to Tell a Flatterer from a Friend* 73C–74C. The purpose of sharp censure is to make one "sound." Cf. Titus 1:13 and 9.

²⁰⁵ Contrast Epictetus, *Discourse* 3.14.9, "Now conceit is removed by cross-examination (τὴν μὲν οὖν οἴησιν ἔλεγχος ἐξαιρεῖ) and this is what Socrates starts with...." Cf. Plato, *Sophist* 229E–231B. On the mixed method see Philodemus, *On Frank Criticism* frs. 58, 71; App. Tab. IV I; fr. 87 Herc.; Ps.-Plutarch, *On the Education of Children* 13D; *How to Tell a Flatterer from a Friend* 72D; Dio Chrysostom, *Discourse* 32.25–28; Maximus of Tyre, *Discourse* 1.3b, 3e–f, 8c–e (4, 22–5, 8; 5, 17–6, 9; 14, 10–15,3 Hobein); Seneca, *On Anger* 2.21.1–3, *Herm. Sim.* 9.2.5 and 7. Admonition reflects previous evaluation and judgment (cf. Tit 3:10–11). See pp. 42–43, 86, 127 and 155, above.

²⁰⁶ For the possible meaning of ἐπιτιμία in 2 Cor 2:6, see V. P. Furnish, *2 Corinthians*, p. 155.

²⁰⁷ Paul never uses ἐπιτίμησις, ἐπιτιμάω (2 Tim 4:2), κατανεμέσησις, ἐπίπληξις, ἐπιπλήσσω (1 Tim 5:1), μέμψις, μεμψιμοιρία, διάσυρσις, and ὀνειδίζω. He uses λοιδορέω once in a peristasis catalogue (1 Cor 4:12) and λοίδορος twice, in vice lists (1 Cor 5:11; 6:10. Λοιδορία occurs in 1 Pet 3:9; 1 Tim 5:14). Ὀνειδισμός occurs once in a quotation of LXX Ps 68:10 in Rom 15:3 (cf. Heb 10:33), and ἐλέγχω once, of the result of prophetic speech in 1 Cor 14:24. See pp. 202–203, above.

²⁰⁸ Rom 15:14; 1 Thess 5:12, 14; 2 Thess 3:15.

²⁰⁹ See 1 Cor 10:1–15; v. 12, "Therefore let the man who thinks he stands beware lest he fall;" v. 11, ἐγράφη δὲ πρὸς νουθεσίαν ἡμῶν. Νουθεσία = hapax legomenon; cf. Eph 6:4; Tit 3:10. See Clement, *Ped.* 76.1 (GCS 134, 17 Stählin-Treu, ἡ γραφὴ νουθετεῖ); Aristotle, *Rhetoric* 1416b–1417a.

for a more overt shame. In the ironic list of hardships in 4:10, Paul identifies himself with the "fools," while the Corinthians are the sensible ones (φρόνιμοι); "we are weak; but you are strong." The wise Corinthians are the honored, strong and wise of this world; as such, they have the right and duty to correct and shame others. To suggest otherwise would indeed question their mature status. This is precisely what Paul does; the Corinthians are faulty in their judgment with regard to the weak as well as their own maturity. Every man, Paul says, will receive his praise from God (4:5). In 1:27–29 Paul also uses the contrast between the wise and strong and the folly of the world and the weakness of the world, and claims that God has chosen the latter in order to shame the former. God, in his demolition of the existing order by choosing "mere nothings," has shamed the wise and strong in Corinth. Later in the letter, Paul employs the same verb, namely καταισχύνω, in order to characterize the "humiliation" of those who "have nothing" by those well off in Corinth.[210] Such a behavior Paul says he cannot commend.

Besides the gentle approach Paul advocates for the weak and his accommodation to the different segments of the community, he also uses a more stringent approach recognizing the need for a friend to be emphatic in his use of frank speech when checking the pride and inconsiderate harshness of the "wise."[211] Admonition is a form of blame and did, in the mind of some, have affinities with harsher forms of blame.[212] Paul's use of admonition thus easily slides into harsher forms of blame, the purpose of which is to shame into repentance. What Paul then only contemplates doing when he comes to the Corinthians (4:21), he does so indirectly earlier and explicitly later in the letter. A brief overview of Paul's blame in 1 Cor 5–15 will suffice here.

Paul is cognizant of the effect of his language; what he says is intended to shame his readers. This shows his conscious use of harshness. The purpose of Paul's blame—as is reasonably clear from his

---

[210] 1 Cor 1:27 and 11:22, καταισχύνετε τοὺς μὴ ἔχοντας. See also 1 Cor 11:4 and 5.

[211] As Plutarch notes, it is particularly in good fortune that men have the most need of friends to speak frankly and reduce their excess of pride (*How to Tell a Flatterer from a Friend* 68F).

[212] Col. 1:28; 3:16. Cf. Plutarch, *Sertor.* 19.11 πληγαῖς v. 1 *Clem.* 56.2–4 legitimizes the practice of mutual admonition (ἡ νουθέτησις, ἣν ποιούμεθα εἰς ἀλλήλους. . . .) with scriptural support, quoting for example Prov 3:12 and Ps 118:18 and 141:5, all of which give examples of the "harsh discipline" of the Lord described by such terms as παιδεύω, ἐλέγχω, and, μαστιγόω.

quotation of the proverb φθείρουσιν ἤθη χρήσθ' ὁμιλίαι κακαί—is to change the Corinthians' behavior in light of God's workings.²¹³ Moral carelessness among those who deny the resurrection is inappropriate; others should not cultivate their bad company since it ruins good moral character. Again, as in 1 Cor 5, the goal of good moral conduct is an intramural affair, a goal Paul attempts to achieve through his use of blame and implementation of a practice of shunning. The purpose of shaming in 1 Cor 6:5 is clear, namely, to attempt to change the practice among the Corinthians who were taking their litigations outside the community, instead of doing so intramurally: "I say this to your shame. Is there not a single wise man among you, then, who is able to judge between his brothers?" Paul attempts to change through shame a Corinthian practice and the underlying beliefs of that practice. Similarly, in light of the practice of the incestuous man, Paul condemns the act *in absentia* and asks the Corinthians to execute an appropriate judgment for the erring one.²¹⁴

These explicit forms of blame are coupled with periodic compliments. In 1 Cor 11 we find a clear example of a sequence from praise to blame. Paul first commends the Corinthians for holding onto the traditions as he delivered them and for remembering him in everything.²¹⁵ Paul proceeds to discuss issues relating to the communal gatherings of the Corinthians. With regard to the praying and prophesying by unveiled women Paul appeals to the understanding of his addressees, to what nature teaches, and uses a common topic as in chapter seven, referring to that which is fitting (11:13). With regard to the question of head covering during service, the Corinthians can then judge for themselves on the basis of what nature teaches them and on the basis of their own sense of what is fitting. Paul proceeds to suggest that some in Corinth disagree and are conten-

---

[213] Cf. 15:34, "For some have no knowledge of God; I say this to your shame." The proverb quoted in 15:33 is often assumed to be from Menander's lost comedy *Thais*, but R. Renehan has shown that the words "originally occurred in some tragedy, by Euripides more likely than not" ("Classical Greek Quotations in the New Testament," in *The Heritage of the Early Church*, pp. 29–34).

[214] Heinrici appropriately translates ἐντροπή both as *Beschämung* and *Sinneswendung*. See *Der erste Brief an die Korinther*, pp. 193–94; cf. 180–86. See also Weiss, *Der erste Korintherbrief*, pp. 140–45, 149–50. 1 Cor 15:33–34 should then be compared to 1 Cor 5:9–13. See pp. 260–64, above.

[215] 1 Cor 11:2. Paul's subsequent discussion implies that training in "Christian" conduct was a part of the teaching of the "traditions." Compare 1 Cor 11:23; 15:1; 2 Cor 2:15; 3:6 Rom 6:14; and Gal 1:14. Cf. Epictetus, *Discourse* 2.23.40, referred to by Weiss, *Der erste Korintherbrief*, p. 268.

tious about it and counters with an injunction to the contrary, arguing that neither "we" nor any of the "congregations of God" have such a "habit" (11:16).

Paul apparently refers here to the habit of being contentious.[216] By a reference to some who are "contentious" (φιλόνεικοι), Paul continues his character portrayal of the "wise" and signals a change in his viewpoint to a more explicit censure: "In giving you these injunctions I must mention a practice which I cannot commend."[217] Paul withholds praise because their meetings tend to do more harm than good. When the Corinthians come together, they fall into sharply divided groups. Because of this it is impossible for them to eat the Lord's Supper, because each is in such a hurry to eat his own, that one goes hungry while another has too much to drink. Such behavior displays a contemptuous attitude towards the "church of God"; through such behavior the better off in the community shame its poorer members.[218] "What shall I say"—Paul self-reflectively remarks— "can I commend you? On this point, certainly not!"

Here Paul joins God in his effort to shame the wise of this world.[219] He begins by commending the Corinthians for maintaining the tradition he handed on to them, appeals to their understanding, and refers to what is fitting and what nature itself teaches them. Paul then goes on to blame the Corinthians and will even question later in the letter that they are holding fast to the teaching as he had delivered it, contrary to what he commends them for in this chapter (15:2; 11:2). This progression from praise to blame shows that Paul was cognizant not only of the common requirement of *captatio benevolentiae* but also of the importance of mollifying one's friends before applying to them frank criticism like a tempering bath! The

---

[216] And not to the habit of women praying with their heads uncovered. See H. A. W. Meyer, *Der Paulus erster Brief an die Korinther*, p. 243; Heinrici, *Der erste Brief an die Korinther*, pp. 334–35; Weiss, *Der erste Korintherbrief*, p. 277. See now T. Engberg-Pedersen, "1 Corinthians 11:16 and the Character of Pauline Exhortation," *JBL* 110.1 (1991), 679–89. Paul had, as we have seen, rejected the attempt of the "wise" to influence the "habits" of the weak in 1 Cor 8 but one should, apparently, not shy away from changing the habit of being contentious!

[217] 1 Cor 11:17, τοῦτο δὲ παραγγέλλων οὐκ ἐπαινῶ.... For text critical matters see Heinrici, *Der erste Brief an die Korinther*, pp. 335–36; 338; Weiss, *Der erste Korintherbrief*, p. 278.

[218] 1 Cor 11:22b ἢ τῆς ἐκκλησίας τοῦ θεοῦ καταφρονεῖτε, καὶ καταισχύνετε τοὺς μὴ ἔχοντας; this clashes with the advice given in 1 Cor 10:33. Compare Rom 12:16.

[219] 1 Cor 11:22c, τί εἴπω ὑμῖν; ἐπαινέσω ὑμᾶς; ἐν τούτῳ οὐκ ἐπαινῶ. Cf. 1 Cor 1:27 and Barrett, *A Commentary on the First Epistle to the Corinthians*, p. 264.

exasperated remark, "how dumb can you get," reveals both Paul's piqued attitude because of the tense situation and his view of the "wise" in Corinth.[220]

Paul's use of the common pedagogical method of praise and blame and the typology that emerges of the "wise" in Corinth reveals Paul's view of his critics; they are still immature, in need of blame and correction. Paul's use of blame lodges him squarely within the tradition that valued the use of therapeutic harshness and reveals both Paul's view of the "wise" as immature and as recalcitrant pupils who need to be forcefully led in order to secure their repentance. My focus on the typology that emerges from Paul's description of his critics does not allow us to identify them as a distinct social group; it only allows us to gauge Paul's view of their spiritual status.[221]

### 6.4.3 *Paul's debate with the recalcitrant Corinthians*

Throughout 2 Corinthians Paul answers charges of inconsistency and concealment as well as that of harshness. The source of these charges is, I submit, Paul's polyphonic psychagogy in 1 Corinthians evident in four areas: firstly, an indirect and oblique approach contrasted with more direct commands and advice; secondly, and related to the oblique approach, Paul's guidance through character portrayal, in which he lends the concerns of the "weak" and the "wise" a voice; thirdly, Paul's attentiveness and adaptation to the various constituents of the Corinthian community, his use of "common topics," and his shift of focus from his own opinions to those of the early Christian tradition which he represents; and, finally, Paul's use of the mixed method of praise and blame or the mixture of affable and stringent guidance.

Paul's use of the above techniques vividly demonstrates his use of common pedagogical motifs and pertinent means of adaptation. These methods give us the clearest indication of Paul's view of the spiritual status of Corinthians since they are all recognized by moralists as

---

[220] See 11:2; 4:17; and 15:36, ἄφρων; 2 Cor 11:19–20. Compare Philodemus' use of the term ἄφρων in *On Frank Criticism* cols. 10a6–10; 21b5–7: Those who think they are "wise" and "perfect" are "foolish" (See pp. 132 and 151–52, above).

[221] For some of the complexities of social group identification, see R. L. Rohrbaugh, "'Social Location of Thought' as a Heuristic Construct in New Testament Study," *JSNT* 30 (1987), pp. 103–19; idem, "Methodological considerations in the Debate over the Social Class Status of Early Christians," *JAAR* 52.3 (1984), 519–46. For the possible social implications of the use of the medical analogy in Philodemus, see pp. 152–56, above.

pertinent pedagogical means of psychagogic adaptation in the persuasion of the immature and progressing persons. The presence of these pedagogical traditions indicate that Paul views the "wise" in Corinth and his so-called "opponents" as "students" in need of guidance. In particular, Paul's use of harsh blame and threats reveals that he views the "wise" as "recalcitrant students", difficult to cure and in need of a dose of stringent medicine.[222]

### 6.4.3.1 *Paul's self-depiction as an open, clear, and consistent guide*

That Paul was aware of the tradition associating frank speech with frank criticism and forthrightness as opposed to deceit and concealment is clear from the first chapters of 2 Corinthians. Here, apparently, some in Corinth had charged Paul both with vacillating in conduct and not being forthright in discourse. In his response to the charge of having concealed his true thoughts, Paul gives a distinctly "Christian" twist to the notion of παρρησία. On the one hand, παρρησία continues to be associated with openness and truthfulness in human relationship in both conduct and discourse, as it does in Philodemus' *On Frank Criticism*.[223] On the other hand, it introduces the notion of boldness towards God which we find in Philo and which became important in subsequent Christian usage.[224] Both Paul's response and the charge accentuate the former aspects of παρρησία.

Paul defends himself against charges of fickleness and corruption in connection with his collection activities. Questions of legitimacy become pronounced. Paul rejects the charge that he had been huckstering the word of God and claims that he had acted out of pure motives.[225] He appeals to his own conscience and claims to have

---

[222] Clement, *Ped.* 66.2-3 (GCS 128, 31-129, 2 Stählin-Treu). Sextus Empiricus claims to use a harsh method in his attempt to cure the self-conceit and rashness of the dogmatists in light of their depraved condition. See *Outlines of Pyrrhonism* 3.281. See pp. 72-77, above.

[223] 2 Cor 7:4; Philodemus, *On Frank Criticism* frs. 41.10; 61.9, 11; 65.12; cols. 15 b1; 17 a12. W. C. van Unnik was tempted to sever the ties of παρρησία to friendship: "The Christian's Freedom of Speech in the New Testament," *Sparsa Collecta* II (Leiden, 1983), p. 280.

[224] W. C. van Unnik, "The Semitic Background of Parrêsia in the New Testament," *Sparsa Collecta* II, pp. 290-306; idem, "'With Unveiled Face', An Exegesis of 2 Corinthians iii.12-18," *Sparsa Collecta* I, pp. 194-210; H. Jaeger, "Parrhesia et fiducia, Étude spirituelle des mots," *Studia Patristica* I, 1 (1957), pp. 221-39; G. J. M. Bartelink, "Quelques observations sur parrêsia dans la littérature paléo-cretienne," *Graecitas et Latinitas Christianorum Premaeva* (1970), pp. 5-57. For παρρησία as boldness towards God in 2 Cor 3:12-18, compare Heb 4:16; 10:19; 1 *Clem.* 34.1-8; 35.2; 2 *Clem.* 15.3 (ἵνα μετὰ παρρησίας αἰτῶμεν τὸν θεόν....); and Philo, *Who is the Heir* 5-7.

[225] 2 Cor 1:8, 12-14, 17-18; 2:4, 17; 4:2; 6:3, 11-13; 7:2-4, 8, 15; 10:1, 10;

acted in the world with "candor and godly sincerity"—and "all the more with you."[226] Paul answers the charge of fickleness in 2 Cor 1:17–18:

> Do you think then that, when I made this decision, I was acting with fickleness? The plans I make, do I make them according to the flesh, so as to say at the same time Yes, yes, and No, no? God is to be trusted, and he will bear witness that our word to you is not Yes and No.[227]

Paul has been charged with behaving opportunistically.[228] Paul's answer not only reminds us of the words of Gnatho quoted earlier but, by referring to λόγος, alerts us to issues of concern to the Corinthians.[229] When answering the charge of fickleness, Paul refers to his word as he grounds his own trustworthiness in God's trustworthiness. It is now widely recognized that variance in Paul's conduct is one of the basic inconsistencies spotlighted in charges against Paul.[230] But it is incomplete solely to accentuate Paul's conduct. By doing so we sidestep possible inconsistencies in Paul's speech and the common requirement of conformity of speech to life and sever the close connection of σχῆμα and λόγος. Paul's response to the charge of fickleness occurs just after he has referred to the charge that he has not acted out of candor and sincerity. As an example of his candid approach Paul draws attention to his manner of writing. Apparently the Corinthians thought that Paul's letters were ambiguous:

---

12:14–18; 13:8. See E. Käsemann, "Die Legitimität des Apostels. Eine Untersuchung zu II Korinther 10–13," *ZNW* 41 (1942), pp. 33–71; Furnish, *2 Corinthians*, pp. 52–3. Note ἀ/δόκιμος (1 Cor 3:13; 9:27; 11:19, 28; 16:3; 2 Cor 2:9; 8:2, 8, 22; 9:13; 10:18; 13:3, 5–7) and ἱκανότης (3:5).

[226] 2 Cor 1:12, ὅτι ἐν ἁπλότητι καὶ εἰλικρινείᾳ τοῦ θεοῦ ... περισσοτέρως δὲ πρὸς ὑμᾶς. Later Paul charges his counter-psychagogues with being "crooked in all their practices, masquerading as apostles of Christ" (11:13–15; μετασχηματίζω highlights change and adaptation, or vacillation).

[227] Transl. by Barrett, *A Commentary on the Second Epistle to the Corinthians*, pp. 75–76.

[228] Or in a "worldly manner" (κατὰ σάρκα), i.e., "according to the flesh." This phrase is one of the catch-phrases used by the Corinthians in their critique of Paul which Paul in turn also uses in his critique of the Corinthians. See 2 Cor 1:12; 5:16; 10:2–3; 1 Cor 1:26. Significantly, first person singular predominates in 2 Cor 1:15–2:13. cf. Furnish, *2 Corinthians*, p. 134.

[229] Terence, *Eunuch* 251–53. See p. 24, above. As ἁπλοῦς can refer to words, thoughts, or acts, so can ἁπλότης. BAGD s.v. 1 *Clem.* 60.2 v. l. ἐν ἁ. λέγειν *speak simply, plainly*. Note Philo, *Who is the Heir* 6.

[230] P. Marshall, *Enmity in Corinth*, pp. 175–77, 251–57; Fitzgerald, *Cracks in an Earthen Vessel*, pp. 148–51, 157–58; and Furnish, *2 Corinthians*, pp. 52–53.

> For we write you nothing other than what you can read and also understand; and I hope that you will understand completely, as you have understood us partially....[231]

The charge that Paul had concealed his thought appears also in the complaint that his beliefs were "veiled," to which he replies in 2 Cor 3:12-4:6.[232] The above texts, together with 2 Cor 10:1 and 9-11, show that Paul has been charged with the inappropriate use of language. This would not be the first time Paul has to clarify his writings; in 1 Cor 5:9-11 he had to spell out what he really meant in his previous letter to the Corinthians.[233] The above texts indicate that 1 Corinthians is important in our attempt to evaluate some possible reasons for those charges, since it apparently formed one basis on which the critics charged Paul. These issues are then suggestive for our understanding of Paul's purpose, argument and manner of writing in 1 Corinthians.

Paul's mixing of praise and blame in 1 Corinthians as well as veiled arguments and covert allusions and ironical tone exacerbated the misunderstanding between Paul and the Corinthians. In Paul's polyphonic approach he appeared as a leader like Joseph, drawn in different directions, showing that his speech, mind, and action were not in harmony, and as such was no legitimate wielder of παρρησία.[234] Such accusations conform to standard accusations against a Socratic type of philosopher who, instead of being direct and open in his approach, is indirect and oblique. Paul is like a "simple" friend, but has, like the Epicurean psychagogues, used a "varied and good method" of exhortation. Paul's audience has understood him as a Socratic type of philosopher and charged him with concealment.[235]

---

[231] 2 Cor 1:13-14. See H. Windisch, *Der zweite Korintherbrief* (MeyerK 6; 9th ed.; Göttingen, 1970), pp. 53-59.

[232] Suggested by A. Fridrichsen, *The Apostle and his Message* (Uppsala, 1947), p. 23. Note the frequent use of φανερόω (= *reveal, make known*) in 2 Corinthians (2:14; 4:10-11; 5:10-11; 7:12; 11:6).

[233] Cf. 2 Cor 2:17; 6:7-8. Note 2 Pet 3:16b. Windisch, *Der zweite Korintherbrief*, pp. 56-59; Furnish, *2 Corinthians*, pp. 130-31; 468-69; 478-79.

[234] Philo, *On Dreams* 2.10-14; *Every Good Man is Free* 95-96, 99, 126.

[235] See H. D. Betz, *Der Apostel Paulus und die sokratische Tradition* (Tübingen, 1972), p. 66, on 2 Cor 11:6. In his use of covert allusions, Paul has followed Demetrius' advice that such an approach should be used in the criticism of the "powerful," both because flattery is shameful and adverse criticism dangerous. However, Paul's mixed approach and his more outright blame of the wise aligns him both with the "Socratic 'method" and the contrary method of "Gothic bluntness" (*On Style* 294 and 297). Cf. also *Ep. Anacharsis* 9 (50.0 9 Malherbe). See pp. 42-43, 86, and 155 (fn. 202), above.

The charge of indirection hit home and Paul is at pains rectifying the image. Paul's language of openness is a response to charges of concealment and ambiguity.

Paul attempts to remedy the situation by describing the Corinthians as informed participants and beneficial recipients of his previous and forthcoming travel plans (2 Cor 1:23–2:4). Paul attempts in this way to establish a certain comradeship between himself and the Corinthians and to emphasize his own reliability. He then turns the criticism of his "veiled" expressions against his readers by implying that it was their own "blindness" which hindered them from seeing the truth of his statements (4:2–4). In order to lessen the impact of this rejoinder, Paul emphasizes his and Timothy's openness: "Our mouth is open to you, Corinthians; our heart is wide." This sets the stage for an exhortation to the Corinthian "children" also to display a similar openness towards them: "In return—I speak as to children—widen your hearts also." This request, however, contains an oblique critique of his readers as immature and unforthcoming.[236] Paul emphasizes his guileless and open approach as well as urging the Corinthians in a like fashion to open themselves up to him:

> Open your hearts to us; we have wronged no one, we have corrupted no one, we have taken advantage of no one. I do not say this to condemn you, for I said before that you are in our hearts, to die together and to live together. I am perfectly frank with you. I have great pride in you; I am filled with comfort. With all our affliction, I am overjoyed.[237]

This quote has implications for Paul's past dealings with the Corinthians. It captures some of the main elements associated with the discourse of friendship which excludes concealment and demands complete openness and trust, devoid of all deceptiveness. Paul's own language and conduct had, however, caused a breach in that trust; Paul's conduct had reminded the Corinthians of the affable flatterer and the friend of many.[238] In order to remedy the situation, Paul underscores his faithfulness as he answers the charge of fickleness (1:17–18) and makes use of the proverbial expression, "living and dying together," which highlights the importance of steadfast, faith-

---

[236] 2 Cor 6:11, 13. Note the use of "as" in verse 13 compared to a similar usage in 1 Cor 3:1.

[237] 2 Cor 7:2–4. I use the "I am perfectly frank with you" of the NEB.

[238] Note Paul's confident remark in 1 Cor 7:25–26, and his overly bold statement in 1 Cor 4:3–5.

ful, and dependable friends.²³⁹ Paul underscores the ultimate test of faithfulness. He is willing not only to live but also die with the Corinthians. This language is used in light of a perceived breach of trust in an attempt to reconfirm a relationship in jeopardy. Furthermore, when Paul writes, πολλή μοι παρρησία πρὸς ὑμᾶς, he means to say more than, "I have great confidence in you." If that were the meaning the next phrase, πολλή μοι καύχησις ὑπὲρ ὑμῶν, would be a tautology. A translation like "I am perfectly frank with you" (NEB), correctly draws attention to an implicit critique.²⁴⁰ Paul had been charged with not speaking his mind unreservedly. Now, without reservation, Paul speaks his heart to the Corinthians. As we have seen, παρρησία entails the legitimate use of harshness in the correction of one's friend's faults.

### 6.4.3.2 *The problem of excessive harshness*

Paul has not only been charged with concealing his true thoughts but also with excessive harshness. Instead of correcting the wise by shaming them to repentance, Paul's harshness grieved them excessively. Whether or not Paul refers in 2 Cor 2:3–4, 9 and 7:8 to the canonical 1 Corinthians or some other non-extant letter,²⁴¹ his reflections on "grief" (λύπη) in 2 Cor 2:3–11 and 7:8–13a shows both the intended function of blame, namely, to shame into repentance, and Paul's awareness of both the salutary and destructive nature of blame. It also shows that the reason for Paul's use of harsh means of persuasion is the disobedience of some in Corinth. And, finally, Paul's reflections on harshness reveal that Paul himself has been charged with being unduly harsh. Perhaps the response of some in Corinth to Paul reflected in 2 Corinthians was partly a reaction to Paul's criticism of their harshness in 1 Cor 8. The "wise" bring against Paul the same charge that he had leveled against them, namely, that their harsh approach was not "in accordance with love." In the critics' view, the severity of Paul's letters and his overbearing attitude proved

---

[239] Lucian's *Toxaris* (7 and 37) shows that the phrase "dying and living together" was used to emphasize faithfulness among friends. See F. Olivier, "ΣΥΝΑΠΟΘΝΗΙΣΚΩ, d'un article de lexique à St. Paul, 2 Cor 7:3," *RThPh* 17 (1929), pp. 103–33. Cf. Horace, *Carmina* 3.9.24.

[240] This is argued for by David E. Fredrickson, "Paul's Bold Speech in the Argument of 2 Cor 2:14–7:16," Ph.D. Diss., Yale University, 1990. I have not had access to Fredrickson's dissertation.

[241] See P. Bachmann, *Der zweite Brief des Paulus an die Korinther* (Leipzig, 1909), pp. 95–109.

his "non-loving." The contention is part of the περὶ παρρησίας and περὶ φιλίας topoi, namely, how to correctly apply παρρησία in the company of friends. Paul has been charged with improper use of παρρησία or with being inconsiderately harsh in his criticism of his friends.[242]

As 1 Cor 8:1–11:1 and Rom 14:1–15:14 yield evidence of the mature's grieving and "destruction" of the tender ones, so does 2 Cor 2:5–11. This pericope follows 1:23–2:4, which affirms Paul's reasons for changing his travel plans and introduces the corrective and therapeutic aspects of pain. Paul reflects on his "painful" visit and "tearful" letter written to the Corinthians.[243] He proceeds to note an instance of someone who has caused him and the community pain. In light of the use of the word ἐπιτιμία for the "punishment" administered by the "majority", it probably included a form of harsh censure.[244] Although the punishment in question is not made clear, its consequences are. It wounded the reprimanded one and threatened to overwhelm him with excessive grief. The graphic idiom, "to be swallowed up by grief" (καταπίνομαι λύπῃ), captures the severity of the emotion experienced, indicating that the punishment was destructive. 2 Cor 2:7, 1 Cor 8:12, and Rom 14:15, all concern destructive grievance or excessive harshness which ruins the insecure. Such negative effect of exhortation is warned against by moralists. The "smart" incurred through exhortation should not cause unsalutary injury but should initiate the reformation of the erring one by shaming him. But instead of grieving the "offender" into repentance, the grief in this case was so severe that it threatened to "ruin" rather than "save" him.

When the mature cause destructive grievance they "do not walk in accordance with love" and have failed in their responsibilities as

---

[242] If a strong person's brother is "injured" by what the strong eats, he is not "walking in love"; 2 Cor 2:3–4, 6–8; 1 Cor 8:1; Rom 14:15a. See also Sirach 30:23; Philodemus, *On Frank Criticism* fr. 61.1; col. 15a1, 8; and Plutarch, *How to Tell a Flatterer from a Friend* 66B.

[243] Note Paul's self-reflective remarks on his "tearful letter": "But I never meant to cause you pain; I wanted you rather to know the love, the more than ordinary love, that I have for you" (2 Cor 2:3–4).

[244] I.e., ἐπιτίμησις. 2 Cor 2:6, "this punishment by the majority is enough." W. Doskocil has argued that the punishment was in the form of brotherly reprimand, administered with strictness (*Das Bann in der Urkirche, eine rechtsgeschichtliche Untersuchung* (1958), pp. 80–81). This squares well with the meaning of ἐπιτιμάω as "rebuke." Such "punishment," results in λύπη (Plutarch, *Precepts of Statecraft* 825E; Diodorus Siculus, *Library of History* 3.67.2, πληγαῖς ἐπιτιμηθείς).

friends. In light of the severity of the punishment it probably was, as was Paul's own approach, interpreted by some as "non-loving." Paul urges his readers to assure the disciplined one of their "love for him." Because of the negative impact of the harsh "medicine," a soothing one was in order; forgiveness and comfort were needed to prevent the total ruin of the "patient." The question about grief debated among moralists was: What degree of λύπη should one inflict in order to effect the desired change? How harsh should one be? Paul is obviously acquainted with these issues. The purpose of λυπέω τινά, to grieve or pain someone, is precisely λυπηθῆναι εἰς μετάνοιαν; grief should result in repentance. It should be salutary and beneficial. Paul knows that grief can become destructive, leading to ruin instead of salvation. The censure of the Corinthians caused excessive grief (περισσοτέρα λύπη), threatening to destroy the recipient. But constructive "pain" which grieves into repentance leads to positive results and is not regretful.[245]

The participatory aspects of the corrective, forgiving, and comforting process, are integral to the community life in Corinth. The nature of the wrong addressed in Paul's "painful" letter is not as intriguing as the procedure recommended by Paul *in absentia*. Paul urges the Corinthians to forgive the offender, mediating his own forgiveness through his letter and through the recipients of the letter to the offender (2 Cor 2:10 and 12). Paul says he did not write his letter on account of the one who did the wrong, nor on account of the one who suffered the wrong, but rather "in order that your zeal for us might be revealed in you." Paul refers to the communal ramifications of the offence; it made an impact on the community as a whole and has to be addressed by members themselves: "Any one whom you forgive," Paul writes, "I also forgive!" Here Paul allows the community its own authority apart from him but disagrees with the way

---

[245] 2 Cor 2:2a, 6–8; 7:8–9; Rom 14:15; Furnish, *2 Corinthians*, pp. 155–56. Note the inconsiderate approach of the Epicurean psychagoge in *On Frank Criticism* fr. 61.1; cf. fr. 20; col. 15a1, 8. See Plutarch, *How to Tell a Flatterer from a Friend* 55C; 66B; 70DE; 73DE; *Alcibiades* 23:5; *On Moral Virtue* 452C, νουθεσία should cause λύπη, and ψόγος should cause φόβος; both lead to repentance which is a kind of λύπη and initiate the reformation of the erring one. Discussing λύπη resulting from a dreadful deed, Plutarch notes that reason causes μετάνοια, "since the soul, together with its feeling of shame, is stung and chastised by itself" (*On Tranquility of Mind* 476F; cf. 961D). Cf. *On Exile* 599A–C, on "instruction in grief." Note Ps.-Libanius's remark, "For it is my aim always to heal my friends rather than cause them sorrow." *Epistolary Styles* 66 (Malherbe 76, 24–25).

in which they exercised their authority and warns of its negative consequences. They should now turn to "forgive and comfort" the offender and reaffirm their love for him. This use of the philotropeic method displays, in its repetitiveness in light of failure, its stochastic nature and shows the principle of adaptation to the particular case.

But in the view of some in Corinth, Paul had also failed because of his excessive harshness. He had been unduly harsh, causing excessive grief. Paul's blame was yet another aggravating factor in the estrangement between Paul and the Corinthians. Firstly, if admonition is offered in public, it would almost drive people insane with grief and anger at being taken to task before those with whom they feel it is necessary to stand well. That this captures well the state of mind of the wise in light of Paul's castigation goes without saying. Those who wished to use salutary frank speech must not admonish someone inconsiderately in the presence of others. Secondly, one ought to "hurt a friend only to help him," and ought not by "hurting him to kill friendship."[246] In the early parts of 2 Corinthians, Paul subtly attempts to conciliate his readers because of the grief he has caused them and justifies his own harshness in view of its end result, namely, it grieved the Corinthians into repentance.[247]

That Paul did not shy away from being harsh is clear. Paul emphasizes his right to exercise authority in a stringent manner in both 1 Cor 4:14–21 and 2 Cor 13:1–10 where the threat of "showing no leniency" is put forward in light of an upcoming visit. Also, in his sarcastic tone throughout 1 Corinthians, Paul gives the wise in Corinth the rough side of his tongue. There is furthermore both direct and indirect evidence in 2 Corinthians that Paul had been charged with being too harsh both in his writing and speaking, showing that the contention centered on issues of harsh and gentle means of persuasion. Beneficial harshness is inevitable for improvement but can easily be confused with evil-speaking and not as a sign of good-will.[248] Since Paul's psychagogic status was not uniformly recognized by the

---

[246] For these ideas, see Plutarch, *How to Tell a Flatterer from a Friend* 71BCD; 55C.

[247] 2 Cor 7:9 suggests that the painful letter grieved the Corinthians into repentance. Cf. Ps.-Libanius, *Epistolary Styles* 19 (Malherbe 68, 33–34).

[248] This is understandable since, as Isocrates notes in his defence of harshness, "those who admonish and those who denounce cannot avoid using similar words, although their purposes are as opposite as they can be" (*Concerning Paece* 72). Cf. *To Antipater* 4; *Paneg.* 130; Clement, *Ped.* 66.1 (GCS 128, 26–29 Stählin-Treu). Paul's invective against his Galatian "opponents" (Gal 1:8–9; 3:1; 5:12; contrast 1 Cor 4:12) might also have contributed to a general charge that Paul was harsh. Cf. Phil 3:2.

Corinthians, his behavior and method elicited different responses. This is true also of Paul's use of blame.

That some in Corinth had charged Paul with being too overbearing is evident. Suggestive is Paul's stress on the collaborative nature of his efforts, only after having rejected the charge that "we are domineering over your faith" (2 Cor 1:24). This reference to the "high-handed way a person may deal with others" occurs when Paul rebuts charges of fickleness and concealment.[249] The issue of harshness is evident from the reason Paul gives for having decided not to visit the Corinthians, namely, "in order to spare them."[250] We have here an oblique reference to Paul's imperious manner. That this manner was also evident in Paul's letters is suggested by Paul's response in 2:3–11, by the reference to the "painful letter" in 7:8–12, and by the depiction of Paul's letters as "weighty and strong" (βαρεῖαι καὶ ἰσχυραί; 10:10).

The definitions of Ps.-Demetrius and Ps.-Libanius indicate that the blaming letter was used by one who undertakes not "to seem harsh" and against those who had been insulting or neglectful of others. This is also the focus of Clement's definition of μέμψις.[251] Paul charges the "wise" with being neglectful of others and draws attention to their condescending or "harsh" attitude.[252] In spite of Paul's attempts to mollify the Corinthians through his commendations and his use of the complimentary address of "my beloved", it was the peremptory and harsh tone of 1 Corinthians and Paul's more outright castigation that had a more lasting impact. Contrary to the advice of moralists, Paul had allowed the letter to end on a rather sour note.[253]

---

[249] Furnish, *2 Corinthians*, p. 139. See also Windisch, *Der zweite Korintherbrief*, pp. 75–77.
[250] 1 Cor 1:23, ὅτι φειδόμενος ὑμῶν. Note 2 Cor 2:1 which indicates that Paul's visit had been "painful" and 13:2 where Paul threatens not to spare the Corinthians when he comes to them again.
[251] Ps.-Demetrius, *Epistolary Types* 3, Μεμπτικὸς δέ ἐστιν ὁ μὴ νομίζεσθαι βαρεῖν (32, 27 Malherbe). See Ps.-Libanius, *Epistolary Styles* 53 (74, 14–15 Malherbe) and Clement, *Ped.* 77.3 (GCS 135, 11 Stählin-Treu), Μέμψις δέ ἐστι ψόγος ὡς ὀλιγωρούντων ἢ ἀμελούντων.
[252] 1 Cor 4:6, 10; 6:8; 11:18–22, 32–34; 12:22–25. For the connection of contempt, arrogance, and harshness, see Ariston's *On the Relieving of Arrogance* in Philodemus' *On Vices* (*De Vit.* X, cols. 16.29–33; 19.2–5). Cf. p. 140 (fn. 155), above. Arrogance is defined by Theophrastus as "the despising of all the world but yourself" (*Character* 24.1). The αὐθαδείας is said to display "a harshness of behavior in words" (15.1). The "pain" caused by Paul's harshness might also have contributed to the Corinthians' harshness (Aristotle, *Eudemian Ethics* 1240a34, masters are harsh, when in grief).
[253] 1 Cor 4:14; 10:14; 15:58, ἀδελφοί μου ἀγαπητοί. Note again Paul's remark

Some in Corinth felt that Paul's letters were intended to scare them to death! On such a view Paul had attempted to frighten them with threats into repentance just as if they were slaves! As freeborn, the wise likely felt that such an approach was demeaning.[254] The context which refers to Paul's attempt to frighten the Corinthians by means of his letters also refers to the "upbuilding/destruction" motif, precisely the same contrast found in Paul's critique of the practice of the Corinthian wise towards the weak who felt they had a right to reform the weak.[255] This later use of the dichotomy corroborates our non-apocalyptic reading of 1 Cor 8 and of the salvation-destruction dichotomy.[256] In 2 Cor 10 Paul emphasizes his authority, not only to preach the gospel, but also to command and discipline members of the community.[257] The reason why Paul adds that his authority (ἐξουσία) is "not for your destruction" is precisely because he is countering a charge brought against him in light of the destructive and insolent nature of his own approach.[258] This is confirmed by the reference to Paul's forceful manner of writing following the above statement, which suggests that the criticism Paul had applied to the wise in 1 Cor 8 had been turned against Paul himself.

A further piece of evidence for the issues of harshness is found in 2 Cor 11–12 in Paul's use of the words ἀνέχεσθαι and καταναρκᾶν. Significantly, Paul uses these terms only here, except for the use of ἀνέχεσθαι in a hardship list in 1 Cor 4:12. The final occurrence of ἀνέχεσθαι in 2 Cor 11:19–20 is most significant:

---

towards the end of the letter, "how dumb can you get" (1 Cor 15:36; cf. 11:2–22) and pp. 309–10, above. The progression from praise to blame in 1 Cor 11 is contrary to the common advice that subsequent praise should mitigate the harshness of antecedent blame. See Philodemus, *On Frank Criticism* App. Tab. IV I; Plutarch, *How to Tell a Flatterer from a Friend* 73D; 74D.

[254] 2 Cor 10:9. Cf. 4 Macc 9:5, ἐκφοβεῖς δὲ ἡμᾶς... ἀπειλῶν. Windisch, *Der zweite Korintherbrief*, p. 305. Fear, however, was also recognized as beneficial, even for freeborns as part of a more "stringent remedy" needed in severe cases. Cf. Clement, *Paed.* 83.2 (GCS 138, 21–139, 2) and Ps.-Plutarch, *On the Education of Children* 8F–9A.

[255] 2 Cor 13:9 10; 12:19. Cf. pp. 205 206, above. See Vielhauer, *Oikodome*, p. 73; H. W. Hollander, *Joseph as an Ethical Model in the Testaments of the Twelve Patriarchs* (Leiden, 1981), pp. 121, 128.

[256] As do other 2nd cent. CE texts. See pp. 230–31 (fn. 136), above.

[257] So correctly Furnish, *2 Corinthians*, p. 477. See also ibid., 467.

[258] 2 Cor 10:8, εἰς οἰκοδομὴν καὶ οὐκ εἰς καθαίρεσιν ὑμῶν.... Besides 2 Cor 1:24 and 10:9–10, see also 12:14–16. Compare Plutarch's remark that one should avoid using anger when rendering judgment, "for that adds insolence to authority" (*On the Control of Anger* 462C). See Isocrates, *To Philip* 116: Harshness is "grievous both to those who exercise it and to those upon whom it falls, while gentleness... bears a good name." The one who is gentle is genuine and not counterfeit.

For you gladly put up with fools, being wise yourselves! You put up with it when someone enslaves you, when someone eats you up, when someone takes you in, when someone acts presumptuously, when someone slaps you in the face.[259]

Paul refers here to an actual condition; the "wise" had "put up with" the overbearing attitude of Paul's rival leaders. Paul counters such a tendency with an ironic use of the term ἀνέχεσθαι, caricaturing those rashly submitting to the overbearing intruders: "If only you would put up with me in a little bit of foolishness. Indeed," Paul continues, "do put up with me!"[260] Here, through his literary synkrisis, Paul subtly implies that it is only to him, the founder and spiritual father of the congregation, that the "wise" should submit, and not to the "fools" they tolerate now.

Reverberations of these pedagogical traditions, in particular the "Toleranzvokabel", ἀνέχεσθαι, show that Paul views his rival leaders and those who rashly submit to their leadership as recalcitrant students.[261] The common use of the term ἀνέχεσθαι suggests this. Dio Chrysostom, for example, says that he is afraid that the people of Alexandria may not be able to bear with him and listen to his wholesome discourses which aim at making them better. This is so because Dio reproves them and reveals the "weaknesses of the city." Epictetus notes that our duties are in general measured by our social relationships. Thus, in relation to one's father, one's duty is to bear with and submit to his beatings and reviling even though he is a bad

---

[259] 2 Cor 11:19–20, ἡδέως γὰρ ἀνέχεσθε τῶν ἀφρόνων φρόνιμοι ὄντες· ἀνέχεσθε γὰρ εἴ τις ὑμᾶς καταδουλοῖ... εἴ τις εἰς πρόσωπον ὑμᾶς δέρει (cf. BAGD s.v. ῥαπίζω). Transl. by Furnish, *2 Corinthians*, pp. 485, 488. See *Menandri Sententiae* 573 (ed. Jaekel); Musonius Rufus 10 (53, 4–6 Hense); and Epictetus, *Discourses* 3.22.54; 4.1.118–19. Compare 1 Cor 4:12 with 10:13.

[260] 2 Cor 11:1. Translated by Furnish, *2 Corinthians*, pp. 484–86. I take ἀνέχεσθαι in 11:1b as an imperative, not indicative; εἰ + the present indicative ἀνέχεσθε in v. 4 expresses a real condition (BDF # 372), i.e., the wise had received and put up with the intruders. Paul's ironic use of φρόνιμοι in 2 Cor 11:19, compared with his characterization of the wise in 1 Cor 10:15 (4:10), suggests that the rival leaders found a receptive audience among the critics of 1 Cor.

[261] "Toleranzvokabel" is J. Zmijewski's phrase (*Der Stil der paulinischen 'Narrenrede'* (Köln/Berlin, 1978), pp. 207, 209). Paul continues in his "fool's speech" (11:1–12:13) to answer the charge relating to his manner of writing and speaking. In 11:6 Paul, as he compares himself to the Corinthian intruders, concedes that he is an amateur in public speaking (cf. also 2 Cor 10:1, 10; 11:7; and Plutarch, *To an Uneducated Ruler* 782B). See H. D. Betz, *Der Apostel Paulus und die sokratische Tradition*, pp. 59, 66. For 2 Cor 11 as a literary synkrisis, see C. Forbes, "Comparison, self-praise and irony: Paul's boasting and the conventions of Hellenistic rhetoric," *NTS* 32.1 (1986), pp. 1–30.

father! And, finally, Philodemus' extensive use of the term ἀνέχεσθαι in *On Frank Criticism* reveals its importance in the communal context of mutual psychagogy.[262] Here concerns were raised that not everyone could equally put up with frank criticism. Hence the need for considerate attention to the effect one's discourse has on another. Implicit in the use of the term ἀνέχεσθαι is both authority, or an asymmetrical relationship in corrective discipline, and obedience, or the expected submission to the frank criticism of another.

Paul's use of the term καταναρκᾶν in 2 Cor 11:9; 12:13 and 14, gives an additional nuance to his argumentation. The terms ἀνέχεσθαι and καταναρκᾶν are sometimes used together in a moral context, as for example in Philodemus' *On Frank Criticism* col. 12b6–11.[263] Thus, although Paul uses the term καταναρκᾶν to emphasize that he has not been a financial burden one should not, in light of Paul's expressed concern in these chapters with excessive harshness, exclude other possible connotations. Thus, after having disclaimed that he has been a financial burden to the Corinthians, Paul states, "thus I have kept and I shall keep myself from being a burden to you in any way."[264] Paul employs here the word ἀβαρής. In 2 Cor 12:16 Paul, in even more emphatic a manner, claims the same, now using the word καταβαρέω. Now, as we saw, Paul's letters had been characterized by some of the Corinthians as βαρεῖς and ἰσχυροί. Thus although Paul has not burdened the Corinthians financially, there are other sorts of burdens of which some of them complain.

The topic of disobedience gains importance in light of Paul's use of the terms ἀνέχεσθαι and καταναρκᾶν. One is expected to submit to and bear with the frank criticism of another, if that person is in a position of authority, for example a father or a more mature person. Apparently, Paul's position on this score was ambivalent.[265] Paul,

---

[262] Dio Chrysostom, *Discourse* 32.7–8; Epictetus, *Encheiridion* 30. Compare Epictetus' remark ἀνέχου λοιδορούμενος in *Discourse* 3.4.12 to Paul's remark in 1 Cor 4:12. See also Epictetus, *Discourse* 3.20.9; 3.21.5–6. Cf. Lucian, *Apology* 2, ἐμὲ μὲν σιωπᾶν καὶ ἀνέχεσθαι τεμνόμενον καὶ καιόμενον, εἰ δέοι, ἐπὶ σωτηρίᾳ.... See also the use of ἀνέχεσθαι in Heb 13:22; 2 Tim 4:3, and Plutarch, *How to Tell a Flatterer from a Friend* 72F. See pp. 125 (fn. 93) and 137–39, above.

[263] Philodemus notes that he who instructs others will not at all put up with frank speech from those who are being instructed by him. The text is corrupt and does not allow us to determine in what sense the instructor is "willingly burdened," as Philodemus says. LSJ s.v. καταναρκάω.

[264] 2 Cor 11:9, καὶ ἐν παντὶ ἀβαρῆ ἐμαυτὸν ὑμῖν ἐτήρησα καὶ τηρήσω. Paul also uses καταναρκάω in connection with financial burden in 2 Cor 12:13, 14. Cf. also 12:16.

[265] In such a case, Quintilian's remark would certainly ring true: "the same re-

however, expects the stubborn Corinthians to obey him as their father. They should submit to him and his directives instead of his counter-psychagogues.[266] But the "wise" cannot tolerate and even resist Paul's censure; they are thus "hard to cure."[267] Paul's treatment of the recalcitrants recognizes the use of beneficial harshness which should be therapeutic. Paul claims to destroy the critics' arguments, threatens them and implies that some of them are incurable. The use of "abruptness" is, Paul remarks, given for the sake of restoration, not destruction.[268] Paul thus seeks through stringent means the "restoration" of the Corinthians and, as one would expect in light of the collaborative nature of the endeavor, lays the responsibility on the Corinthians themselves: "put things in order, exhort one another, be of one mind."[269]

Paul appeals to the Corinthians by referring to the "gentleness and kindness of Christ."[270] The term πραΰτης reminds us of the phrase πνεῦμα πραΰτητος used by Paul in Gal 6:1 and 1 Cor 4:21 of the

---

mark will seem freedom of speech in one's mouth, madness in another's, and arrogance in a third" (*Oratorical Institutions* 11.1.37).

[266] 2 Cor 2:9, "For this is why I wrote, that I might test you and know whether you are obedient in everything"; 7:15, "the obedience of you all"; and 10:5–6 "We ... take every thought captive to obey Christ, being ready to punish every disobedience, when your obedience is complete" (Phlm 21). On the difficult verse 10:6, see Furnish, *2 Corinthians*, pp. 463–64. It is misleading (ibid., pp. 162, 459) to sever the intricate connection between obedience to Christ on the one hand and obedience to Paul on the other hand, since the medium of the psychagogue's behavior is considered to be a part of his message. Also, obedience to a higher authority, say Epicurus or Christ, does not obliterate established communal conventions where humans were invested with certain authority in mutual psychagogy.

[267] Or, like Epictetus' "wise fool" (*Discourse* 2.15.14; cf. 2 Cor 11:19), hard to handle and in need of more stringent measures. On the disobedient and "foolish wise" in Philodemus, see *On Frank Criticism* cols. 15a–21b. See Ignatius, *Eph.* 7.1, on the hard to cure heretical preachers.

[268] 2 Cor 10:3–6, 8; 13:10. "Incurable," cf. 2 Cor 11:12–15. Cf. 1 Cor 5:5; 8:1; 14:4, 5, and 17.

[269] 2 Cor 13:9, 11. See Furnish, *2 Corinthians*, p. 581, for καταρτίζεσθε and παρακαλεῖσθε as passives. If we would take the latter as a passive (*pace* Windisch, *Der zweite Korintherbrief*, pp. 424–26), having an equivalent function to Heb 13:22 (ἀνέχεσθε τοῦ λόγου τῆς παρακλήσεως—"Bear with my word of exhortation" RSV), and translate "pay attention to my appeals" (so Furnish, ibid.), it would indeed square well with Paul's use of ἀνέχεσθαι in 2 Cor 11:1, 4, 19 and 20. But, since Paul is acquainted with the word ἀνέχεσθαι, he would have had no problems using it here if he wanted to emphasize the connotation suggested by Windisch. I am thus inclined to see παρακαλεῖσθε as equivalent to παρακαλεῖτε ἀλλήλους in 1 Thess 4:18.

[270] 2 Cor 10:1, παρακαλῶ ὑμᾶς διὰ τῆς πραΰτητος καὶ ἐπιεικείας τοῦ Χριστοῦ.... Cf. R. Leivestad, "'The meekness and gentleness of Christ' II Cor X.1," *NTS* 13 (1964), pp. 156–64; Furnish, *2 Corinthians*, pp. 455–56. In a dissertation in progress at Brown University on πραΰτης, Joane Barnett has found that the word is used almost exclusively

desirable mode of corrective discipline, revealing the intricate connection of "gentleness" and "harshness" in Paul's mind. Paul's use of the term πραΰτης and the phrase πνεῦμα πραΰτητος, as well as his threats in 2 Cor 12:20–13:11 and 1 Cor 4:14–21, all accentuate Paul's rightful power in exercising punishment as well as his restraint. Paul becomes explicit in his threats in 2 Cor 10:6 and particularly 13:2 and 10. The threat is again used in reference to an upcoming visit. Paul explicitly threatens "those who have sinned in the past," and warns "everyone else," that when he comes this time he "will show no leniency."[271]

Such a warning Paul gave the Corinthians when he was with them in person on his second visit and gives it to them now *in absentia*, apparently to scare them into repentance. The function of a threatening letter is precisely to instill fear through the threat of punishment for wrong conduct. The greater the disobedience, the greater the harshness needed. The attitude of the wise in Corinth, his counter-psychagogues, determines the degree of harshness wielded. The Corinthians are becoming more and more recalcitrant and these strained relations can only become worse. Apparently, Paul has no desire anymore to hold back his rightful power to punish the Corinthians and to assuage them by combining his abruptness with mildness.[272]

The presence-absence motif became one additional proof of Paul's inconsistency. To some in Corinth, there was a great discrepancy

---

of those in authority who can exercise punishment but hold back on their rightful power and show restraint.

[271] Compare Paul's threat in 2 Cor 13:2 with his statement in 1:23 that the reason why he had cancelled a visit to Corinth was because he wanted to spare them. See Windisch, *Der zweite Korintherbrief*, pp. 8, 414–16, 425.

[272] 2 Cor 13:10, "My purpose in writing this letter before I come, is to spare myself, when I come, any sharp exercise of authority (ἵνα παρὼν μὴ ἀποτόμως χρήσωμαι)—authority (ἐξουσία) which the Lord gave me for building up and not for pulling down" (NEB). Here Paul openly reflects on the effects he hopes a letter of his will have, where the letter becomes the substitute for the exertion of authority (cf. 1 Cor 4:20–21). See Windisch, *Der zweite Korintherbrief*, p. 425. For ἀποτόμως χρῆσθαι see Tit 1:13; Polycarp, *Phil.* 6.1; Wis 6:5; and Ps.-Libanius, *Epistolary Styles* 38 and 85 (70, 31–32 and 80, 17–20 Malherbe). See pp. 143–46, above, on the "unmixed" approach advocated by Philodemus in the case of recalcitrant students. For the threatening letter see Ps.-Demetrius *Epistolary Types* 8 (36, 1–6 Malherbe) and Ps.-Libanius, *Epistolary Styles* 13 and 60 (68, 23 and 74, 37–39 Malherbe). For 2 Cor 10–13 as a threatening letter, see J. T. Fitzgerald, "Paul, the Ancient Epistolary Theorists, and 2 Corinthians 10–13," in D. L. Balch, E. Ferguson and W. A. Meeks (eds), *Greeks, Romans, and Christians. Essays in Honor of Abraham J. Malherbe* (Minneapolis, 1990), pp. 190–200.

between Paul's servile behavior when present and his overbearing letters when absent.[273] Paul's claim or threat to the contrary could hardly have convinced them, for as Menander said centuries earlier—"A threatening father cannot inspire much fear!"[274] Paul responds to the adversarial use of the present-absent motif and uses it to underline his authority in connection with his upcoming visit.[275] Although Paul's use of this motif is polemical, it should not be abstracted from its customary setting in the friendly letter. Such a suggestion might appear disjointed in light of Paul's castigation of the Corinthians, but Paul gives us in 2 Cor 10–13 an example of a corrective discipline in writing which in its appeal proceeds from the "meekness" and "gentleness" of Christ (2 Cor 10:1). And, as in 1 Cor 1:10, an appeal is again made in 2 Cor 13:11 using the proverbial friendship expression τὸ αὐτὸ φρονεῖτε. We would be mistaken if we failed to see Paul's threats as fundamentally philophronetic in nature! In his use of harshness, Paul appears in the role of a frank friend and a loving but stern father who attempts by means of more stringent forms of persuasion to change the self-deceptive and arrogant wise in Corinth.

Paul's phraseology suggests that he views the wise and his rival leaders as recalcitrant students who should submit to his authority. Charges and counter-charges relating to harshness in moral exhortation show that the dispute centered on the appropriate mode of spiritual guidance. Paul's critique of the recalcitrants reveals his theory of blame or the use of harshness in psychagogy, and his view of the Corinthian critics. Contrary to a common view, perhaps there were no "opponents" of Paul in Corinth, but simply, seen from Paul's perspective, recalcitrant and disobedient "students." I have stressed texts both in 1 and 2 Corinthians which yield information concerning a debate between Paul and some in Corinth on harshness and gentleness in moral guidance. These texts reveal a dispute between Paul and the recalcitrants both over Paul's leadership qualifications and style and the appropriate methods of correcting others in the

---

[273] Contrast the wise Calanus who, according to Philo, displayed a consistency in his frankness towards Alexander both in his presence as well as in his letters when absent (*Every Good Man is Free* 95–96).
[274] See 2 Cor 10:1, 11, and Menander, 454K, πατὴρ δ' ἀπειλῶν οὐχ ἔχει μέγαν φόβον. See also Menender 662K.
[275] 2 Cor 10:2, 11; 13:2, 10. Cf. Bünker, *Briefformular*, pp. 30–31. Note also 1 Cor 5:3.

community. This debate in Corinth of the desirable mode of guidance is analogous to the debate among the Epicureans at Herculaneum which I documented in chapter three, and forms a part of a wider debate among moralists relating to the appropriate treatment of different types of humans in their reformation.

## 6.5 *Pauline Pedagogy*

We are now in a position to define more closely Paul's leadership model in view of Pauline psychagogic practice. Paul's leadership style is best explicated in light of the psychagogic traditions of harsh and gentle guidance. As a spiritual patron and father Paul recognizes the value of the mixed approach, or the use of beneficial harshness with the periodic interjection of more soothing measures.[276] Paul's affable approach reminds us of a gentle philosopher whose practice displays commonly noted features of flatterers and obsequious persons, namely, softness, abject servility, and adaptation. In his harsh approach evident in the image of the rod and the use of patriarchal imagery, Paul also displays characteristics of the austere, rigorous type of philosopher who stood his ground, inflexible. This combination of patriarchal and demagogic imagery forms part of a widespread leadership motif, emphasizing the importance of a versatile appoach in light of human diversity and psychagogic adaptation in light of the human disposition which might require both flexible and more stringent guidance. Such an hypothesis takes seriously Paul's continual use of patriarchal imagery as he adjusts and accommodates himself to the different constituents of his encoded audience.

Paul's psychagogic leadership is one of a benevolent "spiritual patriarch" who can be both harsh and accommodating, depending on the condition of those under his care. Undue emphasis on the populist model of leadership unnecessarily downplays Paul's use of patriarchal imagery in the very same correspondence in which he employs demagogic imagery. The combination of gentle and stringent guidance is inherent in the patriarchal paradigm and integral to Paul's self-presentation as a guide. In spite of his use of the dema-

---

[276] Ps.-Plutarch, *On the Education of Children* 13D, "As physicians, by mixing bitter drugs with sweet syrups, have found that the agreeable taste gains access for what is beneficial, so fathers should combine the abruptness of their rebukes with mildness."

gogic topos, Paul continues to speak of himself as the "father" of the Corinthians. A gentle and all accommodating father is not very different from the cunning employer in Varro's and Columella's descriptions, who has recognized the need of benevolence in order to keep his employees content.[277] Both take an egalitarian stand in order not to unsettle those insecure because of their tender disposition; both have the psychological condition of those under their charge in view. The condition of the recipients determines the nature of the approach. Patriarchal imagery is evoked when the recipients are disobedient; it opens the door for harsh discipline or censure. An egalitarian approach is more appropriate for insecure students; it is mild, set forth in light of the tender condition of the "weak."

It has been suggested that Paul's use of the populist model of leadership reflects the position of a visionary egalitarian and not of a benevolent patriarch.[278] The accommodation of the latter is not "real" but only pretended for tactical purposes; the accommodation of the demagogue is, on the other hand "real." Paul's own social self-lowering, exemplified by his trade, for example, had a tangible social dimension. But 1 Cor 9:19-23 does surely not yield information concerning the social "reality" of Paul's adaptation. Paul's connection of "weakness" with "knowledge" and "consciousness" also shows that his concern is cognitive rather than social. The fact that Paul's adaptation is a form of literary adaptation should also make us be on our guard against any facile attempt to determine the social tangible "reality" of Paul's accommodation. We cannot step outside of Paul's own intertextuality!

Paul's advice to the Corinthians is modeled both on the advice of a frank friend and the guidance of a loving but stern father. This twofold standing of a friend and a father—common representatives of types of leadership—displays a contrasting relationship, namely, one of symmetry and asymmetry. Any attempt to downplay one at the expense of the other fails to see the intricate balance of both in Paul's psychagogic guidance. Paul underscores with the phrase ἀγαπητοί

---

[277] Varro, *On Agriculture* 1.17.4; Columella, *On Agriculture* 1.8.15; 12.1.6.

[278] D. B. Martin, *Slavery as Salvation. The Metaphor of Slavery in Pauline Christianity* (New Haven and London, 1990), pp. xix; xxii; 27-28, 126-29, 147-49. Martin concentrates on the phrases "slave of Christ" and "slave of all" (1 Cor 9:19) as he explicates the function of slavery as a metaphor in the church in Corinth. He has correctly connected the phrase "slave of all" to "types of leadership" but has not recognized the significance of the reference to the "weak" in 9:22.

μου that his stern criticism of the Corinthians is based on their friendly relationship.²⁷⁹ In this Paul is like Horace, who in his satires speaks both as an *amicus* and a *pater*; Plutarch also recognizes as guides for moral behavior, not only a διδάσκαλος, but also a πατὴρ χρηστός and a φίλος ἐπιεικής. Similarly, Philodemus speaks of the friendly teacher in the same breath as an elder and a father. None of them is averse to including criticisms in his instruction.²⁸⁰

Paul's twofold approach of symmetry and asymmetry reflects a conscious pedagogical approach, not irreconcilable entities but rather different modes of guidance appropriate for different types of students. Like Philodemus, Paul uses admonitory pedagogy to correct the recalcitrant "wise" and advocates as well the mixture of praise and blame in communal psychagogy.²⁸¹ We thus find in Paul, as we did in Philodemus' *On Frank Criticism*, a variation of two different types of students, namely, the strong or recalcitrant ones, and the weak or tender ones.²⁸² Paul is gentle towards the weak but more forceful and overbearing in his guidance of the recalcitrant and stubborn students. The only hope to effect a change in these stubborn pupils is to be severe. Paul's use of blame is an attempt of a considerate friend and a loving father to grieve and shame the "wise" in Corinth to repentance.

Paul criticizes the "wise" in Corinth and "powerful" in Rome for their inconsiderate approach towards the insecure. At the same time Paul attempts to effect a change in community members by guidance through character portrayal in which he lends two character types a voice, spotlighting their different behaviors and attitudes. The wise and strong are, despite claims to the contrary, also immature

---

[279] 1 Cor 4:14; 10:14; 15:58. See also 1 Cor 4:17; 2 Cor 7:1; Phil 2:14; 4.1.

[280] Philodemus, *On Frank Criticism* col. 7a1–3; Plutarch, *How to Tell a Flatterer from a Friend* 73D-E; Horace, *Sat.* 1.4.25–32,107–08; 1.3.42–48; cf. Philo, *On the Migration of Abraham* 110–11, 115–17.

[281] Like Paul and Philodemus, Clement also advocates the use of admonitory pedagogy, or the mixture of praise and blame (*Ped.* 94.1–2; 145, 26–146, 6 Stählin-Treu). Cf. Clement's remark that "the sort of education that uses chastisement and censure is suitable for humans" (τὸ ἐπιπληκτικὸν καὶ ψεκτικὸν εἶδος τῆς παιδαγωγίας ἁρμόδιον εἶναι τοῖς ἀνθρώποις; *Ped.* 93.3 (145, 16–26 Stählin-Treu). On admonitory education see Plato, *The Sophist* 230A. See Epicurus, *On Nature* [34.25] 21–34 Arr., on the use of admonitory, reformatory, or retaliatory mode of discourse. See also Seneca, *Epistle* 94.45–46, Ps.-Demetrius, *Epistolary Types* 8 (Malherbe, 34, 31–33), Aristotle, *Pol.* 1260b5–7, Plato, *Laws* 777E, and Epictetus, *Discourse* 3.14.9. See pp. 42–43, 86, 127, and 155, above.

[282] See pp. 139–52, above.

and in need of preceptive guidance appropriate for progressing persons. Paul coaxes both types of persons to a better understanding of the issues and manages to be specific as it relates to guidelines he attempts to implement for interacting behavior. Guidance through character portrayal is then didactic, relating to attitude and behavior. We are misguided if we exclude a pedagogical passion in Paul's nurturing paternity and psychagogic guidance.

In conclusion, I want to underline several points I have made with regard to Pauline psychagogy. Firstly, Paul's leadership role is psychagogic; secondly, Paul's discourse supposes education and growth; and, thirdly, the "weak" and "strong" are not groups but dispositions or character types. Paul's description of people as "weak" and "strong" is an attempt at character portrayal, where typical characteristics of certain dispositions and character types are given voice and dramatized. Paul stresses the interacting obligations of different types of people as he focuses on the behavior of the personified characters of these encoded readers.

What is important is not to be able to identify the origin of the "weak" but rather to tap into the appropriate cultural codes which might help explicate Paul's conceptualization of the issues. Such codes suggest that Paul's vocabulary can be explained in light of material found among moralists of the day as they focus on different types of students, particularly those insecure in their new way of life and the teacher's ways and means of directing these students. Those who, on the other hand, attempt to identify the "weak" in Paul as either gentiles or Jews attempt to explain some of the possible reasons why certain behavior continued among members of the Pauline communities. The approach advocated here is a functional-analogical one; instead of relying on or requiring a strict identification and source of origin in a certain background for the "weak" (= a genealogical approach), is to show the structural and functional similarities in the status of the "weak" in Paul and the "weak" in other "backgrounds," and the similarities and differences in attempting to ameliorate tensions present because of that status.

Often moralists who discuss psychological states of different types of humans and differentiate the treatment appropriate for each have simply been sidestepped. But the issues Paul is concerned with were widely discussed and form part of the milieu in which he operates. Although it is not insignificant if we could discover the possible origin—in the sense of previous associations and activities engaged in—

of any particular "weak" person in Philodemus and Paul, or that a "weak" person was either a Jew or some gentile, for example a Scythian, the functional-analogical approach emphasizes, as do the moralists themselves, not the origin of the weak but their present dilemma and the steps taken in order to counter it. Such a caring for the psychologically weak is present in Hellenistic Jewish writings and became standard fare in early Christian writers subsequent to Paul.[283]

There is a clear difference between such an approach and one that identifies a possible background where the weak originate. Max Rauer's fundamental study, for example, asks us to imagine the "weak" as gentile Christians whose vegetarianism stems from their prior religious background in Gnostic, Hellenistic mystery religions.[284] Others ask us to focus on their ethnic origin in terms of Jews versus non-Jews.[285] Both explain why certain behavior continued among members of the Pauline groups and emphasize ethnicity as important in the identification of the "weak" and the "strong." Instead of requiring an ethnic identification or source of origin, my perspective shows the structural and functional similarities in the status of the "weak" in Paul and other contexts, as well as the similarities and differences in attempting to ameliorate tensions present because of that status.

Also, the issues in both 1 Cor 8 and Rom 14–15 cannot be linked exclusively with either former Jews or pagans. Hence, the equation of the "weak" and "strong" as either Jewish or gentile Christians has

---

[283] Besides the texts referred to in fns. 68–69 on pp. 204–205, above, see Heb 4:15; *T. Benj.* 4.4ef; *T. Zeb.* 6.5; 7.3–4; *T. Sim.* 3.6; *T. Iss.* 5.2; *T. Jos.* 3.5; 20.6. Like Paul, other early Christian authors also use the terms "weak" and "strong" to connote a psychological condition. In such a context we find as well the contrast between salvation and destruction (*Herm. Sim.* 9.23.4). 1 *Clem.* 38.2 ("Let the strong care for the weak and let the weak reverence the strong. Let the rich man bestow help on the poor and let the poor give thanks to God. . . .") and Pol. *Phil.* 6.1 refer both to the "weak" and the "strong" as well as the "rich" and "poor," indicating that the words "weak" and "strong" do not connote a social category. The same is true of *Herm. Vis.* 3.12.2. Cf. *1 Clem.* 59.4 (". . . heal the sick . . . raise up the weak").

[284] M. Rauer, *Die 'Schwachen' in Korinth und Rom nach den Paulusbriefen* (Herder, 1923); Jewett, *Paul's Anthropological Terms*, pp. 42–46. Rauer does, though, point out that the "weak" are individuals and not a "group" (88, 95), as does R. J. Karris, "Romans 14.1–15.13 and the Occasion of Romans," in *The Romans Debate* (rev. exp. ed. by K. P. Donfried; Peabody, MA, 1991), pp. 65–84.

[285] Dunn, *Romans 9–16*, p. 801. Meyer argued that ἕως ἄρτι in 1 Cor 8:7 shows that Paul has in view "gentile Christians," not "Jewish Christians" (*Des Paulus erster Brief an die Korinther*, pp. 181–82).

reached an impasse.[286] Gentiles practiced vegetarianism, and the avoidance of certain food and drink can be seen in Stoic discussions of weakness in the form of unreasonable avoidance and repulsion.[287] And the consideration of one day as more auspicious than another was well known among pagans as Theophrastus' or Plutarch's description of the superstitious person shows.[288] The significant deduction from these considerations is that we cannot restrict ourselves to an either-or dichotomy of "Jews" or "gentiles" in light of the issues Paul discusses. We must rather deduce that when Paul addresses the "weak," "strong" or "wise," he does not wish to accentuate the ethnic identity of his addressees but rather their psychological disposition or character type.[289]

Now if the "weak" and the "strong" refer to dispositions, such a classification presupposes people of different aptitudes and their maturation. Within the parameters of such classification, advice is thus not only given as to how the different types should behave but also how they should make progress.[290] Most moralists presuppose human development and accentuate human achievement and character formation. It is correct that progress towards ἀρετή is not accentuated by Paul, although, I suspect, nobody would claim that Paul devalues good moral behavior. The end goal of shunning the immoral is precisely their betterment. Paul is also primarily interested in ameliorating tensions between members, and the lack of emphasis on character development in Paul can be explicated in light of his positive view of the friendship of many and his attempt to create a community with constituents of diverse behaviors and beliefs. Although Paul does not accentuate maturation, it is intrinsic to his discourse;

---

[286] Murphy-O'Connor, "Freedom or the Ghetto (I Cor viii, 1–13; x, 21–xi, 1)," p. 552; W. A. Meeks, "The Polyphonic Ethics of the Apostle Paul," *The Annual of the Society of Christian Ethics* (1988), p. 25; idem, "Judgment and the Brother: Romans 14.1–15.13," pp. 292–293.

[287] W. G. Kümmel, *Introduction to the New Testament* (London, 1975), p. 310; Dunn, *Word Biblical Commentary. 38B. Romans 9–16*, p. 801; Stowers, "Paul on the Use and Abuse of Reason," *Greeks, Romans, and Christians*, pp. 280–81. The avoidance of wine was also a concern among Hellenistic Jews (P. J. Tomson, *Paul and the Jewish Law* [Assen/Maastricht, Minneapolis, 1990], p. 239).

[288] Theophrastus, *Character* 16; Plutarch, *On Superstition* 167A, 169E, 170E–F. Cf. W. A. Meeks, "Judgment and the Brother: Romans 14:1–15:13," pp. 292–93.

[289] Rom 15:7 is attractive to scholars who identify the weak and the strong with the Jew—gentile dichotomy: Keck: "Christology, Soteriology, and the Praise of God (Romans 15.7–13)," pp. 85–97.

[290] Plutarch *On Progress in Virtue* (75A–86A); Epictetus, *Discourse* 1.4, *On Progress*; and 3.2; Seneca, *Epistles* 71.37; 75.15, 18.

a weak person can become strong, just as a young can become older. Latent in the paraenetic material is a didactic element; inculcation of belief is indirectly pursued through exhortation, precept giving, character portrayal, and behavioral modification.[291]

Although the precise terminology differs, Paul's reference to persons as weak and strong, obedient and disobedient, is on par with other moralists' distinction between different types of students contingent on their disposition. We have seen the emphasis on the interaction of these different types in Paul and Philodemus who both advise against a contemptuous attitude in the pratice of mutual psychagogy. The same is true of other moralists of the period. Each author is of course unique. That holds true also for Paul's interpretation of the story of Jesus, the Christ. "Christianity" is not presented as the solution to the human predicament but rather as God's plan to bring gentiles to God.[292] As such, the end goal of Paul's activity is different from that of his contemporaries. But that activity took place on Greco-Roman soil which had specific cultural codes intact which not only influenced Paul's self-presentation and image and his means and methods of persuasion, but also, we can now add, the way in which he conceptualized the different status and relations of persons in his communities.

---

[291] Many deny the presence of moral and spiritual formation in the Pauline corpus. This is often contrasted with the emphasis of the philosophical schools of the day on character formation and development: J. P. Hershbell, "De Virtute Morali (Moralia 440D–452D)," in *Plutarch's Ethical Writings and ECL* (ed. H. D. Betz, Leiden, 1978), pp. 144–45; H. Conzelmann, *1 Corinthians*, p. 147 n. 17; P. W. Gooch, *Partial Knowledge. Philosophical Studies in Paul* (Notre Dame, Indiana, 1987), pp. 123, 181 n. 28; Gaventa, "The Maternity of Paul: An Exegetical Study of Galatians 4:19," pp. 194–97; and R. Bultmann, *Theology of the New Testament* (London, 1955), vol. 2, p. 222, "There is no thought of character-education, just as there is none of education in general." Such a statement surely cannot be meaningfully applied to Paul and his activities. See Clarence E. Glad, "The Significance of Hellenistic Psychagogy for Our Understanding of Paul," *Studia Theologica Islandica* 10 (1995, forthcoming).

[292] See Stanley K. Stowers, *A Rereading of Romans*. New Haven: Yale University Press, 1994.

CONCLUSION

I shall not give a summary of the many points of detail I have put forward in this book but shall limit myself to the broader issues and larger implications of my reading. The concept of adaptability in psychagogic guidance is central in Paul's letters. This discourse comes from discussions of friendship by philosophers and moralists and from discussions of the opportune moment by rhetoricians. Paul adopted the controversial ideal of adapting one's speech and life-style to the needs of various people. This model is discussed in Greco-Roman psychagogic literature on how and to what extent a psychagogue ("leader of souls") should adapt himself in his educational activities. To his critics in Corinth, Paul's adaptability was seen as duplicity, inconsistency, and weakness; to Paul himself, it meant embodying the very form of the good news of which he was a herald. This ethic of adaptability served not only as a paradigm for social and ethical relations in the communities Paul founded but shaped his self-understanding as an apostle of Christ to the gentiles. This self-understanding was in turn modeled on Paul's understanding of Jesus Christ's adaptable behavior.

Paul's use of labels such as "weak", "strong", "wise", "disobedient", and "obedient" and related vocabulary, is to be understood within a specific arena in Greco-Roman literature which discussed adaptability in psychagogic nurture and moral reformation. Instead of attempting to locate the "weak" and "strong" on a spectrum of "opponents," which reflects a bewildering variety of theological positions, we should understand these words in view of a widespread contemporary meaning denoting dispositions of character. These are not fixed roles but relative categories that would differ for an individual at various times and in regard to the particular behavior or aspect of character in question. Thus "the weak" and "the strong" are not groups or parties or theological positions, as New Testament scholars have thought, but psychological dispositions or character types revealing different aptitudes of students and their maturity. Paul's discussion with his critics does then not reflect a theological *Auseinandersetzung* or apology to some "opponents" for his apostolic self-understanding but rather the proper character of *Seelsorge* or spiritual guidance.

The classic statement of Paul's flexible conduct (1 Cor 9:19–23) belongs to a tradition of Greco-Roman society which underlines the importance of adaptability and a versatile approach in light of human diversity and of psychagogic adaptation in view of different human dispositions. Paul's adaptability has implications for his verbal means of persuasion. Paul adapts to the disposition of different types of students, using gentle speech toward the insecure while being appropriately harsh toward the stubborn ones. In Paul's guidance of the recalcitrant in Corinth we witness the use of benevolent harshness as Paul attempts to secure their obedience and conversion. The purpose of Paul's psychagogic adaptability towards the weak and tender is to counter the attempts of the mature to reform the weak, a practice which grieved the immature and undermined their commitments in their new way of life. Paul argues both in Rom 14 and 1 Cor 8 against the attempt of the mature to reform the immature and dispel their false beliefs by rational arguments and by means of a forceful example, pointing out that this inconsiderate harshness wounded the weak and threatened to destroy them. Here we witness a debate between Paul and the "wise" in Corinth on issues of pedagogy and leadership qualifications and style, issues which center on questions of maturation and harsh and gentle means of persuasion.

Ancient writers connected the use of harshness combined with gentler means of persuasion with issues of pleasure and pain, flexibility and rigidity. The mixed method of praise and blame shows the importance of adaptation to the particular case and underlines that it is in the candid approach to faults that a friend differs from the flatterer. The debate as to the appropriate mode of psychagogic guidance and the proper use of harsh and gentle means of persuasion was widespread. Paul's own psychagogic leadership is that of a benevolent father who can be both harsh and accommodating, depending on the condition of those under his care. Paul's use of the "mixed pedagogical method" or recognition of the need for beneficial harshness, with the periodic interjection of more soothing measures, lodges Paul squarely within a widespread moral tradition. Seeing Paul in this light enables us to understand him as a participant in this common tradition of the Greco-Roman milieu in which issues of versatility and adaptability in moral guidance were debated. The prevalence of the mixed method of exhortation shows that issues of harsh and gentle guidance reach beyond the Cynics and provides a context for understanding the Epicurean material as well as a broader basis from which to view Paul and his activities.

One of the aims of this book has been precisely to expand our horizons with regard to Paul's activities and methods, especially the psychagogic nurture of his communities and the practices he attempts to implement in those communities. In order to achieve that goal I have utilized material, not only from Philodemus, but also from such diverse authors as Plato, Aristotle, Isocrates, Musonius Rufus, Epictetus, Seneca, Plutarch, Dio Chrysostom, Maximus of Tyre, Philo, and Clement of Alexandria. All of these authors discussed "psychagogy" which is a variation of the common practice of the "care of the young" or the reformation of people. Within this common tradition there are certain distinguishing features which bring Paul and Philodemus close together. This includes an epistolary and participatory psychagogy. Participatory psychagogy, in particular, as a social practice, is a defining and constitutive feature of both Epicurean and proto-Christian communities. We have seen that there is a widespread pattern of mutual exhortation, edification and correction in both these communities.

Such a practice reveals both symmetrical and asymmetrical social relations between members. Which relationship is evident depends on the function of members on each particular occasion. If we emphasize the corrective aspect of psychagogy, the asymmetrical relationship comes to the fore, but if the edificatory aspect of psychagogy is emphasized, the asymmetrical relationship fades and a symmetrical one emerges. Epicurean and Pauline communities display, then, a rotational form of psychagogy in which members can assume various psychagogic roles in their care of others. Such a practice of participatory pychagogy, as well as the open-ended nature of the recruitment criteria and admission of members of both communities, has implications for their respective views on friendship. This shared view of friendship includes a positive evaluation of the friendship of many which expands the spectrum of persons, noble or base, with whom one can associate, and the spectrum of persons who can become friends. Among both groups diverse friends participated in mutual psychagogy on the basis of their friendship and shared communal values.

It is important to remember that Epicureans and early Christians were often lumped together by outside observers from the second century of the common era onward. Both groups were charged with atheism, misanthropy, social irresponsibility, secrecy and separateness, disruption of families, sexual immorality and general moral depravity. One additional reason for such a perceived congruity is awareness among outsiders of similarities in the psychagogic practices of these communities. Paul is then not promoting a new type of community education for adults but conforms to a widespread pedagogical pattern witnessed in contemporary Epicurean schools. Such a sociocultural perspective on the contemporary pedagogical models available to and appropriated by Paul helps us appreciate the special affinities that Paul's nurture of the proto-Christian communities, and the participatory psychagogy he attempts to implement in these communities, have with the psychagogic practices of contemporary Epicureans in Athens, Naples, and Herculanaeum.

# BIBLIOGRAPHY

*Texts and Translations*

I. *Lexica and Tools*
Bauer, Walter. *Griechisch-deutsches Wörterbuch zu den Schriften des Neuen Testaments und der frühchristlichen Literatur.* 6., völlig neu bearbeitete Auflage, hrsg. von Kurt Aland und Barbara Aland. Berlin/New York: Walter de Gruyter, 1988.
Bauer, Walter, W. F. Arndt, F. W. Gingrich and F. W. Danker. *A Greek-English Lexicon of the New Testament and Other Early Christian Literature.* 2nd ed.; Chicago: University Press, 1979.
Blass, F., A. Debrunner, and Robert W. Funk. *A Greek Grammar of the New Testament and Other Early Christian Literature.* Chicago and London: The University of Chicago Press, 1961.
Kittel, Gerhard, and G. Friedrich, eds. *Theological Dictionary of the New Testament.* Transl. Geoffrey W. Bromiley. Grand Rapids: Wm. B. Eerdmans Publ. Comp.
Liddell, H. G. and R. Scott. *A Greek-English Lexicon.* Rev. H. S. Jones & R. McKenzie. 9th ed.; Oxford: Clarendon, 1940.
Moulton, J. H., W. F. Howard and N. Turner. *A Grammar of New Testament Greek.* 4 vols.; Edinburgh: T. & T. Clark, 1906-76.
Porter, Stanley E. *Idioms of the Greek New Testament.* Biblical Languages 2: Greek. 2nd ed. Sheffield: JSOT Press, 1994.

II. *Collected Texts and Translations*
Angeli, Anna. *Filodemo, Agli Amici di Scuola (PHerc. 1005).* La Scuola di Epicuro 6. Naples: Bibliopolis, 1988.
Arrighetti, G. *Epicuro, Opere* (2nd ed.). Torino, 1973.
Arnim, H. von, ed. *Stoicorum Veterum Fragmenta.* 4 vols. Leipzig: B. G. Teubner, 1903-24.
Bailey, Cyril, ed. *Epicurus: The Extant Remains.* Oxford: Clarendon, 1926.
Butts, James R. *The Progymnasmata of Theon: A New Text with Translation and Commentary.* Diss., Claremont Graduate School, 1986.
Capasso, M. *Trattato etico epicureo.* Naples, 1982.
Chilton, C. W. *Diogenis Oenoandensis Fragmenta.* Leipzig, Teubner, 1967.
———. *Diogenes of Oenoanda. The Fragments. A Translation and Commentary.* London, 1971.
Decleva Caizzi, F. ed. *Antisthenes fragmenta.* Milan: Cisalpino, 1966.
de Lacy, P. H. and E. A. *Philodemus: On Methods of Inference.* Naples: Bibliopolis, 1978.
———. *Galen, On the Doctrines of Hippocrates and Plato.* Ed., transl. and commentary by P. H. de Lacy. Corpus Medicorum Graecorum V 4.1.2.1-3. Berlin, 1978, 1980, 1982.
Dillon, J. and J. Hershbell. *Iamblichus, On the Pythagorean Way of Life.* Atlanta: Scholars Press, 1991.
Edmonds, J. M., ed./transl. *The Fragments of Attic Comedy.* 3 vols. Leiden: E. J. Brill, 1957-61.
Harkins, P. W. *Galen, On the Passions and Errors of the Soul.* Columbus: Ohio State University Press, 1963.
Hense, 'O., ed. *C. Musonii Rufi reliquiae.* Leipzig: B. G. Teubner, 1905; repr. 1990.
*Herculanensium Voluminum quae supersunt,* Vol. 5, part 2. Naples, 1843.
Hobein, H., ed. *Maximi Tyrii philosophumena.* Leipzig: B. G. Teubner, 1910.

Horst, P. W. van der (ed.) *The Sentences of Pseudo-Phocylides. With Introduction and Commentary.* SVTP 4; Leiden: E. J. Brill, 1978.
Hubbell, H. M. "The Rhetorica of Philodemus," *Transactions of the Connecticut Academy of Arts and Sciences* 23 (1920), 243-382.
Indelli, G. *Polistrato, Sul disprezzo irrazionale delle opinioni popolari.* La Scuola di Epicuro 2. Naples: Bibliopolis, 1978.
―――― *Filodemo, L'Ira.* La Scuola di Epicuro 5. Naples: Bibliopolis, 1988.
Jaekel, S., ed. *Menandri sententiae.* Leipzig: B. G. Teubner, 1910.
Jensen, C., ed. *Philodemi Περὶ οἰκονομίας qui licitur libellus.* Leipzig: Teubner, 1906.
―――― *Philodemi Περὶ κακιῶν liber decimus.* Leipzig, Teubner, 1911.
Jonge, M. de, ed. *The Testaments of the Twelve Patriarchs. A Critical Edition of the Greek Text.* SVTP 1/2. Leiden: E. J. Brill, 1978.
Kidd, I. G. *Posidonius. Volume II. The Commentary.* CCTC 14A (i) Testimonia and Fragments 1-149; CCTC 14B (ii) Fragments 150-293. Cambridge: Cambridge University Press, 1988.
Kindstrand, J. F. *Bion of Borysthenes. A collection of the fragments with introduction and commentary.* Uppsala, 1976.
Kock, T., ed. *Comicorum Atticorum Fragmenta.* 3 vols. Leipzig: Teubner, 1880-88.
Kühn, K. G., ed. *Medicorum Graecorum Opera.* 20 vols. Leipzig: B. G. Teubner, 1821-33.
Long, A. A., and Sedley, D. N. *The Hellenistic Philosophers,* 2 vols. Cambridge: Cambridge University Press, 1987.
Longo Auricchio, F. *Philodemi de Rhetorica libri primus et secundus,* in Sbordone, R., *Ricerche sui papiri ercolanesi* vol. 3. Naples, 1977.
Malherbe, Abraham J., ed. *The Cynic Epistles.* SBLSBS 12. Missoula, Mont.: Scholars Press, 1986 (2).
――――, ed. *Ancient Epistolary Theorists.* SBLSBS 19. Atlanta: Scholars Press, 1988.
May, M. Tallmadge. *Galen on the Usefulness of the Parts of the Body.* 2 vols. Ithaca, New York: Cornell University Press, 1968.
Nauck, A. *Tragicorum Graecorum Fragmenta.* 2nd edition, 1889. Reprinted, with supplement by B. Snell, Hildesheim: G. Olms, 1964.
Olivieri, A., ed. *Philodemi De libertate dicendi.* Leipzig: B. G. Teubner, 1914.
Rabe, Hugo, ed. *Hermogenis Opera.* Leipzig: Teubner, 1913; repr. Stuttgart, 1969.
―――― *Aphthonii Progymnasmata.* Leipzig: Teubner, 1926.
Russell, D. A., and N. G. Wilson, ed. and trans. *Menander Rhetor.* Oxford: Clarendon Press, 1981.
Sbordone, F. *Philodemi Adversus [sophistas]. E papyro Herculanensi 1005.* Naples, 1947.
Sharples, R. W. *Alexander of Aphrodisias On Fate. Text, translation and commentary.* London: Duckworth, 1983.
Spengel, L., ed. *Rhetores Graeci.* 3 vols. Leipzig: B. G. Teubner, 1854-56.
Stählin, Otto, and Ursula Treu. *Clemens Alexandrinus. Erster Band. Protrepticus und Paedagogus.* 3rd ed. GCS; Berlin: Akademie Verlag, 1972.
Sternbach, L., ed. *Gnomologium Vaticanum.* Berlin: Walter de Gruyter, 1963 (repr.).
Sudhaus, S., ed. *Philodemi Volumina Rhetorica* I, II. Teubner: Leipzig, 1892, 1896 (Amsterdam, 1964); Supplementum, Leipzig, 1895.
Usener, H. *Epicurea.* Leipzig, 1887. Reprinted, Rome, 1963.
Ussher, R. G. *The Characters of Theophrastus.* London: Macmillan & Co. Ltd., 1960.
Wachsmuth, C., and O. Hense. *Ioannis Stobaei anthologium.* 5 vols. Berlin: Weidmann, 1884-1912.
Wettstein, J. J. *Novum Testamentum Graecum.* 2 vols. Amsterdam, 1751-52.
White, L. Michael, and John T. Fitzgerald. *The Tabula of Cebes.* SBLTT 24. Chico, California: Scholars Press, 1983.
Wilke, C. *Philodemi De ira liber,* Leipzig, 1914.

## Other Works

Allo, E.-B. *Saint Paul: Première Épître aux Corinthiens*. Ebib. 2nd ed. Paris: Gabalda, 1956.
——— *Saint Paul: Seconde Épître aux Corinthiens*. Ebib. 2nd ed. Paris: Gabalda, 1956.
Amoroso, Filippo. "Filodemo sulla conversazione," *CErc* 5 (1975) 63–76.
Amstutz, J. 'ΑΠΛΟΤΗΣ: *Eine begriffsgeschichtliche Studie zum jüdisch-christlichen Griechisch*. Bonn: Peter Hanstein, 1968.
Annas, Julia. "Epicurean Emotions," *GRBS* 30.2 (1989) 145–164.
Apel, Karl-Otto. *Understanding and Explanation. A Transcendental-Pragmatic Perspective*. Cambridge, Mass.: The MIT Press, 1984.
Arnim, H. von. *Leben und Werke des Dio von Prusa*. Berlin: Weidmann, 1898.
Asmis, Elizabeth. "Psychagogia in Plato's Phaedrus," *ICS* 11.1/2 (1986) 153–172.
——— "Philodemus' Epicureanism," ANRW 2.36.4. Berlin/New York: Walter de Gruyter, 1990, 2369–2406.
Attridge, H. W. *The Epistle to the Hebrews*. Hermeneia; Philadelphia: Fortress Press, 1989.
Bachmann, Philipp. *Der zweite Brief des Paulus an die Korinther*. Zahn's Kommentar zum Neuen Testament 8; 1st & 2nd ed.; Leipzig: Deichert, 1909.
Balsdon, J. P. V. D. *Roman Women: their history and habits*. Oxford, 1974.
Barr, J. *The Semantics of Biblical Language*. Oxford, 1961.
Barrett, C. K. *A Commentary on The First Epistle to the Corinthians*. HNTC; New York: Harper & Row, 1968.
——— *Essays on Paul*. Philadelphia: The Westminster Press, 1982.
Bartchy, S. Scott. *First-Century Slavery and the Interpretation of 1 Corinthians 7:21*. SBLDS 11. Atlanta, Georgia: Scholars Press, 1973.
Bartelink, G. J. M. "Quelques observations sur παρρησία dans la littérature paléocretienne," *Graecitas et Latinitas Christianorum Primaeva*. Supplementa 3. Nimwegen, 1970, 5–57.
Bassler, J. M. *Divine Impartiality: Paul and a Theological Axiom*. SBLDS 59. Chico, California: Scholars Press, 1982.
Baumeister, T. "Ordnungsdenken und charismatische Geistererfahrung in der Alten Kirche," *RQ* 73 (1978) 137–51.
Behm, J. "νουθετέω, νουθεσία," *TDNT* 4 (1967) 1019–22.
Berger, Peter, and Thomas Luckmann. *The Social Construction of Reality: A Treatise in the Sociology of Knowledge*. Garden City, N. Y.: Doubleday & Co., Anchor Books, 1967.
Bergson, L. "Eiron und Eironeia," *Hermes* 99 (1971) 409–22.
Berry, Edmund. "Dio Chrysostom The Moral Philosopher," *GR* 30.1 (1983) 70–80.
Bertram, F. *Die Timonlegende. Eine Entwicklungsgeschichte des Misanthropentypus in der antiken Literatur*. 1906.
Best, E. *Paul and his Converts*. Edinburgh: T. & T. Clark, 1988.
Betz, Hans Dieter. *Der Apostel Paulus und die sokratische Tradition. Eine exegetische Untersuchung zum einer "Apologie" 2 Korinther 10–13*. BHT 45; Tübingen: Mohr, 1972.
——— *Galatians. A Commentary on Paul's Letter to the Churches in Galatia*. Hermeneia; Philadelphia: Fortress Press, 1979.
——— ed. *Plutarch's Ethical Writings and Early Christian Literature*. Studia ad Corpus Hellenisticum Novi Testamenti 4; Leiden: E. J. Brill, 1978.
Billerbeck, M. *Der Kyniker Demetrius: ein Beitrag zur Geschichte der frühkaiserzeitlichen Popularphilosophie*. Philosophia Antiqua 34; Leiden: E. J. Brill, 1979.
Bjerkelund, C. J. *Parakalô: Form, Funktion und Sinn der parakalô-Sätze in den paulinischen Briefen*. BTN 1; Oslo: Universitetsforlaget, 1967.
Black, David Alan. *Paul, Apostle of Weakness. Astheneia and its Cognates in the Pauline Literature*. New York: Peter Lang, 1984.
Bohmenblust, Gottfried. *Beiträge zum Topos ΠΕΡΙ ΦΙΛΙΑΣ*. Diss. Bern; Berlin: Gustav Schade (Otto Francke), 1905.

Bollack, M. Jean. "Les Maximes de l'Amitié," ACGB; Paris, Société d'Édition <Les Belles Lettres> (1969) 221–236.
Bonhöffer, Thomas. *Ursprung und Wesen der christlichen Seelsorge.* BEvT 95; München: Kaiser, 1985.
Bonner, Stanley F. *Education in Ancient Rome. From the Elder Cato to the Younger Pliny.* Berkeley/Los Angeles: University of California Press, 1977.
Booth, A. D. "Punishment, Discipline and Riot in the Schools of Antiquity," *EMC* 17 (1973) 107–114.
—— "Elementary and Secondary Education in the Roman Empire," *Florilegium* 1 (1979) 1–14.
—— "The Schooling of Slaves in First-Century Rome," *TAPA* 109 (1979) 11–19.
Bornkamm, G. "The Missionary Stance of Paul in I Corinthians 9 and in Acts," *Studies in Luke-Acts*. Eds. L. E. Keck and J. L. Martyn (Nashville, 1966), 194–207.
Bowers, Paul. "Paul and Religious Propaganda in the First Century," *NovT* 22.4 (1980) 316–323.
Bowersock, G. W. *Greek Sophists in the Roman Empire*. Oxford: Clarendon, 1969.
Branham, R. B. *Unruly Eloquence. Lucian and the Comedy of Traditions*. Cambridge, Mass.: Harvard University Press, 1989.
Brinckmann, Wolfgang. *Der Begriff der Freundschaft in Senecas Briefen*. Inaugural-Diss. dokt. Univ. Köln, 1963.
Brown, Peter. *The Body and Society: Men, Women and Sexual Renunciation in Early Christianity*. New York: Columbia University Press, 1988.
Brunt, J. C. "Rejected, ignored, or misunderstood? The fate of Paul's approach to the problem of food offered to idols in early Christianity," *NTS* 31 (1985) 113–24.
Brunt, P. A. "*Amicitia* in the Late Roman Republic," *PCPS* n.s. 11 (1965) 1–20.
Burgess, T. C. "Epideictic Literature," *The University of Chicago Studies in Classical Philology* 3. Chicago: The University of Chicago Press (1902) 89–261.
Burkert, W. *Lore and Science in Ancient Pythagoreanism*. Cambridge: Mass.: Harvard University Press, 1972.
Burns, J. McGregor. *Leadership*. New York: Harper & Row, 1978.
Büchner, W. "Über den Begriff der eironeia," *Hermes* 76 (1941) 339–41.
Bünker, Michael. *Briefformular und rhetorische Disposition im 1. Korintherbrief*. GTA 28; Göttingen: Vandenhoeck & Ruprecht, 1984.
Cadbury, H. J. "The Macellum of Corinth," *JBL* 53 (1934) 134–41.
Campenhausen, H. von. *Kirchliches Amt und geistliche Vollmacht in den ersten drei Jahrhunderten*. BHTh 14; Tübingen, 1953 (2nd ed. 1963).
Cancik, Hildegard. *Untersuchungen zu Senecas Epistulae Morales*. Spudasmata 18; Hildesheim: G. Olms, 1967.
Castner, C. J. "Epicurean Hetairai as Dedicants to Healing Divinities," *GRBS* 22 (1982) 51–57.
—— *Prosopography of the Roman Epicureans from the Second Century B.C. to the Second Century A.D.* Stud. z. kl. Phil 34; Frankfurt a. M., 1988.
Chadwick, Henry. "All Things to All Men (I Cor IX.22)," *NTS* 1 (1955) 261–75.
Chow, J. K. *Patronage and Power. A Study of Social Networks in Corinth*. JSNTSS 75; Sheffield: Sheffield Academic Press, 1992.
Clark, A. J. "Child and School in the Early Church," *CER* 66 (1968) 468–79.
Clarke, Andrew D. *Secular and Christian Leadership in Corinth. A Socio-Historical and Exegetical Study of 1 Corinthians 1–6*. AGJU 18. Leiden: E. J. Brill, 1993.
Clarke, M. L. *Higher Education in the Ancient World*. London: Routledge & Kegan Paul, 1971.
Clay, Diskin. *Lucretius and Epicurus*. Ithaca: Cornell University Press, 1983.
—— "The cults of Epicurus," *CErc* 16 (1986) 11–28.
—— "A Lost Epicurean Community," *GRBS* 30.2 (1989) 313–35.

Cohen, S. J. D. "Adolph Harnack's 'The Mission and Expansion of Judaism': Christianity Succeeds Where Judaism Fails," *The Future of Early Christianity. Essays in Honor of Helmut Koester* (ed. B. A. Pearson; Minneapolis: Fortress Press, 1991) 163–69.
Cole, R. W., ed. *Current Issues in Linguistic Theory.* Bloomington & London, 1977.
Conzelman, Hans. "Paulus und die Weisheit," *NTS* 12 (1965–66) 231–44.
——— *1 Corinthians. A Commentary on the First Epistle to the Corinthians.* Hermeneia; Philadelphia: Fortress Press, 1975.
Coune, Michel. "Le problème des idolothytes et l'éducation de la syneidêsis," *RSR* 51 (1963) 497–534.
Coyle, J. K. "The Exercise of Teaching in the Postapostolic Church," *EeT* 15 (1984) 23–43.
Cranfield, C. E. B. *A Critical and Exegetical Commentary on the Epistle to the Romans.* 2 Vols. ICC; Edinburgh: T. & T. Clark, 1975.
Crönert, Wilhelm. *Kolotes und Menedemos.* Studien zur Palaeographie und Papyruskunde VI; Leipzig, 1906; Amsterdam, 1965.
Daube, D. *The New Testament and Rabbinic Judaism.* London, 1956.
Davies, W. D. *Jewish and Pauline Studies.* London: SPCK, 1984.
Day, L. K. K. *The Intermediary World and Patterns of Perfection in Philo and Hebrews.* Missoula, MT, 1975.
Deissmann, G. Adolf. *Bible Studies.* Hendrickson Publ., 1988 [repr. from the T. & T. Clark, ed., 1901].
——— *Light from the Ancient East.* New York: Doran Press, 1927.
de Lacy, Phillip H. "The Patrons of Philodemus." *CP* 34 (1939) 59–65.
——— "Cicero's Invective against Piso," *TAPA* 72 (1941) 49–58.
Delling, G. "ἀναπληρόω," *TDNT* 6 (1968) 305–06.
——— "ἄρτιος, κτλ," *TDNT* 1 (1964) 475–76.
Desideri, P. *Dione di Prusa.* Messina, 1978.
Dibelius, M. James. *A Commentary on the Epistle of James.* Hermeneia; Philadelphia: Fortress Press, 1975.
Diels, Hermann. "Ein epikureischers Fragment über Götterverehrung," *Kleine Schriften zur Geschichte der Antiken Philosophie.* Ed. W. Burkert; Darmstadt, 1969.293–311.
Dihle, Albrect. "Ethik," *RAC* 6 (1966) cols. 646–796.
——— "Posidonius' System of Moral Philosophy," *JHS* 93 (1973) 50–57.
——— "Philosophie—Fachwissenschaft—Allgemeinbildung," *Aspects de la Philosophie Hellénistique.* Fondation Entretiens Hardt 32 (Geneva, 1986) 185–223.
Dill, S. *Roman Society from Nero to Marcus Aurelius.* London: Macmillan, 1904.
Dillon, John M. "Metriopatheia and Apatheia: Some Reflections on a Controversy in Later Greek Ethics," *Essays in Ancient Greek Philosophy.* Edd. by John P. Anton & Anthony Preus; Albany: State Univ. of New York Press, 1983. 2.508–517.
——— & A. A. Long (eds.), *The Question of "Eclecticism." Studies in Later Greek Philosophy.* Berkeley: University of California Press, 1988.
Doskocil, Walter. *Das Bann in der Urkirche, eine rechtsgeschichtliche Untersuchung.* MTS 3.11; 1958.
Dudley, D. R. *A History of Cynicism. From Diogenes to the 6th Century A.D.* London: Methuen & Co. Ltd., 1937.
Dunn, J. D. G. *Romans 1–8. Word Biblical Commentary. Volume 38A. Romans 9–16. Volume 38B.* Dallas, Texas: Word Books Publ., 1988.
Dupont, Jacques. "Syneidesis aux origines de la notion chrétienne de conscience morale," *Studia Hellenistica* 5 (1948) 119–53.
——— *Gnosis. La Connaissance religieuse dans les épîtres de saint Paul.* Paris: J. Gabalda, 1949.
——— "Appel aux faibles et aux forts dans la communauté Romaine (Rom. 14, 1–15, 13)," *Studiorum Paulinorum Congressus Internationalis Catholicus* 1961. AnBib 17, Rome: Pontificio Instituto Biblico, 1.357–66.

Duvernoy, J. F. "Le modèle médical de l'éthique dans l'épicurisme," *Justifications de l'éthique. XIXe Congrès de l'Association de Societés de philosophie de langue française*, Bruxelles-Louvain la Neuve 6–9 Sept. 1982 (Brussels, 1984) 171–77.

——— "Guérir par la philosophie (sur le modèle médical de l'éthique dans l'épicurisme)," *Revue de l'enseignemente philosophique* 34/5 (1984).

Eckstein, H.-J. *Der Begriff Syneidesis bei Paulus.* WUNT 2.10; Tübingen: Mohr, 1983.

Edelstein, L. *Ancient Medicine. Selected Papers of Ludwig Edelstein.* Ed. by O. Temkin & C. L. Temkin; Baltimore: Johns Hopkins University Press, 1987.

Ellison, H. L. "Paul and the Law—'All things to all men'," in *Apostolic History and the Gospel.* Eds. W. W. Gasque and R. P. Martin (The Paternoster Press, 1970) 195–202.

Engberg-Pedersen, Troels. "1 Corinthians 11:16 and the Character of Pauline Exhortation," *JBL* 110.1 (1991) 679–689.

——— ed. *Paul in His Hellenistic Context.* Edinburgh: T. & T. Clark, 1994.

Engels, Donald. *Roman Corinth. An Alternative Model for the Classical City.* Chicago and London: The University of Chicago, 1990.

Falco, V. de. "Appunti sul' Περὶ κολακείας' de Filodemo. Pap erc. 1675." *Rivista Indo-Greco-Italica* 10 (1926) 15–26.

Farrington, B. *The Faith of Epicurus.* London, 1967.

Festugière, André-Jean. *Epicurus and his Gods.* Oxford, 1955; repr. New York 1977.

——— "Lieux communs littéraires et thèmes de folk-lore dans l'Hagiographie primitive," *Wiener Studien. Zeitschrift für klassische Philologie* 73 (1960), 123–52.

Figueira, T. J., and G. Nagy, eds. *Theognis of Megara.* Baltimore, 1985.

Finley, M. I. *The Use and Abuse of History.* Rev. ed. Penguin Books, 1975.

——— *Ancient Slavery and Modern Ideology.* Penguin Books, 1980.

Fiore, Benjamin, S. J. "'Covert Allusion' in 1 Corinthians 1–4," *CBQ* 47 (1985) 85–102.

——— *The Function of Personal Example in the Socratic and Pastoral Epistles.* Analecta Biblica 105; Rome: Biblical Institute Press, 1986.

Fitzgerald, John T. *Cracks in an Earthen Vessel: An Examination of the Catalogues of Hardships in the Corinthian Correspondence.* SBLDS 99; Atlanta, Georgia: Scholars Press, 1988.

——— "Paul, the ancient epistolary theorists, and 2 Corinthians 10–13. The Purpose and Literary Genre of a Pauline Letter," in *Greeks, Romans, and Christians. Essays in Honor of Abraham J. Malherbe.* Ed. by D. L. Balch, E. Ferguson, and W. A. Meeks; Minneapolis: Fortress Press, 1990. 190–200.

——— ed. *Friendship, Flattery, and Frankness of Speech* (NovTSup; Leiden: E. J. Brill, forthcoming).

Forbes, Christopher. "Comparison, Self-Praise and Irony: Paul's Boasting and the Conventions of Hellenistic Rhetoric," *NTS* 32.1 (1986) 1–30.

Forkman, Göran. *The Limits of the Religious Community: Expulsion from the Religious Community within the Qumran Sect, within Rabbinic Judaism, and within Primitive Christianity.* Coniectanea Biblica, NT Series, 5; Lund: Gleerup, 1972.

Fortna, R. T. and B. R. Gaventa, edd. *The Conversation Continues. Studies in Paul & John. In Honor of J. Louis Martyn.* Nashville: Abingdon Press, 1990.

Foucault, Michel. *The Care of the Self.* The History of Sexuality, vol. 3. Trans. R. Hurley. New York: Vintage Books [Random House], 1988.

Frede, Michael. *Essays in Ancient Philosophy.* Minneapolis: University of Minnesota Press, 1987.

Fridrichsen, A. *The Apostle and his Message.* Uppsala, 1947.

Friedländer, L. *Darstellungen aus der Sittengeschichte Roms, in der Zeit von August bis Ausgang der Antonine.* 9th and 10th ed. by G. Wissowa; 4 vols. Leipzig: Hirzel, 1919–21.

Frischer, Bernard D. *The Sculpted Word. Epicureanism and Philosophical Recruitment in Ancient Greece.* Berkeley: University of California, 1982.

Fuchs, Gerhard. *Die Aussagen über die Freundschaft im Neuen Testament, verglichen mit denen des Aristoteles (Nic. Eth. 8/9).* Borna-Leipzig: Robert Noske, 1914.
Funk, R. W. "The Apostolic *Parousia*: Form and Significance," *Christian History and Interpretation: Studies Presented to John Knox.* Eds. W. R. Farmer, C. F. D. Moule and R. R. Niebuhr; Cambridge: Cambridge University, 1967), 249–68.
Funke, Hermann. "Antisthenes bei Paulus," *Hermes* 98 (1970) 459–71.
Furnish, Victor Paul. *II Corinthians. Translated with Introduction, Notes, and Commentary.* The Anchor Bible 32A; New York: Doubleday, 1984.
Gargiulo, T. "PHerc. 222: Filodemo sull'adulazione," *CErc* 11 (1981) 103–127.
Gaventa, B. R. "Apostles as Babes and Nurses in 1 Thessalonian 2:7," *Faith and History. Essays in Honor of Paul W. Meyer.* Edd. J. T. Carroll, C. H. Cosgrove, E. E. Johnson; Atlanta, Georgia: Scholars Press, 1990. 193–207
Georgi, Dieter. *The Opponents of Paul in Second Corinthians.* Philadelphia: Fortress Press, 1986.
Gerhard, G. A. *Phoinix von Kolophon.* Leipzig/Berlin: B. G. Teubner, 1909.
——— "Zur Legende vom Kyniker Diogenes," *ARW* 15 (1912) 388–408.
Geytenbeek, A. C. van. *Musonius Rufus and Greek Diatribe.* Revised ed., transl. by B. L. Hijmans, Jr. Assen: Royal VanGorcum Ltd., 1962.
Gigante, Marcello. "Philodème: Sur la liberté de parole," ACGB; Paris: Société d'Édition <Les Belles Lettres> (1969) 196–217.
——— "'Philosophia Medicans' in Filodemo," *CErc* 5 (1975) 53–61.
——— *Ricerche Filodemee.* Seconda edizione riveduta e accresciuta. Biblioteca della Parola del Passato, 6; Naples: Gaetano Macchiaroli Editore, 1983 (1969 (1)).
——— "La Biblioteca di Filodemo," *CErc* 15 (1985) 5–25.
——— *La Bibliothèque de Philodème et l'Épicurisme Romain.* Paris, 1987.
——— & G. Indelli. "Bione e l'Epicureismo," *CErc* 8 (1978) 124–31.
Gill, C. J. "The Question of Character-development: Plutarch and Tacitus," *CQ* 33 (1983) 469–87.
Glad, Clarence E. "Lestur og ritskýring 1. Korintubréfs 8. Deilur um kennsluaðferðir í Korintuborg," *Studia Theologica Islandica* 9 (1994) 55–106.
——— "The Significance of Hellenistic Psychagogy for Our Understanding of Paul," *Studia Theologica Islandica* 10 (1995, forthcoming).
——— "Frank Speech, Flattery, and Friendship in Philodemus," in John T. Fitzgerald (ed.), *Friendship, Flattery, and Frankness of Speech* (NovTSup; Leiden: E. J. Brill, forthcoming).
Glucker, John. *Antiochus and the Late Academy.* Hypomnemata 56; Göttingen: Vandenhoeck & Ruprecht, 1978.
Gooch, Paul W. "The Ethics of Accommodation: A Study in Paul," *TynBul* 29 (1978) 93–117.
——— "'Conscience' in 1 Corinthians 8 and 10," *NTS* 33 (1987) 244–54.
——— *Partial Knowledge. Philosophical Studies in Paul.* University of Notre Dame Press, 1987.
Goodenough, W. H. "Componential Analysis and the Study of Meaning," *Language* 32 (1956) 195–216.
Grant, R. M. *Greek Apologists of the Second Century.* Philadelphia: The Westminster Press, 1988.
Griffin, Miriam, and Jonathan Barnes, ed. *Philosophia Togata. Essays on Philosophy and Roman Society.* Oxford: Clarendon Press, 1989.
Grimal, Pierre. "L'Épicurisme romain," ACGB; Paris: Société d'Édition <Les Belles Lettres> (1969) 139–68.
Grube, G. M. A. "Theodorus of Gadara," *AJPh* 80.4 (1958) 337–65.
Grundmann, W. "Die NHΠIOI in der Urchristliche Paränese," *NTS* 5 (1959) 188–205.
Guerra, A. T. "Filodemo sulla Gratitudine," *CErc* 7 (1977) 96–113.
Gutierrez, Pedro. *La Paternité Spirituelle selon Saint Paul.* Paris: J. Gabalda, 1968.

Haber, L. L. *Prokope: Stoic Views on Moral Progress in the Context of Stoic Developmental Psychology*. Diss., University of California at Berkeley, 1973.
Hadot, Ilsetraut. *Seneca und die griechisch-römische Tradition der Seelenleitung*. QSGP 13; Berlin: Walter de Gruyter & Co., 1969.
───── "Epicure et l'enseignement philosophique hellenistique et romain," ACGB; Paris: Société d'Édition <Les Belles Lettres> (1969) 347–354.
───── *Arts Libéraux et Philosophie dans la Pensée Antique*. Paris: Études Augustiniennes, 1984.
───── "The Spiritual Guide," *Classical Mediterranean Spirituality Egyptian, Greek, Roman*. World Spirituality, Vol. 15; Ed. A. H. Armstrong; New York: Crossroad, 1986. 436–459.
Hadot, Pierre. *Exercices Spirituels et Philosophie Antique*. Deuxième édition revue et augmentée; Paris: Études Augustiniennes, 1987.
Hahm, D. E. "The Diaeretic Method and the Purpose of Arius' Doxography," *On Stoic and Peripatetic Ethics: The Work of Arius Didymus*. Ed. W. W. Fortenbaugh; New Brunswick, NJ: Transaction, 1983. 15–37.
Hainz, Josef. *Ekklesia. Strukturen paulinischer Gemeinde-Theologie und Gemeinde-Ordnung*. BU 9. Regensburg: Verlag Friedrich Pustet, 1972.
Hall, J. *Lucian's Satire*. New York, 1981.
Harder, G. "στηρίζω, κτλ.", *TDNT* 7 (1971) 653–57.
Hartlich, Paulus. *De Exhortationum a Graecis Romanisque Scriptarum Historia et Indole*. Leipziger Studien zur Classischen Philologie, 11.2; Leipzig: S. Hirzel, 1889.
Hays, R. B. "Christology and Ethics in Galatians: The Law of Christ," *CBQ* 49.2 (1987) 268–290.
Heinrici, G. *Der erste Brief an die Korinther*. MeyerK 5; 8th ed.; Göttingen: Vandenhoeck & Ruprecht, 1896.
───── *Der zweite Brief an die Korinther*. MeyerK 6; 8th ed.; Göttingen: Vandenhoeck & Ruprecht, 1900.
Helm, R. *Lucian und Menipp*. Leipzig/Berlin: B. G. Teubner, 1906.
Héring, J. *La première épître de Saint Paul aux Corinthiens*. CNT 7; Neuchâtel/Paris: Delachaux & Niestlé, 1949.
Heylbut, G. *De Theophrasti libris Περὶ φιλίας*. Bonner Dissertation, 1876.
Hijmans, B. L. *Askesis. Notes on Epictetus' Educational System*. Assen: Van Gorcum, 1959.
Hock, R. F. *The Social Context of Paul's Ministry: Tentmaking and Apostleship*. Philadelphia: Fortress Press, 1980.
───── "'By the Gods, It's My One Desire to See an Actual Stoic': Epictetus' Relations with Students and Visitors in His Personal Network," *Semeia* 56; ed. L. Michael White; Scholars Press, 1992. 121–142.
Hoïstad, R. *Cynic Hero and Cynic King. Studies in the Cynic Conception of Man*. Uppsala, 1948.
Hollander, Harm W. *Joseph as an Ethical Model in the Testaments of the Twelve Patriarchs*. SVTP 6; Leiden: E. J. Brill, 1981.
───── and M. de Jonge (eds.). *The Testaments of the Twelve Patriarchs. A Commentary*. SVTP 8; Leiden: E. J. Brill, 1985.
Holmberg, Bengt. *Paul and Power: The Structure of Authority in the Primitive Church as Reflected in the Pauline Epistles*. Lund, 1978.
Horowits, M. "Modes of Representation of Thought." *Journal of the American Psychological Association* 20 (1972), 793–819.
Horsley, R. A. "Pneumatikos vs. Psychikos: Distinctions of Spiritual Status among the Corinthians," *HTR* 69 (1976) 269–288.
───── "Wisdom of Word and Words of Wisdom in Corinth," *CBQ* 39 (1977) 224–39.
───── "'How can some of you say there is no resurrection of the dead?' Spiritual Elitism in Corinth," *NovT* 20 (1978) 203–31.
───── "Consciousness and Freedom among the Corinthians: 1 Corinthians 8–10," *CBQ* 40 (1978) 574–89.
───── "Gnosis in Corinth: 1 Cor 8.1–6," *NTS* 27 (1981) 32–51.

Howe, H. M. "Amafinius, Lucretius, and Cicero," *AJPh* 77 (1951) 57–62.
Hugedé, Norbert. *La Métaphore du Miroir dans les Épîtres de Saint Paul aux Corinthiens*. Paris/Neuchâtel: Delachaux et Niestlé S. A., 1949.
Hunter, R. L. "Horace on Friendship and Free Speech (Epistles 1.18 and Satires 1.4)," *Hermes* 113 (1985) 480–90.
Hurd, Jr., J. C. *The Origin of 1 Corinthians*. New York: Seabury Press, 1965.
Hyldahl, Niels. "The Corinthian 'Parties' and the Corinthian Crisis," *Studia Theologica* 45 (1991) 19–32.
Ihm, M., "Zu Philodem Περὶ κολακείας," *Rh. Mus.* 51 (1896) 315–318.
Ingenkamp, Heinz Gerd. *Plutarchs Schriften über die Heilung der Seele*. Hypomnemata Heft 34; Göttingen: Vandenhoeck & Ruprecht, 1971.
Jaeger, H. "Parrhesia et fiducia, Étude spirituelle des mots," *Studia Patristica* I, 1 (1957) 221–39.
Jaeger, Werner. *Paideia. The Ideals of Greek Culture*. Vols. 1–3; New York/Oxford: Oxford University Press, 1939–1944.
——— *Early Christianity and Greek Paideia*. Cambridge, Mass.: Harvard University Press, 1961.
Jensen, C. "Ariston von Keos bei Philodem," *Hermes* 46 (1911) 393–406.
——— "Die Bibliothek von Herculaneum," *Bonner Jahrbücher* 135 (1930) 49–61.
——— *Ein neuer Brief Epikurs*. Berlin: Weidmannsche Buchhandlung, 1933.
Jeremias, Joachim. "Zur Gedankenführung in den paulinischen Briefen," in J. N. Sevenster and W. C. van Unnik, eds., *Studia Paulina in honorem Johannis de Zwaan septuagenarii*. Haarlem: De Erven F. Bohn, 1953. 146–154.
Jewett, Robert. *Paul's Anthropological Terms. A Study of their Use in Conflict Settings*. Leiden: E. J. Brill, 1971.
Johann, Horst-Theodor, hrsg. *Erziehung und Bildung in der Heidnischen und Christlichen Antike*. Darmstadt: Wissenschaftliche Buchgesellschaft, 1976.
Joly, Robert. *Le vocabulaire chrétien de l'amour est-il original? Φιλεῖν et Ἀγαπᾶν dans le grec antique*. Brussels: Presses Universitaires de Bruxelles, 1968. 2nd ed. 1971.
Jones, Howard. *The Epicurean Tradition*. London and New York: Routledge, 1989.
Joos, M. "Semantic Axiom Number One." *Language* 47 (1972) 258–265.
Jordan, Mark D. "Ancient Philosophic Protreptic and the Problem of Persuasive Genres." *Rhetorica* 4 (1986) 309–333.
Judge, Edwin A. "The Early Christians as a Scholastic Community," *JRH* 1 (1960) 4–15; 2 (1961) 125–137.
——— "St. Paul and Classical Society," *JAC* 15 (1972) 19–36.
——— "Paul as a Radical Critic of Society," *Interchange* 16 (1974) 191–203.
——— "The Reaction Against Classical Education in the New Testament," *Journal of Christian Education Papers* 77 (1983) 7–14.
——— "Cultural Conformity and Innovation in Paul," *TynBul* 35 (1984) 3–24.
Jungkuntz, Richard. *Epicureanism and the Church Fathers*. Diss. Univ. of Wisconsin. Ann Arbor, Mich., 1961.
——— "Fathers, Heretics and Epicureans," *JEH* 17 (1966) 3–10.
Käsemann, Ernst. "Die Legitimität des Apostels. Eine Untersuchung zu II Korinther 10–13," *ZNW* 41 (1942) 33–71.
Kahrstedt, U. *Kulturgeschichte der römischen Kaiserzeit*. Bern: Francke, 1958 (2).
Kakridis, T. "Die Bedeutung von πολύτροπος in der Odyssee," *Glotta* 11 (1921) 288–91.
Kaster, Robert A. "Notes on 'Primary' and 'Secondary' Schools in Late Antiquity," *TAPA* 113 (1983) 323–46.
Kennedy, George. *The Art of Persuasion in Greece*. Princeton, New Jersey: Princeton University Press, 1963.
Kerferd, G. B. "Two Problems Concerning Impulses," *On Stoic and Peripatetic Ethics: The Work of Arius Didymus*. Ed. W. W. Fortenbaugh; New Brunswick, NJ: Transaction, 1983. 87–93.

Kertelge, K. ed. *Das Kirchliche Amt im Neuen Testament.* Darmstadt: Wissenschaftliche Buchgesellschaft, 1977.
Kidd, I. G. "Moral actions and rules in Stoic ethics," In *The Stoics*, ed. J. M. Rist. Berkeley/London, 1978. 247–58.
────── "Euemptosia-Proneness to Disease," In *On Stoic and Peripatetic Ethics: The Work of Arius Didymus.* Ed. W. W. Fortenbaugh; New Brunswick, NJ: Transaction, 1983. 107–17.
Kindstrand, J. F. "Demetrius the Cynic., *Philologus* 124 (1980) 83–98.
King, J. M. "Patterns of Enculturation in Communal Society," *The Anthropological Study of Education.* Ed. C. J. Calhoun and F. A. J. Ianni; The Hague and Paris, 1976. 75–104.
Kitzberger, I. *Bau der Gemeinde: Das paulinische Wortfeld οἰκοδομή/ (ἐπ)οἰκοδομεῖν.* FB 53; Würzburg: Echter, 1986.
Knögel, W. *Der Peripatetiker Ariston von Keos bei Philodem.* Leipzig, 1933.
Köhler, L. *Die Briefe des Sokrates und der Sokratiker herausgegeben, übersetzt und kommentiert.* Philologus suppl. B. 20, 2; Leipzig: Dieterich, 1928.
Körte, A. "Augusteer bei Philodem." *Rh. Mus.* 45 (1890) 172–77.
Kondo, Eiko. "I 'Caratteri' di Theofrasto nei Papiri Ercolanesi," *CErc* 1 (1971) 73–87.
────── "Per l'interpretazione del pensiero filodemeo sulla adulazione nel PHerc. 1457," *CErc* 4 (1974) 43–56.
Konstan, D. *Some Aspects of Epicurean Psychology.* Leiden: E. J. Brill, 1973.
────── "Frankness, Flattery and Friendship," in John T. Fitzgerald (ed.), *Friendship, Flattery, and Frankness of Speech* (NovTSup; Leiden: E. J. Brill, forthcoming).
Koskenniemi, Heikki. *Studien zur Idee und Phraseologie des griechischen Briefes bis 400 n.Chr.* Annales Academiae Scientiarum Fennicae; ser. B; vol. 102.2. Helsinki: Suomalaisen Kirjallisuuden Kerjapaino, 1956.
Kuck, D. W. *Judgment and Community Conflict. Paul's Use of Apocalyptic Judgment Language in 1 Corinthians 3:5–4:5.* NovTSup 66; Leiden: E. J. Brill, 1992.
Kümmel, W. G. *Introduction to the New Testament.* London, 1975
La Bonnardière, A.-M., "Portez les fardeaux les uns des autres: exégèse augustinienne de Gal. 6:2," *Didaskalia* I (1971) 201–15.
Lain-Entralgo, P. *The Therapy of the Word in Classical Antiquity.* New Haven, CT/ London: Yale University Press, 1970.
Lampe, G. W. H. "Church Discipline and the Interpretation of the Epistles to the Corinthians," *Christian History and Interpretation: Studies presented to John Knox.* Eds. W. R. Farmer, C. F. D. Moule, R. R. Niebuhr; Cambridge: Cambridge University, 1967. 337–61.
Lang, F. *Die Briefe an die Korinther.* NTD 7. Göttingen: Vandenhoeck & Ruprecht, 1968.
Lausberg, Heinrich. *Handbuch der literarischen Rhetorik. Eine Grundlegung der Literaturwissenschaft.* 2 vols. 2nd rev. ed. München: Max Hueber, 1973.
Leivestad, Ragnar. "'The Meekness and Gentleness of Christ' II Cor X.1," *NTS* 13 (1964) 156–64.
Liebich, W. *Aufbau, Absicht, und Form der Pragmateiai Philodems.* Berlin, 1960.
Liefeld, W. *The Wandering Preacher as a Social Figure in the Roman Empire.* Diss., Columbia University. Ann Arbor: University Microfilms, 1967.
Lightfoot, J. B. *The Epistle of St. Paul to the Galatians.* Grand Rapids: Zondervan, 1976.
Lim, Timothy H. "'Not in Persuasive Words of Wisdom, but in the Demonstration of the Spirit and Power'," *NovT* 29.2 (1987) 137–149.
Lindblom, J. "Zur Begriff 'Anstoss' im Neuen Testament," *Strena Philologica Upsaliensis* (1922) 1–6.
Linde, P. "Homerische Selbsterläuterungen." *Glotta* 13 (1924) 223–24.
Long, Anthony A. "Pleasure and Social Utility—The Virtues of Being Epicurean," *Aspects de la Philosophie Hellénistique*, Entretiens Fondation Hardt 32 (Geneva, 1986), 282–316 (Discussion, 317–324).

―――― "Socrates in Hellenistic Philosophy," *CQ* 38.1, n.s. (1988) 150–71.
Longo Auricchio, F. "La scuola di Epicuro," *CErc* 8 (1978) 21–37.
―――― "Sulla Concezione Filodemea dell'Adulazione," *CErc* 16 (1986) 79–91.
―――― and Tepedino Guerra, A. "Aspetti e problemi della dissidenza epicurea," *CErc* 11 (1981) 25–40.
Lüdemann, Gerd. *Paul, Apostle to the Gentiles: Studies in Chronology*. Transl. F. Stanley Jones; Philadelphia: Fortress Press, 1984.
Lührmann, Dieter. "Freundschaftsbrief trotz Spannungen. Zu Gattung und Aufbau des Ersten Korintherbriefes," *Studien zum Text und zur Ethik des Neuen Testaments. Festschrift zum 80. Geburtstag von Heinrich Greeven*. Hrsg. W. Schrage; Berlin/New York: Walter de Gruyter, 1986. 298–314.
Lütgert, W. *Freiheitspredigt und Schwarmgeister in Korinth. Ein Beitrag zur Charakteristik der Christuspartei*. BFCT XII, 3; Gütersloh: Bertelsmann, 1908.
Lund, N. W. *Chiasmus in the New Testament. A Study in the Form and Function of Chiastic Structures*. Peabody, MA: Hendrickson Pub., 1992.
Lutz, Cora E. "Musonius Rufus 'The Roman Socrates'," *YClS* 10 (1947) 1–147.
Lyons, J. *Language and Linguistics*. Cambridge, 1981.
MacMullen, Ramsay. *Enemies of the Roman Order*. Cambridge, Mass.: Harvard University Press, 1966.
Mack, Burton L. & Vernon K. Robbins, *Patterns of Persuasion in the Gospels*. Sonoma, California: Polebridge Press, 1989.
Malherbe, Abraham J. *Social Aspects of Early Christianity*. Second Ed. Enlarged. Philadelphia: Fortress Press, 1983.
―――― *Moral Exhortation. A Greco-Roman Sourcebook*. Philadelphia: The Westminster Press, 1986.
―――― *Paul and the Thessalonians. The Philosophic Tradition of Pastoral Care*. Philadelphia: Fortress Press, 1987.
―――― *Paul and the Popular Philosophers*. Minneapolis: Fortress Press, 1989.
―――― "Greco-Roman Religion and Philosophy and the New Testament," *The New Testament and its Modern Interpreters*. Ed. by E. J. Epp and G. W. MacRae; Atlanta: Scholars Press, 1989. 3–26.
―――― "Hellenistic Moralists and the New Testament," ANRW 2.26.1; Berlin/New York: de Gruyter, 1992. 267–333.
―――― "Determinism and Free Will in Paul: The Argument of 1 Corinthians 8 and 9," *Paul in His Hellenistic Context*. Ed. Troels Engberg-Pedersen. Edinburgh: T. & T. Clark, 1994. 231–55.
Malina, Bruce J. *The New Testament World: Insights from Cultural Anthropology*. Atlanta, 1981.
Maly, Karl. *Mündige Gemeinde. Untersuchungen zur pastoralen Führung des Apostels Paulus im 1. Korintherbrief*. SBM 2; Stuttgart: Katholische Bibelwerk, 1967.
Markantonato, G. "On the Origin and Meanings of the Word εἰρωνεία," *Riv. Filol. Istr. Cl.* 103 (1975) 16–18.
Marrou, Henri Irénée. *Histoire de l'éducation dans l'antiquité*. Paris, 1948.
Marshall, Peter. *Enmity in Corinth: Social Conventions in Paul's Relations with the Corinthians*. WUNT 23; Tübingen: J. C. B. Mohr (Paul Siebeck), 1987.
Martin, Dale B. *Slavery as Salvation. The Metaphor of Slavery in Pauline Christianity*. New London and London: Yale University Press, 1990.
Martin, J. *Antike Rhetorik: Technik und Methode*. Handbuch der Altertumswissenschaft II, 3; Münich: Beck, 1974.
Martin, R. P. "The Opponents of Paul in 2 Corinthians: An Old Issue Revisited," *Tradition and Interpretation in the New Testament. Essays in Honor of E. Earle Ellis*; Ed. G. F. Hawthorne with O. Betz; Grand Rapids: Wm B. Eerdmans/Tübingen: J. C. B. Mohr [Paul Siebeck], 1987. 281–87.
Martínez, Florentino García. *The Dead Sea Scrolls Translated. The Qumran Texts in English*. Transl. by Wilfred G. E. Watson. Leiden: E. J. Brill, 1994.
Maslowski, T. "The Chronology of Cicero's Anti-Epicureanism," *Eos* 62 (1974) 55–78.

———— "Cicero, Philodemus, Lucretius," *Eos* 66 (1978) 215–226.
McKnight, S. *A Light among the Gentiles. Jewish Missionary Activity in the Second Temple Period.* Minneapolis: Fortress Press, 1990.
Meeks, Wayne A. "'Since Then You Would Need To Go Out Of The World': Group Boundaries in Pauline Christianity," *Critical History and Biblical Faith: New Testament Perspectives* (ed. T. J. Ryan; Villanova, Pa.: College Theology Society, 1979) 4–29.
———— *The First Urban Christians. The Social World of the Apostle Paul.* New Haven and London: Yale University Press, 1983.
———— "Judgment and the Brother: Romans 14:1–15:13," *Tradition and Interpretation in the New Testament. Essays in Honor of E. Earle Ellis.* Ed. G. F. Hawthorne with Otto Betz; Grand Rapids: Wm. B. Eerdmans; Tübingen: J. C. B. Mohr [Paul Siebeck], 1987. 290–300.
———— "The Polyphonic Ethics of the Apostle Paul," *The Annual of the Society of Christian Ethics* (1988) 17–29.
Mendelson, Alan. *Secular Education in Philo of Alexandria.* Cincinnati: Hebrew Union College Press, 1982.
Méndez, E. A. "PHerc. 1089: Filodemo 'Sobre la Adulación'," *CErc* 13 (1983) 121–38.
Meyer, H. A. W. *Die Paulus erster Brief an die Korinther.* MeyerK 5; Göttingen: Vandenhoeck & Ruprecht, 1856.
Michels, A. K. "Παρρησία and the Satire of Horace," *CP* 39 (1944) 173–77.
Minar, E. L. "Pythagorean Communism," *TAPA* 75 (1944) 34–46.
Mitchell, Alan C. "Rich and Poor in the Courts of Corinth: Litigiousness and Status in 1 Corinthians 6.1–11," *NTS* 39 (1993), 562–586.
Mitchell, Margaret M. "Concerning ΠΕΡΙ ΔΕ in 1 Corinthians," *NovT* 31.3 (1989) 229–256.
———— *Paul and the Rhetoric of Reconciliation: An Exegetical Investigation of the Language and Composition of 1 Corinthians.* HUT 28; Tübingen: Mohr-Siebeck, 1991.
———— "New Testament Envoys in the Context of Greco-Roman Diplomatic and Epistolary Conventions: The Example of Timothy and Titus," *JBL* 111.4 (1992) 641–62.
Mitsis, P. *Epicurus' Ethical Theory. The Pleasures of Invulnerability.* Ithaca and London: Cornell University Press, 1988.
Moles, J. L. "The Career and Conversion of Dio Chrysostom," *JHS* 98 (1978) 79–100.
———— "'*Honestius Quam Ambitiosius?*'—an Exploration of the Cynic's Attitude to Moral Corruption in his Fellow Men," *JHS* 103 (1983), 103–23.
Momigliano, A. D. Review of *Science and Politics in the Ancient World* by B. Farrington, *Journal of Roman Studies* 31 (1941), 149–157 (repr. in *Secondo contributo alla storia degli studi classici*, Rome, 1960, 375–388).
Müller, K. *Anstoss und Gericht: Eine Studie zum jüdischen Hintergrund des paulinischen Skandalon-Begriffs.* Münich, 1969.
Munck, Johannes. *Paul and the Salvation of Mankind.* Atlanta: John Knox Press, 1977.
Murphy O'Connor, J. "I Cor. VIII, 6: Cosmology or Soteriology?" *RB* 85.2 (1978) 253–67.
———— "Freedom or the Ghetto (I Cor viii, 1–13; x, 23–xi, 1)," *RB* 85.4 (1978) 543–74.
———— "Corinthian Slogans in 1 Cor 6:12–20," *CBQ* 40 (1978) 391–96.
———— "Food and Spiritual Gifts in 1 Cor 8:8," *CBQ* 41.2 (1979) 292–298.
———— "'Being at Home in the Body we are in Exile from the Lord' (2 Cor 5:6b)," *RB* 93.2 (1986) 214–21.
———— "Pneumatikoi and Judaizers in 2 Cor 2:14–4:6," *ABR* 34 (1986) 42–58.
———— "Pneumatikoi in 2 Corinthians," *PIBA* 11 (1988) 59–66.
———— "Philo and 2 Cor 6:14–7:1," *RB* 95.1 (1988) 55–69.
———— "Another Jesus (2 Cor 11:4)," *RBi* 97.2 (1990) 238–251.

Nagy, G. *The Best of the Achaeans. Concepts of the Hero in Archaic Greek Poetry*. Baltimore: Johns Hopkins University Press, 1979.
Neymeyr, Ulrich. *Die Christlichen Lehrer im Zweiten Jahrhundert. Ihre Lehrtätigkeit, ihr Selbstverständnis und ihre Geschichte*. VCSup 4; Leiden: E. J. Brill, 1989.
Newman, Robert J. "*Cotidie meditare*. Theory and Practice of the *meditatio* in Imperial Stoicism," ANRW 36.3; Berlin-New York: Walter de Gruyter, 1989. 1473–1517.
Nickelsburg, G. W. E. ed. *Studies in the Testament of Joseph*. SBLSCS 5; Missoula: Scholars Press, 1975.
Nilsson, Martin P. *Die Hellenistische Schule*. München: C. H. Beck, 1955.
Nock, Arthur Darby. *Early Gentile Christianity and its Hellenistic Background*. New York: Harper Torchbooks, 1964.
Nolland, J. "Classical and Rabbinic Parallels to 'Physician, heal yourself' (Lk. IV 23)," *NovT* 21.3 (1979), 193–209.
Norden, Eduard. "Beiträge zur Geschichte der griechischen Philosophie," *Jahrbücher für classische Philologie* Supplementband 19, 2 (1893) 368–462.
―――― *Agnostos Theos*. Darmstadt, 1956.
Nussbaum, Martha C. "Therapeutic Arguments: Epicurus and Aristotle," in *The Norms of Nature. Studies in Hellenistic Ethics*, edited by Malcolm Schofield and Gisela Striker. Cambridge University Press, 1986. 31–74.
―――― *The Therapy of Desire. Theory and Practice in Hellenistic Ethics*. Princeton, New Jersey: Princeton University Press, 1994.
Obbink, D. D. "POxy. 215 and Epicurean Religious Theôría," *Atti del XVII Congresso Internz. di Papirologica*, Vol. II (1984) 607–19.
Obens, W. *Qua aetate Socratis et Socraticorum epistulae, quae dicuntur, scriptae sunt*. Münster i. W. Aschendorff, 1912.
O'Brien, P. T. *Introductory Thanksgivings in the Letters of Paul*. NovTSup 49; Leiden: E. J. Brill, 1977.
O'Connor, D. K. "The Invulnerable Pleasure of Epicurean Friendship," *GRBS* 30.2 (1989) 165–86.
Oden, Thomas C. *Care of Souls in the Classic Tradition*. Philadelphia: Fortress, 1984.
Olivier, Frank. "ΣΥΝΑΠΟΘΝΗΣΚΩ; d'un article de lexique a Saint Paul, 2 Cor 7:3," *Revue de théologie et de philosophie* 17 (1929), 103–33.
Ollrog, Wolf-Henning. *Paulus und seine Mitarbeiter*. Neukirchen-Vluyn, 1979.
Olson, Stanley N. "Epistolary Uses of Expressions of Self-Confidence," *JBL* 103.4 (1984) 585–97.
Oster, Richard E., Jr. "Use, Misuse and Neglect of Archaeological Evidence in Some Modern Works on 1 Corinthians (1 Cor 7, 1–5; 8, 10; 11, 2–16; 12, 14–26)," *ZNW* 83.1/2 (1992) 52–73.
Pagels, E. H. *The Gnostic Paul. Gnostic Exegesis of the Pauline Letters*. Philadelphia: Fortress Press, 1975.
―――― *The Gnostic Gospels*. New York: Vintage Books, 1989.
Painter, J. "Paul and the Πνευματικοί at Corinth," *Paul and Paulinism. Essays in Honour of C. K. Barrett*. Eds. M. D. Hooker and S. G. Wilson; London: SPCK, 1982. 237–50.
Paratore, E. "La problematica sull'epicureismo a Roma," ANRW 1.4; Berlin-New York: de Gruyter, 1973. 116–204.
Pavlovskis, Z. "Aristotle, Horace and the Ironic Man," *CP* 63 (1968) 312–19.
Pearson, B. A. *The Pneumatikos-Psychikos Terminology in 1 Corinthians. A Study in the Theology of the Corinthian Opponents of Paul and Its Relation to Gnosticism*. SBLDS 12. Missoula, MT, 1973.
Perdue, L. G., and J. G. Gammie, eds. *Paraenesis: Act and Form. Semeia 50*. Society of Biblical Literature, 1990.
Peristiay, J. G., ed. *Honour and Shame: The Values of Mediterranean Society* Chicago: University of Chicago Press, 1966.
Petersen, Norman R. *Rediscovering Paul. Philemon and the Sociology of Paul's Narrative World*. Philadelphia: Fortress Press, 1985.

Peterson, Erik. *ΕΙΣ ΘΕΟΣ*. Göttingen: Vandenhoeck & Ruprecht, 1926.
——— "Zur Bedeutungsgeschichte von Παρρησία," *Reinhold Seeberg-Festschrift*, Vol. I. Zur Theorie des Christentums. Ed. by Wilhelm Koerr; Leipzig: Scholl, 1929. 283–297.
Philippson, Robert. "Die Rechtsphilosophie der Epikureer," *Archiv für Geschichte der Philosophie* 23 (1910) 433–46.
——— Review of Olivieri's ed. of Philodemus' Περὶ παρρησίας. *Berliner Philologische Wochenschrift* (1916) cols. 677–688.
——— "Philodems Buch Über den Zorn," *Rh. Mus.* 71 (1916) 425–60.
——— "Philodemos," *Realencyclopädie* 19.2 (1938) cols. 2444–2482.
——— "Papyrus Herculanensis 831," *AJP* 64 (1943) 148–162 = idem, *Sudien zu Epikur und den Epikureern*, 1983. 284–298 [Transl. by Dr. Philip de Lacy].
Pierce, C. A. *Conscience in the New Testament*. SBT 15; London: SCM Press, 1955.
Pigeaud, J. *La maladie de l'âme. Étude sur la relation de l'âme et du corps dans la tradition médico-philosophique antique.* Paris, 1981.
Plessis, P. J. du. *ΤΕΛΕΙΟΣ. The Idea of Perfection in the New Testament*. Kampen: J. H. Kok, 1959.
Price, A. W. *Love and Friendship in Plato and Aristotle*. Oxford: Clarendon Press, 1989.
Rabbow, Paul. *Antike Schriften über Seelenheilung und Seelenleitung auf ihre Quellen untersucht*. Vol. 1, *Die Therapie des Zorns*. Leipzig, 1914.
——— *Seelenführung. Methodik der Exerzitien in der Antike*. München: Kösel, 1954.
Rabel, R. J. "Diseases of the soul in Stoic psychology." *GRBS* 22 (1981) 386–93.
Rauer, M. *Die 'Schwachen' in Korinth und Rom nach den Paulusbriefen*. BibS (F) 21, 2/3. Freiburg im Breisgau: Herder, 1923.
Reitzenstein, R. *Die hellenistischen Mysterienreligionen*. Stuttgart: Teubner, 1927.
Renehan, Robert. "Classical Greek Quotations in the New Testament," *The Heritage of the Early Church. Essays in honor of Georges Vasilievich Florovsky*. Eds. D. Neiman & M. Schatkin; Roma: Pont. Instit. Stud. orientalium, 1973. 17–46.
Ribbeck, Otto. "Über den Begriff des εἴρων," *RhM* 31 (1876) 381–400.
——— *ALAZON. Ein Beitrag zur antiken Ethologie*. Leipzig: Teubner, 1882.
——— "*KOLAX*. Eine Ethologische Studie," Abhandlungen der philologisch-historischen Klasse der Kgl.-Sächsischen Gesellschaft der Wissenschaften 9 (1884) 1–114.
Richardson, Peter. "Early Christian Sources of an Accommodation Ethic—From Jesus to Paul," *TynBul* 29 (1978) 118–142.
——— "Pauline Inconsistency: 1 Corinthians 9:19–23 and Galatians 2:11–14," *NTS* 26 (1980) 347–62.
Riley, M. T. "The Epicurean Criticism of Socrates," *Phoenix* 34 (1980) 63–66.
Rist, J. M. "Epicurus on Friendship," *CP* 75.2 (1980) 121–29.
Rodis-Lewis, Geneviève. *Épicure et son école*. Paris, 1975.
Rohrbaugh, Richard L. "Methodological Considerations in the Debate over the Social Class Status of Early Christians," *JAAR* 52.3 (1984) 519–46.
——— "'Social Location of Thought' as a Heuristic Construct in New Testament Study," *JSNT* 30 (1987) 103–19.
Rydbeck, Lars. *Fachprosa, Vermeintliche Volkssprache und Neues Testament. Zur Beurteilung der sprachlichen Niveauunterschiede im nachklassischen Griechisch*. Acta Universitatis Upsaliensis. Studia Graeca Upsaliensia 5; Lund: Berlingska Boktryckeriet, 1967.
Saller, R. *Personal Patronage under the Early Empire*. Cambridge: Cambridge University Press, 1982.
Saussure, F. de. *Course in General Linguistics*. London: Fontana/Collins, 1974.
Sbordone, Francesco. "Il Quadrifarmaco Epicureo," *CErc* 13 (1983) 117–19.
Scarpat, Guiseppe. *Parrhesia. Storia del termine e delle sue traduzioni in Latino*. Brescia: Paideia, 1964.
Schächter, R. "Philodemus quid de psychagogia docuerit," *Eos* 30 (1927), 170–73.
Schenkeveld, D. M. "Hoi kritikoi in Philodemus," *Mnemosyne* 21 (1968) 176–215.

Schlüchter, W. ed., *Max Webers Sicht des antiken Christentums*. Frankfurt, 1985.
Schmid, Wolfgang M. "Contritio und 'ultima linea rerum' in neuen Epikureischen Texten," *Rh. Mus.* N. F. 100 (1957), pp. 301–27.
——— "Epikur," *RAC* 5 (1962) cols. 681–819.
Schmithals, W. *Die Gnosis in Korinth: Eine Untersuchung zu den Korintherbriefen*. FRLANT 66 [NF 48]. Göttingen: Vandenhoeck & Ruprecht, 1959 (3); ET: *Gnosticism in Corinth*. Nashville: Abingdon, 1971.
Schmitz-Stählin. "παρακαλέω, παράκλησις," *TDNT* 5 (1967) 773–99.
Schneider, J. "σχῆμα, μετασχηματίζω," *TDNT* 7 (1971), pp. 954–58.
Scholes, R. *Protocols of Reading*. New Haven: Yale University Press, 1989.
Schrijvers, P. H. "Eléments psychagogiques dans l'oeuvre de Lucrèce," ACGB; Paris: Société d'Édition <Les Belles Lettres> (1969) 370–376.
Schütz, John Howard. *Paul and the Anatomy of Apostolic Authority*. SNTSMS 26; Cambridge: Cambridge University Press, 1975.
Sedley, David. "Epicurus, On Nature Book XXVIII," *CErc* 3 (1973) 5–83.
Sergiovanni, Thomas J., and Robert J. Starratt. *Supervision. Human Perspectives*. New York: McGraw-Hill Publishing Company, 1988 (4).
Sevenster, J. N. "Waarom spreekt Paulus nooit van vrienden en vriendschap?" *Nederlands Theologisch Tijdschrift* 9 (1954/55) 356–363.
——— *Paul and Seneca*. NovTSup 4; Leiden: E. J. Brill, 1961.
Shanor, Jay. "Paul as Master Builder. Construction Terms in First Corinthians," *NTS* 34 (1988) 461–71.
Simpson, Adelaide D. "Epicureans, Christians, Atheists in the Second Century," *TAPA* 72 (1941) 372–81.
Smolders, D. "L'audace de l'apôtre selon saint Paul, La thème de la parrêsia," *Collectanea Mechliniensia* 43, N. S. 28, 1958, 16–30, 117–133.
Snell, B. *The Discovery of the Mind in Greek Philosophy and Literature*. New York: Dover Publications, Inc., 1982.
Soden, Hans von. "Sakrament und Ethik bei Paulus," *Urchristentum und Geschichte*; Tübingen: Mohr, 1951. 239–75.
Spicq, Ceslas. "La conscience dans le Nouveau Testament." *RB* 47 (1938) 50–80.
Spina, L. "Il trattato di Filodemo su Epicuro e altri (PHerc. 1418)," *CErc* 7 (1977) 43–83.
Stanford, W. B. *The Ulysses Theme. A Study in the Adaptability of a Traditional Hero*. 2nd ed. revised; New York: Barnes and Noble, 1968.
Stanton, G. R. "Sophists and Philosophers: Problems of Classification," *American Journal of Philosophy* 94 (1973), 350–64.
Stählin, G. "παραμυθέομαι, κτλ," *TDNT* 5 (1967), pp. 816–18.
Ste. Croix, M. de. *The Class Struggle in the Ancient Greek World, from the Archaic Age to the Arab Conquests*. Ithaca: Cornell University Press, 1981.
Stegemann, W. "Theon." PW, RE 5A (1934), cols. 2037–54.
Stelzenberger, J. *Syneidesis im Neuen Testament*. Paderborn, 1961.
Stowers, Stanley Kent. "A 'Debate' over Freedom: 1 Corinthians 6.12–20," *Christian Teaching: Studies in Honor of LeMoine G. Lewis*; ed. Everett Ferguson; Abilene, TX: Abilene Christian University, 1981. 59–71.
——— *The Diatribe and Paul's Letter to the Romans*. SBLDS 57; Chico: Scholars Press, 1981.
——— "Social Status, Public Preaching and Private Teaching: The Circumstances of Paul's Preaching Activity," *NovT* 26 (1984) 59–82.
——— *Letter Writing in Greco-Roman Antiquity*. Library of Early Christianity Vol. 5; Philadelphia: The Westminster Press, 1986.
——— "Paul on the Use and Abuse of Reason," *Greeks, Romans, and Christians. Essays in Honor of Abraham J. Malherbe*. Ed. by D. L. Balch, E. Ferguson and W. A. Meeks; Minneapolis: Fortress Press, 1990. 253–286.
——— "Romans 7:7–25 as a Speech-in-Character (προσωποποιία)," *Paul in His*

*Hellenistic Context.* Ed. Troels Engberg-Pedersen. Edinburgh: T. & T. Clark, 1994. 180–202.

———— *A Rereading of Romans. Justice, Jews, & Gentiles.* New Haven: Yale University Press, 1994.

Stuhlmacher, P. "The Hermeneutical Significance of 1 Cor 2:6–16," *Tradition and Interpretation in the New Testament. Essays in Honor of E. Earle Ellis.* Ed. G. F. Hawthorne with O. Betz; Grand Rapids: Wm B. Eerdmans/Tübingen: J. C. B. Mohr [Paul Siebeck], 1987. 328–47.

Sudhaus, S. "Epikur als Beichtvater," *ARW* 14 (1911) 647–48.

Summey, J. L. *Identifying Paul's Opponents. The Question of Method in 2 Corinthians.* JSNTSS 40; Scheffield: JSOT Press, 1990.

Tait, J. I. M. *Philodemus' Influence on the Latin Poets.* Diss., Bryn Mawr, 1941.

Theissen, Gerd. *The Social Setting of Pauline Christianity: Essays on Corinth.* Philadelphia: Fortress Press, 1982.

———— "Vers une théorie de l'histoire sociale du christianisme primitif," *ETR* 63 (1988) 199–225.

———— *Social Reality and the Early Christians. Theology, Ethics, and the World of the New Testament.* Transl. Margaret Kohl. Minneapolis: Fortress Press, 1992.

Thraede, Klaus. *Grundzüge griechisch-römischer Brieftopik.* Zetemata 48. Munich: C. H. Beck, 1970.

Thrall, Margaret E. "The Pauline Use of συνείδησις," *NTS* 14 (1967–68) 118–25.

———— "The Offender and the Offence: A Problem of Detection in 2 Corinthians," *Scripture: Meaning and Method. Essays Presented to Anthony Tyrrell Hanson for His Seventieth Birthday.* Ed. by B. P. Thompson; Hull University Press, 1987. 65–78.

Tomson, Peter J. *Paul and the Jewish Law: Halakha in the Letters of the Apostle to the Gentiles.* CRINT III.1; Maastricht: Van Gorcum; Minneapolis: Fortress, 1990.

Tuilier, A. "La notion de φιλία dans ses rapports avec certains fondements sociaux de l'épicurisme," ACGB; Paris, Société d'Édition <Les Belles Lettres> (1969) 318–29.

Turner, V. *The Forest of Symbols: Aspects of Ndemby Ritual.* Ithaca, N. Y.: Cornell University Press, 1977.

Unnik, W. C. van. "Die Rücksicht auf die Reaktion der Nicht-Christen als Motiv in der altchristlichen Paränese." *Judentum-Urchristentum—Kirche, Festschrift für Joachim Jeremias.* BZNW 26; Berlin: 1960; 1964 (2), 221–34.

———— *Sparsa collecta* I. The Collected Essays of W. C. van Unnik. NovTSup 30; Leiden: E. J. Brill, 1980; *Sparsa collecta* II. NovTSup 31; Leiden: E. J. Brill, 1983.

Valantasis, R. J. *Spiritual Guides of the Third Century. A Semiotic Study of the Guide-Disciple Relationship in Christianity, Neoplatonism, Hermetism, and Gnosticism.* HDR 27; Minneapolis: Fortress Press, 1991.

Vanhoye, A., ed. *L'Apôtre Paul. Personnalité, Style et Conception du Ministère.* BETL 73; Leuven University Press, 1986.

Vetschera, R. *Zur griechischen Paränese.* Smichow/Prague: Rohlicek & Sievers, 1912.

Vielhauer, Ph. *Oikodome. Das Bild vom Bau in der christlichen Literatur vom Neuen Testament bis Clemens Alexandrinus.* TBü 65. Münich: Kaiser, 1979.

Voelke, André-Jean. "La fonction thérapeutique du Logos selon Chrysippe," *Études de Lettres* 4 (1981) 57–71.

———— "Santé de l'âme et bonheur de la raison. La fonction thérapeutique de la philosophie dans l'épicurisme," *Études de Lettres* 3 (1983) 67–87.

———— "Opinions vides et troubles de l'âme: la médication épicurienne," *Jeux et Contre-Jeux. Mélanges offerts à Pierre-André Stucki.* Édités par Pierre Bühler. Neuchâtel: Université de Neuchâtel (1986), 8–16.

Vogel, C. J. de. *Pythagoras and Early Pythagoreanism: An Interpretation of Neglected Evidence on the Philosopher Pythagoras.* Assen: Van Gorcum, 1966.

Volz, Carl A. *Pastoral Life and Practice in the Early Church*. Minneapolis: Augsburg Fortress, 1990.
Wallace-Hadrill, A. ed. *Patronage in Ancient Society*. London/New York: Routledge, 1989.
Walsh, Joseph J. "On Christian Atheism," *VC* 45 (1991) 255–77.
Walzer, Richard. "New Light on Galen's Moral Philosophy," *CQ* 43 (1949) 82–96.
Watson, D. F. "1 Corinthians 10.23–11.1 in the Light of Greco-Roman Rhetoric," *JBL* 108.2 (1989) 301–18.
Weinfeld, Moshe. *The Organizational Pattern and the Penal Code of the Qumran Sect: A Comparison with Guilds and Religious Associations of the Hellenistic-Roman Period*. Novum Testamentum et orbis antiquus, 2; Freiburg, Switzerland: Universitätsverlag; Göttingen: Vandenhoeck & Ruprecht, 1986.
Weiss, Johannes. *Die Aufgaben der neutestamentlichen Wissenschaft in der Gegenwart*. Göttingen: Vandenhoeck & Ruprecht, 1908.
——— *Der erste Korintherbrief*. MeyerK 5; 9th ed.; Göttingen: Vandenhoeck & Ruprecht, 1910 [repr. 1970].
Welty, Eudora, and Ronald A. Sharp, eds. *The Norton Book of Friendship*. New York-London: W. W. Norton & Company, 1991.
Wette, W. M. L. de. *Kurze erklärung der Briefe an die Corinther*. Leipzig: Weidmann, 1841.
White, P. "Amicitia and the Profession of Poetry," *JRS* 68 (1978) 74–92.
Wilckens, U. *Weisheit und Torheit. Eine exegetisch-religionsgeschichtliche Untersuchung zu 1. Kor. 1 und 2*. BHT; Tübingen: J. C. B. Mohr [Paul Siebeck], 1959.
——— "Zu 1 Kor. 2, 1–16," *Theologia Crucis-Signum Crucis. Festschrift für Erich Dinkler zum 70. Geburtstag*. Hrgs. C. Andresen und G. Klein; Tübingen, 1979. 501–37.
Willis, W. L. *Idol Meat in Corinth: The Pauline Argument in 1 Corinthians 8 and 10*. SBLDS 68; Chico: Scholars Press, 1985.
——— "An Apostolic Apologia? The Form and Function of 1 Corinthians 9," *JSNT* 24 (1985) 33–48.
Wilson, R. McL. "Gnosis at Corinth," *Paul and Paulinism. Essays in honour of C. K. Barrett*. Eds. M. D. Hooker & S. G. Wilson; London: SPCK, 1982. 102–14.
Windisch, Hans. *Der zweite Korintherbrief*. MeyerK 6; 9th ed. Göttingen: Vandenhoeck & Ruprecht, 1924 [repr. ed. Georg Strecker, 1970].
Winter, Martin. *Pneumatiker und Psychiker in Korinth: Zum religionsgeschichtlichen Hintergrund von 1. Kor. 2, 6–3, 4*. MThSt 12. Marburg: Elwert, 1975.
Wire, A. C. *The Corinthian Women Prophets. A Reconstruction through Paul's Rhetoric*. Minneapolis: Fortress Press, 1990.
Witt, N. W. de. "Parresiastic Poems of Horace," *CP* 30 (1935) 312–319.
———. "Epicurean Contubernium," *TAPA* 67 (1936) 55–63.
——— "Organization and Procedure in Epicurean Groups," *CP* 31 (1936) 205–211.
——— "Epicurean Doctrine in Horace," *CP* 34 (1939) 127–134.
——— *St. Paul and Epicurus*. Minneapolis: University of Minnesota Press, 1954.
Xenakis, J. *Epictetus, Philosopher-Therapist*. The Hague, 1969.
Zeller, E. *Die Philosophie der Griechen in ihrer geschichtlichen Entwicklung*. Vol. III.1: *Die nacharistotelische Philosophie*. 2 vols.; 6th ed.; Darmstadt: Wissenschaftliche Buchgesellschaft, 1963.
Zimmermann, A. F. *Die urchristlichen Lehrer. Studien zum Tradentenkreis der διδάσκαλοι im frühen Christentum*. WUNT 2, 12; Tübingen: J. C. B. Mohr (Paul Siebeck), 1984.
Zmijewski, Josef. *Der Stil der paulinischen "Narrenrede."* BBB 52; Köln/Berlin: Peter Haustein, 1978.

# INDEX OF AUTHORS

Allo, E.-B.   297 n. 179, 339
Amoroso, F.   109 n. 36, 114 n. 51, 339
Amstutz, J.   97 n. 150, 339
Angeli, A.   115 n. 55, 337
Annas, J.   122 n. 83, 137 n. 132, 147 n. 176, 150 n. 188, 339
Apel, K.-O.   9 n. 17, 339
Arnim, H. von   6, 337, 339
Arrighetti, G.   337
Asmis, E.   18, 59 n. 20, 102 n. 3, 103 nn. 6 & 9, 107 n. 27, 144 nn. 53 & 56 & 58 & 59, 117 n. 63, 135 n. 125, 140 n. 153, 144 n. 166, 149 n. 183, 157 n. 204, 162 n. 4, 172 n. 50, 339
Attridge, H. W.   39 n. 90, 339

Bachmann, P.   315 n. 241, 339
Bailey, C.   337
Balsdon, J. P. V. D.   170 n. 41, 339
Barnes, J.   8 n. 14, 102 n. 1, 343
Barnett, J.   323 n. 270
Barr, J.   275, 339
Barrett, C. K.   192 n. 25, 199 n. 41, 250 n. 47, 253 n. 56, 309 n. 219, 312 n. 227, 339
Bartchy, S. S.   271 n. 106, 339
Bartelink, G. J. M.   311 n. 224, 339
Bassler, J. M.   225 n. 120, 339
Baumeister, T.   339
Behm, J.   202 n. 49, 339
Bendix, R.   186 n. 5
Berger, P.   187 n. 13, 339
Bergson, L.   339
Bertram, F.   92 n. 133, 339
Best, E.   188 n. 13, 339
Betz, H. D.   180 n. 74, 187 n. 7, 236 n. 2, 237 n. 4, 243 n. 29, 271 n. 105, 298, 299 n. 185, 313 n. 235, 321 n. 261, 339
Billerbeck, M.   339
Bjerkelund, C. J.   202 n. 48, 296 n. 172, 339
Black, D. A.   274 n. 113, 339
Bohnenblust, G.   107 n. 23, 166 n. 22, 339
Bollack, M. J.   161 n. 3, 340
Bonhöffer, T.   191 n. 22, 340

Bonner, S. F.   48 n. 113, 340
Booth, A. D.   279 n. 124, 340
Bornkamm, G.   340
Bowers, P.   241 n. 20, 340
Bowersock, G. W.   57 n. 15, 340
Branham, R. B.   75 n. 78, 98 n. 151, 105 n. 15, 340
Brinckmann, W.   163 n. 7, 166 n. 22, 170 n. 41, 340
Brown, P.   11 n. 21, 191 n. 22, 340
Brunt, J. C.   340
Brunt, P. A.   31 n. 58, 340
Bultmann, R.   332 n. 291
Burgess, T. C.   61 nn. 24 & 25, 340
Burkert, W.   11 n. 20, 340
Burns, J. McGregor   56 n. 13, 340
Butts, J. R.   48 n. 113, 337
Büchner, W.   340
Bünker, M.   245 n. 33, 296 n. 172, 325 n. 275, 340

Cadbury, H. J.   291 n. 163, 340
Calvin   288 n. 157
Campenhaus, H. von   209 n. 80, 340
Capasso, M.   102 n. 4, 337
Castner, C. J.   103 n. 8, 172 n. 48, 340
Chadwick, H.   340
Chilton, C. W.   337
Chow, J. K.   270 n. 103, 340
Clark, A. J.   340
Clarke, A. D.   340
Clarke, M. L.   340
Clay, D.   8 n. 14, 104 nn. 13 & 15, 107 n. 25, 137 n. 133, 140 n. 154, 158 nn. 209 & 210, 165 n. 20, 175 nn. 58 & 60 & 61, 176, 177, 340
Cohen, S. J. D.   241 n. 21, 341
Cole, R. W.   341
Conzelmann, H.   253 n. 57, 282 n. 140, 289 n. 159, 292 n. 167, 332 n. 291, 341
Coune, M.   290 n. 161, 341
Coyle, J. K.   341
Cranfield, C. E. B.   217 n. 99, 226 n. 123, 289 n. 159, 341
Crönert, W.   108 n. 30, 127 n. 101, 341

Daube, D.   252 n. 53, 341
Davies, W. D.   242 n. 24, 287 n. 155, 341
Day, L. K. K.   39 n. 90, 341
Decleva Caizzi, F.   57 n. 15, 69 n. 50, 251 n. 50, 273 n. 110, 337
Deissmann, G. A.   200 n. 42, 202 n. 56, 291 n. 166, 341
De Lacy, E. A.   5 n. 8, 103 n. 9, 107 n. 27, 134 n. 123, 337
De Lacy, P. H.   5 n. 8, 103 n. 9, 107 n. 27, 112 n. 44, 134 n. 123, 337, 341
Delling, G.   202 nn. 51 & 57, 341
Desideri, P.   341
Dibelius, M.   204 n. 68, 341
Diels, H.   8 n. 14, 341
Dihle, A.   58 n. 17, 85 n. 109, 117 n. 63, 341
Dill, S.   241 n. 20, 341
Dillon, J. M.   10 n. 18, 69 n. 50, 85 n. 110, 337, 341
Doskocil, W.   316 n. 244, 341
Dudley, D. R.   341
Dunn, J. D. G.   207 n. 72, 217 n. 99, 231 n. 137, 330 n. 285, 341
Dupont, J.   226 n. 122, 236 n. 1, 276 n. 117, 287 n. 155, 300 n. 189, 341
Duvernoy, J. F.   133 n. 120, 341, 342

Eckstein, H.-J.   287 n. 155, 342
Edelstein, L.   66 n. 40, 134 n. 122, 342
Edmonds, J. M.   337
Ellison, H. L.   342
Engberg-Pedersen, T.   309 n. 216, 342
Engels, D.   188 n. 15, 244 n. 30

Falco, V. de   111 n. 41, 342
Farrington, B.   103 n. 8, 342
Festugière, A. J.   22 n. 26, 139 n. 152, 164 n. 11, 165 n. 20, 342
Figueira, T. J.   27 n. 44, 342
Finley, M. I.   65 n. 38, 211 n. 90, 342
Fiore, B.   6 n. 10, 61 n. 24, 89 n. 125, 296 n. 175, 342
Fitzgerald, J. T.   194 n. 29, 242 n. 25, 296 n. 172, 312 n. 230, 324 n. 272, 338, 342
Forbes, C.   321 n. 261, 342
Forkman, G.   342
Fortna, R. T.   342

Foucault, M.   11, 12 n. 23, 53 n. 3, 54, 160 n. 219, 342
Fowler, D. P.   102 n. 1
Frede, M.   66 n. 40, 134 n. 122, 342
Fredrickson, D. E.   315 n. 240
Friedländer, L.   241 n. 19, 342
Fridrichsen, A.   313 n. 232, 342
Frischer, B.   104 n. 12, 158 n. 209, 165 n. 18, 174 nn. 55 & 56, 342
Fuchs, G.   178 n. 70, 343
Funk, R. W.   343
Funke, H.   272 n. 107, 343
Furnish, V. P.   237 n. 4, 238 n. 7, 306 n. 206, 312 nn. 225 & 228 & 230, 317 n. 245, 319 n. 249, 321 nn. 259 & 260, 323 nn. 266 & 269 & 270, 343

Gammie, J. G.   349
Gargiulo, T.   25 n. 35, 103 n. 10, 109 nn. 33 & 35, 110 n. 39, 112 n. 44, 112 nn. 45 & 46, 123 n. 85, 138 n. 139, 343
Gaventa, B. R.   187 nn. 10 & 11, 332 n. 291, 342, 343
Georgi, D.   186 n. 3, 236 n. 2, 237 n. 4, 241 n. 21, 343
Gerhard, G. A.   89 n. 125, 94 n. 137, 343
Gigante, M.   98 n. 150, 103 n. 9, 107 n. 26, 108 n. 30, 109 n. 32, 122 n. 44, 116, 119 n. 71, 122 n. 84, 128 n. 107, 129 n. 110, 130 n. 112, 131 n. 113, 133 nn. 118 & 120, 134, 135 n. 126, 136 n. 127, 143 n. 163, 143–144 n. 165, 145 nn. 169 & 171, 147 nn. 175 & 177 & 178 & 179, 149 n. 186, 150 n. 188, 153, 154, 155, 158 n. 209, 176 n. 63, 343
Gill, C. J.   29 n. 51, 343
Glad, C. E.   114 n. 49, 332 n. 291, 343
Glucker, J.   159, 159–160 n. 218, 343
Gooch, P. W.   253 n. 56, 287 n. 155, 288 n. 156, 290 n. 161, 291 n. 164, 332 n. 291, 343
Goodenough, W. H.   275 n. 115
Grant, R. M.   53 n. 1, 343
Griffin, M.   8 n. 14, 102 n. 1, 343
Grimal, P.   343
Grube, G. M. A.   51 n. 126, 343
Grundmann, W.   343
Guerra, A. T.   115 n. 53, 116

n. 57, 130 n. 112, 343
Gutierrez, P. 187 n. 9, 296 n. 173, 297 n. 180, 343

Haber, L. L. 67 n. 42, 344
Hadot, I. 53 n. 2, 55, 58 n. 17, 66 n. 41, 140 n. 154, 233 n. 142, 344
Hadot, P. 60 n. 23, 191 n. 22, 344
Hahm, D. E. 344
Hainz, J. 344
Hall, B. 253 n. 56
Hall, J. 57 n. 14, 344
Harder, G. 202 n. 54, 344
Harkins, P. W. 337
Hartlich, P. 60 n. 24, 344
Hays, R. B. 344
Heinrici, C. F. G. 6 n. 12, 282, 289 nn. 157 & 158, 296 n. 174, 308 n. 214, 309 nn. 216 & 217, 344
Helm, R. 22 n. 26, 344
Hense, O. 337, 338
Héring, J. 344
Hershbell, J. P. 69 n. 50, 332 n. 291, 337
Heylbut, G. 166 n. 22, 344
Hijmans, B. L. 11 n. 22, 344
Hirzel, R. 163 n. 7
Hobein, H. 337
Hock, R. F. 11 n. 22, 241 n. 20, 344
Hoistad, R. 19 n. 15, 38 n. 86, 90 n. 127, 94 n. 137, 344
Hollander, H. W. 38 n. 87, 70 n. 58, 274 n. 113, 276 n. 117, 320 n. 255, 344
Holmberg, B. 191 n. 23, 344
Horowits, M. 60 n. 22, 344
Horsley, R. A. 236 n. 1, 281 n. 131, 283 n. 142, 287 n. 155, 300 n. 189, 344
Horst, P. W. van der 338
Howe, H. M. 102 n. 1, 345
Hubbell, H. M. 116 n. 57, 135 n. 125, 338
Hugedé, N. 236 n. 1, 300 n. 188, 301 n. 190, 345
Hunter, R. L. 32 n. 59, 38 n. 85, 112 n. 44, 345
Hurd, J. C. 16 n. 7, 236 n. 2, 242 n. 22, 283 n. 142, 297 n. 176, 345
Hyldahl, N. 345

Ihm, M. 345
Indelli, G. 95 nn. 150 & 151, 103 n. 5, 119 n. 71, 338

Ingenkamp, H. G. 66 n. 41, 345

Jaeger, H. 311 n. 224, 345
Jaeger, W. 65 n. 38, 233 n. 145
Jaekel, S. 338
Jensen, C. 104 nn. 11 & 13, 138 n. 140, 140 n. 155, 158 n. 209, 175 n. 60, 338, 345
Jeremias, J. 285, 345
Jewett, R. 207 n. 73, 282 n. 139, 287 n. 155, 330 n. 284, 345
Johann, H.-T. 345
Joly, R. 271 n. 105, 345
Jones, H. 101 n. 1, 173 n. 52, 345
Jonge, M. de 70 n. 58, 338
Joos, M. 275 n. 114, 345
Jordan, M. D. 61 n. 24, 345
Judge, E. A. 12 n. 24, 186 nn. 3 & 4, 211 n. 90, 214 n. 93, 270 n. 103, 271 n. 105, 345
Jungkuntz, R. 9 n. 16, 345

Käsemann, E. 191 n. 23, 312 n. 225, 345
Kahrstedt, U. 241 n. 20, 345
Kakridis, T. 19 n. 14, 345
Karris, R. J. 330 n. 284
Kaster, R. A. 345
Keck, L. E. 217 n. 99, 331 n. 289
Kennedy, G. 46, 345
Kerferd, G. B. 133 n. 119, 345
Kertelge, K. 346
Kidd, I. G. 85 n. 109, 133 n. 119, 338, 346
Kindstrand, J. F. 338, 346
King, J. M. 59 n. 19, 346
Kitzberger, I. 346
Kleve, K. 121 nn. 78 & 79 & 80
Knögel, W. 140 n. 155, 346
Kock, T. 338
Köhler, L. 6 n. 10, 346
Körte, A. 101 n. 1, 346
Kondo, E. 25 n. 35, 104 n. 13, 108 n. 31, 111 n. 43, 113 n. 48, 123 n. 87, 346
Konstan, D. 158 n. 206, 164 n. 11, 346
Koskenniemi, H. 244 n. 32, 245 n. 33, 346
Kuck, D. W. 281 n. 131, 289 n. 159, 302 n. 193, 346
Kühn, K. G. 338
Kümmel, W. G. 331 n. 287, 346

## INDEX OF AUTHORS

La Bonnardière, A.-M.   191 n. 22, 346
Lampe, G. W. H.   346
Lang, F.   296 n. 172, 346
Lausberg, H.   246 n. 36, 346
Leivestad, R.   323 n. 270, 346
Liebich, W.   176 n. 63, 346
Liefeld, W.   241 n. 20, 346
Lightfoot, J. B.   235 n. 147, 346
Lim, T. H.   298 n. 181, 346
Lindblom, J.   226 n. 122, 346
Linde, P.   19 n. 14, 346
Long, A. A.   10 n. 18, 82 n. 103, 121 n. 79, 163 n. 6, 165 n. 17, 338, 346
Longo Auricchio, F.   25 n. 35, 27 n. 43, 109 n. 34, 110 nn. 38 & 39, 112 n. 44, 112 n. 45, 115 n. 53, 116 n. 57, 122 nn. 82 & 84, 123 n. 88, 128 n. 108, 158 nn. 209 & 211, 159 n. 212, 338, 347
Louw, J. P.   275 n. 115
Luckmann, T.   187 n. 13, 339
Lund, N. W.   250 n. 46, 347
Lüdemann, G.   234 n. 146, 347
Lührmann, D.   245 n. 33, 347
Lütgert, W.   236 n. 1, 347
Lutz, C. E.   347
Lyons, J.   237 n. 3, 275 n. 114, 347

Mack, B. L.   233 n. 142, 347
Malherbe, A. J.   1 n. 1, 4, 5, 6, 7, 9 n. 17, 10 n. 15, 22 n. 27, 46 n. 110, 59 n. 18, 61 n. 26, 69 n. 51, 70 n. 53, 89 n. 125, 91 n. 130, 92, 93–94, 95 n. 140, 96 n. 146, 139 n. 152, 175 n. 57, 187 n. 11, 193 n. 27, 195 n. 31, 200 n. 42, 241 n. 18, 244 n. 31, 264 n. 84, 265 n. 87, 266 nn. 90 & 92, 271 n. 105, 272 n. 107, 287 n. 152, 302 n. 194, 338, 347
Malina, B. J.   213 n. 92, 347
Maly, K.   12 n. 24, 347
Markantonato, G.   347
Marrou, H. I.   347
Marshall, P.   180 nn. 74 & 75, 266 n. 91, 271 n. 105, 281 n. 131, 312 n. 230, 347
Martin, D. B.   187 n. 12, 327 n. 278, 347
Martin, J.   347
Martin, R. P.   347
Martínez, F. G.   11 n. 21, 347

Maslowski, T.   114 n. 54, 170 n. 40, 173 n. 52, 347
May, M. T.   338
McKnight, S.   241 n. 21, 348
Meeks, W. A.   8 n. 15, 56 n. 12, 59 n. 19, 186 n. 5, 188 n. 15, 191 nn. 23 & 24, 196 n. 33, 206 n. 71, 210 n. 82, 217 n. 99, 220 n. 106, 224, 225, 231, 254 n. 59, 331 nn. 286 & 288, 348
Mendelson, A.   40 n. 94, 301 n. 190, 348
Méndez, E. A.   28 n. 49, 109 n. 33, 111 n. 42, 112 n. 45, 127–128 n. 97, 348
Meyer, H. A. W.   284 n. 146, 289 n. 159, 309 n. 216, 330 n. 285, 348
Michels, A. K.   32 n. 59, 348
Millett, P.   31 n. 58, 32 n. 62, 206 n. 71
Minar, E. L.   11 n. 20, 348
Mitchell, A. C.   199 n. 39, 348
Mitchell, M. M.   15 n. 3, 195 n. 31, 245 n. 35, 265 n. 86, 297 n. 176, 348
Mitsis, P.   163 nn. 8 & 9, 165 n. 17, 348
Moles, J. L.   94 n. 136, 348
Momigliano, A. D.   65 n. 38, 103 n. 8, 348
Müller, K.   226 n. 122, 348
Munck, J.   237 n. 4, 348
Murphy-O'Connor, J.   237 n. 4, 248 n. 43, 282 nn. 138 & 139, 283 nn. 142 & 143, 285 n. 148, 289 n. 158, 292 n. 167, 331 n. 286, 348

Nagy, G.   27 n. 44, 91 n. 129, 98 n. 151, 349
Nauck, A.   338
Neymeyr, U.   12 n. 24, 349
Newman, R. J.   62 n. 29, 349
Nickelsburg, G. W. E.   38 n. 87, 349
Nida, E. A.   275 n. 115
Nilsson, M. P.   138 n. 134, 349
Nock, A. D.   349
Nolland, J.   21 n. 25, 349
Norden, E.   89 n. 125, 97, 283 n. 142, 349
Nussbaum, M. C.   133 n. 120, 152, 153, 156, 158 n. 209, 349

Obbinck, D. D.   165 n. 18, 349
Obens, W.   6 n. 10, 349

O'Brien, P. T. 296 n. 174, 349
O'Connor, D. K. 163 n. 8, 349
Oden, T. C. 191 n. 22, 349
Olivier, F. 315 n. 239, 349
Olivieri, A. 4 n. 6, 128 n. 107, 338
Ollrog, W.-H. 349
Olson, S. N. 349
Oster, R. E. 290 n. 162, 349

Pagels, E. H. 209 n. 80, 349
Painter, J. 349
Paratore, E. 349
Pavlovskis, Z. 349
Pearson, B. A. 236 n. 1, 300 n. 189, 349
Perdue, L. G. 59 n. 19, 349
Peristiay, J. G. 349
Petersen, N. R. 209 n. 78, 350
Peterson, E. 106 n. 23, 283 n. 142, 350
Philippson, R. 103 n. 9, 109 n. 31, 118 nn. 69 & 70, 163 n. 9, 350
Pierce, C. A. 287 n. 155, 350
Pigeaud, J. 350
Pitt-Rivers, J. 213 n. 92
Plessis, P. J. du 236 n. 1, 297 n. 178, 350
Porter, S. E. 222 n. 111, 223 n. 114, 337
Price, A. W. 167 n. 27, 350

Rabbow, P. 66 n. 41, 127 n. 102, 191 n. 22, 350
Rabe, H. 48 n. 115, 338
Rabel, R. J. 350
Rauer, M. 330 n. 284, 350
Reitzenstein, R. 236 n. 1, 350
Renehan, R. 241 n. 18, 308 n. 213, 350
Ribbeck, O. 20 n. 20, 25 n. 33, 25 nn. 35 & 36, 27 n. 42, 28 n. 46, 30 n. 57, 31 n. 58, 32 n. 62, 110 n. 38, 114 n. 51, 122 n. 83, 350
Richardson, P. 16 n. 6, 350
Riley, M. T. 121 n. 79, 127 n. 102, 158 n. 209, 350
Rist, J. M. 161 n. 1, 165 n. 20, 350
Robbins, V. K. 233 n. 142, 347
Rodis-Lewis, G. 350
Roetchel, C. R. 302 n. 194
Rohrbaugh, R. L. 153 n. 197, 310 n. 221, 350
Russell, D. A. 51 n. 126, 55 n. 10, 338

Rydbeck, L. 228, 350

Saller, R. P. 31 n. 58, 267 n. 97, 269 n. 101, 350
Sanders, E. P. 259 n. 70
Saussure, F. de 275 n. 114, 350
Sbordone, F. 164 n. 11, 338, 350
Scarpat, G. 107 n. 23, 351
Schächter, R. 351
Schenkeveld, D. M. 18 n. 11, 351
Schlüchter, W. 204 n. 67, 351
Schmid, W. M. 9 n. 16, 127 n. 103, 351
Schmithals, W. 237 n. 4, 351
Schmitz 202 n. 48, 351
Schneider, J. 351
Scholes, R. 214 n. 94, 351
Schrijvers, P. H. 351
Schütz, J. H. 191 n. 23, 351
Sedley, D. 8 n. 14, 82 n. 102, 103 n. 7, 135 n. 125, 165 n. 17, 338, 351
Sergiovanni, T. J. 9 n. 17, 56 n. 13, 351
Sevenster, J. N. 271 n. 105, 351
Shanor, J. 351
Sharp, R. A. 353
Sharples, R. W. 54 n. 4, 82 n. 103, 338
Simpson, A. D. 9 n. 16, 351
Smith, R. B. 275 n. 115
Smolders, D. 351
Snell, B. 20 n. 19, 38 n. 86, 351
Soden, Hans von 351
Spengel, L. 338
Spicq, C. 287 n. 155, 351
Spina, L. 175 n. 59, 351
Stanford, W. B. 1, 19, 20 n. 19, 38, 242 n. 23, 272 n. 109, 351
Stanton, G. R. 57 n. 14, 351
Starratt, R. J. 9 n. 17, 56 n. 13, 351
Stählin, G. 202 nn. 48 & 55, 351
Stählin, O. 338
Ste. Croix, M. de 211 n. 90, 241 n. 16, 279 n. 123, 351
Stegemann, W. 48 n. 113, 351
Stelzenberger, J. 287 n. 155, 351
Sternbach, L. 338
Stowers, S. K. 6 n. 10, 58 n. 16, 121 n. 79, 176 n. 64, 215 n. 95, 233, 234, 235, 237 n. 4, 238 n. 9, 241 n. 20, 244 n. 32, 246 n. 38, 247 n. 41, 256 n. 65, 257 n. 66, 273 n. 111, 281 n. 134, 305

nn. 201 & 203, 331 n. 287, 332 n. 292, 351
Stuhlmacher, P.  352
Sudhaus, S.  127 n. 103, 338, 352
Summey, J. L.  352

Tait, J. I. M.  104 n. 10, 352
Theissen, G.  185 n. 2, 209 n. 81, 210 n. 82, 211 n. 90, 213 n. 93, 241 n. 17, 278 n. 120, 352
Thraede, K.  245 n. 33, 352
Thrall, M. E.  287 n. 155, 352
Tomson, P. J.  331 n. 287, 352
Treu, U.  338
Tuilier, A.  161 n. 3, 352
Turner, V.  59 n. 19, 352

Unnik, W. C. van  105 n. 17, 311 nn. 223 & 224, 352
Usener, H.  338
Ussher, R. G.  338

Valantasis, R. J.  191 n. 22, 352
Vanhoye, A.  352
Vetschera, R.  61 n. 24, 352
Vielhauer, Ph.  187 n. 7, 282 n. 136, 320 n. 255, 352
Voelke, A.-J.  133 nn. 119 & 120, 352
Vogel, C. J. de  11 n. 20, 69 n. 50, 353
Volz, C. A.  191 n. 22, 353

Wachsmuth, C.  338
Wallace-Hadrill, A.  31 n. 58, 269 n. 101, 353
Walsh, J. J.  9 n. 16, 353

Walzer, R.  353
Watson, D. F.  293 n. 168, 353
Weinfeld, M.  10 n. 19, 353
Weil, S.  208 n. 77
Weiss, J.  6, 7, 236 n. 1, 247 n. 42, 250 n. 46, 282, 284 n. 145, 308 nn. 214 & 215, 309 nn. 216 & 217, 353
Welty, E.  353
Wette, W. M. L. de  289 n. 159, 353
Wettstein, J. J.  235 n. 147, 338
White, L. M.  338
White, P.  31 n. 58, 33 n. 63, 267 n. 97, 269 n. 101, 353
Wilckens, U.  236 n. 1, 353
Wilke, C.  108 n. 30, 338
Willis, W. L.  15 n. 2, 248 n. 43, 262 n. 80, 353
Wilson, N. G.  51 n. 126, 55 n. 10, 338
Wilson, R. McL.  353
Windisch, H.  313 nn. 231 & 233, 319 n. 249, 323 n. 269, 324 nn. 271 & 272, 353
Winter, M.  236 n. 1, 353
Wire, A. C.  210 n. 84, 353
Witt, N. W. de  8 n. 14, 32 n. 59, 107 n. 26, 143–144 n. 165, 153, 154, 155, 158 n. 209, 159 n. 218, 176 n. 65, 353

Xanakis, J.  353

Zeller, E.  165 n. 17, 353
Zimmermann, A. F.  12 n. 24, 353
Zmijewski, J.  321 n. 261, 353

# INDEX OF PASSAGES

## OLD TESTAMENT

*Genesis*
2:7 — 300 n. 189
37:3 — 39 n. 91
*Exodus*
12:27 — 276 n. 117
*Leviticus*
11:10 — 259 n. 72
*Deuteronomy*
23:5 — 88
*1 Samuel*
26:24 — 276 n. 117
*Job*
5:22 — 258 n. 68
*Psalms*
6:2 — 274 n. 113
17:7–8 — 276 n. 117
27:5 — 276 n. 117
28:5 — 205 n. 70
32:1 — 257
64:1–2 — 276 n. 117
68:10 — 306 n. 207
93:11 — 223
109:31 — 230 n. 134
118:18 — 307 n. 212
141:5 — 307 n. 212
*Proverbs* — 305
3:11–12 — 278 n. 121
3:12 — 307 n. 212
17:9 — 70 n. 58
23:13–14 — 88 n. 121
*Isaiah*
40:13 — 303
49:17 — 205 n. 70
*Jeremiah*
24:6 — 205 n. 70
31:28 — 205 n. 70
42:10 — 205 n. 70
45:41 — 206 n. 70
*Ezekiel*
36:36 — 205 n. 70

## APOCRYPHAL/DEUTEROCANONICAL BOOKS

JUDITH
8:15 — 276 n. 117
9:11 — 274 n. 113

WISDOM OF SOLOMON
6:5 — 324 n. 272

SIRACH
6:7–17 — 166 n. 22
21:2–3 — 278 n. 121
21:28 — 284 n. 146, 289 n. 157
22:6–7 — 279 n. 122
22:6–8 — 278 n. 121
22:20 — 70 n. 55
22:22 — 106 n. 21, 278 n. 121
30:23 — 230 n. 133, 316 n. 242
51:2–3 — 276 n. 117

1 ESDRAS
4:32–34 — 78 n. 87

3 MACCABEES
3:11–13 — 291 n. 165
3:28 — 291 n. 165
6:6–8 — 276 n. 117

4 MACCABEES
9:5 — 320 n. 254
15:5 — 285 n. 149

## NEW TESTAMENT

*Matthew*
4:21 — 235 n. 145
8:16–17 — 228 n. 127
13:31 — 73 n. 68
25:16 — 251 n. 49
*Luke*
22:32 — 202 n. 54

## INDEX OF PASSAGES

*John*
17:21–23   232 n. 138

*Acts*
4:29   105 n. 18
4:31   105 n. 18
9:27–28   105 n. 18
14:3   105 n. 18
14:15   177 n. 69
14:22   190 n. 20, 202 n. 54
17:4   256 n. 65
17:18   185 n. 1
18:26   105 n. 18
19:8   105 n. 18
20:31   202 n. 49
20:35   203 n. 61, 206 n. 71
23:2   278 n. 121
23:36   278 n. 121
26:12–18   57 n. 13
26:22   185 n. 1
28:31   105 n. 18

*Romans*
1   215 n. 95
1:8–15   217 n. 100
1:11   190, 193
1:12   193, 202 n. 58
1:16   255 n. 63
1:21   223
1:23–24   252 n. 80
2:1–5   238
2:9–10   255 n. 63
2:12   257
3:9   255 n. 63
3:27   258 n. 67
4:7   257
4:19   274 n. 113
4:19–20   228 n. 126
4:20   202 n. 50
5:6   274 n. 113
6   222 n. 111
6:1   222 n. 111
6:13   222 n. 111
6:14   308 n. 215
6:15   222 n. 111
6:19   257, 274 n. 113
7   273 n. 111
7:7–8   262 n. 80
8:2   258 n. 67
8:3   256 n. 64, 274 n. 113
8:16   188 n. 14
8:21   188 n. 14
8:26   274 n. 113
8:29   187 n. 9
9:8   188 n. 14
10:12   255 n. 63
11:25   237 n. 6
12:1   207 n. 72, 215 n. 95, 223
12:1–2   189 n. 17
12:3   246 n. 39
12:3–8   191
12:6   190 n. 20, 246 n. 39
12:6–8   191, 202
12:8   203, 204 n. 66, 207 n. 72
12:9–10   216 n. 96
12:9–21   216
12:10   187 n. 9, 271 n. 105
12:13–15   216 n. 96
12:15   215, 229 n. 132
12:16   216 n. 96, 232 n. 138, 237 n. 5, 309 n. 218
12:17–21   216 n. 96
13:1–7   216 n. 96
13:8–10   216 n. 97, 262 n. 80
14   218, 219 n. 102, 222 n. 111, 225, 228, 233, 234, 238, 283, 289, 334
14–15   214, 231, 293 n. 168
14:1–15:6   218, 232 n. 138
14:1–15:7   217
14:1–15:14   213–235, 214, 215, 217, 235, 263 n. 82, 277, 316
14:1   189 n. 16, 202 n. 50, 217, 218, 219, 220, 221, 222, 223 n. 114, 229, 233 n. 144, 274 n. 113, 281 n. 134, 283
14:1b   219 n. 104, 222, 223, 233
14:1–2   218
14:1–4   220, 222 n. 111
14:2   218, 219, 274 n. 113
14:3   218 n. 101, 219 n. 102, 220, 221, 222, 223
14:3–4   219
14:3b–4   221
14:3–13a   218
14:4   219, 220, 221 n. 110, 230 n. 134, 289 n. 158
14:4b   225 n. 119
14:5   218 n. 101, 220 n. 106, 222
14:5–6a   219 n. 102
14:5a   220
14:5b   220, 224
14:6a   220
14:6b   219 n. 102, 220

# INDEX OF PASSAGES

| | | | |
|---|---|---|---|
| 14:7 | 220 | | 228, 234, 274 n. 113 |
| 14:9 | 260 n. 75 | 15:1–3 | 216 n. 97 |
| 14:10 | 218 n. 101, 220, 230 n. 134, 289 n. 158 | 15:2 | 187 n. 7, 202 n. 52, 217, 222 n. 111 |
| 14:10b | 221 | 15:3 | 216 n. 97, 221, 306 n. 207 |
| 14:11 | 220 | | |
| 14:12 | 221, 222 | 15:4 | 202 n. 48 |
| 14:13 | 227 n. 125 | 15:5 | 202 n. 48 |
| 14:13a | 216, 217, 220 n. 106, 221, 222, 225, 303 | 15:5–6 | 232 n. 138 |
| | | 15:6–8 | 232 n. 138 |
| 14:13b | 220 n. 106, 222 n. 111, 225, 226, 227 | 15:7 | 217, 218, 222 n. 111, 224, 232 n. 138, 331 n. 289 |
| 14:13b–21 | 218, 227 | | |
| 14:13b–15:1 | 225 | 15:7–8 | 216 n. 97 |
| 14:13b–15:6 | 218 | 15:7a | 221 |
| 14:14 | 224, 226, 283 n. 141 | 15:7b | 221, 224 |
| 14:14–16 | 227, 293 | 15:8 | 216 n. 97 |
| 14:15 | 203, 214, 222 n. 111, 226, 227 n. 125, 229, 230, 231 n. 137, 276 n. 116, 289 n. 159, 316, 317 n. 245, 330 | 15:8–13 | 217, 232 n. 138 |
| | | 15:9a | 232 n. 138 |
| | | 15:13 | 217 |
| | | 15:14 | 202 n. 49, 203, 217, 218 n. 101, 232, 306 n. 208 |
| 14:15a | 316 n. 242 | | |
| 14:15–16 | 226 | 15:15a | 217 n. 100 |
| 14:15–21 | 219 n. 102 | 15:15b–22 | 217 n. 100 |
| 14:15b | 226 n. 122 | 15:30 | 207 n. 72 |
| 14:15b–16 | 293 n. 169 | 15:32 | 193 n. 27, 202 n. 53 |
| 14:16 | 222 n. 111, 226, 227, 293 | 16:4 | 255 n. 63 |
| | | 16:16 | 271 n. 105 |
| 14:17 | 227, 284 n. 145 | 16:17 | 207 nn. 72 & 74, 261 n. 77 |
| 14:18 | 218 n. 101, 227 | | |
| 14:19 | 187 n. 7, 202 n. 52, 217, 222 n. 111, 227 | 16:17–19 | 216 n. 96 |
| | | *1 Corinthians* | |
| 14:19–20 | 228 | 1–4 | 295 |
| 14:20 | 222 n. 111, 226 n. 123, 227 n. 125 | 1:1 | 187 n. 9, 245 n. 33 |
| | | 1:1–9 | 296 |
| 14:20–21 | 226 | 1:5 | 232 n. 141, 298 |
| 14:20a | 227 | 1:7 | 190, 195, 289 n. 158 |
| 14:20b | 227 n. 124 | 1:8 | 190 n. 21 |
| 14:21 | 226 n. 122, 227 n. 125, 274 n. 113 | 1:10 | 190 n. 19, 195, 201, 202 n. 48, 244, 296, 304, 325 |
| 14:22 | 218, 219, 230 n. 134, 246 n. 39 | | |
| | | 1:10–4:21 | 297 n. 176 |
| 14:22–23 | 218, 224, 227 | 1:11 | 238 n. 8, 297 n. 176 |
| 14:22–23a | 228 n. 126 | 1:17 | 237 n. 5, 254 n. 60 |
| 14:22a | 219, 227 | 1:18 | 230 n. 135, 254 n. 59, 277 n. 118, 299 |
| 14:22b | 219, 226 n. 123, 228 | | |
| 14:23 | 202 n. 50, 218, 219, 221, 226, 227 | 1:18–21 | 254 n. 60 |
| | | 1:18–31 | 299 |
| 14:23a | 219 n. 102 | 1:18–3:23 | 299 |
| 14:23b | 219 n. 103 | 1:19 | 199 n. 38 |
| 15:1 | 68 n. 49, 189 n. 16, 201, 202 n. 56, 217, 218, 220, 226 n. 123, | 1:20 | 199 n. 38, 299 |
| | | 1:21 | 254 n. 60, 299 |
| | | 1:22 | 255 n. 63 |

| | | | |
|---|---|---|---|
| 1:23 | 254 n. 60, 255 n. 63, 299 | 3:15 | 237 n. 6, 254 nn. 59 & 60 |
| 1:24 | 255 n. 63, 299 | 3:15–18 | 230 n. 135 |
| 1:25 | 199 n. 38, 274 n. 113 | 3:16 | 244 n. 32, 300 |
| 1:25–27 | 236 n. 1 | 3:18 | 199 n. 38, 237 n. 5, 252 n. 55, 299 |
| 1:26 | 199 n. 38, 237 n. 5, 312 n. 228 | 3:18–21a | 300 |
| 1:26–28 | 230 n. 135 | 3:19 | 199 n. 38 |
| 1:27 | 199 n. 38, 307 n. 210, 309 n. 219 | 3:20 | 199 n. 38, 223 |
| | | 3:21 | 237 n. 5 |
| 1:27–29 | 307 | 4:1 | 303 n. 195 |
| 1:28 | 220 n. 107 | 4:3 | 198 n. 37 |
| 1:30 | 299 | 4:3–4 | 202 n. 50, 291 n. 165, 303 n. 196 |
| 1:31 | 237 n. 5 | | |
| 2:1 | 299, 303 n. 195 | 4:3–5 | 198, 303 nn. 195 & 196, 314 n. 238 |
| 2:1–6 | 299 | | |
| 2:2 | 299 | 4:5 | 254 n. 59, 307 |
| 2:2–4 | 220 n. 107 | 4:6 | 237 n. 5, 238 n. 10, 296 n. 175, 319 n. 252 |
| 2:3 | 274 n. 113 | | |
| 2:4 | 254 n. 60, 299 n. 184 | 4:7 | 202 n. 50, 223 n. 113 |
| 2:4–5 | 237 n. 5 | 4:8 | 296 n. 174, 299, 301 n. 192, 303 n. 195 |
| 2:6 | 236 n. 1, 297 n. 179, 299, 302 | | |
| | | 4:8–10 | 236 n. 1 |
| 2:6–3:3 | 189 n. 16 | 4:9–13 | 194 n. 29, 242 |
| 2:6–3:4 | 286 | 4:10 | 237 n. 6, 238 n. 10, 274 n. 113, 301 n. 192, 307, 319 n. 252, 321 n. 260 |
| 2:7 | 303 n. 195 | | |
| 2:7–13 | 299 | | |
| 2:10 | 299 n. 186 | | |
| 2:13 | 303 n. 195 | 4:11 | 243 n. 26 |
| 2:13b | 299 n. 186 | 4:12 | 306 n. 207, 318 n. 248, 320, 321 n. 260, 322 n. 262 |
| 2:13–14 | 300 n. 189 | | |
| 2:13–15 | 302 | | |
| 2:14–15 | 202 n. 50, 236 n. 1 | 4:13 | 244 n. 32 |
| 2:14–16 | 216, 302 | 4:14 | 202 n. 48, 244 n. 32, 296, 305, 306, 319 n. 253, 328 n. 279 |
| 2:15 | 198, 200 n. 44, 201, 213, 234 n. 145, 291 n. 165, 299 n. 186, 302, 203, 304 n. 197 | | |
| | | 4:14–17 | 188 n. 14 |
| | | 4:14–21 | 76, 92, 189 n. 16, 239 n. 13 |
| 2:15–16 | 303 n. 195 | | |
| 2:16 | 246 n. 40 | 4:15 | 187 nn. 9 & 10, 252 n. 55, 254 n. 60 |
| 2:16b | 303 n. 196 | | |
| 3:1 | 236 n. 1, 237 n. 5, 314 n. 236 | 4:16 | 202 n. 48, 244 n. 32, 305 |
| 3:1–2 | 297 n. 179 | 4:16–21 | 304 |
| 3:1–3 | 187 n. 10, 211 n. 89, 299 | 4:17 | 187 n. 9, 195 n. 32, 244 n. 32, 310 n. 220, 328 n. 279 |
| 3:1–4 | 302 | | |
| 3:1–21 | 300 | 4:17–21 | 296 n. 173 |
| 3:3 | 238 n. 8, 297 n. 179 | 4:18 | 237 n. 5 |
| 3:5 | 187 n. 12, 237 n. 6 | 4:18–21 | 245 n. 33, 304 n. 199 |
| 3:6–9 | 187 n. 7 | 4:19 | 237 n. 5 |
| 3:9–17 | 187 n. 7 | 4:20 | 305 |
| 3:10 | 199 n. 38 | 4:20–21 | 88, 324 n. 272 |
| 3:13 | 312 n. 225 | 4:21 | 239 n. 13, 307, 323 |

## INDEX OF PASSAGES 365

| | | | |
|---|---|---|---|
| 5 | 197, 260, 301, 308 | 6:18 | 262 n. 79, 277 n. 119 |
| 5–6 | 261 | 6:18a | 248 |
| 5–7 | 258 | 6:18b | 248 |
| 5–14 | 238 n. 8 | 6:19 | 244 n. 32 |
| 5–15 | 295, 299, 307 | 6:19–20 | 261 n. 76 |
| 5:1–11:1 | 215, 216 n. 96, 240, 247, 294 | 6:20b | 248 |
| | | 7 | 246, 247, 248 |
| 5:1–13 | 199 n. 41, 216 | 7:1 | 245, 297 n. 176 |
| 5:1–8 | 297 n. 176 | 7:4 | 247 n. 41, 281 n. 132 |
| 5:1–5 | 260 | 7:6 | 246 n. 40 |
| 5:1 | 297 n. 176 | 7:8 | 245 |
| 5:2 | 237 n. 5 | 7:8–12 | 247 |
| 5:3 | 245 n. 33, 325 n. 275 | 7:10 | 244 n. 32 |
| 5:5 | 203 n. 62, 254 n. 60, 323 n. 268 | 7:12–15 | 255 n. 63 |
| | | 7:12–16 | 260 n. 74, 262 |
| 5:6 | 237 n. 5, 244 n. 32, 245 | 7:15 | 245 n. 33 |
| | | 7:16 | 254 n. 60 |
| 5:8 | 261 n. 76 | 7:16a | 203 n. 62 |
| 5:9 | 199, 207 n. 74, 208 n. 76, 245 n. 33, 256 n. 65, 260, 261 n. 77 | 7:17 | 246 n. 39 |
| | | 7:20–24 | 252 n. 55 |
| | | 7:21 | 247 n. 41 |
| 5:9–11 | 260, 261, 313 | 7:22 | 247 n. 41 |
| 5:9–13 | 261, 308 n. 214 | 7:23 | 271 n. 106 |
| 5:11 | 187 n. 9, 199, 203 n. 65, 208 n. 76, 245 n. 33, 261, 263, 306 n. 207 | 7:25 | 245 n. 33, 297 n. 176 |
| | | 7:25–26 | 314 n. 238 |
| | | 7:26 | 245, 246 |
| | | 7:29–31 | 252 n. 55 |
| 5:12 | 105 n. 17, 185 n. 2, 245 | 7:35 | 245, 246 |
| | | 7:36 | 245 |
| 5:13b | 297 n. 176 | 7:37 | 245, 247 n. 41 |
| 6 | 260, 301 | 7:38 | 245 |
| 6:1 | 262 | 7:39 | 247 n. 41 |
| 6:1–7 | 198, 216 | 7:40 | 246 n. 40, 303 n. 196 |
| 6:2 | 244 n. 32 | 8 | 203, 206, 215, 226, 231, 233, 239 n. 14, 240, 248, 263, 264, 265, 266 n. 91, 277, 278, 283, 287 n. 151, 289, 290, 291 n. 162, 293 n. 168, 295, 298, 309 n. 216, 315, 320, 330, 334 |
| 6:3 | 244 n. 32 | | |
| 6:4 | 220 n. 107 | | |
| 6:5 | 200 n. 44, 202 n. 50, 305 n. 202, 308 | | |
| 6:5b | 199 | | |
| 6:6 | 255 n. 63, 262 | | |
| 6:8 | 319 n. 252 | | |
| 6:9 | 237 n. 5, 244 n. 32, 258, 261 n. 76 | | |
| | | 8–9 | 197, 272 |
| 6:9–10 | 261 | 8–10 | 290 |
| 6:10 | 203 n. 65, 306 n. 207 | 8–14 | 258 |
| 6:11 | 261 n. 76 | 8:1–11:1 | 214, 215, 216, 235, 247, 316 |
| 6:12 | 247 n. 41, 248, 294 | | |
| 6:12–11:1 | 247 n. 41 | 8:1–8 | 287 |
| 6:12–20 | 245 n. 33, 247, 248, 260, 262 | 8:1–13 | 225, 277–295 |
| | | 8:1 | 237, 245 n. 33, 276, 283, 285, 297 n. 176, 316 n. 242, 323 n. 268 |
| 6:12–18 | 289 | | |
| 6:13ab | 248 n. 43 | | |
| 6:15 | 244 n. 32 | 8:1b | 282 n. 137 |
| 6:16 | 244 n. 32 | 8:1–3 | 296 n. 174 |

| | | | |
|---|---|---|---|
| 8:4 | 283, 284, 285, 291 n. 162 | 9:12a | 265 |
| 8:5–6 | 283, 284 | 9:12b | 265 n. 88, 266 |
| 8:6 | 260 n. 75, 286 | 9:13 | 244 n. 32 |
| 8:7 | 234 n. 245, 274 n. 113, 276, 283, 284, 287, 288, 330 n. 285 | 9:14 | 244 n. 32, 254 n. 60 |
| | | 9:15 | 266 |
| | | 9:15–18 | 15 |
| | | 9:15a | 265 n. 88 |
| 8:7–10 | 189 n. 16, 256 n. 65, 288 | 9:16 | 254 n. 60 |
| | | 9:18 | 247 n. 41, 254 n. 60, 294 n. 171 |
| 8:7–11 | 68 n. 49, 219 n. 103 | | |
| 8:7–12 | 16, 274, 275, 278, 284, 288, 290 | 9:18–19 | 267 |
| | | 9:18a | 266 n. 89, 269 |
| 8:8 | 195, 230 n. 134, 283, 284, 285, 286, 287, 289 n. 158, 292 | 9:18b | 265 n. 88 |
| | | 9:19 | 187 n. 12, 250, 251, 252, 254, 267, 269, 327 n. 278 |
| 8:9 | 226 n. 121, 234 n. 145, 247 n. 41, 265, 274 n. 113, 287 n. 152, 288 | 9:19–22 | 97, 250 n. 46, 267 |
| | | 9:19–22a | 16 |
| 8:10 | 234 n. 145, 254 n. 59, 274 n. 113, 282, 287, 290 n. 162 | 9:19–23 | 1, 2, 3, 15, 16 n. 6, 17, 43–45, 87, 88, 240, 244, 245, 249–277, 252, 253, 258, 263, 272, 273, 274, 276, 294, 295, 327, 334 |
| 8:10–12 | 276 | | |
| 8:10–13 | 292 | | |
| 8:10b | 288 | | |
| 8:11 | 214, 226 n. 121, 230, 234 n. 145, 237 n. 5, 276, 277, 282, 288, 289 n. 159 | 9:19–27 | 254 n. 60 |
| | | 9:20 | 251, 252, 253, 256 |
| | | 9:20–21 | 255 |
| | | 9:20–22 | 250 n. 46, 258 |
| 8:11–12 | 274 n. 113 | 9:20–22a | 250, 255 |
| 8:11–13 | 238 n. 10 | 9:20a | 250 n. 46 |
| 8:12 | 234 n. 145, 277, 280, 292, 316 | 9:20b | 250 n. 46, 253, 267 |
| | | 9:21 | 250 n. 46, 251, 253, 257, 267 |
| 8:13 | 226 n. 121, 263 | | |
| 9 | 15, 44, 105, 248, 263, 264, 265 n. 86, 268, 271, 289 | 9:21a | 250 n. 46 |
| | | 9:21–22 | 216 n. 97 |
| | | 9:22 | 68 n. 49, 189 n. 16, 230, 234 n. 145, 253, 254, 273 n. 111, 274, 275, 277, 327 n. 278 |
| 9–10 | 258 | | |
| 9:1 | 57 n. 13, 247 n. 41, 263 n. 85, 267 n. 93, 269 | | |
| | | 9:22a | 16, 250 n. 46, 251, 252, 276 |
| 9:1–5 | 266 | | |
| 9:3 | 198 n. 37, 202 n. 50, 291 n. 165, 303 n. 196 | 9:22b | 1, 15, 16, 203 n. 62, 242, 250, 251, 252, 254 nn. 59 & 60, 256 n. 65, 260 n. 74, 278 |
| 9:3–12 | 265, 269 | | |
| 9:4 | 247 n. 41, 265, 266 n. 91 | | |
| | | 9:23 | 251, 254 n. 60 |
| 9:5 | 245 n. 33, 247 n. 41, 265 | 9:23b | 16, 252 |
| | | 9:24 | 244 n. 32 |
| 9:6 | 247 n. 41 | 9:24–27 | 190 n. 21, 248, 252, 256, 284 |
| 9:10 | 247 n. 41 | | |
| 9:11–12 | 265 | 9:24–10:13 | 248, 290 n. 160 |
| 9:12–18 | 16 | 9:25 | 256 n. 65 |
| 9:12 | 247 n. 41, 254 n. 60, 265, 269, 294 n. 171 | 9:27 | 254 n. 60, 312 n. 225 |
| | | 10 | 215 n. 95, 288, 291 |

# INDEX OF PASSAGES

| | | | |
|---|---|---|---|
| | n. 162, 293 n. 168 | 11:2 | 245 n. 33, 308 n. 215, |
| 10:1–13 | 248, 262 | | 309, 310 n. 220 |
| 10:1–15 | 306 n. 209 | 11:2–22 | 320 n. 253 |
| 10:1–22 | 262, 290 | 11:3 | 244 n. 32 |
| 10:6 | 262 | 11:4 | 307 n. 210 |
| 10:7–10 | 262 n. 80 | 11:5 | 307 n. 210 |
| 10:9 | 254 n. 59 | 11:10 | 244 n. 32 |
| 10:9–12 | 230 n. 135 | 11:13 | 308 |
| 10:11 | 262, 306 | 11:13–16 | 247 |
| 10:12 | 306 n. 209 | 11:16 | 309 |
| 10:13 | 321 n. 259 | 11:17 | 244 n. 32, 297 n. 176, |
| 10:14 | 248, 263, 290 n. 162, | | 309 n. 217 |
| | 296 n. 175, 319 n. 253, | 11:17–34 | 199, 297 n. 176 |
| | 328 n. 279 | 11:18–22 | 319 n. 252 |
| 10:14–22 | 248, 262 | 11:19 | 312 n. 225 |
| 10:15 | 237 n. 6, 238 n. 10, | 11:22 | 307 n. 210 |
| | 251 n. 48, 306, 321 | 11:22b | 309 n. 218 |
| | n. 260 | 11:22c | 309 n. 219 |
| 10:19 | 245 n. 33 | 11:23 | 308 n. 215 |
| 10:20 | 244 n. 32 | 11:27–34 | 230 n. 135, 276 n. 117 |
| 10:21 | 290 n. 162 | 11:28 | 312 n. 225 |
| 10:23 | 245, 247 n. 41, 248, | 11:29 | 202 n. 50 |
| | 262 | 11:30 | 274 n. 113 |
| 10:23–11:1 | 245 n. 33 | 11:31 | 202 n. 50 |
| 10:23b | 202 n. 52 | 11:32 | 202 n. 50, 245 n. 33 |
| 10:23–24 | 294 | 11:32–34 | 319 n. 252 |
| 10:24 | 249 n. 44 | 11:34 | 245 n. 33, 304 n. 199 |
| 10:24–11:1 | 290–295 | 12:1 | 245 n. 33, 297 n. 176 |
| 10:25 | 198 n. 37, 202 n. 50, | 12:4–7 | 191, 192 |
| | 254 n. 59, 290, 291 | 12:7 | 245 |
| | nn. 163 & 165 | 12:8 | 296 n. 174, 299 n. 183 |
| 10:25–28 | 290, 291, 292, 293 | 12:8–10 | 191, 202, 203 |
| 10:25–29 | 274 | 12:10 | 202 n. 50, 222, 223 |
| 10:27 | 198 n. 37, 202 n. 50, | | n. 113 |
| | 254, n. 59, 262, 290 | 12:9 | 192 n. 25 |
| 10:28 | 291, 292 | 12:13 | 255 n. 63 |
| 10:28–29a | 291 | 12:22 | 211, 274 n. 113 |
| 10:28–31 | 254 n. 60 | 12:22–25 | 319 n. 252 |
| 10:29 | 247 n. 41 | 12:28 | 191, 192, 203 n. 61 |
| 10:29b–30 | 292–293 | 12:28–30 | 191, 202, 203 |
| 10:31–11:1 | 294 | 12:29 | 192 |
| 10:32 | 255 n. 63, 256, 294 | 12:29–30 | 192, 204 |
| | n. 171 | 12:30 | 192 |
| 10:32–33 | 15, 43, 88, 244, 248, | 12:31 | 192 n. 25 |
| | 249, 255 | 13 | 216 n. 97 |
| 10:32–11:1 | 216 n. 97, 294, 295 | 13:1–2 | 296 n. 174 |
| 10:33 | 16 n. 6, 190, 203 | 13:2 | 303 n. 195 |
| | n. 62, 249 n. 44, 254, | 13:4 | 237 |
| | 309 n. 218 | 13:5 | 245 |
| 10:33–11:1 | 216 n. 97 | 13:8–9 | 296 n. 174 |
| 10:33b | 254 n. 60, 260 n. 74 | 14 | 194, 195, 197, 256, 258 |
| 11 | 308, 320 n. 253 | 14:1 | 193 n. 26 |
| 11:1 | 15, 248, 258, 259, 294 | 14:1–6 | 190 |
| | n. 171 | 14:2 | 303 n. 195 |

367

368    INDEX OF PASSAGES

| | | | |
|---|---|---|---|
| 14:2–3 | 196 | 15:44–46 | 300 n. 189 |
| 14:2–4 | 196 | 15:51 | 303 n. 195 |
| 14:3 | 197, 198 n. 36, 202 nn. 48 & 52 & 55, 244 n. 32 | 15:58 | 190 n. 21, 206 n. 175, 319 n. 253, 328 n. 279 |
| | | 16:1 | 245 n. 33, 297 n. 176 |
| 14:3–5 | 187 n. 7 | 16:3 | 312 n. 225 |
| 14:4 | 196, 202 n. 52, 323 n. 268 | 16:5–7 | 245 n. 33, 304 n. 199 |
| | | 16:10–11 | 190 n. 21, 195 n. 32 |
| 14:4–6 | 198 n. 36 | 16:11 | 220 n. 107 |
| 14:5 | 198, 202 n. 52, 323 n. 268 | 16:12 | 187 n. 9, 245 n. 33, 297 n. 176 |
| 14:6 | 192 n. 25, 196, 203 | 16:15–16 | 202 n. 48, 206, 244 n. 32, 270 n. 103 |
| 14:10 | 198 n. 36 | | |
| 14:12 | 187 n. 7, 198 n. 36, 202 n. 52 | 16:17 | 202 n. 57, 206 n. 71 |
| | | 16:17–18 | 190 n. 19, 202 n. 53 |
| 14:13–15 | 196 | 16:18 | 193 |
| 14:14–17 | 196 | 16:20 | 271 n. 105 |
| 14:15 | 196 n. 34 | 16:22 | 271 n. 105 |
| 14:16–17 | 196 | *2 Corinthians* | |
| 14:17 | 198 n. 36, 202 n. 52, 323 n. 268 | 1 | 194 |
| | | 1:1 | 187 n. 9 |
| 14:19 | 196, 198 n. 36 | 1:1–2:13 | 194 n. 30 |
| 14:20 | 196, 252 n. 55 | 1:3 | 194 n. 30, 202 n. 48 |
| 14:21 | 202 n. 52 | 1:3–7 | 194 |
| 14:22 | 196, 197 | 1:4 | 194, 202 n. 48 |
| 14:22–24 | 255 n. 63, 262 | 1:5 | 194 nn. 29 & 30, 202 n. 48 |
| 14:23–24 | 105 n. 17, 185 n. 2 | | |
| 14:23–25 | 197 | 1:6 | 194, 202 n. 48, 276 n. 117 |
| 14:24 | 198, 203, 254 n. 59, 291 n. 165, 306 n. 207 | 1:7 | 194 nn. 29 & 30, 202 n. 48 |
| 14:24–25 | 197 | | |
| 14:25 | 260 n. 75 | 1:8 | 194 n. 29, 311 n. 225 |
| 14:26 | 187 n. 7, 192 n. 25, 196 n. 34, 198 n. 36, 203, 245 n. 33 | 1:12 | 312 nn. 226–7, 228 |
| | | 1:12–14 | 311 n. 225 |
| | | 1:13–14 | 313 n. 231 |
| 14:26–33 | 197 | 1:15–2:13 | 312 n. 228 |
| 14:29 | 202 n. 50 | 1:17 | 297 n. 179 |
| 14:31 | 196, 198 n. 36, 202 n. 48, 244 n. 32 | 1:17–18 | 311 n. 225, 312, 314 |
| | | 1:19 | 254 n. 60 |
| 15:1 | 308 n. 215 | 1:23–2:4 | 314, 316 |
| 15:1–2 | 254 n. 60 | 1:23 | 319 n. 250, 324 n. 271 |
| 15:1–3 | 254 n. 60 | 1:24 | 238 n. 11, 319, 320 n. 258 |
| 15:2 | 254 n. 60, 309 | | |
| 15:6 | 251 n. 48 | 2 | 239 n. 14 |
| 15:8–10 | 57 n. 13 | 2:1 | 194 n. 29, 239 n. 11, 319 n. 250 |
| 15:11 | 254 n. 60 | | |
| 15:12 | 236 n. 1, 254 n. 60 | 2:2 | 194 n. 29 |
| 15:14 | 254 n. 60 | 2:2a | 317 n. 245 |
| 15:33 | 308 n. 313 | 2:3 | 194 n. 29 |
| 15:33–34 | 308 n. 313 | 2:3–4 | 315, 316 nn. 242 & 243 |
| 15:34 | 261 n. 77, 305 n. 202, 308 n. 213 | | |
| | | 2:3–11 | 315, 319 |
| 15:35 | 245 n. 33 | 2:4 | 194 n. 29, 311 n. 225 |
| 15:36 | 310 n. 220, 320 n. 253 | 2:5 | 194 n. 29 |
| 15:43 | 274 n. 113 | 2:5–9 | 207 |

## INDEX OF PASSAGES

| Passage | Pages |
|---|---|
| 2:5–10 | 216 |
| 2:5–11 | 199, 316 |
| 2:6 | 203 n. 65, 306 n. 206, 316 n. 244 |
| 2:6–8 | 316 n. 242, 317 n. 245 |
| 2:7 | 194, 199 n. 41, 202 n. 48, 316 |
| 2:8 | 202 n. 48 |
| 2:9 | 208 n. 76, 312 n. 225, 315, 323 n. 266 |
| 2:10 | 317 |
| 2:12 | 317 |
| 2:13 | 202 n. 53 |
| 2:14 | 313 n. 232 |
| 2:15 | 277 n. 118, 308 n. 215 |
| 2:17 | 311 n. 225, 313 n. 233 |
| 3:1–3 | 269 n. 101 |
| 3:5 | 190 n. 21, 312 n. 225 |
| 3:6 | 308 n. 215 |
| 3:12–4:6 | 313 |
| 3:12–18 | 311 n. 224 |
| 3:18 | 189 n. 17 |
| 4:2 | 269 n. 101, 311 n. 225 |
| 4:2–4 | 314 |
| 4:3 | 277 n. 118 |
| 4:4 | 255 n. 63 |
| 4:5 | 187 n. 12 |
| 4:8–9 | 194 n. 29, 242 |
| 4:10–11 | 313 n. 232 |
| 4:16–18 | 187 n. 17 |
| 4:17 | 194 n. 29 |
| 5:10–11 | 313 n. 232 |
| 5:12 | 237 n. 5, 269 n. 101 |
| 5:16 | 312 n. 228 |
| 5:17 | 187 n. 17 |
| 5:20 | 202 n. 48 |
| 5:20–21 | 256 n. 64 |
| 6:1 | 202 n. 48 |
| 6:3 | 311 n. 225 |
| 6:3–4 | 187 n. 12 |
| 6:3–10 | 194 n. 29, 242 |
| 6:7–8 | 313 n. 233 |
| 6:10 | 194 n. 29 |
| 6:11 | 314 n. 236 |
| 6:11–13 | 311 n. 225 |
| 6:13 | 188 n. 14, 314 n. 236 |
| 6:14 | 257 |
| 6:14–15 | 255 n. 63 |
| 7:1 | 328 n. 279 |
| 7:2–4 | 311 n. 225, 314 n. 237 |
| 7:3 | 195 |
| 7:4 | 105 n. 18, 194 nn. 29 & 30, 202 n. 48, 311 n. 223 |
| 7:4–13 | 194 |
| 7:5 | 194 n. 29 |
| 7:5–16 | 194 n. 30 |
| 7:6 | 194, 202 n. 48 |
| 7:7 | 194 n. 30, 202 n. 48 |
| 7:8 | 194 n. 29, 311 n. 225, 315 |
| 7:8–9 | 317 n. 245 |
| 7:8–12 | 319 |
| 7:8–13 | 208 n. 76 |
| 7:8–13a | 315 |
| 7:9 | 194 n. 29, 239 n. 14, 318 n. 247 |
| 7:10 | 194 n. 29 |
| 7:11 | 194 n. 29 |
| 7:12 | 313 n. 232 |
| 7:13 | 193 n. 27, 194 n. 30, 202 nn. 48 & 53 |
| 7:15 | 208 n. 76, 311 n. 225, 323 n. 266 |
| 8:2 | 194 n. 29, 312 n. 225 |
| 8:4 | 187 n. 12, 202 n. 48 |
| 8:6 | 202 n. 48 |
| 8:7 | 296 n. 174 |
| 8:8 | 312 n. 225 |
| 8:9 | 256 n. 64 |
| 8:13 | 194 n. 29 |
| 8:14 | 190 n. 19 |
| 8:17 | 202 n. 48 |
| 8:19 | 187 n. 12 |
| 8:20 | 187 n. 12 |
| 8:22 | 312 n. 225 |
| 9:6–14 | 187 n. 7 |
| 9:13 | 312 n. 225 |
| 9:22 | 253 |
| 10 | 233 n. 143, 320 |
| 10–13 | 92, 237 n. 4, 324 n. 272, 325 |
| 10:1 | 202 nn. 47 & 48, 239 n. 13, 311 n. 225, 313, 321 n. 261, 323 n. 270, 325 |
| 10:2 | 325 n. 275 |
| 10:2–3 | 297 n. 179, 312 n. 228 |
| 10:3–6 | 205 n. 70, 323 n. 268 |
| 10:5 | 237 n. 5 |
| 10:5–6 | 208 n. 76, 323 n. 266 |
| 10:6 | 239 n. 13, 323 n. 266, 324 |
| 10:7 | 237 n. 5 |
| 10:8 | 187 n. 7, 202 n. 52, 205 n. 70, 276 n. 117, 320 n. 258, 323 n. 268 |
| 10:9–10 | 238 n. 11, 313 |
| 10:9–11 | 320 n. 258 |
| 10:10 | 220 n. 107, 274 n. 113, |

# INDEX OF PASSAGES

| | | | |
|---|---|---|---|
| | 311 n. 225, 319, 321 n. 261 | 12:19 | 187 n. 7, 202 n. 52, 205 n. 70, 320 n. 255 |
| 10:11 | 325 nn. 274 & 275 | 12:20 | 237 n. 5 |
| 10:15 | 187 n. 17, 237 n. 5 | 12:20–21 | 238 n. 7 |
| 10:18 | 312 n. 225 | 12:21 | 239 n. 13 |
| 11 | 321 n. 261 | 12:20–13:11 | 324 |
| 11–12 | 320 | 13.1–10 | 318 |
| 11:1–12:13 | 321 n. 261 | 13:1–2 | 239 n. 13 |
| 11:1 | 239 n. 12, 321 n. 260, 323 n. 269 | 13:1–4 | 87, 88 |
| | | 13:2 | 324, 325 n. 275 |
| 11:1b | 321 n. 260 | 13:3 | 274 n. 113, 312 n. 225 |
| 11:4 | 239 n. 12, 254 n. 60, 321 n. 260, 323 n. 269 | 13:4 | 274 n. 113 |
| | | 13:5–7 | 312 n. 225 |
| 11:5 | 238 | 13:5–11 | 189 n. 17 |
| 11:6 | 296 n. 174, 313 n. 232, 313 n. 235, 321 n. 261 | 13:8 | 312 n. 225 |
| | | 13:9 | 190 n. 19, 200 n. 44, 201, 202 n. 51, 235 n. 147, 323 n. 269 |
| 11:6a | 298 n. 181 | | |
| 11:7 | 321 n. 261 | | |
| 11:7–12 | 269 n. 101 | 13:9–10 | 205 n. 70, 239 n. 13, 320 n. 255 |
| 11:8 | 187 n. 12 | | |
| 11:9 | 239 n. 12, 322 | 13:10 | 187 n. 7, 202 n. 52, 276 n. 117, 323 n. 268, 324, 325 n. 275 |
| 11:10–12 | 266 | | |
| 11:12–15 | 323 n. 268 | | |
| 11:13 | 236 n. 238 | 13:11 | 195, 201, 202 nn. 48 & 51, 235 n. 147, 245 n. 33, 323 n. 269, 325 |
| 11:13–15 | 260 n. 73, 312 n. 226 | | |
| 11:17–19 | 238 n. 10 | | |
| 11:18 | 297 n. 179 | 13:11–13 | 194 n. 30 |
| 11:19 | 237 n. 6, 239 n. 12, 321 n. 260, 323 n. 269 | 13:12 | 271 n. 105 |
| | | *Galatians* | |
| 11:19–20 | 310 n. 220, 320, 321 n. 259 | 1:8–9 | 318 n. 248 |
| | | 1:14 | 308 n. 215 |
| 11:20 | 237 n. 5, 239 n. 12, 278 n. 121, 323 n. 269 | 1:10 | 16 n. 6 |
| | | 2:3 | 255 n. 63 |
| 11:21 | 274 n. 113 | 2:8 | 190 n. 21 |
| 11:22 | 236 | 2:11–14 | 258 |
| 11:23 | 236, 279 n. 125 | 2:12 | 255 n. 63 |
| 11:23–29 | 194 n. 29, 242 | 2:12–13 | 259 n. 71 |
| 11:26 | 243 n. 26 | 2:14 | 255 n. 63, 259 n. 71 |
| 11:26–27 | 242 n. 25 | 3:1 | 299, 318 n. 248 |
| 11:28 | 186 n. 6 | 3:13 | 256 n. 64 |
| 11:29 | 274 n. 113 | 3:26 | 188 n. 14 |
| 11:30 | 274 n. 113 | 3:28 | 255 n. 63 |
| 12:5 | 274 n. 113 | 4:3–5 | 216 n. 97 |
| 12:7 | 237 n. 5 | 4:4–5 | 260 n. 73 |
| 12:9–10 | 274 n. 113 | 4:5 | 256 |
| 12:10 | 237 n. 5, 274 n. 113 | 4:8–10 | 260 n. 75, 286 |
| 12:11 | 269 n. 101 | 4:9 | 274 n. 113 |
| 12:13 | 239 n. 12, 322 | 4:12 | 243 |
| 12:14 | 188 n. 14, 237 n. 5, 239 n. 12, 322 | 4:12–20 | 180 n. 74 |
| | | 4:13 | 274 n. 113 |
| 12:14–16 | 239 n. 11, 320 n. 258 | 4:14 | 220 n. 107 |
| 12:14–18 | 312 n. 225 | 4:19 | 187 n. 10, 188 n. 14 |
| 12:15 | 186 n. 6, 266 n. 89 | 5:12 | 318 n. 248 |
| 12:16 | 322 | 5:13–15 | 193 n. 26 |

# INDEX OF PASSAGES

| | | | |
|---|---|---|---|
| 5:16–24 | 262 n. 80 | 4:10–20 | 259 n. 101 |
| 5:26 | 193 n. 26 | 4:11–14 | 243 n. 26 |
| 6:1 | 187 n. 9, 190 n. 19, 195, 200, 201, 202 n. 51, 206, 234, 235 n. 147, 239 n. 13, 323 | 4:12 | 289 n. 158 |
| | | 4:18 | 289 n. 158 |
| | | *Colossians* | |
| | | 1:28 | 202 n. 49, 307 n. 212 |
| 6:1–3 | 189 n. 16, 212, 214, 217, 225, 232 n. 139, 234 n. 146, 302 | 2:16 | 221 |
| | | 2:18 | 221 n. 109, 237 n. 5 |
| | | 3:11 | 255 n. 63 |
| 6.1–5 | 213, 216 | 3:16 | 196 n. 33, 202 n. 49, 307 n. 212 |
| 6:2 | 201, 202 n. 56, 218, 234, 257 | | |
| | | 3:18–4:1 | 206 n. 71 |
| 6:3 | 232 n. 139 | 4:8 | 202 n. 48 |
| 6:6 | 187 n. 8 | *1 Thessalonians* | |
| 6:7–9 | 187 n. 7 | 1:9 | 260 n. 75, 286, 289 |
| 6:10 | 105 n. 17, 185 n. 1, 193 n. 26 | 2 | 92 |
| | | 2:2 | 16 n. 5, 105 n. 18 |
| 6:11 | 105 n. 17, 185 n. 2 | 2:3 | 202 n. 48 |
| *Ephesians* | | 2:5 | 16 n. 5 |
| 2:19 | 105 n. 17, 185 n. 1 | 2:7 | 187 n. 11 |
| 4:11 | 187 n. 8, 192 n. 25 | 2:11 | 188 n. 14 |
| 4:12 | 200 n. 44, 201 | 2:12 | 202 nn. 48 & 55 |
| 5:18–20 | 196 n. 34 | 2:13 | 190 n. 21 |
| 5:21 | 206 n. 71 | 3:2 | 190 n. 20, 195, 202 nn. 48 & 54 |
| 5:22–6:9 | 206 n. 71 | | |
| 6:4 | 202 n. 49, 306 n. 209 | 3:7 | 202 n. 48 |
| *Philippians* | | 3:10 | 189 n. 17, 190 n. 19, 195 n. 31, 200 n. 44, 201, 202 n. 51, 235 n. 147 |
| 1:6 | 190 n. 21 | | |
| 1:8–9 | 189 n. 17 | | |
| 1:12 | 189 n. 17, 190 n. 21 | | |
| 1:21 | 252 n. 53 | 3:12 | 189 n. 17, 193 n. 26 |
| 1:25 | 189 n. 17, 190 n. 21 | 3:13 | 203 n. 54 |
| 2:1 | 202 n. 48 | 4:1 | 189 n. 17, 202 n. 48 |
| 2:5–11 | 216 n. 97, 256 n. 64, 260 n. 73 | 4:9 | 187 n. 9, 271 n. 105, 302, 303 n. 195 |
| 2:6–11 | 196 n. 34 | 4:9–10 | 193 n. 26 |
| 2:12 | 195 | 4:10 | 189 n. 17 |
| 2:12b | 190 n. 21 | 4:12 | 105 n. 17, 185 n. 2 |
| 2:13 | 190 n. 21 | 4:18 | 200 n. 42, 202 n. 48, 323 n. 269 |
| 2:14 | 328 n. 279 | | |
| 2:15 | 188 n. 14 | 5:8–10 | 194 n. 28 |
| 2:19 | 193 n. 27, 202 n. 59 | 5:11 | 187 n. 7, 194 n. 28, 200 n. 42, 202 nn. 48 & 52 |
| 2:26–27 | 274 n. 113 | | |
| 2:29–30 | 206 n. 71 | | |
| 3:2 | 318 n. 248 | 5:11–15 | 194, 195 |
| 3:5 | 253 | 5:12 | 206, 306 n. 208 |
| 3:7–9 | 252 n. 53 | 5:12–13 | 206 |
| 3:12–16 | 297 n. 179 | 5:12–14 | 206 |
| 3:12–18 | 189 n. 17 | 5:14 | 200, 203, 202 nn. 48 & 55, 203 nn. 60 & 61, 206, 234 nn. 145 & 146, 235 n. 148, 274 n. 113, 306 n. 208 |
| 3:14–16 | 189 n. 16 | | |
| 3:21 | 189 n. 17 | | |
| 3:30 | 202 n. 57 | | |
| 4:1 | 328 n. 279 | | |
| 4:2 | 202 n. 48 | 5:15 | 193 n. 26 |

| | | | |
|---|---|---|---|
| 5:23 | 194 n. 28 | 4:15 | 330 n. 283 |
| 5:23–24 | 194 | 4:16 | 311 n. 224 |
| 5:26 | 193 n. 26 | 5:14 | 222 n. 112 |
| *2 Thessalonians* | | 6:1 | 301 n. 191 |
| 2:7 | 202 n. 48 | 10:19 | 311 n. 224 |
| 2:16 | 202 n. 48 | 10:33 | 306 n. 207 |
| 2:17 | 190 n. 20, 202 nn. 48 & 54 | 10:39 | 230 n. 136 |
| | | 12:5–6 | 278 n. 121 |
| 3:6 | 199 n. 40, 207 n. 74, 261 n. 77 | 13:13 | 125 n. 93 |
| | | 13:22 | 322 n. 262, 323 n. 269 |
| 3:12 | 202 n. 48 | | |
| 3:14–15 | 199 n. 40, 200 n. 43, 207 n. 75, 261 n. 77 | *James* | |
| | | 1:6–8 | 228 n. 126 |
| 3:15 | 187 n. 9, 202 n. 49, 306 n. 208 | 2:4 | 223 |
| | | 2:9 | 223 n. 115 |
| *1 Timothy* | | 3:13–18 | 237 n. 6 |
| 4:16 | 203 n. 62 | 4:11–12 | 230 |
| 5:1 | 210 n. 83, 306 n. 207 | 4:13 | 251 n. 49 |
| 5:14 | 306 n. 207 | 5:10 | 70 n. 58 |
| 5:19–20 | 204 n. 68 | 5:13–19 | 230 n. 136 |
| *2 Timothy* | | 5:14–20 | 204 |
| 3:5 | 207 n. 74 | 5:20 | 203 n. 62 |
| 4:2 | 94 n. 139, 306 n. 207 | 5:19 | 148 n. 181 |
| 4:3 | 322 n. 262 | *1 Peter* | |
| *Titus* | | 1:14 | 206 n. 71 |
| 1:9 | 202 n. 48, 203 n. 62, 306 n. 204 | 1:17 | 206 n. 71 |
| | | 1:22 | 206 n. 71 |
| 1:11 | 251 n. 49 | 2:2 | 301 n. 191 |
| 1:13 | 203 n. 62, 306 n. 204, 324 n. 272 | 2:13 | 206 n. 71 |
| | | 2:18 | 90 n. 126, 206 n. 71 |
| 3:10 | 202 n. 49, 306 n. 209 | | |
| 3:10–11 | 207 n. 75, 218 n. 101, 261 n. 77, 306 n. 205 | 3:1 | 206 n. 71, 252 n. 53 |
| *Philemon* | | 3:9 | 306 n. 207 |
| 4 | | 4:8 | 70 n. 58 |
| 6–7 | 193 n. 27 | 4:10 | 209 n. 80 |
| 7 | 193 n. 27 | 5:5 | 206 n. 71 |
| 10 | 187 n. 10 | 5:10 | 202 n. 54 |
| 16 | 187 n. 9 | *2 Peter* | |
| 20 | 193 n. 27 | 3:16b | 313 n. 233 |
| 21 | 323 n. 266 | *Jude* | |
| *Hebrews* | | 5–7 | 230 n. 135 |
| 1:1 | 51 | 17–19 | 237 n. 6 |

## NON-CANONICAL WRITINGS

**AELIUS ARISTIDES**
*Orations*
41 (4).2        21 n. 22

**AESCHYLUS**
*Prometheus bound*
469–77        21 n. 25

**ALCIPHRON**
II 42, 3        31 n. 58
II 62, 3        31 n. 58
III 44, 2        25 n. 36

**ALEXANDER OF APHRODISIAS**
*On Fate*
XXXII 204.25–28        54 n. 4

| | | | |
|---|---|---|---|
| XXXIV 206.25–30 | 82 n. 103 | 1233b30 | 25 n. 33 |
| XXXV 207.5–7 | 82 n. 103 | 1233b30–32 | 109 n. 34, 111 n. 40 |
| XXXV 207.12–22 | 82 n. 103 | | |
| XXXVI 210.8–10 | 82 n. 103 | 1233b30–39 | 26 n. 39 |
| | | 1233b34–39 | 27 n. 42 |
| EPISTLE OF ANACHARSIS | | 1233b38–1234a3 | 121 n. 76 |
| 9 | 313 n. 235 | 1234a4–23 | 31 n. 59 |
| 9.50.5–11 | 91 n. 129 | 1237b8–1238a3 | 168 n. 31 |
| | | 1238a8–10 | 167 n. 28 |
| ANAXANDRIDES | | 1239a27 | 27 n. 42 |
| *The Lady from Samos* | | 1239b11–12 | 179 n. 72 |
| ii.155 (Kock) | 25 n. 35 | 1240a33–35 | 229 n. 132, 271 n. 105 |
| ANAXIMENES | | 1240a39–1240b1 | 229 n. 132 |
| *Rhetorica ad Alexandrum* | | 1240a34 | 319 n. 252 |
| 1421b23–26 | 246 n. 36 | 1241b25–1243b39 | 212 n. 91 |
| 1427b39–41 | 246 n. 36 | 1242b35–1243a14 | 68 n. 46, 106 n. 22 |
| 1428a1–2 | 246 n. 36 | | |
| | | 1243b15–40 | 106 n. 22 |
| ANTIPHON | 31 n. 58 | 1244a24–25 | 229 n. 132 |
| | | 1245b20–26 | 168 n. 31, 173 n. 51 |
| ANTISTHENES | | | |
| *Fragments* | | 1245b26–1246a25 | 229 n. 132 |
| 14 | 251 n. 50 | 1249a27 | 27 n. 42 |
| 15 | 57 n. 15, 251 n. 50 | | |
| | | *Great Ethics* | |
| 51 | 69 n. 50, 273 n. 110 | 1100a14–18 | 26 n. 40 |
| | | 1187a19–21 | 82 n. 101 |
| | | 1192b30–36 | 27 n. 42 |
| APULEIUS | | 1192b30–39 | 26 n. 39 |
| *Metamorphoses* | 45 | 1193a20–22 | 109 n. 34, 111 n. 40 |
| 10.11 | 70 n. 88 | | |
| | | 1193a20–28 | 26 n. 39 |
| EPISTLE OF ARISTEAS | | 1193a28–35 | 121 n. 76 |
| 125 | 107 n. 23 | 1199a14–18 | 27 n. 42 |
| | | 1208b22 | 26 n. 39 |
| ARISTON | | 1209b11–19 | 168 n. 32 |
| *On the Relieving of Arrogance* | | 1210a7–16 | 168 n. 33 |
| | 140 n. 155, 319 n. 252 | 1213b2–18 | 78 n. 87, 168 n. 31 |
| | | 1213b18–30 | 68 n. 46, 106 n. 22 |
| ARISTIOPHANES | | | |
| *Birds* | | *Nicomachean Ethics* | |
| 1555 | 18 n. 10 | 1102b33–1103a2 | 305 n. 201 |
| *Clouds* | | 1103a17–18 | 29 n. 51 |
| 102 | 121 n. 78 | 1103a17–19 | 63 n. 36 |
| 968 | 278 n. 121 | 1107a28–1108b10 | 26 n. 30 |
| | | 1108a9–10 | 121 n. 76 |
| ARISTOTLE | | 1108a19–21 | 121 n. 76 |
| *Eudemian Ethics* | | 1108a23–26 | 31 n. 59 |
| 1220b21–1221b27 | 26 n. 39 | 1108a26 | 25 n. 33 |
| 1221a1–3 | 121 n. 76 | 1108a26–30 | 38 n. 85 |
| 1221b10–16 | 90 n. 128 | 1109b31 | 82 n. 101 |
| 1223a10 | 2 n. 101 | | |

## 374 INDEX OF PASSAGES

| | | | |
|---|---|---|---|
| 1113b23–25 | 82 n. 101 | *Poetics* | |
| 1115a25–1128b36 | 26 n. 39 | 1447a28 | 63 n. 36 |
| 1121a20 | 75 n. 75 | | |
| 1124b28–30 | 125 n. 94 | *Politics* | |
| 1125a1–3 | 26 n. 41 | 1260b5–7 | 60 n. 21, 328 n. 281 |
| 1125b26–1126b10 | 90 n. 128 | | |
| 1126b11–16 | 38 n. 85 | 1266a31 | 138 n. 139 |
| 1126b12–15 | 25 n. 33 | 1292a22–24 | 268 n. 100 |
| 1126b20–29 | 38 n. 85 | | |
| 1126b36–1127a3 | 38 n. 85 | *Rhetoric* | |
| 1127a3–6 | 38 n. 85, 88 n. 122 | 1358b1–7 | 51 n. 128 |
| | | 1358b23 | 246 n. 36 |
| 1127a7–9 | 25 n. 33 | 1359a | 82 n. 101 |
| 1127a13–1127b33 | 121 n. 76 | 1359a38 | 246 n. 36 |
| 1137a14–25 | 21 n. 24 | 1362a18 | 246 n. 36 |
| 1137a29 | 151 n. 190 | 1365b | 246 n. 36 |
| 1146a10–17 | 285 n. 147 | 1371a22 | 26 n. 38 |
| 1146a17–22 | 38 n. 86 | 1377b24–27 | 47 n. 112 |
| 1146a34 | 75 n. 75 | 1388b32–1389a2 | 47 n. 112 |
| 1146a34–35 | 285 n. 147 | 1390a | 47 n. 112 |
| 1150a21–23 | 285 n. 147 | 1391b21 | 51 n. 128 |
| 1150a23 | 151 n. 190 | 1408a | 50 n. 124 |
| 1150b19–22 | 285 n. 147 | 1408ab | 51 n. 127 |
| 1150b29–35 | 285 n. 147 | 1416b25 | 20 n. 18 |
| 1151a12–15 | 285 n. 147 | 1416b–1417a | 306 n. 209 |
| 1155a12–16 | 106 n. 22, 229 n. 130 | 1451a | 297 n. 177 |
| 1155a28–30 | 167 n. 26 | *Topica* | |
| 1156a13 | 271 n. 105 | 100b21 | 286 n. 151 |
| 1158a1–10 | 167 n. 27 | | |
| 1158a10–16 | 167 n. 29 | **ATHENAEUS** | |
| 1158a16 | 271 n. 104 | *Sophists at Dinner* | |
| 1158b11–1159b24 | 212 n. 91 | 162B | 78 n. 85 |
| 1158b23–28 | 212 n. 91 | 182A | 111 n. 44, 125 n. 91 |
| 1159a33–1159b2 | 212 n. 91 | | |
| 1159b2–4 | 168 n. 33 | 211A–215C | 117 n. 66 |
| 1159b12–15 | 168 n. 33 | 211D | 118 n. 67 |
| 1162a34–1165b36 | 68 n. 46 | 220A | 98 n. 151, 117 n. 66, 127 n. 104 |
| 1163b11–12 | 212 n. 91 | | |
| 1165b18–23 | 151 n. 190 | 236D | 25 n. 33 |
| 1170b20–1171a20 | 167 n. 26 | 236EF | 28 n. 45, 39 n. 89 |
| 1171a7–13 | 167 n. 28 | 237A | 25 n. 33 |
| 1171a13–15 | 167 n. 30 | 237B–F | 30 n. 57 |
| 1171a15–20 | 167 n. 30 | 238B | 25 n. 36 |
| 1171a21–1172a15 | 106 n. 22 | 239E | 24 n. 31 |
| 1171a21–b27 | 229 n. 132 | 248D | 25 n. 33 |
| 1171a29 | 229 n. 132 | 255A | 25 n. 35 |
| 1173b31 | 25 n. 33 | 255C | 27 n. 43, 166 n. 21 |
| 1173b33–1174a2 | 26 n. 38 | | |
| 1179b11–15 | 305 n. 203 | 258A | 28 n. 47 |
| 1180a1–5 | 305 n. 203 | 258AB | 27 n. 43 |
| 1180a6–14 | 86 n. 113, 106 n. 22, 148 n. 181 | 260D | 267 n. 95 |
| | | 279F | 111 n. 44 |
| | | 316A–318F | 27 n. 43, 28 n. 45 |

| | | | |
|---|---|---|---|
| 317D | 211 n. 88 | 50 | 170 n. 42 |
| 588A | 37 n. 83 | 51–52 | 171 n. 46 |
| | | 52 | 171 n. 44 |
| BARNABAS | | 61 | 170 n. 42 |
| 5.14 | 279 n. 125 | 62–63 | 171 n. 45 |
| 10.5 | 259 n. 72 | 64 | 229 n. 129 |
| 19.4 | 210 n. 83 | 65 | 171 n. 45 |
| 19.12 | 205 n. 68 | 76–100 | 170 n. 41 |
| 21.4 | 205 n. 68 | 85 | 166 n. 22, 171 n. 45 |
| | | 85–86 | 174 n. 54 |
| CHRYSIPPUS | | 88–95/100 | 174 n. 54 |
| *On the Passions* | 73 n. 67, 118 n. 69 | 89 | 70 n. 56 |

CICERO
*Academica*
1.5          102 n. 1, 172 n. 47

*De Inventione*
97           297 n. 177
2.155–58     246 n. 36

*On Duties*
1.53         170 n. 41
1.56         77 n. 83
1.58         77 n. 83
1.88         90 n. 126
1.136–137    77 n. 84
3.10.43      77 n. 11
3.45         170 n. 41

*Letters to His Friends*
15.16.1      102 n. 1
15.19.2      102 n. 1, 172 n. 47

*Orator ad M. Brutum*
21–23        50 n. 123
25.85        49 n. 120

*On Ends*
1.65         171 n. 46, 177 n. 69
1.66–70      115 n. 53, 163 n. 5
1.68         163 nn. 8 & 10
1.71–72      139 n. 152
1.78–85      163 n. 5
1.80–82      172 n. 46
2.25         115 n. 53
2.30–31      115 n. 53
2.79         170 n. 41
2.119        102 n. 2
5.43         285 n. 149

*The Making of an Orator*
50
2.82         246 n. 36
3.204–205    48 n. 119
3.205        49 n. 120
3.210–212    50 n. 123

*Against Piso*
68–71        112 n. 44
70           112 n. 44
70–71        105 n. 16

*Stoic Paradoxes*  267 n. 94

*On Friendship*
7–10         84 n. 106, 297 n. 179
15           170 n. 41
18–23        170 n. 41
19           170 n. 42
21           84 n. 106
22           20 n. 129
28           170 n. 42
30           170 n. 42
32           170 n. 42
45           171 n. 43
45–47        171 n. 46
46           78 n. 87, 170 n. 41
46–47        171 n. 44
48–51        170 n. 42

*Tusculan Disputations*
3–4          118 n. 69
4.26         285 n. 149
4.3.7        103 n. 8
4.7          102 n. 1, 172 n. 47
4.10.23      66 n. 40
4.11.26      66 n. 40
4.15         285 n. 149
4.27.58      66 n. 40
4.31–32      66 n. 39
4.29.42      285 n. 149

[CICERO]
*ad Herennium*
1.4.6        296 n. 175

| | | | |
|---|---|---|---|
| 3.2.3 | 246 n. 36 | 74.2–3 | 73 n. 70 |
| 3.3.8 | 246 n. 36 | 74.2–4 | 63 n. 33 |
| 4.1.63 | 48 n. 117 | 74.3 | 63 n. 32 |
| 4.53.66 | 49 nn. 117 & 120 | 75.1 | 62 n. 31, 63 n. 32, 79 n. 90, 87 n. 118 |

CLEARCHUS
*Gergithios*
Fragments

| | | | |
|---|---|---|---|
| | | 75.3 | 63 n. 32 |
| 19–20 | 27 n. 42 | 76.1 | 120 n. 75, 305 n. 201, 306 n. 209 |
| 20 | 28 n. 47 | 76.1–4 | 62 n. 31 |
| | | 77.1 | 305 n. 202 |
| | | 77.1–2 | 62 n. 31 |

*On Proverbs*

| | | | |
|---|---|---|---|
| | | 77.3 | 62 n. 31, 319 n. 251 |
| ii.318 FHG | 28 n. 45 | 78.1 | 62 n. 31, 305 n. 202 |
| | | 78.2–4 | 62 n. 31 |

*Clitarchi sent.*

| | | | |
|---|---|---|---|
| | | 79.1 | 62 n. 31 |
| 88–89 (ed. Elter) | 166 n. 23 | 79.2 | 62 n. 31 |
| | | 80.1 | 62 n. 31 |

CLEMENT OF ALEXANDRIA
*Exhortation of the Greeks*

| | | | |
|---|---|---|---|
| | | 80.2 | 62 n. 31 |
| | | 80.3 | 62 n. 31 |
| | 59 n. 18 | 81.1 | 62 n. 31, 305 n. 202 |
| | | 81.2 | 62 n. 31 |

*Exhortation to Endurance*

| | | | |
|---|---|---|---|
| | | 81.3 | 278 n. 121 |
| | 59 n. 18 | 81.3–83.2 | 305 n. 200 |
| | | 82.1 | 88 n. 121 |

*The Pedagogue*

| | | | |
|---|---|---|---|
| | 51, 62, 72 | 82.2 | 62 n. 31, 278 n. 121 |
| 1.1–2 | 63 n. 36 | 83.2 | 63 n. 33, 73 n. 68, 320 n. 254 |
| 1.4 | 63 n. 36 | | |
| 1.4–2.2 | 63 n. 34 | 85.4 | 62 n. 31 |
| 3.3 | 73 n. 67, 79 n. 88 | 88.1 | 62 n. 31 |
| 3.8 | 72 n. 66 | 89.1 | 63 n. 34 |
| 25.1–52.3 | 303 n. 195 | 89.1–4 | 63 n. 36 |
| 43.2 | 17 n. 8, 72 n. 66 | 89.3–4 | 63 n. 34 |
| 62.1 | 73 n. 70 | 89.4 | 63 n. 32 |
| 64.1 | 62 n. 31 | 90.2–93.1 | 63 n. 35 |
| 64.3 | 73 n. 70 | 91.1 | 63 n. 32 |
| 64.4–65.1 | 73–74 n. 70 | 93.1 | 125 n. 91 |
| 64.4–66.4 | 63 n. 33 | 93.2–94.1 | 74 n. 171 |
| 65.1 | 62 n. 31 | 93.3 | 328 n. 182 |
| 65.2 | 62 n. 31 | 94.1 | 75 n. 75, 84 n. 108, 139 n. 152, 301 n. 191, 303 n. 195 |
| 66.1 | 63 n. 36, 70 n. 54, 318 n. 248 | | |
| 66.1–5 | 74–75 n. 73 | 94.1–2 | 328 n. 281 |
| 66.2 | 51 n. 129, 62 n. 31, 231 n. 137, 276 n. 117, 279 nn. 122 & 126 | 94.2 | 62 n. 31, 217 n. 98, 305 n. 201 |
| | | 96.1–2 | 73 n. 68 |
| | | 97.3 | 63 n. 32 |
| 66.2–3 | 311 n. 222 | | |
| 66.3 | 278 n. 121 | *Who Is the Rich Person Who Will Be Saved?* | |
| 66.4 | 63 n. 32 | | |
| 66.4–5 | 51 n. 129 | 2 | 139 n. 147 |
| 66.5 | 62 n. 31 | 16 | 276 n. 117 |
| 72.1 | 62 n. 31 | 20 | 258 n. 68 |
| 74.2 | 120 n. 75, 252 n. 54 | 23 | 258 n. 68 |
| | | 35 | 205 n. 68 |

# INDEX OF PASSAGES

1 CLEMENT
| | |
|---|---|
| 6.2 | 78 n. 87 |
| 13.1 | 237 n. 6 |
| 14.1 | 237 n. 6 |
| 16.4–5 | 228 n. 127 |
| 16.13 | 258 n. 68 |
| 18.13 | 258 n. 68 |
| 34.1–8 | 311 n. 224 |
| 34.5–7 | 232 n. 138 |
| 35.2 | 311 n. 224 |
| 35.5 | 258 n. 68 |
| 35.9 | 258 n. 68 |
| 37.1–38.2 | 211 n. 87 |
| 38.1–2 | 206 n. 71, 209 n. 80 |
| 38.2 | 237 n. 6, 330 n. 283 |
| 39.1 | 237 n. 6 |
| 45.4 | 258 n. 68 |
| 48.5 | 223 n. 112 |
| 48.6 | 249 n. 44 |
| 56.2–4 | 307 n. 212 |
| 56.10 | 279 n. 126 |
| 56.11 | 258 n. 68 |
| 59.4 | 205 n. 69, 330 n. 283 |
| 60.2 | 312 n. 229 |

2 CLEMENT
| | |
|---|---|
| 15.1 | 205 n. 69, 230 n. 136 |
| 15.3 | 311 n. 224 |
| 17:1–2 | 230 n. 136 |
| 17.2 | 205 n. 69 |
| 19.1 | 205 n. 69 |
| 19.2 | |

COLUMELLA
*On Agriculture*
| | |
|---|---|
| 1.8.15 | 327 n. 227 |
| 12.1.6 | 327 n. 227 |

DEAD SEA SCROLLS
*1 QS*
| | |
|---|---|
| V 20–VI 1 | 11 n. 21 |
| V 23 | 11 n. 21 |
| V 24 | 11 n. 21 |
| VI 2b | 11 n. 21 |
| VI 3b–4 | 11 n. 21 |
| VI 8–9a | 11 n. 21 |
| VI 13–23 | 11 n. 21 |

DEMETRIUS
*On Style*
| | |
|---|---|
| 191 | 296 n. 175 |
| 216 | 43 n. 103 |
| 240 | 78 n. 85 |
| 259–61 | 43 n. 103 |
| 261 | 98 n. 151 |
| 265 | 273 n. 112 |
| 265–66 | 49 n. 120 |
| 279 | 127 n. 102 |
| 292–98 | 296 n. 175 |
| 294 | 313 n. 235 |
| 296–98 | 43 n. 103 |
| 297 | 313 n. 235 |

PSEUDO-DEMETRIUS
*Epistolary Types*
| | |
|---|---|
| 30, 3–4 Malherbe | 61 n. 27 |
| 30, 20 Malherbe | 61 n. 27 |
| 1 | 244 n. 32 |
| 3 | 319 n. 251 |
| 5 | 200 n. 42 |
| 6 | 306 n. 204 |
| 7 | 60 n. 21, 70 n. 57 |
| 8 | 324 n. 272, 328 n. 281 |

DIDACHE
| | |
|---|---|
| 4.14 | 205 n. 68 |
| 15.3 | 205 n. 68, 207 n. 75 |

DIO CHRYSOSTOM
*Discourses*
| | |
|---|---|
| 3.32–39 | 90 n. 127 |
| 12.17 | 298 n. 181 |
| 13 | 57 n. 13 |
| 13.9–13 | 54 n. 7 |
| 13:11 | 243 n. 26 |
| 13.18 | 57 n. 15 |
| 13.28 | 57 n. 14 |
| 14 | 267 n. 94 |
| 15 | 267 n. 94 |
| 15.18–19 | 279 n. 127 |
| 15.21–23 | 267 n. 95 |
| 16.11 | 229 n. 131 |
| 17.2 | 57 n. 15 |
| 21[38].21 | 223 n. 114 |
| 27.7–10 | 54 n. 7, 57 n. 15, 66 n. 40 |
| 32 | 92 |
| 32.7–11 | 72 n. 65 |
| 32.8 | 125 n. 93 |
| 32.10 | 252 n. 10 |
| 32.11 | 93 |
| 32.11–12 | 92 n. 134 |
| 32.11–13 | 120 n. 74 |

| | | | |
|---|---|---|---|
| 32.17–19 | 72 n. 65, 87 n. 118 | **PSEUDO-DIOGENES** | |
| 32.17–20 | 74 n. 72, 79 n. 89 | *Epistles* | |
| 32.18 | 79 n. 90 | 27.18 | 93 n. 136 |
| 32.25–28 | 76 n. 79, 90 n. 127, 306 n. 205 | 29.1–3 | 251 n. 51 |
| | | 29.1–29 | 79 n. 90 |
| 32.26 | 87 n. 118 | 29.14–26 | 87 n. 117 |
| 32.30 | 74 n. 72, 79 n. 89 | | |
| 32.33 | 74 n. 72, 79 n. 89 | **DIOGENES LAERTIUS** | |
| 39.3 | 229 n. 131 | *Lives of Eminent Philosophers* | |
| 40.20 | 78 n. 86 | 1.60 | 166 n. 23 |
| 40.21 | 78 n. 87 | 2:66 | 243 n. 27 |
| 40.35–36 | 90 n. 127 | 2.91–93 | 170 n. 42 |
| 42.3 | 298 n. 181 | 3.85 | 134 n. 121 |
| 43.10 | 79 n. 88 | 4.24 | 160 n. 219 |
| 49.13–14 | 21 n. 25 | 4.47 | 19 n. 12 |
| 54.1 | 298 n. 181 | 6.4 | 91 n. 131 |
| 66.26 | 16 n. 4 | 6.13 | 97 n. 150 |
| 70 | 22, 45 n. 107 | 6:22 | 91 n. 131, 243 n. 27 |
| 70.2 | 57 n. 14 | 6.30 | 57 n. 15 |
| 70.6 | 22 n. 26 | 6.51 | 16 n. 4 |
| 70.7 | 22 n. 28 | 6.72 | 20 n. 20 |
| 71 | 22, 45 n. 107, 272 n. 108 | 7.12 | 125 n. 93 |
| | | 7.111 | 118 n. 69 |
| 71.2 | 21 n. 22 | 7.111–14 | 85 n.111 |
| 71.6 | 22 n. 28 | 7.117 | 90 n. 128 |
| 72 | 23, 43 n. 104 | 7.124 | 166 n. 24, 170 n. 42 |
| 72.1 | 23 n. 30 | 7.127 | 67 n. 42, 127 n. 101 |
| 72.2 | 23 n. 30 | 10.4–5 | 111–112 n. 44 |
| 72.9 | 23 n. 30, 57 n. 14 | 10.5 | 105 n. 17 |
| 72.10 | 23 n. 30 | 10.6 | 154 n. 199 |
| 72.11–16 | 54 n. 7 | 10.11 | 126 n. 99 |
| 73 | 125 | 10.16–21 | 160 n. 210, 175 n. 58 |
| 74.1 | 125 n. 94 | 10.24–25 | 118 n. 68, 161 n. 3 |
| 74.11–12 | 125 n. 95 | 10.26 | 116 n. 57 |
| 77/78.33 | 37 n. 83 | 10.27–28 | 161 n. 3 |
| 77/78.35 | 267 n. 95 | 10.35–36 | 140 n. 154 |
| 77/78.38 | 72 n. 62, 92, 93 | 10.83 | 140 n. 154 |
| 77/78.39 | 22 n. 26 | 10.120 | 127 n. 101 |
| 77/78.40 | 87 n. 118 | 10.120b | '177 n. 69 |
| 77/78.42 | 72 n. 64 | 10.135 | 140 n. 154, 165 n. 17 |
| 77/78.43 | 72 n. 63 | | |
| 77/78.43–45 | 66 n. 40 | **DIOGENES OF OENOANDA** | |
| 77/78.45 | 79 n. 88 | *Fragments* | |
| | | 1 | 130 n. 111 |
| **DIODORUS SICULUS** | | 2 | 130 n. 111 |
| *Library of History* | | 2, V–VI | 130 n. 111 |
| 3.67.2 | 316 n. 244 | 20, II 4–5 | 138 n. 139 |
| 10.4.6 | 224 n. 116, 259 n. 73 | 32 | 82 n. 102 |
| 16.54.4 | 79 n. 88 | 51, III.7–8 | 175 n. 61 |
| | | | |
| **DIOGENES** | | **DIOGNETUS** | |
| *Fragment* | | *Epistle of Diognetus* | |
| 35 | 98 n. 151 | 9.3–6 | 258 n. 68 |
| | | 9.5 | 70 n. 58 |

| | | | |
|---|---|---|---|
| 10.5–6 | 228 n 127 | 3.21.17–20 | 21 n. 23, 57 n. 13 |
| 10.6 | 232 n. 139 | 3.21.18–24 | 2 n. 3, 43 n. 103 |
| | | 3.21.19–20 | 43 n. 103 |

DIONYSIUS OF HALICARNASSUS
*On the Arrangement of Words*
12          46 n. 108
*Rhet*
9.323.1 U.  296 n. 175

| | | | |
|---|---|---|---|
| 3.21.23 | 18 n. 11 |
| 3.22.48 | 364 n. 85 |
| 3.22.50 | 95 n. 142 |
| 3.22.54 | 321 n. 259 |
| 3.22.77 | 95 n. 143 |
| 3.22.81–82 | 95 n. 141 |

DIOSCORIDES
*Materia medica*
5.11        136 n. 127

| | |
|---|---|
| 3.22.82 | 95 n. 143 |
| 3.22.93 | 95 n. 143 |
| 3.22.94 | 84 n. 112, 281 n. 132 |
| 3.22.95 | 95 n. 143 |
| 3.22.96–97 | 95 n. 144 |
| 3.22.101 | 78 n. 85 |
| 3.23.27 | 21 n. 23, 43 n. 103, 165 n. 18 |

ENNODIUS 59 n. 18

EPICTETUS
*Discourses*

| | | | |
|---|---|---|---|
| 1.4 | 67 n. 42, 331 n. 290 | 3.23.30 | 71 n. 59 |
| 1.4.4 | 301 n. 190 | 3.23.30–32 | 21 n. 23 |
| 1.8.8 | 81 n. 98, 301 n. 188 | 3.23.30–34 | 43 n. 103 |
| 1.15.29 | 81 n. 98 | 3.23.36 | 55 n. 8 |
| 1.18.8 | 81 n. 97 | 3.24.12–14 | 98 n. 150 |
| 1.18.10 | 127 n. 104 | 4.1 | 267 n. 94 |
| 1.26.16 | 81 n. 99 | 4.1.118–19 | 321 n. 259 |
| 2.9.22 | 228 n. 128 | 4.2.8–10 | 261 n. 77 |
| 2.11 | 81 n. 99 | 4.4.44 | 11 n. 21 |
| 2.15.14 | 73 n. 69 | 4.5.34 | 81 n. 99 |
| 2.15.20 | 81 n. 99, 285 n. 149 | 4.8 | 43 n. 104 |
| 2.16.6–7 | 82 n. 101 | 4.8.1–9 | 11 n. 21 |
| 2.17.1–2 | 82 n. 101 | 4.9.13–18 | 80 n. 95 |
| 2.17.10 | 82 n. 101 | 4.9.16–18 | 80 n. 96 |
| 2.18 | 96 n. 144 | 4.13 | 126 n. 97 |
| 2.18.2–4 | 96 n. 144 | 4.13.10 | 270 n. 102 |
| 2.19.29 | 67 n. 45 | 4.13.16 | 126 n. 98, 229 n. 130 |
| 2.22.15–16 | 249 n. 44 | 4.13.23 | 126 n. 98 |
| 2.22.24 | 126 n. 97 | | |
| 2.22.26–27 | 249 n. 44 | *Encheiridion* | |
| 2.22.28 | 98 n. 151 | 5 | 11 n. 21 |
| 2.22.30 | 126 n. 97 | 20 | 280 n. 128 |
| 2.22.34 | 126 n. 97 | 30 | 125 n. 93 |
| 2.22.36 | 90 n. 128, 281 n. 132 | 51.1–3 | 300 n. 188 |
| 2.23.40 | 308 n. 215 | 51.2 | 81 n. 97 |
| 2.24.26 | 98 n. 150 | | |
| 3.2 | 67 n. 45, 331 n. 290 | *Gnomologium* | |
| 3.4.12 | 125 n. 93, 249 n. 45 | 63 | 120 n. 75 |
| 3.6.9–10 | 66 n. 39, 67 n. 45 | | |
| 3.13.22–23 | 96 n. 144 | EPICURUS | |
| 3.14.9 | 306 n. 205, 328 n. 281 | *Fragments* | |
| | | Usener | |
| 3.14.18 | 126 n. 97 | 51 | 143 n. 163 |
| 3.16 | 127 n. 97 | 56 | 125 n. 91 |
| 3.19.6 | 81 n. 98, 300 n. 188 | 71, 3 | 74 n. 71 |
| 3.21.5 | 125 n. 93 | 87, 23–28 | 104 n. 10 |
| 3.21.8–9 | 21 n. 23 | 106–107 | 104 n. 10 |

| | | | |
|---|---|---|---|
| 131–164 | 175 n. 61 | 18 | 165 n. 16 |
| 135–136 | 175 n. 61 | 23 | 163 n. 10, 164 n. 14 |
| 138 | 175 n. 60 | | |
| 143 | 175 n. 62 | 28 | 165 n. 19 |
| 152 | 149 n. 186 | 29 | 104 n. 15 |
| 187 | 16 n. 4, 113 n. 48 | 34 | 125 n. 93, 163 n. 10, 104 |
| 192 | 67 n. 44, 139 n. 151 | 37 | 78 n. 87, 231 n. 137 |
| 220 | 114 n. 50 | | |
| 221 | 133 n. 120 | 39 | 125 n. 93, 164 n. 15 |
| 227b | 143 n. 163 | | |
| 521 | 127 n. 101 | 54 | 114 n. 50 |
| 522 | 128 n. 106, 130 n. 111 | 56–57 | 125 n. 93, 164 n. 15 |
| 531 | 128 n. 106 | 61 | 163 n. 10, 164 |
| Arrighetti | | 64 | 113 n. 48, 133 n. 120 |
| (2) [59], 3 | 175 n. 60 | 66 | 163 n. 10 |
| (2) [59], 3–4 | 175 n. 61 | 67 | 113 n. 48 |
| | | 70 | 163 n. 10 |
| *Letter to Herodotus* | 140 | 74 | 109 n. 36, 117 n. 64 |
| | | 78 | 177 n. 69 |

*Letter to Menoeceus*  140 n. 154, 165
122        133 n. 120
133        82 n. 102

*Letter to Pythocles*  85, 175 n. 61

*On Nature*     140
[34.25] 21–34   82 n. 102, 328 n. 281

*Principal Doctrines*   59 n. 20
1       148, 163 n. 8
6       163 n. 10
7       163 n. 10
11      161 n. 1
13      161 n. 1, 163 n. 10
14      163 n. 10, 164 n. 12
17      163 n. 10
27      163 n. 10
28      163 n. 10
29      163 n. 10
31–35   125 n. 95, 163 n. 10
38      163 n. 10
39      163 n. 10
40      163 n. 10

*Symposium*     125 n. 91

*Vatican Sentences*
1       163 n. 8
7       163 n. 10

EPITOME MONACENSIS
26, 1–2      25 n. 33
26, 11–12    25 n. 33

EUPOLIS
*The Flatterers*
*Fragment*
159, 9       24 n. 32
159, 12      25 n. 36

EURIPIDES
*Fragments*
362      25 n. 36, 26 n. 37
364      25 n. 36
403, 6   134 n. 121

*Medea*
809–810      20 n. 19

*Phoenecian Women*
1688     75 n. 77

EUSEBIUS
*Praep. Ev.*
14.5     177 n. 69

GALEN
*De compositione medicamentorum per genera*
2.14     228 n. 127

*On the Doctrines of Hippocrates and Plato*
2.5.3–7      53 n. 3
298.31–34    66 n. 40

| | | | |
|---|---|---|---|
| *On the Passions and Errors of the Soul* | | HERMOGENES | |
| | 75 n. 78 | *Progymnasmata* | |
| 1.1 | 53 n. 3 | 9 | 48 n. 115 |
| 3.6–10 | 53 n. 3 | | |
| 8 | 53 n. 1 | *On Stasis* | |
| | | 1 | 51 n. 127 |
| GNOMOLOGIUM BYZANTINUM | | | |
| 59 | 69–70 n. 53 | HERODOTUS | |
| | | *Histories* | |
| GORGIAS | | 4.70 | 167 n. 25 |
| *Palamedes* | | | |
| 22 | 46 n. 108 | HESIOD | |
| | | *On Works and Days* | |
| HEGESIPPUS | | 353 | 20 n. 19 |
| *Fragments* | | | |
| 1 | 26 n. 37 | HIPPOCRATES | |
| 2 | 26 n. 37 | *The Art* | |
| | | 6.1–3 | 78 n. 85 |
| HELIODORUS | | | |
| *Ethiopian Story* | | PSEUDO-HIPPOCRATES | |
| 8.8.57 | 257, 258 n. 68 | *Epistles* | |
| | | 17.28 | 93 n. 136 |
| PSEUDO-HERACLITUS | | 17.43 | 93 n. 136 |
| *Epistles* | | | |
| 2.4–5 | 93 n. 136 | HOMER | |
| 7 | 93 n. 136 | *Iliad* | |
| | | 4.218 | 145 n. 171 |
| SHEPHERD OF HERMAS | | 5.171 | 75 n. 77 |
| *Visions* | | 11.515 | 145 n. 171 |
| 1.3.1–2 | 205 n. 69 | 11.833–35 | 21 n. 25 |
| 3.5.4 | 138 n. 134 | 12.267 | 71 n. 60 |
| 3.6.1 | 258 n. 68 | 13.116 | 75 n. 77 |
| 3.6.4 | 258 n. 68 | | |
| 3.6.6 | 18 n. 11 | *Odyssey* | |
| 3.12.2 | 339 n. 283 | 1.1 | 19 |
| 3.13.4 | 138 n. 134 | 6.184 | 20 n. 19 |
| 4.2.6 | 279 n. 126 | | |
| | | HORACE | |
| *Mandates* | | *Carmina* | |
| 8.10 | 205 n. 69 | 3.9.24 | 315 n. 239 |
| 12.6.3 | 230 n. 136 | | |
| | | *Epistles* | |
| *Similitudes* | | 1.17 | 31–32, 268 n. 100 |
| 5.5.3 | 258 n. 68 | 1.17.19 | 28 n. 46 |
| 6.2.1–4 | 231 n. 136 | 1.17.13–32 | 243 n. 27 |
| 6.2.5 | 278 n. 121 | 1.18 | 31–32 |
| 6.2.7 | 278 n. 121 | 1.18.1–16 | 26 n. 40, 32 n. 60, 91 |
| 6.3.1–4 | 278 n. 121 | | n. 131, 272 n. 108 |
| 9.2.5 | 306 n. 205 | 1.18.14 | 28 n. 46 |
| 9.2.7 | 306 n. 205 | | |
| 9.9.1 | 258 n. 68 | *Satire* | |
| 9.23.4 | 230 n. 136, 330 | 1.3.42–48 | 328 n. 28 |
| | n. 283 | 1.4.25–32 | 328 n. 28 |
| | | 1.4.107–108 | 328 n. 28 |
| | | 2.7 | 267 n. 94 |

382    INDEX OF PASSAGES

| | |
|---|---|
| 2.7.81–82 | 267 n. 96 |

**IAMBLICHUS**
*The Life of Pythagoras*

| | |
|---|---|
| 17.71–74 | 11 n. 20 |
| 9.49 | 69 n. 50 |
| 30.180–183 | 69 n. 50 |

**IGNATIUS**
*Letter to the Ephesians*

| | |
|---|---|
| 7.1 | 323 n. 267 |
| 7.1–2 | 228 n. 127 |
| 20.2 | 228 n. 127 |
| 21.1 | 228 n. 127 |

*Letter to Polycarp*

| | |
|---|---|
| 1.2–3 | 228 n. 128 |

**IGNATIUS OF LOYOLA**

| | |
|---|---|
| *Exercitia spiritualia* | 191 n. 22 |

**ISOCRATES**

| | |
|---|---|
| *Against the Sophists* 18 | |

*Antidosis*

| | |
|---|---|
| 147–148 | 127 n. 104 |
| 206–208 | 57 n. 13 |
| 206–214 | 86 n. 113, 106 n. 22 |
| 208 | 67 n. 44, 303 n. 195 |
| 288–290 | 86 n. 113 |
| 289–290 | 55 n. 8, 106 n. 22, 209 n. 80 |
| 290 | 54 n. 6 |
| 293–294 | 298 n. 182 |

*To Antipater*

| | |
|---|---|
| 3–4 | 106 n. 22 |
| 4 | 318 n. 248 |
| 3–6 | 86 n. 113 |
| 5–6 | 90 n. 126 |
| 6 | 79 n. 90 |
| 7 | 106 n. 22 |
| 9 | 106 n. 22 |

*Concerning Peace*

| | |
|---|---|
| 14–15 | 106 n. 22 |
| 70 | 106 n. 22 |
| 72 | 70 n. 54, 86 n. 113, 88 n. 123, 106 n. 22, 318 n. 248 |

*To Demonicus*

| | |
|---|---|
| 1 | 168 n. 31 |
| 1–6 | 106 n. 22 |
| 3 | 2 n. 3 |
| 3–5 | 55 n. 8 |
| 3–6 | 86 n. 113 |
| 6 | 2 n. 3 |
| 11–12 | 106 n. 22 |
| 17 | 249 n. 45 |
| 20 | 106 n. 22 |
| 20–31 | 107 n. 23 |
| 22 | 79 n. 88, 86 n. 113, 106 n. 22, 128 n. 105 |
| 24 | 128 n. 105 |
| 24–26 | 106 n. 22 |
| 29–31 | 106 n. 22 |
| 30–31 | 86 n. 113, 238 n. 10 |
| 45–46 | 86 n. 113, 106 n. 22 |

*Letter to Philip*

| | |
|---|---|
| 1.1 | 34 n. 69, 86 n. 113 |
| 1.22 | 86 n. 113, 249 n. 45 |

*To Nicocles*

| | |
|---|---|
| 2 | 86 n. 113, 106 n. 22 |
| 3 | 107 n. 23 |
| 4 | 303 n. 195 |
| 12 | 106 n. 22 |
| 28 | 86 n. 113, 106 n. 22 |
| 42–43 | 86 n. 113, 106 n. 22 |
| 45 | 249 n. 45 |
| 45–49 | 106 n. 22 |
| 47 | 127 n. 104 |
| 48–53 | 86 n. 113 |
| 49 | 18 n. 11 |
| 50 | 249 n. 45 |

*Nicocles or the Cyprians*

| | |
|---|---|
| 55 | 89 n. 124, 106 n. 22 |
| 55–57 | 90 n. 126 |
| 57 | 106 n. 22, 209 n. 80 |

*Panegyricus*

| | |
|---|---|
| 130 | 318 n. 248 |

*To Philip*

| | |
|---|---|
| 72 | 107 n. 23 |
| 116 | 238 n. 10, 320 n. 258 |
| 116–117 | 90 n. 126 |

**JOSEPHUS**
*Jewish Antiquities*

| | |
|---|---|
| 2.6.9 | 193 n. 27 |
| 7.372 | 125 n. 93 |
| 10.8.3.142 | 39 n. 91 |
| 10.11 | 38 n. 87, 259 n. 73 |
| 17.342 | 125 n. 93 |

## JULIAN
*Orations*
| | |
|---|---|
| 6.201A | 94 n. 137 |
| 6.201B | 94 n. 137 |
| 7.214BC | 22 n. 26 |

## JUSTIN MARTYR
*Dialogue with Trypho*
| | |
|---|---|
| 2.3–6 | 53 n. 1 |

## PSEUDO-JUSTIN
*Paraenetic Address to the Greeks*
59 n. 18

## PSEUDO-LIBANIUS
*Epistolary Styles*
| | |
|---|---|
| 9 | 296 n. 175 |
| 13 | 324 n. 272 |
| 19 | 318 n. 247 |
| 34 | 306 n. 204 |
| 38 | 324 n. 272 |
| 45 | 71 n. 61 |
| 53 | 319 n. 251 |
| 60 | 324 n. 272 |
| 66 | 317 n. 245 |
| 81 | 306 n. 204 |
| 85 | 324 n. 272 |
| 92 | 98 n. 151 |

## LUCIAN
*Alexander the False Prophet*
| | |
|---|---|
| | 104 |
| 17 | 104 n. 15 |
| 25 | 37 n. 83, 104 n. 15 |
| 25, 38 | 9 n. 16 |
| 61 | 104 n. 15 |

*Apology for the 'On Salaried Posts in Great Houses'*
| | |
|---|---|
| 2 | 77 n. 84 |
| 9 | 268 n. 99 |
| 11–12 | 268 n. 99 |

*Demonax*
| | |
|---|---|
| 3 | 22 n. 26 |
| 10 | 95 n. 139, 97 n. 149 |

*The Fisherman*
| | |
|---|---|
| 19 | 37 n. 83 |

*Hermotimus*
| | |
|---|---|
| 1–2 | 54 n. 6 |

*The Parasite*
| | |
|---|---|
| 2 | 26 n. 37 |

| | |
|---|---|
| 4 | 26 n. 37 |
| 15 | 26 n. 37 |
| 19 | 26 n. 37 |
| 20 | 26 n. 37 |
| 22 | 268 n. 98 |
| 23 | 26 n. 37 |
| 30 | 26 n. 37 |

*The Parliament of the Gods*
| | |
|---|---|
| 2 | 37 n. 83 |

*The Passing of Peregrinus*
| | |
|---|---|
| 19 | 22 n. 26 |

*On Salaried Posts in Great Houses*
| | |
|---|---|
| 1 | 268 n. 98 |
| 4–6 | 268 n. 98 |
| 19–20 | 268 n. 98 |

*Slander*
| | |
|---|---|
| 19 | 285 n. 149 |

*Toxaris*
| | |
|---|---|
| | 125 |
| 7 | 315 n. 239 |
| 29–34 | 259 n. 73 |
| 37 | 125 n. 96, 166 n. 21, 167 n. 25, 315 n. 239 |

## LUCRETIUS
*On the Nature of Things*
| | |
|---|---|
| 2.16–19 | 163 n. 10 |
| 3.37–39 | 163 n. 10 |
| 4.11 | 73 n. 69 |
| 5.1020 | 125 n. 95 |
| 5.1020–26 | 163 n. 10 |

## MAXIMUS OF TYRE
*Discourses*
| | |
|---|---|
| 1 | 22 n. 27, 23, 41 n. 95, 45 n. 107, 46 n. 109, 87 n. 120 |
| 1.1a–c | 41 n. 96 |
| 1.1b–h | 41 n. 97 |
| 1.2 | 18 n. 11 |
| 1.2a | 41 n. 97 |
| 1.2b | 41 n. 97 |
| 1.2f | 41 n. 97 |
| 1.3a | 41 n. 97 |
| 1.3b | 146 n. 174, 306 n. 205 |
| 1.3bc | 96 n. 147 |
| 1.3e–f | 96 n. 147, 146 n. 174, 306 n. 205 |
| 1.5c | 42 n. 98 |
| 1.5h | 42 n. 98 |
| 1.8a | 42 n. 98 |

| | | | |
|---|---|---|---|
| 1.8c–e | 42 n. 98, 76 n. 79, 146 n. 174 | 10 | 280 n. 128, 321 n. 259 |
| 1.9a–d | 42 n. 99 | 16 | 66 n. 39 |
| 1.10a–f | 42 n. 101 | 36 | 21 n. 24, 80 n. 93 |
| 1.10e–f | 42 n. 102 | 46 | 65–66 n. 39 |
| 2.2 | 78 n. 87 | 49 | 62 n. 31 |
| 3e–f | 278 n. 122, 280 n. 129 | | |

NICOLAUS
*Fragments*

| | | | |
|---|---|---|---|
| 4.5a | 78 n. 87, 85 n. 109 | 66–67 | 293 n. 168 |
| 7 | 151 n. 190 | IV 570 M. V. 36 | 25 n. 36 |
| 8c–e | 306 n. 205 | | |
| 10.5 | 303 n. 195 | | |

ORIGEN
*Against Celsus*

| | | | |
|---|---|---|---|
| 14.1 | 25 n. 36, 28 n. 49, 33 n. 64 | 3.66 | 98 n. 150 |
| 14.4 | 33 n. 65 | | |
| 14.6 | 25 n. 33, 166 n. 21, 169 n. 38 | *Com. Rm.* | |
| 14.7 | 169 n. 38, 170 n. 39 | 6.9 [1086A] | 273 n. 111 |
| 14.8g–i | 37 n. 82 | | |

OVID
*The Art of Love*

| | | | |
|---|---|---|---|
| 20.3 | 166 n. 22 | 1.146–162 | 28 n. 46 |
| 25 | 22 n. 27 | | |
| 25.4ab | 33 n. 66 | *Metamorphoses* | 45 |
| 25.4f–6d | 81 n. 100 | | |
| 25.5 | 279 n. 122 | PAPYRUS LOND. | |
| 25.5–6 | 33 n. 66 | 971, 4 | 78 n. 87 |

MENANDER
*Sententiae*

PAPYRUS PAR.

| | | | |
|---|---|---|---|
| 432 (ed. Kauk) | 156 n. 203 | 10 | 291 n. 166 |
| 454 | 325 n. 274 | | |
| 534 | 229 n. 129 | PATROLOGIA GRAECA | |
| 545 | 37 n. 83, 125 n. 92 | 21:644B | 210 n. 84 |
| 662 | 87 n. 118, 325 n. 274 | PHILO | |
| 689 | 30 n. 54 | *On Abraham* | |
| 695 | 125 n. 92 | 16 | 301 n. 192 |
| 708 | 73 n. 69 | 20 | 114 n. 50 |
| 573 (ed. Jaekel) | 279 n. 124, 321 n. 259 | 22 | 114 n. 50 |
| | | 26 | 78 n. 85, 301 n. 192 |
| *Thais* | 261 n. 77, 308 n. 213 | 52 | 301 n. 192 |
| | | 176–77 | 79 n. 88 |

MENANDER RHETOR
*On Farewell Speeches*

*Allegorical Interpretation*
39

| | | | |
|---|---|---|---|
| 395.1–32 | 55 n. 10 | 1.45 | 301 n. 190 |
| 395.4–12 | 55 n. 10 | 1.74–78 | 22 n. 28 |
| 395.12–20 | 55 n. 11 | 1.94 | 301 n. 190 |
| | | 1.108 | 301 n. 190 |

MUSONIUS RUFUS
*Fragments*

| | | | |
|---|---|---|---|
| | | 3.25 | 301 n. 190 |
| | | 3.100 | 301 n. 190 |
| 1 | 22 n. 27, 65 n. 39 | 3.131 | 301 n. 190 |
| 2 | 78 n. 86 | 3.140 | 301 n. 190 |
| 9 | 281 n. 132 | 3.144 | 301 n. 190 |

| | | | |
|---|---|---|---|
| 3.147 | 301 n. 190 | 56 | 40 n. 92 |
| 3.159 | 301 nn. 190 & 192 | 165 | 301 n. 192 |
| 3.179 | 40 n. 92 | | |
| 3.207 | 301 n. 190 | *On Joseph* | 39–40 |
| | | 32 | 39 n. 88 |
| *On the Cherubim* | | 32–34 | 39 n. 91, 40 |
| 75 | 301 n. 190 | 33–34 | 40 n. 92 |
| | | 34 | 192 n. 25 |
| *On the Confusion of Tongues* | | 62 | 37 n. 82 |
| 71 | 40 n. 92 | 67–69 | 40 n. 93 |
| | | 70–85 | 301 n. 192 |
| *On the Contemplative Live* | | 73 | 40 n. 93 |
| 31 | 22 n. 28 | 73–79 | 87 n. 120 |
| | | 74 | 40 n. 94, 280 n. 128 |
| *On Dreams* | | 75 | 40 n. 93 |
| 1.102–114 | 301 n. 192 | 75–79 | 40 |
| 1.210 | 39 n. 88 | 76 | 40 n. 93 |
| 2.9–10 | 301 n. 190 | 168–170 | 301 n. 192 |
| 2.10 | 301 n. 191 | 230 | 22 n. 28 |
| 2.10–14 | 300 n. 189, 313 n. 234 | | |
| 2.10–16 | 39 n. 90 | *On the Migration of Abraham* | |
| | | 29 | 301 n. 190 |
| *On Drunkenness* | | 38 | 301 n. 190 |
| 35 | 40 n. 92 | 85 | 22 n. 28 |
| 82–86 | 40 n. 92 | 110–111 | 87 n. 120, 88 n. 123, 328 n. 280 |
| 170 | 41 n. 97 | | |
| | | 115–117 | 328 n. 280 |
| *Every Good Man is Free* | | 116–117 | 106 n. 20 |
| | 267 n. 94 | 115–118 | 88 n. 123 |
| 12 | 55 n. 8 | 118 | 87 n. 120 |
| 20 | 55 n. 8 | 124 | 79 n. 88 |
| 63 | 55 n. 8 | 152–153 | 39 n. 90, 300 n. 189 |
| 64 | 55 n. 8 | 171 | 22 n. 28 |
| 95–96 | 22 n. 28, 301 n. 192, 313 n. 234, 325 n. 273 | *Moses* | |
| 99 | 22 n. 28, 301 n. 192, 313 n. 234 | 1.117 | 41 n. 97 |
| | | 2.289 | 39 n. 90, 300 n. 189 |
| 126 | 22 n. 28, 301 n. 192, 313 n. 234 | *On Noah's Work as a Planter* | |
| 155 | 22 n. 28 | 44 | 39 n. 90, 300 n. 189 |
| | | 104–106 | 25 n. 36 |
| *Who is the Heir* | | 105–106 | 271 n. 105 |
| 5–7 | 311 n. 224 | 168 | 301 n. 90 |
| 6 | 312 n. 229 | | |
| 10 | 303 n. 195 | *On the Posterity and Exile of Cain* | |
| 14–21 | 301 n. 192 | 88 | 300 n. 189 |
| 19 | 106 n. 19, 114 n. 50, 301 nn. 190 & 191 | 132 | 301 n. 192 |
| 21 | 106 n. 19 | *On the Preliminary Studies* | |
| 302 | 22 n. 28 | 36 | 301 n. 192 |
| 313–314 | 301 n. 190 | | |
| | | *On the Sacrifices of Abel and Cain* | |
| *On Husbandry* | | 7 | 301 n. 190 |
| 8–9 | 301 n. 192 | 8 | 301 n. 190 |
| 9 | 301 n. 190 | 11 | 301 n. 190 |

| | | | |
|---|---|---|---|
| 43 | 301 n. 190 | 38.1–3 | 114 n. 49 |
| 65 | 301 n. 190 | 38.7 | 98 n. 151, 136 n. 128 |
| 121 | 301 n. 190 | 41.8 | 98 n. 151, 136 n. 128 |
| | | 42.30–31 | 114, n. 49 |
| *On Sobriety* | | 43.14–41 | 149 n. 183, 172 n. 49 |
| 9–10 | 301 n. 190 | 44.9–22 | 137 n. 132, 147 n. 176 |
| 14 | 40 n. 92 | 44.15–27 | 114 n. 49 |
| | | 44.27 | 132 n. 114 |
| *The Worse Attacks the Better* | | p. 54 (Wilke) | 128 n. 105 |
| 7 | 40 n. 92 | | |
| 69–78 | 22 n. 28 | *On Arrogance* | |
| 178 | 74 n. 72 | PHerc 1008 | 102 |
| **PHILODEMUS** | 5 n. 8 | *Comparetti Ethics* | |
| *On Anger* | 102, 108 n. 30 | PHerc 1251 | 102 n. 4 |
| Pherc 182 | | | |
| Columns | | *On Death* | 102 |
| 1.7–20 | 119 n. 71 | PHerc 1050 | |
| 1.8–27 | 114 n. 49 | Columns | |
| 1.21–27 | 119 n. 72 | 17.33 | 127 n. 101 |
| 2.21 | 117 n. 64 | 23.2–15 | 172 n. 50 |
| 3.13 | 119 n. 72 | 23.8 | 127 n. 101 |
| 4.4–23 | 153 n. 196 | 23.9 | 138 n. 139 |
| 4.15–16 | 119 n. 72 | 25.37–39 | 117 n. 64 |
| 9.21 | 145 n. 171 | 31.12 | 138 n. 139 |
| 12.18 | 98 n. 151, 135 n. 128 | 33.23–24 | 117 n. 64 |
| | | 35.24–34 | 172 n. 50 |
| 13.5–11 | 278 n. 122 | 35.28 | 138 n. 139 |
| 13.23–30 | 278 n. 122 | 37.23–25 | 172 n. 50 |
| 19.11 | 160 n. 219 | 37.27–29 | 172 n. 50 |
| 19.12–17 | 145 n. 170 | 38.8 | 117 n. 64 |
| 19.12–27 | 114 n. 49 | 39.1–25 | 172 n. 50 |
| 19.14–27 | 126 n. 100 | | |
| 19.15–16 | 160 n. 219 | *On Epicurus* | 102 n. 3 |
| 19.17–21 | 145 n. 171 | PHerc 1232/1289 | |
| 19.19 | 132 n. 114, 160 n. 219 | Fragment | |
| | | 8, col. 1.6–12 | 104 n. 13 |
| 19.25–26 | 109 n. 36 | 9, col. 1.8–9 | 128 n. 108 |
| 19.25–27 | 114 n. 64, 145 n. 168 | *Epitome on Conduct and Character* | |
| 24.1 | 114 n. 50 | | 102, 108–109 |
| 26.24–25 | 104 n. 13 | | |
| 27.19–39 | 114 n. 49 | *On Flattery* | 102, 110–111 |
| 27.19–21 | 114 n. 49 | PHerc 222 | 110, 111, 112 n. 44 |
| 28.39 | 132 n. 114 | Columns | |
| 31–32 | 122 n. 83 | 1.3–4 | 37 n. 83 |
| 31.28 | 122 n. 83 | 2 | 112 n. 45 |
| 31.31–32 | 122 n. 83 | 2.1–12 | 112 n. 46 |
| 35.18–36.6 | 150 n. 189 | 2.4–7 | 123 n. 85 |
| 35.18–39.7 | 114 n. 49 | 2.20–21 | 112 n. 46, 123 n. 85 |
| 35.19 | 108 n. 29 | 4 | 112 nn. 45 & 46 |
| 35.22–23 | 150 n. 189 | 4.6–7 | 138 n. 139 |
| 36.24–25 | 108 n. 30 | PHerc 223 | 110 n. 39 |
| 37.19 | 98 n. 151, 136 n. 128 | Fragment | |
| | | 3 | 98 n. 150 |

INDEX OF PASSAGES 387

| | | | |
|---|---|---|---|
| *PHerc 1082* | 109, 110 n. 39, 111 | 5.7 | 203 n. 60 |
| Columns | | 6–10 | 146, 150 |
| 1.1–7 | 108 n. 30 | 6.1–4 | 145 |
| 2.1–3 | 104 n. 14 | 6.1–8 | 142 n. 161 |
| 2.1–4 | 109 n. 34, 117 n. 65 | 6.7–8 | 132 n. 114, 151 n. 156, |
| 2.1–14 | 109 n. 35, 261 n. 77 | | 144, 159 n. 212 |
| *PHerc 1089* | 110 n. 39, 111 | 7 | 186 n. 6 |
| Columns | | 7.1–5 | 137 n. 133 |
| 3.1–2 | 112 n. 46 | 7.1–6 | 149 n. 185 |
| 5.2 | 112 n. 46 | 7.2–3 | 145 |
| 5.6–7 | 126 n. 102 | 7.5–11 | 142 n. 161 |
| 7.5–6 | 114 n. 51 | 7.6 | 145 |
| 7.17 | 28 n. 48 | 7.9–11 | 145 |
| *PHerc 1457* | 110, 111, 122 n. 84, | 8.4–11 | 129 |
| | 123 | 8.9–11 | 156, 173 n. 52 |
| Fragments | | 8.10 | 138 n. 142 |
| 12.5–6 | 110 n. 37 | 10 | 144 n. 165, 145, 146 |
| 16.3–5 | 104 n. 13, 117 n. 65 | | n. 173 |
| Columns | | 10.1 | 122 |
| 1.5–7 | 25 n. 36 | 10.1–2 | 123 n. 89 |
| 1.23–24 | 110 n. 37 | 10.1–7 | 143 |
| 4.7–9 | 25 n. 36 | 10.4 | 143 n. 165 |
| 5.19–21 | 25 n. 35 | 10.4–5 | 145 |
| 8.1–3 | 112 n. 46 | 10.5–9 | 145 n. 173 |
| 8.19–21 | 179 n. 71 | 10.7 | 145 |
| 10 | 138 n. 137 | 10.9 | 145, 149 n. 185 |
| 10.11–13 | 113 | 10.10 | 127 n. 101 |
| 10.17–19 | 112 n. 46 | 13.7–8 | 127 n. 101, 147 |
| 11.10–15 | 112 n. 46 | | n. 178 |
| 11.16 | 113 | 15.6–10 | 159 n. 212 |
| 11.16–25 | 113 n. 47 | 16.2–3 | 136 n. 128 |
| *PHerc 1675* | 110, 111 | 16.3–5 | 135 |
| Column | | 18.1 | 138 n. 140 |
| 11 | 123 n. 88 | 18.3–5 | 282 n. 137 |
| | | 18.5 | 203 n. 61 |
| *On Frank Criticism* | | 19.1–5 | 147 n. 177 |
| *PHerc 1471* | 4 n. 6, 86–87, 102, | 20 | 281 n 133, 317 |
| | 107 n. 25, 108 n. 31 | | n. 245 |
| Fragments | | 20.1–2 | 132 n. 114 |
| 1 | 130 n. 111, 135 | 20.5–6 | 141 n. 158 |
| | n. 125, 154, 164 n. 15, | 21 | 281 n. 133 |
| | 173 n. 51 | 22 | 127 n. 101 |
| 1.2–3 | 173 n. 51 | 23.1–5 | 141 n. 158 |
| 1.5–9 | 134 n. 124 | 25 | 142 n. 160 |
| 2 | 281 n. 133 | 25.3–8 | 130 n. 112, 142 |
| 2.1–7 | 132, 141 | 25.6 | 138 n. 135 |
| 2.3 | 138 n. 135 | 26.2–4 | 142 |
| 2.6 | 125 n. 93 | 26.4–7 | 120 n. 75 |
| 3.8–10 | 104 n. 12 | 26.8 | 132 n. 114 |
| 4.4–10 | 162 n. 4 | 26.9 | 136 n. 128 |
| 4.9 | 130 n. 111 | 26.11 | 123 n. 86, 261 n. 77 |
| 5 | 144 n. 167 | 28 | 108, 128 n. 107, 163 |
| 5–10 | 145 | 28.1–10 | 162 |
| 5.1–4 | 159 n. 212 | 31.1 0 | 139 n. 150 |
| 5.4–8 | 139 n. 150, 144 | 31.2 | 138 n. 134 |

## INDEX OF PASSAGES

| | | | |
|---|---|---|---|
| 31.9–12 | 142 | 45.8–11 | 157 n. 204 |
| 31.11 | 159 n. 213 | 45.9–11 | 158 n. 208 |
| 32.7–9 | 136 n. 128 | 46 | 155, 172 nn. 48 & 49, |
| 33.3 | 127 n. 101 | | 181 n. 133, 297 n. 179 |
| 34.3 | 130 n. 111 | 46.3 | 159 n. 213 |
| 34.3–4 | 251 n. 49 | 46.4–5 | 155 n. 202 |
| 34.3–8 | 139 n. 147 | 46.5–11 | 132 n. 116, 141 n. 158, |
| 35 | 154 | | 156 |
| 35.8 | 143 n. 165 | 49 | 128, 156, 291 n. 165 |
| 35.8–9 | 143 n. 165 | 49.2–7 | 127 n. 103 |
| 36.1–2 | 130 n. 111, 251 n. 49 | 49.7–10 | 129 |
| 36.2–4 | 130 | 50.1 | 142 n. 160 |
| 36.4–9 | 137 n. 133, 157 n. 205, | 50.3–10 | 129 |
| | 172 n. 48 | 50.7 | 138 n. 142 |
| 36.5 | 138 n. 134 | 50.10–12 | 129 n. 109 |
| 37 | 117 n. 61, 281 n. 133 | 51–52 | 156 |
| 37.4 | 117 n. 64 | 51.1 | 128 n. 107 |
| 37.5–9 | 141 n. 157 | 51.2–5 | 129 |
| 38 | 132 n. 114 | 51.5–10 | 129 |
| 38.1–6 | 141 n. 156 | 52 | 281 n. 133 |
| 39 | 133 n. 118 | 52.1–3 | 129 |
| 39–40 | 135 n. 125 | 52.2 | 132 n. 114 |
| 39.2 | 159 n. 213 | 52.2–5 | 130 |
| 39.2–4 | 152 | 52.2–3 | 147 n. 177 |
| 39.4–5 | 133 n. 118 | 52.4 | 138 n. 134 |
| 40 | 153 n. 196 | 52.4–5 | 157 n. 205 |
| 40.5–9 | 158 n. 208 | 52.6 | 159 n. 213 |
| 40.8 | 130 n. 111, 158 n. 209 | 52.6–9 | 122 n. 84 |
| 41 | 154, 157 | 52.6–12 | 129 n. 110 |
| 41.2–8 | 128 n. 108 | 52.12 | 138 n. 141 |
| 41.4–10 | 151 n. 192 | 53.2 | 109 n. 36 |
| 41.7 | 138 n. 142 | 53.4 | 138 n. 135 |
| 41.7–8 | 158 n. 208 | 53.7 | 138 n. 135 |
| 41.10 | 311 n. 223 | 53.10–13 | 141 |
| 42 | 128, 141, 156, 291 | 54.1 | 104 n. 12 |
| | n. 165 | 54.2–6 | 130 |
| 42.1–7 | 128 | 54.11 | 138 n. 141 |
| 42.2 | 138 n. 141 | 55 | 130, 157 n. 204 |
| 42.5 | 159 n. 213 | 55–56 | 232 n. 140 |
| 42.6 | 120 n. 75 | 55.3 | 138 n. 135 |
| 43 | 120, 141, 172 nn. 48 & | 55.5–6 | 131 |
| | 49, 173 n. 52 | 55.7 | 138 n. 142 |
| 43.1–8 | 141 | 55.8 | 132 n. 116 |
| 43.1–4 | 86 n. 115 | 56 | 297 n. 179 |
| 43.4 | 204 n. 66 | 56.1–3 | 135, 201 n. 46, 235 |
| 43.4–8 | 86 n. 116 | | n. 147 |
| 43.7 | 203 n. 61 | 56.8–13 | 135 |
| 44 | 154 | 57 | 120, 135 n. 125 |
| 44.6–9 | 156, 172 n. 48 | 57.4–5 | 135 n. 126, 208 |
| 44.7 | 104 n. 12 | 57.5–11 | 135 |
| 45 | 154 n. 201, 232 n. 140 | 58 | 144 n. 165, 306 |
| 45.1–6 | 131 | | n. 205 |
| 45.5 | 159 n. 213 | 58–60 | 205 n. 69 |
| 45.7–11 | 137 n. 133 | 58.5–6 | 144 n. 165 |

# INDEX OF PASSAGES

| | | | |
|---|---|---|---|
| 58.5–9 | 149 | 70.3 | 138 n. 142 |
| 58.6–9 | 123 n. 90 | 70.4 | 159 n. 213 |
| 58.7–8 | 143 n. 165, 144 n. 165 | 70.5–7 | 139 n. 150 |
| 58.7–9 | 143 | 70.8 | 138 n. 143 |
| 58.9–10 | 149 | 71 | 146, 306 n. 205 |
| 59 | 119, 150 | 71.1–6 | 142 n. 160 |
| 59–60 | 150, 289 n. 15 | 71.2 | 138 n. 135 |
| 59.1–2 | 119 n. 73 | 71.8 | 138 n. 134 |
| 59.9–11 | 119 n. 73 | 74.1–2 | 123 n. 86, 142 n. 159 |
| 60 | 35 n. 74, 92 n. 135, 145 | 74.5–9 | 132 n. 116 |
| | | 75 | 142 |
| 60.1–7 | 119 | 75.1–8 | 157 n. 205 |
| 60.8–12 | 120, 122 n. 82 | 75.3 | 159 n. 213 |
| 61 | 113 n. 48, 120, 131, 138 n. 143, 156 | 75.4–5 | 138 n. 136, 160 n. 219 |
| | | 76.1 | 159 n. 213 |
| 61.1–10 | 131 n. 113 | 76.3 | 138 n. 135 |
| 61.1 | 316 n. 242, 317 n. 245 | 78.6 | 130 n. 111 |
| 61.2 | 138 n. 137 | 79 | 281 n. 133 |
| 61.6–12 | 129 | 79.1–4 | 130 |
| 61.9 | 311 n. 223 | 79.2–3 | 138 n. 136, 160 n. 219 |
| 61.11 | 311 n. 223 | 79.8–12 | 120 n. 74 |
| 62.1–4 | 142 | 79.9–12 | 141 n. 157 |
| 63 | 155 | 80.2 | 159 n. 213 |
| 63–65 | 135 n. 125 | 80.5 | 125 n. 93 |
| 63–69 | 137 | 80.7–11 | 282 n. 137 |
| 63.3–11 | 136 | 81 | 107 n. 27 |
| 63.6–7 | 135 n. 126 | 81.1–4 | 130 |
| 64 | 155 | 81.3 | 138 n. 142 |
| 64.2–5 | 135 | 81.8 | 138 n. 142 |
| 64.5–8 | 136 | 82 | 122 n. 83 |
| 64.8–12 | 136 | 83.7–10 | 143 n. 162 |
| 65 | 136, 205 n. 69 | 83.8 | 138 n. 134 |
| 65–66 | 96 n. 145, 147 | 84 | 142 n. 160 |
| 65.8–11 | 148 n. 181 | 84.2 | 138 n. 142 |
| 65.9–11 | 136, 137 n. 133 | 84.8–14 | 145 n. 169 |
| 65.11–13 | 151 n. 192 | 85.1–4 | 142 n. 160 |
| 65.12 | 311 n. 223 | 85.7 | 159 n. 213 |
| 66 | 281 n. 133 | 85.7–9 | 114 n. 51, 129 n. 109 |
| 66.2–10 | 147 n. 179 | 85.9 | 132 n. 114 |
| 66.13 | 147 n. 189 | 86.1 | 157 n. 205 |
| 66.13–15 | 151 n. 192 | 86.2–4 | 147 n. 189 |
| 67 | 144 | 86.2–7 | 122 n. 82 |
| 67.5–9 | 147 n. 180 | 86.5–7 | 123 n. 89 |
| 67.8–9 | 203 n. 61 | 86.6–7 | 20 n. 21, 143 |
| 67.9–11 | 139 n. 150 | 86.7 | 203 n. 61 |
| 68 | 144 n. 165 | 86.7–8 | 142 n. 160 |
| 68.1 | 20 n. 21 | 87.1–3 | 123 n. 86 |
| 68.1–2 | 122 | 87.1–4 | 138 n. 138, 142 n. 159 |
| 68.1–7 | 123 n. 89, 143 | 88 | 114 n. 50 |
| 68.3–7 | 123 n. 165 | 77 Herc. | 128 n. 107 |
| 69 | 135 n. 125 | 79 Herc. | 128 n. 107 |
| 69.4–10 | 135 n. 126, 145 | 79.2–4 Herc. | 130 n. 112 |
| 70 | 120, 144 | 79.9 Herc. | 128 n. 107 |
| 70.1–4 | 173 n. 52 | 84 Herc. | 128 n. 107 |

## INDEX OF PASSAGES

| | | | |
|---|---|---|---|
| 87 Herc. | 128 n. 107, 146, 306 n. 205 | 10a10 | 125 n. 93 |
| 91 Herc. | 128 n. 107, 147 n. 178 | 10b8 | 125 n. 93 |
| 93 Herc. | 128 n. 107, 149 | 11b1 | 138 n. 139 |
| 93.4–6 Herc. | 149 n. 186 | 12a5–6 | 172 n. 48 |
| Columns | | 12b6–9 | 157 n. 205, 172 n. 48 |
| | | 12b6–11 | 322 |
| 1 | 114 n. 50 | 12b7 | 138 n. 135 |
| 1–2 | 114 | 12b8 | 125 n. 93 |
| 1a | 116 n. 60 | 13a3 | 282 n. 137 |
| 1a1–4 | 114 n. 50 | 13a7–9 | 142 n. 160 |
| 1b5–13 | 114 n. 51, 261 n. 77 | 13a7–11 | 173 n. 52 |
| 1b13 | 114 n. 51 | 13a10 | 138 nn. 142 & 143 |
| 2a1–9 | 114 n. 51 | 13a12–13 | 137 n. 133, 158 n. 208 |
| 2a7–8 | 116 n. 60 | 13b3–6 | 123 n. 90 |
| 2b | 114 n. 50, 120, 146 | 13b4 | 108 n. 30 |
| 2b3–7 | 137 n. 131 | 13b11 | 125 n. 93 |
| 3a1–3 | 114 n. 50 | 13b12 | 120 n. 75 |
| 4a1–8 | 140 n. 155 | 13b13 | 123 n. 90 |
| 4a1–6a8 | 86 n. 115 | 14a | 172 n. 48 |
| 4a7–8 | 142 n. 160 | 14a3–10 | 157 n. 205 |
| 4b8–9 | 132 n. 114 | 14a6–10 | 175 n. 48 |
| 5a7–10 | 158 n. 209 | 14a10–11 | 104 n. 13 |
| 5a9 | 159 n. 213 | 14b9–11 | 127 n. 101 |
| 5b1–2 | 159 n. 213 | 15a–21b | 144, 151 n. 191 |
| 5b4–6 | 142 n. 160 | 15a1 | 316 n. 242, 317 n. 245 |
| 6a1–8 | 142 n. 160 | 15a8 | 316 n. 242, 317 n. 245 |
| 6a4–8 | 138 n. 145 | 15a8–10 | 151 n. 191 |
| 6a6 | 138 n. 134 | 15b1 | 311 n. 223 |
| 6a8–15 | 123 n. 86 | 15b7–14 | 151 n. 192 |
| 6b1–3 | 139 n. 152, 251 n. 49 | 16a6–12 | 131 |
| 6b3 | 130 n. 111 | 16a8 | 132 n. 114 |
| 7a1–2 | 138 n. 146 | 16a10 | 138 n. 134 |
| 7a1–3 | 159 n. 217, 328 n. 280 | 16a10–12 | 151 n. 191 |
| 7a2 | 159 n. 213 | 16b1–2 | 151 n. 192 |
| 7a2–3 | 104 n. 12 | 16b2–9 | 114 n. 50 |
| 7a7–10 | 138 n. 144, 157 n. 205 | 16b6–7 | 151 n. 192 |
| 7a8–10 | 172 n. 48 | 17a | 120, 131, 135 n. 125, 142, 150 n. 188 |
| 7b1 | 131 | | |
| 8a2–9 | 132 n. 116 | 17ab | 131 |
| 8a8–9 | 117 n. 61 | 17a2–3 | 151 n. 192 |
| 8a9 | 117 n. 64 | 17a4–10 | 136 n. 128 |
| 8b–9a | 209 n. 79 | 17a8–13 | 151 n. 192 |
| 8b2 | 104 n. 12 | 17a12 | 311 n. 223 |
| 8b6–13 | 130 | 17b1–6 | 142 n. 160 |
| 8b8 | 149 n. 186 | 17b6–9 | 151 |
| 8b11–12 | 136 n. 128 | 18a–b | 138 |
| 8b12 | 132 n. 114 | 18b2–10 | 151 |
| 9a | 149 | 18b7–10 | 151 n. 192 |
| 9a1–8 | 130 | 18b13–14 | 132 n. 115, 151 n. 192 |
| 9a1–8 | 132 n. 116 | 19a1–3 | 146 n. 172 |
| 10a1–5 | 117 n. 61 | 19a5–8 | 151 n. 193 |
| 10a2 | 117 n. 64 | 19a11 | 138 n. 143 |
| 10a6–10 | 151 n. 194, 310 n. 220 | 19b7–9 | 123 n. 115 |
| 10a8–10 | 132 n. 116 | 19b8–9 | 151 n. 192 |

# INDEX OF PASSAGES 391

| | | | |
|---|---|---|---|
| 19b10–11 | 132 n. 143 | *On the Good King according to Homer* | |
| 20a | 144 | *PHerc 1507* | 102 n. 3 |
| 20a1–5 | 107 n. 27, 139 n. 150, 157 | *On Gratitude* | |
| 20a3–4 | 150 n. 213 | *PHerc 1414* | |
| 20a5–10 | 151 n. 193 | Column | |
| 20a5–12 | 144 n. 166 | 10 | 130 n. 12 |
| 20a8–12 | 157 n. 205 | 15.14 | 146 n. 173 |
| 21b4–7 | 157 | 16 | 130 n. 112 |
| 21b5–7 | 151 n. 193, 310 n. 220 | 16.9 | 127 n. 101 |
| 21b7–8 | 136 n. 128 | | |
| 21b12–14 | 107 n. 27, 138 n. 145 | *On Household Management* | |
| 22a | 149 n. 184 | *PHerc 1424* | 102, 103, 162 |
| 22a–b | 139 n. 148, 149, 172 n. 48 | Columns | |
| | | 7.10–26 | 147 n. 176 |
| 22a7 | 136 n. 128 | 9.14–16 | 138 n. 139 |
| 22b | 78 n. 87, 281 n. 133 | 23.11–18 | 164 n. 12 |
| 22b1 | 78 n. 87 | 23.22–36 | 103 n. 6, 109 n. 37, 116 n. 59 |
| 22b2–4 | 141 n. 158 | | |
| 22b5 | 149 n. 185 | | |
| 22b10–13 | 138 n. 144 | 24.19–25.4 | 162 n. 4 |
| 22b10–24a6 | 172 n. 48 | 26.1–14 | 161 n. 2, 162 n. 4 |
| 23a–b | 107 n. 27, 139 n. 149 | | |
| 24a | 149, 281 n. 133 | 26.18–28 | 161 n. 2, 162 n. 4 |
| 24a–b | 139 n. 149 | | |
| 24a4–8 | 138 n. 146 | 27.6–9 | 161 n. 2, 162 n. 4 |
| 24a7–9 | 107 n. 27, 138 n. 146 | | |
| 24b1–12 | 138 n. 146 | | |
| 24b10 | 138 n. 140 | *Index Academicorum* | |
| App. Tab. | | *PHerc 164/1021* | 102 n. 3 |
| II D2 | 130 n. 111 | | |
| III F | 104 n. 13 | *Index Stoicorum* | |
| III G | 141 n. 157, 149 nn. 185 & 187 | *PHerc 1018* | 102 n. 3 |
| | | Column | |
| III H | 104 n. 12 | 17.10 | 138 n. 139 |
| IV I | 136 n. 128, 143 n. 164, 149, 306 n. 205, 320 n. 253 | 17.57 | 138 n. 139 |
| | | *On Music* | |
| IV J | 141 n. 157, 141 n. 158 | *PHerc 1497* | 102 n. 3 |
| XII ib. 1–2 | 136 n. 129 | | |
| | | *On Phenomena and Inferences* | |
| *To Friends of the School* | | *PHerc 1065* | 102 n. 3 |
| *PHerc 1005* | 102 n. 3, 115 | | |
| Columns | | *On Piety* | 102 |
| 4.10–14 | 164 n. 11 | *PHerc 1428* | |
| 8 | 115 n. 56 | 123, 17 | 37 n. 83 |
| 13.3–15 | 59 n. 20, 140 n. 153 | | |
| 14–15 | 115 n. 53 | *On Poems* | 102 n. 3 |
| 17.6–9 | 59 n. 20 | | |
| | | *On Praise* | 116 |
| *On the Gods* | 102 | | |
| *PHerc 26* | | *Rhetoric* | 102 n. 3 |
| 3, fr. 84 col. 13, 36–9, 36 165 n. 17 | | Sudhaus | |
| | | 1, 19 col. 1 | 135 n. 125 |

| | | | |
|---|---|---|---|
| 1, 216–224 | 116 n. 57 | 22.2–4 | 121 n. 78 |
| 1, 219 col. 38a24–25 | | 22.27–32 | 121 n. 78 |
| | 116 n. 58 | 23.23–26 | 121 n. 78 |
| 1, 237 col. 8 | 113 n. 48 | 24.1–21 | 140 n. 155 |
| 1, 247, 11–12 | 134 n. 124 | | |
| 1, 267 col. 30.34–36 | 138 n. 134, | *On the Way of Life of the Gods* | |
| | 172 n. 46 | PHerc 152/157 | 102 n. 3 |
| 1, 269 col. 32.2–10 | 116 n. 58 | | |
| 1, 270 col. 32.32–37 | 116 n. 58 | *Works on the Records of Epicurus and* | |
| 1, 369 | 135 n. 126 | *Some Others* | 102 n. 3 |
| 1, 373 col. 94 | 113 n. 48 | *PHerc 310* | |
| 1, 373 | 135 n. 126 | *PHerc 1418* | |
| 2, 1 | 108 n. 30 | Columns | |
| 2, 17 col. 23 | 113 n. 48 | 2.6–15 | 115 n. 56 |
| 2, 18–19 col. 24 | 113 n. 48 | 15.3–13 | 115 n. 56 |
| 2, 74–75 | 27 n. 43 | | |
| 2, 74 fr. XII | 45 n. 106, 116 n. 57 | *PHerc 176* | 175 n. 59 |
| 2, 77 fr. IV | 97 n. 150 | *PHerc 312* | 101 n. 1 |
| 2, 106 frs. XIII, XIV | 45 n. 106, 116 n. 57 | *PHerc 346* | 102 n. 4 |
| 2, 115 fr. VI | 45 n. 106 | Fragment | |
| 2, 127 fr. XII | 116 n. 57 | 3 IV.b.7 | 158 n. 209 |
| 2, 157 fr. XVII | 113 n. 48 | IV.24–28 | 158 n. 209 |
| 2, 214 col. 30a19 | 51 n. 127 | VII.24 | 158 n. 209 |
| 2, 219–223 cols. 15–18 | 113 n. 48 | | |
| 2, 256–263 | 116 n. 57 | *PHerc 831* | 115, 118 |
| 4, col. 30a19–32a8 | 116 n. 58 | Column | |
| 4, col. 32a6–8 | 82 n. 101 | 5.9–11 | 118 n. 70 |
| 5, fr. 11.4–6 | 290 n. 161 | | |
| Longo Auricchio | | *PHerc 1389* | 108 n. 31 |
| 2, XLI 35–XLII 1 | 114 n. 51 | | |
| | | *PHerc 1573* | |
| *On the Stoics* | 102 n. 3 | Fragment | |
| PHerc 155/339 | | 12 | 27 n. 43 |
| 17.23 | 127 n. 101 | | |
| | | **PHILOSTRATUS** | |
| *On Vices and the Opposing Virtues* | | *On the Hero* | |
| | 102, 110 | 19.3 | 51 n. 127 |
| Columns | | | |
| 2.32–35 | 104 n. 13 | **PSEUDO-PHOCYLIDES** | |
| 8.15 | 138 n. 140 | *Sentences* | |
| 8.28–30 | 104 n. 13 | 150 | 149 n. 184 |
| 10.10–16.28 | 140 n. 155 | | |
| 10.11–13 | 147 n. 180, 238 n. 10 | **PHRYNICHUS** IId; 371 | 117 n. 62 |
| 16.29–17.17 | 140 n. 155 | | |
| 16.29–33 | 319 n. 252 | **PINDAR** | |
| 17.17–19.2 | 140 n. 155 | *Fragment* | |
| 19.2–5 | 319 n. 252 | 43 (Snell) | 28 n. 45 |
| 20.3–37 | 140 n. 155 | | |
| 21.1–37 | 140 n. 155 | *Pythian Odes* | |
| 21.37–38 | 121 n. 77 | 2.52–53 | 98 n. 151 |
| 21.37–23.37 | 121 n. 77, 140 n. 155 | 4.219 | 279 n. 126 |

## INDEX OF PASSAGES

PLATO
*Epistle*
13.360D             29 n. 51

*Gorgias*           18
461B–466A           26 n. 37
463A                18 n. 10
464C                134 n. 122
464D                37 n. 82
465B                37 n. 82
477A                75 n. 73
482C–486D           294 n. 171
487A                37 n. 84, 63 n. 32
488B                294 n. 171
492C                20 n. 19
500B                37 n. 82
500E–501D           26 n. 37
501A                37 n. 82
502B–503A           26 n. 37
513B                46 n. 108
520C–522E           37 n. 82
521D                26 n. 37
525A–C              86 n. 113
525A                121 n. 78
525B                106 n. 22
525BC               74 n. 72, 87 n. 118
526B                148 n. 181

*Laches*
179C                25 n. 33

*Laws*
659E                138 n. 134
777DE               294 n. 171
777E                328 n. 281
791D–793A           86 n. 114
908A                224 n. 116
909A                79 n. 90, 224 n. 116
951D–E              138 n. 134, 224 n. 116

*Lesser Hippias*    20
364BCE              20 n. 17
365B                20 n. 17
368B–D              22 n. 28

*Ion*
532CD               298 n. 181

*Lysis*
215A                271 n. 105
215DE               168 n. 33

*Phaedrus*          18
240B                26 n. 37
245A                149 n. 185

260E–272B           17 n. 9
261A                17 n. 9, 47 n. 111
270D–271D           47 n. 111
271A                46 n. 108
271C                2 n. 4
272A                47 n. 111
277BC               17 n. 9, 51 n. 125

*Philebus*
55E–56B             134 n. 122

*Protagoras*
325AB               74 n. 72, 86
                    n. 113, 106 n. 22,
                    148 n. 181

*Republic*
2.357               163 n. 6
362B                20 n. 19
404C–D              37 n. 82
406D                134 n. 121
407D                134 n. 121
410A                148 n. 181
462A–B              177 n. 69
464D                177 n. 69
492A                81 n. 96
492A–B              270 n. 102
560C                121 n. 78
582E                117 n. 63

*Sophist*           86
221C–D              138 n. 139
222D–223A           26 n. 37
229E                87 n. 119
229E–230A           86 nn. 113 & 114
229E–231B           306 n. 205
230A                87 n. 119, 233
                    n. 142, 328
                    n. 281
230B–231B           86 n. 114
230C–D              155 n. 202

*Statesman*
298C                134 n. 121

*Theaetetus*
146D                20 n. 17

PLAUTUS
*The Bragging Soldier*  24
11–12               24 n. 31
20–22               24 n. 31
24–25               24 n. 31
33–37               24 n. 31
70                  24 n. 31

# INDEX OF PASSAGES

PLUTARCH
*Advice to Bride and Groom*
142B                35 n. 73

*Alcibiades*
2.1                 30 nn. 54 & 56
23.4                28 n. 45, 30
                    n. 54, 34 n. 72,
                    87 n. 117,
                    173 n. 52
23.5                28 n. 50, 30
                    n. 55, 229 n. 132,
                    317 n. 245
23.3–5              30 n. 56
26.5                30 n. 54

*On Being a Busybody*
521E                127 n. 104

*On Brotherly Love*  210
480F                210 n. 85
481A                22 n. 25, 78 n. 85
482B                166 n. 22
484C–486A           210 n. 85
484D                210 n. 85, 224
                    n. 116
484F                211 n. 86
485B–C              211 n. 86
486A                211 n. 90
486B–491C           211 n. 86
487A–C              211 n. 87
487C                280 n. 130
488A                211 n. 87
490E                168 n. 34
492D                210 n. 85

*Brutus*
34                  92 n. 132

*Can Virtue be Taught?*
439A–440C           60 n. 23

*Comparison of Alcibiades and Coriolanus*
1.4                 30 n. 54
3.2                 30 n. 54
4.5                 29 n. 52, 30 n. 54

*On Compliancy*
532D                247 n. 42

*Concerning Talkativeness*
                    126
502B–515A           126 n. 97

*On the Control of Anger*
453D                136–137 n. 129
453DE               80 n. 93
453E                145 n. 171, 148
                    n. 182
455C                145 n. 171
462C                320 n. 258
463B–D              126 n. 97
463D                28 n 51, 78
                    n. 87, 84 n. 107

*On Curiosity*      126
515B–523B           126 n. 97

*On the Delays of the Divine Vengeance*
549F–550A           51 n. 128
551E                74 n. 72
551EF               29 n. 51
562D                51 n. 129

*The Dinner of the Seven Wise Men*
155B                28 n. 50

*On Exile*
599A–C              317 n. 245

*On Having Many Friends*
88F                 78 n. 85
93C                 166 n. 21
93CDEF              168 n. 35
94A                 32 n. 61
94ABEF              168 n. 35
94B                 166 n. 22
95AB                158 n. 35
96–97               174 n. 54
96A                 173 n. 53
96A–D               259 n. 73
96ACDF              169 n. 36
96F–97A             27 n. 43
96F–97B             35 n. 72
97A                 28 n. 44, 20 n. 53
97ABE               169 n. 36

*How to Profit by One's Enemies*
88D                 22 n. 25
89B                 80 n. 94
90C                 80 n. 94

*How to Study Poetry*
25D                 51 n. 125

*How to Tell a Flatterer from a Friend*
                    31 n. 58
47E                 160 n. 219

| | | | |
|---|---|---|---|
| 49B | 20 n. 20, 112 n. 45 | 67BE | 35 n. 75 |
| 49C | 25 n. 33, 32 n. 61, 268 n. 100 | 67D–74D | 69 n. 52 |
| | | 68AC | 35 n. 75 |
| 49D | 166 n. 22 | 68D–74D | 35 n. 76 |
| 49E | 34 n. 67 | 68F–69C | 35 n. 78 |
| 49EF | 71 n. 59 | 68A–70D | 98 n. 151 |
| 50B | 34 n. 70 | 68EF | 36 n. 79 |
| 50C | 35 n. 73 | 68F | 307 n. 211 |
| 50F–51D | 28 n. 48 | 69CD | 35 n. 77, 92 n. 132 |
| 51A–C | 169 n. 37 | 70B | 35 n. 77, 92 n. 132 |
| 51B | 25 n. 33, 177 n. 69 | 70DE | 36 n. 79, 317 n. 245 |
| 51C | 20 n. 20, 34 n. 70 | 70E | 148 n. 181, 159 n. 214 |
| 51D | 20 n. 52 | | |
| 51F | 28 n. 48 | 70F | 36 n. 80, 126 n. 97 |
| 52A | 160 n. 38 | 71A–D | 36 n. 80 |
| 52A–C | 20 n. 21 | 71BCD | 318 n. 246 |
| 52A–53B | 169 n. 37 | 71E | 281 n. 132 |
| 52AF | 28 n. 45 | 71F | 22 n. 25 |
| 52C | 98 n. 150 | 72A | 22 n. 25, 98 n. 151 |
| 52DE | 30 n. 54 | 72AB | 303 n. 195 |
| 52E | 37 n. 83 | 72B | 36 n. 80 |
| 52F | 27 n. 43 | 72B–D | 36 n. 80, 75 n. 77 |
| 52FAB | 29 n. 52 | 72D | 306 n. 205 |
| 53A–B | 20 n. 53 | 72F | 209 n. 80 |
| 53B | 98 n. 150 | 73A | 35 n. 71 |
| 53C–D | 35 n. 72 | 73C | 35 n. 71 |
| 53D | 27 n. 43 | 73C–74C | 306 n. 204 |
| 53F | 365 n. 80 | 73D | 320 n. 253 |
| 53F–54A | 127 n. 105 | 73DE | 36 n. 81, 317 n. 245, 328 n. 280 |
| 54C | 170 n. 39 | | |
| 55A | 25 n. 36 | 74A | 118 n. 69 |
| 55AB | 34 n. 68 | 74AC | 36 n. 81 |
| 55B | 81 n. 100, 120 n. 75, 136 n. 128 | 74B | 98 n. 150 |
| | | 74C | 80 n. 93 |
| 55B–E | 71 n. 59 | 74D | 106 n. 21, 320 n. 253 |
| 55C | 317 n. 245, 318 n. 246 | 74DE | 36 n. 81, 141 n. 156 |
| 55D | 25 n. 36, 246 n. 37 | 74E | 209 n. 80 |
| 55DE | 34 n. 69 | | |
| 55F–59A | 34 n. 69 | *Is 'Live Unknown' a Wise Precept?* | |
| 56B–D | 20 n. 20 | 1128D–E | 126 n. 97 |
| 58E | 24 n. 32 | 1128F–1129A | 103–104 n. 10 |
| 59B | 20 n. 20, 68 n. 52 | | |
| 59C | 98 n. 151 | *Isis and Osiris* | |
| 59D–60C | 34 n. 71 | 381C | 136 n. 127 |
| 59F | 166 n. 21 | | |
| 60D–61D | 35 n. 71 | *Life of Aegis* | |
| 62B–65A | 35 n. 73 | 795E | 35 n. 73 |
| 62C | 20 n. 20 | | |
| 64C | 35 n. 73 | *On Listening to Lectures* | |
| 65A | 92 n. 135, 168 n. 34 | | 79 |
| 66A | 35 n. 74, 120 n. 74 | 46C–47E | 68 n. 47 |
| 66B | 35 n. 75, 316 n. 242, 317 n. 245 | 46DE | 79 n. 91 |
| | | 46E | 80 n. 92, 119 n. 73, 289 n. 159 |
| 66F–67A | 98 n. 150 | | |

## On Moral Virtue
| | |
|---|---|
| 443C | 29 n. 51 |
| 451C | 142 n. 160 |
| 452C | 85 n. 111, 142 n. 160, 317 n. 245 |
| 452C–D | 85 n. 112, 281 n. 132 |
| 452D | 76 n. 79, 80 n. 94 |

## The Obsolescence of Oracles
| | |
|---|---|
| 410F | 150 n. 214 |

## Precepts of Statecraft
| | |
|---|---|
| 799C | 37 n. 83, 40 n. 92 |
| 800A | 28 n. 48, 30 n. 56 |
| 800AB | 37 n. 83, 40 n. 92 |
| 800B | 96 n. 144, 268 n. 100 |
| 802E | 268 n. 100 |
| 802EF | 40 n. 92 |
| 802F | 87 n. 120 |
| 807A | 268 n. 100 |
| 808D–809B | 37 n. 83, 90 n. 126 |
| 810C | 40 n. 92, 76 n. 79, 90 n. 127, 96 n. 144, 120 n. 74, 142 n. 160 |
| 815B | 40 n. 92, 87 n. 120 |
| 825D–F | 40 n. 92, 87 n. 120 |
| 825E | 316 n. 244 |

## Progress in Virtue
| | |
|---|---|
| 75A–86A | 331 n. 290 |
| 78AB | 119 n. 73, 289 n. 159 |
| 78B | 80 n. 93 |
| 82A | 54 n. 6, 80 n. 93, 144 n. 167, 151 n. 190 |
| 82AB | 128 n. 106 |

## Reply to Colotes
| | |
|---|---|
| 1117D | 121 n. 79 |

## Sertor.
| | |
|---|---|
| 19.11 | 307 n. 212 |

## On Superstition
| | |
|---|---|
| 167A | 331 n. 288 |
| 169E | 331 n. 288 |
| 170E–F | 331 n. 288 |

## Table Talk
| | |
|---|---|
| 628B | 32 n. 61 |
| 632E | 94 n. 137 |
| 719F | 159 n. 215 |
| 736D | 159 n. 214 |

## That a Philosopher ought to Converse especially with Men in Power
| | |
|---|---|
| 776B | 32 n. 61 |
| 777E | 271 n. 105 |
| 777E–778B | 32 n. 61 |

## Themistius
| | |
|---|---|
| 32.4 | 159 n. 214 |

## On Tranquility of Mind
| | |
|---|---|
| 456F | 80 n. 94 |
| 457B | 80 n. 94 |
| 468A | 98 n. 151 |
| 472F | 110 n. 37 |
| 474E | 28 n. 51 |
| 476F | 37 n. 82, 239 n. 13, 317 n. 245 |
| 533B–C | 28 n. 51 |

## Whether the Affections of the Soul are worse than those of the Body
| | |
|---|---|
| 500CD | 28 n. 50 |

## To an Uneducated Ruler
| | |
|---|---|
| 782B | 321 n. 261 |

# PSEUDO-PLUTARCH
## The Education of Children
| | |
|---|---|
| | 75 |
| 3A | 29 n. 51 |
| 6B | 270 n. 102 |
| 8F–9A | 75 n. 78, 279 n. 125, 320 n. 254 |
| 11E | 76 n. 79 |
| 12B–D | 76 n. 79 |
| 13D | 76 n. 79, 306 n. 205, 326 n. 276 |
| 13F | 146 n. 174 |
| 14A–B | 157 n. 205 |

# POLYBIUS
| | |
|---|---|
| 18.28.3 | 223 n. 114 |

# POLYCARP
## Letter to the Philippians
| | |
|---|---|
| 6.1 | 205 n. 69, 324 n. 272, 330 n. 283 |
| 6.1–2 | 230 n. 136 |
| 11.4 | 205 n. 69, 207 n. 75 |

# POLYSTRATUS
## On Irrational Contempt
PHerc 336/1150

INDEX OF PASSAGES 397

| | | | |
|---|---|---|---|
| Column | | 11.1.45 | 50 n. 122 |
| 18.2–4 | 18 n. 11, 122 n. 81 | 11.1.86 | 50 n. 122 |
| | | 11.1.90 | 77 n. 80 |
| PORPHYRY | | SAPPHO | |
| *On Abstinance* | | 25.6 | 20 n. 19 |
| 1.42 | 289 n. 157 | | |
| 1.56 | 75 n. 75 | SENECA | |
| | | *On Anger* | 77 |
| *Ad Marc.* | | 1.6.1–2 | 77 n. 82 |
| 31 | 133 n. 120 | 1.6.3 | 77 n. 82 |
| | | 1.15.1 | 77 n. 81, 148 n. 181 |
| QUINTILIAN | | | |
| *Oratorical Institutions* | 48 | 1.16.3 | 148 n. 181 |
| 1.9.3 | 50 n. 122 | 2.21.1–3 | 77 n. 81, 306 n. 205 |
| 1.3.13–14 | 77 n. 80 | | |
| 2.2.4 | 77 n. 80 | 2.21.1–7 | 76 n. 79 |
| 2.2.7 | 77 n. 80 | 3.10.3 | 145 n. 171 |
| 2.2.14 | 77 n. 80 | | |
| 2.2.1–14 | 68 n. 48 | *On Beneficence* | |
| 2.3.10 | 68 n. 48 | 2.2.1 | 166 n. 22 |
| 2.4.8–12 | 68 n. 48, 77 n. 80 | | |
| | | *De Brev. Vitae* | |
| 2.8 | 51 n. 127 | 2.7 | |
| 2.8.1 | 68 n. 48 | | |
| 2.13.2 | 50 n. 123, 51 n. 127 | *Epistles* | |
| | | 3.2 | 166 n. 22 |
| 2.13.16 | 51 n. 127 | 4.2 | 301 n. 190 |
| 2.17.22–25 | 51 n. 126 | 6.5–6 | 22 n. 26 |
| 3.1.4 | 73 n. 69 | 6.6 | 154 n. 199, 171 n. 46, 177 n. 69 |
| 3.4.3 | 64 n. 37 | | |
| 3.4.6 | 64 n. 37 | 7 | 258 n. 69 |
| 3.4.6–16 | 51 n. 125 | 7.11 | 175 n. 60 |
| 3.4.16 | 246 n. 36 | 9.6 | 166 n. 22 |
| 3.7.1–28 | 51 n. 125 | 9.17 | 170 n. 41 |
| 3.7.28 | 246 n. 36 | 25.4–5 | 158 n. 210 |
| 3.8.1–70 | 51 n. 126 | 33.4 | 158 n. 210 |
| 3.8.22–25 | 246 n. 36 | 42.1 | 53 n. 2 |
| 3.8.35 | 50 n. 122 | 45.7 | 20 n. 20 |
| 3.8.38 | 50 n. 122 | 47.1 | 170 n. 42 |
| 3.8.49–52 | 50 n. 122 | 47.15–19 | 170 n. 42 |
| 9.2.29–37 | 48 n. 115, 49 | 48.1–4 | 170 n. 42 |
| 9.2.30 | 40 n. 121, 62 n. 31 | 48.3 | 170 n. 41 |
| 9.2.58 | 40 n. 120 | 50.9 | 285 n. 149 |
| 9.2.65 | 296 n. 175 | 52.2 | 53 n. 2 |
| 9.3.99 | 49 n. 120 | 52.3–4 | 67 n. 44, 139 n. 151 |
| 11.1 | 49 | 52.3–6 | 68 n. 46 |
| 11.1.1–2 | 50 n. 124 | 52.12–14 | 71 n. 59 |
| 11.1.4 | 50 n. 123 | 64.8–9 | 46 n. 109 |
| 11.1.8–9 | 246 n. 36 | 71 | 83 |
| 11.1.14 | 246 n. 36 | 71.19–20 | 83 n. 105, 139 n. 151, 303 n. 195, 304 n. 197 |
| 11.1.37 | 323 n. 265 | | |
| 11.1.41–43 | 50 n. 122 | 71.26 | 83 n. 105 |

| | | | |
|---|---|---|---|
| 71.26–27 | 67 n. 42 | 108.35–37 | 22 n. 26 |
| 71.29 | 297 n. 179 | 124.10 | 301 n. 190 |
| 71.29–30 | 83 n. 105, 304 n. 198 | | |
| 71.37 | 331 n. 290 | *On Providence* | |
| 72.6–11 | 67 n. 42 | 5 | 186 n. 6 |
| 72.6 | 67 n. 42 | | |
| 75.5 | 71 n. 59 | ANONYMUS SEQUERIANUS | |
| 75.7–8 | 67 n. 42 | 30–32 | 51 n. 126 |
| 75.8–18 | 67 n. 42 | | |
| 75.9 | 67 n. 43 | SEXTUS EMPIRICUS | |
| 75.10–12 | 67 n. 42, 285 n. 149 | *Against the Dogmatics* | |
| 75.13–14 | 67 n. 43 | 1.12 | 83 n. 104 |
| 75.15 | 67 n. 42, 68 n. 46, 331 n. 290 | | |
| | | *Outlines of Pyrrhonism* | |
| 75.18 | 331 n. 290 | 1.20 | 75 n. 74 |
| 82.11 | 158 n. 210 | 1.164 | 75 n. 74 |
| 90.4–5 | 294 n. 171 | 1.177 | 75 n. 74 |
| 90.5–7 | 84 n. 108 | 3.32 | 75 n. 74 |
| 94 | 82 | 3.239–40 | 60 n. 23 |
| 94–95 | 82–83 | 3.32.280 | 87 n. 117 |
| 94.1 | 83 | 3.280 | 75 n. 74 |
| 94.2 | 83 n. 104 | 3.281 | 75 n. 75, 311 n. 222 |
| 94.5–17 | 83 n. 104 | | |
| 94.17 | 73 n. 69 | | |
| 94.21 | 83 n. 104 | PSEUDO-SOCRATES | |
| 94.30 | 83 n. 104 | *Epistles* | |
| 94.31 | 83 | 8.14–16 | 73 n. 69 |
| 94.32 | 83 n. 104 | | |
| 94.39 | 62 n. 31, 83 n. 104 | SOLON | |
| 94.42 | 83 n. 104 | 1.5 | 20 n. 19 |
| 94.44–45 | 83 n. 104 | | |
| 94.45–46 | 328 n. 281 | SOPHOCLES | |
| 94.48–52 | 304 n. 198 | *"Iphigenia"* | |
| 94.49 | 62 n. 31 | Fragment | |
| 94.51 | 84 n. 106, 297 n. 179 | 286 | 28 n. 45 |
| 95 | 83 | | |
| 95.4–6 | 84 n. 107 | *Oedipus Coloneus* | |
| 95.10–17 | 84 n. 107 | 378 | 224 n. 116 |
| 95.17 | 97 n. 148 | | |
| 95.29 | 84 n. 107 | SOSIPATER | |
| 95.29–32 | 97 n. 148 | *Fragment* | |
| 95.31 | 84 n. 107 | 1 | 26 n. 37 |
| 95.34 | 62 n. 31, 84 n. 107, 97 n. 148 | | |
| | | STOBAEUS | |
| 95.36 | 139 n. 152, 303 n. 195 | *Anthology* | |
| 95.36–37 | 84 n. 108, 287 n. 153 | 2.33.7 | 166 n. 24, 169 n. 36 |
| 95.55 | 84 n. 107 | | |
| 95.64 | 84 n. 108 | 2.35 | 20 n. 20 |
| 95.65 | 62 n. 31 | 2.198 | 301 n. 190 |
| 95.65–66 | 84 n. 109 | 3.41 | 128 n. 105 |
| 95.66 | 48 n. 118 | 4.659 | 166 n. 22 |
| 95.72 | 84 n. 107 | | |
| 97.15–16 | 128 n. 106 | STOICORUM VETERUM FRAGMENTA | |
| 103 | 258 n. 69 | | |
| 108.23 | 117 n. 62 | 1.67 | 285 n. 149 |

| | | | |
|---|---|---|---|
| 1.383 | 137 n. 130 | 17.1–4 | 70 n. 58 |
| 2.1000 | 82 n. 103 | 20.6 | 330 n. 283 |
| 3.177 | 285 n. 149 | | |
| 3.407–20 | 85 n. 111 | *Testament of Simeon* | |
| 3.411 | 142 n. 160 | 3.6 | 330 n. 283 |
| 3.458 | 73 n. 67, 73 n. 65 | 4.6 | 70 n. 58 |
| 3.460 | 73 n. 67, 118 n. 69 | | |
| 3.471 | 66 n. 40, 73 n. 67 | *Testament of Zebulun* | |
| 3.513 | 38 n. 86 | 6.5 | 330 n. 283 |
| 3.631 | 170 n. 42 | 7.3–4 | 330 n. 283 |

**SYNESIUS**
*Epistle*
5                289 n. 157

**THEMISTIUS**
*Orations*
327D             166 n. 22

**TELES**
*Fragment*
10, 7 (Hense)    229 n. 131

**THEOGNIS**
*Elegy*
213–218          27 n. 44

**TERENCE**
*Andria*
1.1.41           70 n. 56

**THEON**
*Progymnasmata*

| | | | |
|---|---|---|---|
| | | | 48 |
| *The Eunuch* | 24 | 8.1–2 | 48 n. 114 |
| | | 8.9–10 | 293 n. 168 |
| 1–3 | 24 n. 31 | 8.9–15 | 48 n. 116 |
| 247–49 | 24 n. 32 | 8.11–37 | 42 n. 114 |
| 251–53 | 312 n. 229 | 8.16–29 | 49 n. 117 |
| 254 | 24 n. 31 | 8.34–37 | 50 n. 124 |
| 391–453 | 24 n. 31 | 8.34–42 | 48 n. 117 |
| 771–817 | 24 n. 31 | 8.43–50 | 61 n. 28, 246 n. 36 |
| 1053–93 | 24 n. 31 | 8.75–76 | 48 n. 116 |

**THEOPHRASTUS**
*Characters*

**TERTULLIAN**
*De praescr.*
3                289 n. 157

| | | | |
|---|---|---|---|
| | | | 25 n. 33, 31 n. 58, 110 |
| | | 2.1 | 25 n. 33 |
| **TESTAMENTS OF THE TWELVE PATRIARCHS** | | 5 | 111 |
| | | 5.1 | 25 n. 34 |
| | | 5.3 | 25 n. 34 |
| *Testament of Benjamin* | | 15.1 | 319 n. 252 |
| 3.4–5 | 276 n. 117 | 16 | 331 n. 288 |
| 4.4ef | 330 n. 283 | 20 | 114 n. 50 |
| | | 23.1 | 121 n. 78 |
| *Testament of Issachar* | | 24 | 238 n. 10 |
| 5.2 | 330 n. 283 | 24.1 | 319 n. 252 |

*Testament of Job*
25.10            274 n. 113

*On Flattery*    25 n. 33, 31 n. 58

*Testament of Joseph*
                 38, 70
1.6              274 n. 113
3–9              38 n. 87, 259 n. 73
3.5              330 n. 283
9.2–16.6         38 n. 87
11.2             70 n. 58

*Fragment*
74 (ed. Wimmer)  166 n. 22

*On Friendship*  31 n. 58

*Historia Plantarum*
5.4.5            75 n. 75

THUCYDIDES
*Histories*
1.70.1                281 n. 132

VARRO
*On Agriculture*
1.17.4                327 n. 277

XENOPHON
*Memorabilia*         20
2.1.21–25             33 n. 66
2.7.1–14              229 n. 129

2.9
3.5.5
4.1.3–4
4.2.14–16
4.2.32
4.2.35

*On Household Management*
13.6–9

13.6–12
14.8

31 n. 58
158 n. 207
65 n. 39
20 n. 18
231 n. 137
231 n. 137

146
106 n. 22,
147 n. 175
86 n. 113
86 n. 113

# INDEX OF SUBJECTS

Abraham; and the "strong" and "weak"  228
Absent; vs. present  244, 308, 324–25
Abuse  72, 76, 88–89, 93, 114
Accusation  62
Actions  63; right and wrong  82
Adaptability  1, 2, 7, 74–75, 86–87, 112, 134; chameleon-like  19, 23; character portrayal and  48–50; Christ's  216, 257–58, 333; in communal psychagogy  215; in conduct and speech  1, 2–3, 23, 28, 272, 273; defence of  41–42; diversity of exhortation and  60–64; ethic of  215, 216, 333; expressed in 1 Cor 9:19–23  1–4, 15–17, 43–45, 87–88, 105–105, 178–81, 240, 247–77; and harshness  34; and hypocrisy  1; literary  327; and servility to the great  30–33, 264–72; and leadership style  43–43; psychagogic  1, 39, 41, 277–95; in the unreserved association with all  38–43; valued by orators, philosophers, and moralists  24–52
Adjudication; divine  216, 217, 231
Admonition  62, 68, 70, 72, 74, 77, 83, 84, 85, 90, 120, 131, 142, 147, 200, 203, 206, 207, 232, 296, 305, 306; definition of  60, 106, 217 n. 98; described as a dissection  136; engenders shame and repentance  142, 200, 305; *examplum* as an  306; authority and submission in  207; mutual  124–32, 213; purpose of  142; and reproach  69, 70; Rom 14:1–15:14 as an example of the practice of  217; symbol used as an  262; teaches conduct  83; type of blame  200, 305–306, 307; unmixed  36, 75
Admonitory education  86–87, 232, 305–306; and cross-examination  86 n. 114, 155 n. 202, 305–306
Advantage; communal vs. personal  240, 249, 252, 254, 294

Advice(r)  63, 72, 80, 90, 117, 306; general  246; precepts and dogmas as  83; specific  246
Aesop; fables of  54
Aetiology  84
Agency; human and divine  190, 194, 195
Ambition  66, 85; thwarts progress  145
Amputation  77
Analogical-functional approach  3, 329–30
Analogy; of beating and harsh criticism  142–43; of biting and blame/harsh censure  97–98, 136; of bodily ailment vs. psychological frailty  73, 78, 133; of students as children  189; of community as a body  191, 211, 215; of conjectural art and medical practice  108, 133–37; of the curb and the spur  77, 90; medical  21, 66, 75; of purgatives  155; of purificators of souls vs. physicians of the body  155 n. 202; of steersmen  251; of taming practices  42, 122, 146; of wormwood and frank speech  137
Anger  66, 73, 77, 80, 86, 118–19, 135, 137, 142, 163; Epicurean view of  148, 172; Peripatetic view of  122; thwarts progress  126, 140–41, 145
Animal analogies  27 n. 43, 146–147, 259; chameleon  27, 30; cuttlefish  30, 169, 259; foals  146; lamprey  259; lapdogs  146; octopus  27; polyp  27, 259; sea-god Proteus  27, 28, 30, 41; (noble) steed  90
Antisthenes  4, 19, 97, 272; as paradigm of the milder Cynics  91; a "simple hound"  97
Apology; 1 Cor 9 as  15, 105, 265 n. 86
Apostle(s)  264–65; of Christ  333; false  236, 237; super  237
Aptitude(s)  65, 66, 67, 68, 76, 84,

139, 160; spiritual 300, 302
Argumentation; resources of 61
Argument(s); anti-determinist 82;
of 1 Cor 8:1–8 285–86, 287;
destroyed 205; philosophical 117;
rational 226, 233, 235, 239;
therapeutic 152; veiled 313, 314
Arrogance 116, 237–38, 304, 325
Art 116, 134; of censure 74;
conjectural 108, 133–37; Epicurus'
definition of 143; of healing 110,
133, 134; of living 53, 60, 117; of
moral guidance 107; of mutual
concession 211; of navigation 110,
133, 134; of persuasive speech 298;
of psychagogy 123; of
rhetoric 133; vs. science 134; of
therapeutic healing of souls 135
Asclepius 33, 54
Assistance; the need for 53, 84, 139
Association 26–27, 44, 38–43, 91, 96,
97, 112; with all 1, 2, 44, 86, 179;
with different character types 16,
29, 30; expressed in 1 Cor 9:19–23
1–4, 15–17, 43–45, 87–88, 105–105,
178–81, 240, 247–77; and the
friendship of many 174; with the
immoral/base 97, 258–63; limits
of 289–90; in patronage 263–72;
and recruitment 174; purpose
of 44; as a source of pleasure
26, 34
Attitude(s) 60, 65, 68;
conceited 202; contemptuous
224, 238, 278, 280, 281, 332;
enlightened 281; forthcoming
108, 162–63, 291; judgmental 224;
modified 220, 233, 306;
moral 58; overweening 297;
patriarchal 297; religious 58; of
the "wise" 237
Audacity; of rashness 106; of
courage 106
Authority; achieved 55, 157, 213;
ambiguous 188; attributed 157,
213; corrective vs. edificatory 206;
and discipline 320; ethical 246;
and friendship 55; functional 213;
in nurture and correction 205; and
obedience 152–60, 205–208;
personal 213; recognized 55, 157;
submission to 188; used in a
stringent manner 318
Avarice 66
Aversion; to food 225, 283, 285

Babbler 126
Barking; the Cynics and 92
Βαστάζω; therapeutic and
non-therapeutic connotations
of 228
Beating; harsh criticism compared
to 142–43, 280 n. 128; of a (bad)
father 321–21; physical 279, 280;
mental 279, 280
Beguilement; vs. sincere guidance
17–21, 240
Behavior; appropriate 227; contrasting
modes of 90–92, 118;
diverse 263; divine sanction
of 215, 219, 228, 229, 230, 231,
277, 289; modified 60, 233, 263,
290, 292, 294, 332; relativized 248;
servile 24; "soft" 24;
ungodly 261; unified code of 263;
viewed holistically 22–23
Belief(s); and behavior 284, 290;
(basic) Christian 283, 286; different
inferences of 283, 286; dispute over
acceptable 231, 286;
eradicated 278, 287; false 226,
231; firmly held 226, 233, 281,
292; inculcation of 60, 332;
inferential 285, 286; intense 285;
irrational 215, 287; mistaken 83,
278; modified 263; true 286;
unified 263; uninformed 285;
variance in 224, 263; weak
in 217–221, 224; in wrong
ideas 84
Benediction 63
Biting; form of blame 97–98; the
Cynics and 92, 98; metaphor for
harsh censure 136
Blame 71, 73; destructive 69, 315;
different forms and function of 70,
305, 307–308; disparaging 62, 89;
and dissuasion 62–63; function
of 85, 307; harshest form of 93;
salutary 315; terms of
hortatory 62–63 n. 31, 108 n. 28;
used among friends 70
Blasphemy 93
Blessing(s) 88
Blows 75, 278, 279; metaphorical
sense of 279
Boldness 92; towards God 311
Brother 95, 189
Brotherly love 210–12
Burden(s) 218, 229, 322;
financial 322

## INDEX OF SUBJECTS 403

Busybody 95

Care; correct kind of 85; freedom from 171; of humans 6, 73, 194; intracommunal 195; of the soul 54, 58, 133, 161; of the young 2, 11–12, 21, 43, 71, 81–82, 85, 138, 335; of the (psychologically) weak 200, 330
Castigation 62, 190, 318, 319, 325
Catharsis 147
Cautery 40, 72, 77
Censure 62, 70, 74, 75, 85; art of 74; engenders shame and repentance 142; moderate 142, 149; and reproach 76; sting of 149
Change 82; attained through harshness 142; attained through shame 305
Character(s); -education 332 n. 291; (re)formation 79, 106, 174, 178, 263, 331–32; noble 86; test 162, 166, 171, 173, 178, 263; types of 65; wicked 86
Character portrayal 48–50, 61, 273; in exhortation 61–62; function of 84, 273–74; Paul's use of 238, 253, 273–74, 292–93, 310, 328–29, 332
Charisma; functional vs. personal 186, 204 n. 67;
Charlatans 37, 121, 241
Charmers 20, 119, 122; flatterers and 122 n. 82
Christ('s); adaptability 216, 257–58, 333; servants of 236
Circumstantial requirements 52, 69
Cognitive; vs. social 327
Comfort 77, 194, 317, 318
Common topics 245–46, 247, 308, 310
Community; of "active perception" 168, 173, 178; alternative 104; ethos 11, 176; founding of 105; and individual 175–81, 185
Compassion 79
Complaisance 70
Conceit 81, 306
Concealment; ideal of non- 162; Paul charged with 311–15, 319; a sin 164
Conduct; speech and 2–3, 18, 20–23, 42–43, 44, 300, 311–13, 314, 318

Confession 54, 292; communal 141; and reporting 124–32; of sins 204
"Confessional practice" 124, 161, 291
Conscience 287–88, 290–91; bad 227; built up 278; defiled 286; polluted 284, 288; weak 273, 284, 287, 288; wounded 207, 277, 288
Consistency; of words and deeds 21–22
Consolation 83, 84, 194, 195
Contentiousness 66, 308–309
Conversation 77, 109; assenting 112; divine friendship and 165; frank speech as a type of 109; ingratiating 112
Conversion 54
Conviction(s); behavior contrary to 226, 227; to eat everything 227; rational 227
Correction (of faults) 71, 82, 105, 108; among friends 70, 106; mutual 124–32, 198, 199, 200, 204, 216
Cowardice 93
Counsel 77
Counsellor(s) 87 n. 120
Courage 97
Cross-examination 62, 106, 305; and "admonitory education" 86 n. 114, 155 n. 202, 305–306; vs. plain teaching 127 n. 102
Culpability of all 156, 160, 201, 213
Cultural codes/cues 17, 329–30
Culture; alternative 175
Cure(s); of beliefs 232; beyond the hope of 95 nn. 139 & 140, 96, 97; of bodily ailments 75; difficult to 74, 119, 145, 311, 323; easy to 71, 75; of the emotions 118–120; through fear and shame 69; of fickleness 118; harshness needed for 96; harshness rejected for 119; of moral ills 114, 133; by means of an example 227; plain 84; rational 227; of souls 51 n. 128, 54; of the weak 233–35, 287
Curse(s) 88–89
Cynic(s) 35, 266; debate among 91, 101; dogs 98; gentle vs. rigoristic 4, 89–98, 101; harshness of the 71; ideal 72, 92, 93, 95
Cynicism 35; father of 91

## INDEX OF SUBJECTS

Deliberation 284–85
Deliberative genre 64
Demagogue(s) 45, 57, 267, 268, 327
Demagogy 114; and leadership 326–27
Democracy 90
Denunciation 74
Desires; put on evil things 262
Destruction 74, 78; (non-) apocalyptic 215, 230, 231, 277; eschatological 278; psychological 277–89, 292, 293, 316–17; salvation and 78, 79, 80, 81, 214, 229, 230, 275–77, 320; theological 230; vs. upbuilding 205–206, 320, 323
Determinism 82; soft- 82
Diagnosis 153, 208; incorrect 136; and prognosis 208; uncertain 135
Διάσυρσις; defined 305
Diogenes; father of Cynicism? 91; a paradigm of the rigorous Cynics 91
Diogenes of Oenoanda 129
Director; of souls 55; spiritual 134
Discourse(s); admonitory 82; aim of a 245–46; consolatory 63; contentious 110 n. 37; demagogic 116; of friendship 314; hortatory 63–65; insinuating 123; likened to taming practices 42; on moral education 86; paraenetic 59, 63; philosophical 103, 110 n. 37, 116; protreptic 59, 63; psychagogic 62, 65, 245; reformatory 82; retaliatory 82; of self-mastery 257, 284; sophistic 110, 116; sycophantic 112, 116; therapeutic 63; wholesome 321
Discipline 76, 280, 320; corrective 239, 322, 324, 325; moral 278; severe 304, 327
Disclosure 54
Disobedience 156, 157, 304, 322–26; and harshness 315–26
Disposition 1, 65, 79, 139; psychological 78; punished 96
Dissuasion; type of blame in 62–63
Divine commissioning 56
Doctor 21, 54, 152, 155, 156, 157, 160; can fail 155
Doctor's office; the lecture room of the philosophers as a 21; and school of philosophy 43

Dogmas; vs. precepts 82–85
Dogmatists 75
Drugs 21, 43, 76, 134
Duplicity 17–21

Eating 219, 220, 221, 222; and drinking 226, 227; of idol meat 280, 281, 282, 283, 286, 289, 290
Edification 105, 282, 282; collective 124–32, 190, 196, 197, 198, 204, 227, 256, 294; individual 190, 196, 197, 198, 256, 294; sham 288
Education(al); admonitory 86–87, 189, 232, 305–306; adult 12 n. 24, 58, 214 n. 93, 336; advanced 140; beastly 146–47; community 12 n. 24, 214 n. 93, 336; Hellenic 298; moral 86, 106; practice 279; private 159; types of 59 n. 20, 74; theory 279; using rebuke and censure 74, 232
Eloquence; and knowledge 298, 299, 300
Encouragement 63, 74, 75, 84
Enculturation 175
Enemy/Enmity 207, 208, 216
Epicurus; purifier of all 157; the (only) savior 8, 152, 154, 158 n. 209, 178; his symposia 111
Epicurean(s) 4, 5, 6, 7, 8, 9, 53; in Athens 102, 116, 123, 174, 185, 231, 291, 336; and Christians 9, 104, 105, 178–81; critique of Socrates 121; critique of Stoic pedagogy 127; debate among 102, 112, 113–124, 137, 151–52; "dissident" 115; fellowship 161; (importance of) friendship among 111, 115, 162–63; harsh and gentle 98, 114–24; at Herculanaeum 101, 103, 112, 123, 231, 326, 336; "hero cult" and religious aspects of their communities 8–9, 176–78; Latin exponents 101, 172; mutual support group 172; in Naples 101, 103, 116, 123, 174, 185, 231, 291, 336; recruitment practices 174–75; of the Rhodian school 116; social organization of their groups 153–55
Epideictic; genre 64, 71; oratory 116

Ἐπίπληξις; defined 305
Epistolary; psychagogy 53, 175–76, 178, 185, 193, 195; types 61
Ἐπιτίμησις 150; defined 305 n. 202; harsher than νουθεσία 142; a type of παρρησία 142
Evaluation 223; mutual 200, 213, 216
Example; forceful 239; pedagogical use of 281–82
Exercise(s); ascetic 247–48; elementary 48, 61; meditational 66 n. 41; for self-edification 197; for self-healing 66 n. 41; (collective/individual/(non-)rational) spiritual 60 n. 23, 62, 66 n. 41, 196, 197, 198, 256, 258, 262
Exhortation 59–60, 63, 72, 74, 83, 105; appropriate mode of 76, 114; destroys or saves 81; diversity of 60–65; harsh 306; moral 52, 66; resourcefulness of 75; and teaching 65; types of 42–43

Family; of friends 162; surrogate 104 n. 12
Farmer 57; his pruning-hook 76
Father(s) 33, 36, 40, 76, 86, 87, 94, 95, 321–22, 327; harsh 76; loving but stern 327; stern 189, 325; threatening 325; wise 76
Fault(s); candid approach to 69; correction of 70, 71, 76; -finding 62; concealment of 54, 70
Fear 85, 161, 163–64, 325; of gods 163–64, 287; of humans 164; mental 161; of punishment 76, 324
Flatterer(s) 23–36; and cooks 37; and demagogues 113; and friends 3, 26, 29, 30, 31, 32, 33, 34, 35, 69, 110; and the friend of many 169, 179, 180; the greatest 86; and the ironic person 121; and psychagogues 122–23; their "psychagogy" 122
Flattery 23–36, 110–13; characteristics of 109; and enmity 26, 109, 111; and frank speech 16, 109; and friendship 109; and obsequiousness 111; rhetoric and 26; and tragic poetry 26; vices akin to 111

Flogging 76, 279; physical 280
Folly; rescue from 93
Food 248; avoided 225, 283, 285; and drink 224, 331; milk vs. solid 300–301; moral and religious significance of 284, 289; profane 215, 216
Fools 307, 321; the "wise" as 73 n. 69
Forgiveness 63, 74, 199, 317, 318
Frank counselor 37, 86; and the simple, forthright and truthful person 37
Frank criticism; and friendship 161, 316; and the friendship of many 165–75
Frankness (of speech); aim of 134, 164; bitter 131; its effect on people of different professions, sex, age, and disposition 138–39; vs. flattery 16; and friendship 105–106, 109–10; harsh and gentle 73; and moral education 106; real vs. counterfeit 114–115; salutary 36; simple 145, 146; as a stochastic method 110; twofold perspective of 104, 105, 109; and unequal friendship 158; varied 87
Freeborns 75–76, 320
Freedom 266–67; as basis of frank speech 92; restricted 292–94; and slavery 267–70; and shamelessness 93
Friend(s) 26, 189; and enemies 80, 111; everybody's 97; most excellent of 156, 157; faithful 125, 166–68, 229, 314–15; and flatterers 3, 26, 29, 30, 31, 32, 33, 34, 35, 69; a like 165; testing a 161–62, 165–75
Friend of many 45, 105, 161, 165–75, 178, 179, 180
Friendship 26, 109, 154; aristocratic 169, 170, 180; associational type of 165; of character 166, 168, 169, 170; contractual type of 165; divine 165; ethic of 108, 160; exclusive 179; fraternal 180; language of 28, 34, 106; of many 165–75, 179, 185, 263, 270, 331, 335; mean between flattery and enmity 111; and openness and trust 162–65; paradigmatic

model of loyal 166–67, 170, 171; paternal 180; patronal 180, 267–68, 270–72; perfect 166, 180, 181; proportional 211–212; psychagogy and 161–181; terms of 108 n. 29; testing in 161–62, 165–75; types of 167–169, 173–74; "unemotional" 38, 179; valued by Epicureans 161; and virtue 166, 167, 168, 169, 170, 173, 174, 179, 270; "vulgar" 173

Generals 33
Gentiles 223, 225, 243, 255, 257, 329, 330, 331
Gentle(ness) 94–95, 323–24; of Christ 323, 325; philosophers 89–98; vs. harsh(ness) 71–77, 324; needed for the weak and tender 307
Gift(s) 191–92; spiritual 190
God(s); accountability towards 222; adapts himself to humans 51; church of 249, 255, 309; master of all 230; -fearers 256; impartiality of 217, 221, 225; mysteries of 286, 299, 301, 302, 303; nature of the 105; judgement seat of 221; as physician 51; spirit of 246, 301, 302; -taught 302; unable to save 80; wise and perfect 74
Golden age 84
Goodwill 106, 114, 122, 130, 142, 154, 318; and friendship 170
Gospel; of Christ 265, 269; Epicurean 103; Paul's 190, 249, 251; preaching of the 16, 105, 320
Gratitude 154
Greed 66
Greeks 249, 255
Grief 85, 194, 229, 239, 315–19; excessive 207, 315; and repentance 142
Group(s); of friends 231; mutual support 194; of people in 1 Cor 9:1–23 250, 252, 253, 254, 255–58, 267, 274; -sessions 160; study approach 165; the "weak" and "strong" not 333
Growth 65, 160, 190; human 301; spiritual 256–57; stunted 76; in understanding and belief 217
Guardians 40, 87; of all who can be saved 79

Guidance; of converts 3; harsh and gentle 62, 326; moral 107, 108; preceptual 83, 85, 282, 287, 328–29; rejected 302; of the soul 2, 71, 72; spiritual 186, 238, 294, 301, 302; through example 282, 287; of the weak 3; of the young 77
Guide(s); the authority of 64; God as 301; human 301; mature 53–58; moral 55; psychological 55; of souls 71; spiritual 55, 57, 176, 179, 189

Habit(s) 63, 284–85; eating 229; evil 84; fetters of old 284; (non-)contentious 247, 308–309; weakness and 284
Habituation 277, 287
Harsh(ness) 27, 35, 62–63, 74, 77, 87; beneficial 69, 72, 75, 85–89, 94–95; in the correction of faults 113–24; philosophers 89–98; destructive 71, 78–81; dispute on 239, 315–24; excessive 315–24; vs. gentle(ness) 71–77; and Greek educational theory 239; legitimate wielders of 33, 87 n. 120, 255, 280; purpose of 93–94, 96; therapeutic 310, 323; un/salutary 63, 72, 79, 315; of value in moral guidance 70, 239
Health; restoration of 75
Hebrews 236
Hellebore 34, 73, 96, 134, 136
Heracles 142; as model 91, 97
Hierarchy 209; functional 201–202; lack of emphasis on 212; social 153–54
Hippias of Elis 22
Homo duplex; vs. simplex 19–22
Hortatory terms 62–64, 202–203, 245; defined 305 nn. 201 & 202, 319 n. 251; the psychagogic use of 62, 245
Hortatory; department of philosophy 64; means 66, 82, 84; nature of 1 Cor 244; tradition in antiquity 244, 305
Household; ancient 187; of Epicurus 185; of faith 185; setting 231
Human(s); care of 6, 73, 194; culpable 82; described in

INDEX OF SUBJECTS 407

psychological and ethical terms 86–87, 238; different types of 1, 44, 68; predicament 66, 247–48; typology of 286
Human condition 41, 61, 66, 71, 86; depraved 84, 85, 97; diverse views of the 71, 91, 93, 96, 97, 132, 144
Huntsman 57
Hypocrisy; charge of 45; vs. truthful guidance 17

Ideology; Corinthian 236
Idolatry 284; dangers of 262
Idol(s) 286, 292; belief in 277, 285, 288; food offered to 215, 248, 262, 264, 266, 271–72, 277, 290, 292; worship 262, 289
Imagery; demagogic 326; familial 224; fraternal 208; friendship 224; patriarchal 326, 327
Imitation 248, 259, 294
Impetuosity 285
Imposters 122
Improvement 66, 79, 88, 92, 93–94 n. 136, 281
Inconsistency; Paul charged with 310–13, 324–25
Incontinence; two types of 285
Incurable 54, 65, 74, 96, 97, 119, 135, 137, 141, 144, 145, 150–51, 323
Indignation 62
Individual; and community 175–81, 185, 190, 194, 196, 197
Individualism; radical 95 n. 140
Informant 291–92
Insiders; and outsiders 104, 105, 113, 117, 123, 185, 196, 197, 198, 247, 254, 258, 260–63
Instruction 62, 76, 79; dogmatic 60; methods of 107; paraenetic 59
Irony 282, 288, 296, 313, 321
Israelites 236

Jew(s) 225, 240, 241, 249, 250, 252, 253, 255, 256, 329, 330, 331
Judgement; criterion for friendship 231, 232; God's 216, 217, 221, 224; faulty 297–98; about reasonings 219, 222, 223, 224; in the Roman community 216–26
Kerygma 299
Kinship terms; fictive 188

Knowledge 283–84, 285, 299; and eloquence 298, 299, 300

Language; of becoming 252–53; of friendship 28, 34, 106; of openness 314; plain 88, 106; of progress 189; of servility 268; stringent 305
Leaders; different types of 39
Leadership; ambiguous 188–89; charismatic 186; debate on 151–52, 272, 295; institutional 186; model(s) 3, 240, 295, 326; in Paul 44, 186, 189, 240, 326–29, 331–32, 334; populist model of 326, 327; psychagogy as 56, 58, 186, 189, 240; qualification(s) 151–52, 205, 238–39, 295, 325–26; in recruitment 240; style 151–52, 238–39, 295, 325–26; transformational 56
Lecture-room 79
Lecturer; touring 58
Letter(s); admonishing 70; blaming 319; friendly 325; painful 317, 319; Paul's 316, 317, 319, 320, 322, 324, 325; tearful 316; threatening 324; weighty and strong 319
Likeness; of purpose/pursuits 10, 11, 165; and friendship 165, 169–70, 180
"Liminality" 59, 175
Living together 168, 173, 178
Λόγος 299; Paul's 97; and σχῆμα 2–3, 20–23, 42–43, 253, 273–74
Λοιδορία 150; confused with παρρησία 92, 119–20; and ὀνειδισμός 92; used by philosophers 92, 93, 94–95
Love 315, 316, 317; of fame and glory 103, 111
Lust 66

Magistrates 88
Maturity; and immaturity 130–31, 238, 295, 300–304; moral/spiritual 56
Mature (person) 76, 301–304; vs. child 81, 211, 295, 300–302; concern with self-mastery and moral achievement 216; fail 81, 120, 130, 135; vs. the progressing person 81, 130–31, 301, 303–304;

responsibility of the 202, 214, 218, 225, 228, 229, 232, 234–35, 302
Meddler 95
Medical analogy/imagery 21, 66, 75, 108, 120; implications of the 132, 133, 137, 152, 153, 155, 156; and the stochastic method 133–37
Medicine(s) 73, 96; harsh 317; sweet and bitter 134
Μέμψις; defined 319
Metaphor; agricultural 288, 189; of the body 191; building 189
Mind; sick 285; uninformed 285
Misanthrophy 92, 93
Mistakes; pardonable 156
Mixed method 36, 42, 71, 72–77, 84, 87–88, 93, 123, 143–46; adaptability and the 69–77; as admonitory education 86; the care of the young and 71; description of the 90 n. 127; of exhortation 44, 52, 62; implications of the 98, 101; in Paul 240, 245, 246, 296–97, 304, 308–310, 311, 324, 326–29, 334; purpose of the 72
Modes of representation; enactive 60; imagistic 60; lexical 60
Modesty 79–80; beginning of salvation 80
Money 103
Moralist(s) 7, 60, 70, 78, 87, 96, 97, 105, 129, 230, 316, 319, 326, 329, 330, 332; classification of 57; common term/theme among 65, 238, 251; concern for the weak 79; on different types of students 65–69; as guide of soul 71; proponents of an "art of living" 60; protreptic goal of 7; task of benefiting humans 87
Mother(s) 33, 87, 187
Multitude 112, 113

Neighbours 113
Neophyte(s)/Novice(s) 2, 10, 11, 140, 197, 198, 254; concept of 175; exhorted by precepts 59; nurture of 11, 196
Nurse(s) 33, 35, 76, 87, 94, 187; gentle as a 92
Nurture 3; vs. correction 190; of neophytes 11; psychagogic 12

Obedience 152–60, 205–208; call to 296

Obsequious person(s) 23–30
Obsequiousness 112–114; and flattery 111, 122; positive 110, 112, 113, 120, 122–23; sly and persuasive vice 113
Occupations 103; reputable 162
Odes; spiritual 196, 197, 203
Odysseus; and Achilles 19–20; and Ajax 19 n. 15, 251; ambiguous character 1; charges against 1; as described by Antisthenes 4, 19, 91, 251, 272; father of Cynicism? 91; Homer's traditional hero 1; as a homo duplex 19; "a magnificent liar" 38; a "man of many turns" 19; as model 91, 97; and Paul 1, 243; his versatility 1, 38
"Office" 155, 157, 213
On Frank Criticism 102, 107–109; translation of 108; reason for its existence 161–62
Openness 152–53; vs. concealment 124–32, 311–15; emphasis on 163, 164, 173, 177–78; in Epicurean friendship 108, 162–65; ideal of 151, 291; needed for correct diagnosis 163; and trust 162–65
Opponents; as disobedient students 311, 325, 333
Opportune moment 35–36, 51, 52, 69, 106

Paideia 58, 232, 233, 298 n. 182
Pain 35–36, 73, 85, 316, 317, 318, 319; bearers of 33; beneficial 34, 74, 85; corrective 316; leads to true pleasure 85; vs. pleasure 25–26, 33–34, 37, 71 n. 59, 85; therapeutic 316; unsalutary 35, 131
Paraenesis 59, 60, 83, 118; vs. protrepsis 59
Paraenetic; instruction 59; terms 64
Parasite(s) 24–25, 30, 32; epithet of 122 n. 83
Parents 40, 70, 88
Παρρησία; "Christian" 311; harsh dimension of 305; a form of blame 108; legitimate wielders of 301; use of the word 105–107; as a way of life 109
Passion(s)/Emotion(s) 63, 67, 80, 85 n. 111, 267; of arrogance 147; censure of the 118; curing of

the   53, 73, 287; not to be
extirpated   142; at their
height   146, 148; need a therapy
and an education   142; progressive
deliverance of   147; swollen   148
Patient(s)   21, 77, 317
Patriarch; benevolent   327;
spiritual   326
Patron(age)   110; Philodemus and
Piso   101, 102, 103, 105, 111, 112,
157 n. 205, 172, 264; Paul and the
Corinthian   178-79, 180-81,
263-72, 294; spiritual   326
Paul('s); adaptability in conduct and
speech   1, 179, 240-49; ambiguous
character/status   1, 322; approach
towards the recalcitrant   295-326;
as a brother/friend   88, 208, 209;
as a casuist   247, 290;
characterization of people   68, 211,
238, 295; characterization of the
recalcitrant   297-304, 311, 325,
333; charges against   1, 2-3, 15,
237, 239, 241, 310-16, 318-19,
320; community organizer   241;
and contemporary moralists   186,
329, 332; debate with the "wise"/
his critics   3, 16, 233, 236, 237,
295, 310-26; as a (spiritual)
father   88, 208, 209, 296, 297,
304, 321, 323, 325, 326, 327, 328;
as a friend and father   327-28; on
harshness and gentleness   88, 94,
238-39, 295; Hellenistic literary and
religious context   7, 242; imagery
applied to   187, 241, 243; itinerant
recruiter   241; knowledge of the
hortatory tradition   305;
leadership   186, 187, 189, 236-37,
239, 278, 300, 310-11, 321-22,
326-32, 334; likeness to flatterers
and obsequious persons   15-17, 88,
252; nurturing paternity   187, 329;
and Odysseus   1, 243, 272; as an
open and consistent guide   311-15;
opportunism   15, 312; and
patronage   178-79, 180-81,
263-72, 294; philosophic
contemporaries   4, 7; the
psychagogue   186-90; stringent
guidance   304-310; a
sychophant   16; travels   242-43;
view of the human condition   97;
use of the language of the
Corinthians   234, 236

Paulus christianus; vs. Paulus
hellenisticus   4-5
Pedagogue(s); common   154;
divine   73; false   116;
philantropic   72
Pedagogy   58-59; admonitory   233,
328, 305-306; communal   107;
debate on   294-95; didactic element
in   232-33; and examples   281-82;
informal nature of   159-60; moral
instruction and   58-60;
Pauline   189, 236-37, 239, 278,
300, 310-11, 321-22, 326-32, 334;
philanthropic   63
People; bad   90 n. 128;
immoral   207, 240, 257, 258-63;
ironic   120, 121; irresolute   81;
lawless   250, 257-58; lay-   81;
rough   90 n. 128; self-learnt   301;
spiritual   200, 201, 218, 225, 234,
299, 302, 303; stubborn   27; types
of   66, 74, 79, 173-74, 189; of
worth   106
Perfect person   64, 74, 83, 301; vs.
child   300, 301, 302; Pauls view of
the   297-98; can progress   297; vs.
a progressing person   64, 74, 301
Perfection   67, 82, 156; and spiritual
guidance   297; twofold   40
Personification   48-50, 52, 61-62, 84
Persuasion   72, 83, 84; vs.
dissuasion   52-63; different forms
and degree of   63, 75, 84, 85, 93,
96, 97, 98, 114-15, 116; non-lexical
mode of   299; philosophical   116;
rational   214, 224, 283, 287;
rhetorical   116
Philanthropy   95 n. 140
Philodemus of Gadara   5, 101; his
writings   102; works on
flattery   110-111, 112
Philosopher(s)   57, 87 n. 120; a
bad   72, 79; and demagogues   57;
"fellow-"   175; house-   103;
ideal   93; "mixed"   93; as a
physician   21; and prostitutes   37;
resident   58; and sophists   57;
"harsh" and "gentle"   71, 89-98;
use different forms of
exhortation   42-43
Philosophy; beginning students
of   138; deserted   79, 119, 137,
149; hidden truths of   84; "noble"
171; philology and   116;
recommended as a cure for

## INDEX OF SUBJECTS

fickleness 118; recent converts of 138; starting point of 81
Philotropeic method 85–89, 141, 179–80, 318
Physician(s) 21, 35, 36, 39–40, 72, 73, 76, 77, 87, 91, 110, 122, 208, 252; aid of a 122, 123; his art 41, 110; and cooks 33, 37; and frank counselors 37; moral 108; most philanthropic 33, 75
Pilot(s) 33, 39–40, 41, 87 n. 120
Pleasure; and/in friendship 162–63, 167, 168; vs. pain 25–26, 33–34, 37, 42, 71 n. 59, 85; result of pain 85
Poetry; tragic 26
Poets; comic 35
Politicians 255; pilots, physicians and 39–40; resentful of frank criticism 138
Power 56, 90
Praise; and blame 63, 65, 69, 71, 74, 76, 81–85, 91 n. 129, 116, 123; mock 296; and persuasion 63
Prayer(s) 88, 196
Precepts 82–85, 332; and character portrayal 49, 84, 273; used in exhortation 59–60; situational 60; like symbols 300
Pretentious person 37, 114–15, 121, 122, 144; thinks he is perfect 144, 151
Pretentiousness 66, 120–21, 132
Proctors 88
Prodicus myth 33
Progress 54, 81, 186; all 132; in faith 190; lost or saved 81; making no 145; means of 130; moral 66–68; thwart or aid 81, 205, 214, 276–77, 278; of the weak 230, 280; in wisdom 127; of the young 80
Progressing person 49, 64, 67 n. 42, 71, 74, 79, 81–85, 123; vs. the perfect person 64
Progymnastic writers 48, 61
Proofs 83, 84
Prostitute(s) 37, 262, 289
*Protrepsis* 59; protreptic terms 64
Psychagogic; discourse 62, 65, 245; metatext 214; perspective 53–69; practice 107; "proxy" 195; theory 107; terms 202–204

Psychagogue(s) 57, 58, 94; ambiguous status of 58; counter- 323, 324; as friend 60; as parent 60; his self-presentation 22–23; his skill 59
Psychagogy; and beguilement 3; and "care of the young" 335; communal 8, 12, 86, 126, 178, 185, 190–235; the concept of 17–23; conjectural method in 148; in 1 Cor 8 277–90; in 1 Cor 9:19–23 253, 254, 272–77; corrective 82, 151, 172–73, 178–79, 205, 207, 208, 218, 301–302; definition of 2, 17, 56, 57, 58, 60, 64–65; destructive 207; different types of humans and 210; edificatory 205, 208; as "enculturation" 59; epistolary 53, 175–76, 178, 185, 193, 195; and friendship 161–75; function of 58–59, 161; harshness in 3; history of 58 n. 17; implications of 160, 212; and moral instruction 58–60; non-dogmatic 10; participatory 8, 10–11, 124–32, 177–78, 185–86, 192–205, 335; Pauline 186–92, 202–204, 329–32; as pedagogy 233; polyphonic 310, 313; preceptive 10; and recruitment 59; right and wrong 120; as a "rite of passage" 59; as "Seelenheilung" 66; as "Seelenleitung" 66; rotational 101, 124, 160, 161, 209, 213 n. 93, 232, 335; system of 5; tensions in 209–10; twofold aspect of (Pauline) 189–90; and versatility 44; of the wise 283–87
Public speakers 58, 241
Punishment 73, 74, 76, 77, 79, 82, 88, 137, 146–47, 156, 199, 205, 316–18, 324; fear of 76, 324; purpose of 77; and reward 146
Purification 155; of mistakes 155–56; of the sick 155

Quietness 164
Qumran 11 n. 21

Railing 62, 93; divine pedagogue's use of 73
Reading of 1 Cor 8; non-

apocalyptic 295, 320;
pedagogical 295
Reason 81, 83, 85, 233, 234; calms
the soul 79, 89; as a principle of
social hierarchy 234
Reasoning(s) 75, 84, 223, 224;
dialectical 286, 298; faulty 223,
231, 233; ill founded 219;
together 109; true 286
Rebuke 62, 68, 70, 72, 74;
defined 305 n. 201; letter of 305
Recruiters; religious and
philosophical 241
Recruitment 2, 44, 105, 171–75, 180,
240, 260, 262, 269, 272; and
psychagogy 16–17, 174–75,
196–98, 240, 253–54;
unregulated 162, 263, 335
Recruits 59, 165, 174; education
of 59, 175; formation of 103;
psychologically alienated 175;
youngest 153
Reform(ation) 80 126; moral 2, 7,
64, 79, 80, 106, 124, 126, 174, 178,
261–63, 331–32; of the weak 206
Reformatory ethic 11, 78, 79, 82, 88,
214, 276, 284
Refutation 155; principal form of
purification 155 n. 202
Rein(s) 76, 90, 146
Relationship(s); with an hierarchical
and egalitarian axis 212, 213, 216
Relief; mental 126, 163, 164;
mutual 194; varied 143
Religion; and morality 214, 230, 281;
mystery 299, 330
Remedies 74, 75; mild and
stringent 73, 75, 77
Repentance 63; achieved through
blame, grief and shame 85, 142,
199, 207, 208, 239, 261, 305, 307,
310, 315, 316, 317, 318; a kind of
pain or grief 142; and threats 320
Reporting; of errors 128–29, 132,
135, 201
Reproach 62, 72, 88, 93, 119, 305;
and admonition 69; boldly 106;
and censure 70; divine pedagogue's
use of 73
Reproof 77, 81
Responsibility; and fate 82
Reviling 88, 93; of a (bad)
father 321–22; tactless 95 n. 14,
96, 119

Reward 82; hope of 76; and
punishment 146
Rhetoric 18, 50–51, 64, 298; and
adaptability 46–47, 116; as
art 47, 51, 116; deliberative 123;
of demonstration 298, 299; and
navigation 51; and medicine 51;
as flattery 18; of persuasion 299;
as ψυχαγωγία 18; rules of 50;
of self-examination 300;
sophistic 116
Rhetorical questions 265, 292–93
Rod; imagery of 73, 88, 304, 326;
silver 91
Role(s); fraternal 65, 188;
functional 160; leadership 191,
202; or office 155; parental
188–89; paternal 65, 188–89, 304;
Paul's many 187–89; of a
"psychagogue" 161; (recognized)
social 160, 212, 213; status
implications of 188; "weak" and
"strong" not fixed 333
Rulers 87; harsh an gentle 89–90

Sailor 57
Salvation 68, 73, 74, 79, 89, 129–30,
134, 138–39, 194, 248, 249, 251–52,
254, 317; (non-) apocalyptic 215,
230, 231, 277; destruction and 78,
79, 80, 81, 214, 229, 230, 275–77,
320; eschatological 278;
psychological 277–89, 292, 293,
316–17; reciprocal 154;
theological 230
Sarcasm 76
Savior(s) 8, 79, 152, 154, 158 n. 209,
178
Sceptic 75
Scholar(s) 117; literary 117
School(s); philosophical 53
Schoolmasters 88, 279
Scythians; proverbial bluntness of 90
Self(-); advantage 249; assertive
Corinthians 280, 281;
awareness 290; benefit 249; care
of 53, 54; conceit 74, 75;
condemnation 221; control 80;
correction 132; cultivation 11;
deception 151, 295, 306, 325;
definition 59; delusion 298;
depictions 311–15; deprecator 37,
121; disguise 38, 259;
discipline 248, 252, 284, 290;

## INDEX OF SUBJECTS

edification 190, 196, 197, 256, 290, 294; effort 81; estimation 288; examination 300; healing 66 n. 41; identity 252; praise 298; presentation 266, 326, 332; reform 81; respect 80; scrutiny 80; sufficiency 26, 170; taught 74, 139, 302; willed person 27
Self-mastery 216, 247–48, 256–57, 284, 290; ascetic vs. intellectual 248, 290
Seniors 87, 88
Servility; to the great 110, 111, 271
Shame 305, 306, 307, 308, 309; and fear 85, 305; rebuke/reproach and 305; and repentance 305
Shameless(ness) 80, 83; as freedom 93
Shepherd 57, 96
Shunning; practice of 199, 207, 208; purpose of 261, 308, 331
Sickness 66, 71; diagnosis and prescribed cure of 118; easily cured 71; human predicament as 66; human vices as 66; of pupils 108; in remission 96, 148; severe 73, 74, 75, 96, 97; of the young 208; visualized 119
Simple method 143–46
Sin(s) 248, 324; against Christ 292; against a weaker brother 292; prevention of 63; rebuked 70, 143; not recognized 151, 238; shame of 73
Slaves 75, 165, 173, 210, 221, 320
Slavery; voluntary 27, 251, 252, 254
Slogans 283, 284, 286, 294
Socrates; a conjurer of souls 18; true rhetorician 18; true psychagogue 18; as teacher 54 n. 7
Social; vs. cognitive 327; contexts of psychagogues 58; setting 241
Softness 24, 97, 179, 185
Solicitude 87
Solidarity; diastratic 157, 213 n. 93
Solutions to the human predicament; ascetic 247–48; conceptual-intellectual 247–48
Sophists 57, 116
Soul(s) 47, 80, 83, 117, 171, 186; care of 54, 58, 133, 161; contest of the 41; director of 55; diseases of 54–55, 66–67; compound 47;

grown callous 73; cure of 51 n. 128, 54; improvement of 88, 106; leader of 333; -rust 84; -search 21–22; service 11, 54; sick 81, 285; simple 47, 51; therapeutic healing of 110
Speaking; plain 70
Speech(es); different forms of 195–96; discrimination in 42, 45, 52, 273; farewell 55; harsh 79, 82; propriety of 49–51; revelatory 299; unimpressive 298
Spirit; troubled 36; taught by the 301, 302
Spur 147
Spying 124
Statesmen 87, 255
Status; achieved 186; acquired 157, 159; advanced 56; advisory 55, 208; ambiguous 55–56, 208, 209–10; attributed 186; of the "doctor" 155; hidden 259–60; local-community 56; mature 56; moral 3; oriented society 56; people of diverse 174–75, 210; social 3, 56, 209; (different) spiritual 56, 196, 310–11
Stoic(s); bent of the "wise" in Corinth; criticized 281; paradox 248
Strong 42, 68, 137, 329–32; vs. weak 78, 80, 148–49, 211, 214
Student(s); appropriate treatment of 124; aptitude of 59; classification of 3; different disposition of 43; dilemma of 64; disobedient 68, 119, 137, 146–48; mature 140; obedient 68, 137, 140, 189; private 159; psychology of 64; recalcitrant 68, 135, 136, 137, 140, 189, 208; teacher relationship 64, 69, 118; tutorial 159; types of 22, 43, 46, 52, 60, 65–69, 137–52, 328–329; weak and tender 68, 78–81
Style; admonishing 62 n. 30; advisory 62 n. 30; angry 62 n. 30; blaming 62 n. 30; consoling 62 n. 30; consorious 62 n. 30; didactic 62 n. 30; encouraging 62 n. 30; friendly 62 n. 30; ironic 62 n. 30; mixed 62 n. 30; paraenetic 62 n. 30; praising 62 n. 30; reproving 62 n. 30; sympathetic 62 n. 30;

threatening  62 n. 30;
vituperative  62 n. 30
Superiority; cognitive  280; vs. inferiority  55
Support; financial  265–66, 269, 270, 272; means of support  103
Surgery  40, 72, 73, 96, 131, 136, 137; See also Cautery; Medical imagery; Physician
Symbols  299, 300; like precepts  300
Symmetry; in social relations  56, 152; vs. asymmetry  152–60, 186, 189, 205–212, 297, 304, 327–28, 335
Sympathy  120, 141
Symposium  117–118

Tasks; communal  191–92, 203–204
Teacher(s)  33, 36, 40, 76, 87, 118, 131–32; as an elder or a father  159, 328; and flatterers  122; God as  301; parental attitude of  76
Teaching; of nature  246, 247, 308, 309; relation to psychagogy  58–60; by example  226
Temperaments; untrained  80
Therapeutic; aid  156; arguments  152; contexts  234; harshness  310, 323; healing of souls  110; model  34, 66, 133–34, 228, 233, 235, 247–48, 285; terms  234, 235; treatment  130, 152–53
Therapy  63; purgative  79, 134, 155; surgical  79, 134; varied  143; of vice  79
Threats  62, 73, 74, 76, 93; Paul's use of  88, 206, 239, 304, 318, 320, 323–24, 325; philophronetic  325
Tradition; "syndrome" of  92
Trainer; gymnastic  80, 279
Treatment  77; admonitory  145; appropriate  124; correctional  145; ill-  75; of students  64, 137; therapeutic  130, 152–53; of the weak  233–35
Trust  162–65; and distrust  124–32
Tutor; home  88; private  159
Typology; of the Corinthian critics  238–39; of Philodemus' critics  150–52; of the "weak" as insecure students  239; of the "wise" as recalcitrant students  239, 295, 310, 311, 325, 333

Ulysses; tradition of  19. See also Odysseus
Unbeliever(s)  196, 197, 198, 254
Uneducated  81
(Un)initiated  84, 154, 299

Versatility  39; defence of  41–42; impediment to a permanent relationship  169, 180; needed in recruitment and psychagogy  17, 65–69
Vice(s)  67, 199, 238, 260–61; therapy of  79
Virtue(s);  83, 109; of character  26; as a leader  33; a medium between two vices  109, 110–111; of social life  26
Virtue and vice (lists)  82, 116
Vocational terms  188

Way of life  53, 60
Weak(ness)  42, 44, 68, 71, 73, 76, 78, 80, 84, 119, 135, 141, 148–50, 228–29, 233, 234, 253–54, 329–32; destroyed  205, 206, 214; discourse of self-mastery and  257, 284; educated  214, 277–87; in faith/belief  217–21, 224;  guidance of the  3; and habit  284; knowledge, conscience and  276, 284, 287, 288, 327; Paul on  274–77; predicament of the  234–35; psychological(ly)  78, 254, 256, 276, 278, 330; and the reformatory ethic  284; reformed  206; social(ly)  78, 278; in spirit  229; vs. strong/strength  78, 80, 148–49, 211, 214; and the therapeutic model  233; treatment of  233–35; a type of incontinence  285; of the will  80
Well-being  193, 244; physical  161, 162; spiritual  161, 162
Whip(ping)  279; very painful  251; of sharp words  278
Wine  226; employed for medical purposes  90 n. 128
Wisdom (of God)  299, 300, 301; cannot be taught  299; words of  299
Wise  83, 110, 130, 301; can err  154; Epicurean  111, 112, 116, 121; and flatterers  123; as judges  198, 199; as (not)

perfect 132; progress of the 130; susceptible to anger 137
Withdrawal 103
Women 149, 165, 173, 210; helpless 171; promiscuous 166; resentful of frank criticism 138–39
Word(s); of the cross 299; and deeds 2–3, 18, 20–23, 42–43, 44, 300, 311–13, 314, 318; divine 93; persuasive 299; picture 299; (whip of) sharp 74, 278

Wormwood 73, 96, 120, 134, 136, 137, 146; compared to frank speech 137
Worship; rational 215; unified 247; put in jeopardy 23
Wound(ing) 207, 277, 288
Wrongdoing; habitual 79

"Young" 137–38, 153

Zeus; servant of 95

www.ingramcontent.com/pod-product-compliance
Lightning Source LLC
Chambersburg PA
CBHW021351290426
44108CB00010B/190